ASCENT®

CENTER FOR TECHNICAL KNOWLEDGE

Creo Parametric 11.0
Introduction for Non-Designers

Learning Guide
Edition 1.0

ASCENT - Center for Technical Knowledge®
Creo Parametric 11.0
Introduction for Non-Designers
Edition 1.0

Prepared and produced by:

ASCENT Center for Technical Knowledge
630 Peter Jefferson Parkway, Suite 175
Charlottesville, VA 22911

866-527-2368
www.ASCENTed.com

Lead Contributor: Mark Potrzebowski

ASCENT - Center for Technical Knowledge (a division of Rand Worldwide Inc.) is a leading developer of professional learning materials and knowledge products for engineering software applications. ASCENT specializes in designing targeted content that facilitates application-based learning with hands-on software experience. For over 25 years, ASCENT has helped users become more productive through tailored custom learning solutions.

We welcome any comments you may have regarding this guide, or any of our products. To contact us please email: feedback@ASCENTed.com.

Contents

Chapter 4: Sketching Geometry   4-1

Chapter 8: Model Information   8-1

Chapter 9: View Manager   9-1

Appendix A: Customizing Creo Parametric — A-1

Preface

The *Creo Parametric 11.0: Introduction for Non-Designers* guide provides reviewers or downstream users of Creo Parametric data with the knowledge to investigate, manipulate, and annotate existing models. It is targeted at users who require less training in geometry creation techniques. The user learns to open models for the purpose of providing feedback, verification, image capture, and taking data into specialized modules. This learning guide provides a good introduction to Creo Parametric for users who are evaluating the software or need a high-level understanding of the software's capabilities.

This content was developed using Creo Parametric 11.0.

Topics Covered

* Creo Parametric interface

* Obtaining model information

* Display control

* Creating datum features

* View manager

* 3D annotations

* Creating planar and offset cross-sections

* View creating and detailing

* File management

* Exporting and importing data

Prerequisites

* Access to the Creo Parametric 11.0 version of the software, to ensure compatibility with this guide. Future software updates that are released by the manufacturer may include changes that are not reflected in this guide. The practices and files included with this guide might not be compatible with prior versions (e.g., 10.0.0). The practice files included with this guide are compatible with the commercial version of the software, but not the student edition.

Note on Software Setup

This guide assumes a standard installation of the software using the default preferences during installation. Lectures and practices use the standard software templates and default options for the Content Libraries.

Note on Learning Guide Content

ASCENT's learning guides are intended to teach the technical aspects of using the software and do not focus on professional design principles and standards. The practices aim to demonstrate the capabilities and flexibility of the software, rather than following specific design codes or standards, which can vary between regions.

Lead Contributor: Mark Potrzebowski

Mark is a seasoned trainer and curriculum designer with more than 15 years of experience in the PLM industry. With a primary focus on CATIA, Creo, and PLM systems, Mark uses his Instructional Design skills and comprehensive CAD experience to develop training products at ASCENT, including learning content for print and web, as well as instructional videos and presentations.

Mark holds a bachelor's degree in Computer Graphics Technology from Purdue University, West Lafayette, Indiana.

Mark has been the Lead Contributor for *Creo Parametric: Introduction for Non-Designers* since 2022.

In This Guide

The following highlights the key features of this guide.

Feature	Description
Practice Files	The Practice Files page includes a link to the practice files and instructions on how to download and install them. The practice files are required to complete the practices in this guide.
Chapters	A chapter consists of the following: Learning Objectives, Instructional Content, Practices, Chapter Review Questions, and Command Summary. • **Learning Objectives** define the skills you can acquire by learning the content provided in the chapter. • **Instructional Content**, which begins right after Learning Objectives, refers to the descriptive and procedural information related to various topics. Each main topic introduces a product feature, discusses various aspects of that feature, and provides step-by-step procedures on how to use that feature. Where relevant, examples, figures, helpful hints, and notes are provided. • **Practice** for a topic follows the instructional content. Practices enable you to use the software to perform a hands-on review of a topic. It is required that you download the practice files (using the link found on the Practice Files page) prior to starting the first practice. • **Chapter Review Questions**, located close to the end of a chapter, enable you to test your knowledge of the key concepts discussed in the chapter.
Appendices	Appendices provide additional information to the main course content. It could be in the form of instructional content, practices, tables, projects, or skills assessment.

Practice Files

To download the practice files for this guide, use the following steps:

1. Type the URL *exactly as shown below* into the address bar of your Internet browser to access the Course File Download page.

   Note: If you are using the ebook, you do not have to type the URL. Instead, you can access the page by clicking the URL below.

   https://www.ascented.com/getfile/id/pantlingiaPF

2. On the Course File Download page, click the **DOWNLOAD NOW** button, as shown below, to download the .ZIP file that contains the practice files.

3. Once the download is complete, unzip the file and extract its contents.

   The recommended practice files folder location is:
   C:\Creo Parametric Introduction for Non-Designers Practice Files

   Note: It is recommended that you do not change the location of the practice files folder. Doing so may cause errors when completing the practices.

Stay Informed!
To receive information about upcoming events, promotional offers, and complimentary webcasts, visit:
www.ASCENTed.com/updates

Introduction to Creo Parametric

Understanding the construction of Creo Parametric models and their response to changes is essential for designing robust and intelligent models. Additionally, familiarizing oneself with the Creo Parametric working environment is important as it comprises various components such as toolbars, tabs, and menus. Interacting effectively with all these components can enhance modeling efficiency.

Learning Objectives

- Understand how Creo Parametric models are constructed using a feature-based approach.
- Describe the five key attributes of Creo Parametric and how they contribute to creating robust parts and assemblies.
- Understand design intent and how dimensioning contributes to building a robust model.
- Navigate the ribbon, toolbars, menus, and selection methods to locate and execute commands.
- Open existing files and create new files.
- Pan, zoom, rotate, and look at specific objects in a model using the various model orientation commands.
- Assign display styles to your models to accurately visualize them in your working environment.
- Explore object selection techniques to efficiently select objects in your models.

1.1 Solid Modeling

Solid modeling is the creation and manipulation of solid, 3D representations of a model. Creo Parametric is used to design solid 3D part models, resulting in a digital prototype of your product.

Creo Parametric can produce two kinds of 3D models: Solid and Surface.

Note: Surface models are covered in the Creo Parametric: Surface Design guide.

You can create drawings of parts, as shown in Figure 1−1. The part models and drawings can then be used for manufacturing.

Part model is referenced to create drawing views

Figure 1−1

Additionally, you can place existing models relative to one another in an assembly. The assemblies can then be referenced by a drawing, as shown in Figure 1−2.

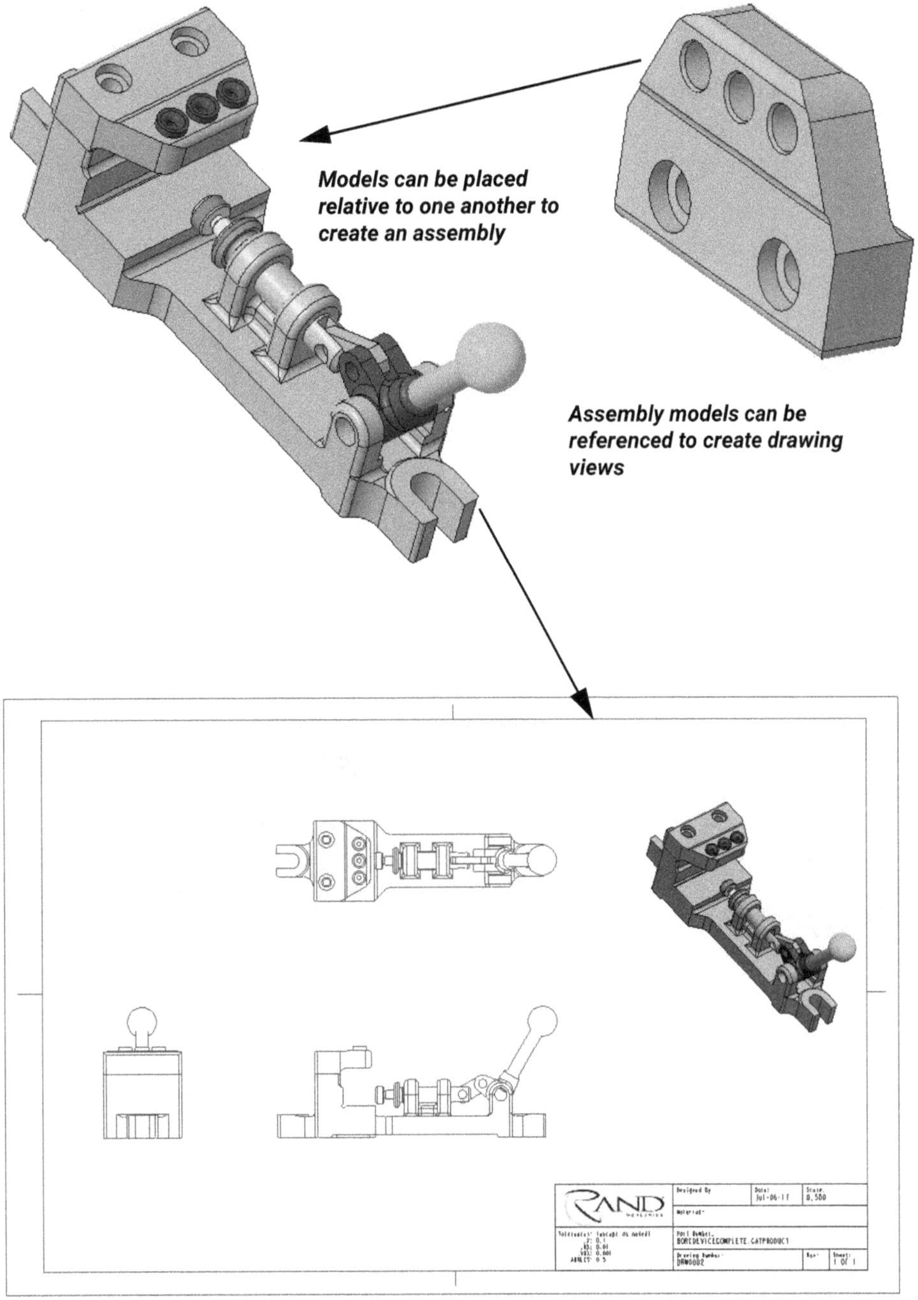

Models can be placed relative to one another to create an assembly

Assembly models can be referenced to create drawing views

Figure 1–2

1.2 Creo Parametric Fundamentals

Creo Parametric has the following four key attributes:

- Feature-based
- Parametric
- Associative
- Relations

Feature-Based

Creo Parametric is a feature-based modeling program, which means that a part evolves by creating features one by one until it is complete. Each feature is individually recognized by the system. Figure 1–3 shows a part model consisting of several individual features.

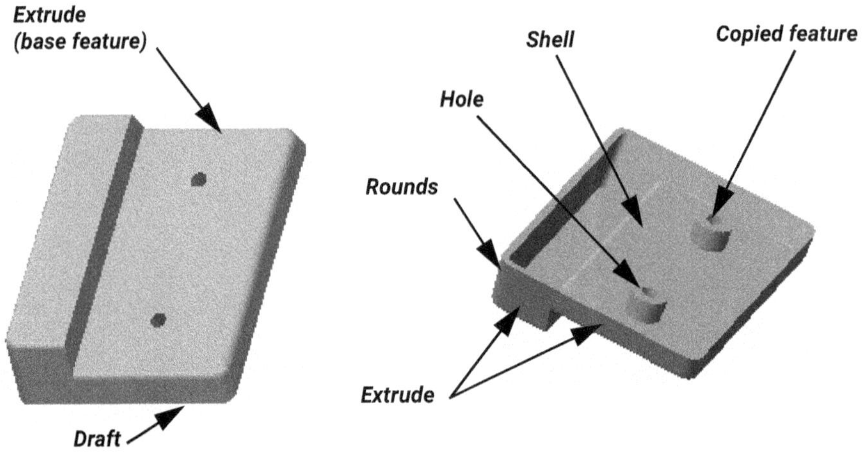

Figure 1–3

To start a design, create a simple extruded base feature that approximates the shape of the part and continue to add additional features until the part is complete, as shown in Figure 1–4.

1st (Base) Feature: Extrude

2nd Feature: Drafts

3rd Feature: Rounds

4th Feature: Shell

5th Feature: Extrude

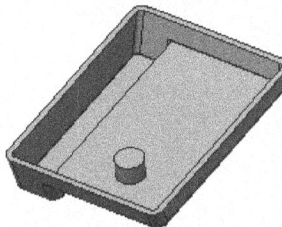

6th Feature: Hole

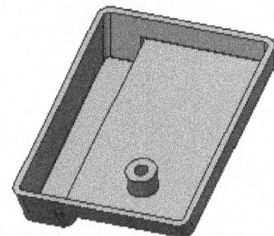

7th Feature: Copy

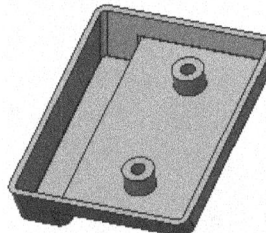

Figure 1–4

Note: Extruded features can either add or remove material from the model. Extrusions that remove material are commonly referred to as cuts. The following primary feature types are discussed in this guide:

- Sketched
- Engineering

Sketched Features

A sketched feature is created by sketching its shape or profile and it can be any shape and size. To create a sketched feature, you must sketch a 2D cross-section on the placement surface and then add dimensions to define and locate the sketched geometry with respect to the model, as shown in Figure 1-5.

Figure 1-5

Engineering Features

An Engineering feature is a feature for which a shape is predefined. For example, the cross-section of a hole feature is a circle. To create an Engineering feature, you must define the location of the feature and the references required to locate the feature with respect to the existing geometry. Figure 1-6 shows an example of a hole feature.

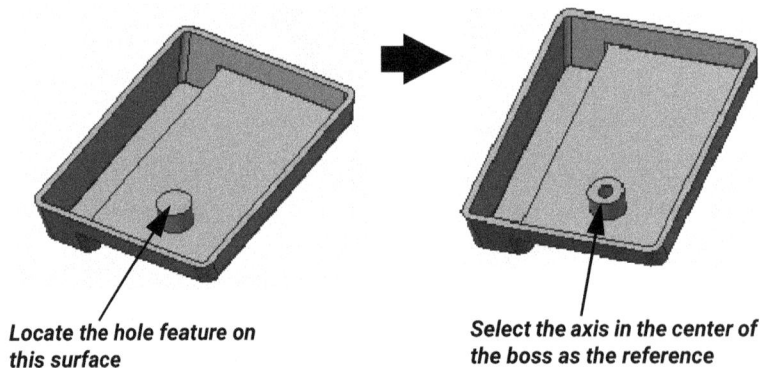

Locate the hole feature on this surface

Select the axis in the center of the boss as the reference

Figure 1-6

Parent/Child Relationships

Feature-based modeling requires that features be added one by one. As a result, *parent/child relationships* are created as new features reference existing features. For example, the hole shown in Figure 1−6 cannot exist without the cylindrical extruded feature because the hole's placement references exist in the extrusion. Parent/child relationships are created with all features.

Parametric

Creo Parametric is a parametric modeling tool. When creating geometry, precise dimensions are not required; only a conceptual idea of the shape of the object is required.

Geometry is said to be dimension-driven because dimensions are automatically applied to a part in the Creo Parametric software. However, you can change the applied dimensions and redimension as required. Dimension values can be modified to incorporate changes in a model, as shown in Figure 1−7.

Figure 1−7

*Note: Creo Parametric automatically assigns names (e.g., d1, d2) to dimensions. You can display either the name or value of the dimension. To switch between these two display modes, select **Model Intent>Switch Dimensions** in the Model tab.*

Dimensioning is an important step in the modeling process. In addition to the dimensions that are created automatically, you can create your own dimensions.

- When creating dimensions, consider those to be shown in drawings and be aware of any resulting parent/child relationships. Consider changes that might be made to the model in the future and how easily the dimensions facilitate these changes.

- Periodically modify the dimensions to test *what if* scenarios. This is called *flexing the model* and helps to eliminate future problems by verifying that the model behaves as expected when changes are incorporated.

Associative

Creo Parametric is fully associative, which enables you to work with the same model in different modes (e.g., Part mode, Assembly mode, or Drawing mode) and changes made to a model in any of the modes propagate to all other modes, as shown in Figure 1–8.

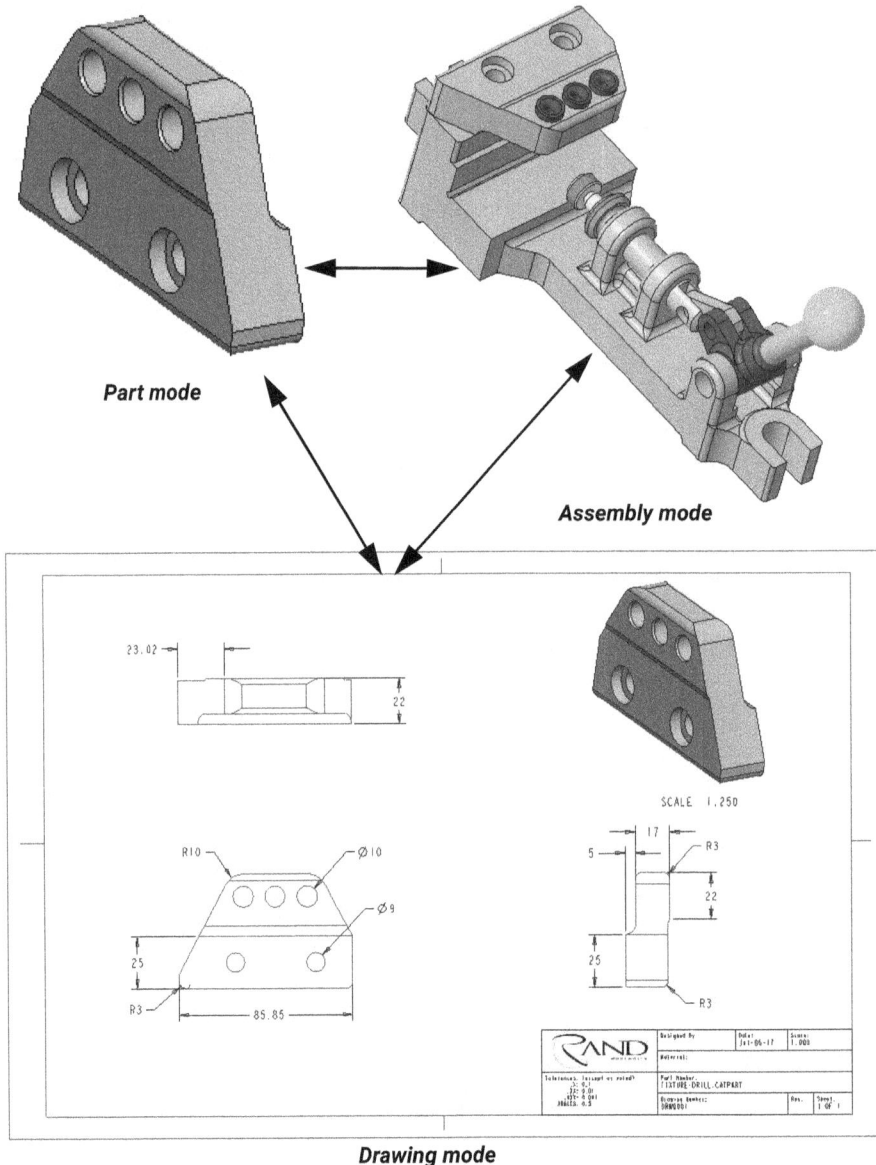

Part mode

Assembly mode

Drawing mode

Figure 1–8

Assembly Relationships

Models built in Creo Parametric Part mode can be used as components in assemblies. Assemblies are created by constraining components with respect to one another, rather than constraining them relative to one global position. The addition of these constraints incorporates parent/child relationships between components and builds intelligent assemblies.

Relations

Creo Parametric relations are user-defined mathematical equations used to capture and control design intent. Relations are created by writing equations using dimensions or parameters from the model, and help establish robust models.

For example, the following relation can be used to keep a hole centered on a block, as shown in Figure 1−9:

/* Relations to center hole
d6=d1/2
d7=d2/2

Figure 1−9

1.3 Design Intent

The key to building robust, parametric, feature-based, solid models is to construct them so that their behavior is flexible and predictable. The result of constructing them this way is known as the *design intent*.

- Design intent can be captured in a variety of ways. When creating models in the Creo Parametric software, pay special attention to the features used, how they are created (Engineering or Sketched), and the dimensioning scheme.

- The parent/child relationships established during feature creation and the explicit relations set up after feature creation are also important for incorporating design intent.

- There are various ways to incorporate the design intent into a models.

   Note: Creo Parametric also provides tools that enable you to change your design intent.

Dimensioning Scheme

One method of capturing design intent is to determine the feature's dimensioning scheme. Figure 1–10 shows an example of a part with a hole. When the base feature increases in length, the design intent of the hole determines how it behaves. If the hole is dimensioned to the outside face of the base feature, the hole moves, but remains 3.00 from that end. If the hole is dimensioned to the inside face, it remains 6.00 from that face.

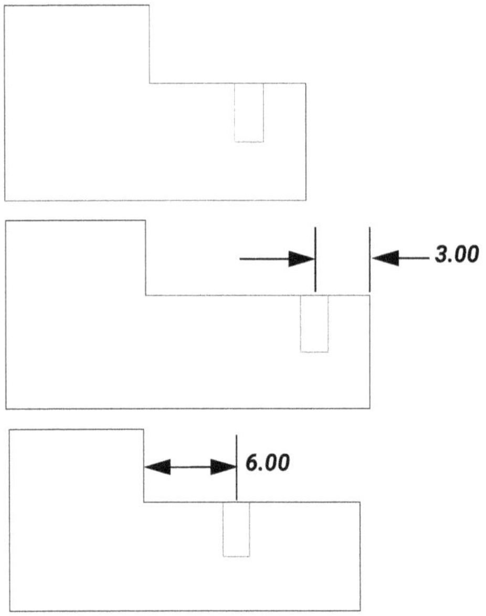

Figure 1–10

Symmetrical Geometry

A second method is to create symmetrical geometry. The design intent for the part shown in Figure 1-11 is to have the extruded cut remain at the center of the part. Constraining the cut from either end of the base feature does not capture the design intent. It is recommended to construct the base feature and cut relative to a center datum reference, or to use relations to capture this design intent.

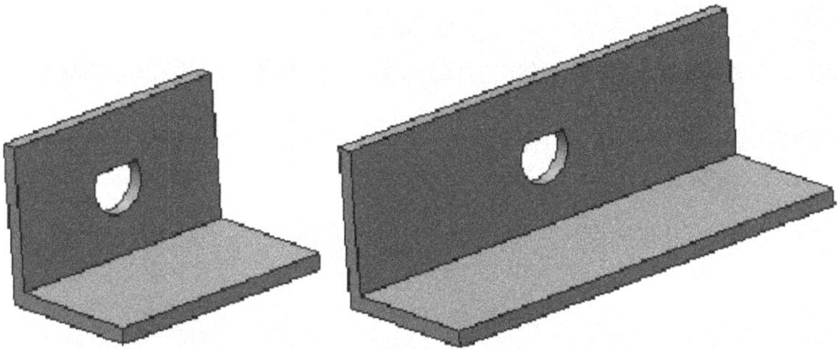

Figure 1-11

Depth Options

A third method is to determine the type of depth required for your feature. Figure 1-12 shows a part a part with a hole, whose design intent is for the hole to pass through the entire model. When the base feature changes from **5.00** to **6.00**, the resulting geometry displays differently depending on the depth option set for the hole. If the hole is given a blind depth value of **5.00**, it no longer passes through the entire part. Therefore, the hole depth must also be changed to maintain the design intent. A better solution is to set the depth option for the hole to **Through All**. In this scenario, the hole always passes through the part, regardless of the height of the base feature.

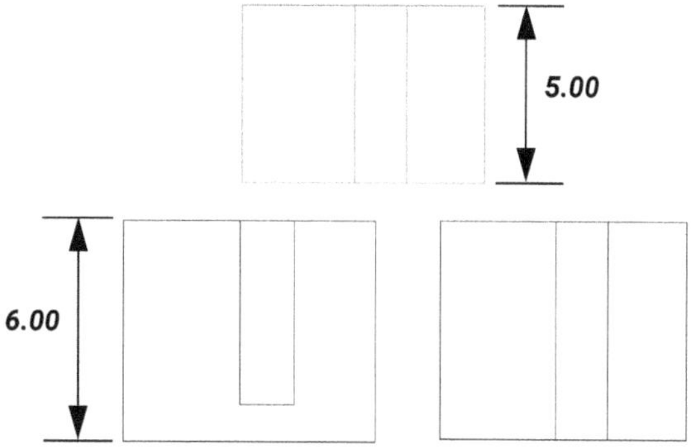

Figure 1-12

1.4 Creo Parametric Interface

The Creo Parametric user interface enables you to work with your models in a variety of ways using a ribbon style interface with tabs. Its development addresses ease of use, accessibility, and efficiency. Figure 1–13, Figure 1–14, and Figure 1–15 show the current layout of the Creo Parametric software interface.

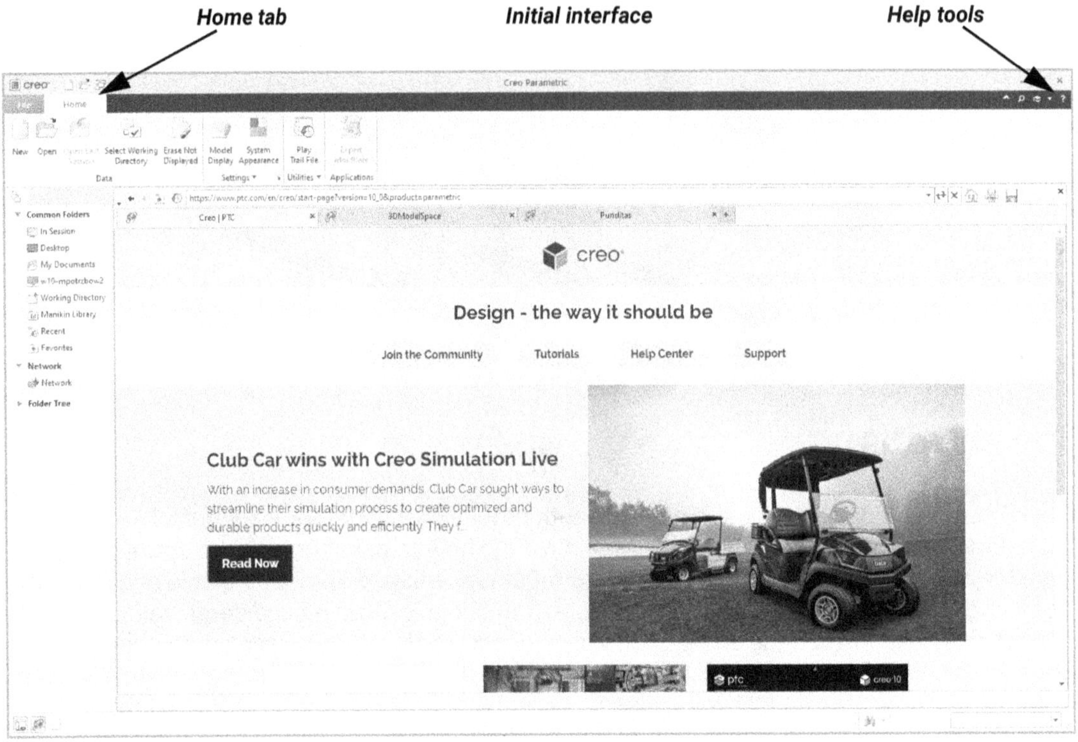

Figure 1–13

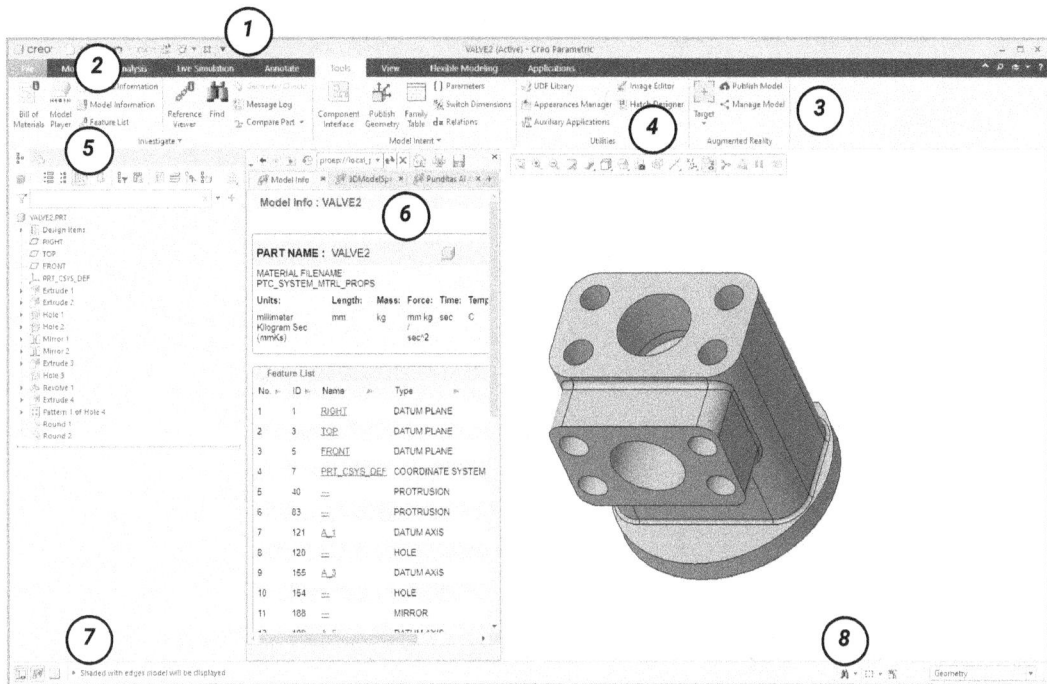

Figure 1-14

1. Quick Access Toolbar	Used for quick access to frequently used icons.
2. Tabs	Contain collections of related icons.
3. Ribbon	Contains collections of functions grouped together in tabs.
4. Groups	Used to further organize related ions in the tabs.
5. Navigator	Contains multiple tabs for the Model Tree, Folder Browser, and Favorites.
6. Creo Parametric Browser	Displays the contents of the embedded web browser and other pages such as feature information.
7. Status Bar	Displays the regeneration status. Also has icons for controlling the display of the navigator and browser.
8. Selection Filter	The options in this drop-down list enable you to refine what you can select in the model.

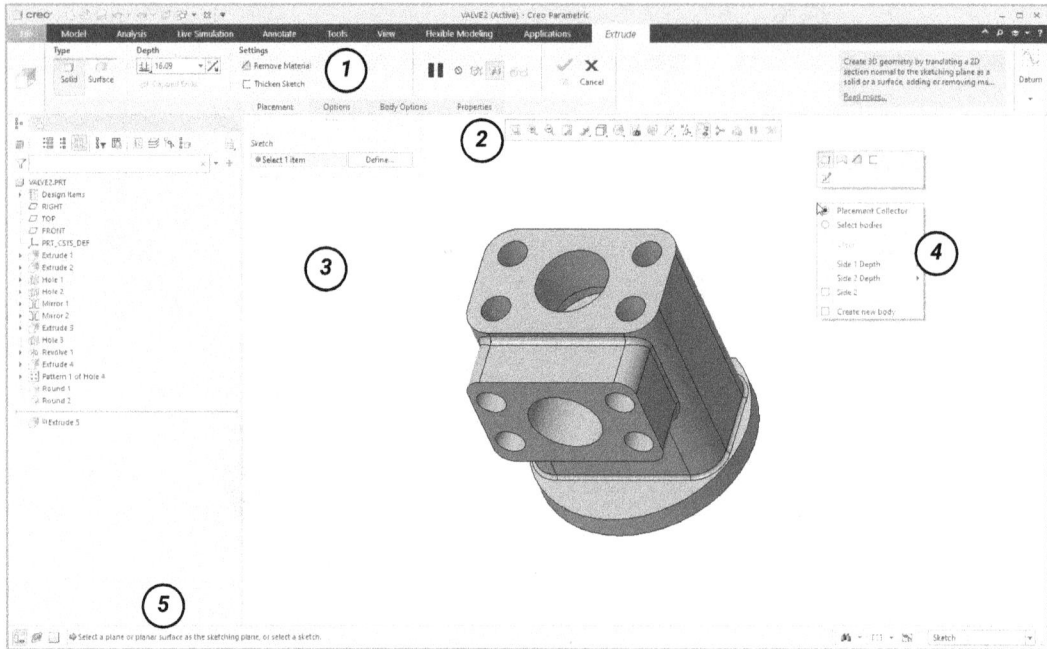

Figure 1–15

1. **Dashboard**	Contains options used when creating features.
2. **In-graphics Toolbar**	Contains icons to control the display of the model.
3. **Graphics (Main) Window**	Displays the model.
4. **Contextual Menu**	Can be displayed by right-clicking.
5. **Message Window**	System messages and prompts display in the multi-line message window.

Menus

In the Creo Parametric software, menus are used to create and manipulate a model. Examples of the different menu types are described as follows:

- Group Overflow Buttons: Display additional options in the Ribbon, as shown in Figure 1–16.

- Menu Manager: In limited cases, the menu manager (shown in Figure 1–17) is used to run specific operations and displays at the right side of the main window.

Figure 1–16   **Figure 1–17**

- Mini Toolbar: The *mini* toolbar displays when you select an entity (shown in Figure 1–18) either directly from the model, or from the Model Tree.

  Important: *The mini toolbar displays when you left-click on an entity. If you right-click on an entity, in addition to the typical right-click options, the mini toolbar also displays.*

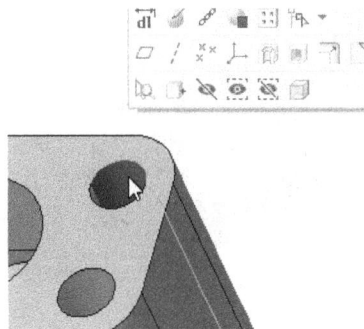

Figure 1–18

The *mini* toolbar provides access to common tools that you can use, based on the selected entity. For example, if you select a face of the model, ✐ (Extrude) will be one of the available tools, but if you select an edge, ⤳ (Round) will be one of the options. These options will be covered later in this course.

- Contextual Menus: Select a feature in the model or Model Tree and right-click to display the *mini* toolbar as well as contextual menus, as shown in Figure 1-19.

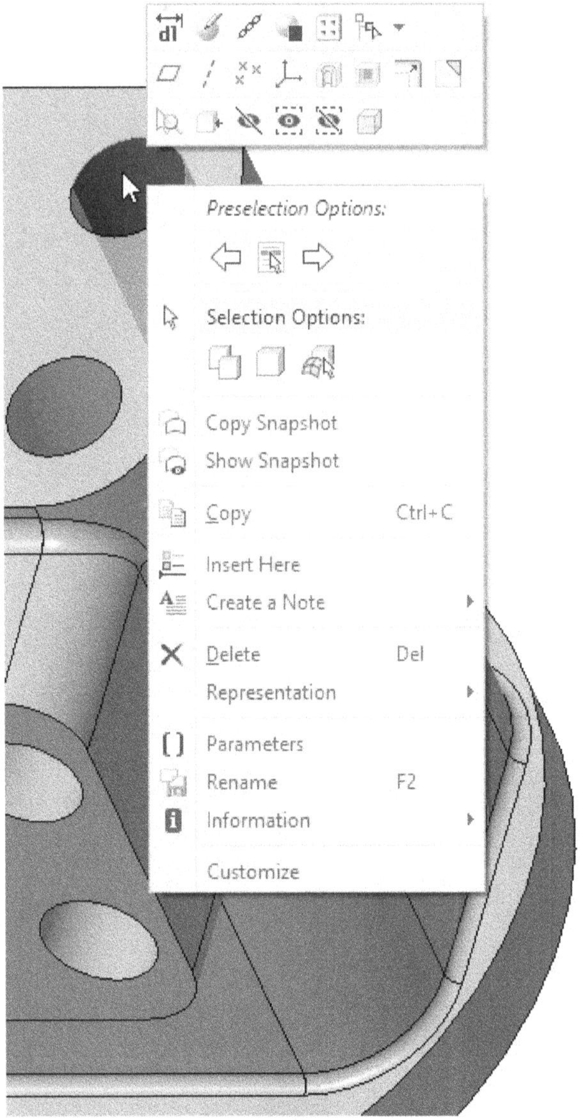

Figure 1-19

- When the option is selected, it highlights in blue, indicating that it is the active option. Options that are dimmed or grayed are not available for selection, indicating they are not applicable to the action being performed. Some selections in the menus display additional options. Figure 1–20 shows the additional menus associated with the **Information** option.

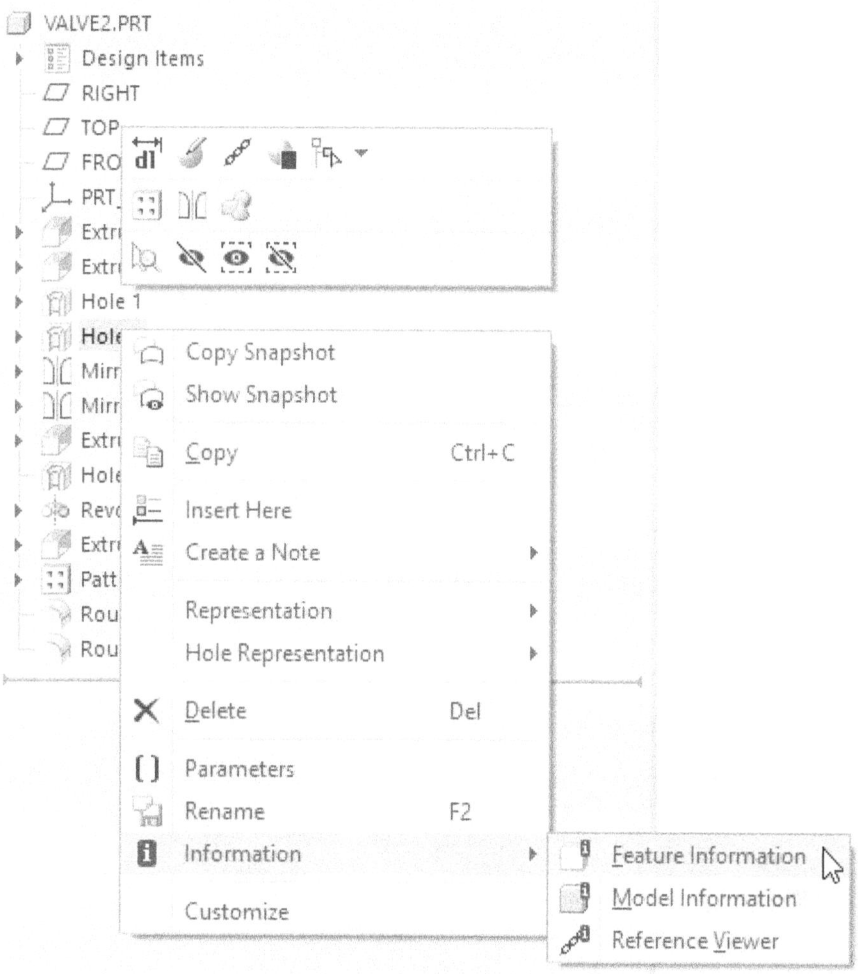

Figure 1–20

Toolbars

The shortcut icons, available in the toolbars, enable you to select commonly used options with one click of the mouse.

In-Graphics Toolbar

The default icons found in the *In-graphics* toolbar are listed as follows:

Icon	Description	Icon	Description
	Refit		Saved Orientations
	Zoom In		View Manager
	Zoom Out		Perspective View
	Repaint		Datum Display Filters
	Rendering Options		Annotation Display
	Display Style		Spin Center
	Simulate		Animation Options

Quick Access Toolbar

The default icons found in the Quick Access toolbar are listed as follows:

Icon	Description	Icon	Description
	New		Regenerate
	Open		Windows
	Save		Close
	Undo		Customize Quick Access Toolbar
	Redo		

Tabs and Ribbons

The Creo Parametric software uses a ribbon style interface with tabs. Tasks are grouped under tabs and common icons related to the task are grouped under the tab. For example, all icons related to the display, orientation, and model setup are located in the *View* tab, as shown in Figure 1–21.

- The ribbon can be collapsed for more viewing space by clicking ▲ or by double-clicking on a tab. When the ribbon is collapsed, click once on the tab to temporarily display it. To return the ribbon to the default display, click ▼ or double-click on the tab.

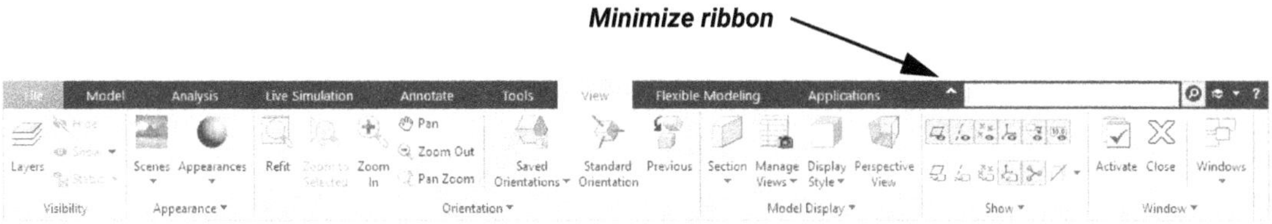

Figure 1–21

File Tab

The *File* tab contains menu choices that enable you to perform some basic tasks, as shown in Figure 1–22. Previously opened files are also listed in the *File* tab, enabling you to quickly access the files.

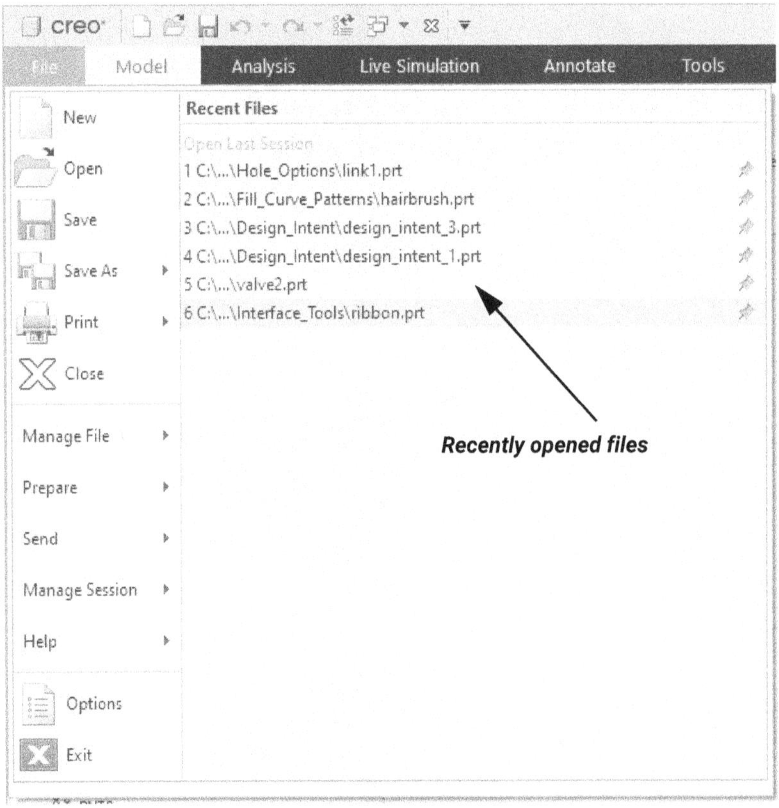

Figure 1–22

Creo Parametric Browser

By default, the software launches with a browser window that covers the main graphics window. The browser provides you with the standard capabilities of any internet browser. The default address opens PTC's Creo Parametric 11.0 Home page (**https://www.ptc.com/en/**). The page contains links to tools to help you learn and become productive. Several other tabs may be present:

- **PARTcommunity 3D CAD manufacturer catalogs** is a webpage that enables you to search for free 3D CAD models and 2D drawings. You can download the files to your system.

- **3DModelSpace** is a webpage located in one of the default tabs of the software. It is a web search engine for 3D and 2D CAD files of purchased items. These CAD files can be used by engineers in their product designs.

- **Punditas** is an Artificial Intelligence (AI) driven Knowledge Platform for CAD, PLM, IoT, and other Enterprise Applications.

  *Note: To change the default browser address, set the **configuration option** (discussed later in this guide) **web_browser_ homepage** to the required URL.*

How To: Disable the Default Browser from Opening Each Time Creo Parametric Is Launched

1. Expand the *File* tab and select **Options**. The *Creo Parametric Options* dialog box opens.
2. Select **Window Settings**.
3. In the *Browser settings*, clear the **Expand the browser during startup** option.
4. Click **OK** to close the dialog box.

The browser's size can be set as a percentage (%) of the window's width by setting the **Set Browser width as a percentage of main window to be** option to a value between **25** and **100**.

Figure 1–23 shows the browser icons and how to deactivate the browser.

PART Community tab   *3DModelSpace tab*   *Punditas*

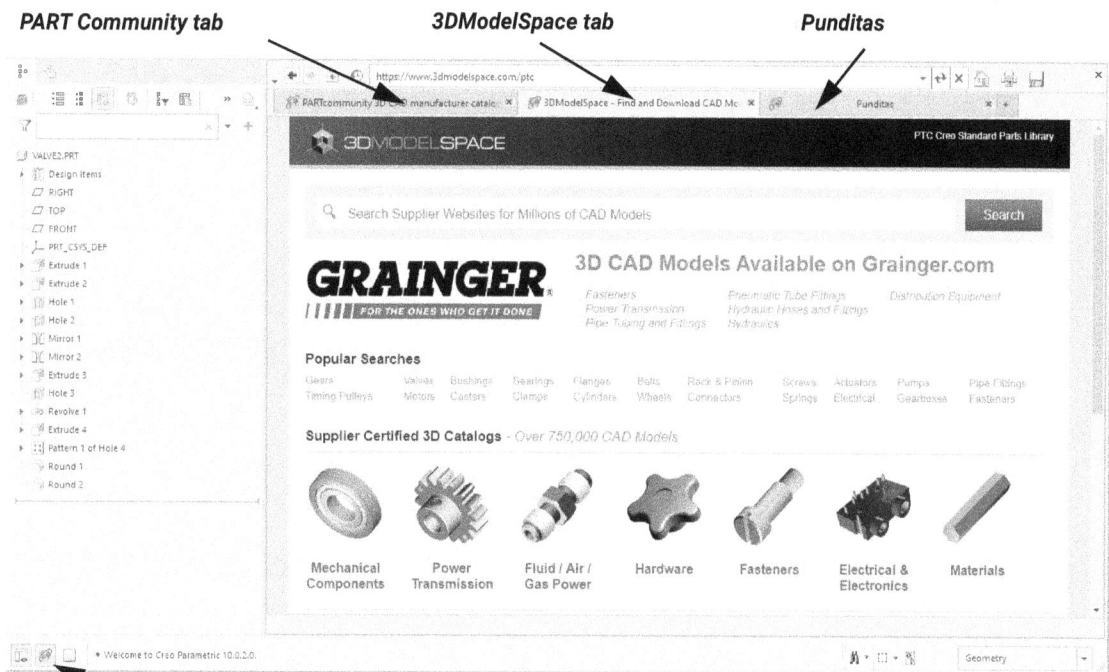

To close the browser, select this button. Use it to expand it, once it has been closed.

Figure 1–23

Some of the icons in the *Tools* tab provide feedback in the browser (e.g., ⬚ (Feature Information) or ⬚ (Model Information)). Certain information is provided with a hyperlink (blue font and underlined) to the model, as shown in Figure 1−24. This enables you to highlight the information directly in the model for easier identification. Click ⬚ (Show Browser) in the lower left of the window to hide the browser.

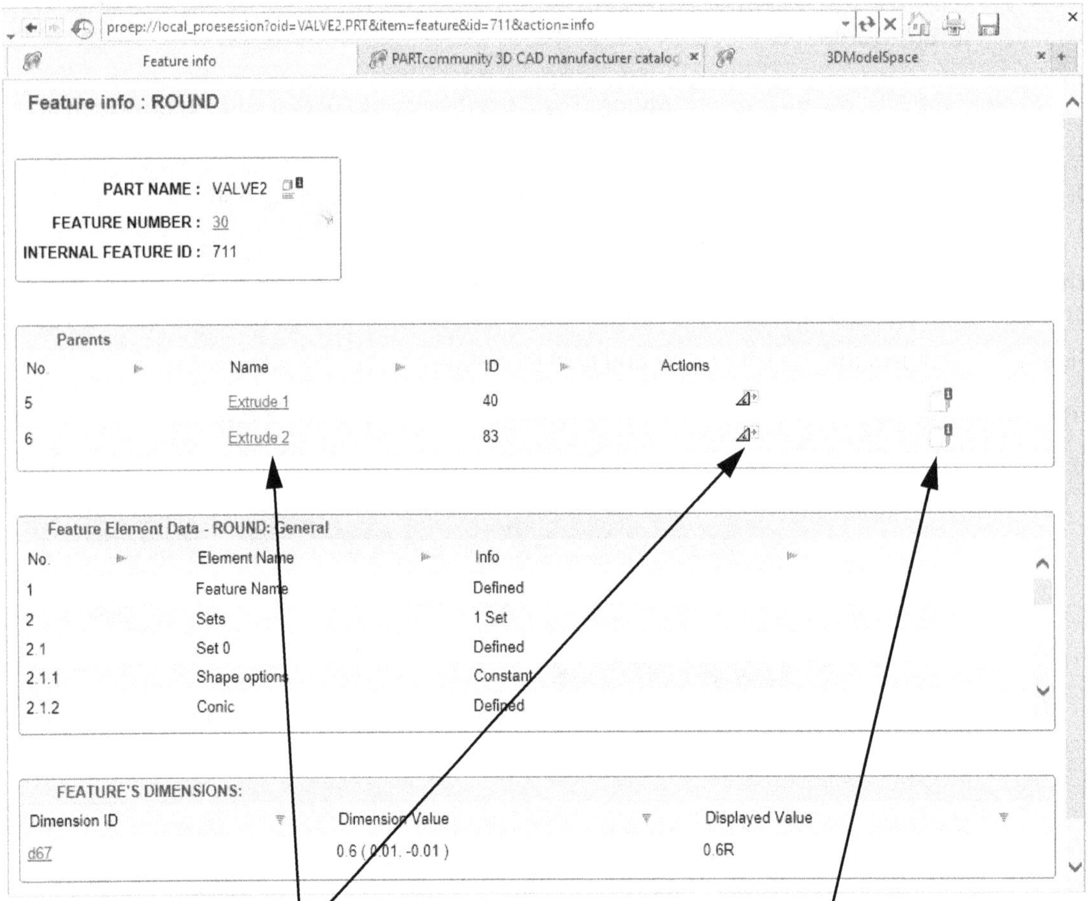

Select this hyperlink or icon to highlight the feature on the model

This icon provides additional information on the listed feature

Figure 1−24

Navigator

The Navigator, found on the left section of the interface, includes the following components:

- Folder Browser
- Model Tree

Folder Browser 🗀

The *Folder Browser* is the default tab that displays when you launch Creo Parametric. It enables you to browse the local file system and local network. When you select one of the directories listed in the Folder Navigator, the browser is replaced with detailed information about the directory and its files, as shown in Figure 1–25. You can set the working directory by right-clicking on the directory and selecting **Set Working Directory** or by clicking 🗀 (Select Working Directory) in the *Home* tab.

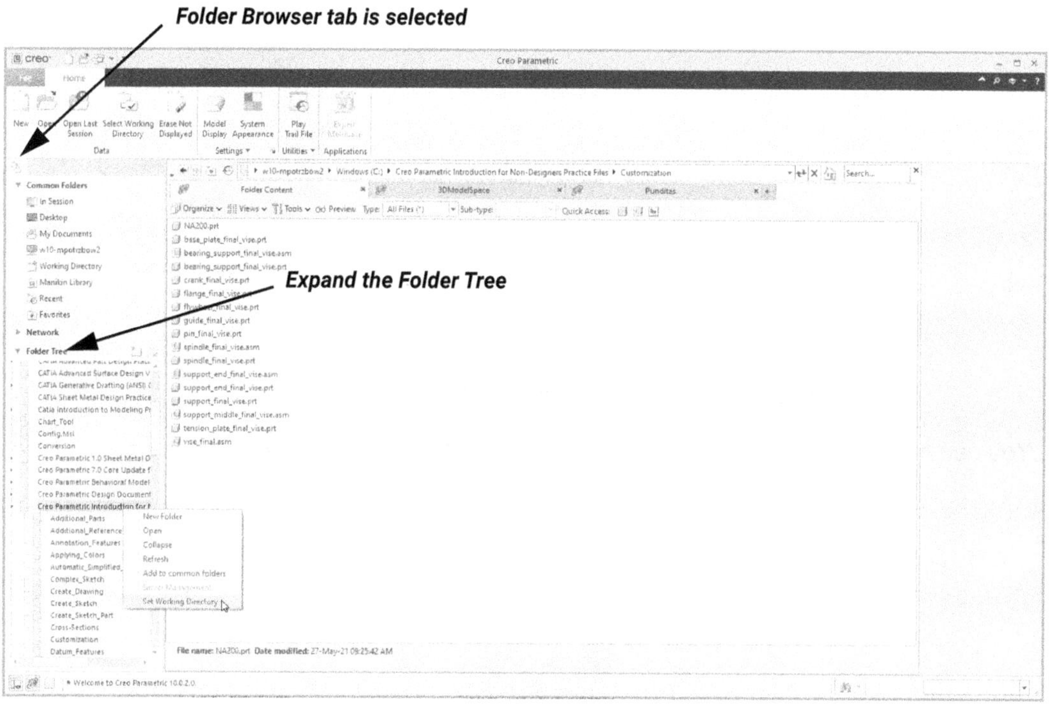

Figure 1–25

*Note: Additional locations such as Windchill servers, ftp locations, etc. can be added to the Folder Navigator by selecting **File>Manage Session>Server management**.*

Select the filename in the directory and then select 👓 **Preview** at the top-center to preview models using ProductView Express (installed by default with the Creo Parametric software).

The model displays at the bottom of the browser, as shown in Figure 1–26. Select 👓 **Preview** again when you have finished viewing the model.

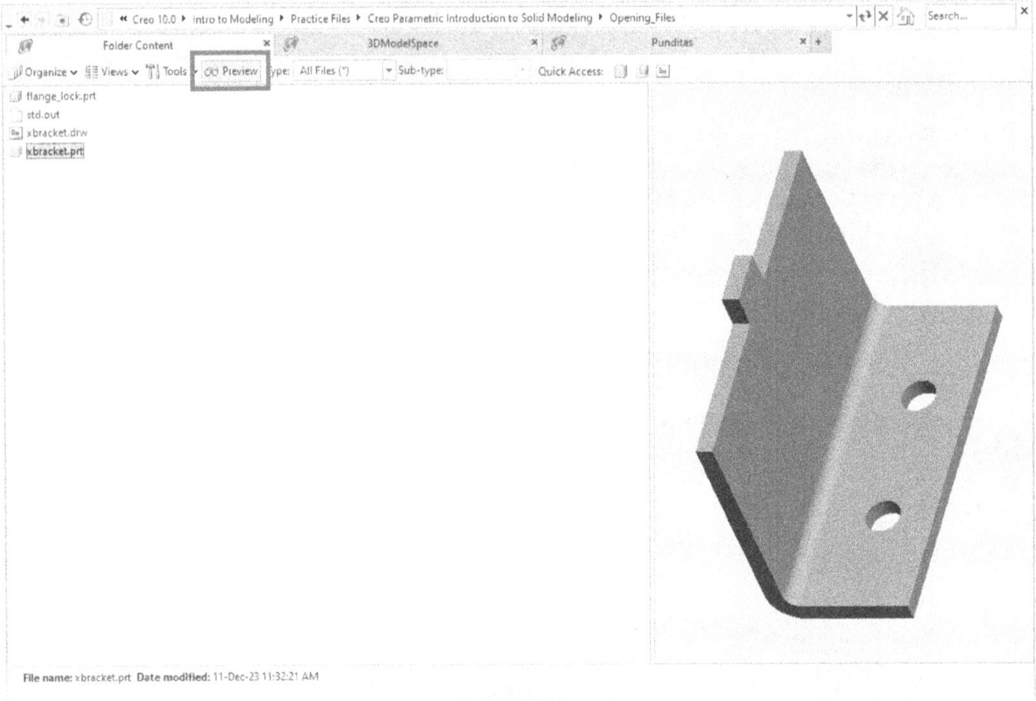

Figure 1–26

- You can open files directly from the directory listing by double-clicking on them.

Navigation Trees ⣿

The Navigation Trees is activated by default in the Navigator when a file is opened, as shown in Figure 1−27. This tab displays a number of different information trees available within Creo. These custom tree structures are differentiated by icons and allow for specific objects of the file to be focused on based on the tree type that is displayed. The tree structure can include but is not limited to Model Tree, Design Tree, Layer Tree and Drawing Tree.

The Navigation Tree tab is selected

The Model Tree icon

Select this icon to Hide/Show the NavigationTree

VALVE2.PRT
▸ Design Items
RIGHT
TOP
FRONT
PRT_CSYS_DEF
▸ Extrude 1
▸ Extrude 2
▸ Hole 1
▸ Hole 2
▸ Mirror 1
▸ Mirror 2
▸ Extrude 3
Hole 3
▸ Revolve 1
▸ Extrude 4
▸ Pattern 1 of Hole 4
Round 1
Round 2

Figure 1−27

Icon	Name	Description
	Model Tree	List of model features organized in a hierarchical structure. Shown by default when a part is open.
	Design Tree	Separates the Design Items node of the model tree so it can be displayed in its own list.
	Layer Tree	Allows for the creation and manipulation of layers, their associated items, and their display status.
	Drawing Tree	Displays the sheets, views and annotations created in the drawing file.

Note: *The Model Tree will be focus of this chapter, however all four will be discussed later in the training material.*

The Model Tree displays all of the features contained in your models. All objects are listed in the order of creation. It is a powerful tool that can be used for any of the following actions:

- Selecting features and bodies
- Renaming features and bodies
- Accessing commonly used options (e.g., **Delete** or **Edit Definition**)
- Searching
- Creating and editing parameters
- Editing features
- Viewing information on features
- Changing the order of features (click and drag)
- Inserting features or bodies
- Opening components in an assembly

To the right of the model tree icon is a set of options that allow customization of the model tree display. The number of icon options displayed depends on the width you have the Navigator. Figure 1-28 shows what the navigator looks like when the width is smaller than the number of options available. Select the " (Expand) icon to see all hidden icons temporarily. The Navigator can also be widened by clicking and dragging the left side of the window.

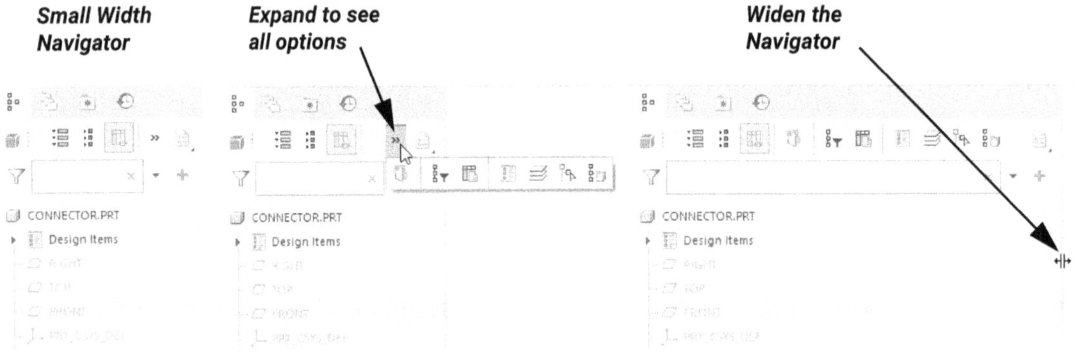

Figure 1-28

A table of all the available Model Tree options are shown below.

Icon	Description	Icon	Description
	Expand by Level		Design Tree
	Collapse All		Layer Tree
	Hide or Show Columns		Select Related
	Create Custom Group		Quilt/Body Evolution Tree
	Tree Filter		Model Tree Settings
	Tree Columns		

Note: The options for the Design Tree, Layer Tree and Drawing Tree can and will be different.

To customize the Model Tree to show or remove specific information (e.g., remove all suppressed features), select the ⓣ (Tree Filters). Select the required options in the Tree Filters dialog box, as shown in Figure 1-29.

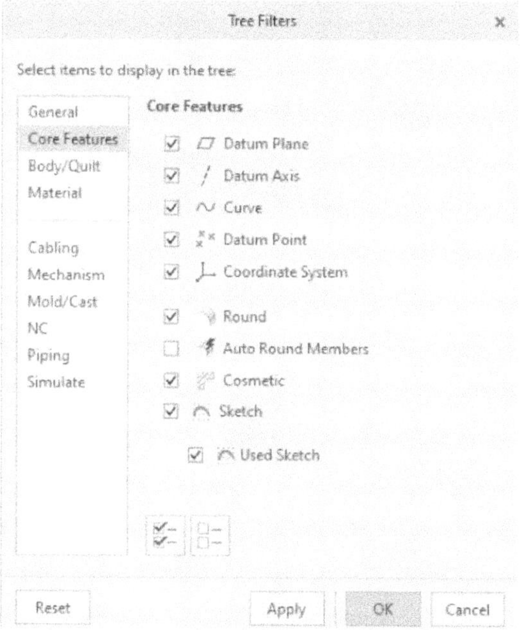

Figure 1-29

The display of the columns of the Model Tree can also be customized to include additional information on your model. To add or remove columns to the Model Tree, select the 🔳 (Tree Columns).

The *Model Tree Columns* dialog box displays, as shown in Figure 1–30. Select an option in the *Type* drop-down list menu to add column information.

Some common Type options are described as follows:

Options	Description
Info	Enables you to add columns of information regarding your model (Status, Feat #, Feat ID, Feat Type, Feat Name).
Model Params	Enables you to add a column in the Model Tree that displays the model's parameters and their values.
Feat Params	Enables you to add a column in the Model Tree that displays the feature parameters and their values.
Simplified Reps	Enables you to add a column in the Model Tree indicating the simplified representation name and the features/components that were selected to create it.
Layer	Enables you to add a column to the Model Tree that indicates layer names and their status.
Note	Enables you to add a column to the Model Tree that displays information on a note (Note ID, First Line, Note Display, URL, Note Type).

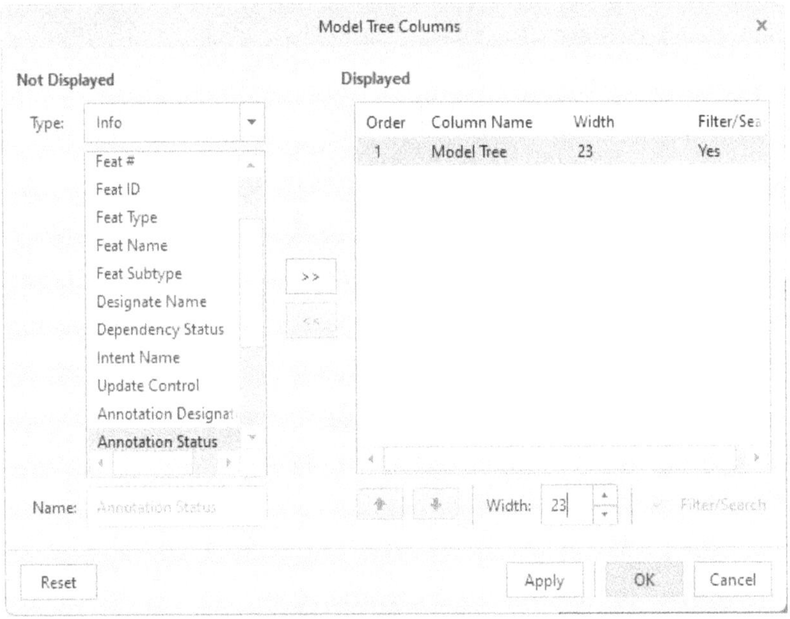

Figure 1–30

Favorites ✳

By default, the *Favorites* area in the Navigator is disabled. To enable it, access the browser and click ✳ (Favorites). Once enabled, this area provides you with a list of all of the websites that have been previously saved as Favorites, as shown in Figure 1−31.This tab enables you to bookmark your favorite websites, as shown in Figure 1−31.

The Favorites tab is selected

Add...   Organ...   ✕

Personal Favorites

▾ Online Resources

3DModelSpace

User Area

User Group

ptc.com

Technical Support

Rand Worldwide

Figure 1−31

*Note: Favorites are saved each time the Creo Parametric software is closed. An alternative way to enable Favorites is to select **File>Options>Windows Settings> Navigation Tab Settings>Show Favorites tab**.*

- To add bookmarks to your list, access the webpage and click ⬚ (Add Favorite). By default, all bookmarks are included at one level.

- Click ⬚ (Organize Favorites) and use the *Organize Favorites* dialog box to create, rename, and delete folders.

History ⊕

By default, the *History* area in the Navigator is disabled. To enable it, access the browser and click ⊕ (History). Once enabled, this area provides you with a list of all of the websites that have been previously visited, as shown in Figure 1–32.

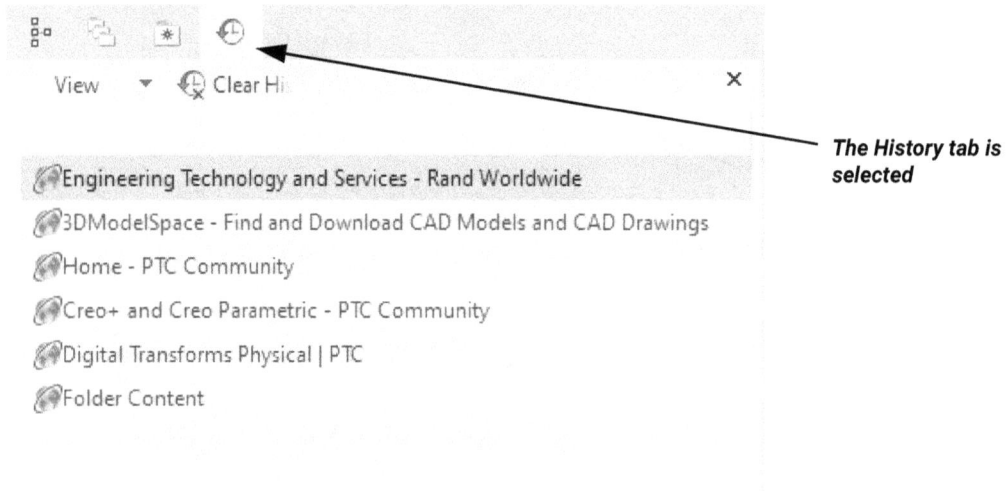

The History tab is selected

Figure 1–32

Note: The History Browser is not the same as the history list created in your standard browser.

Click **View** in the History Browser to display the history according to the following criteria:

- By Date
- By Site
- By Most Visited
- By Order Visited Today

To clear all of the history recorded from your browser, click ⊕ (Clear History). To disable the History Browser, click ✕ in the top right corner of the Navigator.

*Note: The **config.pro** option, web_browser_history_days, enables you to specify the number of days to store the history record.*

Toggle Full Screen

To provide more working area, you can toggle the Full Screen mode by pressing <F11>, or by clicking ☐ (Full Screen) in the lower left of the Creo Parametric window. The window expands to fill the entire screen, while the ribbon, the Model Tree, and the message bar disappear from the display, as shown in Figure 1-33.

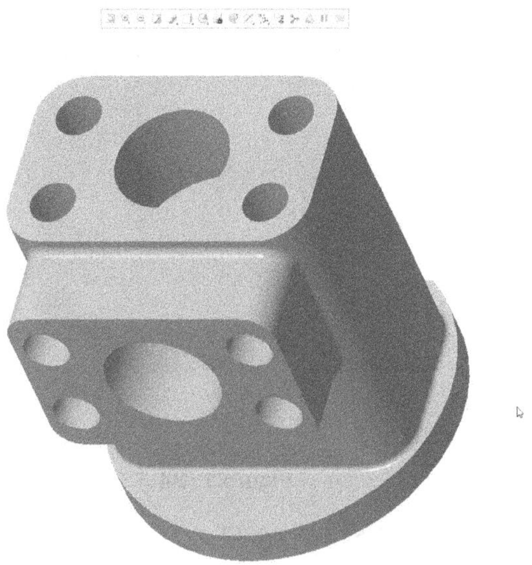

Figure 1-33

To view the ribbon, the Model Tree, or the message bar when in the Full Screen mode, move the cursor to the appropriate location and the corresponding item displays until you move the cursor off of it.

For example, move the cursor to where the Model Tree is located, and the Model Tree displays, as shown in Figure 1–34.

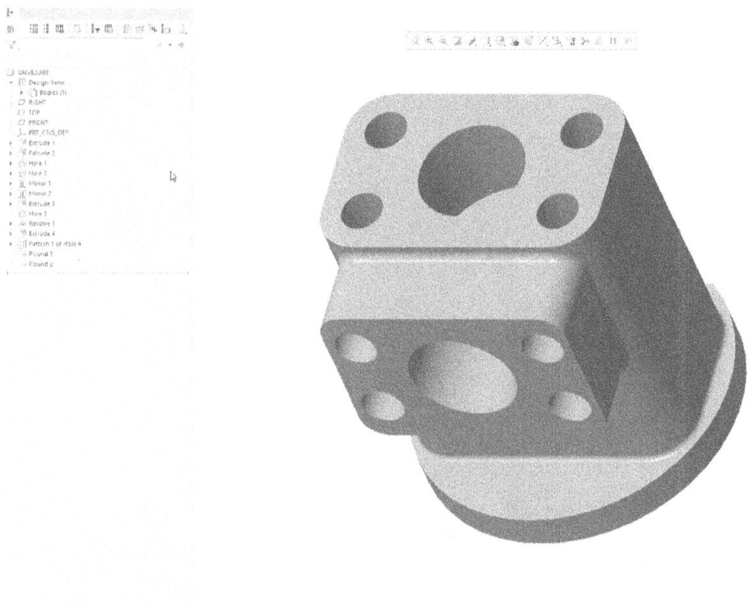

Figure 1–34

To exit the Full Screen mode, press <F11> again.

Feature Creation Controls

When you create a feature, you can define a variety of elements or properties, such as sketch, direction, and depth. To define these elements, you use either the ribbon interface or a feature dialog box.

Dashboard

When creating most features, a tab that corresponds to the feature being created displays in the ribbon at the top of the Creo Parametric window. This tab is referred to as the feature dashboard. All elements can be defined using the available icons and panels. Figure 1–35 shows the dashboard that is used to create an **Extrude** feature. The options in the tab vary depending on the feature being created. Features such as extrusions and rounds are created using this dashboard interface.

Figure 1–35

Panels display when you click the labels in the bottom row of the dashboard and enable you to select references, define additional elements, and modify the properties of the feature. The options that display in the main area of the dashboard vary according to the feature being defined. For example, the *Options* panel for an extrude feature is shown in Figure 1−36.

Figure 1−36

The icons that display on the right side of the dashboard are accessible for all features and are described in the table below:

Icon	Description
❙❙	Pauses feature creation and enables you to access other features.
▶	Resumes feature creation.
⊘	Removes the preview from the view window.
🔲	Displays an outline of the new geometry before the feature is finalized.
🔲	Displays a preview of the geometry and enables you to continue to make changes to the geometry.
🔲	Displays a preview of new geometry before the feature is finalized. Allows you to verify that the geometry will regenerate given the current parameters.
✓	Completes the feature. Results are displayed in the main window.
✕	Exits or cancels out of a dashboard.

Message Window

The message window at the bottom of the main window displays information and prompts. It can provide information and require you to enter information, as shown in Figure 1–37.

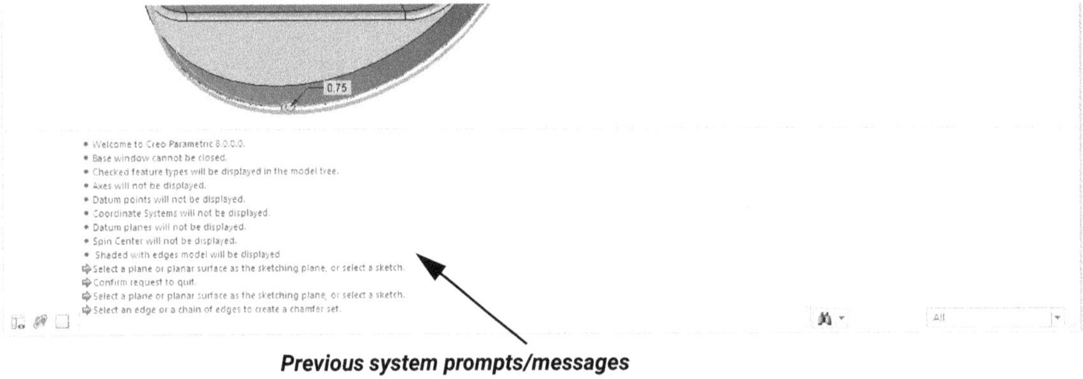

Previous system prompts/messages

Figure 1–37

The system presents the current prompt at the bottom of the message window, and near the cursor when you move the cursor away from geometry, as shown in Figure 1–38.

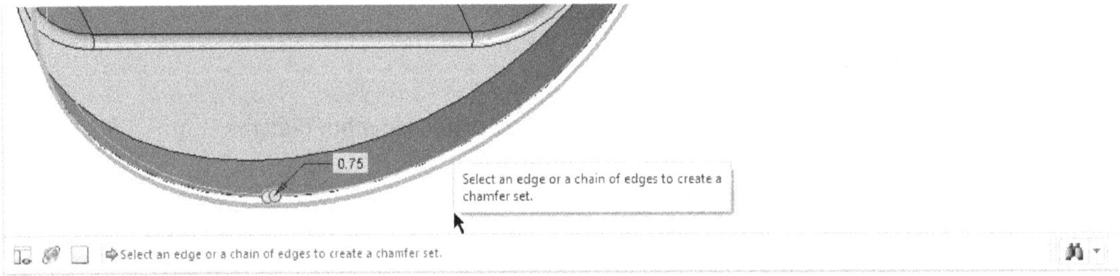

Figure 1–38

Old prompts can be found by scrolling up in the message window. You can use the scroll bars on the right side of the message window to display the old prompts. You can also click

 (Message Log) in the *Tools* tab to display older message lines. By default, the number of visible message lines is set to two. To change this, select the top border of the message window and once ÷ is displayed, drag up or down as required.

Help Options

Several help tools are available at the top right corner of the main window, as shown in Figure 1–39. These options can help provide direction when you are using a new tool or trying to locate the tool.

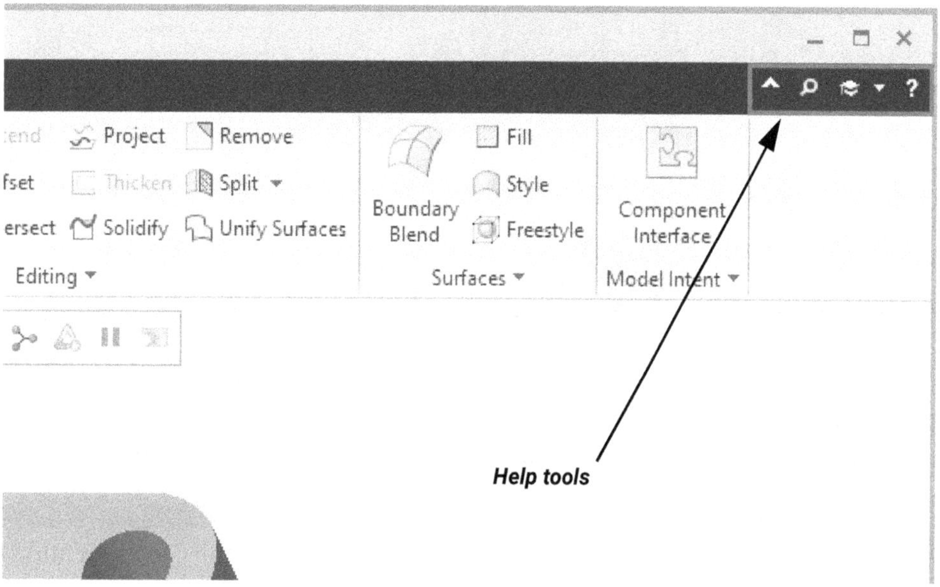

Help tools

Figure 1–39

The icons available are described as follows:

Icon	Description
🔍	Command search helps you to find an existing command in Creo Parametric.
☁	The **PTC Learning Connector** option requires you to set up an account and enables you to search for topics.
❓	Creo Help tool enables you to search for topics.

- 🔍 (Command Search): Launches the command search, as shown in Figure 1–40.

Figure 1–40

If you type the name of the command that you are looking for, the tool lists one or more commands that match your search. If you hover over the listed command, the location for that tool highlights in the associated tab and location, as shown in Figure 1–41.

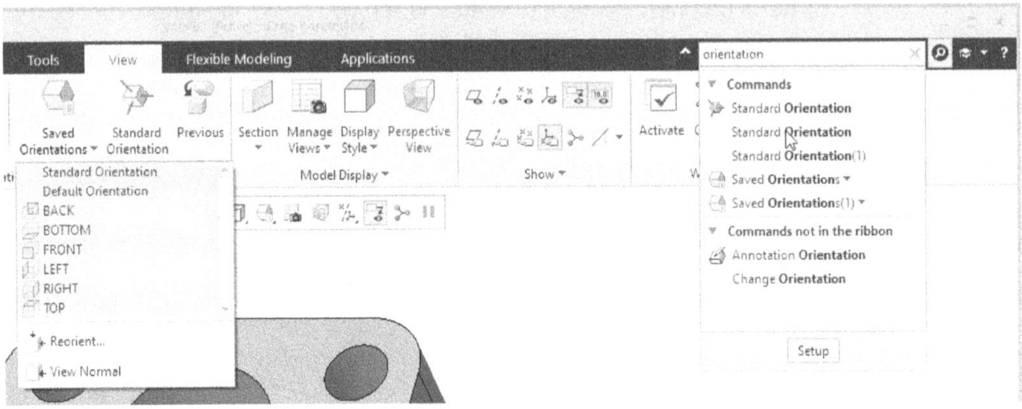

Figure 1–41

* ❓ (PTC Creo Parametric Help): Opens the *Creo Help* dialog box, as shown in Figure 1–42. You can select a topic or search for a topic by typing key words and clicking **Search**.

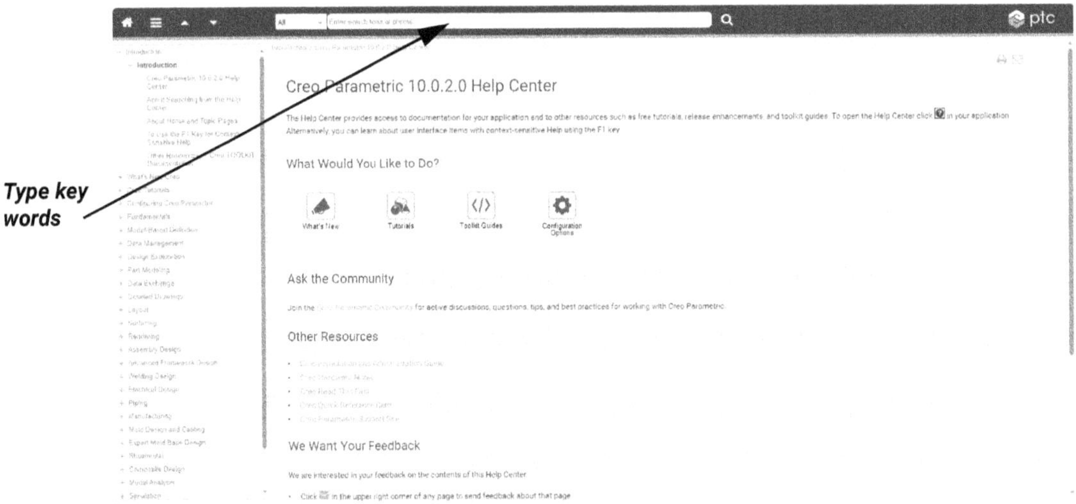

Figure 1–42

Commands

Icons can be of different sizes, depending on the size of the main window. When the window becomes smaller, the icons might lose their labels and the large icons become smaller, as shown in Figure 1–43. This enables the entire ribbon to be displayed. Icons called *split icons* contain an arrow indicating that other commands are available in the flyout, as shown in Figure 1–44. Clicking an icon that contains an arrow launches the command. Clicking the arrow next to the icon opens the corresponding flyout menu, as shown in Figure 1–45.

Icons without labels	**Icons with labels**	**Icon with flyout options**
Figure 1–43	**Figure 1–44**	**Figure 1–45**

- Hovering the cursor over an icon opens a tool-tip containing a brief description of any item, such as a menu option, icon, or model geometry.

- Hotkeys are another method that you can use to select tabs or commands. You can display the hotkeys for the tabs and other commands by pressing <Alt>. The hotkeys display below the command or tab, as shown in Figure 1–46. To remove the display of hotkeys, select anywhere on the screen or press <Alt> again.

Press <Alt>+<1> to activate the new file command

Click <T> to activate the Tools tab

Note that the hotkey for repaint is <Alt>+<ZD>

Figure 1–46

Note: *Traditional hotkeys also work. For example, you can press <Ctrl>+<Z> to undo a previous task.*

1.5 Manipulating a Model

Modes

This guide covers the following four basic modes of operation in Creo Parametric:

- Sketcher mode
- Part mode
- Assembly mode
- Drawing mode

To work in these modes, click ☐ (New) to create a new file. Alternatively, you can click ☖ (Open) to open an existing file. When you create a new file, you must select a type of file to create in the *New* dialog box. This determines the Creo Parametric mode. All existing files are stored with mode-specific extensions. The *New* and *File Open* dialog boxes are shown in Figure 1–47.

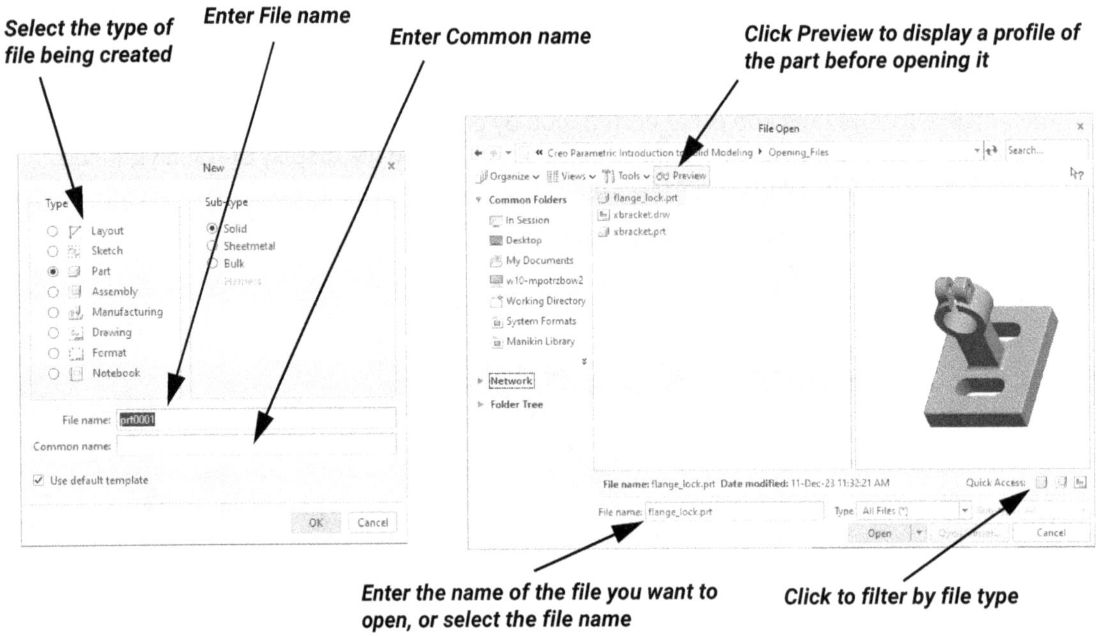

Select the type of file being created

Enter File name

Enter Common name

Click Preview to display a profile of the part before opening it

Enter the name of the file you want to open, or select the file name

Click to filter by file type

Figure 1–47

*Note: The **New** and **Open** options are also available using <Ctrl>+<N> and <Ctrl>+<O> respectively.*

The File menu displays the most recently opened files. They can be quickly retrieved by selecting the name of the file.

Multiple Windows

Multiple files can be opened in a Creo Parametric session. The first file that is opened displays in the main graphics window. If this file is not closed before another file is opened, the next file is displayed in a separate window. Both windows contain the same menu options.

- When a file is opened, it becomes the active window. To activate a previously active window, expand ⌹ ▾ (Windows) in the Quick Access Toolbar and select the name of the file, as shown in Figure 1−48.

  Note: Alternatively, you can activate an open window by selecting it.

- ✓ in front of the filename indicates the active file.

Figure 1−48

- If you no longer need to have a file open, you can remove it from the display. To remove a file from the graphic display, select **File>Close**. The model is no longer displayed but is still in memory.

File Naming

Files created in the various modes are given different filename extensions. When you create a new file or open an existing file into any mode, Creo Parametric automatically knows the correct extension. You do not need to enter the extension with the filename.

Creo Parametric permits a maximum of 31 characters in a filename. Periods and spaces are not permitted. Certain operating systems might not permit other characters in filenames. All files are stored in lowercase regardless of whether they are entered with uppercase letters.

The extensions used for the four modes discussed in this guide are listed as follows:

Mode	Extension	Example
Sketcher	.SEC	groove.sec
Part	.PRT	key.prt
Assembly	.ASM	padlock.asm
Drawing	.DRW	padlock.drw

Model Orientation Using Two Planar Surfaces

The model does not have an explicit top, bottom, right, left, front, or back, but you can orient a model in 3D space by assigning directions to two perpendicular planar surfaces. The system orients the selected surfaces in the assigned directions, relative to your monitor, as shown in Figure 1–49.

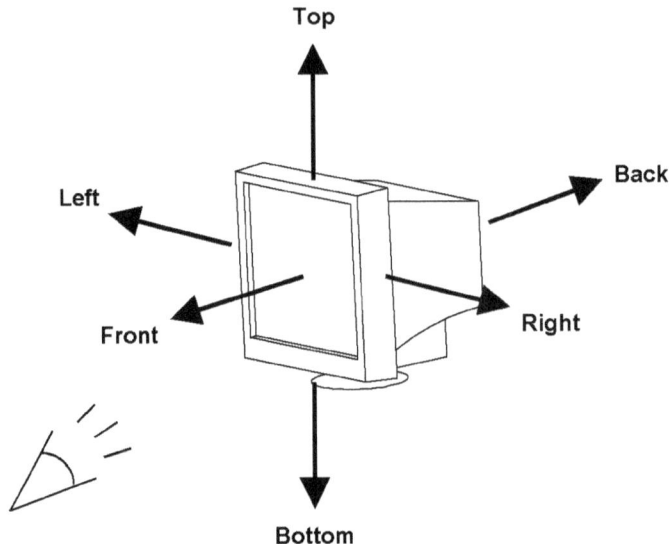

Figure 1–49

You can orient the model using the surfaces shown in Figure 1–50.

Select this surface to face the Front of the monitor

Select this surface to face the Bottom of the monitor

The resulting orientation

Figure 1–50

Note: Press <Ctrl>+<D> or click ⬚ (Saved Orientations) and select Standard Orientation to return to the default orientation.

View Normal

You can quickly orient the model into a planar orientation by clicking ⬚ (Saved Orientations) from the *In-graphics* toolbar, and then clicking ⤴ (View Normal). Select a planar surface, and the system will automatically define a second reference so that the selected surface is oriented parallel to the screen, as shown in Figure 1–51.

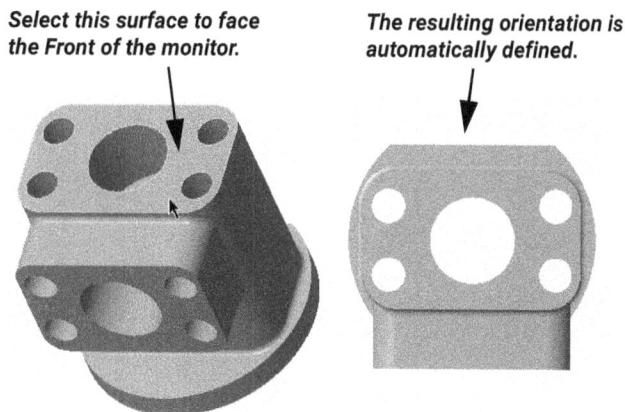

Select this surface to face the Front of the monitor.

The resulting orientation is automatically defined.

Figure 1–51

Designing in Perspective

You can maintain perspective display mode when working in Part and Assembly modes, as shown in Figure 1–52.

Standard Orientation   **Perspective View**

Figure 1–52

To activate perspective display mode, click ⬚ (Perspective View) in the *In-graphics* toolbar or in the *View* tab.

The use of perspective helps designers plan and visualize products in a realistic view, as they would appear to the eye. The perspective display is controlled using the *Perspective* tab in the *View* dialog box, as shown in Figure 1–53.

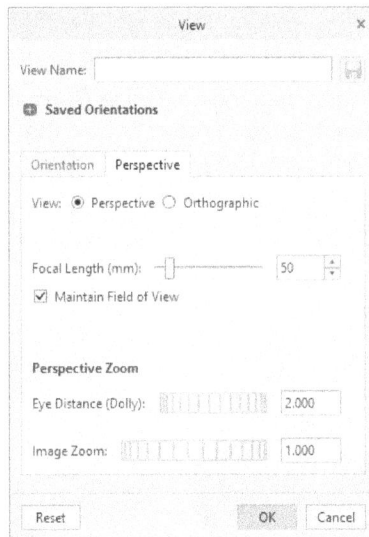

Figure 1–53

The *View* dialog box provides control over the **Focal Length (mm)**, **Eye Distance (Dolly)**, and **Image Zoom** to fine tune the perspective display.

Spin, Pan, Zoom

The three standard controls for spinning, panning, and zooming work as follows:

- To spin the model, press and hold the middle mouse button and move the mouse as required to spin the model. When the ⤙ (Spin Center) is displayed, the system spins the model about this location. Otherwise, the model is spun about a selected location. The selected location can be anywhere in the main graphics window, including selected geometry (entities, edges, or vertices). To select geometry, you can use the Geometry selection filter.

- To pan the model, press and hold <Shift> and the middle mouse button and move the mouse as required.

- To zoom the model, press and hold <Ctrl> and the middle mouse button and move the mouse up or down as required. You can also use the mouse scroll wheel to zoom the model.

- To zoom in on a specific area of the model, press and hold <Ctrl>, press and release the middle mouse button, and drag the bounding box to define the zoom area.

- To turn the model, press and hold <Ctrl> and the middle mouse button and move the mouse right or left as required.

Practice 1a
Open and Manipulate a Part

Practice Objectives

- Open part and drawing files and navigate between them using the **Windows** command in the Quick Access Toolbar.

- Change the visual style and orientation views of the model for improved visualization.

- Delete features and modify dimension values associated with a model to verify associativity between a part and its drawing file.

In this practice, you will practice using the Creo Parametric interface before you begin creating new models. You will then use the **Zoom**, **Pan**, and **Rotate** commands to orient the model shown in Figure 1-54.

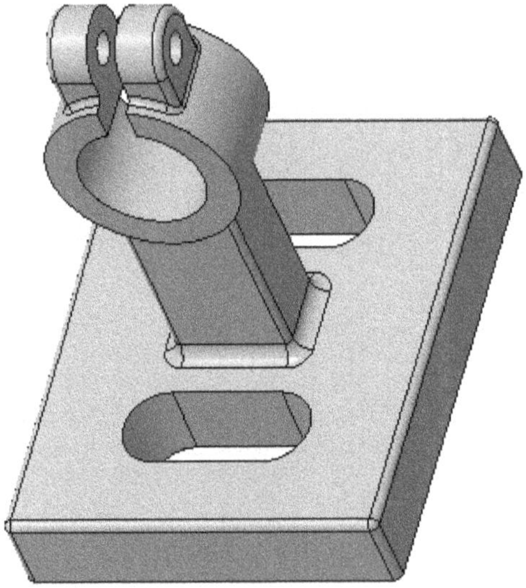

Figure 1-54

Task 1: Open the model called flange_lock.prt.

1. Set the current working directory by selecting **File>Manage Session>Select Working Directory**.

    Note: You can also set the working directory by clicking ⬚ *(Select Working Directory) in the Home tab.*

2. Navigate to the Practice Files, select the **Opening_Files** folder and click **OK**.

3. In the *Quick Access* Toolbar at the top of the main window, click 🗁 (Open).

   *Note: To open files, you can also select **File>Open**.*

4. In the *File Open* dialog box, select **flange_lock.prt** and click **Open**. The model displays in the main window and the Model Tree displays all of the features in the model, as shown in Figure 1–55.

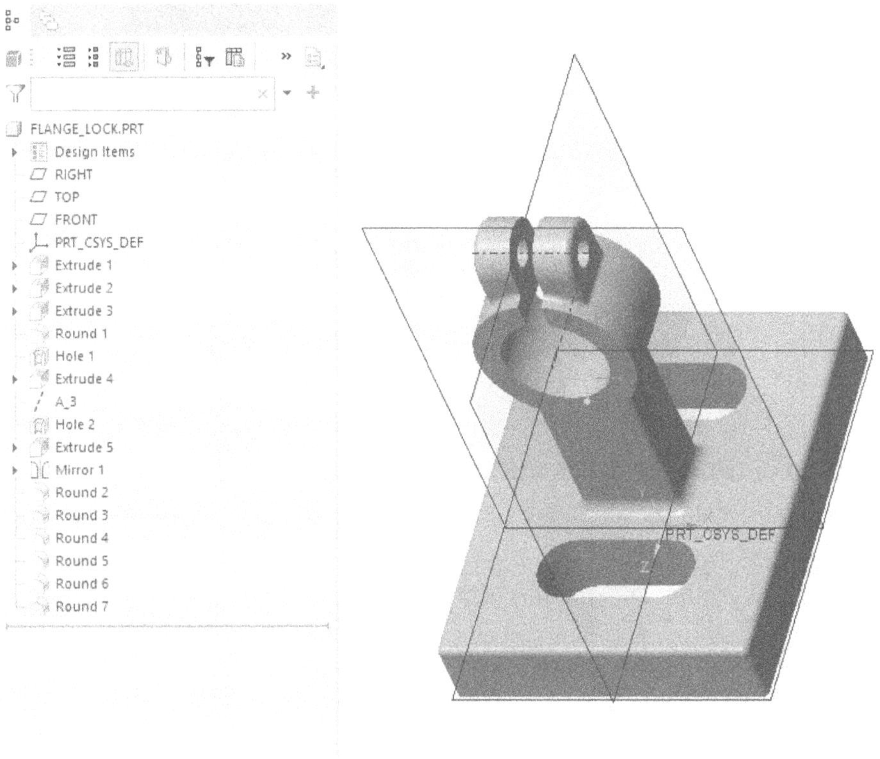

Figure 1–55

Note that the model name is displayed in the header of the Creo Parametric window and at the top of the Model Tree listing. The name in the Model Tree identifies the model as a part (.PRT) file. The model consists of solid geometry and datum features that were used as references when creating the solid geometry.

Task 2: Zoom in and out on the model.

1. While holding <Ctrl>, press and hold the middle mouse button.

2. Move the mouse toward you to zoom in and away from you to zoom out.

3. Release <Ctrl> and the middle mouse button.

4. If the cursor has a scroll wheel, use it to zoom in and out on the model.

5. In the *In-graphics* toolbar at the top of the view window, click ⌕ (Refit) to refit the model in the center of the screen, as shown in Figure 1–56.

    Note: To refit the model to the screen, you can also click ⌕ (Refit) in the Orientation group in the View tab.

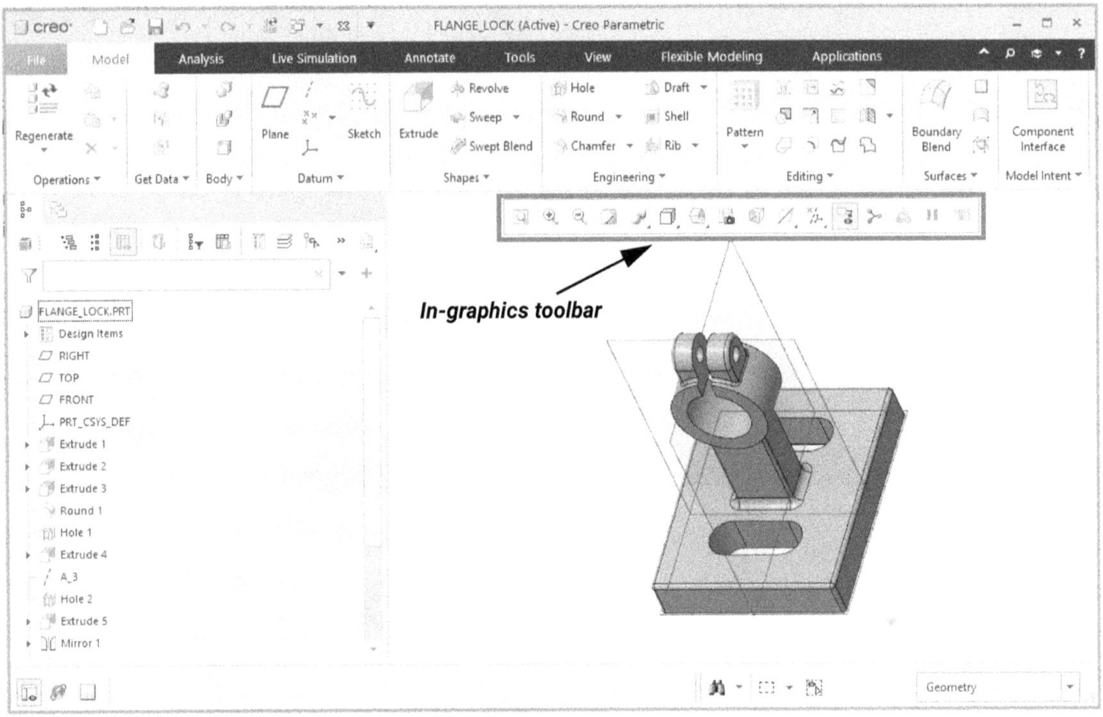

Figure 1–56

6. Press and hold <Ctrl>.

7. Hold the middle mouse button.

8. Move the mouse right or left to rotate the model.

9. In the *In-graphics* toolbar, click ⌕ (Refit) to refit the model in the center of the screen.

    Note: You can also click ⌕ (Refit) in the View tab of the ribbon.

10. In the *In-graphics* toolbar, click ⊡ (Saved Orientations) and select **Standard Orientation** to return to the standard isometric orientation.

    Note: You can also press <Ctrl>+<D> or click ⋗ (Standard Orientation) in the Orientation group in the View tab.

Task 3: Zoom in to an area of the model and zoom out on the model.

1. In the *In-graphics* toolbar, click ⊕ (Zoom In).

2. Select a location on the model using the mouse button to define a corner of the bounding box zoom area.

3. Move the mouse to draw a box over the area to zoom.

4. Press and release the mouse button again when the box is the required size.

5. In the *In-graphics* toolbar, click ⊖ (Zoom Out). The Creo Parametric software automatically zooms out on the model. Continue to click this icon to zoom out further on the model.

6. In the *In-graphics* toolbar, click ⊙ (Refit).

7. If the cursor has a scroll wheel, move the cursor over the model, then scroll up to zoom out and scroll down to zoom in.

8. Move the cursor to the right of the model and scroll up and down. Note that the system zooms in and out on the location under the cursor, as shown in Figure 1–57.

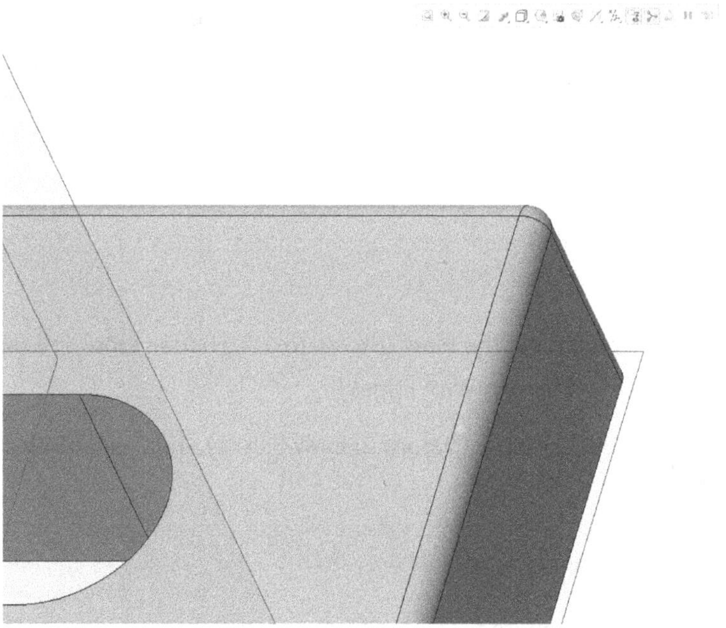

Figure 1–57

9. Click ⊙ (Refit).

Task 4: Pan the model on the screen.

1. Press and hold <Shift>.
2. Hold middle mouse button.
3. Move the mouse to drag the model.
4. Click ⛶ (Refit).

Task 5: Spin the model around the tri-colored spin center.

1. Hold the middle mouse button on any location in the main window.
2. Move the mouse to spin the model. The Spin Center can be used as an orientation reference.
3. Press <Ctrl>+<D> to return to standard orientation.

Task 6: Manipulate the view display of the model.

The ability of a system to spin a shaded model depends on the quality of the graphics hardware. By default, the model display is set as shaded (⬚ (Shading) is selected in the *In-graphics* toolbar at the top of the view window).

1. In the *In-graphics* toolbar, expand ⬚ (Display Style) and click ⬚ (No Hidden) from the flyout menu to set the *View Display* to **No Hidden**.

    Note: You can also select different model display options by clicking ⬚ (Display Style) in the Model Display group in the View tab.

2. Repeat the previous step to set the *View Display* to ⬚ (Hidden Line), ⬚ (No Hidden), ⬚ (Wireframe), and ⬚ (Shading With Edges).

3. In the *In-graphics* toolbar, click ⤬ (Datum Display Filters), then click **(Select All)** to toggle off the display of all datum entities.

    Note: Datum planes, axes, points, and coordinate systems are features that can exist in the model. They are discussed later in this guide.

4. In the *In-graphics* toolbar, ensure that ⬚ (Shading With Edges) is selected.

5. In the *In-graphics* toolbar, click ⤙ (Spin Center) to disable it.

Task 7: Orient the model by selecting two orientation constraints.

1. In the *In-graphics* toolbar, expand ⬚ (Saved Orientations) and click ⬚ (Reorient). The *View* dialog box opens, as shown in Figure 1–58.

    *Note: When orienting models, two perpendicular surfaces must be selected. **Front** and **Top** are the default reference options.*

2. For the **Front** surface, select the surface shown in Figure 1–59.

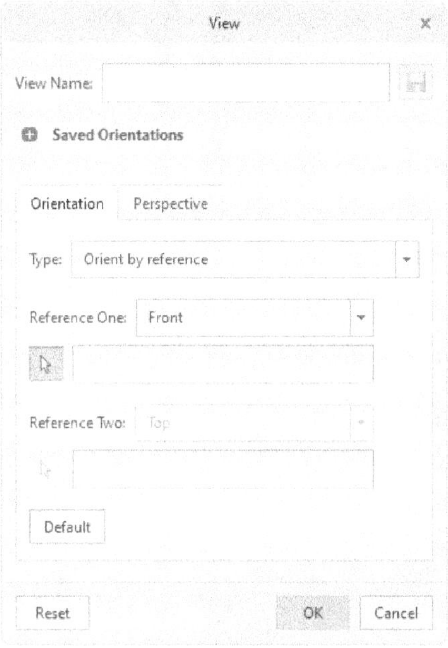

Figure 1–58

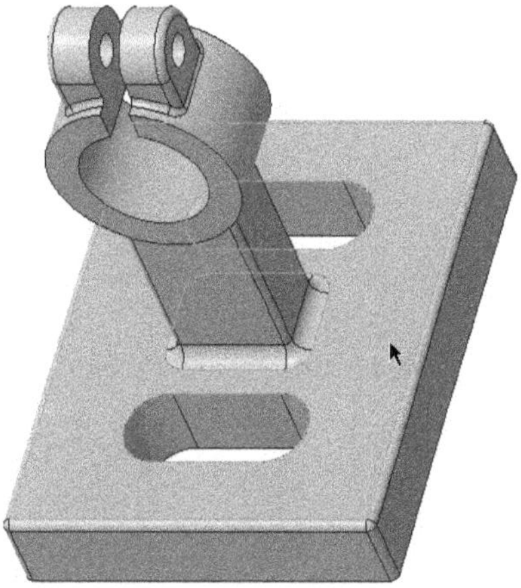

Figure 1–59

3. In the *Reference Two* area, select **Bottom** from the drop-down list, and then select the surface shown in Figure 1–60.

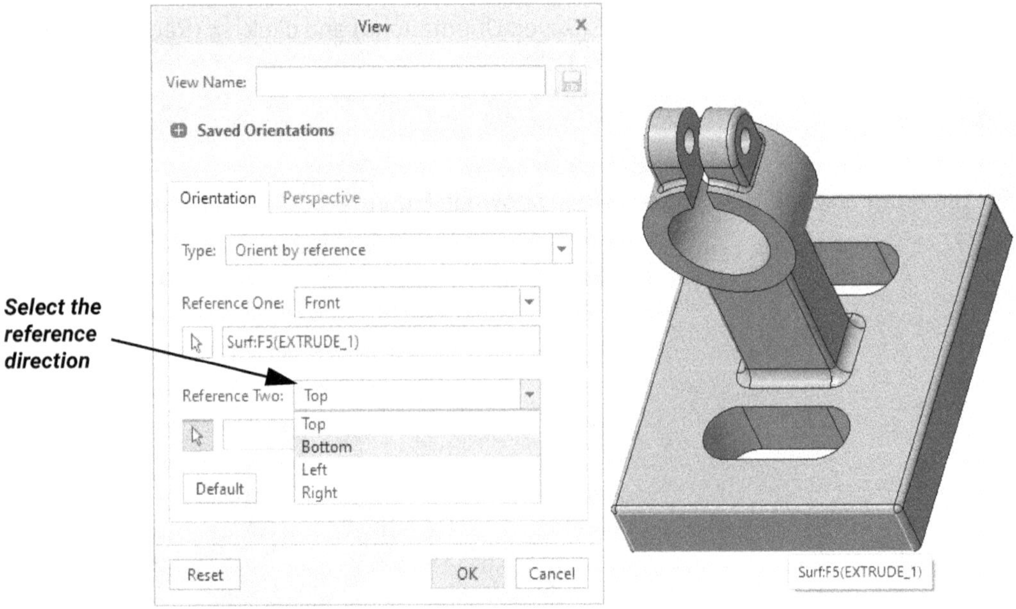

Figure 1–60

The model automatically reorients, as shown in Figure 1–61.

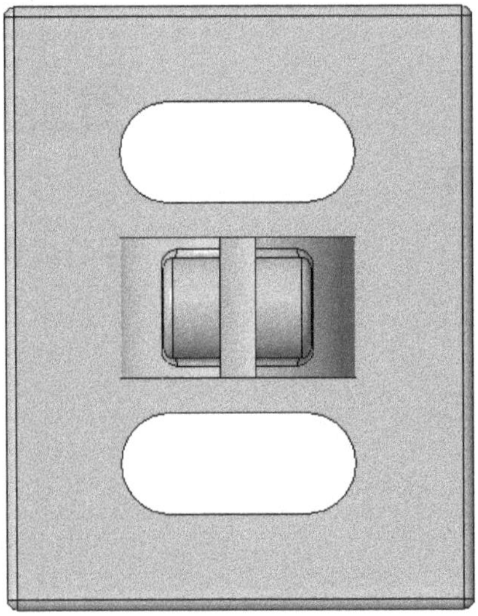

Figure 1–61

4. In the *View* dialog box, in the *View Name* field, enter **view1**, as shown in Figure 1–62.

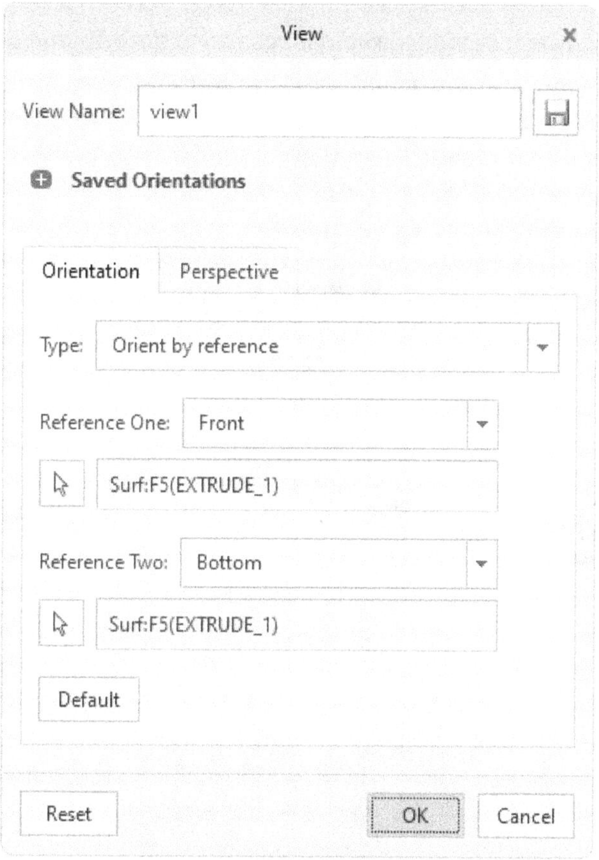

Figure 1–62

5. Click 🖫 (Save) to save the view.

6. Expand the **Saved Orientations** area to see the views stored in the model, as shown in Figure 1–63.

   Note: To retrieve a saved orientation without accessing the View dialog box, expand ⊟ *(Saved Orientations) in the In-graphics toolbar and select the associated name.*

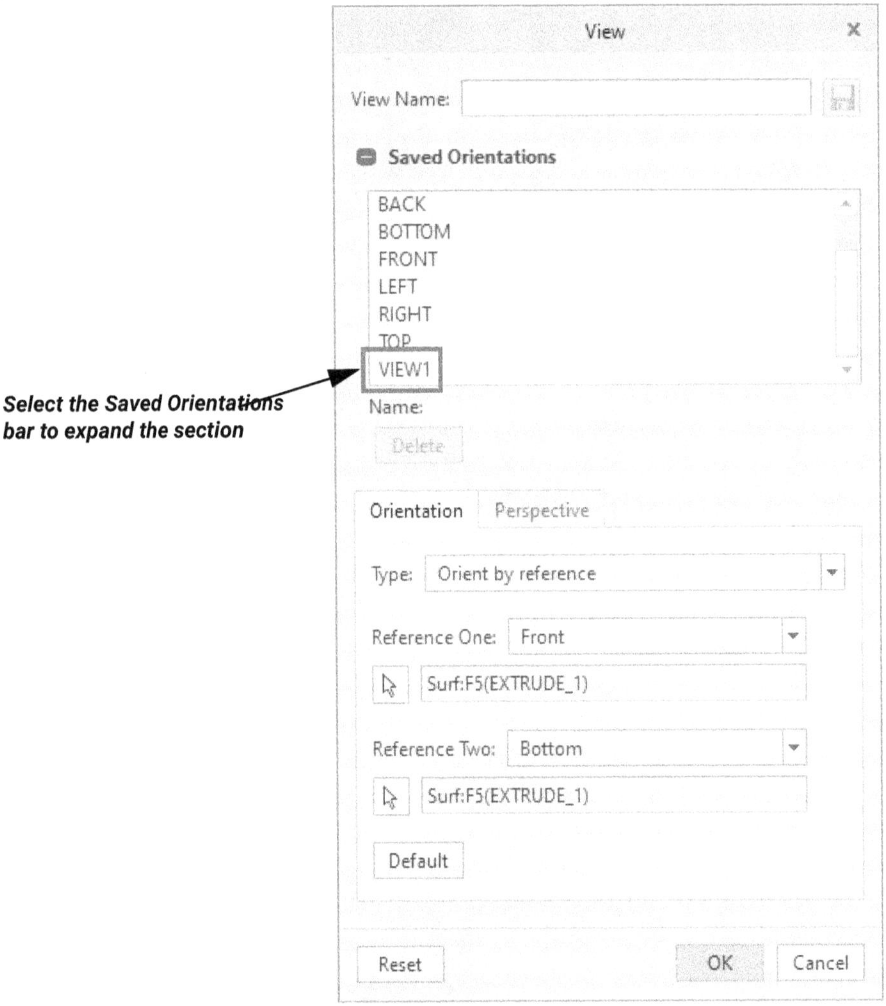

Select the Saved Orientations bar to expand the section

Figure 1–63

7. Click **Reset** to return to the default orientation.

Task 8: Practice orienting the model.

1. Select any two orientation constraints to define the views shown in Figure 1–64.

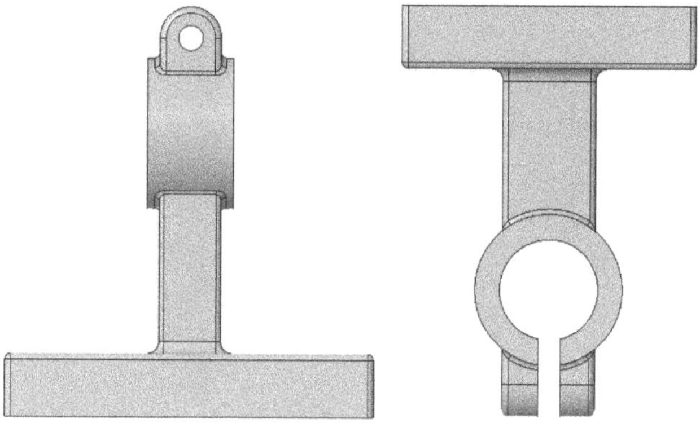

Figure 1–64

2. In the dialog box, click **Reset** to return the model to the default view.

3. Click **OK** to close the *View* dialog box.

4. In the *In-graphics* toolbar, expand (Saved Orientations) and click (View Normal).

5. Select the surface shown in Figure 1–65. The model automatically reorients, as shown in Figure 1–66.

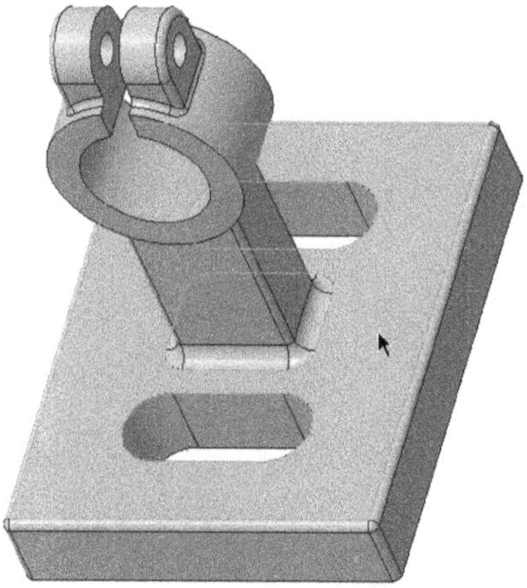

Figure 1–65

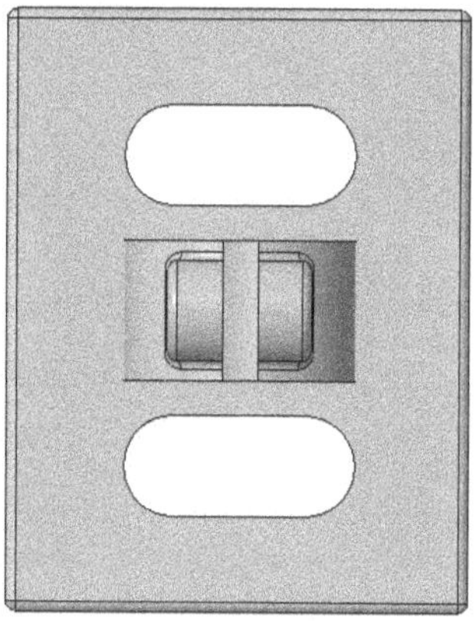

Figure 1–66

6. Press <Ctrl>+<D>.

7. In the *In-graphics* toolbar, expand (Saved Orientations) and click (View Normal).

8. Select the surface shown in Figure 1–67 to reorient the model.

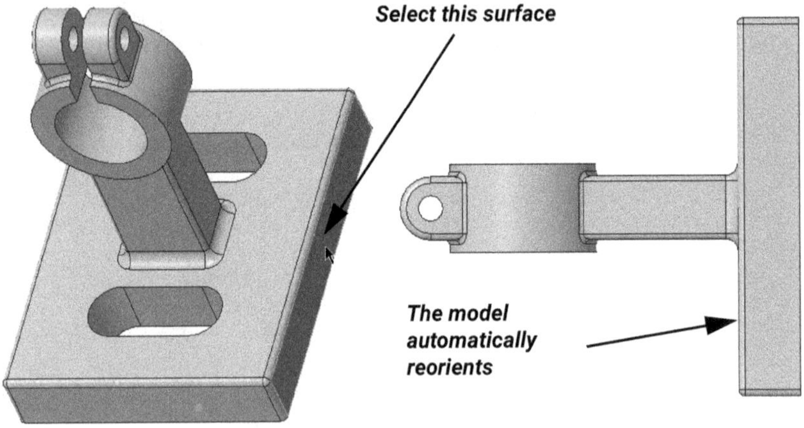

Select this surface

The model automatically reorients

Figure 1–67

9. Press <Ctrl>+<D>.

Task 9: Edit feature dimensions on the model.

1. In the Model Tree, select **Hole 1**.

2. In the *mini* toolbar, select ⟷ (Edit Dimensions).

3. In the main window, double-click on the **80.00** diameter dimension.

4. Set the new value to **50.00**, as shown in Figure 1–68. Press <Enter>.

5. Click on the screen twice (two slow, distinct clicks) and the size of the hole updates as the model regenerates.

Note: When the model regenerates, the system recalculates the model geometry. The length of regeneration time depends on the complexity of the model.

6. In the model, select **Round 3**, and select ⟘ (Edit Dimensions) in the *mini* toolbar, as shown in Figure 1–69.

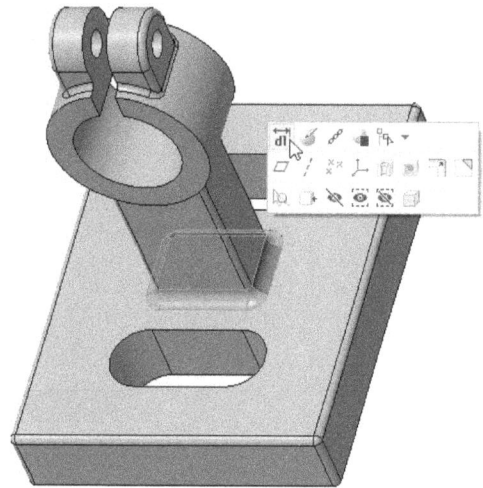

Figure 1–68   Figure 1–69

7. Set the radius round to **15** and click two times on the screen to regenerate.

8. As an alternative to entering the dimensional value, you can dynamically drag the green arrows of the dimension. Double-click on the oblong cut (**Extrude 5**). Note that the dimension locating the oblong cut is *77.50*, as shown in Figure 1–70.

9. Select the bottom arrow shown in Figure 1–71 and drag the position of the oblong cut to approximately **88**.Change the post height (**Extrude 2**) from *275* to **350 units** using either method.

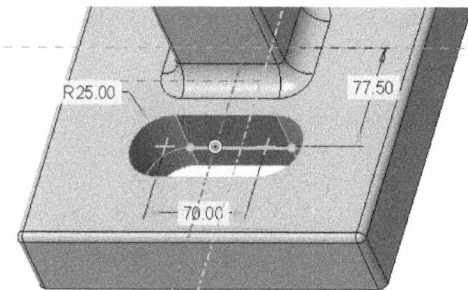

Figure 1–70

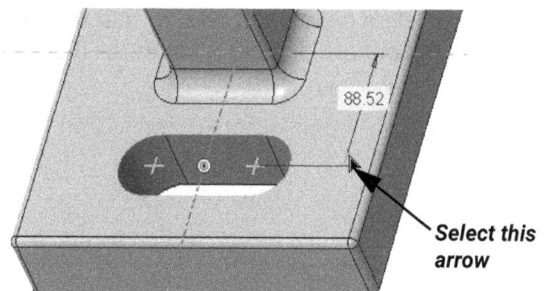

Figure 1–71

10. Click twice on the screen or click ▒ (Regenerate) in the Quick Access Toolbar to regenerate the model. The model displays, as shown in Figure 1−72.

Figure 1−72

11. In the *Quick Access* Toolbar, click ▤ (Save).

    *Note: To save files, you can also select **File>Save** or press <Ctrl>+<S>.*

Task 10: Delete features from the model.

1. Select **Hole1** directly on the model, hold the right mouse button, and select **Delete**. The *Delete* dialog box is displayed, as shown in Figure 1−73.

   Note: You can use <Ctrl> to select multiple features at the same time in your model.

2. In the *Delete* dialog box, ensure that the **Delete all** option is enabled. Then, click **OK**. The hole and cut are deleted. The model displays, as shown in Figure 1−74.

3.

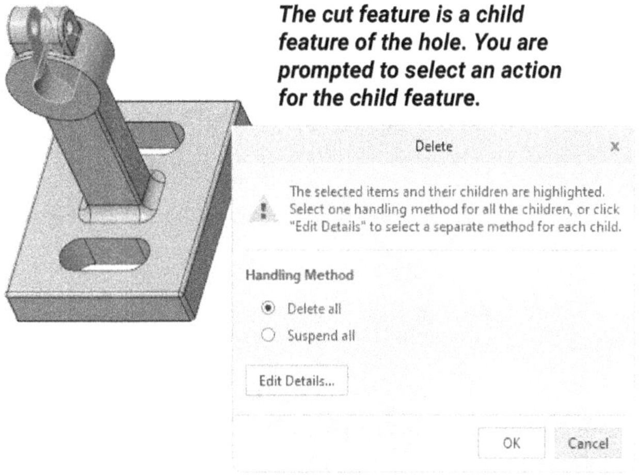

The cut feature is a child feature of the hole. You are prompted to select an action for the child feature.

Delete   ✕

The selected items and their children are highlighted. Select one handling method for all the children, or click "Edit Details" to select a separate method for each child.

Handling Method

◉ Delete all

○ Suspend all

Edit Details...

OK   Cancel

Figure 1–73 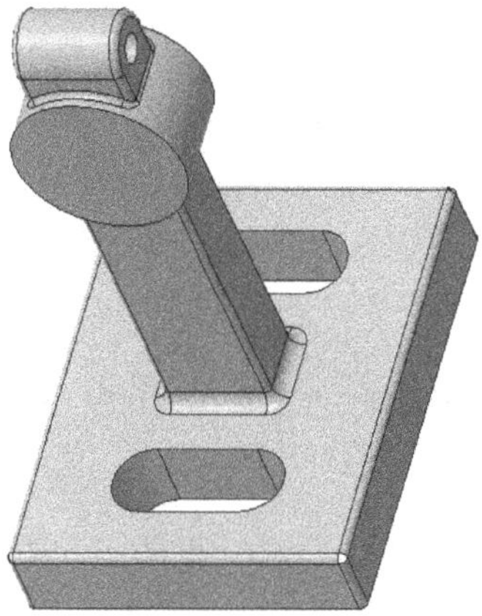   Figure 1–74

4. To close the active working window, select **File>Close**. The model is no longer displayed but is still in memory.

   Note: Alternatively, you can click ⌧ (Close) in the Quick Access Toolbar.

Task 11: Open files.

1. In the *Home* tab, click 📂 (Open).

2. If required, click 🗂 (Working Directory) in the *Common Folders* area of the *File Open* dialog box.

3. Double-click on **flange_lock.prt**. The model was not saved with the deleted features. However, the **flange_lock** file (with the deleted features) still remains in the active working memory until it is erased. This active working memory is termed *in session*.

   Note: The previous files that were opened are listed in the File tab on the right, under Recent Files. This enables you to quickly access these files without using the Open dialog box.

4. Select **File>Manage Session>Erase Current** to erase the file from memory. This does not affect the file saved on the system disk.

5. In the *Erase Confirm* dialog box, click **Yes**.

6. Open **flange_lock.prt** again. The model displays with all of its features because it was not saved after the features were deleted.

7. In the *Quick Access* Toolbar, click ⌧ (Close).

Task 12: Open multiple Creo Parametric windows.

The Creo Parametric environment enables you to work with multiple open windows.

1. Open **xbracket.drw**. The header of the main window displays the name of the drawing. The word **Active** after the name indicates that this is the active window.

2. Open **xbracket.prt**. A second window opens containing the drawing model.

   *Note: You can also open the drawing model by selecting the model in the Model Tree, right-clicking and selecting **Open**.*

3. The window containing **xbracket.drw** is still open. In the *Quick Access* Toolbar, click
   ⊐ ▾ (Windows).

   The xbracket.drw and **xbracket.prt** are listed but **xbacket.prt** is the active file. These can be selected to activate the appropriate window.

Task 13: Delete the rectangular tab protrusion on the model.

1. In the *Quick Access* toolbar, expand 🗗 ▾ (Windows) and verify that **xbracket.prt** is the active file.

2. In the Model Tree or main window, select the rectangular tab protrusion as shown in Figure 1–75, press and hold the right mouse button and select **Delete**.

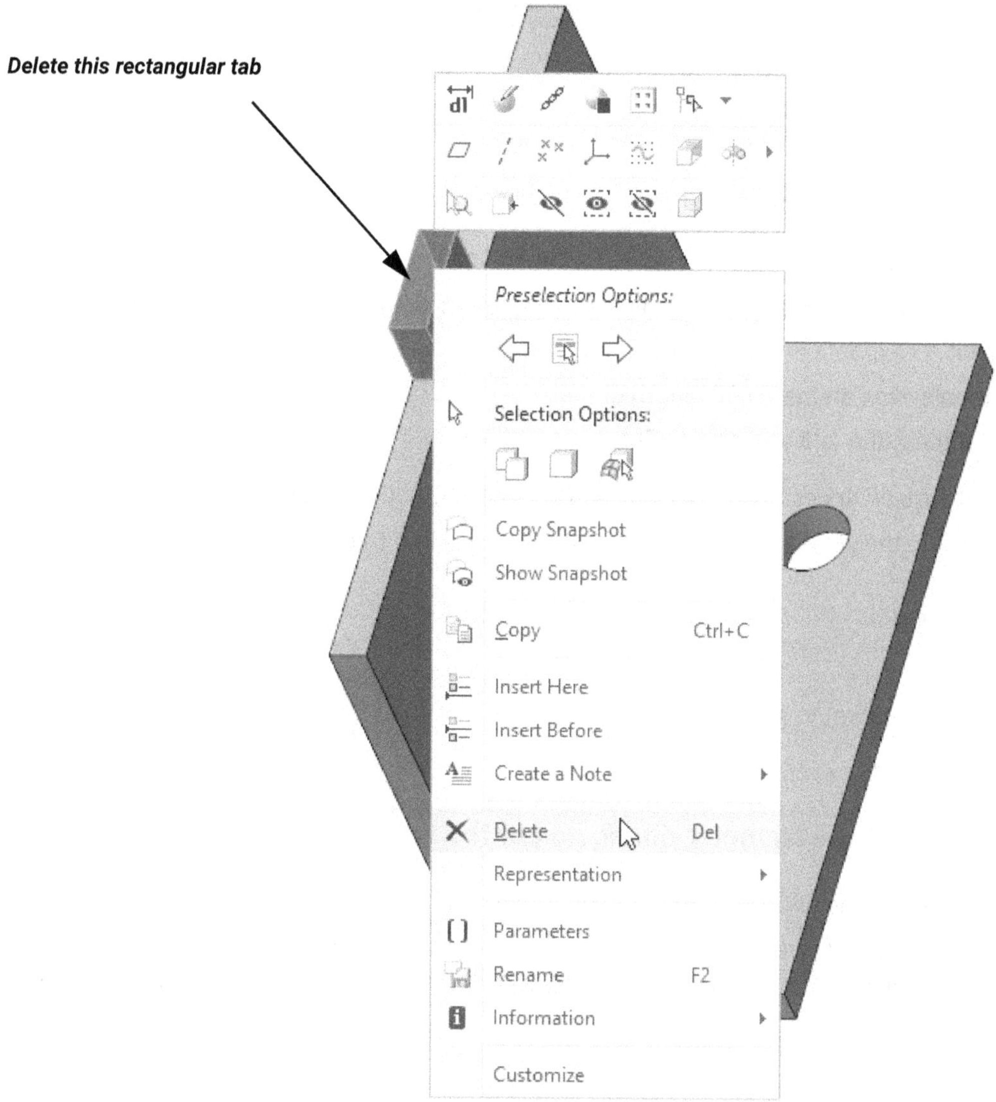

Delete this rectangular tab

Figure 1–75

3. Click **OK** to confirm the removal of the tab.

Task 14: Edit the length of the bracket in the drawing.

1. In the *Quick Access* toolbar, expand ⛶ ▾ (Windows) and select **XBRACKET.DRW** to activate the drawing, as shown in Figure 1–76.

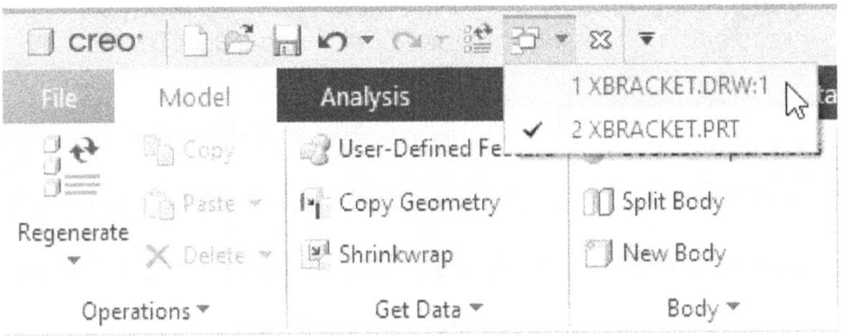

Figure 1–76

2. The drawing updates now that the tab protrusion has been deleted. If it does not update, click ⛶ (Update Sheets) in the *Review* tab.

3. Double-click on the **10.00** length dimension.

4. *Edit* the value to **8** and press <Enter>.

5. In the *Quick Access* Toolbar, click ⛶ (Regenerate Active Model) to regenerate the model.

6. Activate the window containing the part to verify that the model has changed.

    Note: To repaint the model you can click ⛶ (Repaint). This option refreshes the work area by eliminating residual graphics or returning graphics that might have disappeared.

7. Click ⛶ (Save) to save the model.

8. Click ⛶ (Close) close the part file.

Task 15: Edit the diameter dimension of the hole in the drawing.

1. Ensure that the window containing the drawing is active.

2. Set the hole *Diameter* to **0.5** and regenerate the model. Note that the diameter of both holes has updated simultaneously. This is because the holes were created using the **Pattern** option.

Task 16: Save the drawing and close the window.

1. Save the drawing and close the window.

2. In the *Home* tab, click ✎ (Erase Not Displayed) and click **OK** to erase all of the files from memory.

End of practice

Practice 1b
Model Tree Manipulation

Practice Objectives

- Manipulate the Model Tree display.
- Select and operate on features from the Model Tree.

Task 1: Open a model and set the display so that your model matches the images in this practice.

1. In the *Home* tab, in the ribbon, click ⛁ (Select Working Directory) and navigate to the *Model_Tree_Manipulation* folder. Click **OK**.

2. In the *Home* tab at the top of the main window, click 🗁 (Open).

3. In the *File Open* dialog box, select **valve2.prt** and click **Open**.

Design Considerations

To ensure that your images match those in a given practice, from this point forward, one of your first steps will be to set the model display. You will see a note similar to that shown in Figure 1-77.

Set the initial display as follows:

- ⁺⁄ (Datum Display Filters): All Off
- ⅌ (Spin Center): Off
- ▭ (Display Style): ⬜ (Shading With Edges)

Figure 1-77

4. Set the initial display by doing the following:

- In the *In-graphics* toolbar, select ⁺⁄ (Datum Display Filters) and disable the display of all datum entities.

- In the *In-graphics* toolbar, select ⅌ (Spin Center) to toggle the display off.

- In the *In-graphics* toolbar, select ▭ (Display Style) and select ⬜ (Shading With Edges).

The model displays, as shown in Figure 1–78.

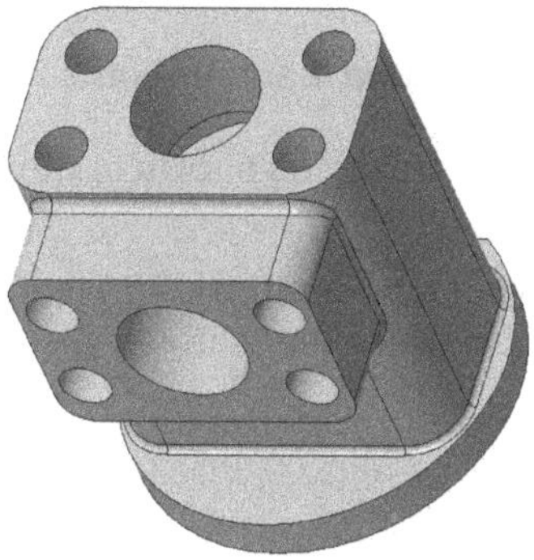

Figure 1–78

Task 2: Toggle the display of the Model Tree on and off.

1. To remove the Model Tree from the display, click (Show Navigator) in the lower left corner of the Creo Parametric window. Removing the Model Tree from the display gives you more room to work with your model.

2. To return the Model Tree to the display, click (Show Navigator) again.

3. To resize the Model Tree, click and hold the cursor on the right-side border of the Model Tree. The cursor changes, as shown in Figure 1–79.

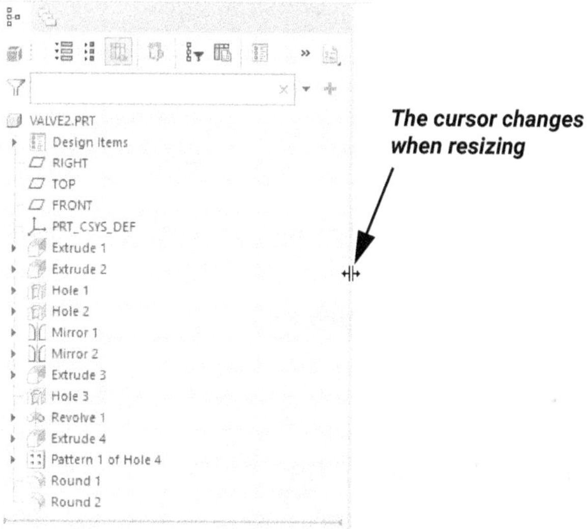

The cursor changes when resizing

Figure 1–79

4. Drag the border right to increase the Model Tree width, and left to decrease it.

Task 3: Conduct a feature operation directly in the Model Tree.

1. Press and hold <Ctrl> and select **Round 1** and **Round 2** from the Model Tree.

2. In the *mini* toolbar, select ◼ (Suppress), as shown in the left of Figure 1−80. The *Suppress* dialog box displays.

3. Click **OK** to confirm suppression of the features. The features are removed from the model, and the Model Tree updates to indicate the features are suppressed, as shown (on the right) in Figure 1−80.

   Note: Feature suppression is covered later in this guide.

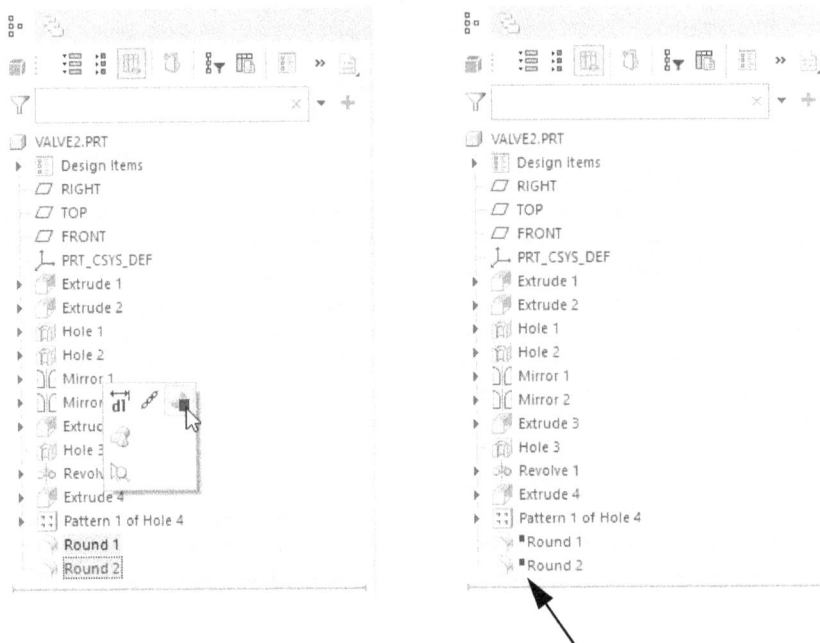

The black squares next to the Rounds indicate they are suppressed

Figure 1−80

Task 4: Manipulate the display of the items in the Model Tree.

1. In the Model Tree, select ⁸⊤ (Tree Filters). The *Tree Filters* dialog box displays.

2. With **General** selected, Uncheck **Suppressed** under the **Items by State** node, to hide any suppressed features in the Model Tree.

3. Select **Core Features** from the list on the left. In the *Core Feature* section of the dialog box, deselect **Datum plane** and **Coordinate system**.

4. Select **OK** and close the *Tree Filters* dialog box. The Model Tree displays, as shown in Figure 1–81.

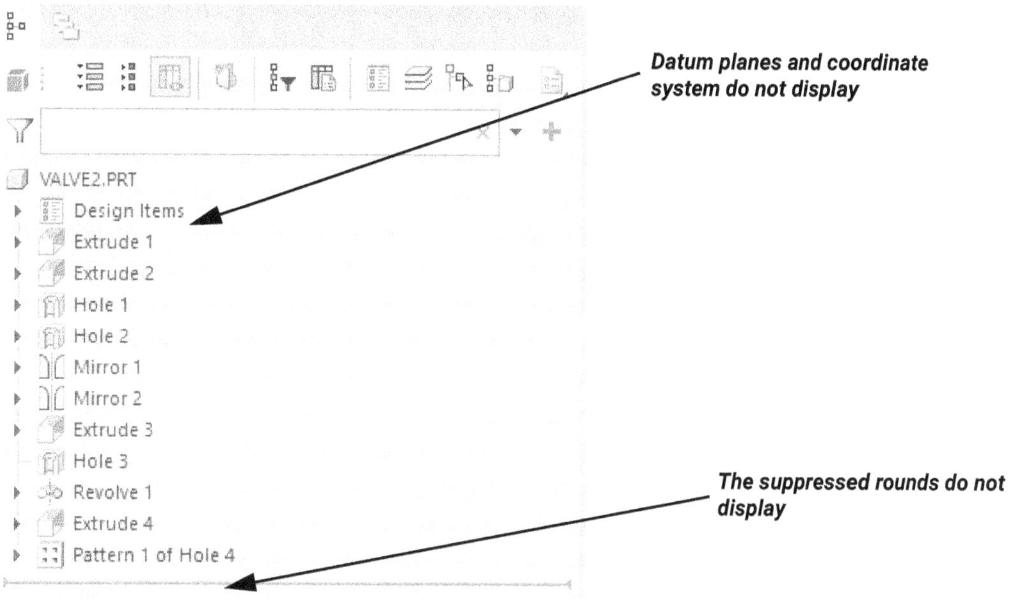

Datum planes and coordinate system do not display

The suppressed rounds do not display

Figure 1–81

5. Return the Model Tree to default display. In the Model Tree, click ⁝▼ (Tree Filters).

6. Select **General** from the list on the left, then click **Suppressed** to add the check-mark.

7. Select **Core Feature** from the list on the left. In the *Core Feature* area of the dialog box, click **Datum plane** and **Coordinate system** to enable them.

8. Click **OK**.

Task 5: Manipulate the column display of the Model Tree.

1. In the Model Tree, select ▦ (Tree Columns). The *Model Tree Columns* dialog box displays.

2. Select **Feat #** from the *Not Displayed* list.

3. Select to ≫ (Add column) to add the feature number to the *Displayed* column.

4. Repeat the preceding two steps for **Feature Status** and **Feat Type**.

5. In the *Type* drop-down list, select **Layer**. Each item in this list enables you to add additional columns to the Model Tree. Add **Layer Names** to the *Displayed* column.

Note: Layers are discussed later in this guide.

6. Select **OK** to close the *Model Tree Columns* dialog box and update the Model Tree.

7. Resize the Model Tree window and drag the column dividers to display the columns and Model Tree, as shown in Figure 1–82.

	Feat #	Feature Status	Feat Type	Layer Names
VALVE2.PRT				
▶ Design Items				
RIGHT	1		Datum Plane	01___PRT_ALL_DTM_PLN, 01___PRT_DEF_DTM_PLN
TOP	2		Datum Plane	01___PRT_ALL_DTM_PLN, 01___PRT_DEF_DTM_PLN
FRONT	3		Datum Plane	01___PRT_ALL_DTM_PLN, 01___PRT_DEF_DTM_PLN
PRT_CSYS_DEF	4		Coordinate Syst	05___PRT_ALL_DTM_CSYS, 05___PRT_DEF_DTM_CSYS
▶ Extrude 1	5		Protrusion	
▶ Extrude 2	6		Protrusion	
▶ Hole 1	8		Hole	02___PRT_ALL_AXES
▶ Hole 2	10		Hole	02___PRT_ALL_AXES
▶ Mirror 1	11		Mirror	
▶ Mirror 2	14		Mirror	
▶ Extrude 3	20		Protrusion	
Hole 3	21		Hole	02___PRT_ALL_AXES
▶ Revolve 1	22		Cut	02___PRT_ALL_AXES
▶ Extrude 4	24		Cut	
▶ Pattern 1 of Hole 4	25		Pattern	
Round 1	<None>	Suppressed (1)	Round	
Round 2	<None>	Suppressed (1)	Round	

Figure 1–82

Note: The Model Tree, Model Tree filters and Model Tree columns can be used to select objects and entities efficiently.

In a later chapter, you will learn how Creo Parametric saves your Model Tree settings so the Model Tree opens the same way every time.

8. Return the Model Tree to its default settings. In the Model Tree, select ▤ (Model Tree Settings)>**Settings>Reset Tree Settings in Mode**.

9. In the *Quick Access* Toolbar, click ⌧ (Close).

10. In the *Home* tab, in the ribbon, click ✐ (Erase Not Displayed) and click **OK.**

End of practice

Practice 1c
Interface Tools

Practice Objectives

- Manipulate the ribbon display.
- Investigate commands and groups in the ribbon.
- Use Full Screen mode.

Task 1: Open a model.

1. Set the working directory to the *Interface_Tools* folder.

2. In the *Quick Access* Toolbar, click 🖾 (Open).

3. In the *File Open* dialog box, select **ribbon.prt** and click **Open**.

4. Set the initial display as follows:

   - ⅍ *(Datum Display Filters)*: All Off

   - ⅀ *(Spin Center)*: Off

   - ⬜ *(Display Style)*: ⬜ (Shading With Edges)

   The model displays, as shown in Figure 1–83.

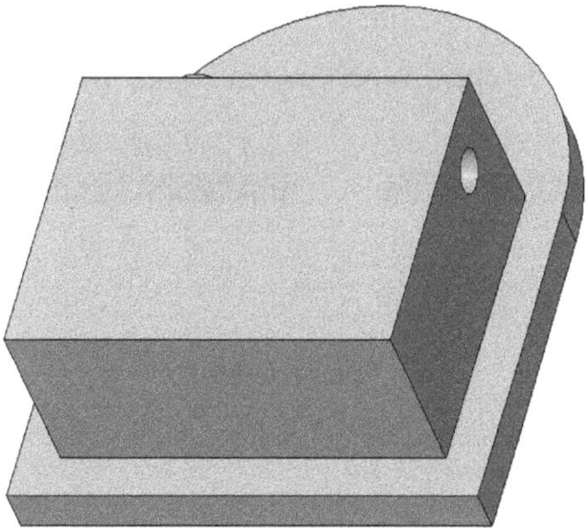

Figure 1–83

Note: Refer to the steps in the previous practice if you are unsure as to how to apply the display settings.

Task 2: Review the ribbon interface.

1. In the ribbon, click the various tabs such as *Analysis*, *Annotate*, *Tools* and so on to view the contents.

2. Select the *Model* tab.

3. In the upper-right corner of the Creo Parametric window, click ▲ to close the ribbon, as shown in Figure 1–84.

Figure 1–84

Note: The tabs are still visible, but you have more room to work on the model.

4. Select the *Model* tab again to temporarily display the ribbon.

5. Click on the screen and the ribbon closes again.

6. Double-click one of the tabs or, in the upper-right corner of the Creo Parametric window, or click ▼ to permanently display the ribbon.

7. Select the *View* tab, which displays, as shown in Figure 1–85.

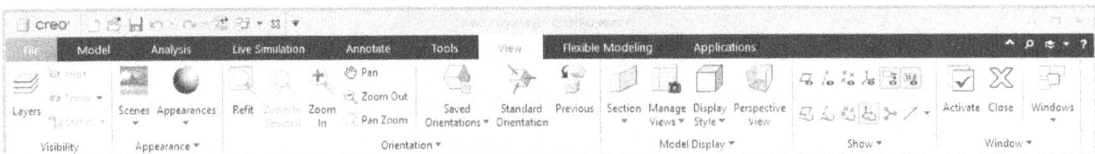

Figure 1–85

8. Resize the Creo Parametric window, as shown in Figure 1–86 and note that the most commands are reduced to icons only.

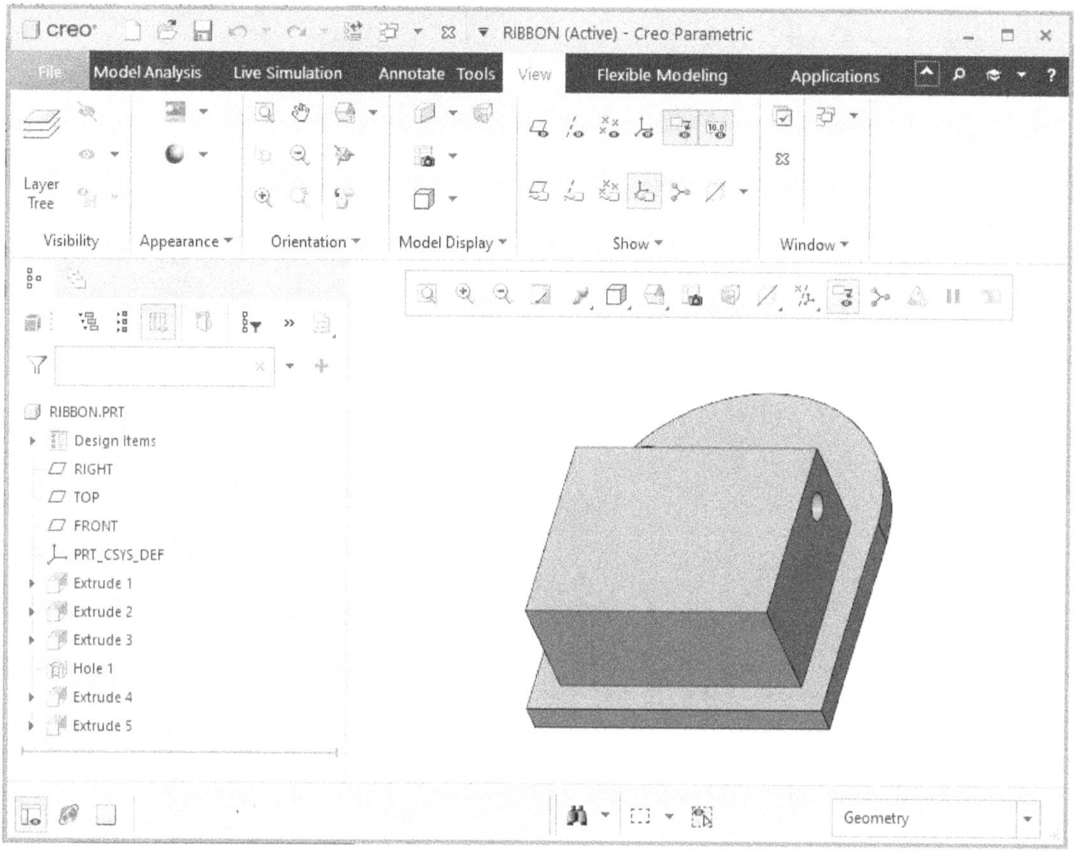

Figure 1–86

9. Resize the Creo Parametric window until all groups expand fully.

10. Note that most groups in the ribbon have an arrow indicating they can be expanded to access additional commands. Click the *Window* group to expand it and click **Default Size**, as shown in Figure 1–87.

Figure 1–87

Note: In general, the most commonly used commands display as icons in groups in the ribbon, and the less frequently used commands are found in the group drop-downs.

11. Commands found in the ribbon also have sub-commands. In the *Model Display* group, expand ⬜ (Section) to see the various *Section* types, as shown in Figure 1–88.

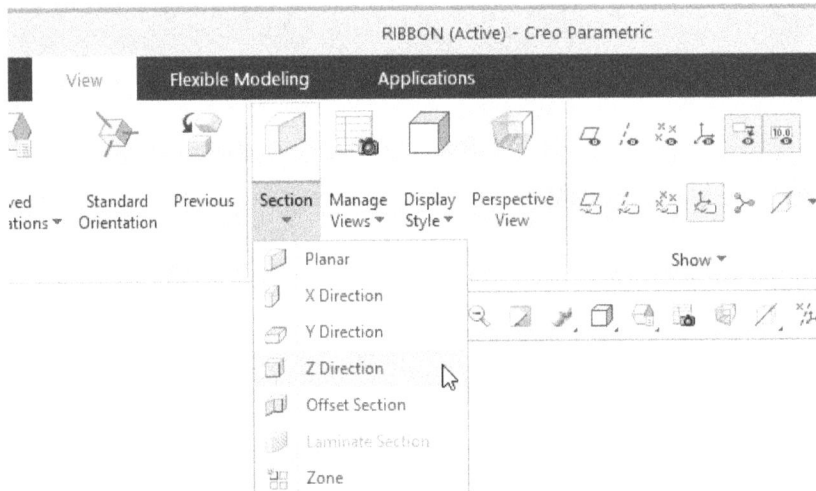

Figure 1–88

Note: Cross sections are covered in a later chapter in this guide.

12. Click on the screen to close the *Section* list.

Task 3: Apply Full Screen mode to provide maximum screen space while modeling.

1. In the lower-left corner of the Creo Parametric window, click ▢ (Full Screen). The graphics area encompasses the entire screen, and the ribbon, Model Tree, and message window are hidden, as shown in Figure 1−89.

Figure 1−89

2. Press <F11> to toggle the Full Screen mode off.
3. Press <F11> again to toggle the Full Screen mode on.

4. Move the cursor to the top of the screen and note that the ribbon becomes visible, as shown in Figure 1-90.

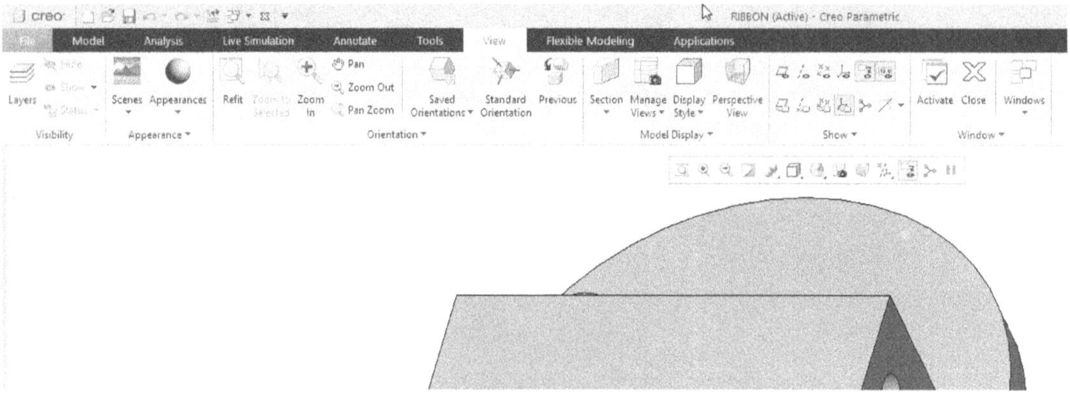

Figure 1-90

5. Move the cursor to the far left of the screen and note that the Model Tree displays.

6. Move the cursor to the bottom of the screen and note that the message area displays.

7. Press <F11> again to toggle the Full Screen mode on.

8. In the *Quick Access* toolbar, click 🖫 (Save) to save the model.

9. In the *Quick Access* toolbar, click ⌧ (Close) close the part file.

10. In the *Home* tab, in the ribbon, click 🖌 (Erase Not Displayed) and click **OK**.

End of practice

Chapter Review Questions

1. Which of the following are the key attributes of the Creo Parametric software?

   a. Feature-based

   b. Parametric

   c. Associative

   d. All of the above

2. Which of the following represent features for which a shape is predefined? (Select all that apply.)

   a. Sketched

   b. Engineering

   c. Extrude

   d. Revolve

3. After editing the dimensions of a part model, you must open all of the drawings referencing that part to make the same dimension changes.

   a. True

   b. False

4. Which of the following actions can be initiated in the Model Tree? (Select all that apply.)

   a. Select features

   b. Search

   c. Insert features

   d. View feature information

5. Creo Parametric part files have the _____ filename extension.

   a. .asm

   b. .prt

   c. .drw

   d. .sec

6. The ⬦ (View Normal) option orients a selected surface parallel to the screen.

   a. True

   b. False

7. To spin the model, which mouse button do you need to click and hold?

   a. Left

   b. Middle

   c. Right

8. Which of the following answers describes the purpose of the ⬦ (Regenerate) option?

   a. It refreshes the screen after spinning the model.

   b. It changes the display mode of the model from hidden line to shaded.

   c. It re-calculates the geometry after dimension changes.

   d. It opens a new model.

9. Which of the following orientation option combinations can be used to orient a model? (Select all that apply.)

   a. Right and Top

   b. Front and Back

   c. Back and Left

   d. Top and Back

10. **File>Manage Session>Erase Current** option erases the current file from your system's hard disk.

   a. True

   b. False

Answers: 1d, 2b, 3b, 4abcd, 5b, 6a, 7b, 8c, 9acd, 10b

Managing Your Creo Parametric Session and Files

File management options in Creo Parametric enable you to organize your files. Managing your files is important for effectively controlling your design data. In addition to PDM (Product Data Management), these file management options offer methods for saving, duplicating, and deleting files.

Learning Objectives

- Understand how files are stored and retrieved.
- Explore the different options in the *File* tab.
- Learn about part versions and how to display them in the File dialog box.
- Differentiate between the erase commands.

2.1 Managing Creo Parametric Files

Most companies have some form of PDM (Product Data Management) system setup in their organizations. Most of the capabilities discussed in this chapter are handled via the PDM system.

It is important to understand how Creo handles files when not using a PDM system, in the event you are ever working offline. This chapter covers how Creo Parametric handles files when working with them locally.

All work done in the Creo Parametric software uses the system's memory (RAM). RAM is considered temporary storage (or In Session working memory) and the system hard drive is considered permanent storage. Files are only stored to the system's hard drive when the file is saved, as shown in Figure 2-1.

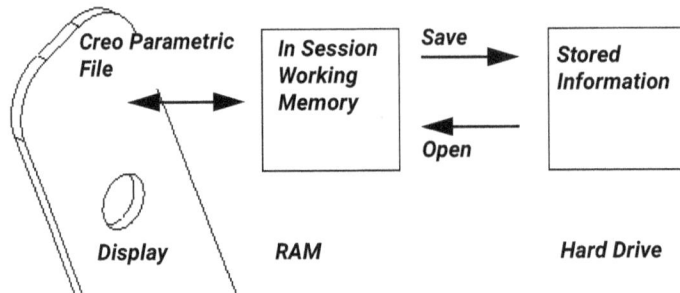

Figure 2-1

Files remain in RAM until one of the following occurs:

- Files are erased using one of the **Erase** options.

- The Creo Parametric session is closed.

General Steps

Once a design has been created or changes have been made to the model, it is recommended to store the files in a permanent location on your hard drive. Files can be saved using any of the following options:

- Save

- Rename

- Save a Copy

- Save a Backup

Save

To save a model, click ⊟ (Save) in the *Quick Access* Toolbar or select the **File>Save**. When saving a new file that has not been saved before, the *Save Object* dialog box opens, as shown in Figure 2–2.

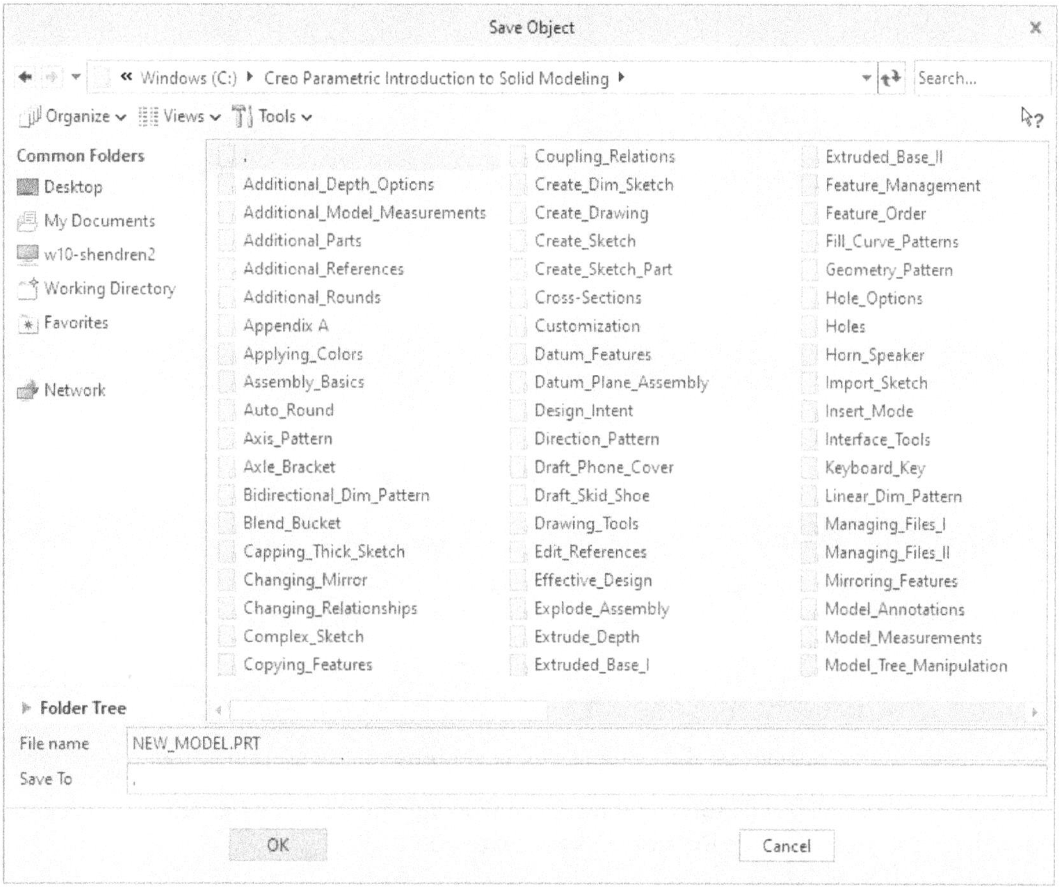

Figure 2–2

Note: You can also press <Ctrl>+<S>.

- Press <Enter> or click **OK** in the *Save Object* dialog box to store the file on the hard drive.

  Note: You can also click the middle mouse button at this point, to store the file on the hard drive.

- When you save a file using **File>Save**, the model is automatically saved to the current working directory (for a new file) or the directory from which it was retrieved (for an existing file).

Rename

To rename the existing file, select **File>Manage File>Rename**. The *Rename* dialog box opens, as shown in Figure 2–3. Enter a new name for the model and select whether to rename the file in session and on disk or only in session.

Rename	✕
Model: LINK-B.PRT	
New file name: LINK-B	
Common name: link-b.prt	
⦿ Rename on disk and in session	
○ Rename in session	
OK	Cancel

Figure 2–3

Rename In Session

If you rename the file in session, the file is only renamed in RAM. Subsequently, selecting **File>Save** creates a new file in the directory in which the original model is stored. The original model remains unchanged.

Rename On Disk and In Session

This option depends on whether the original model is stored in the current working directory:

- If the original model is not stored in the current working directory, the **Rename on disk and in session** option acts like the **Rename in session** option.

- If the original model is stored in the current working directory, the file is renamed in RAM and on the hard drive. All versions of the original model take the new name.

If the file you are renaming is associated with other files (i.e., assemblies or drawings), you must bring all of them into session by opening them. This ensures that all of the associated files are updated with the correct model name, once the file is renamed. For example, if an assembly is comprised of several part models and you rename one of those parts without the assembly in session, the part will be considered missing when you later open the assembly. Once the associated file is renamed, all of the reference files must be re-saved to ensure that the change is applied.

Save a Copy

You can copy an existing file to a new name while retaining the existing file using the **Save a Copy** tool. This enables you to explore different design options. To save a copy of an existing file, select **File>Save As>Save a Copy**. The *Save a Copy* dialog box opens, as shown in Figure 2–4.

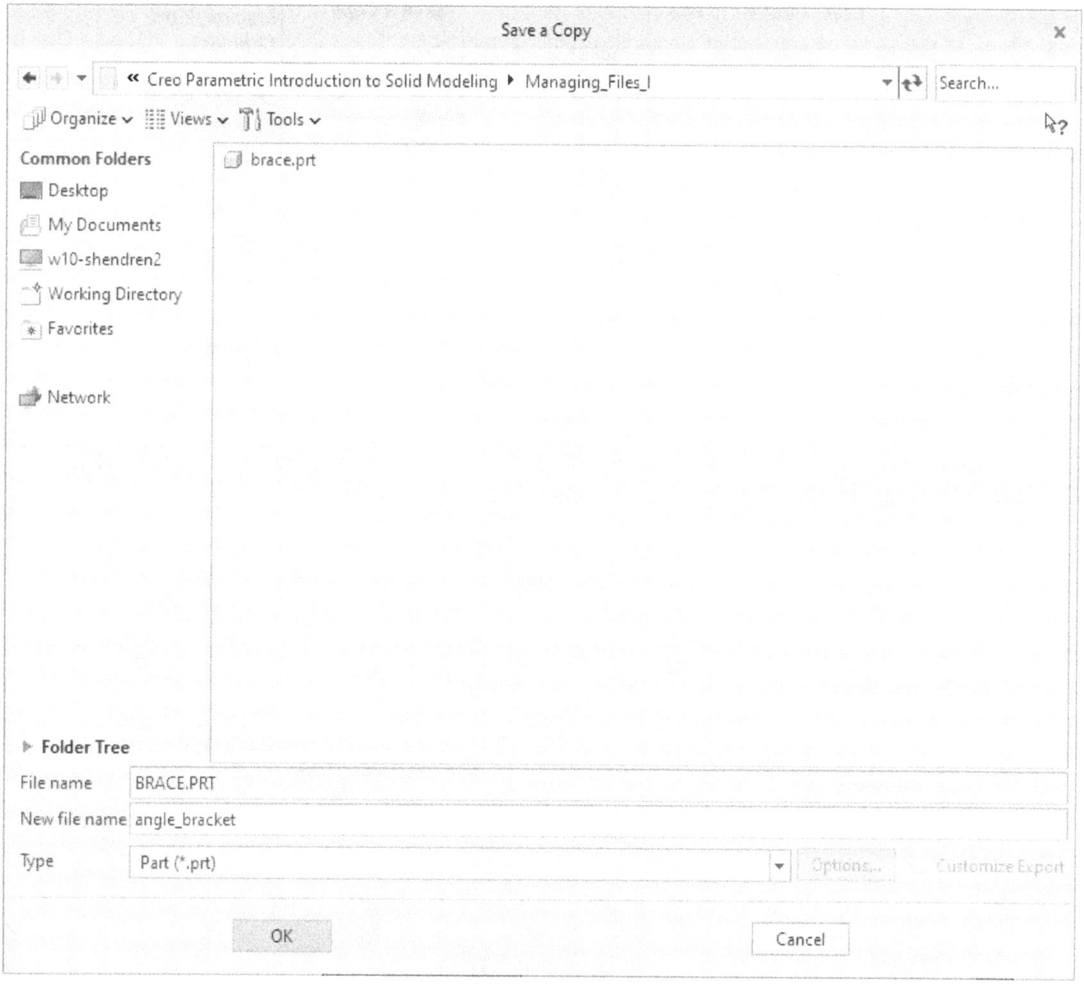

Figure 2–4

- Enter a new name for the file and click **OK** to save it to the hard drive. Note that the original file remains in the active window, so you must open the new file to work with it. If you do not want to save changes in the original file, erase it from the session without saving.

  Note: By default, the copied file is stored in the current working directory. You can select a different directory in which to save the file, by navigating to the appropriate folder.

- In the example shown in Figure 2–5, the part **bracket_2.prt** originally contained two holes. A design change requires the model to have four holes. Once the holes are created, the file is saved as **bracket_4.prt** using the **Save a Copy** option. As a result, the current file in RAM is still **bracket_2.prt** and **bracket_4.prt** is saved to the hard drive. To ensure that the additional holes do not display in the original file, it is erased without saving.

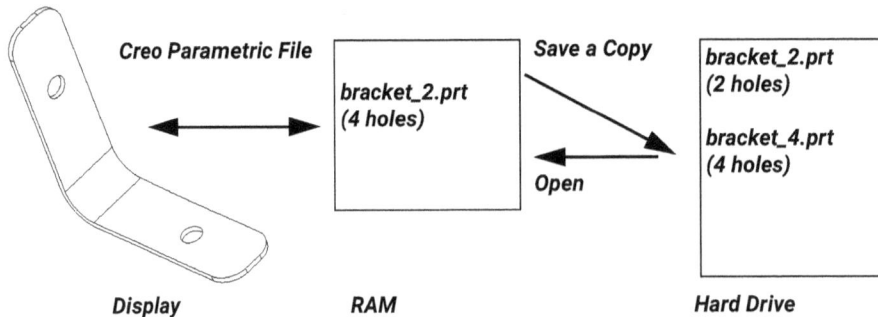

Figure 2–5

Backup

To avoid losing your work, you can create a backup copy of your file by selecting **File>Save As>Save a Backup**. The *Backup* dialog box opens, as shown in Figure 2–6.

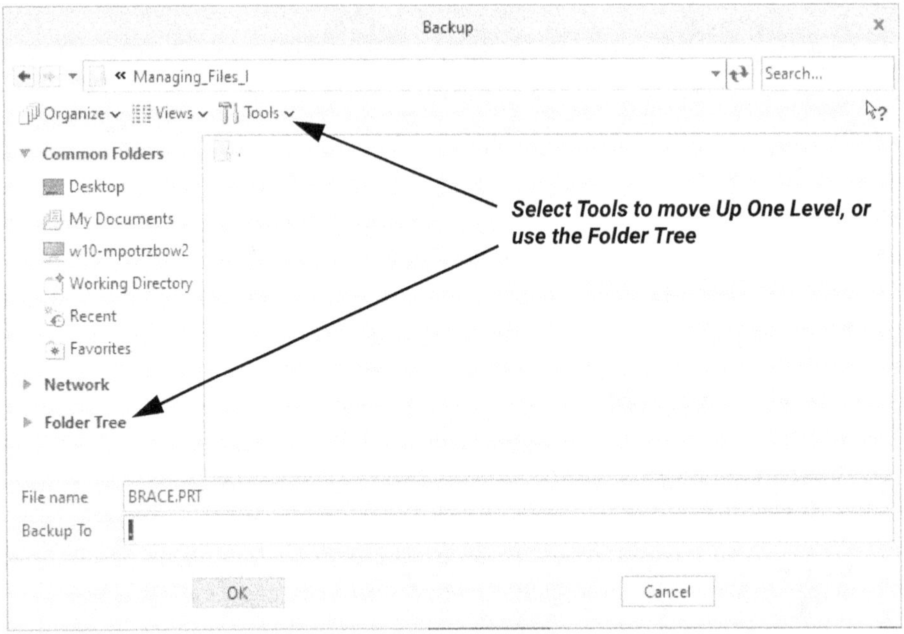

Figure 2–6

- Browse to the target directory. The original filename is maintained and the backup copy is stored in the new directory. The original model remains in the active window. The changes saved to the backup file remain independent to the original file.

- It is recommended to save your changes often and/or create a backup file. The software does not have an automatic save function and does not prompt you to save your files when exiting the program.

  Note: Backup also saves the backups of any associated files to the backup directory.

Each time a file is saved, an updated version of that file is stored on the hard drive. For example, if **brace.prt** is saved three times, it is stored as three different files in the directory. Each version of the saved file has a numbered extension appended to the end of the filename. The highest numerical extension represents the most recently saved model, as shown in Figure 2–7.

brace.prt has been saved three times

Figure 2–7

To display a list of versioned files, select **Tools>All Versions**, as shown in Figure 2–8.

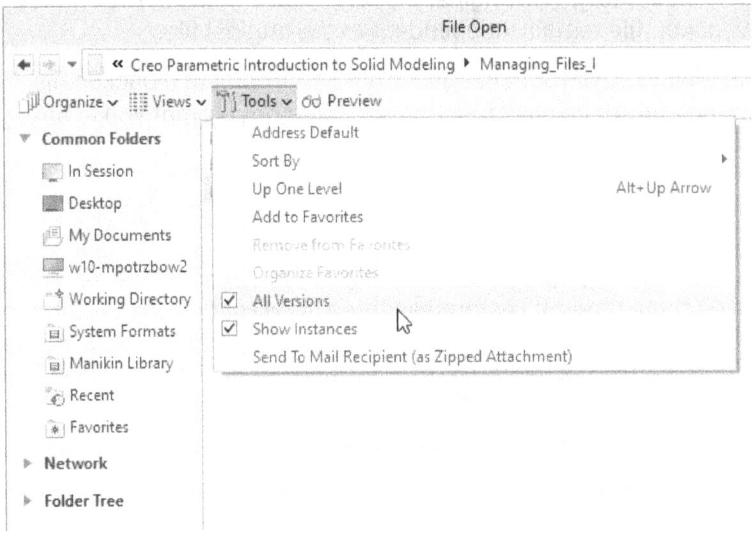

Figure 2–8

To help manage the number of files that you have stored on the hard drive, it is recommended that you delete any unwanted versions of your models.

Delete Old Versions

Retaining older versions of a file is useful if you need to retrieve them later. However, each new file takes up additional disk space. If retaining older versions is no longer required, select **File>Manage File>Delete Old Versions** to remove all but the most recent version of the file.

Delete All Versions

If a file is no longer required, remove it and all of its versions from your hard drive by selecting **File>Manage File>Delete All Versions**. This permanently deletes the files from the hard drive and RAM. It is recommended to use this option with extreme caution.

When a file is opened in Creo Parametric, it is displayed in the active window. If you accidentally close a window without saving, you can retrieve it from RAM without losing your work. The information on the hard disk is not accessed.

- (In Session): Enables you to review the files in RAM. It can be found in the Common Folders list. You can also open the files in the dialog box.

Once the files have been saved, it is recommended that you erase them to clear your RAM. Files can be erased from the current display or erased from memory if their window has already been closed.

Erasing Current Files

Files can be erased from the current display in the active window by selecting **File>Manage Session>Erase Current**. Ensure that all of the changes are saved before erasing the file as erasing it completely removes it from RAM. Only the last saved version of the model can be accessed.

Erasing Not Displayed Files

Files that were previously closed still exist in RAM. To erase these files, select **File>Manage Session>Erase Not Displayed**. Erasing files ensures that only the required ones are in session. Try to erase files when you have finished working with them to minimize the amount of information stored in RAM. Too much information in RAM slows down the system. If you are not sure which files are currently in session, click ▨ (In Session) in the *Common Folders* list.

- For example, three parts (**bracket_2.prt**, **bracket_4.prt**, and **bracket_6.prt**) are in session, as shown in Figure 2–9. Suppose **bracket_2.prt** and **bracket_4.prt** have previously been saved and **bracket_6.prt** has not yet been saved. If you close all three windows and select **File>Manage Session>Erase Not Displayed**, **bracket_6.prt** would no longer exist, while **bracket_2.prt** and **bracket_4.prt** would remain because they were previously saved.

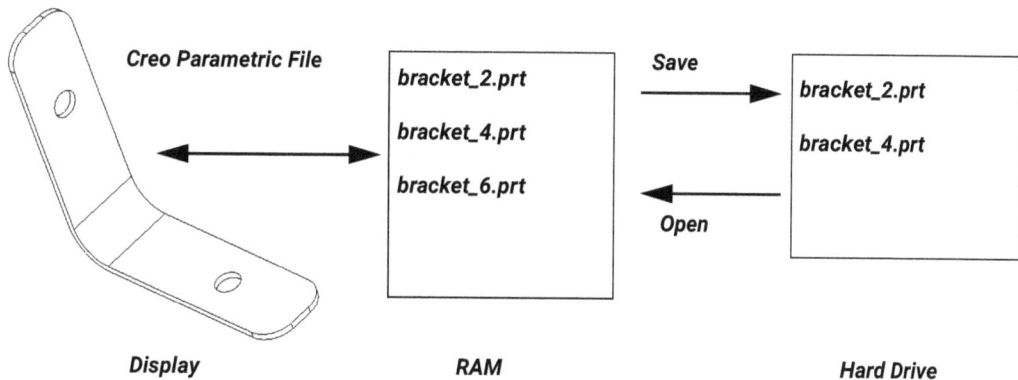

Figure 2–9

Practice 2a
Manage Files I

Practice Objectives

- Display the different versions of a part.
- Rename a part, save a copy, or erase files from memory using the *File* tab.

In this practice, you will open a model with which multiple saved versions are associated and practice using the file management options covered in this chapter.

Task 1: Open a part file.

1. Set the working directory to the *Managing_Files_I* folder.

2. In the Creo Parametric Navigator, click ▱ (Folder Browser), if required. In the *Common Folders* list, select **Working Directory**. The Browser displays, as shown in Figure 2–10.

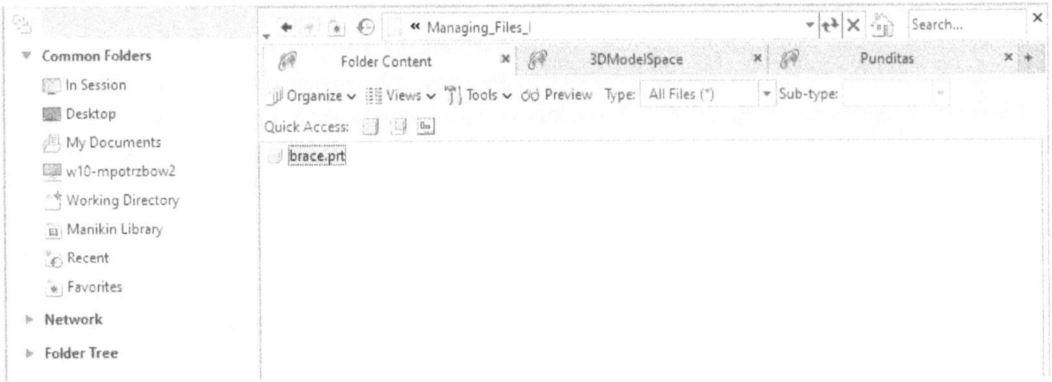

Figure 2–10

This is an alternative way to browse the contents of directories.

3. Select **brace.prt** and select **Preview**, as shown in Figure 2–11.

Select Preview to display a preview of the selected file

Figure 2–11

Note: *If the preview window is too small or the model is not zoomed in far enough, some of the model details will not be visible.*

You can spin, zoom, and pan the model inside the Preview window.

4. In the Browser, select **Tools>All Versions**, as shown in Figure 2–12. The file structure displays all of the saved versions of the models. There are several different versions of **brace.prt**.

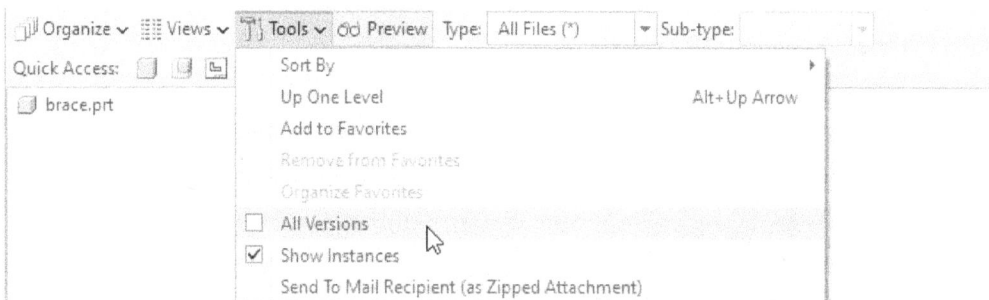

Figure 2–12

5. Click **brace.prt.1**. Note that the original version of the model displays in the *Preview* area.

Note: *If a previous version is opened, modified, and saved, it becomes the latest version of the part.*

6. Double-click on **brace.prt.3** to open the latest version of the model.

7. Set the model display as follows:

   - ⅍ *(Datum Display Filters)*: All Off

   - ⸚ *(Spin Center)*: Off

   - ▱ *(Display Style)*: ▱ (Shading With Edges)

   The model displays, as shown in Figure 2–13.

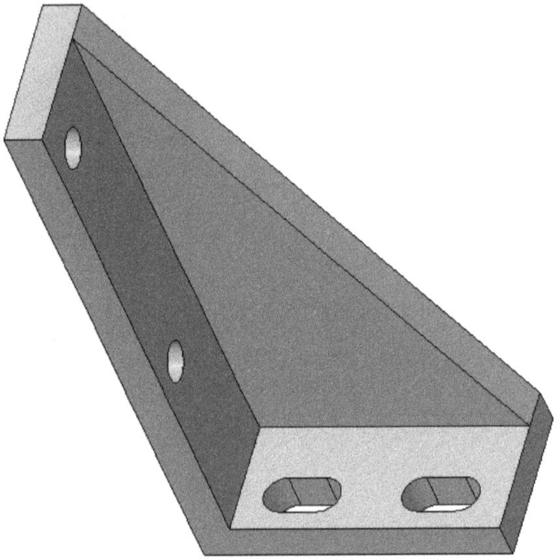

Figure 2–13

Task 2: Rename the part.

1. Select **File>Manage File>Rename**.

2. Edit the name from *BRACE* to **holder**.

3. Select the **Rename on disk and in session** option. This will rename the part in the current session as well as permanently rename it on the hard drive.

4. Click **OK**.

5. Use the Browser to display the working directory and confirm that all versions of the part have been renamed as **holder.prt**, as shown in Figure 2–14.

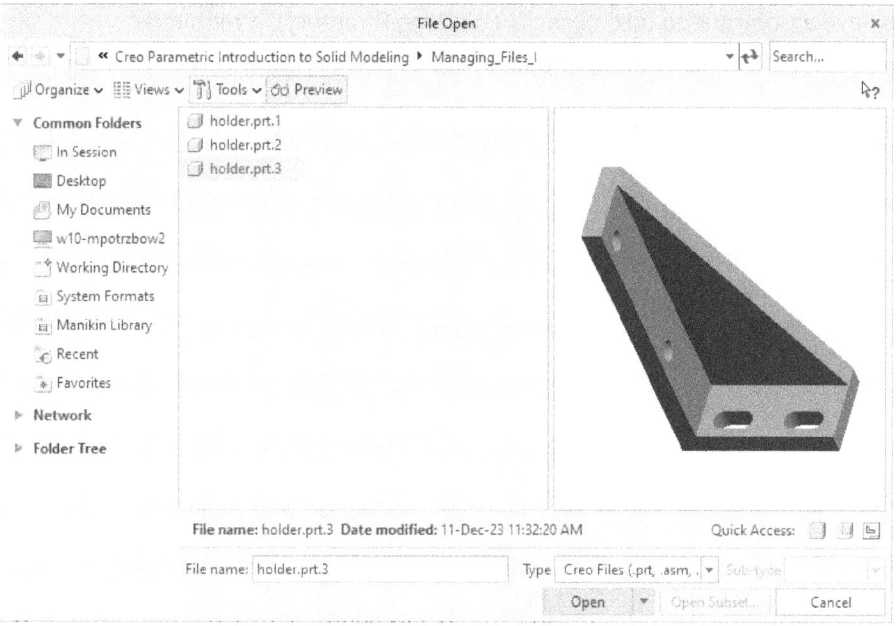

Figure 2-14

6. To close the browser window, click ✖ in the top right corner.

Task 3: Modify and save the part with a new name.

1. Click ⣿ (Navigation Trees) in the Navigator, if required.

2. Right-click **Extrude3** in the Model Tree and click ✖ (Delete).

3. Click **OK** in the *Delete* dialog box. The part displays, as shown in Figure 2-15.

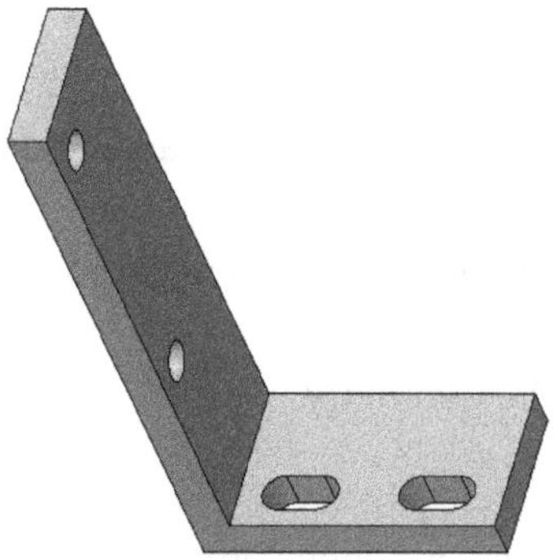

Figure 2-15

4. Select **File>Save As>Save a Copy** to save the changes made in the model.

5. In the *Save a Copy* dialog box, click ⬒ (Working Directory), if required.

6. In the *New file name* field, enter **stabilizer**, as shown in Figure 2–16.

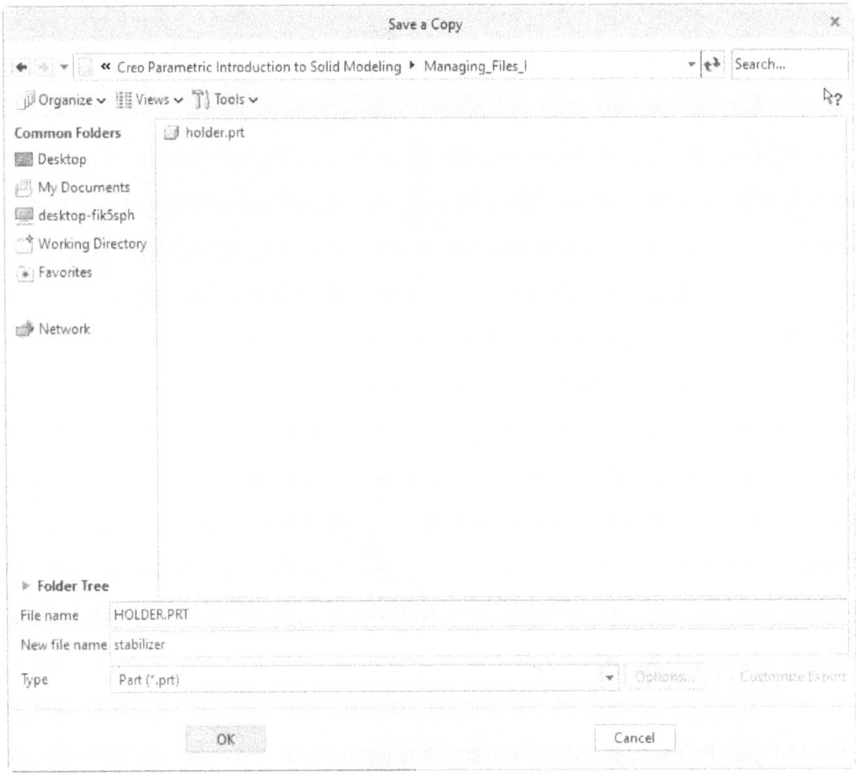

Figure 2–16

7. Click **OK**.

Task 4: Erase a single file from RAM.

1. Select **File>Manage Session>Erase Current** to erase **holder.prt** from RAM. Click **Yes** to confirm.

2. Open **holder.prt**. The model contains the original geometry. The changes were only saved in **stabilizer.prt**.

3. Open **stabilizer.prt**. Observe the geometry.

4. Close all files.

5. In the *Home* tab, click ✎ (Erase Not Displayed) to remove all files from memory.

End of practice

Practice 2b
Manage Files II

Practice Objective

* Rename a file used in a drawing to see the effect on the drawing.

Task 1: Open a drawing.

1. Set the working directory to the *Managing_Files_II* folder.
2. Open **xbracket.drw**. The drawing displays, as shown in Figure 2–17.

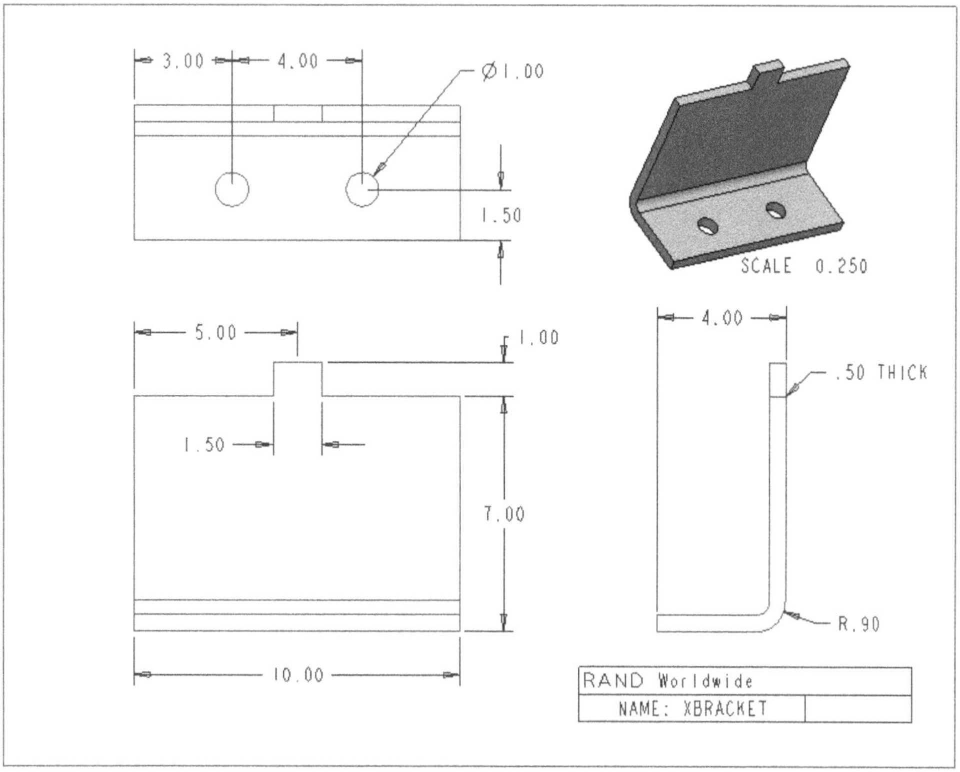

Figure 2–17

In this practice, you will rename the part associated with a drawing when the drawing is and is not in session, to see the effect.

3. In the Model Tree, note that the model used is **XBRACKET.PRT**, as shown in Figure 2–18.

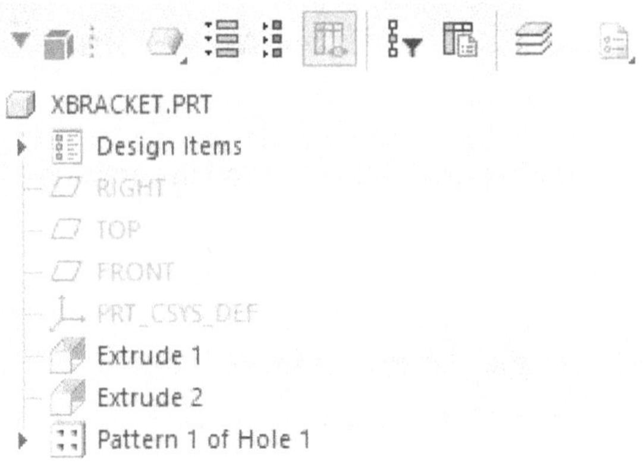

Figure 2–18

4. Click **File>Manage Session>Object List**.

5. The *INFORMATION WINDOW* opens, listing the objects that are in memory. Note that the **XBRACKET** part and XBRACKET drawing are in memory, as shown in Figure 2–19.

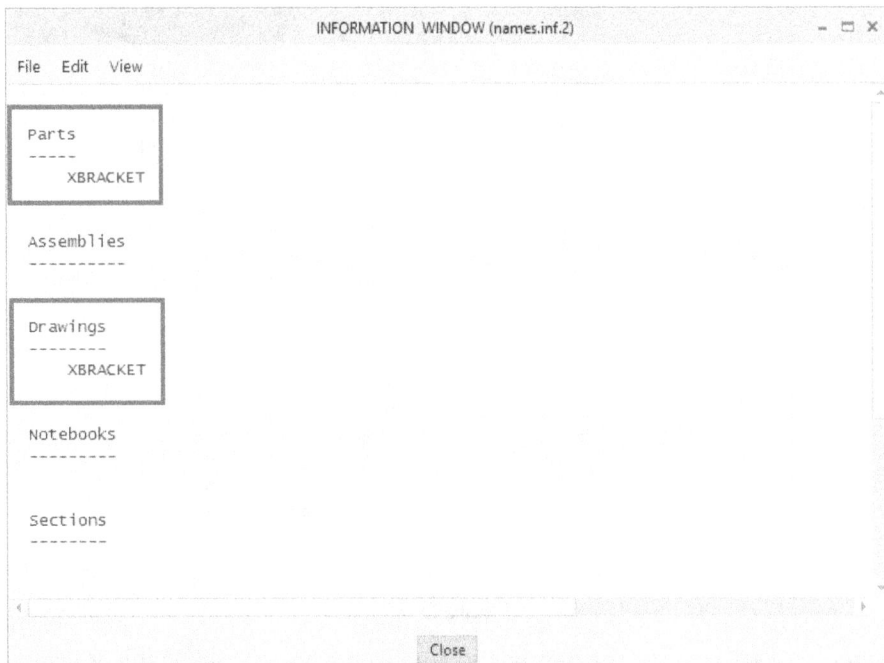

Figure 2–19

*Note: When the drawing was opened, the system knew to also open **xbracket.prt**. When a drawing or assembly is opened, the system searches the working directory for the associated objects and brings them into session (memory) as well.*

6. Click **Close** in the *INFORMATION WINDOW*.

7. In the *Quick-Access* toolbar, click ⌧ (Close). Ensure that no files are open.

8. In the *Home* tab, click 🖉 (Erase Not Displayed) to remove all files from memory.

Task 2: Open the xbracket part file and rename it without the drawing in session.

---

1. Open **xbracket.prt**.

2. Set the model display as follows:

   - ⅍ *(Datum Display Filters)*: All Off

   - ⅀ *(Spin Center)*: Off

   - ⬚ *(Display Style)*: ⬚ (Shading With Edges)

   The model displays, as shown in Figure 2–20.

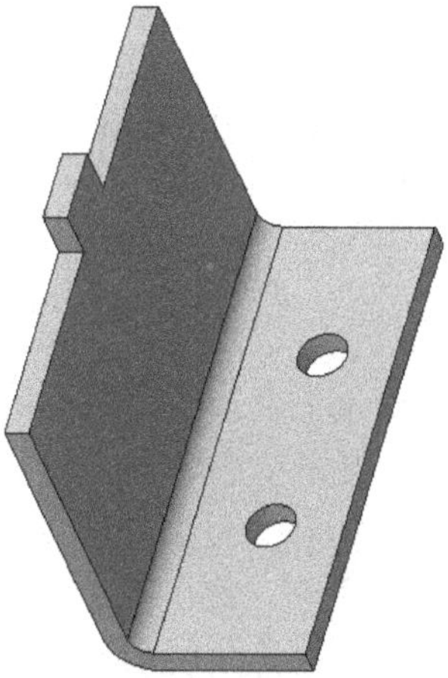

Figure 2–20

3. Click **File>Manage File>Rename**, and set the name to **XBRACKET2**, as shown in Figure 2–21.

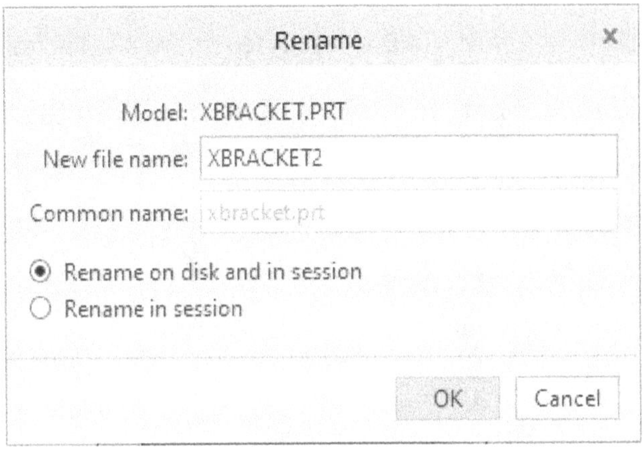

Figure 2–21

4. Click **OK**.

5. Open **xbracket.drw**.

6. The *Message* dialog box opens, indicating the part required for the drawing is not in the current directory, as shown in Figure 2–22.

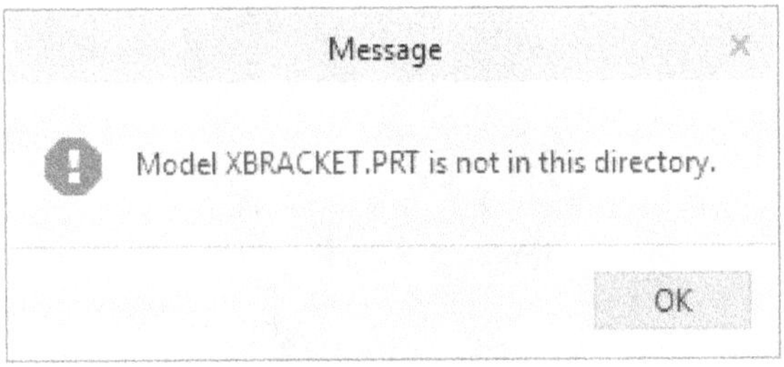

Figure 2–22

*Note: The drawing is still looking for **XBRACKET.PRT**.*

7. Click **OK**.

8. Click **File>Manage File>Rename** and set the name back to **XBRACKET**.

Task 3: **Open the xbracket drawing, and rename the part while the drawing is in session.**

---

1. Open **xbracket.drw**. The drawing opens correctly this time since it is again able to find the part file.

2. In the *Quick Access* toolbar, expand ⮹ ▾ (Windows) and select **XBRACKET.PRT**.

---

3. In the part window, click **File>Manage File>Rename**, set the name to **XBRACKET2**, and click **OK.**

4. Switch back to the drawing window.

5. Note that the Model Tree now refers to **XBRACKET2.PRT**, as shown in Figure 2-23.

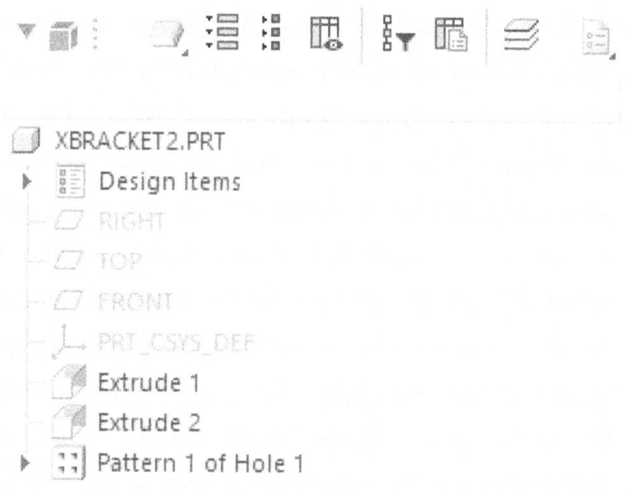

Figure 2-23

6. Save the drawing and close all files.

7. In the *Home* tab, click (Erase Not Displayed) to remove all files from memory.

Note: When renaming objects used in drawings and assemblies, it is important to ensure the files that refer to them are in session when the rename is conducted.

End of practice

Chapter Review Questions

1. Which of the following statements is true regarding saving a file? (Select all that apply.)

    a. Click ⊞ (Save) to save a file.

    b. When you save a file for the first time, it automatically prompts you for the directory in which you want to save it.

    c. When saving a file using ⊞ (Save), the current name can be changed by entering the new name in the Save dialog box.

    d. Each time a file is saved, an updated version of the file is stored on the hard disk.

2. If you open a file and make changes, then decide you want to reject the changes and start over, select **File>Close** and reopen the part.

    a. True

    b. False

3. Which of the following statements is true regarding the **Save a Copy** option?

    a. Any files that reference the file being copied must be in session.

    b. The copied file becomes the active model once saved.

    c. The copied file must be stored in the current working directory.

    d. The **Save a Copy** option is the same as renaming the file.

4. Which of the following options enables you to create a duplicate of a model by saving it under a new name?

    a. Save

    b. Rename

    c. Save a Copy

    d. Save a Backup

5. Which of the following options enables you to create a copy of a model in another directory while maintaining the original name?

    a. Save

    b. Rename

    c. Save a Copy

    d. Save a Backup

6. Closing a file removes it from RAM.

    a. True

    b. False

7. Select **File>Manage File>Delete Old Versions** to remove all of the versions of a model from the system disk.

    a. True

    b. False

8. Which of the following series of menu selections must be made to save the current file to a new name and erase the original file without saving it?

    a. Select **File>Save As>Save a Copy**, enter a new filename, and click **OK**. Select **File> Manage Session>Erase Current**.

    b. Select **File>Save As>Save a Copy**, enter a new filename, and click **OK**. Select **File> Manage Session>Erase Not Displayed**.

Answers: 1abd, 2b, 3a, 4c, 5d, 6b, 7b, 8a

Selection

Working with 3D models requires the selection of entities when creating, editing, or redefining geometry. Due to the potential complexity of the models, you may have to select hidden geometry, multiple features or multiple entities. This chapter covers the various scenarios and tools you will encounter while modeling in Creo Parametric.

Learning Objectives

- Employ various selection methods for selecting geometry.
- Understand how to select hidden geometry.
- Apply geometry filters to narrow your selection options and make selection easier.
- Explore how to select chains of edges.
- Use box-selection to select multiple entities.
- Use Find to search for and select entities.

3.1 Selecting Entities

To interact with the model, you must select entities such as surfaces, edges, and datums. Multiple methods are available to help you select the entities you want to work with.

Selection Filter

Creo Parametric uses a Selection Filter to decide the types of entities available for selection. By default, the **Geometry** option is selected, as shown in Figure 3–1.

My Filter
Geometry
Edge
Surface
Datums
Curve
Quilt
Body
Annotation
Table Object
Vertex
Sketch Region
Feature
Geometry ▼

Figure 3–1

If you leave the default option selected, you can select any of the listed geometry types. For complex models, you can specify any of the available options (such as **Edge**, **Surface**, **Curve**, etc.) to restrict your selection to the specified type. If you have selected a specific type in the selection filter, you can press and hold <Alt> to select entities outside of the current selection filter scope.

Surface Region Selection Options

The Region Selection options are available for both Part and Assembly files. Located in the lower right corner of the graphic window near the selection filter. These tools allow for different techniques for quickly selecting multiple surfaces. One options is always active, but any of the three can be switched to be expanding the fly-out next to the current selection and choosing the desired region selection option as shown in Figure 3–2.

Figure 3-2

Three Surface Region Selection options are available.

Type	Description
Trace	Used to select surfaces by tracing with the cursor over the Model. Only visible surfaces that make contact with the traced curve will be selected.
Lasso	Used to select surfaces by tracing a free form curve using the cursor. Only visible surfaces that are fully contained by the curve will be selected.
Box	Used to select surfaces by drawing a rectangle over the model using the cursor. This is the default option of the three types so if unchanged expect Creo surface selection to work in this manner. Creating the rectangle from left to right means surface fully enclosed by the rectangle will be selected. Creating the rectangle from right to left means surface that crosses into the rectangle's en-closer will be selected.

With the Box option ⬚(Only visible surface) can also be used by toggling it ON/OFF. When On only the surfaces that can be seen will be selected, while when Off hidden surfaces will be included in the selection box as well. |

Preselection Highlighting

As you move the cursor over the model, selectable entities will highlight. Figure 3-3 shows that the system highlights the available entities based on the selection filter setting, and you can select whichever entity is appropriate.

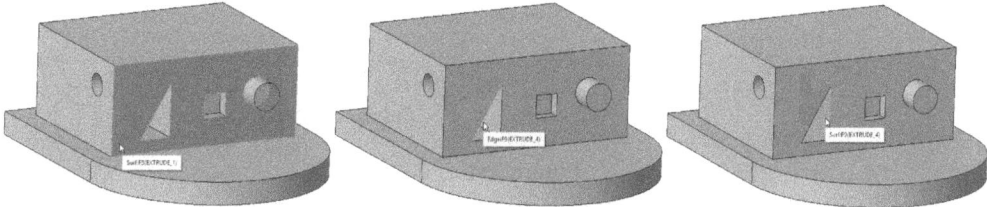

Figure 3-3

When you select an entity, it highlights in green. In the *mini* toolbar or the ribbon, you can select commands that apply to the entity selected, such as ⬚ (Extrude), 🔳 (Hole), etc. as shown on the left in Figure 3–4. If you select a command that applies to the parent feature, such as 🔀 (Edit Dimensions), 🖌 (Edit Definition), etc. then the entire feature highlights, as shown on the right in Figure 3–4.

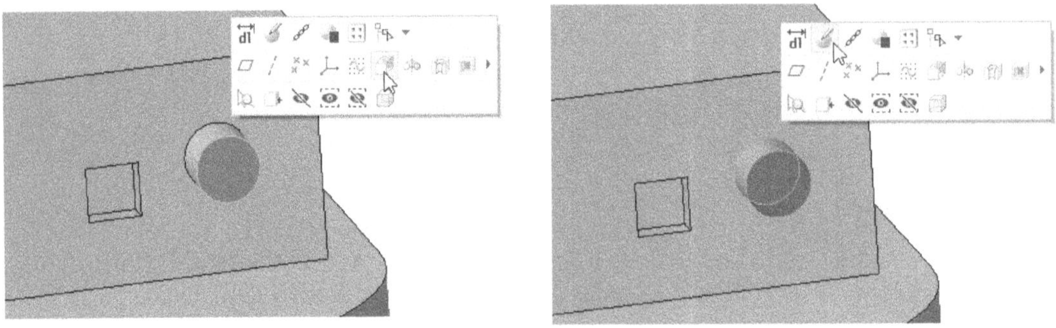

Figure 3–4

Multiple entities can be selected at once by holding <Ctrl> while selecting. The system creates a selection set, and indicates the number of selected entities in the **Selected Items** area in the lower right corner of the Creo Parametric window as shown in Figure 3–5.

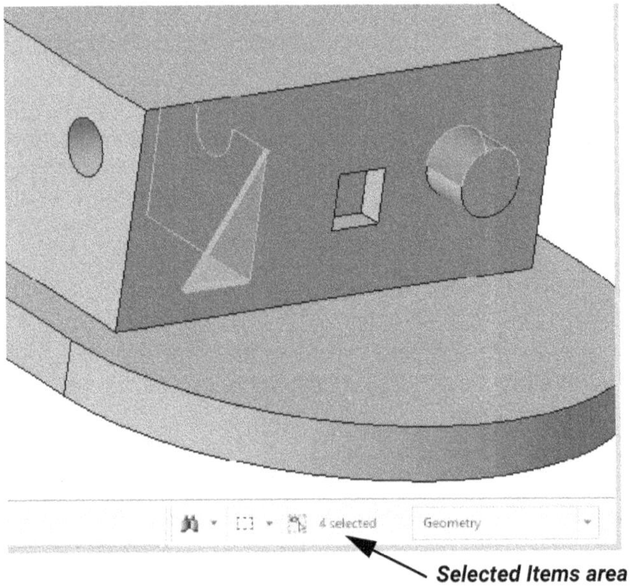

Selected Items area

Figure 3–5

If you double-click the **Selected Items** area, the Selected Items dialog box displays, as shown in Figure 3–6.

Figure 3–6

Select any entities in the list and click **Remove** to remove them from the selected items set.

3.2 Selection in the Model Tree

You can directly select features in the Model Tree by clicking the feature name. To ensure highlighting, click 📋 ▾ (Model Tree Settings) in the Model Tree and enable **Highlight Geometry**. Any feature selected in the Model Tree will then highlight in the model, as shown in Figure 3–7.

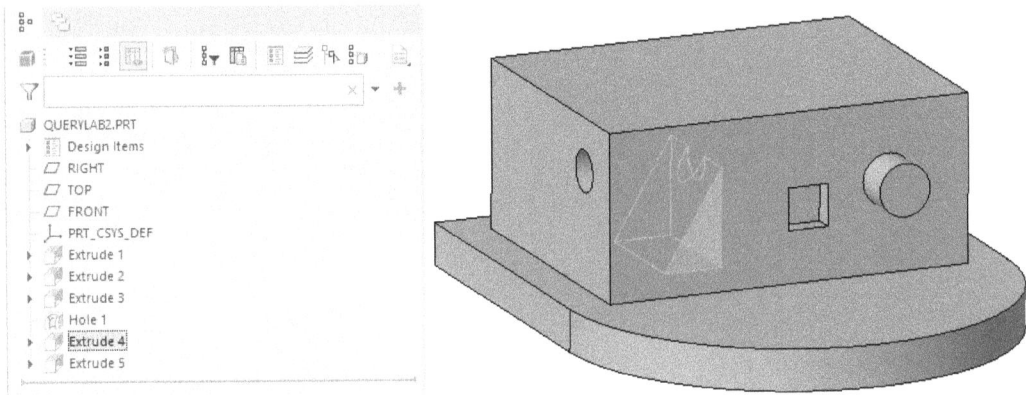

Figure 3–7

- You can also have the system highlight features in the model as you move the cursor over them in the Model Tree by clicking click 📋. (Model Tree Settings) and enabling **Preselection Highlighting**.

- In the Model Tree, you can use <Ctrl> and <Shift> in the same fashion you would with a Microsoft Office application. Press and hold <Ctrl> to select multiple, individual features.

- Select a feature, press and hold <Shift> and select another feature, and the system will select the two features, plus all features in between, as shown in Figure 3–8.

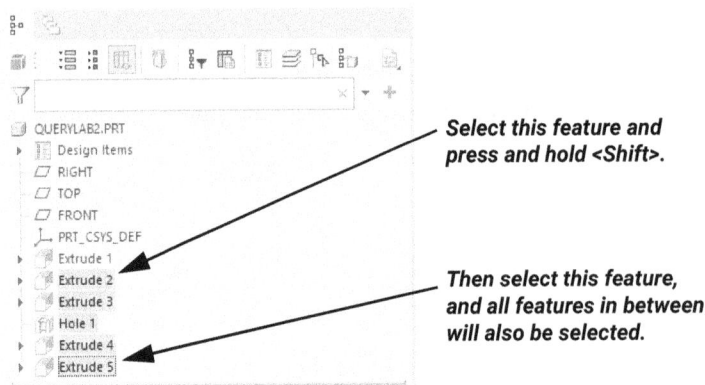

Figure 3–8

Auto Locate

You can use the **Auto Locate in Tree** option to highlight objects in the Model Tree that have been selected in the graphics window, as shown in Figure 3-9.

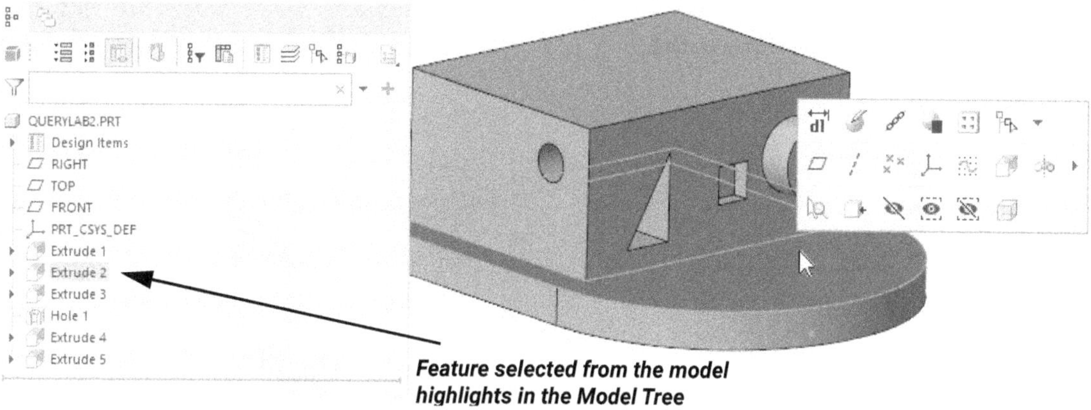

Feature selected from the model highlights in the Model Tree

Figure 3-9

In the Model Tree, click ⬛ (Model Tree Settings) and select **Auto Locate in Tree** to activate it, as shown in Figure 3-10.

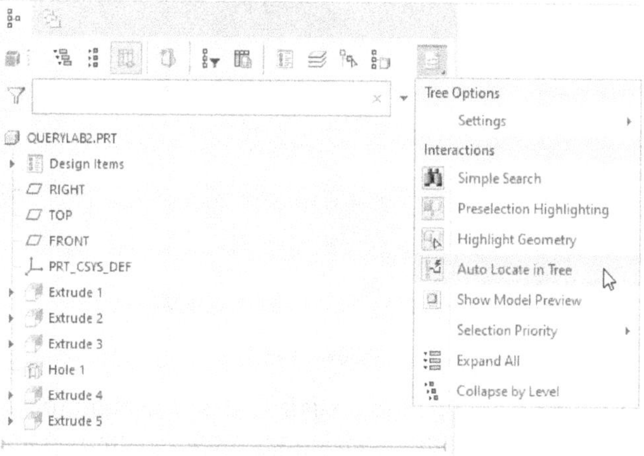

Figure 3-10

If **Auto Locate in Tree** is not enabled, you can select an object on the model, right-click and select **Locate in Model Tree**.If **Auto Locate in Tree** is enabled, **Locate in Model Tree** is removed from the right-click context menu.

With either method, the relevant branch in the Model Tree expands to the selected feature and its node is highlighted. Note that feature display must be enabled for assemblies to highlight features within components.

Note on Model Tree Features

In legacy versions of the Creo Parametric (Pro/ENGINEER) software, features were labeled in the Model Tree differently than they are currently. Figure 3–11 shows a model created with a legacy version, while Figure 3–12 shows a model recreated in the Creo Parametric software.

Legacy Model Tree Listing

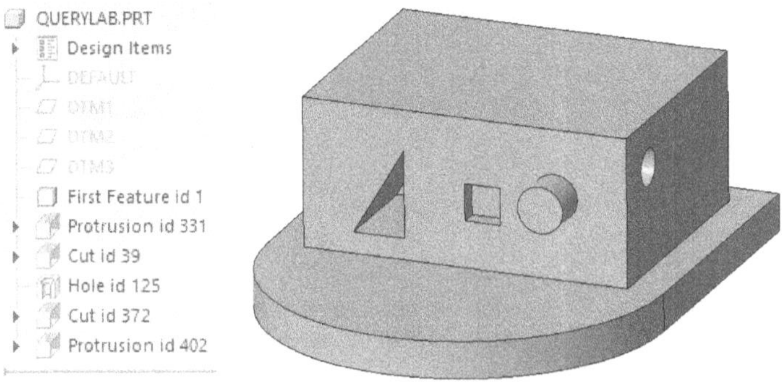

Figure 3–11

Modern Creo Parametric Model Tree Listing

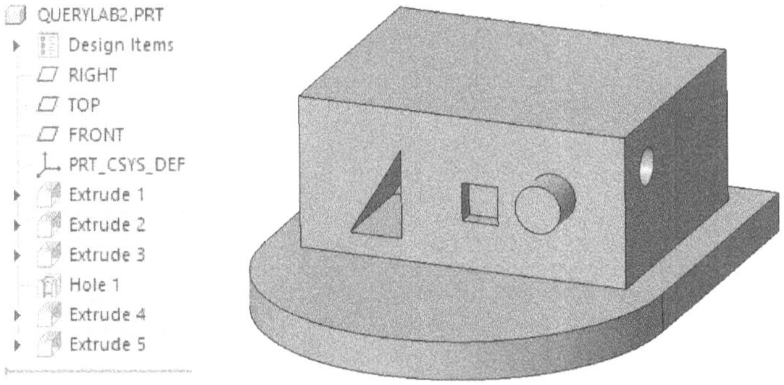

Figure 3–12

Although this course will focus on the modern listing, it is important to be aware of the difference, as you will likely have to work on a legacy model at some point. For that reason you will see both listings used in this course. Whether legacy or modern, features are selected and edited in the same manner.

3.3 Model Tree Search

When using the *Model Tree search* tool, the Model Tree filters and updates dynamically as you type letters in, as shown in Figure 3–13.

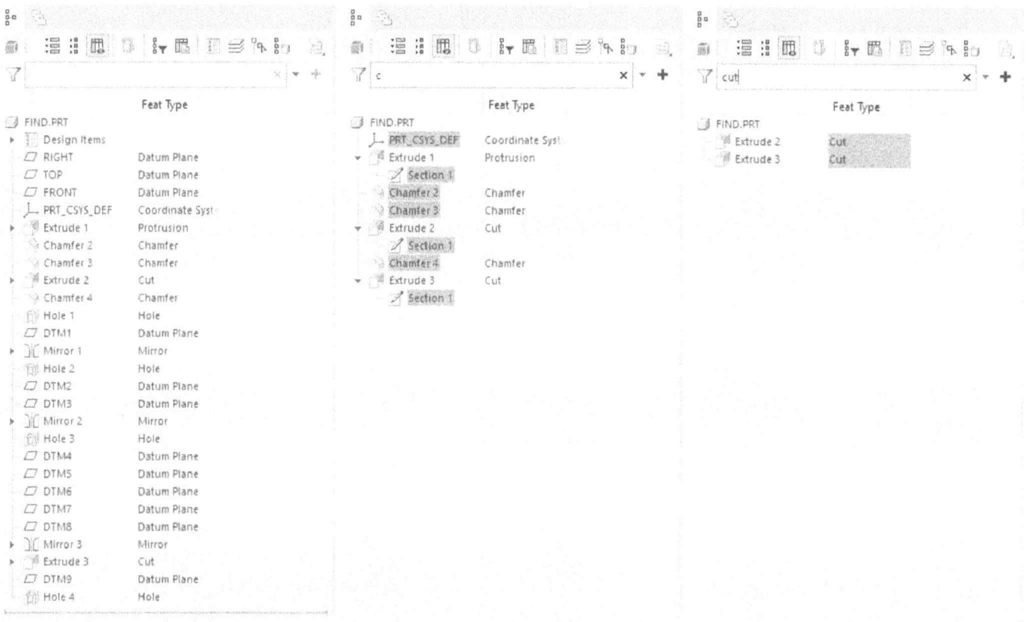

Figure 3–13

In addition to searching text, you can also search for conditions, query types, and wild cards. By default, the Model Tree filters as you type and also highlights objects in the graphics area. These settings can be controlled by right-clicking in the Search bar and enabling or disabling the **Dynamic Filter/Search** or **Highlight in Graphics** (Assembly mode only) options, as shown in Figure 3–14.

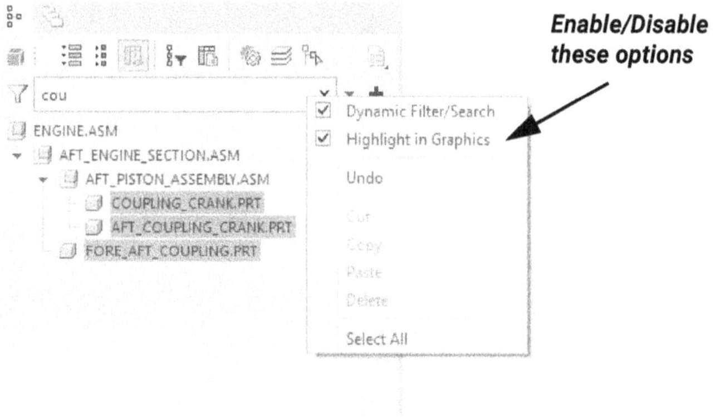

Figure 3–14

You can also filter on values from any columns you add to the Model Tree display. If you add columns to the Model Tree (as shown in Figure 3–15), you can right-click in the search box and select one or more of those columns from the shortcut menu.

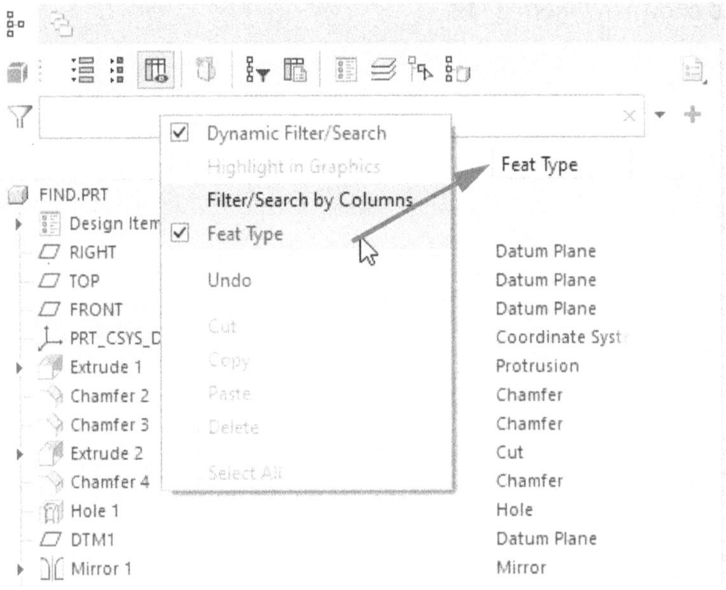

Figure 3–15

When you type values in the search field, the Model Tree filters based on the columns you selected, as Figure 3–16.

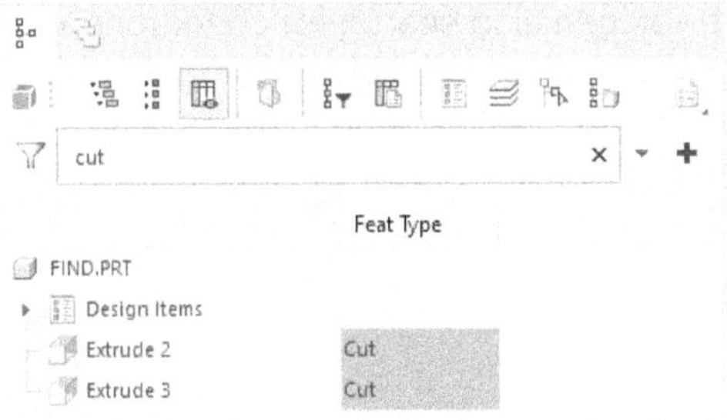

Figure 3–16

To select the objects that are highlighted by your search, click ✚ (Add marked components to selection buffer) in the Model Tree.

If you want to search without filtering, you can click the ▽ (Filter) next to the search bar. The icon changes to 🔍 (Search) and the found objects highlight but no longer filter, as shown in Figure 3-17.

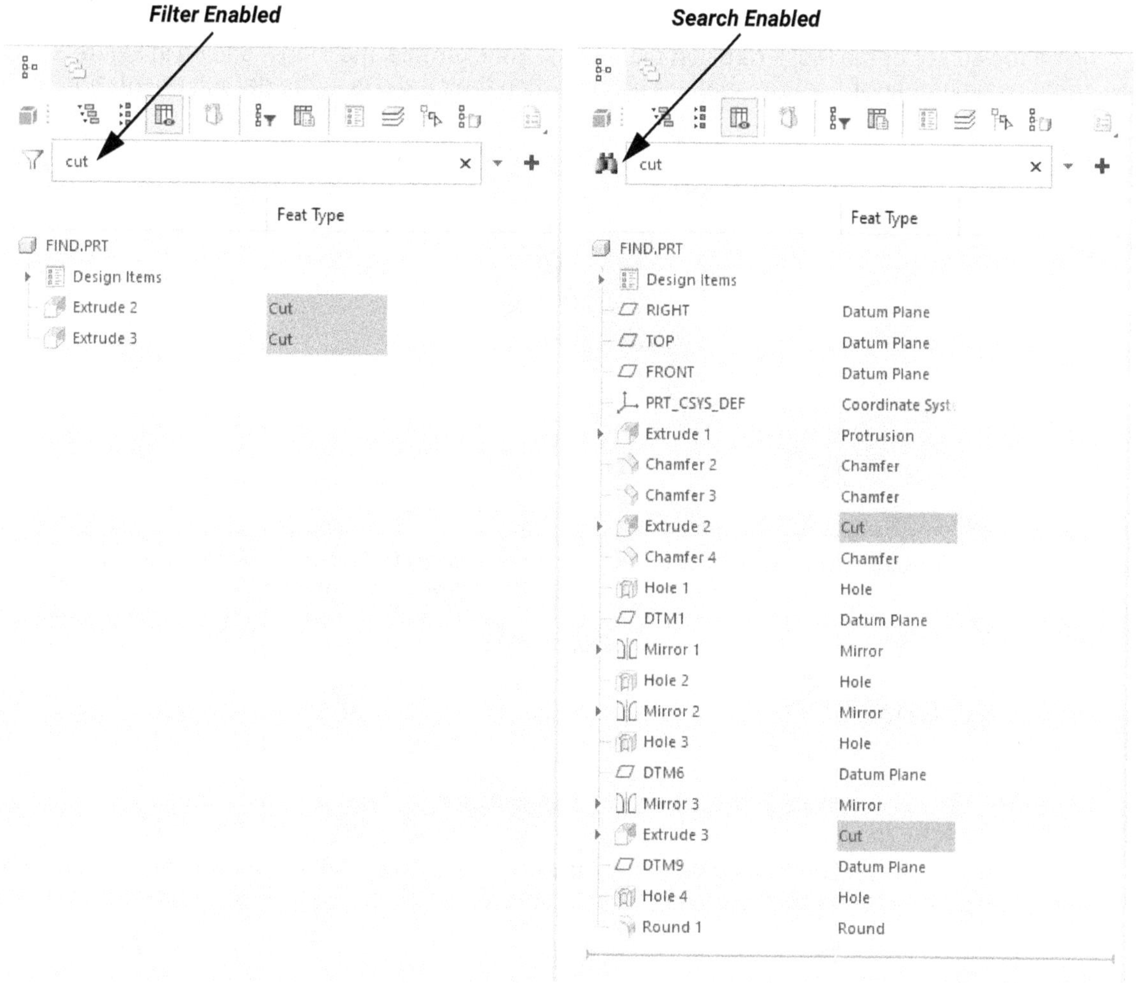

Figure 3-17

3.4 Selecting Hidden Entities

In some model orientations, features are hidden. To select these features or the entities that comprise them, you can reorient the model so that the features are no longer hidden. However, this technique is not efficient. To select hidden entities, you should query through the model using the cursor or the Pick From List dialog box. For example, the model shown in Figure 3–18 contains a number of features that are hidden when the model is in the default orientation.

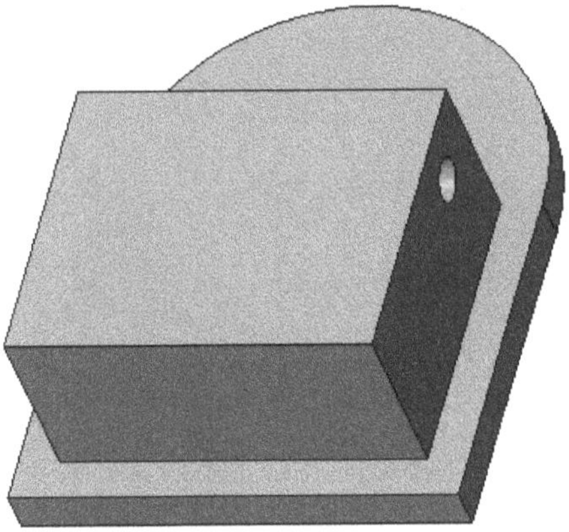

Features hidden when shaded

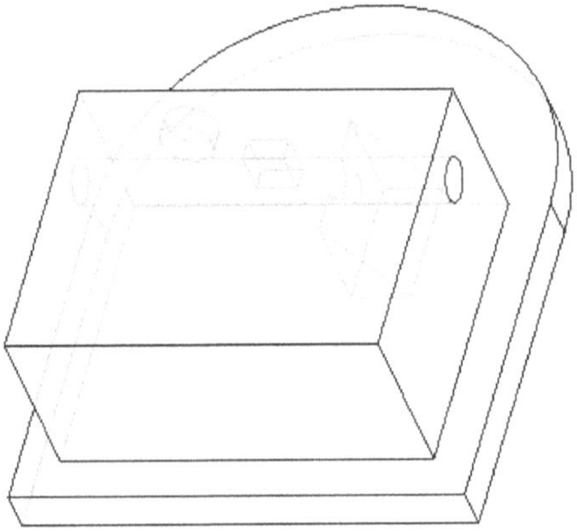

Features display in Hidden Line mode, but still cannot be selected directly

Figure 3–18

Query Selection

How To: Select Hidden Entities Using the Mouse

1. Hover the cursor directly over an entity (as set in the selection filter), even if it is hidden. The entity directly below the cursor highlights.

   Note: You can set the model display to hidden line to help identify the location of the feature.

2. Right-click to toggle through to the next entity in the model. Repeat the click action to step through all entities that lie directly below the cursor.

3. Once the entity you want is highlighted, click to select it.

Pick From List

It is recommended to review a list of all of the entities that can be queried based on where the cursor is located.

How To: Review All of the Features

1. Position the cursor directly over an entity, even if it is hidden. The feature number and type display in a tooltip, indicating the current feature.

2. Hold the right mouse button and select ⬚ (Pick From List). The *Pick From List* dialog box opens, as shown in Figure 3–19.

Figure 3–19

Note: The features that display in the Pick From List dialog box depend on the location of the mouse when you select ⬚ (Pick From List).

3. Select the entity in the selection list or use the up and down arrows to navigate to the required entity.

4. Click **OK** to accept the selected entity.

3.5 Selecting Chains

Chains

Chains consist of a collection of edges or curves that are related either by tangency or by a common vertex. When you establish a chain you are collecting edges or curves into a group to more efficiently perform modeling actions.

- To create curve chains, you select an entity, press and hold <Shift>, and then select the additional entity or entities.

- There are two types of chains: Non-rule based and Rule-based.

Non-rule Based

The two types of Non-rule based chains are described as follows:

- **One-by-One Chain:** A chain of individual curves and edges that you select. Typically, you would create a One-by-One chain if the entities you select are from different features or exist across multiple features. If you hover over the entities, a box displays indicating the chain type, as shown in Figure 3–20.

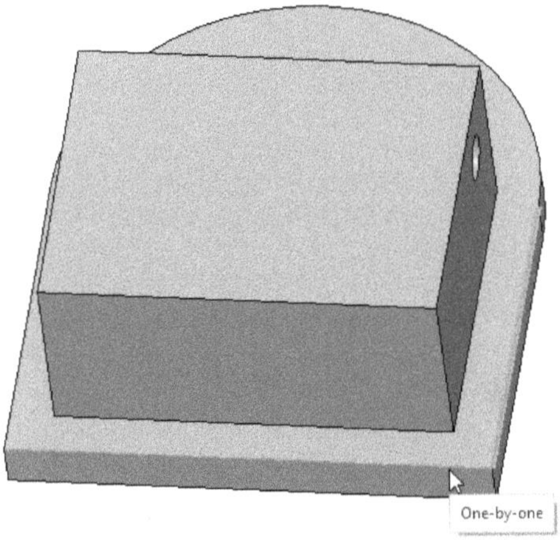

One-by-one

Figure 3–20

- **Intent Chain:** When features are created in Creo Parametric, they result in new edges and surfaces. These edges and surfaces can then be used as references for additional features, and so on. Changes to the original features can result in lost references and feature failures.

An Intent Chain is established and preserved by the feature that created it, not by the entities of that feature. Consider the example shown in Figure 3–21.

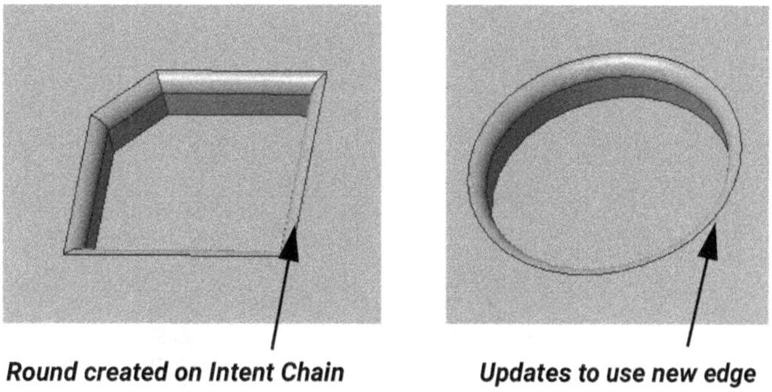

Round created on Intent Chain   **Updates to use new edge**

Figure 3–21

The round is created on the Intent Chain of edges formed by the cut. When the section is redefined to have a circular section, the round simply updates to use it. Without intent edges, the round would have failed after the edit.

Rule Based

The three types of Rule based chains are described as follows:

- **Partial Loop Chain:** A chain that begins at a start-point, follows an edge, and ends at the end-point of a selected edge or curve. This is also known as a From-To chain. If there is a possibility of multiple chains, you can right-click to step through the possibilities, as shown in Figure 3–22.

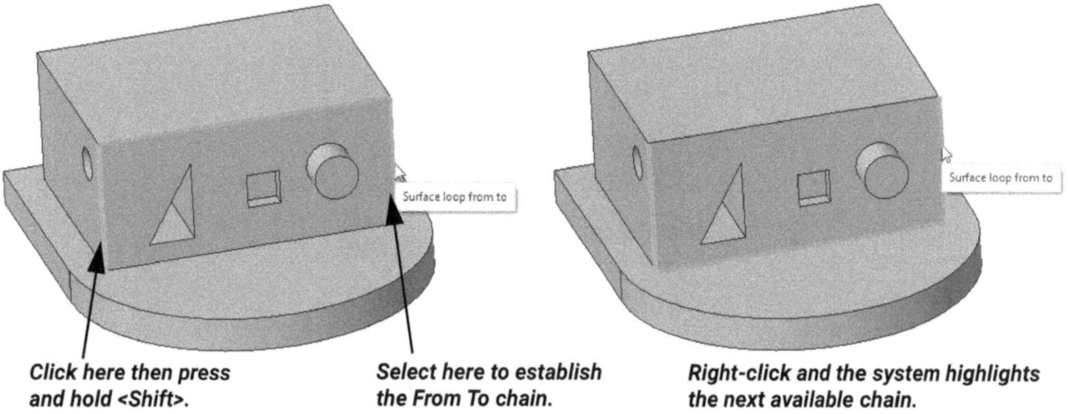

Click here then press and hold <Shift>.   **Select here to establish the From To chain.**   **Right-click and the system highlights the next available chain.**

Figure 3–22

- **Complete Loop Chain:** A chain that contains a loop of curves or edges that encompasses the curve, quilt, or solid surface it belongs to.

By right-clicking a third time, they system highlights the surface loop, as shown in Figure 3–23.

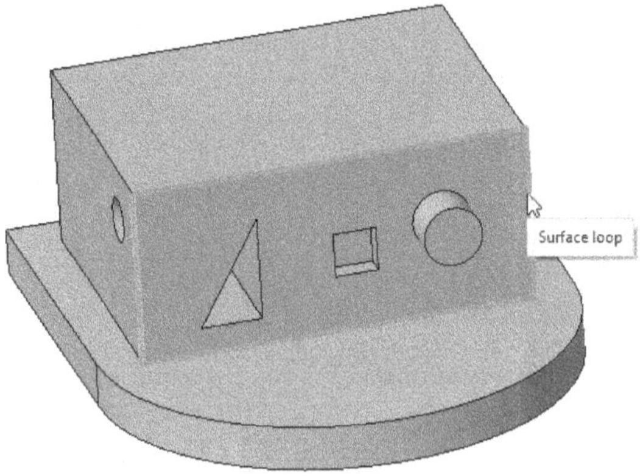

Figure 3–23

- **Tangent Chain:** A chain defined by the selected entity and the end of the adjacent tangent entities, as shown in Figure 3–24.

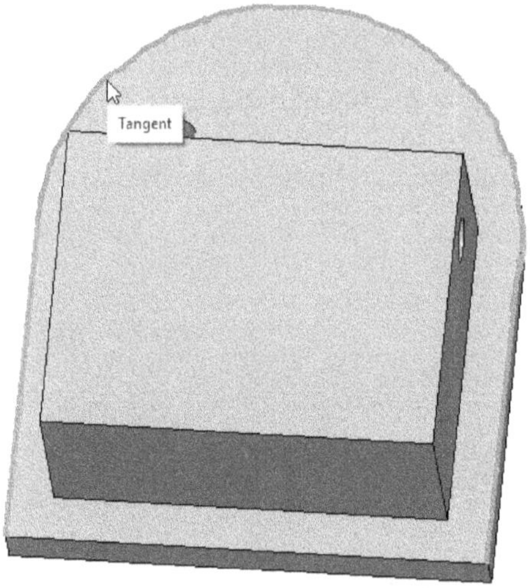

Figure 3–24

3.6 Box Selection

When using an object/action workflow, you can use 2D box selection in combination with the selection filter settings to quickly choose objects of the type applicable to the active filter.

When using 2D box selection and dragging the box from left to right, all items entirely located within the box are selected. When dragging the box from right to left all items touched and surrounded by the 2D box are selected, as shown in Figure 3–25.

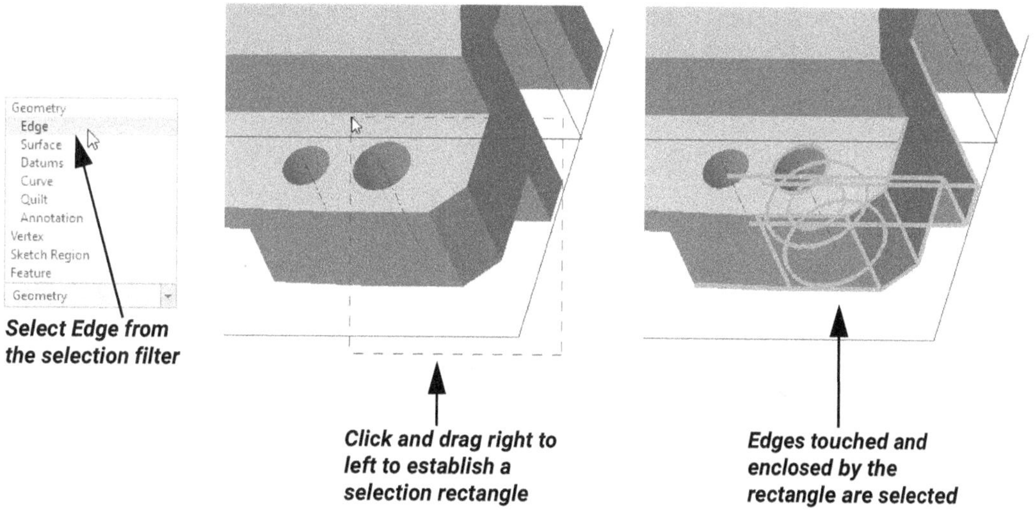

Select Edge from the selection filter

Click and drag right to left to establish a selection rectangle

Edges touched and enclosed by the rectangle are selected

Figure 3–25

You can press and hold <Ctrl> and perform multiple 2D box selection operations. To remove objects from the selection, press and hold <Ctrl> and then click the individual objects.

3.7 Using Search

When models are very complex, or you need to select many features or entities, you can use the *Search Tool* shown in Figure 3–26.

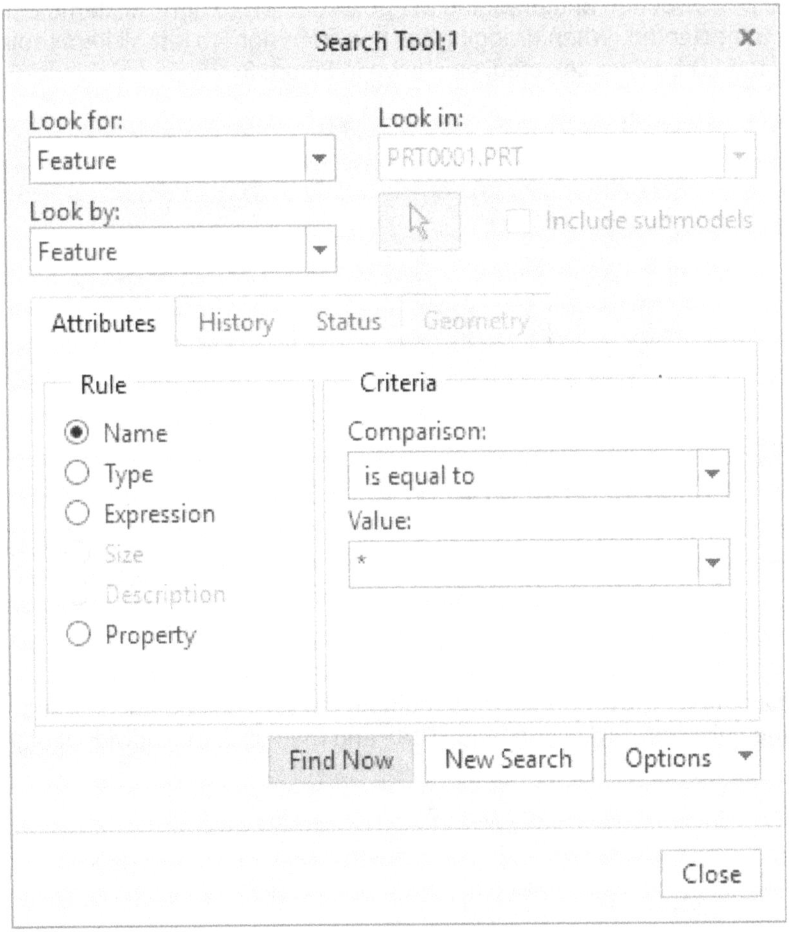

Figure 3–26

You can open the *Search Tool* by clicking 🔍 (Find) in the lower-right of the Creo Parametric window. In the Search Tool, select the type of entity that you want to look for (**Feature**, **Edge**, **Surface**, etc.), then set the search options such as searching by **Name**, **Type**, **Size**, etc. Once you have established the search criteria, you can click **Find Now** to see the results.

For example, if you were to search the model shown in Figure 3–27 for all holes, you would set the options as shown and click **Find Now** to see the results.

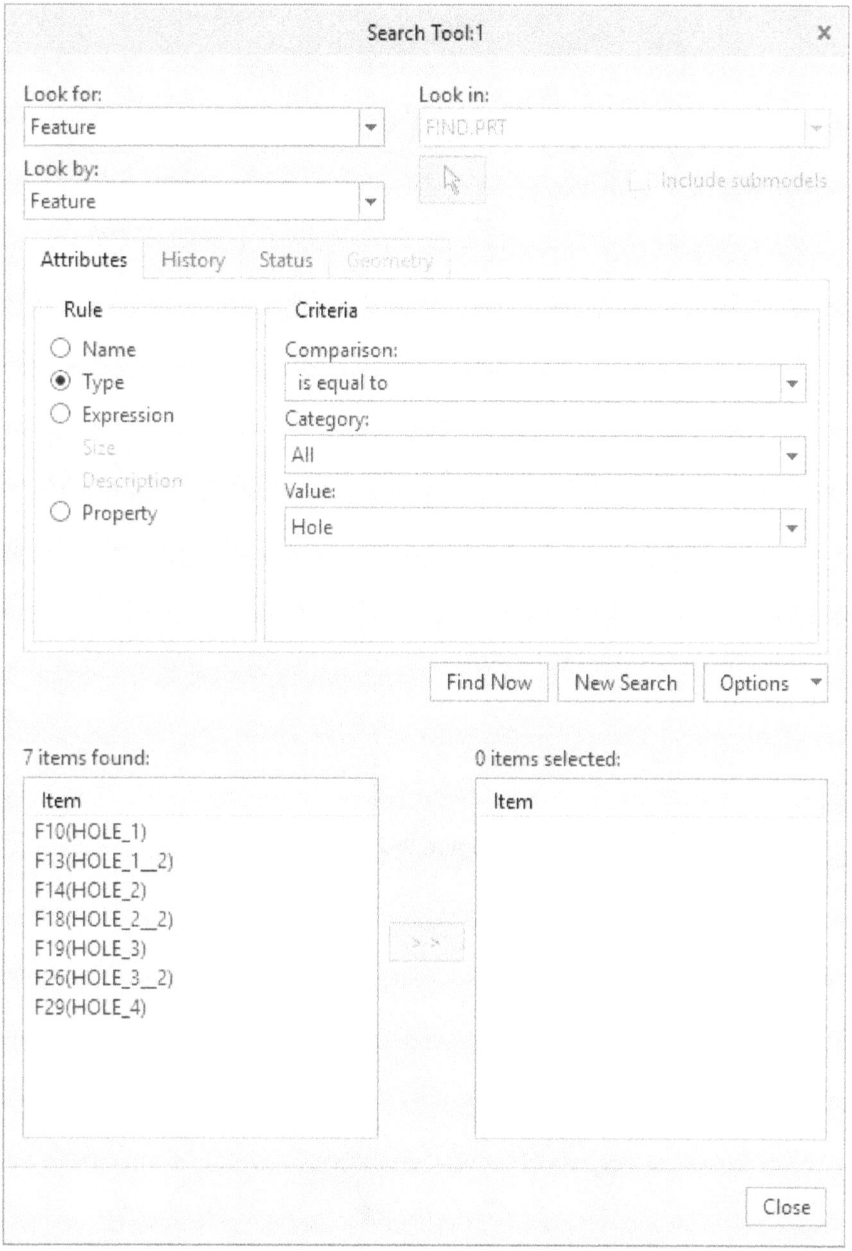

Figure 3–27

You can then select one or more of the entities returned by the search, and click >> (Add Item) to add them to the list of selected items.

You can also run searches that contain multiple search criteria by creating a Query. In the *Search Tool* dialog box, click **Options>Build Query** and the *Query Builder* area of the dialog box displays, as shown in Figure 3–28.

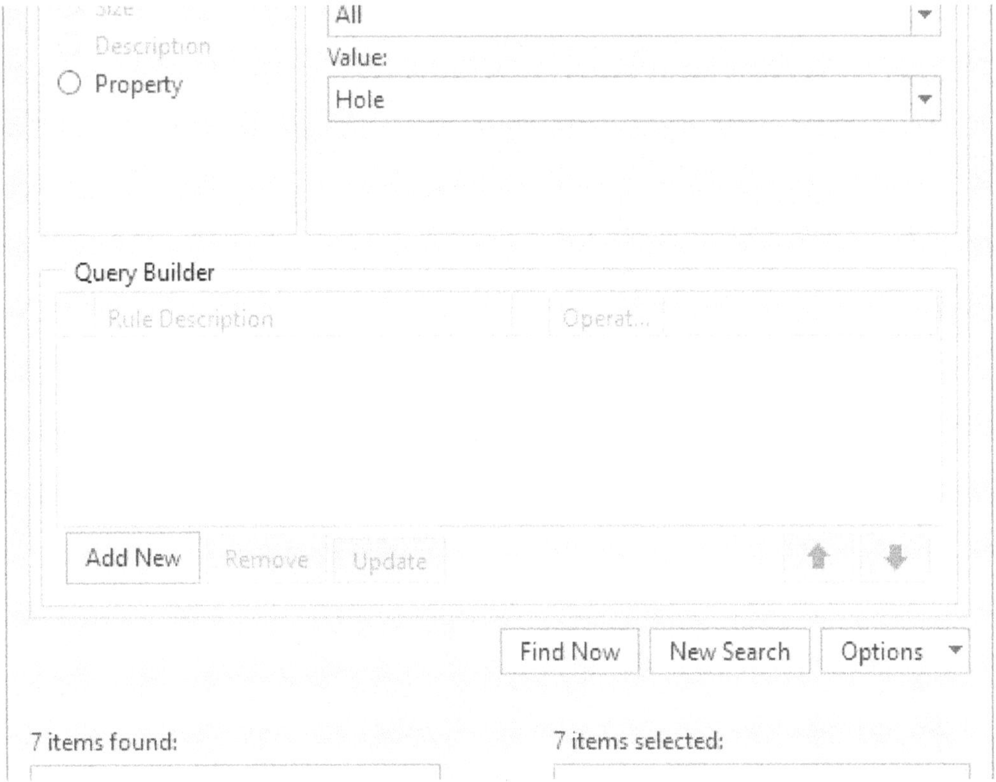

Figure 3–28

With the *Query Builder* open, you can set your search criteria and click **Add New** to add the search to the query. You can then set an additional criteria and add it to the query. For example, if you wanted to search for all datums between **DTM1** and **DTM9**, you could create the query shown in Figure 3–29.

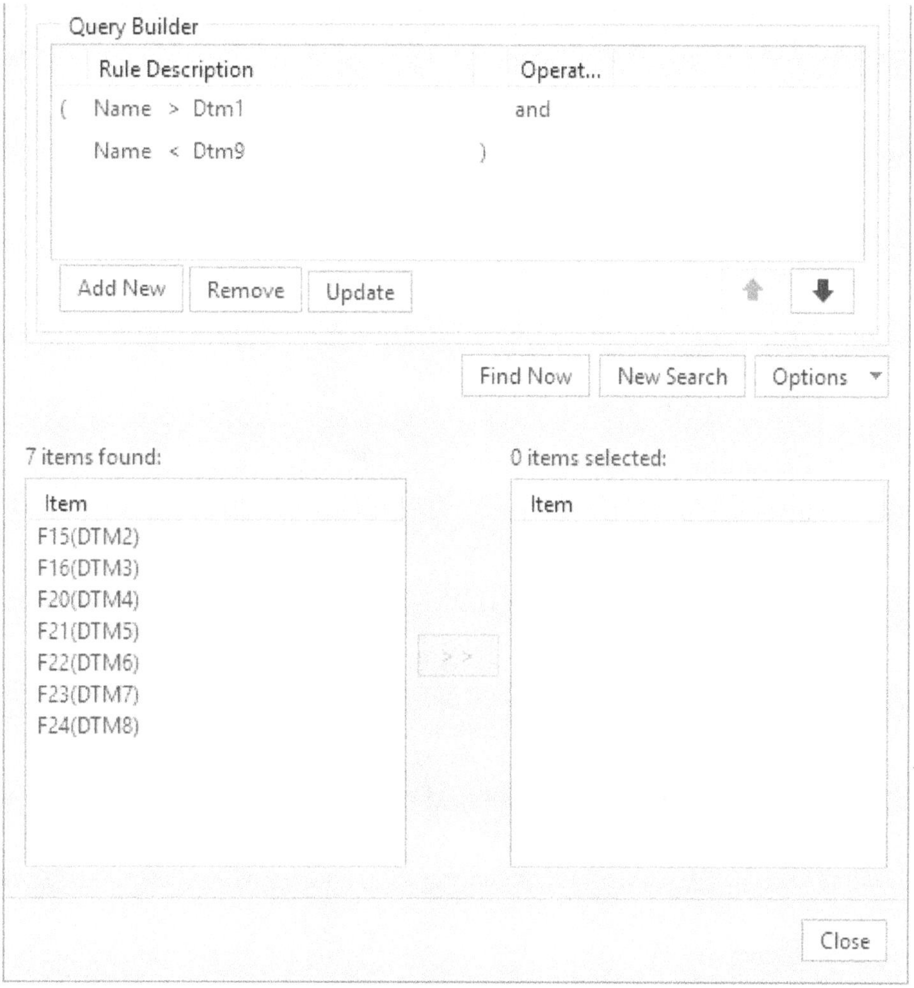

Figure 3–29

Practice 3a
Select Geometry I

Practice Objective

- Select hidden features in a model using the Pick from List option and the mouse buttons.

In this practice, you will edit the dimensions associated with the two hidden features, as shown in Figure 3–30. To edit these features you will use selection techniques for quickly selecting hidden features without having to reorient the model.

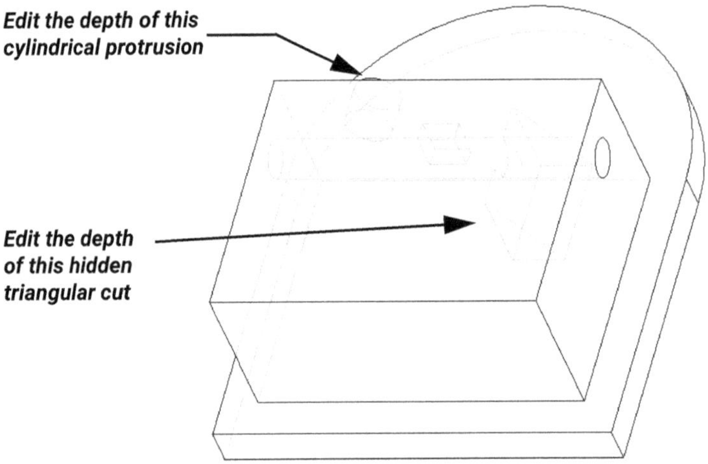

Edit the depth of this cylindrical protrusion

Edit the depth of this hidden triangular cut

Figure 3–30

Task 1: Open the querylab2.prt model and set the initial display.

---

1. In the *Home* tab, click ⌞ (Select Working Directory) and select the *Selecting_Geometry_I* folder.

2. Open **querylab2.prt.**

3. Set the model display as follows:

    - ⁺ᣟ⌞ *(Datum Display Filters)*: All Off

    - ⤳ *(Spin Center)*: Off

    - ⌞ *(Display Style)*: ⬚ (Hidden Line)

Task 2: Use the geometry selection filters.

1. Move the cursor to the location shown in Figure 3–31. Note that only the surface highlights.
2. Move the cursor to the location shown in Figure 3–32. Note again that only the edge highlights.

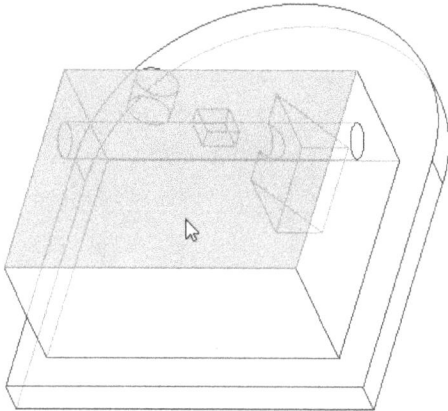

Figure 3–31

Figure 3–32

3. Set the *Selection Filter* to **Feature**, as shown in Figure 3–33.

Figure 3–33

4. Move the cursor to the location shown in Figure 3−34 and note that the entire feature highlights.

5. Move the cursor to the location shown in Figure 3−35 and note again that the entire feature highlights.

Figure 3−34

Figure 3−35

6. Select **Geometry** from the Selection Filter, as shown in Figure 3−36.

Geometry
　Edge
　Surface
　Datums
　Curve
　Quilt
　Body
　Annotation
Vertex
Sketch Region
Feature

Feature

Figure 3−36

Task 3: Edit the depth of the hidden triangular cut.

1. Hover the cursor over the model. Once an entity is recognized, it highlights and a help line displays indicating the entity. Hover the cursor over the surface shown in Figure 3–37.

2. Right-click and the surface of the cut feature located directly below the original mouse location is highlighted, as shown in Figure 3–38.

Figure 3–37

Figure 3–38

Note: Keep the model in its default orientation at all times.

3. Keeping the cursor in the same location, click the left mouse button to select the surface. The surface of **Extrude 4** highlights in green and the *mini* toolbar opens, as shown in Figure 3–39.

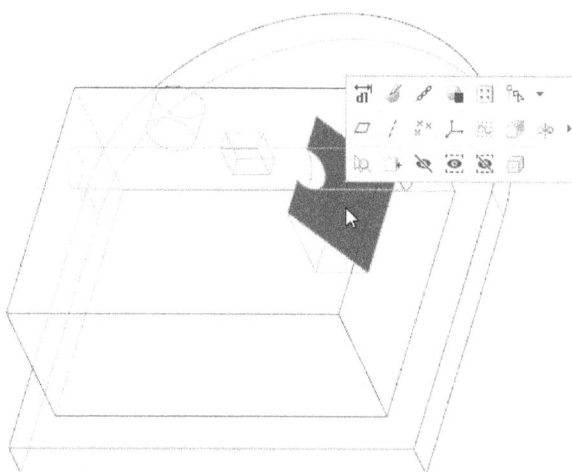

Figure 3–39

4. Move the cursor over any icons in the middle or bottom row, and note that only the selected surface is highlighted, as shown in Figure 3−40. This is because these commands use the surface as a reference, so the surface, not the feature, remains highlighted.

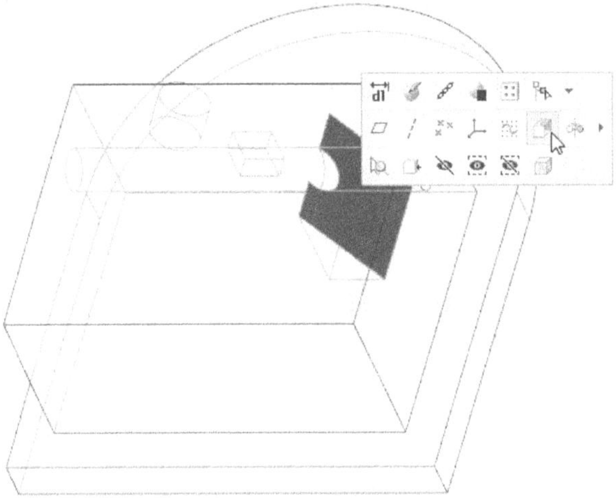

Figure 3−40

5. Move the cursor over any icons in the top row and note that the entire feature is highlighted, as shown in Figure 3−41. This is because these commands apply to the entire feature, so the system highlights the feature.

    Note that if you move off the model, the *mini* toolbar closes. Simply repeat the previous steps to reopen it.

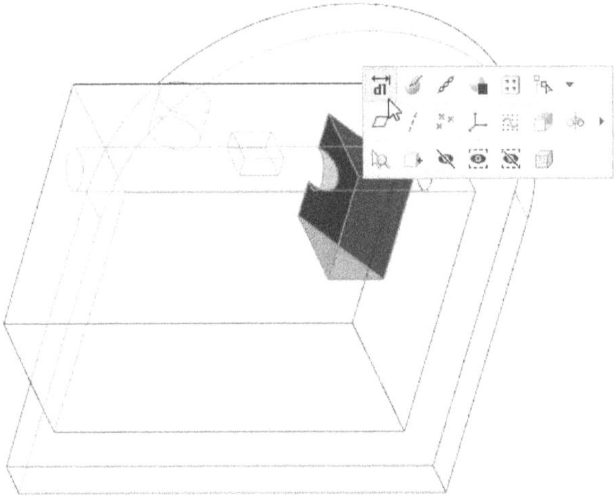

Figure 3−41

6. In the *mini* toolbar, select ⃗d1⃗ (Edit Dimension). All of the dimensions associated with this feature display.

7. Double-click on the 30 depth dimension and enter **50**.

8. Click twice (two distinct clicks) on the screen to regenerate the model. Alternatively, click ⌗⇌ (Regenerate) in the *Quick-access* toolbar.

Task 4: Edit the diameter of the circular extrusion.

1. Hover the cursor over the location shown in Figure 3–42.

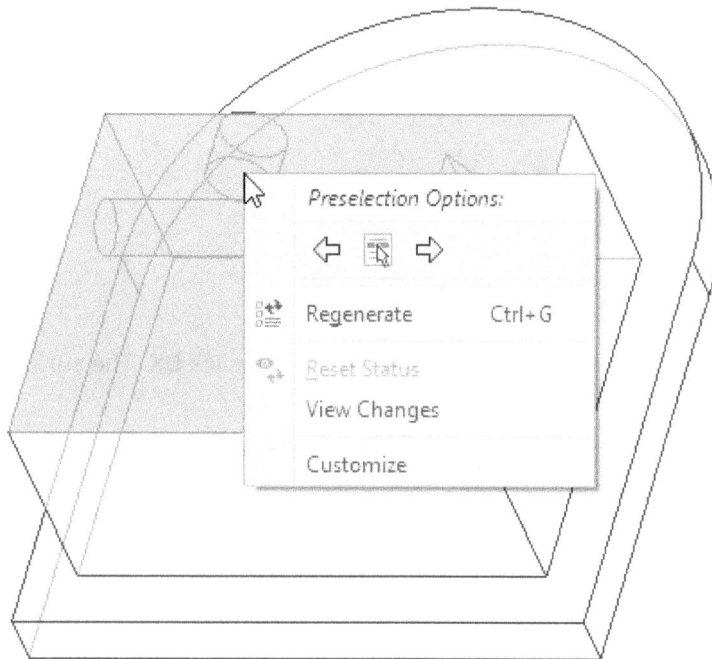

Figure 3–42

Note: The Pick From List dialog box is an alternative to right-clicking to toggle through the selectable entities.

2. Hold the right mouse button, and select ▦ (Pick From List). The *Pick From List* dialog box opens, as shown in Figure 3−43.The features that display in the *Pick From List* dialog box might vary depending on where the cursor is located when you select ▦ (Pick From List). The *Pick From List* dialog box lists all of the entities that lie beneath the selected location.

Figure 3−43

3. In the selection list, select **Surf:F10(EXTRUDE_5)** and click **OK**. The surface of the cylindrical protrusion highlights in green.

4. Hold the right mouse button and select ⊢d1⊣ (Edit Dimensions). All of the dimensions associated with the feature display on the model.

5. Double-click on the **12.5** diameter dimension, and enter **20**.

6. Click twice on the screen to regenerate the model.

Task 5: Select edges to create rounds.

1. Select the edge highlighted in Figure 3−44. Then, press and hold <Shift>.

2. Move the cursor to the position shown in Figure 3−45 and note the **One by One** curve highlights.

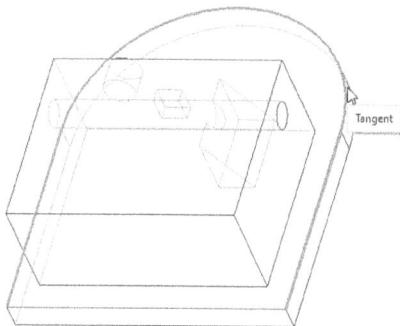

Figure 3−44

Figure 3−45

3. Right-click once and the Tangent chain highlights, as shown in Figure 3−46.

4. Right-click again and the From To chain highlights, as shown in Figure 3−47.

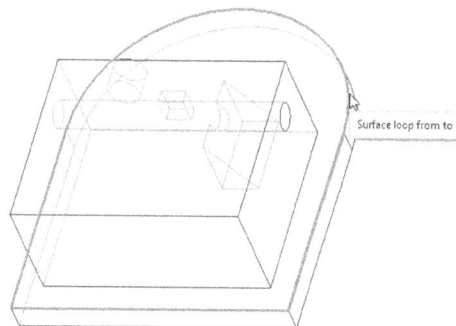

Figure 3−46

Figure 3−47

5. Right-click again and the next From To chain highlights, as shown in Figure 3–48.

6. Right-click again and the Surface Loop chain highlights, as shown in Figure 3–49.

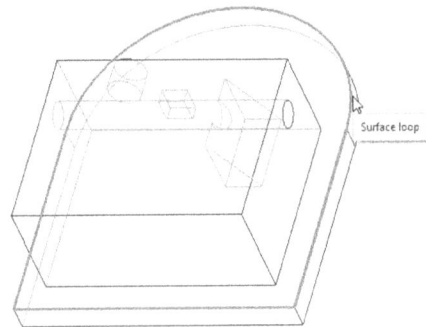

| Figure 3–48 | Figure 3–49 |

7. Press and hold the right mouse button, and select ⬚ (Pick From List).

8. Click through the list and note that the same chains highlight as the previous few steps.

    Note: The Pick From List tool is an efficient way to step through multiple selection option.

9. Select the **Surface loop** chain, as shown in Figure 3–50.

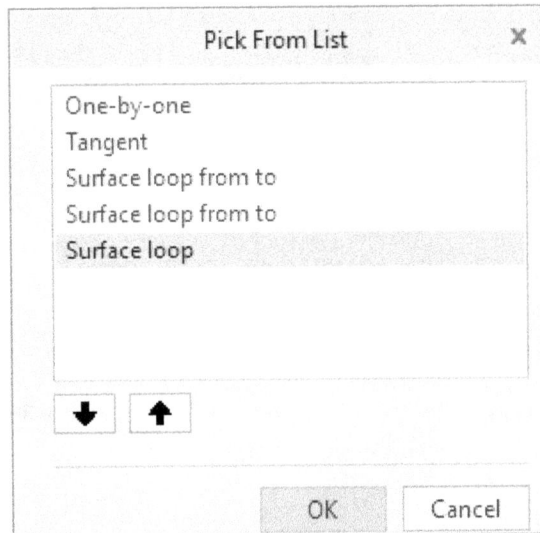

Figure 3–50

10. In the *Pick From List* dialog box, click **OK**.

11. In the *mini* toolbar, click ⌇ (Round), as shown in Figure 3–51.

   Note: *Rounds are covered in detail in later chapters.*

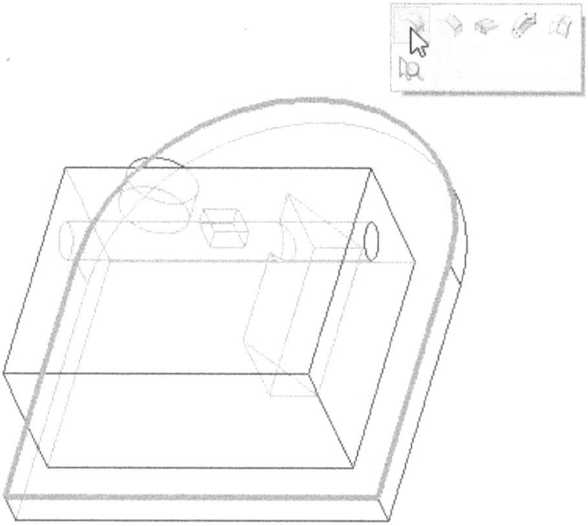

Figure 3–51

12. Set the *Radius* to **2.00**.

13. Click ✓ (Complete Feature).

14. Set the display to ▱ (Shading With Edges) and review the model.

15. Save the model.

16. In the *Quick Access* Toolbar, click ✕ (Close).

17. In the *Home* tab, click ⌇ (Erase Not Displayed) to erase all of the models from memory.

End of practice

Practice 3b
Select Geometry II

Practice Objectives

- Select geometry using the selection rectangle.

- Select features using the Search Tool.

In this practice, you will use the box selection method to select multiple edges on which to add a round feature. You will also use the Search Tool to select multiple datum planes so you can delete them.

Task 1: Open the querylab2.prt model and set the initial display.

1. In the *Home* tab, click ⬙ (Select Working Directory) and select the *Selecting_Geometry_II* folder.

2. Open **find.prt.**

3. Set the model display as follows:

- ⁺⁄⁎ *(Datum Display Filters)*: All Off

- ⋟ *(Spin Center)*: Off

- ⬚ *(Display Style)*: ⬚ (Shading With Edges)

Task 2: Use the selection tools to add rounds to the model.

1. Select the surface shown in Figure 3–52 and click ⬦ (View Normal).

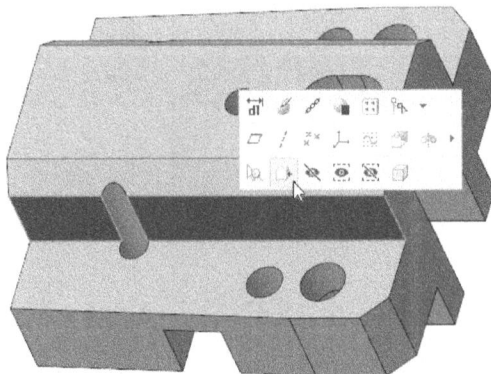

Figure 3–52

The model reorients, as shown in Figure 3–53.

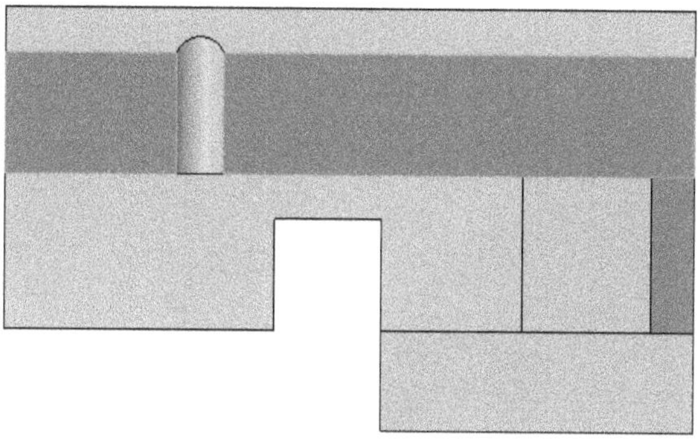

Figure 3–53

2. Click on the screen to clear the selection of the surface.

3. Drag a rectangle from right to left, around the geometry shown in Figure 3–54.

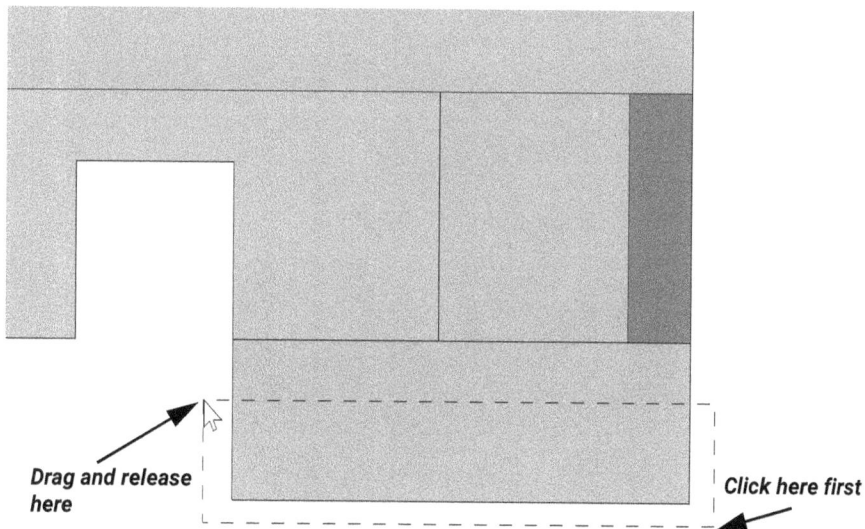

Drag and release here

Click here first

Figure 3–54

- Note that all of the geometry within the rectangle, including surfaces and edges are selected.

4. Click on the screen to clear the selection of the extrude.

5. In the lower right of the Creo Parametric window, expand the selection filter and select **Edge**, as shown in Figure 3–55.

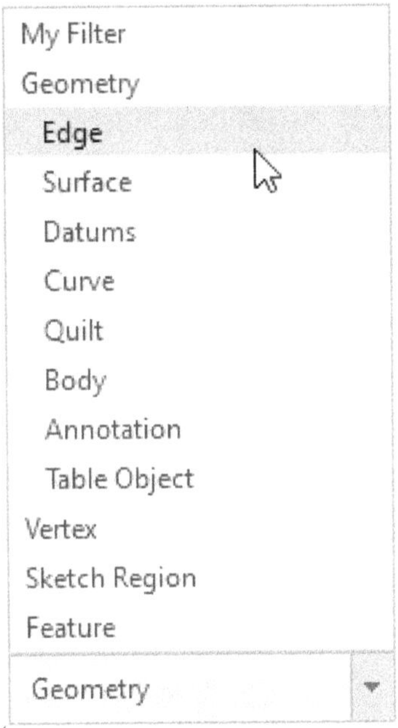

| My Filter |
| Geometry |
| **Edge** |
| Surface |
| Datums |
| Curve |
| Quilt |
| Body |
| Annotation |
| Table Object |
| Vertex |
| Sketch Region |
| Feature |
| Geometry ▼ |

Figure 3–55

6. Click and drag a selection rectangle from left to right, as shown in Figure 3–56.

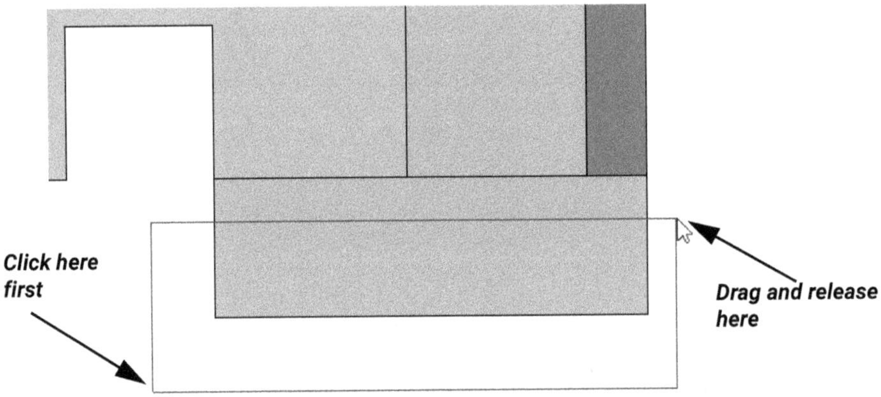

Click here first

Drag and release here

Figure 3–56

Note: The rectangle is solid. This indicates that only entities found in the rectangle will be selected.

7. Press <Ctrl>+<D> to return to default orientation.

8. Only the edges completely within the box are selected, as shown in Figure 3−57.

Figure 3−57

9. Click on the screen to clear the selection of the entities.

10. Select the edge shown in Figure 3−58 and click ╬ (View Normal).

Figure 3−58

11. Click on the screen to clear the selection of the edge.

12. Click and drag a selection rectangle from right to left, as shown in Figure 3–59.

Drag and release here   Click here first

Figure 3–59

13. Press <Ctrl>+<D> to return to default orientation.

• The edges crossed by and inside the box are selected, as shown in Figure 3–60.

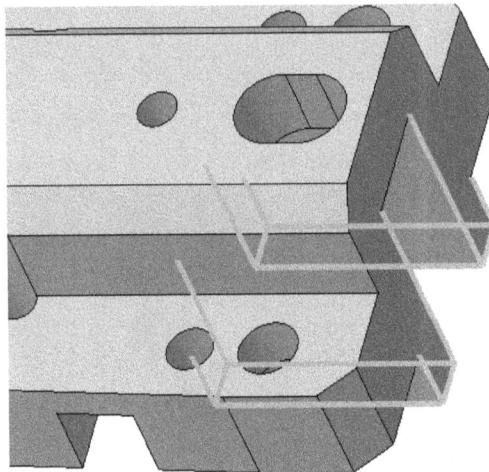

Figure 3–60

14. Press and hold <Ctrl> and select the four edges shown in Figure 3–61 so that they are removed from the set.

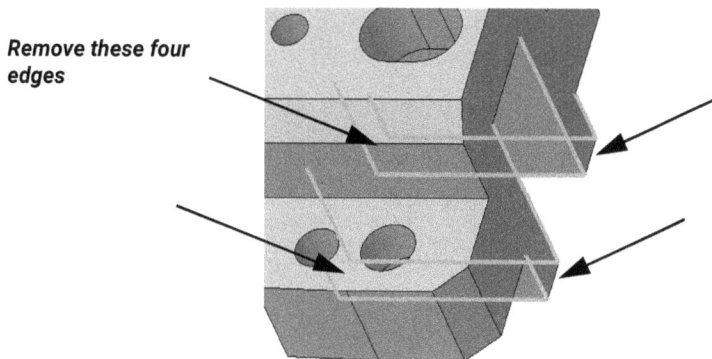

Figure 3–61

15. In the *Engineering* group of the ribbon, click ⟡ (Round).

16. Edit the radius to **0.5** and press <Enter>.

17. Press the middle mouse button to complete the round feature.

Task 3: Use the search tool to select multiple datum features for deletion.

The assumption for this task is that you need to delete all datum planes between **DTM1** *and* **DTM9**, *except* **DTM6**.

1. In the *In-graphics* toolbar, enable 🔩 (Plane Display).

2. The model, with multiple unused datum planes, displays, as shown in Figure 3–62.

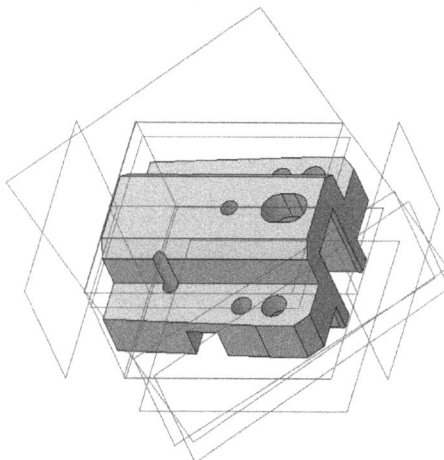

Figure 3–62

Note: If the planes display with a translucent brown shading, turn it off by clicking on

🔩 *(Plane Fill Display) in the In-graphics toolbar.*

3. In the lower-right of the Creo Parametric window, click 🔍 (Find). The *Search Tool* dialog box opens, as shown in Figure 3–63.

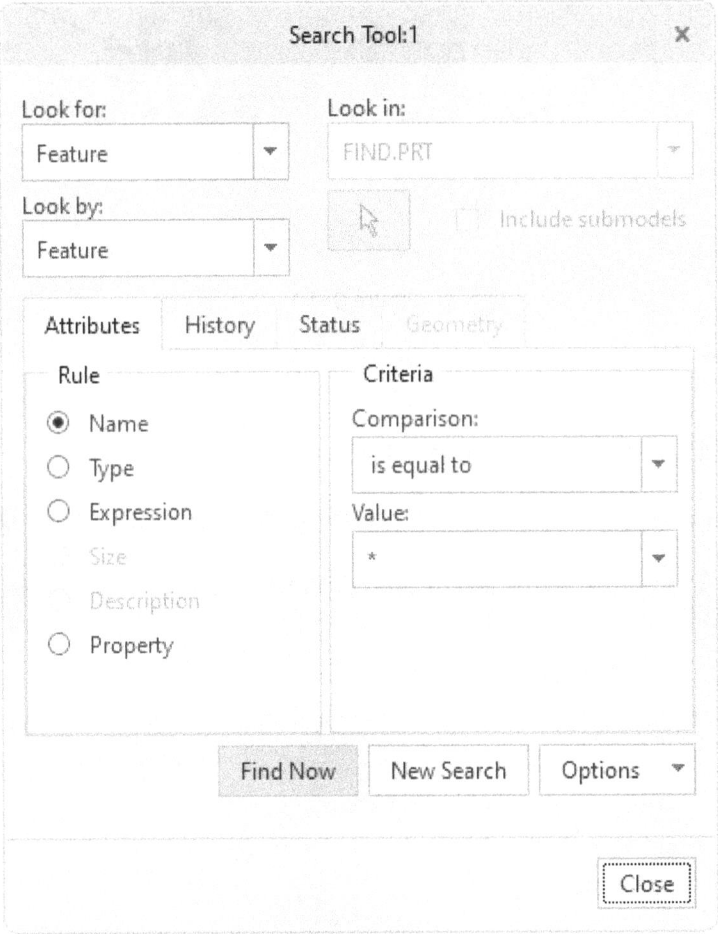

Figure 3–63

4. In the *Search Tool* dialog box, select "**is greater than**" from the *Comparison* drop-down list.

5. Select **DTM1** from the *Value* drop-down list.

6. Click **Options>Build Query**.

7. Click **Add New** and the *Search Tool* dialog box updates, as shown in Figure 3–64. This will select all datums with names greater than (alphanumerically) DTM1.

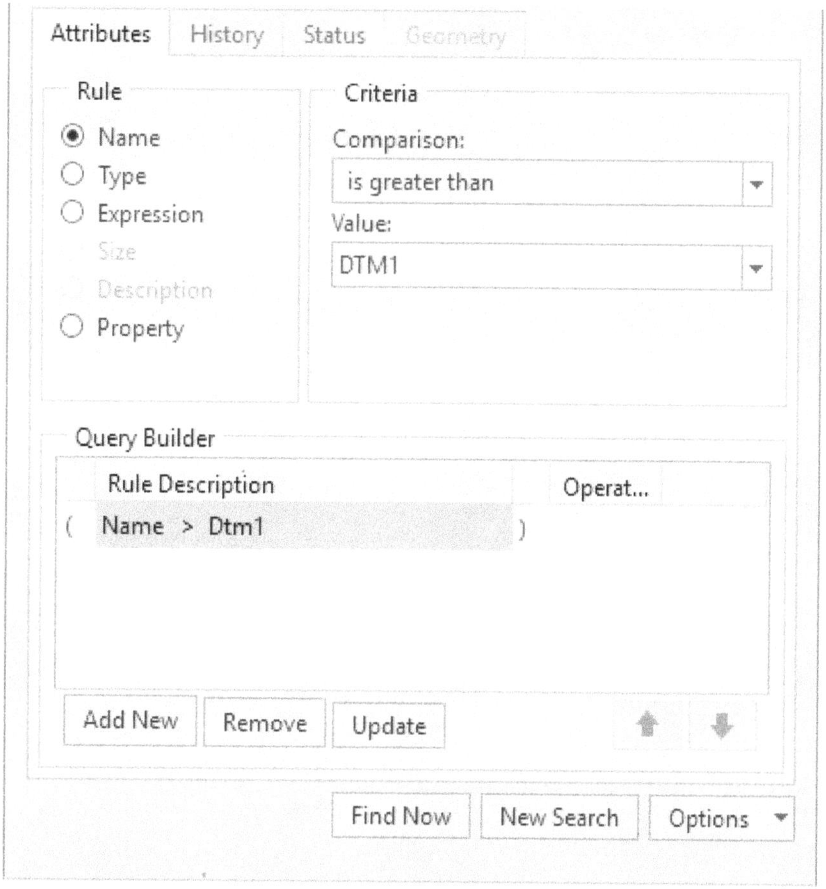

Figure 3–64

8. Select **is less than** from the *Comparison* drop-down list.
9. Select **DTM9** from the *Value* drop-down list.

10. Click **Add New** and the *Search Tool* dialog box updates, as shown in Figure 3–65. This will select all datums with names less than (alphanumerically) DTM9.

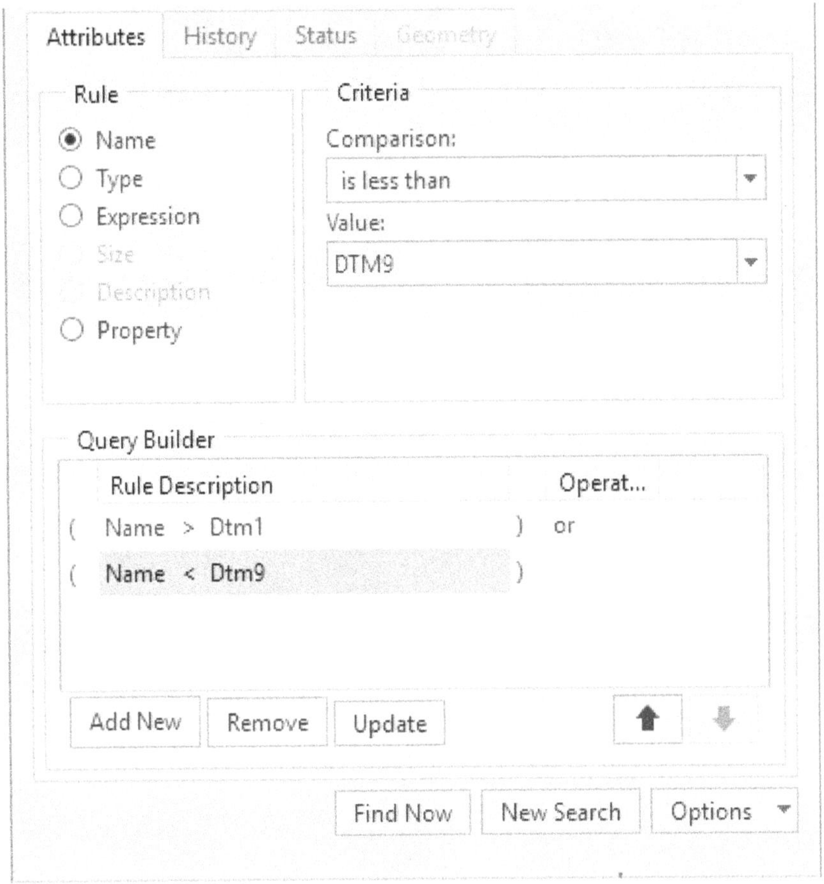

Figure 3–65

11. Click **Find Now** and review the search results, shown in Figure 3–66.

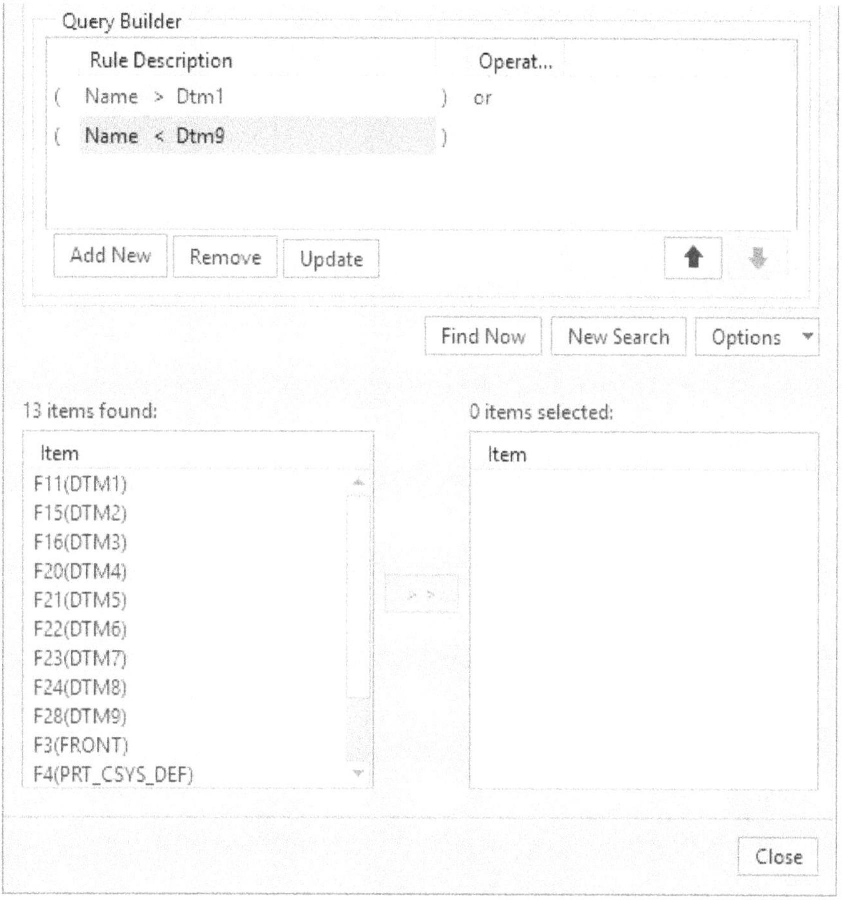

Figure 3–66

12. Scroll to the bottom of the list, and note that the default datum planes, which are alphanumerically greater than **DTM9**, were included in the search results. Why? Note the Operator between the two search criteria is set to **or**, as shown in Figure 3–67.

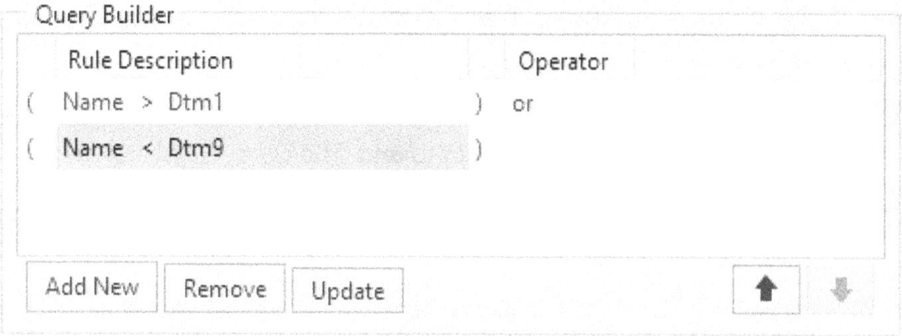

Figure 3–67

13. In the *Query Builder*, edit the *Operator* to **and**, click **Find Now**, and review the search results, shown in Figure 3-68.

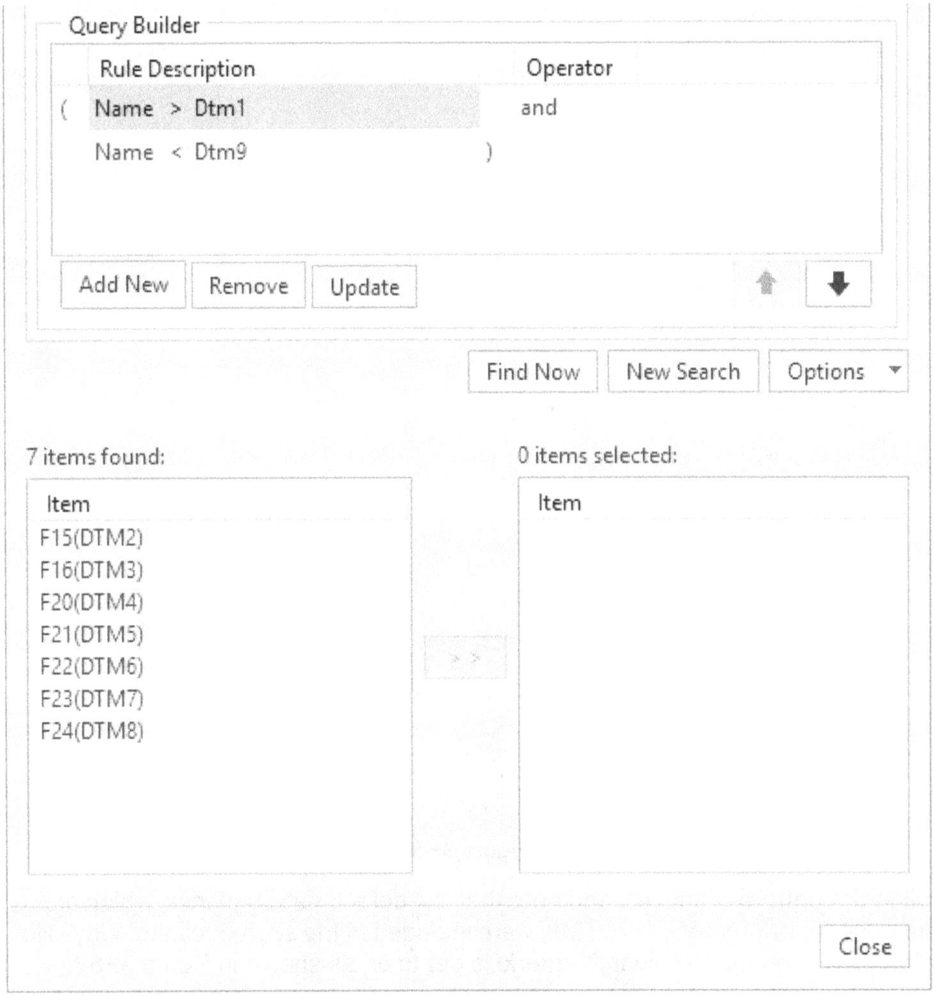

Figure 3-68

14. Select **is not equal to** from the *Comparison* drop-down list.

15. Select **DTM6** from the *Value* drop-down list.

16. Click **Add New** and edit the second Operator to **and**. The *Query Builder* should display, as shown in Figure 3-69.

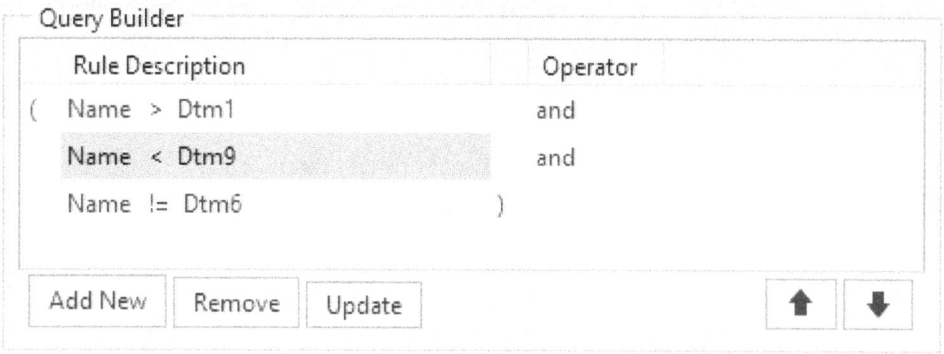

Figure 3–69

17. Click **Find Now**, and the list of objects updates, as shown in Figure 3–70.

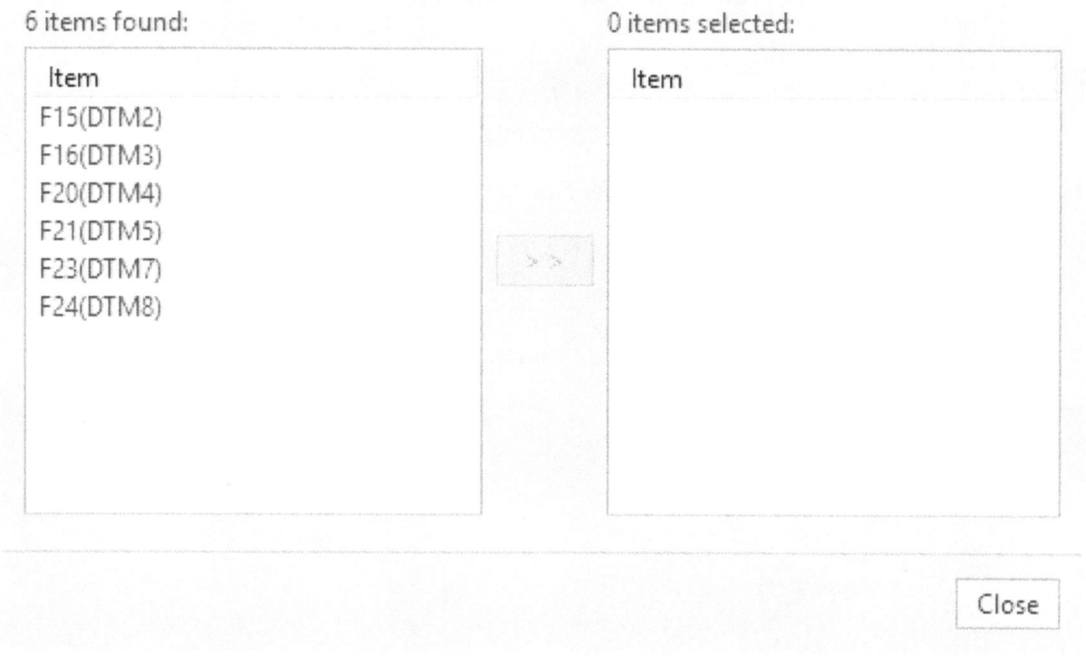

Figure 3–70

18. Select the listed datum planes, and click ≫ (Add Item) to add them to the list of selected items.

19. Click **Close**.

20. Press <Delete> on your keyboard and the *Delete* dialog opens, as shown in Figure 3–71.

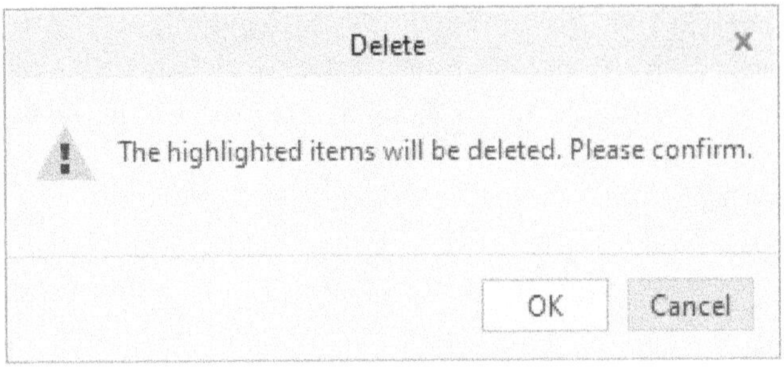

Figure 3–71

21. Click **OK** to remove the datum planes.

Task 4: Use the Model Tree to search for cuts.

1. In the Model Tree, click ▦ (Tree Columns).

2. In the *Model Tree Columns dialog* box, select **Feat Type** in the *Not Displayed* list.

3. Click ≫ (Add Columns) and the *Model Tree Columns* dialog box displays, as shown in Figure 3–72.

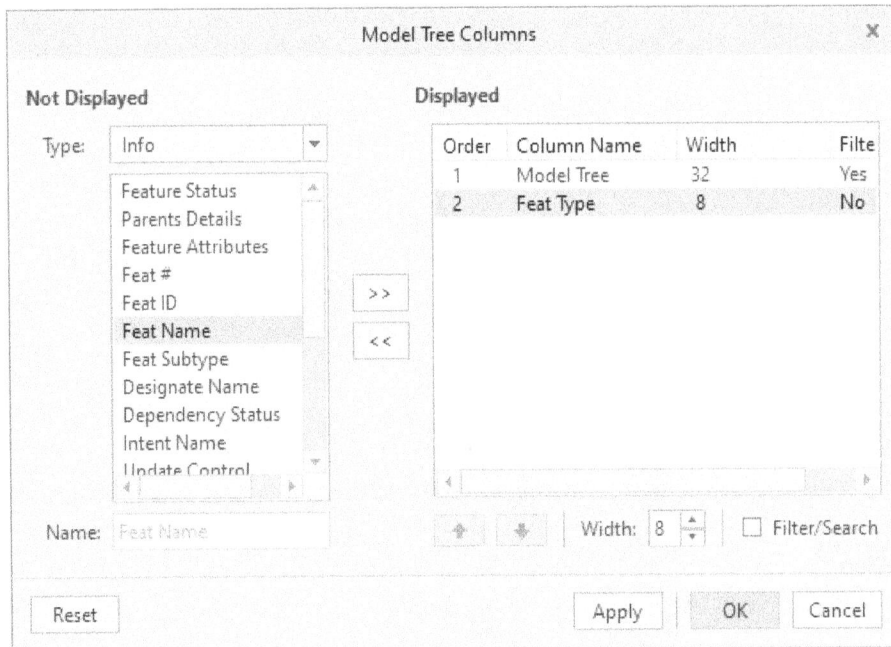

Figure 3–72

4. Click **OK**.

5. In the *Model Tree search* field, type the letter **c** and note that the Model Tree filters to features containing the letter c, such as Chamfer, PRT_CSYS_DEF and so on, as shown in Figure 3–73.

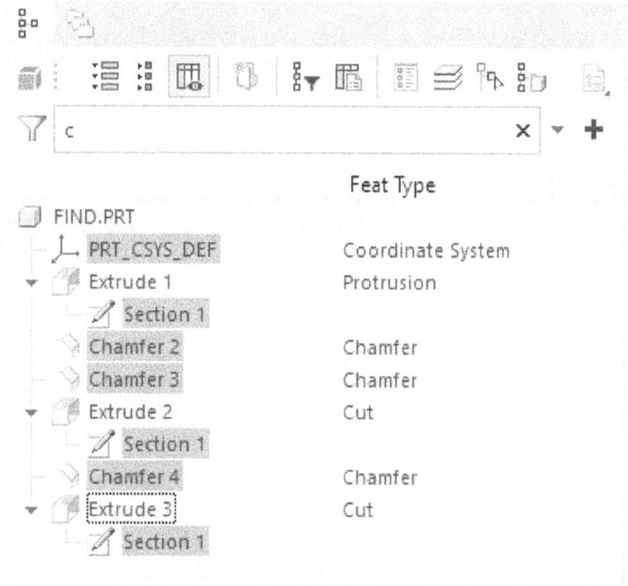

Figure 3–73

6. Complete typing cut and note that there are no matching selections, as shown in Figure 3–74. There are no matching selections because the search filter defaults to the feature names and does not search by columns.

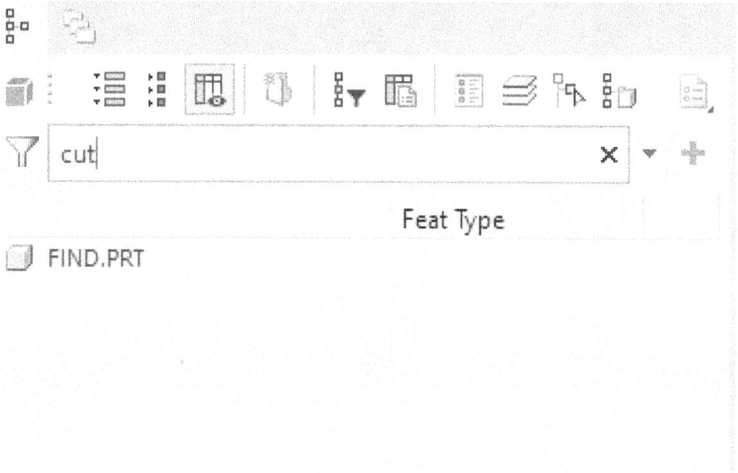

Figure 3–74

7. Right-click in the *Model Tree search* field and select **Feat Type**, as shown in Figure 3–75. This will allow you to search the *Feat Type* column.

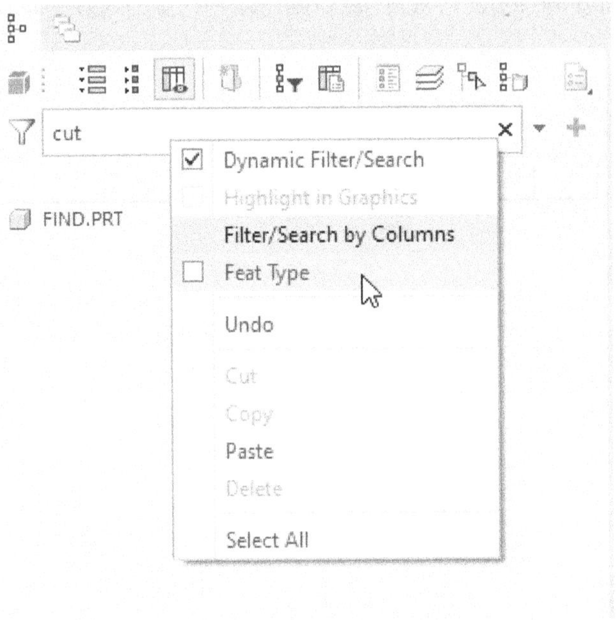

Figure 3–75

8. Note that now your search is also applied to the *Feat Type* column and the two cuts are included, as shown in Figure 3–76. As your models become more complex, being able to refine searches of features in parts or components in assemblies will be a very useful tool.

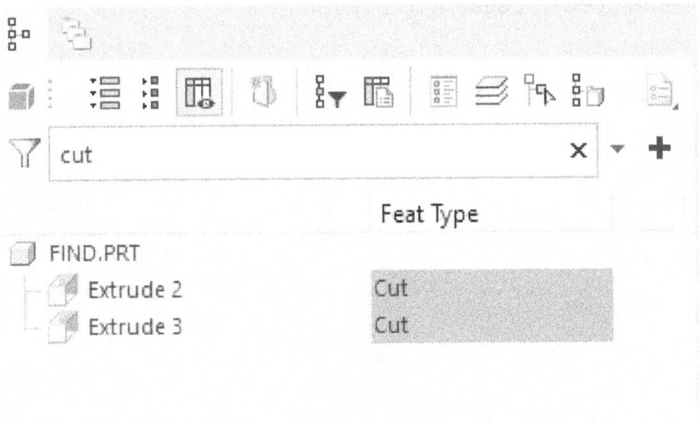

Figure 3–76

9. Right-click **Extrude 3** in the Model Tree and select ✕ (Delete).

10. Click **OK** in the *Delete* dialog box.

- Note that if you had clicked ✚ (Add Marked), it would have selected both cuts.

11. Save the model.

12. In the *Quick Access* Toolbar, click ✖ (Close).

13. In the *Home* tab, click 🖌 (Erase Not Displayed) to erase all of the models from memory.

End of practice

Chapter Review Questions

1. Features can be selected on the model or in the Model Tree.
   a. True
   b. False

2. The system will highlight features as you mouse-over the model. This is referred to as:
   a. Selection
   b. Query Select
   c. Preselection Highlighting
   d. Selection Filter

3. When you prehighlight a feature, you can right-click to step through all features in the model lying under the cursor.
   a. True
   b. False

4. If you were to select the edge on the right, hold <Shift> and place your cursor over the curved edge, the most efficient **Chain** option for selecting the three edges shown in Figure 3–77 is:

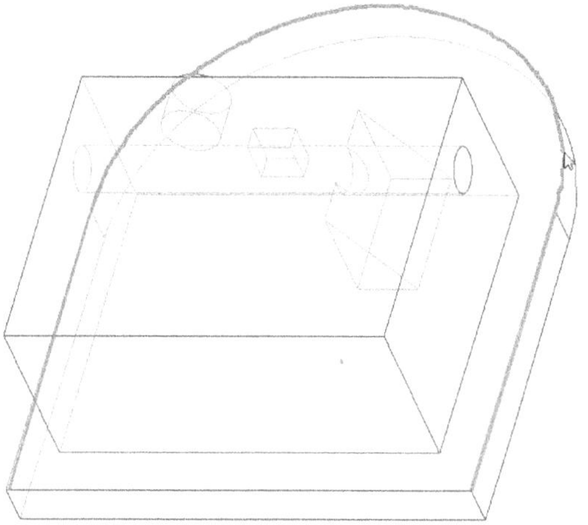

Figure 3–77

a. Surface loop from to

b. Surface loop

c. One-by-one

d. Tangent

5. If you want to select entities that are outside the scope limited by the Selection Filter, you can press and hold _____ while making selections:

a. <Ctrl>

b. <Alt>

c. <Shift>

d. <Tab>

Answers: 1a, 2c, 3a, 4d, 5b

Sketching Geometry

Sketching is the foundation for creating many different feature types. Sketches can be created in a solid feature, or you can create them independently as 2D geometry. When a sketch feature is created on its own, it can later be selected to generate 3D geometry.

Learning Objectives

- Sketch geometry using the basic sketch tools.
- Sketch the geometry using additional tools in the *Sketch* tab.
- Dimension and constrain 2D entities, and use construction geometry in a sketch to capture the design intent for the feature.

4.1 Sketching Tools

Many features require a sketched section to define the profile of the geometry. These are referred to as Sketched Features, and include Extrude, Revolve and Sweep features, among others.

You can create a stand alone sketch, then select that as your profile, or you can create the sketch while defining the feature. This chapter discusses the basic tools available in the *Sketch* tab of the ribbon. In later chapters, you will learn how to use sketches to create solid geometry.

Sketches are non-solid 2D geometry features. The sketching tools used to create a sketch are the same as those used to create any sketched feature. This section focuses on creating sketches.

To create a sketch, click ▨ (Sketch) in the *Datum* group in the *Model* tab.

Once you have started the creation of the sketch, you must define the sketch plane and sketch orientation in the Sketch dialog box shown in Figure 4−1.

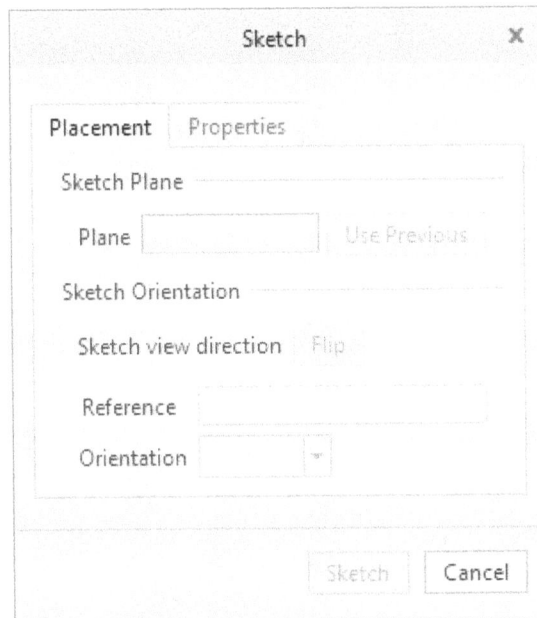

Figure 4−1

Note: *The selection of a sketch orientation reference is optional.*

Sketch Plane

Select the sketch plane first. You can select a datum plane or planar surface as the sketch plane. The 2D sketch is sketched on this reference.

Sketch Orientation

Once a sketch plane has been defined, Creo Parametric automatically selects a default sketch orientation plane. The sketch orientation reference is used to orient the model into 2D for sketching. It is similar to selecting the sketch orientation reference for a base feature. If the default selection is not the required orientation, you can use any of the following methods in the Sketch dialog box to change or override the reference:

- Change the Sketch view direction by clicking **Flip**.

- Change the Reference in the Sketch dialog box, by selecting the default Reference and selecting the required reference plane or surface in the model.

- Change the **Orientation** option in the Sketch dialog box, using the drop-down list.

- Once the sketch orientation has been defined, click **Sketch** to enter Sketcher mode.

If you click **Sketch** to start your sketch and realize it is not oriented correctly, you can use any of the following options in the *Sketch* tab to change or override the references:

- Select **Setup>Section Orientation>Flip sketching plane**.

- Select **Setup>Section Orientation>Flip section orientation**.

- Change the Reference by selecting **Setup>Section Orientation>Set horizontal reference**.

- Change the Reference by selecting **Setup>Section Orientation>Set vertical reference**.

- If enough default sketching references are available to fully place the sketch, you can begin sketching immediately. If required, you can access the *References* dialog box by clicking ⬚ (References) in the *Setup* group, in the *Sketch* tab of the ribbon. The *References* dialog box opens, as shown in Figure 4–2.

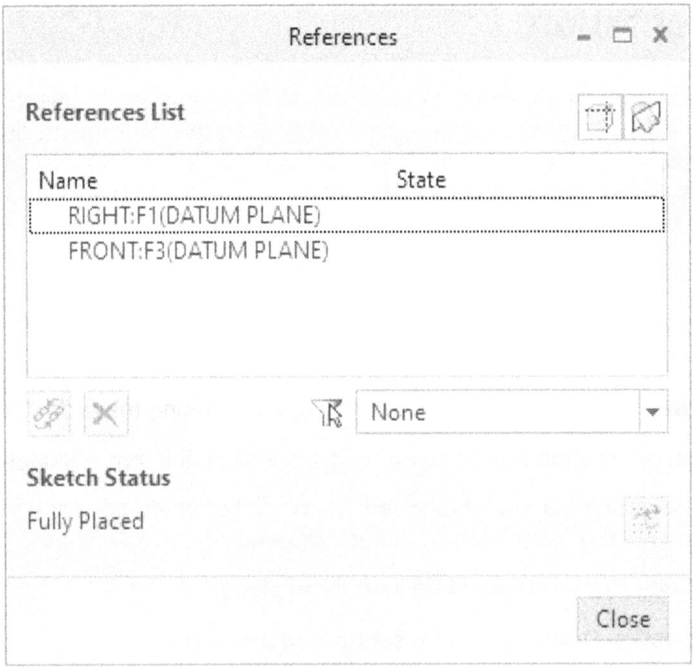

Figure 4–2

Note: The selection of the sketch orientation reference is optional. If you start sketching without an orientation reference, Creo Parametric uses a projection of the X-axis of the default coordinate system for the horizontal orientation of the sketch.

Once the references are defined, click **Close**. This is entirely optional, as references can be added automatically as you select entities while sketching.

4.2 Sketching Geometry

With the references selected, you are now ready to sketch the geometry using the geometry creation tools in the *Sketching* group of the *Sketch* tab, shown in Figure 4-3. The options available for sketching are described in detail as follows.

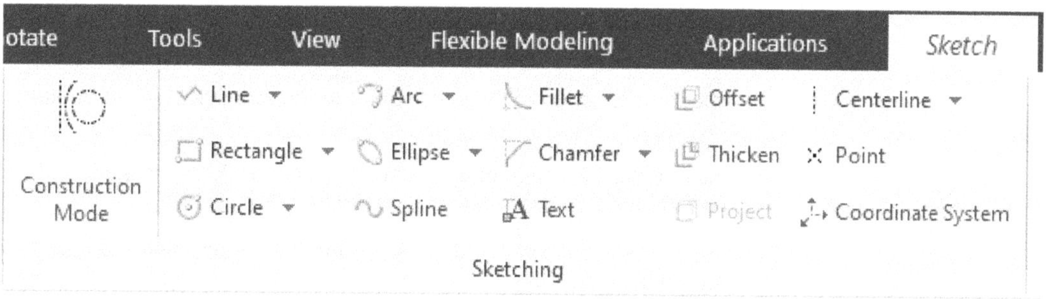

Figure 4-3

Icon	Procedure
⌄ (Line Chain)	Select the location required as the start of the line. A rubber band line displays, attached to the cursor. You can then select the location for the end of the line. Continue selecting locations to create additional attached lines. Click the middle mouse button to complete the line creation.
⟍ (Line Tangent)	Select the location required for a line to be tangent to an entity. A rubber band line displays, attached to the cursor. Select a second location required for a line to be tangent to an entity. Click the middle mouse button to complete the line.
⌐ (Corner Rectangle)	Select the location of the first vertex and drag the rectangle to the required size. Click to place the other vertex and complete the rectangle creation.
◇ (Slanted Rectangle)	Creates a rectangle at any angle.
⊡ (Center Rectangle)	Select a center point and a corner to create the center rectangle.
▱ (Parallelogram)	Creates a parallelogram.
⊙ (Center and Point)	Select the location of the centerpoint and drag the circle to the required size. Click to complete the circle creation.
◎ (Concentric)	Select a reference circle or arc to define the centerpoint (the selected reference circle can be a sketched entity or model edge). A rubber band circle displays, attached to the cursor. Drag the mouse until the circle is the required diameter. Click the left mouse button to create the circle.
◯ (3 Point)	Creates a circle by selecting three points along the circle.

Icon	Procedure
(3 Tangent)	Creates a circle by selecting three entities that you want the circle to be tangent to.
(3-Point / Tangent End)	**3-Point Arc:** Select the locations for the endpoints of the arc. Select an additional point for the radius. **Tangent End Arc:** Select an endpoint of an existing entity to define tangency. Select a location for the endpoint of the arc.
(Center and Ends)	Select the location of the centerpoint of the arc. Select the endpoints of the arc.
(3 Tangent)	Select a start location on an existing arc or circle. Select a second and third location on two other arcs or circles.
(Concentric)	Select a reference circle or arc to define the centerpoint (the selected reference circle can be a sketched entity or model edge). A rubber band circle displays, attached to the cursor. Drag to the required diameter. Click to start the arc, drag the mouse around the diameter, and click again to complete the arc.
(Conic)	Select the location of each endpoint, then click to locate the peak of the conic arc.
(Centerline)	Creates a construction centerline used to help define geometry. No solid geometry will be created. Select the location where you want to intersect the centerline. A centerline displays, attached to the cursor. Select a second location through which the centerline passes.
(Centerline Tangent)	Creates a construction centerline that is tangent to two sketched arcs or circles.

Construction Geometry

As with centerlines, construction entities are used as a reference and do not create solid geometry. To create construction geometry, click (Construction Mode) in the Sketching group in the *Sketch* tab. Once it has been toggled on, any geometry that is created becomes construction geometry and is not shown when exiting sketch mode.

- Any entity can be converted to a construction entity by selecting the entity, right-clicking, and then selecting **Construction**. Figure 4–4 shows an example of a construction geometry that has been used to sketch a hexagon with only one dimension.

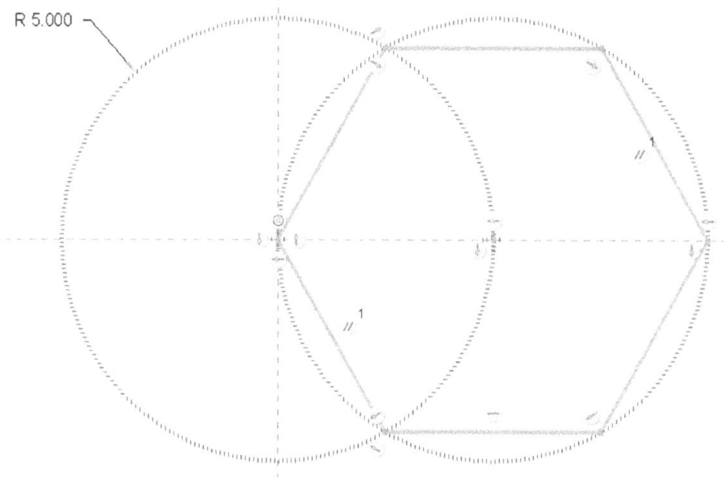

Figure 4–4

*Note: To toggle a construction entity back to solid geometry, select the geometry, right-click and select **Solid**.*

Creo Parametric provides easy-to-use sketcher editing and modification tools, so you are not required to sketch precisely. You can easily make changes using some of the following editing tools.

Tools for editing sketch geometry are accessible in the *Editing* group in the *Sketch* tab, as shown in Figure 4–5.

Figure 4–5

Divide

To divide an entity into two, click ⌐ (Divide). You can also select at the intersection of two entities and divide both of them. The sketch shown in Figure 4–6 is created by sketching a line and dividing it along its length.

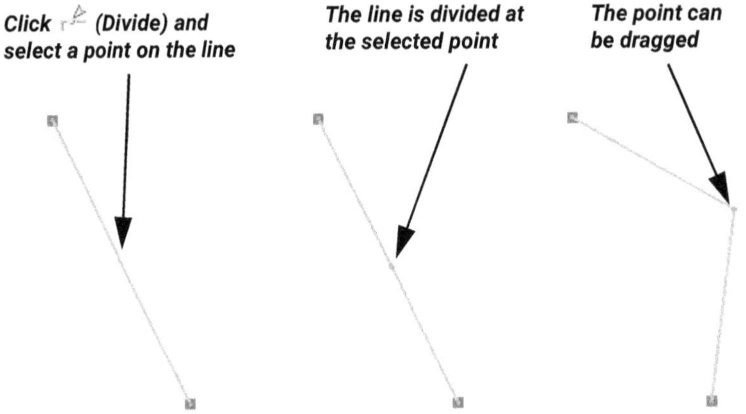

Click ⌐ (Divide) and select a point on the line

The line is divided at the selected point

The point can be dragged

Figure 4–6

Corner

To trim two entities with respect to each other to form a corner, click ⌐ (Corner). The **Corner** sketching tool trims or extends the entities, as required. Select an entity on the segment that you want to remain unchanged.

The sketches shown in Figure 4–7 are created by sketching a rectangle using the **Line** geometry tool and using the **Corner** sketching tool to create the final geometry.

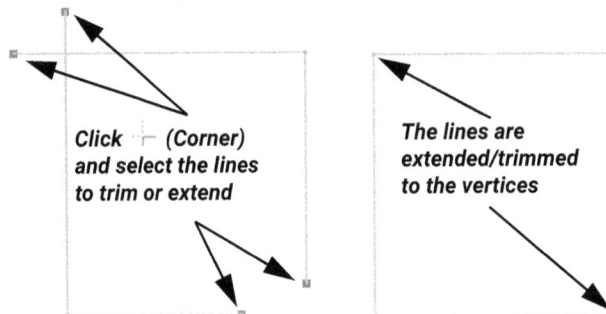

Click ⌐ (Corner) and select the lines to trim or extend

The lines are extended/trimmed to the vertices

Figure 4–7

Note that by default, when a chain of entities creates a closed loop, the system shades the interior of that loop, as shown in Figure 4–8.

Figure 4–8

In many of the images that follow, the shading will be toggled off for clarity.

Delete Segment

To dynamically trim segments on your sketch, click ✂ (Delete Segment). This tool temporarily divides all of the entities at their intersection points with other entities. You can select individual segments to delete. Alternatively, you can press and hold the left mouse button and drag a spline through those segments to delete multiple segments at the same time.

*   For example, the sketch shown on the right in Figure 4–9 is created by sketching the geometry on the left and trimming the inside section of the circle, as shown in the middle sketch.

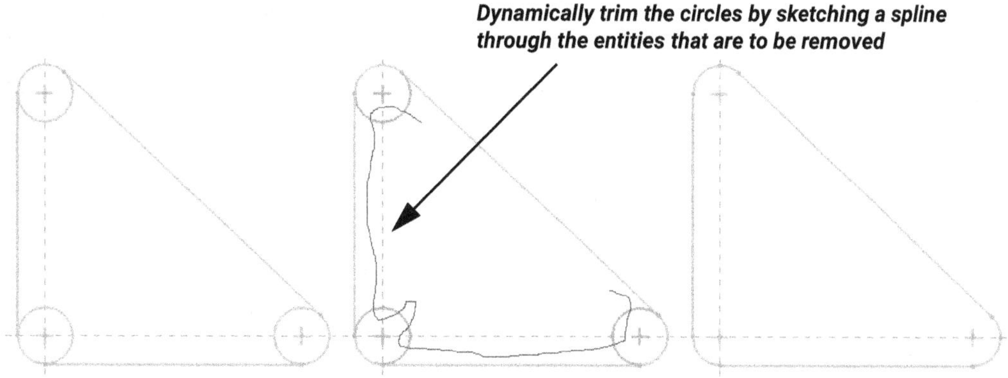

Dynamically trim the circles by sketching a spline through the entities that are to be removed

Figure 4–9

Mirror

To mirror selected entities, select the entity(ies) to be mirrored, click ⬚ (Mirror), and select a sketched entity such as a line or centerline, or a part edge. The sketch is created using the **Mirror** sketching tool, as shown in Figure 4–10.

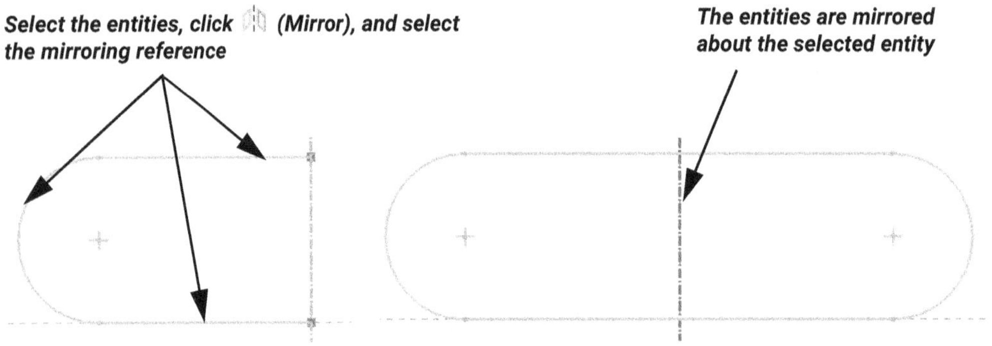

Select the entities, click ⬚ (Mirror), and select the mirroring reference

The entities are mirrored about the selected entity

Figure 4–10

Fillet Tools

When you have two entities that come together to form a corner, you can round off the corner using one of the ⌐ (Fillet) tools in the *Sketching* group of the ribbon.

Fillet Option	Procedure
⌐ (Circular)	Select two entities. A fillet arc with a circular profile is created between the two entities, with construction lines that extend to the intersection point.
⌐ (Circular Trim)	Select two entities. A fillet arc with a circular profile is created between the two entities. The center of the arc is located by dimensions.
⌐ (Elliptical)	Select two entities. A fillet arc with an elliptical profile is created between the two entities, with two construction lines that extend to the intersection point and two that extend to the center of the elliptical arc.
⌐ (Elliptical Trim)	Select two entities. A fillet arc with an elliptical profile is created between the two entities. The center of the ellipse is located by dimensions.

4.3 Constraining Sketches

Constraints control how sketched entities behave. For example, if two lines are constrained to be equal in length, they remain equal even when the geometry of the sketch changes. If the new geometry does not accommodate the constraints, the Resolve Sketch dialog box opens, indicating where you must resolve the constraints or the changes.

As you sketch geometry, Creo Parametric automatically defines constraints as the cursor drags, in a certain tolerance. You can add or delete constraints, as required.

The following describes some basic constraints.

Horizontal and Vertical

The lines are constrained to be horizontal (—) and vertical (|), as shown in Figure 4–11.

Figure 4–11

Tangent

The arc is constrained to be tangent (🔍) to the geometry line at its endpoint and tangent to the horizontal centerline, as shown in Figure 4–12.

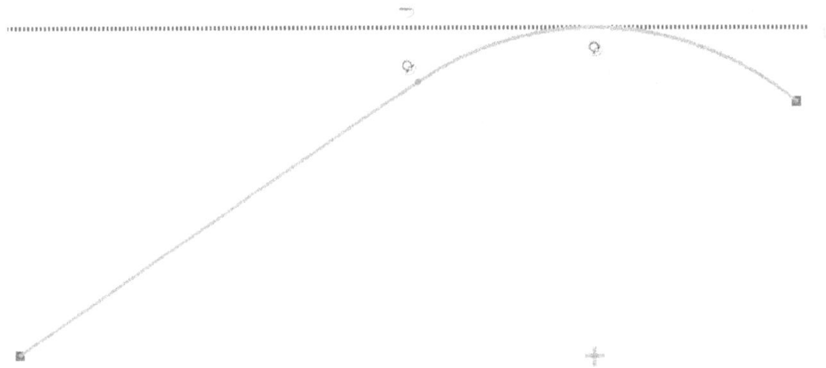

Figure 4–12

Equal Length

The lines are constrained to be equal in length, as shown in Figure 4–13. Lines with the equal length constraint display the same =# symbol.

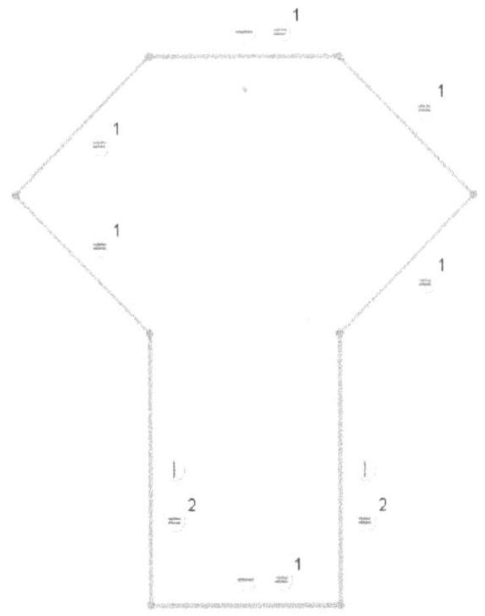

Figure 4–13

Equal Dimensions

The horizontal dimension is constrained to be equal to the vertical dimension, as shown in Figure 4–14. Dimensions with the equal dimension constraint display the same E1 symbol.

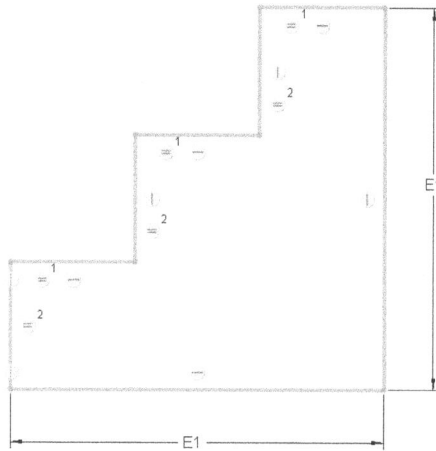

Figure 4–14

Coincident (Point on Entity)

The centerpoint of the large arc is constrained to lie on the horizontal line (⌒), as shown in Figure 4–15.

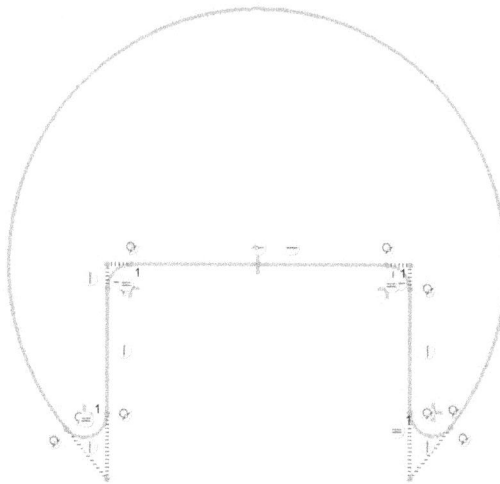

Figure 4–15

Equal Radius/Diameter

The two fillet arcs are constrained to have equal radii ($=_1$), while the radius of the larger arc ($=_2$) is constrained to be equal to the diameter of the construction circle, as shown in Figure 4–16.

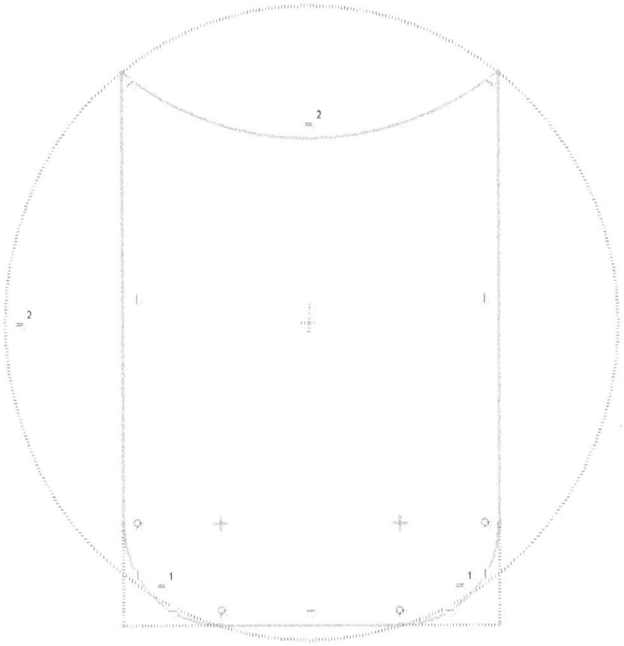

Figure 4–16

Horizontal and Vertical Alignment

The two vertices are constrained to line up horizontally (···), while the circle centerpoints are constrained to line up vertically (▮), as shown in Figure 4–17.

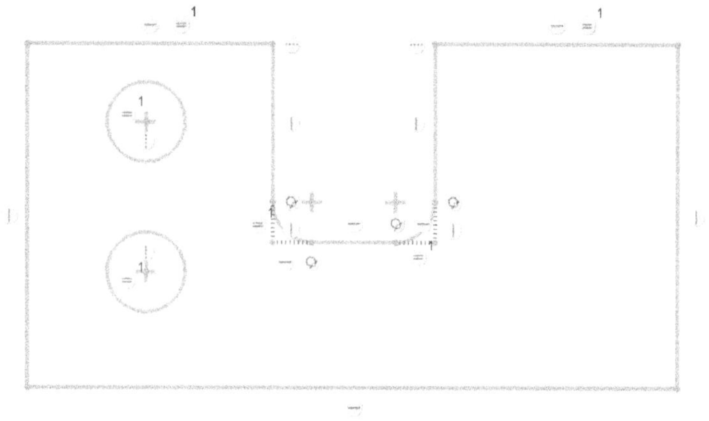

Figure 4–17

Mid-point

The end of the arc is constrained to lie on the mid-point of the adjacent line, as indicated by ◔, shown in Figure 4–18.

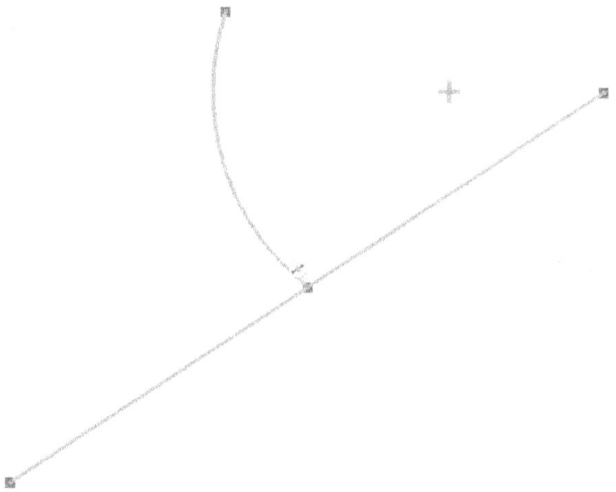

Figure 4–18

Symmetry

Vertices with the ⊹ and ⊹ symbols are constrained to be symmetric about a sketched line or centerline, sketch reference, or part edge. Symmetry about a centerline is shown in Figure 4−19.

Figure 4−19

Note: *The symmetry icons orient perpendicular to the mirroring entity.*

Parallel and Perpendicular

Parallel and perpendicular lines are indicated by the // and ⊥ symbols, as shown in Figure 4−20.

Figure 4−20

Constraint Control

You can control the constraints as you sketch the geometry. Before you select the final location for the entity, you can control a constraint in the following ways:

*   Right-clicking consecutively toggles the status of the highlighted constraint between locking, disabling, and enabling.

*   When a constraint is disabled, Creo Parametric does not automatically define that constraint while sketching. To enable a constraint, right-click again. For example, the graphic on the left side of Figure 4-21 shows the equal length constraint as locked, so although you can move the end of the curve, the length remains fixed. The graphic on the right shows the equal length constraint disabled, so you can continue to drag the entity, but the lengths no longer remain equal.

*   <Shift> can also be used while you drag a sketched entity to automatically disable constraints.

*   When the sketch is complete, the disabled and locked constraint symbols no longer display in the sketch.

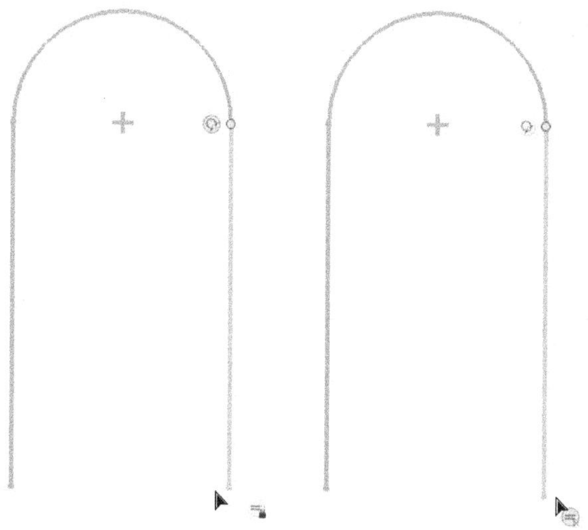

Figure 4-21

Assigning Constraints

When entities have been sketched, you can manually add constraints to the geometry. These constraints are located in the Constrain group in the *Sketch* tab. Additionally, tools for defining sketch constraints are accessible in the *Constrain* group in the *Sketch* tab, as shown in Figure 4–22.

+ Vertical	9 Tangent	+|+ Symmetric
— Horizontal	↖ Mid-point	= Equal
⊥ Perpendicular	-○- Coincident	// Parallel
	Constrain ▾	

Figure 4–22

Note: You can also access the constraints using the contextual menu. Select the sketch entities and right-click to display the relevant constraints in the contextual menu.

The constraint options are described as follows:

Icon	Description
| (Vertical)	Makes a line vertical.
— (Horizontal)	Makes a line horizontal.
⊥ (Perpendicular)	Makes two entities perpendicular.
9 (Tangent)	Makes two entities tangent.
↖ (Mid-point)	Places a point in the middle of a line.
-○- (Coincident)	Creates the same points, points on entity, or collinear constraints.
+|+ (Symmetric)	Makes two points or vertices symmetric about a centerline.
= (Equal)	Creates equal lengths, equal radii, equal dimensions or same curvature constraints.
// (Parallel)	Makes two lines parallel.

Depending on the type of constraint you want to assign, you are prompted to select the entities to which the constraint is going to apply.

Figure 4–23 shows an example of two arcs that were sketched and automatically dimensioned so that they have two independent radius dimensions. Figure 4–24 shows an example where the equal radii constraint is applied to the section by clicking ═ (Equal) and selecting the arcs. Both arcs are of equal radius as indicated by the ═₁ symbol.

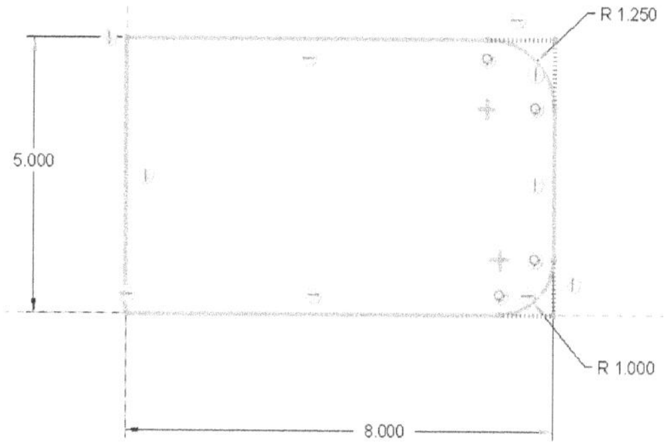

Figure 4–23

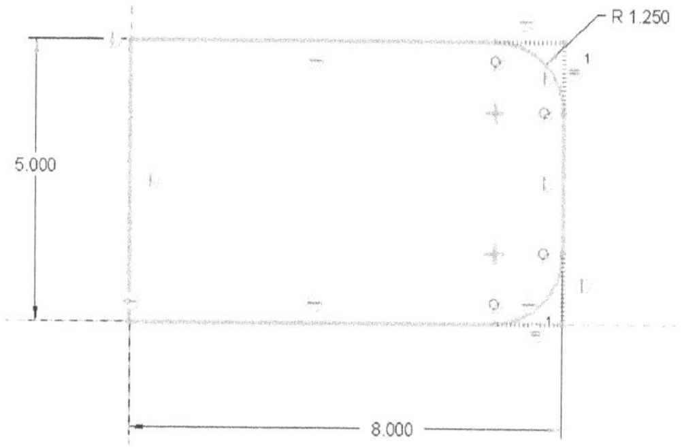

Figure 4–24

Figure 4–25 shows another sketch before being fully constrained.

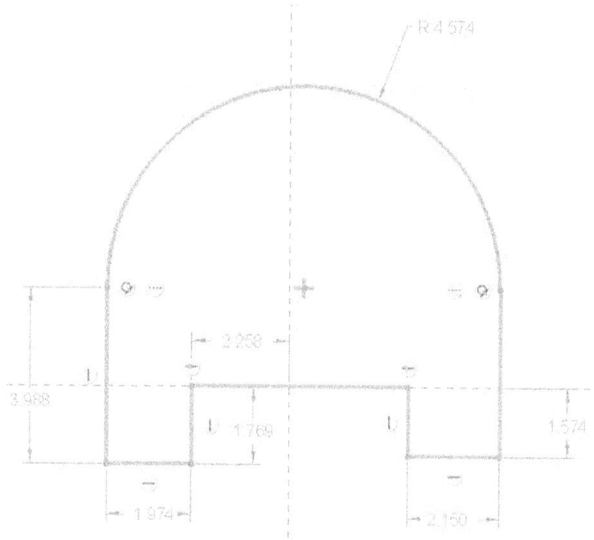

Figure 4–25

Figure 4–26 shows the sketch after being constrained. The center of the arc is aligned with the horizontal entity. The constraint is assigned by clicking ⊸ (Coincident) in the *Constrain* group of the ribbon, and selecting the center-point and horizontal line.

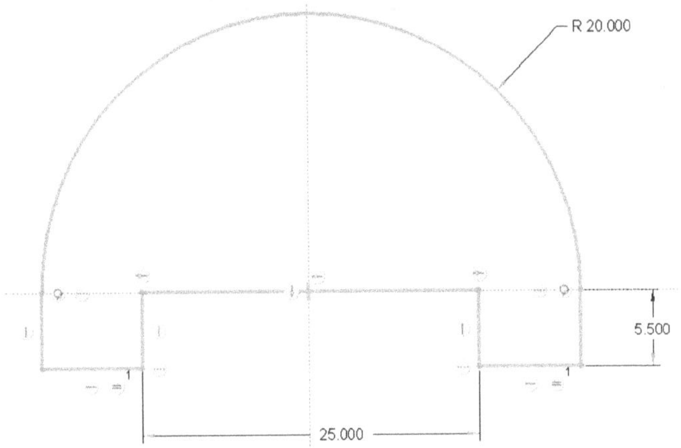

R 20.000

5.500

25.000

Figure 4–26

Automatic Snapping

When sketching entities on existing geometry, the system will dynamically snap the sketched entities to the geometry as you hover the cursor over them. In addition to snapping to free locations along the entities, mid-line and end-line snap locations also display, as shown in Figure 4–27.

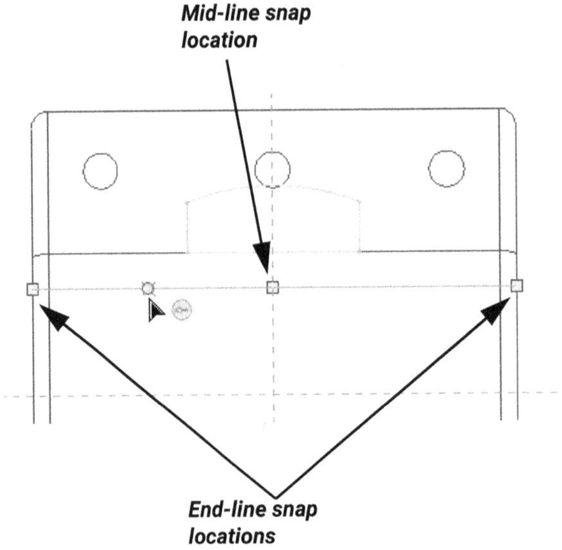

Mid-line snap location

End-line snap locations

Figure 4–27

Note that when you select existing geometry, it is automatically turned into a sketcher reference, as shown in Figure 4–28.

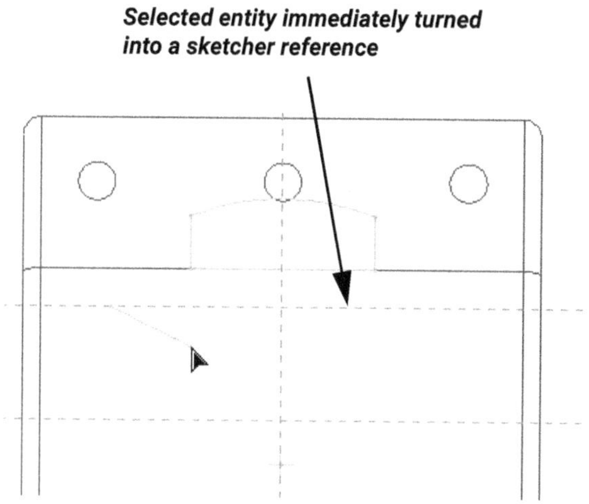

Selected entity immediately turned into a sketcher reference

Figure 4–28

When sketching entities, the system displays a dotted line as a guide in circumstances where entities align, as shown in Figure 4–29.

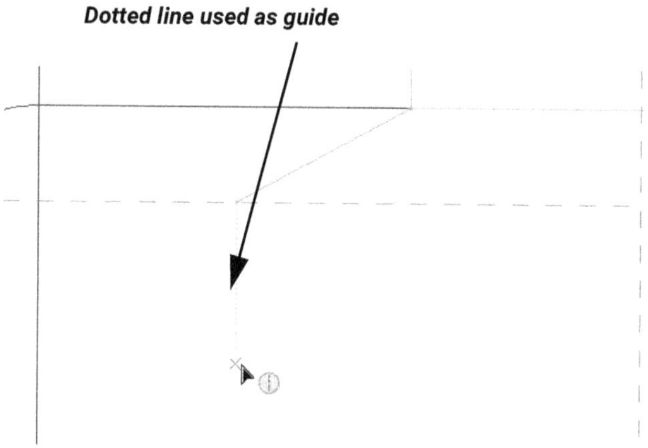

Dotted line used as guide

Figure 4–29

The sketch constraints are highlighted by green boxes to make them stand out visually. The color of closed sections has also been updated, as shown in Figure 4–30.

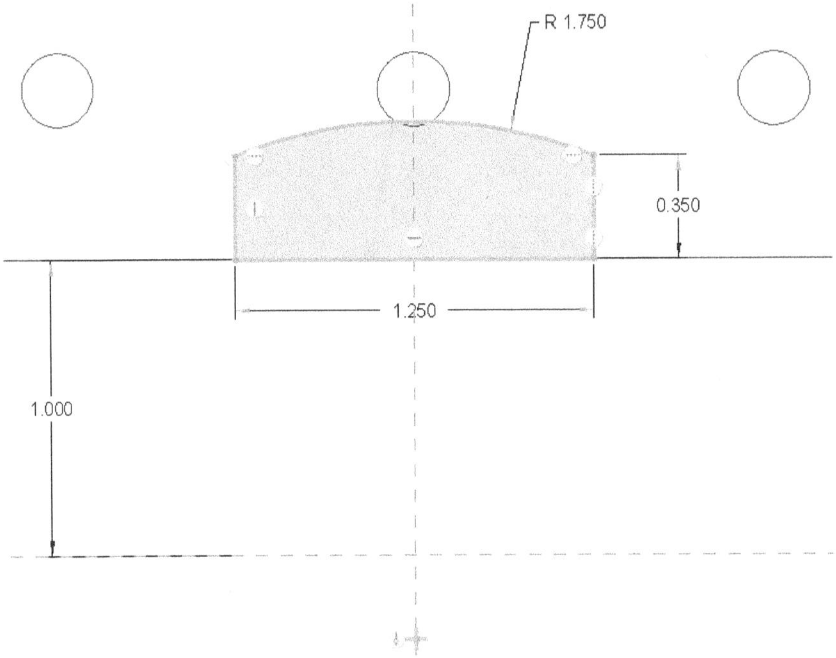

Figure 4–30

4.4 Dimensioning Sketches

As you sketch, dimensions are added and removed automatically so the geometry is always located with respect to the references but is not over-dimensioned. Dimensions created by Creo Parametric are referred to as *weak* dimensions. As you sketch additional geometry, the system automatically removes them to avoid over-dimensioning.

The dimension icons can be found in the *Dimension* group in the *Sketch* tab, as shown in Figure 4–31.

Figure 4–31

To create additional dimensions, click ⟷ (Dimension), select the entities to dimension, and click the middle mouse button to place the dimension. Once the dimensions have been created, they can be immediately changed to the required values. Dimensions that you create are referred to as *strong* dimensions and cannot be automatically removed from the sketch. Strong dimensions are considered required dimensions. Strong and weak dimensions display, as shown in Figure 4–32.

> *Note: You can also create dimensions by selecting the entity, right-clicking and selecting* **Create Dimension**.

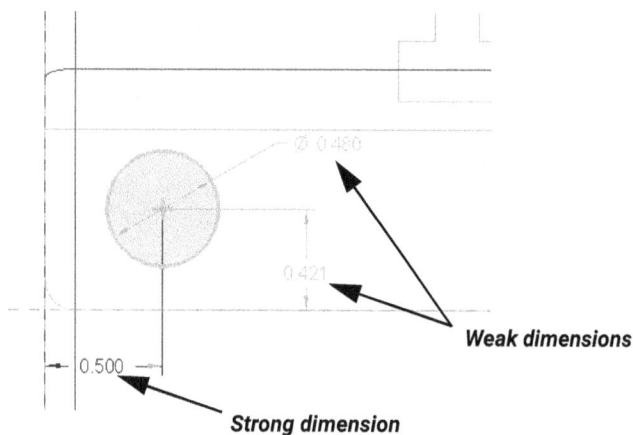

Figure 4–32

Note: Weak dimensions display in light blue. Strong dimensions display in blue.

By default, the dimensions are rounded. You can select a dimension, right-click, and disable **Round Display Value**, as shown in Figure 4–33.

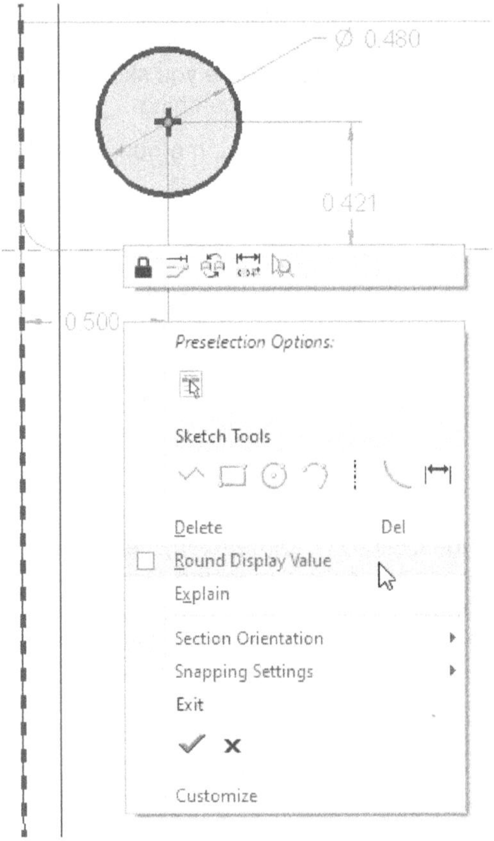

Figure 4–33

Note: Your system administrator may have this option disabled by default. Later in this chapter, we will discuss how to control this option.

Weak dimensions that are important to your design intent should be made strong to ensure that the dimension value is not removed by the system as you continue to sketch geometry.

- To make a weak dimension strong, select the dimension value and select 〰 (Strong) in the *mini* toolbar. A weak dimension also becomes strong when you modify its dimension value. To modify the dimension value, double-click on the value and enter a new one in the field that displays.

- Since the default setting is to round the display of dimension values, you should edit the dimension values to ensure they are correct.

- There are several common types of dimensions that can be created in Sketcher mode. These are described in the following discussion.

Linear Dimensions

To create a linear dimension, click |↔| (Dimension) and select the entity(ies) to dimension using the left mouse button. Move the cursor to the required location and place the dimension using the middle mouse button. The different methods for dimensioning the linear entities are shown in Figure 4–34.

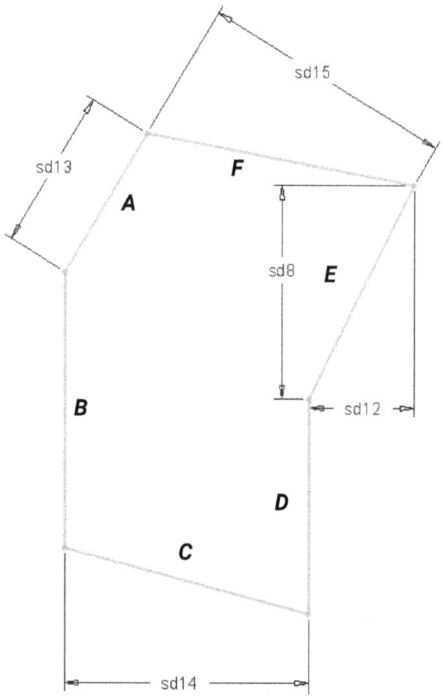

Figure 4–34

Note: The placement of the dimension determines whether it is a horizontal or vertical dimension. Keep the design intent in mind when considering the dimensioning scheme.

Dimension	Procedure
To place dimension sd13	Select line **A**. Position the cursor where you want to place the dimension and click the middle mouse button.
To place dimension sd14	Select lines **B** and **D**. Position the cursor where you want to place the dimension and click the middle mouse button.
To place dimension sd15	Select line **A** and the vertex between lines **E** and **F**. Position the cursor where you want to place the dimension and click the middle mouse button.
To place dimensions sd8 and sd12	Select the two vertices at the ends of line **E**. Position the cursor where you want to place the dimension and click the middle mouse button.

Center/Tangential Dimensions

To dimension the distance between circles and arcs, click ⊬ (Dimension) and select the two entities. Move the cursor to the required location and place the dimension using the middle mouse button. To place a slanted dimension, place the dimension at a point along a line that joins the two entities that are being dimensioned. A sketch with center/tangential dimensions is shown in Figure 4−35.

Figure 4−35

Radius/Diameter Dimensions

To create a radius dimension, click ⊢⇥⊣ (Dimension) and select an arc or a circle. Move the cursor to the required location and place the dimension using the middle mouse button. To create diameter dimensions, select an arc or circle twice and place the dimension using the middle mouse button. A sketch with radius/diameter dimensions is shown in Figure 4–36.

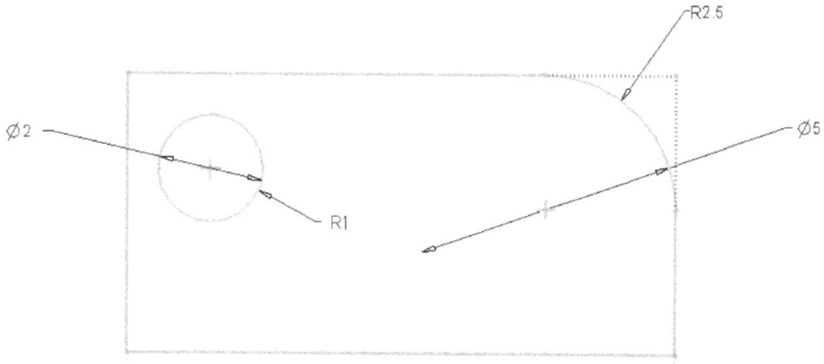

Figure 4–36

You can also change a Radial dimension to a Diameter dimension by clicking the dimension and selecting ⊘ (Diameter) in the *mini* toolbar, as shown in Figure 4–37. The same process can change a Diameter dimension to a Radial dimension.

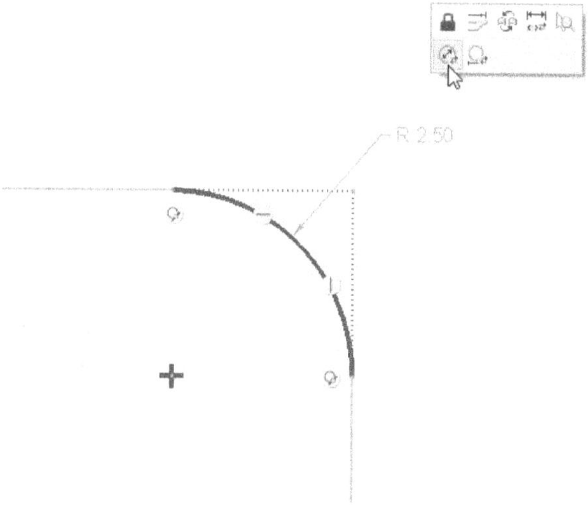

Figure 4–37

Angular Dimensions

For an angular dimension, select lines **A** and **B** and place the dimension using the middle mouse button. The resulting angle is dependent on the placement location of the dimension, as shown in Figure 4–38.

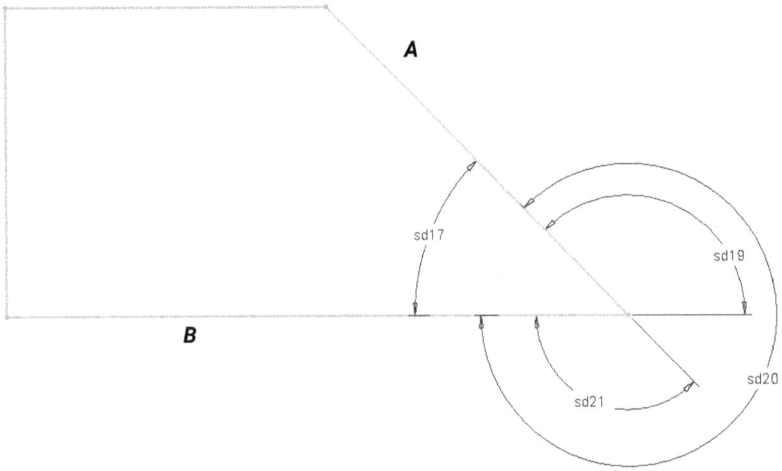

Figure 4–38

To dimension an arc angle, select the arc (the selected arc turns green) and the two end points and place the dimension using the middle mouse button, as shown in Figure 4–39.

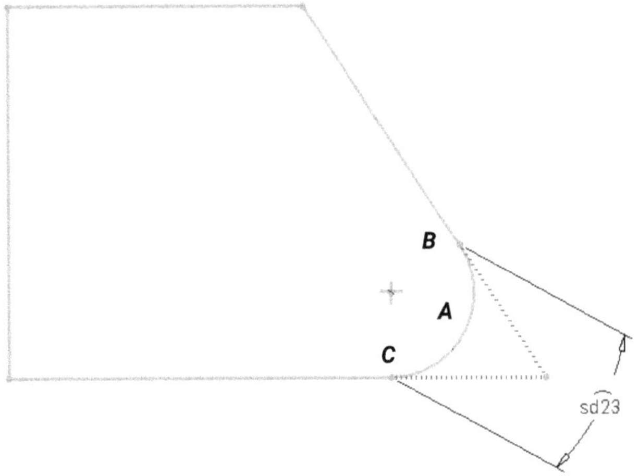

Figure 4–39

Revolved Section Dimensions

Only half of the cross-section of a revolved feature needs to be sketched. It is then revolved about the centerline at a specified angle. You can use any combination of the following selections to create a diameter dimension on the section of a revolved feature. In the example shown in Figure 4–40, the **sd7** dimension is created by selecting the geometry, selecting the centerline, and then selecting the geometry again. The **sd8** dimension is created by selecting the centerline, vertex, and centerline again. In both cases, click the middle mouse button to place the dimension. Using either of these selection techniques results in a diameter dimension.

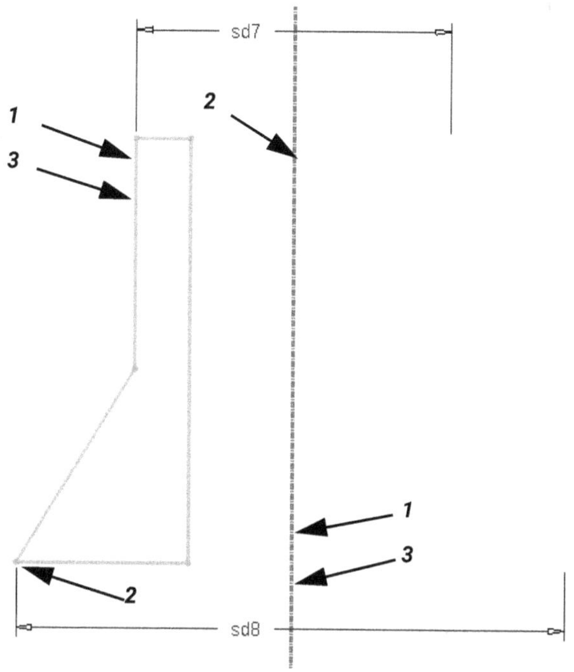

Figure 4–40

> **Note:** *This type of dimensioning scheme can also be used to dimension symmetrical entities.*

Once dimensions have been placed, modify them to suit your design intent. You can modify a dimension in the sketch by double-clicking on the dimension value and entering a new one in the field that displays.

> **Note:** *You can also modify multiple dimensions on a sketch using the Modify Dimensions dialog box.*

Once you are satisfied with the geometry, dimensions, and constraints, exit the Sketcher mode and complete the sketch by clicking ✓ (**OK**). A completed sketch is shown in Figure 4–41.

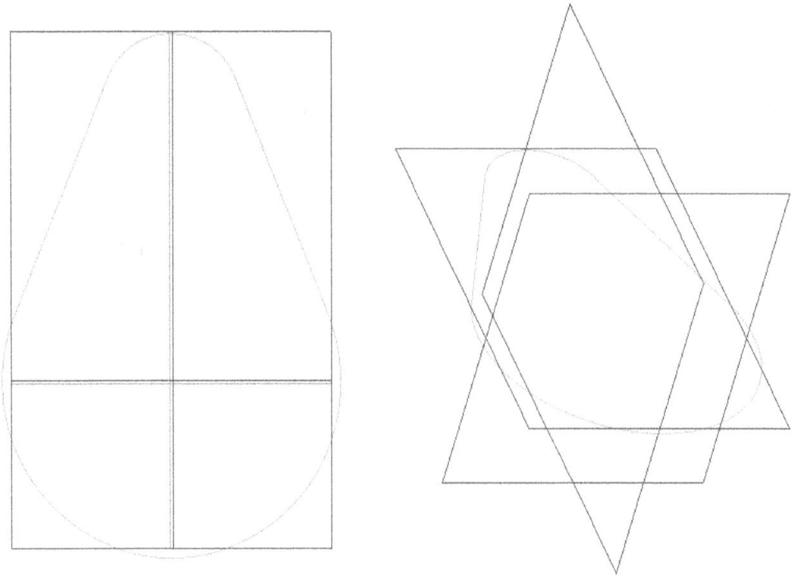

2D   **3D**

Figure 4–41

*Note: If you have accessed Sketcher independently (through **File>New>Sketch**), select **File>Save** to save the file with the .SEC extension. Sketches display in light blue. You can modify the color by selecting **File>Options>System Appearance>Global Colors>Graphics**.*

Highlighting Constraints and Dimensions

When you place the cursor over a dimension, the dimensioned entities are temporarily highlighted, as shown in Figure 4–42. If you select the dimension, the dimensioned entities remain highlighted until you make another selection.

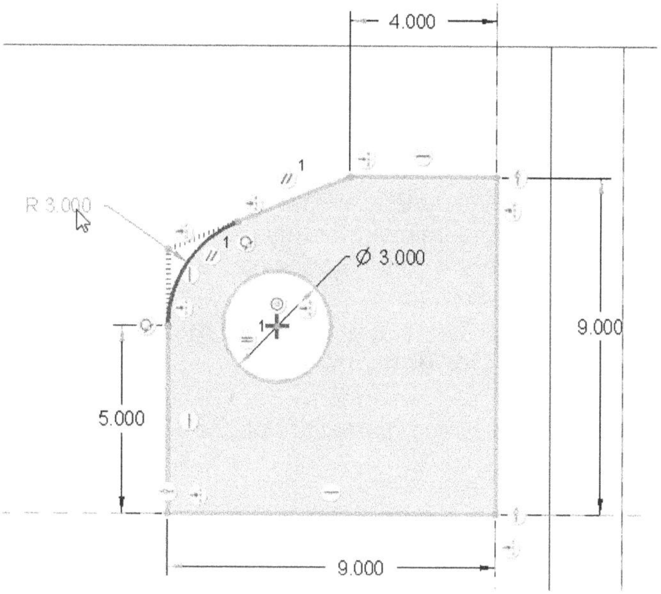

Figure 4–42

When you place the cursor over a constraint, the constrained entities and any matching constraints, such as the symmetry constraint shown in Figure 4–43, are temporarily highlighted.

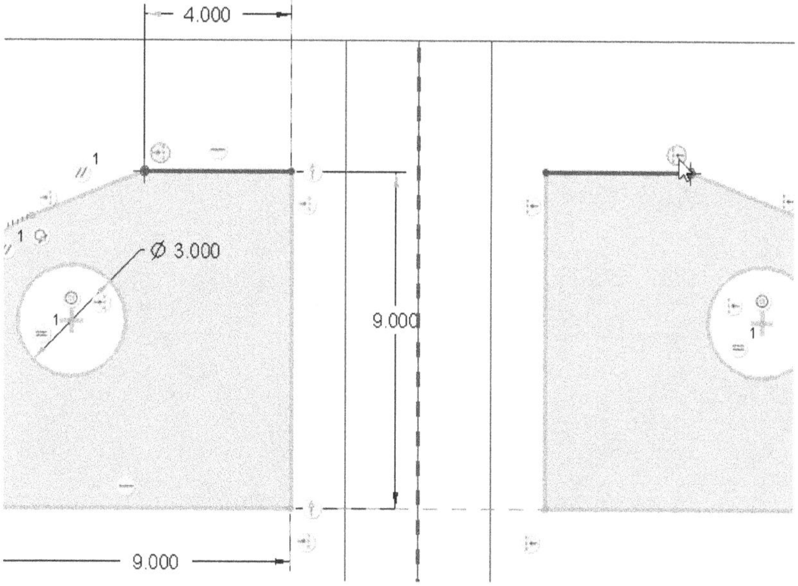

Figure 4–43

4.5 Configuring Sketcher

Automatic Dimension Rounding

As previously discussed, the default sketcher settings are set such that the dimensions display rounded to zero decimal places. The dimensions track up to 12 decimal places, but do not, by default, display them. Your system administrator might already have your system set up such that decimal places display. There is a configuration file (**config.pro**) that can be created or edited to control Creo Parametric Settings.

How To: Change the Default Configuration

1. Click **File>Options** to open the *Creo Parametric Options* dialog box, as shown in Figure 4–44.

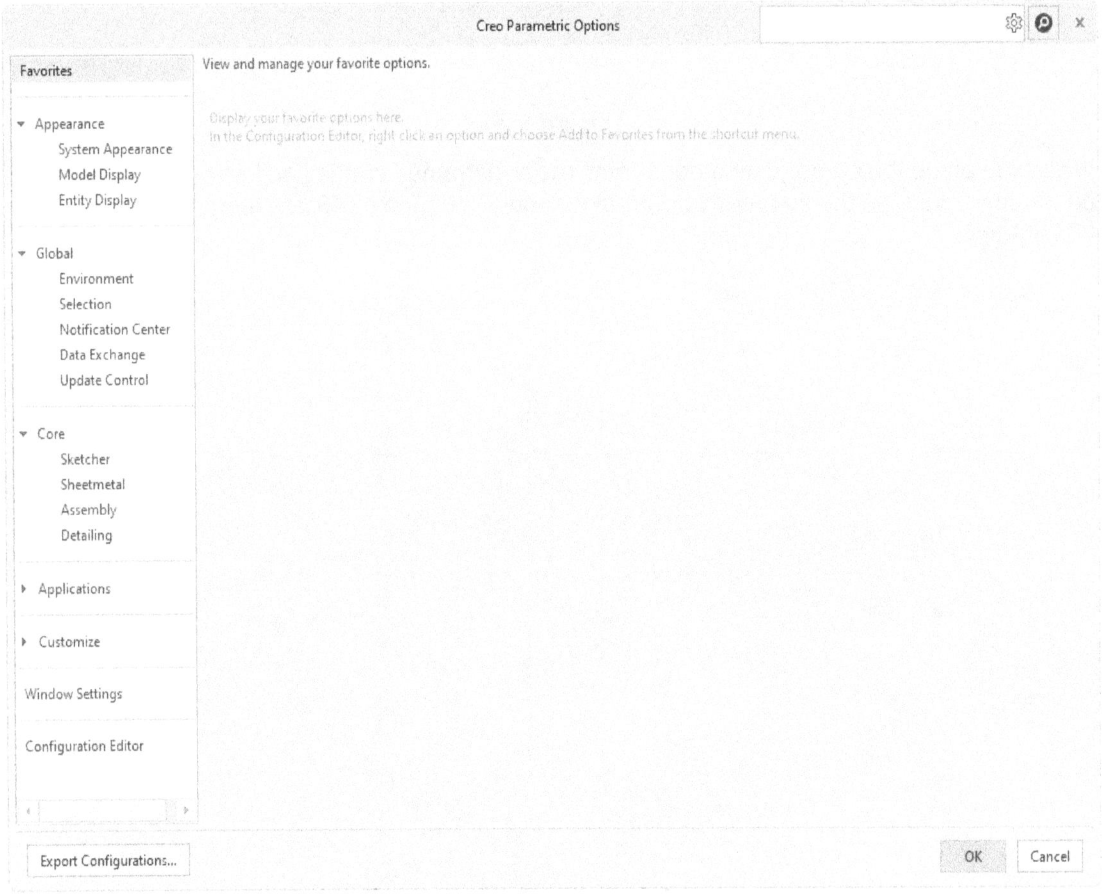

Figure 4–44

2. In the list of categories on the left, select **Sketcher**.

3. In the *Accuracy and Sensitivity* area, edit the *Number of decimal places for dimensions*, as shown in Figure 4–45.

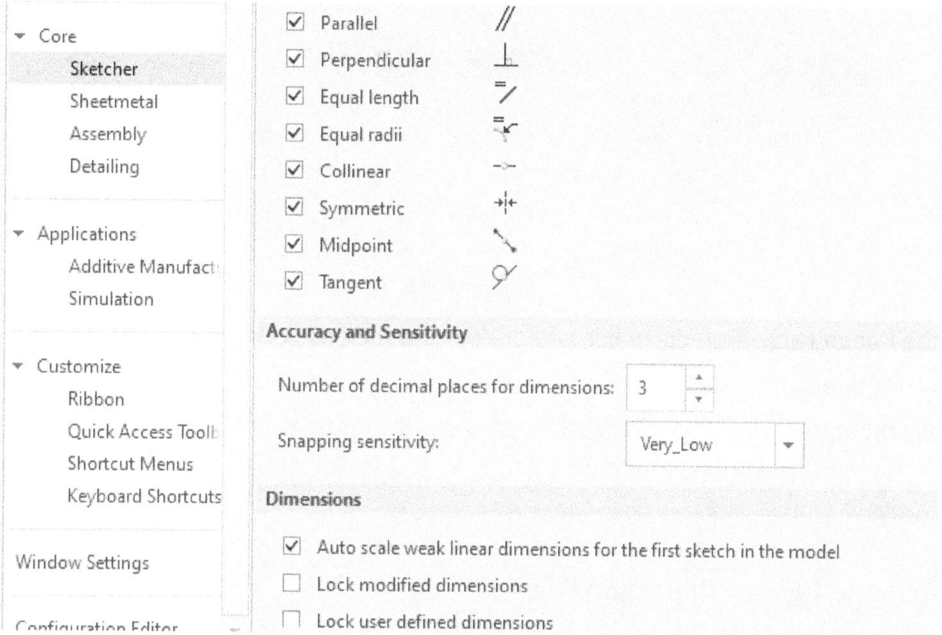

Figure 4–45

4. Click **OK**.

5. When prompted, click **Yes** to save the options and store the configuration file.

6. Navigate to the folder in which Creo Parametric launches, and click **OK**.

Dynamic Refit

By default, when you edit dimensions, the geometry increases or decreases in size based on the edits. This can result in sketches that are too large or too small to see, requiring you to manually select (Refit) from the *In-graphics* toolbar.

You can set Creo Parametric to refit dynamically by setting the configuration option **sketcher_refit_after_dim_modify** to **yes**.

How To: Enable Dynamic Refit

1. Open the *Creo Parametric Options* dialog box by clicking **File>Options**.

2. In the list of categories on the left, select **Configuration Editor**.

3. Click **Add**.

4. In the *Option name* field, type **sketcher_refit**. Note that the field automatically completes as **sketcher_refit_after_dim_modify**, as shown in Figure 4−46.

Figure 4−46

5. In the *Option value* drop-down list, select **Yes**, and then click **OK**.

6. Click **OK** again.

7. When prompted, click **Yes** to save the options and store the configuration file.

   Note: The configuration file and settings are covered in detail in a later section. A configuration file has been set up for this course.

How To: Load the Configuration File

1. Open the *Creo Parametric Options* dialog box by clicking **File>Options**.

2. In the list of categories on the left, select **Configuration Editor**.

3. In the bottom-right area of the dialog box, expand the *Options* drop-down list, and select **Import Configuration File**.

4. In the *File Open* dialog box, navigate to the *Creo Parametric Introduction to Solid Modeling Practice Files* folder.

5. Double-click on **config.pro**.

6. Click **OK** in the *Creo Parametric Options* dialog box.

Practice 4a
Create a Sketch

Practice Objectives

- Create a 2D sketch object.
- Use multiple sketch tools in the *Sketch* tab.
- Add additional constraints and dimensions to the sketch to ensure that it captures the required design intent.

In this practice, you will create a stand alone sketch to learn how to create geometry, add dimensions, and add constraints. You will create the sketch shown in Figure 4–47.

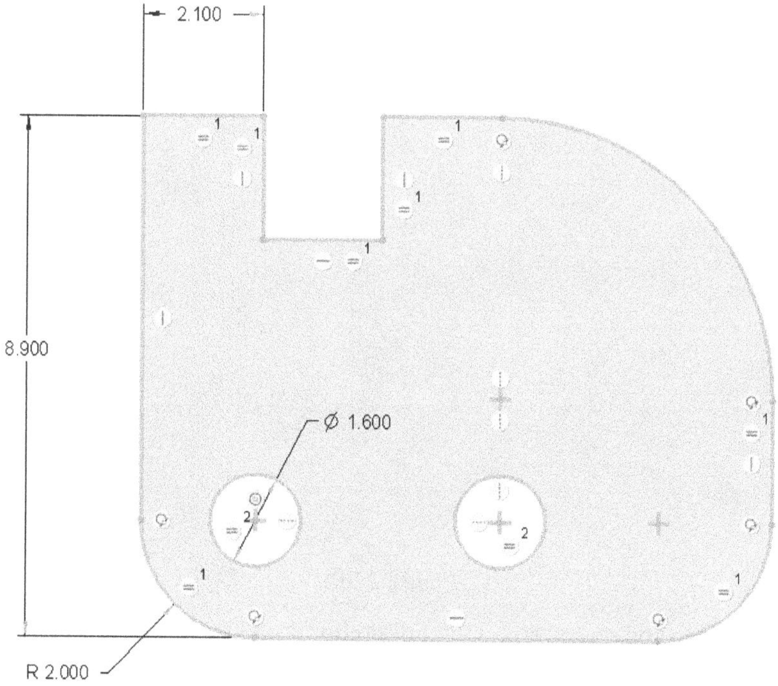

Figure 4–47

Task 1: Create a new sketch.

1. Set your working directory to the *Create_Sketch* folder.

2. Click ☐ (New).

3. Select **Sketch**.

4. Edit the *Name* to **sketch** and click **OK**.

5. Click **File>Options** to open the *Creo Parametric Options* dialog box, as shown in Figure 4–48.

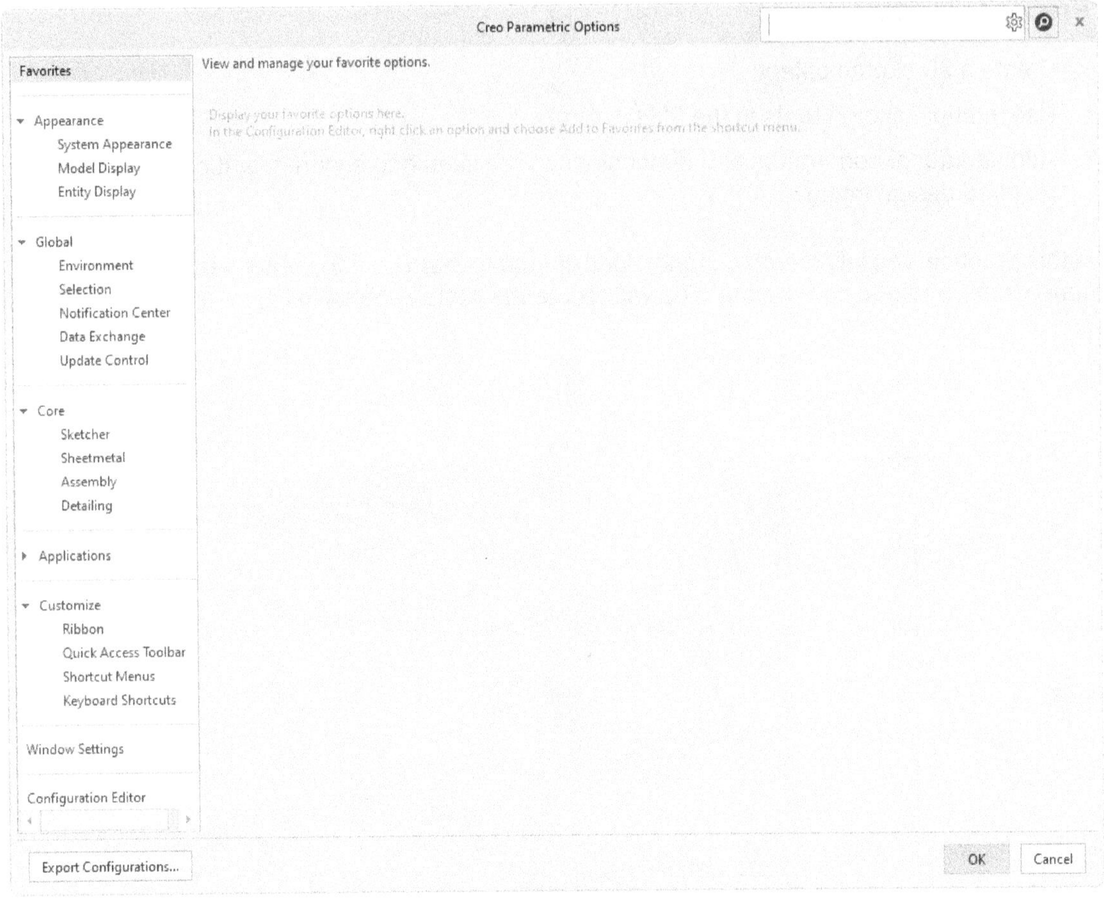

Figure 4–48

6. In the list of categories on the left, select **Sketcher** under the *Core* node.

7. In the *Accuracy and Sensitivity* area, edit the *Number of decimal places for dimensions to **3***, as shown in Figure 4–49.

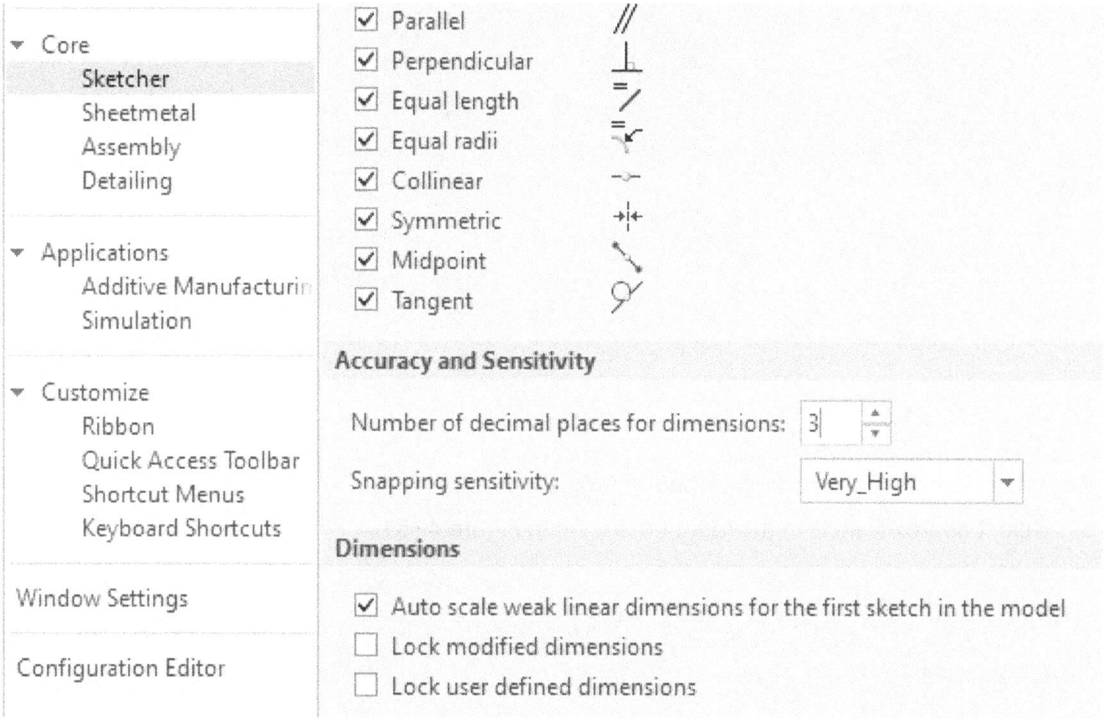

▼ Core	☑ Parallel	//
Sketcher	☑ Perpendicular	⊥
Sheetmetal	☑ Equal length	=
Assembly	☑ Equal radii	
Detailing	☑ Collinear	
	☑ Symmetric	+⊦+
▼ Applications	☑ Midpoint	
Additive Manufacturin	☑ Tangent	
Simulation		

Accuracy and Sensitivity

Number of decimal places for dimensions: 3

Snapping sensitivity: Very_High

Dimensions

☑ Auto scale weak linear dimensions for the first sketch in the model
☐ Lock modified dimensions
☐ Lock user defined dimensions

Customize
  Ribbon
  Quick Access Toolbar
  Shortcut Menus
  Keyboard Shortcuts

Window Settings

Configuration Editor

Figure 4–49

8. Click **OK**.

9. If prompted to save the options and store the configuration file, click **Yes**.

10. Click **OK** in the *Save As* dialog box to save to the default location.

Task 2: Toggle on the grid and start sketching.

1. In the *In-graphics* toolbar, select ⠿ (Sketcher Display Filters).

2. Select ⠿ (Disp Grid) to toggle on the grid display.

3. The display filters should be set, as shown in Figure 4–50.

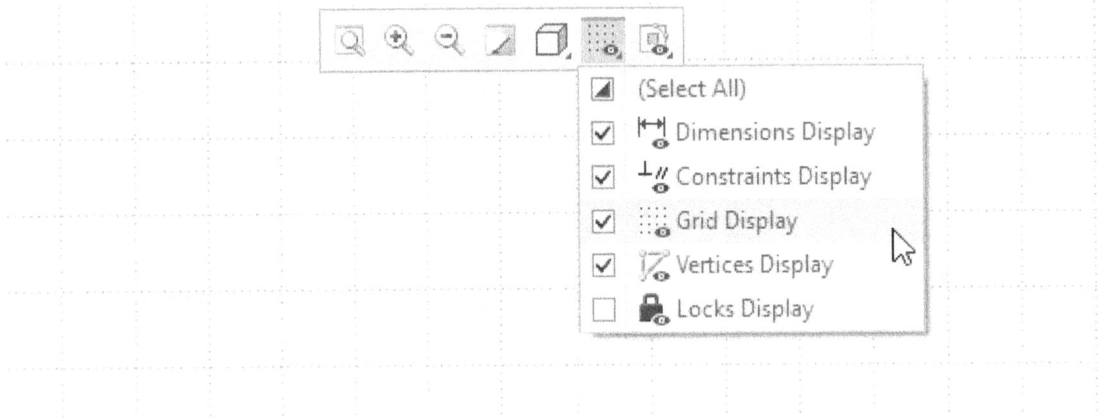

Figure 4–50

4. In the *Sketching* group of the ribbon, click ⌄ (Line).

5. Select approximately in the location shown in Figure 4–51.

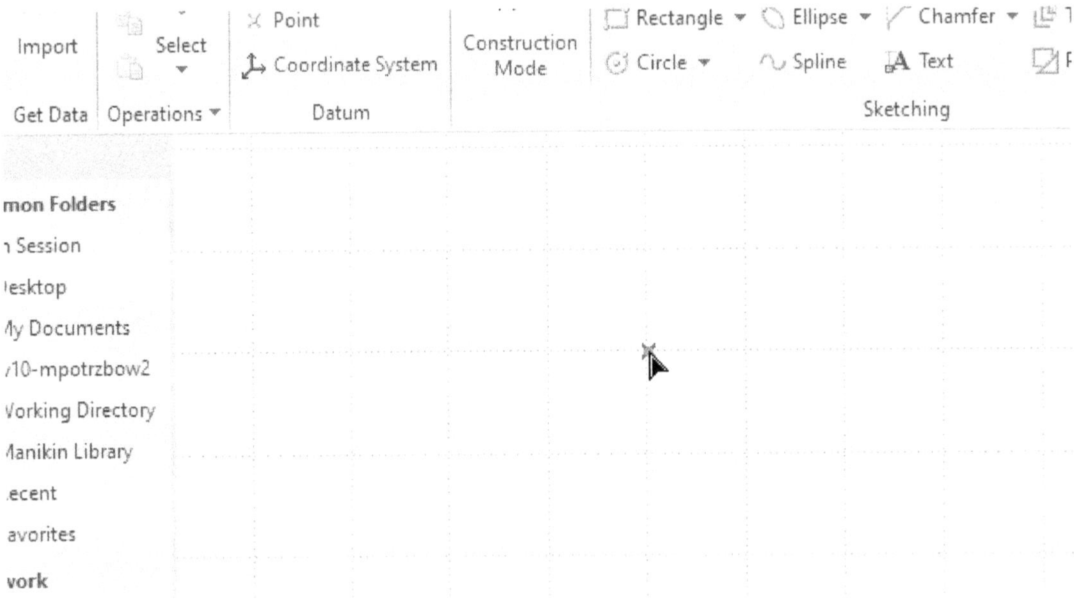

Figure 4–51

6. Note how the line "rubber bands" but snaps to the Vertical position, as shown in Figure 4–52. Click the location shown to complete the first line.

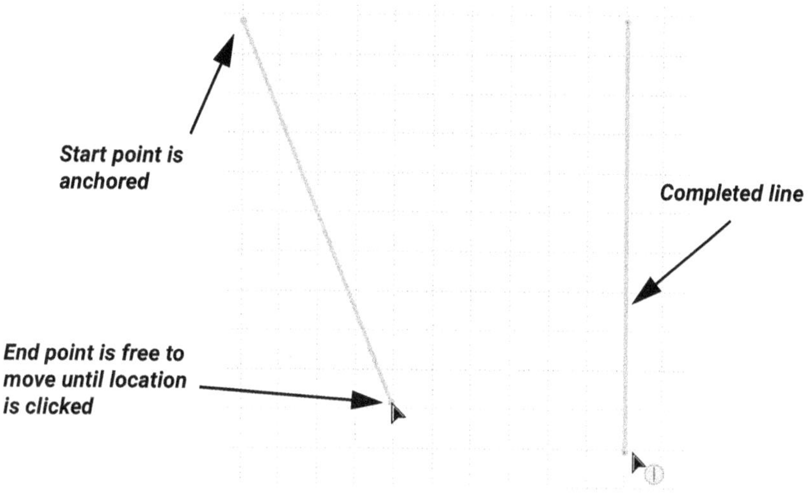

Start point is anchored

Completed line

End point is free to move until location is clicked

Figure 4–52

7. Move the cursor to the right until the ⊖ symbol displays and click the location shown in Figure 4–53 to complete the second line.

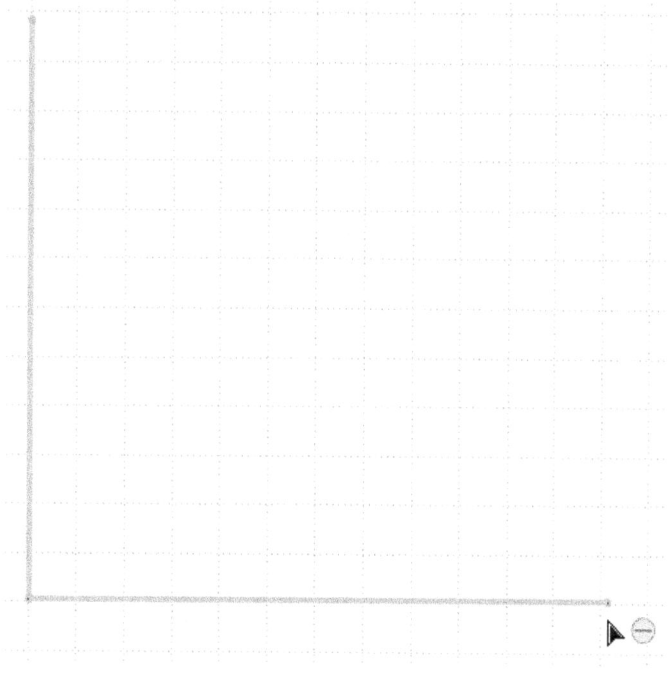

Figure 4–53

8. Click the location shown in Figure 4-54 to complete the third line.

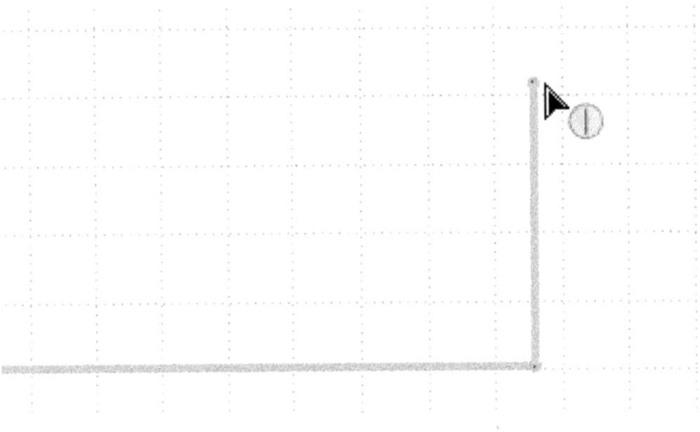

Figure 4-54

9. Click and hold the right mouse button and select ⤻ (3-Point / Tangent End), as shown in Figure 4-55.

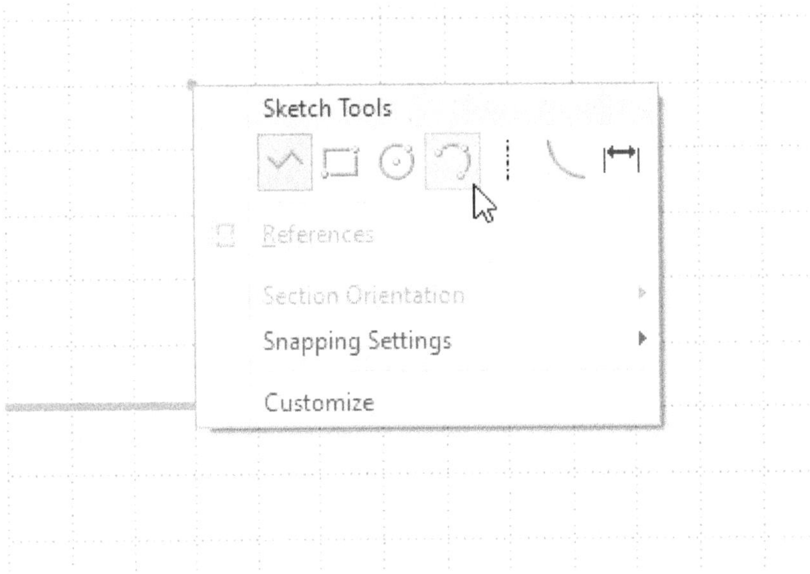

Figure 4-55

10. Click the end locations, as shown in Figure 4–56.

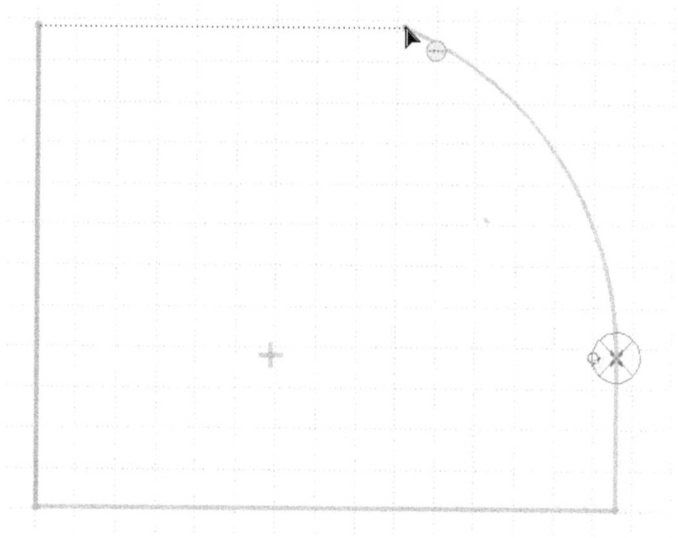

Figure 4–56

11. Right-click and select ⌄ (Line Chain).

12. Click the open end of the arc, and create the two lines shown in Figure 4–57.

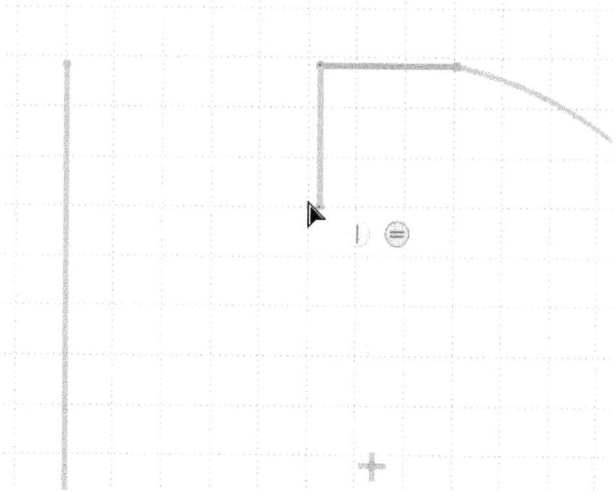

Figure 4–57

Note: Note the equal length constraints that are automatically established if you sketch the lines roughly equal.

13. Sketch the remaining three lines as shown in Figure 4–58. Ensure the final point snaps to the endpoint of the first line.

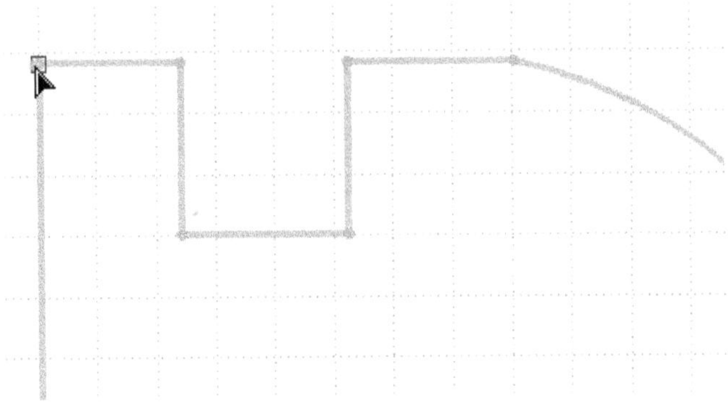

Figure 4–58

14. Click the middle mouse button twice to complete the sketch. The sketch displays approximately as shown in Figure 4–59.

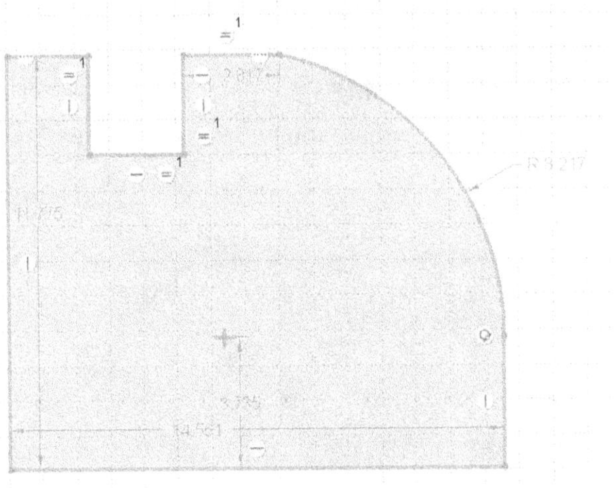

Figure 4–59

Note: *Your constraints and dimensions will be different than those shown, depending on how you created the sketch.*

Task 3: Ensure the large arc is tangent to the adjacent lines.

1. Zoom in on the upper area of the sketch, as shown in Figure 4−60.

Figure 4−60

2. In the *Constrain* group in the ribbon, click ⌒ (Tangent).

3. Select the line and arc shown and note that the ◔ icon displays, as shown in Figure 4−61.

Figure 4−61

4. Repeat the previous two steps for the other end of the arc, as shown in Figure 4−62.

Figure 4−62

Task 4: Add the filleted corners.

1. Right click and select ⌐ (Fillet).
2. Select the location shown in Figure 4−63.

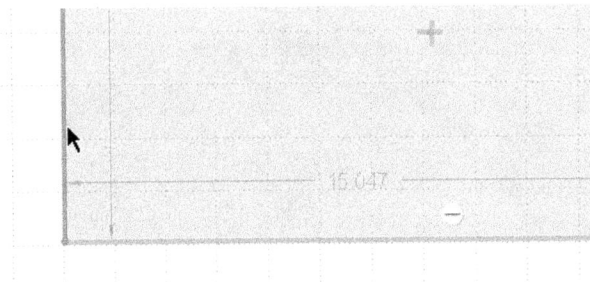

Figure 4−63

3. Select the location shown in Figure 4-64.

Figure 4-64

4. The system creates a radius as shown in Figure 4-65.

Figure 4-65

Note: The radius is defined by the point selected in Figure 4-65, which is closest to the corner.

5. With ⌐ (Fillet) still enabled, select the location shown in Figure 4-66.

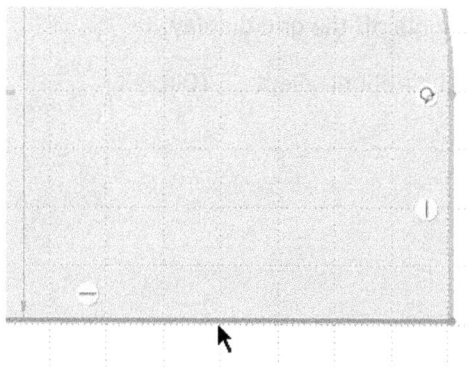

Figure 4-66

6. Select the location shown in Figure 4–67.

Figure 4–67

7. The system creates a radius as shown in Figure 4–68.

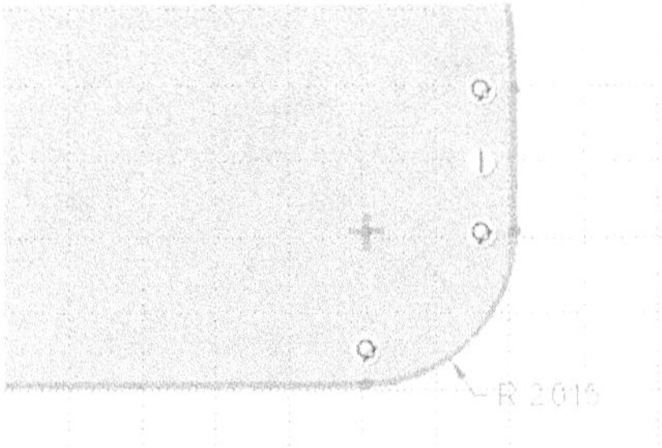

Figure 4–68

Task 5: Add the two circles.

1. In the *In-graphics* toolbar, select ▦ (Sketcher Display Filters).

2. Select ▦ (Disp Grid) to toggle off the grid display.

3. In the *Sketching* group in the ribbon, select ⊘ (Circle).

4. Move the cursor until it *snaps* to the center of the arc shown in Figure 4−69 and left click to start placing the circle.

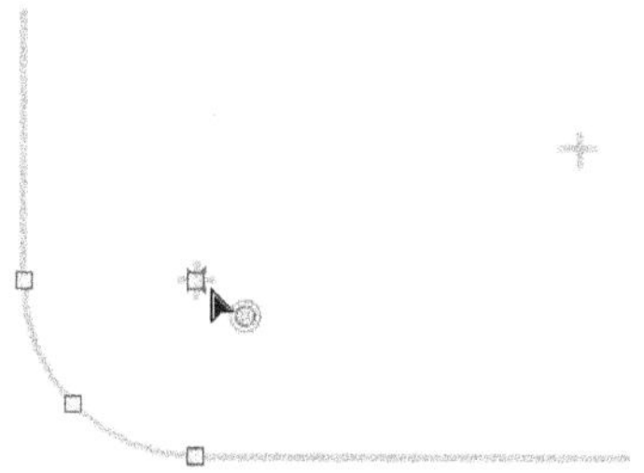

Figure 4−69

5. Move the cursor to the approximate position shown in Figure 4−70 and left-click to complete the circle.

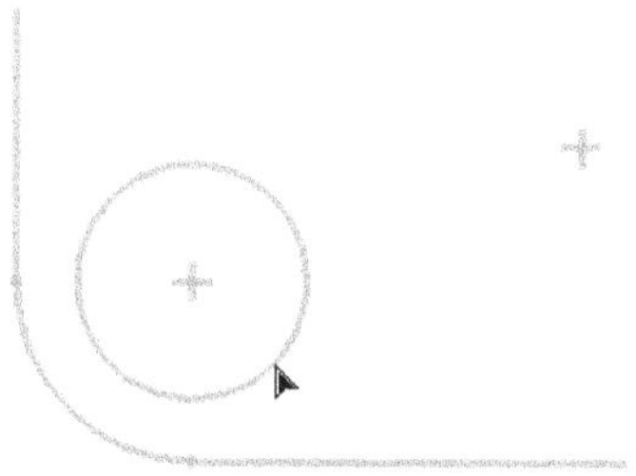

Figure 4−70

6. Create another circle in the approximate position shown in Figure 4−71. Ensure no automatic constraints are applied.

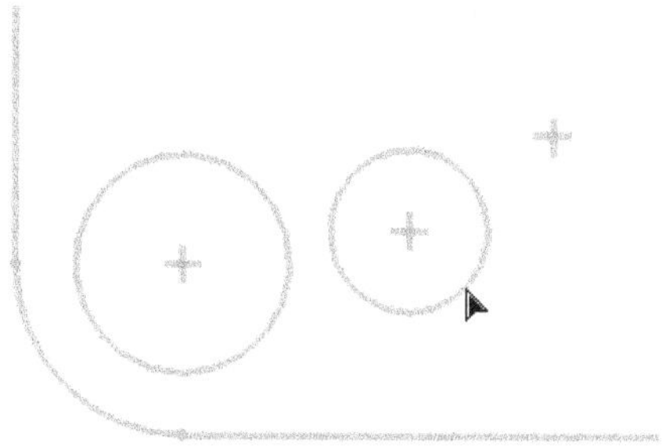

Figure 4−71

7. Click the middle mouse button to stop sketching. The model should display approximately as shown in Figure 4–72. Do not be concerned if your dimensions and constraints are different.

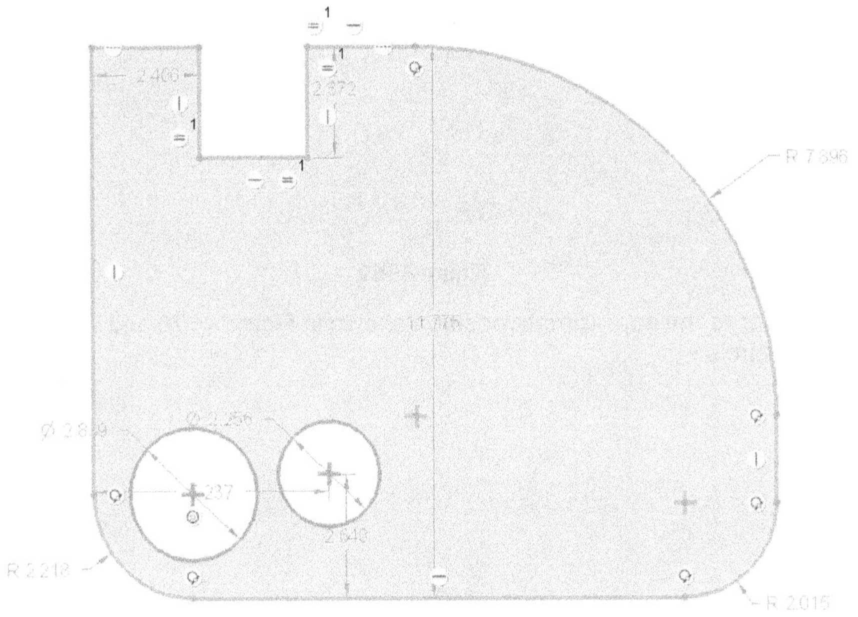

Figure 4–72

Task 6: Add constraints to remove dimensions.

1. In the *Constrain* group in the ribbon, click — (Horizontal) and select the center of each circle. The circles align horizontally, as shown in Figure 4–73.

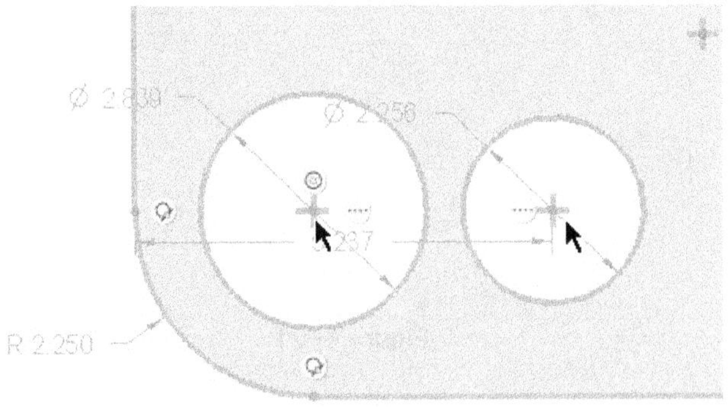

Figure 4–73

2. Click ⊥ (Vertical) and select the center of the large arc in the top-right of the shape and the center of the right circle. The model updates, as shown in Figure 4–74.

Figure 4–74

3. Click ⊥ (Vertical) and select the center of the large arc and the endpoint of the line, as shown in Figure 4–75.

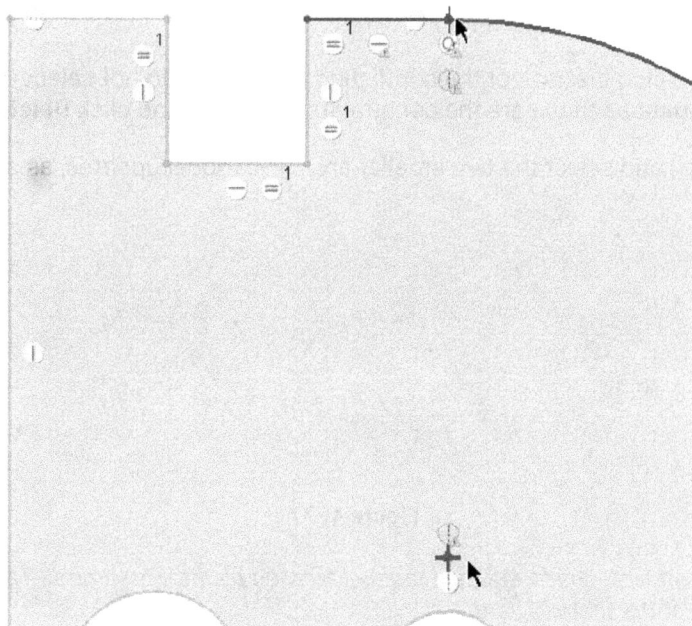

Figure 4–75

4. Depending on your constraints, the *Resolve Sketch* dialog box may open, as shown in Figure 4–76, indicating that there are conflicting constraints.

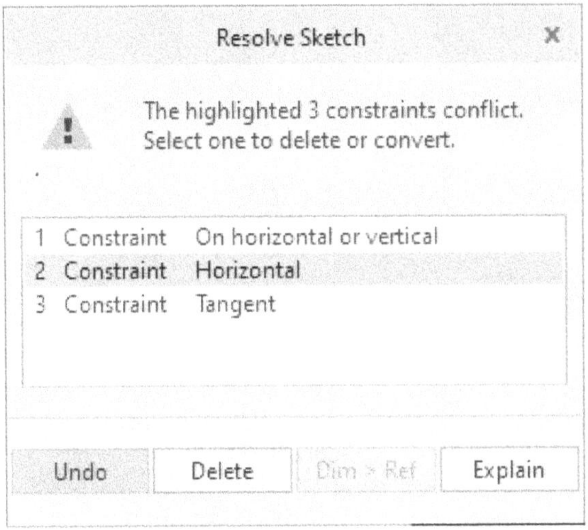

	Resolve Sketch ✕

⚠ The highlighted 3 constraints conflict. Select one to delete or convert.

```
1  Constraint   On horizontal or vertical
2  Constraint   Horizontal
3  Constraint   Tangent
```

Undo	Delete	Dim > Ref	Explain

Figure 4–76

Note: Your dialog box may list slightly different conflicts.

5. If you see this dialog box, select the conflicting constraint (do not select **On horizontal or vertical** or **Tangent** as those are the constraints you want) and click **Delete**.

6. Click ꞊ (Equal) and select the two smaller arcs. The model updates, as shown in Figure 4–77.

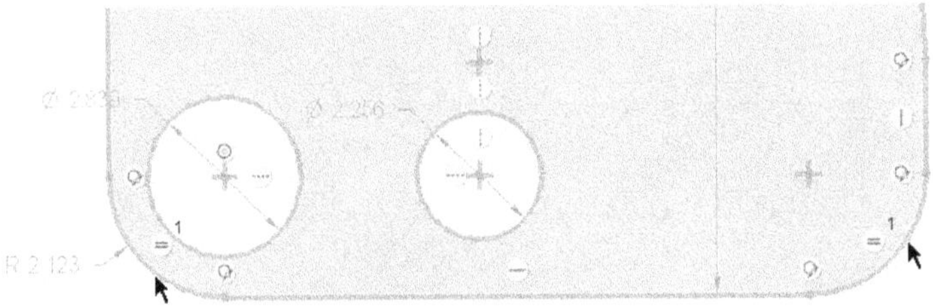

Figure 4–77

Note: The two arcs are made equal in radius, denoted by the ꞊ symbol. The sketch uses the dimension of the first arc selected.

7. Click ꞊ (Equal) again so you can select new entities; otherwise, you will continue making entities equal to the first arc.

8. Select the two circles and the system makes them equal, as shown in Figure 4–78.

Figure 4–78

9. Click = (Equal) again so you can select new entities.

10. Select the top left horizontal line, then select one of the short vertical lines. Repeat for any other lines that are not marked with the = symbol until all lines are equal, as shown in Figure 4–79.

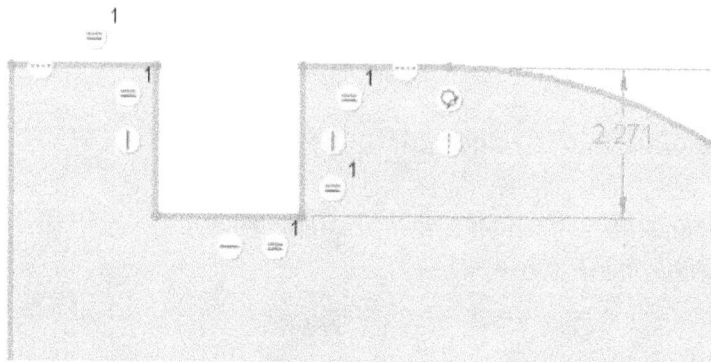

Figure 4–79

11. Click = (Equal) and select one of the small lines from the previous step and the small vertical line on the right of the sketch, as shown in Figure 4–80.

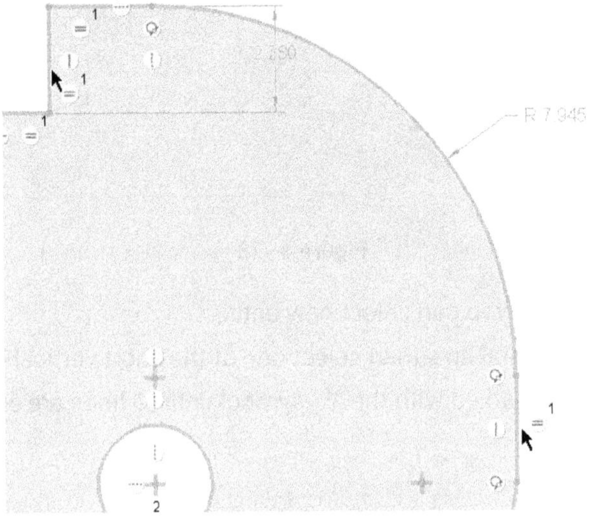

Figure 4–80

Task 7: Edit the dimensions to complete the sketch.

1. In the *Dimension* group in the ribbon, click ⟷ (Dimension).
2. Select the line shown in Figure 4–81.

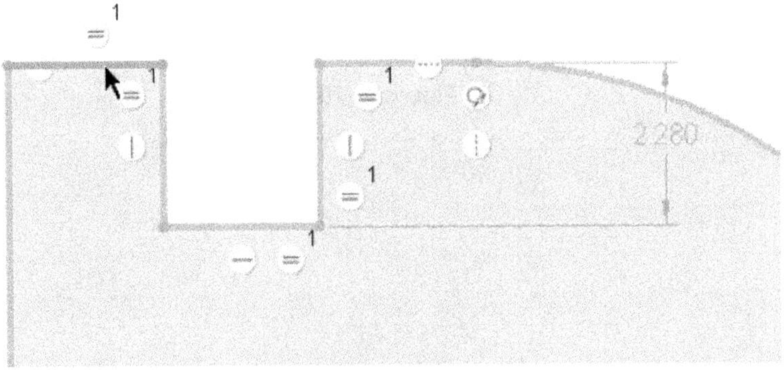

Figure 4–81

3. Move the cursor to the location shown in Figure 4–82 and click the middle mouse button to place the dimension. Set the dimension value to **2.1,** and then press <Enter>.

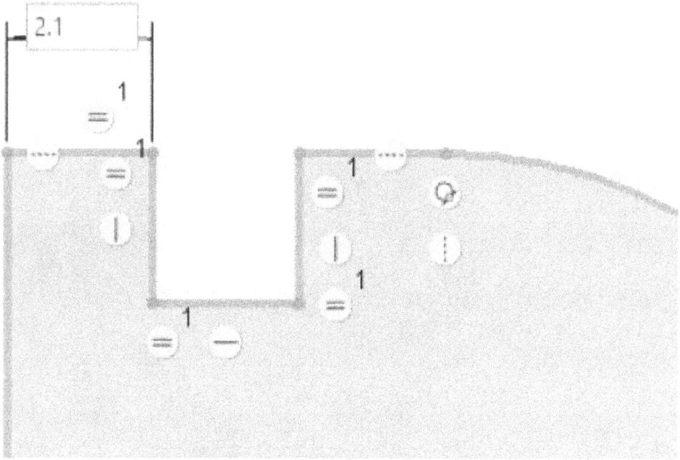

Figure 4–82

4. Select the two lines shown in Figure 4–83.

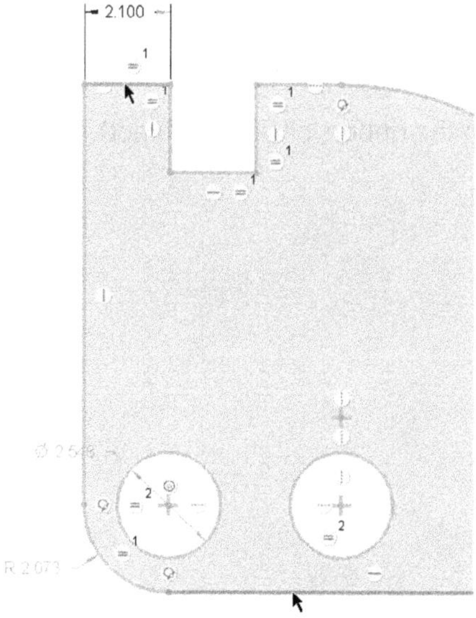

Figure 4–83

5. Move the cursor to the location indicated in Figure 4–84, click the middle mouse button, set the value to **8.9**, and press <Enter>.

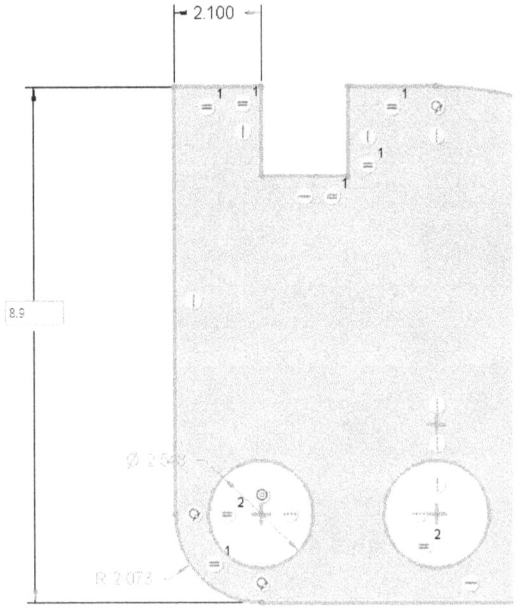

Figure 4–84

6. In the *Operations* group in the ribbon, click � (Select).

7. Double-click on the **radius** dimension for the lower left arc. Note that although it displayed to 3 decimal places, its value is actually carried through to 12 decimal places, as shown in Figure 4–85.

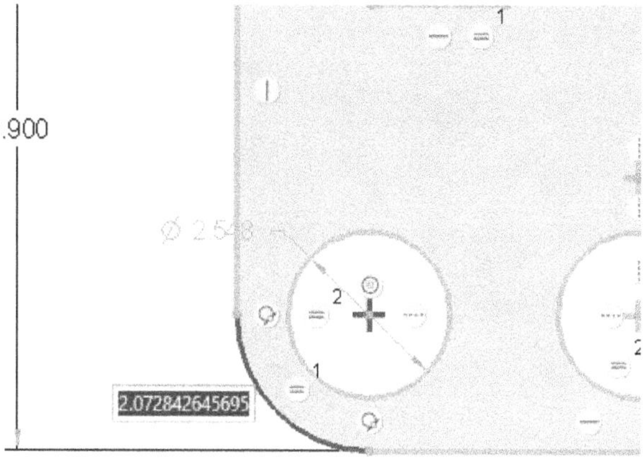

8.900

2.072842645695

Figure 4–85

Note: The value on your system will be slightly different depending on where you clicked to create the fillet. Always ensure that you edit your dimensions and that you do not leave them as weak.

8. Edit the dimension to **2**. Press <Enter>.

9. Double-click on the **diameter** dimension for the holes and set the value to **1.6**. Press <Enter>.

Note: Directly editing a weak dimension will convert is to strong.

10. The completed sketch displays, as shown in Figure 4-86.

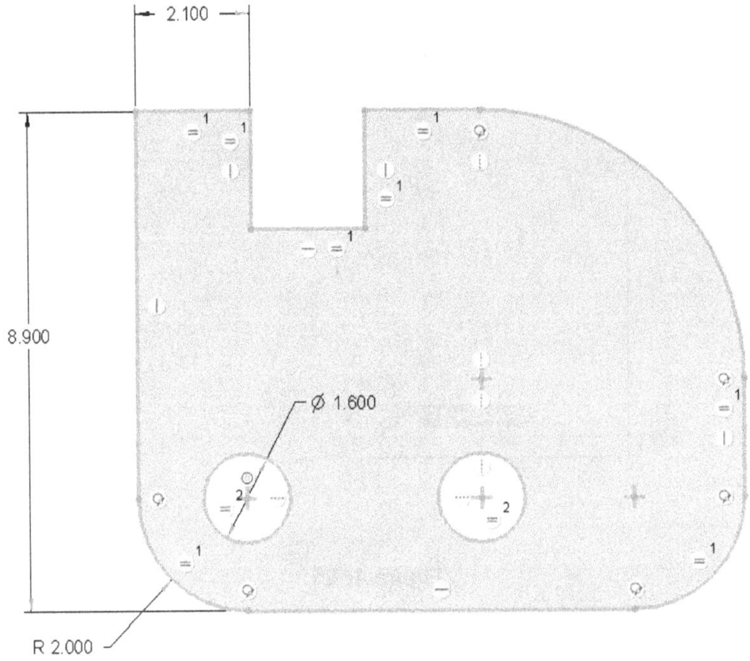

Figure 4-86

11. Close the file and erase it from memory.

End of practice

Practice 4b
Create a Sketch in a New Part

Practice Objectives

- Create a 2D sketch in a new part using references.
- Create a 2D geometry using the line, arc, tangent line, and trim tools in the *Sketch* tab.
- Add additional constraints and dimensions to the sketch to ensure that it captures the required design intent.

In this practice, you will create the sketches shown in Figure 4–87.

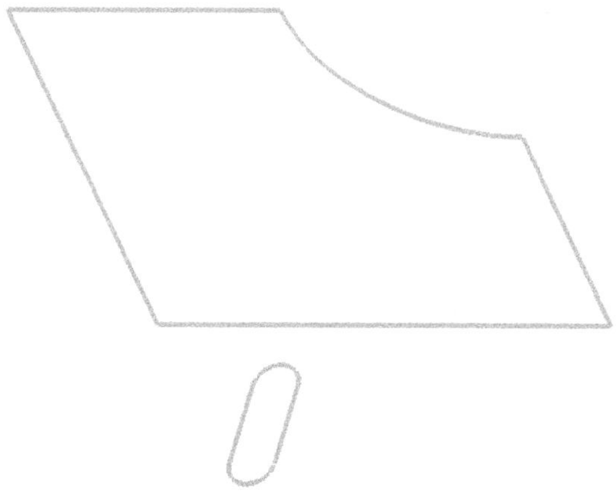

Figure 4–87

Task 1: Create a new part.

1. Set your working directory to the *Create_Sketch_Part* folder.

2. Click ⬜ (New) to create a new part.

3. Verify that **Part** and **Use default template** are selected. Set the *Name* to **gauge**.

4. Click **OK**.

5. Set the model display as follows:

   - ⁺⁄⁺. *(Datum Display Filters)*: Only 🔲 (Plane Display)

   - ⋟ *(Spin Center)*: Off

   - 🔲. *(Display Style)*: 🔲 (Shading)

6. Select datum plane **FRONT** from the Model Tree as the sketch plane for the first sketch.

7. In the *mini* toolbar or the *Datum* group in the *Model* tab, click ⬚ (Sketch) to begin creating the sketch. The *Sketch* tab becomes active.

   Note: Always review the default selections made by Creo Parametric. They might not meet your design requirements.

8. In the *Setup* group in the ribbon, click ⬚ (Sketch Setup) to investigate how the sketch plane has been established. The *Sketch* dialog box opens, as shown in Figure 4–88.

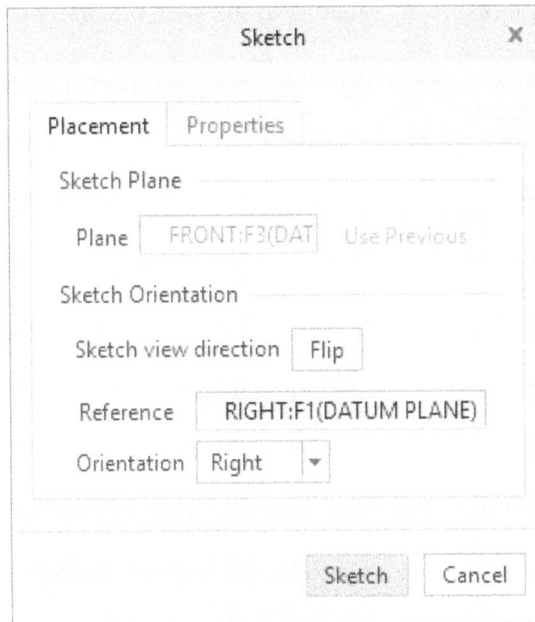

Figure 4–88

9. Note that the Sketch Plane you selected is listed, and datum plane **RIGHT** has been selected as the sketch orientation reference plane for this feature. You could select different references here if required. Click **Cancel** to return to the sketch.

Task 2: Sketch a rectangular section.

1. In the *Setup* group in the ribbon, click ⬚ (Sketch View) to orient the model to the sketch view if needed.

   Note: You can sketch in 3D as well, but in this task you will be using 2D until you are more familiar with the tools.

   *Note: Sketch View will be applied automatically to the sketch if the **Make the sketching plane parallel to the screen** option (under **Tools>Options>Core>Sketcher>Sketcher Startup**) was enabled.*

2. Click ▭ (Rectangle) to sketch a corner rectangle.

3. Start the rectangle at the intersection of datum planes **RIGHT** and **TOP** and move the cursor to the top-right quadrant, as shown in Figure 4–89. If the horizontal and vertical lines become close to the same length, they will turn green and the ⁼ symbol will display, indicating that the automatic equal length constraint has been added. When this symbol displays, click the left mouse button to complete the rectangle.

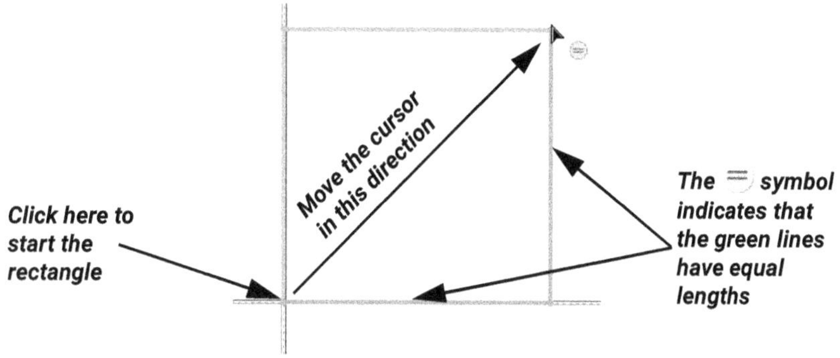

Move the cursor in this direction

Click here to start the rectangle

The ⁼ symbol indicates that the green lines have equal lengths

Figure 4–89

4. Modify the dimension of the rectangle. Click ⬚ (Select), double-click on the dimension, and enter **1.5**. Press <Enter> to complete the modification.

5. In the *In-graphics* toolbar, click ⬚ (Refit).

6. Move the dimension closer to the sketch, if necessary, and click ⬚ (Refit) again. The sketch updates, as shown in Figure 4–90.

1.500

Figure 4–90

Task 3: Set the sketcher to automatically refit after modification and to display 3 decimal places.

1. Open the *Creo Parametric Options* dialog box by clicking **File>Options**.

2. In the list of categories on the left, select **Configuration Editor**.

3. Click **Add**.

4. In the *Option name* field, type **sketcher_refit**. Note that the field automatically completes as **sketcher_refit_after_dim_modify**, as shown in Figure 4−91.

Figure 4−91

5. In the *Option value* drop-down list, select **Yes**, and then click **OK**.

6. Select the **Sketcher** node under the *Core* category in the Creo Parametric Options dialog box.

7. Set the *Number of decimal places for dimensions* to **3**, as shown in Figure 4−92.

Figure 4−92

8. Click **OK**.

9. When prompted to save the options and store the configuration file, click **Yes**.

10. Save the file to the *Practice Files* folder.

Task 4: Sketch a center-and-ends arc.

1. In the *Sketching* group in the ribbon, expand the ⌒ (Arc) flyout and select ⌒ (Center and Ends) to create a center-and-ends arc.

2. Select the vertex in the upper right corner of the rectangle. This vertex is the center of the arc.

3. Sketch the arc from the top horizontal edge to the right edge of the rectangle, as shown in Figure 4–93.

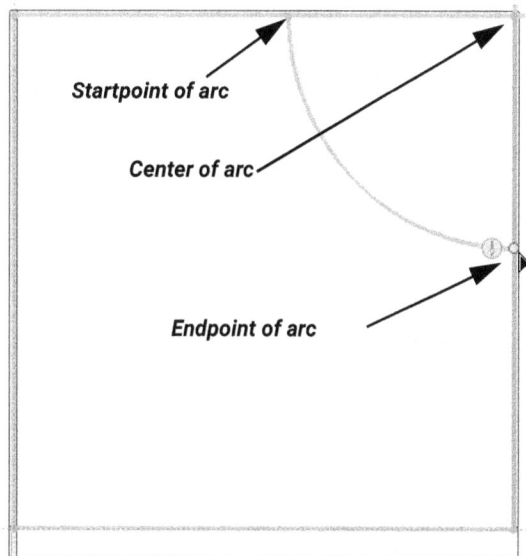

Figure 4–93

The arc displays, as shown in Figure 4−94.

Figure 4−94

Note: The highlighted vertices and the sketch are no longer filled in due to the multiple loops. In the next task, these entities will be trimmed.

4. Modify the value of the *Radius* dimension to **0.60**.

Task 5: Corner trim the arc and edges of the rectangle.

1. In the *Editing* group, click ⊢ (Corner) to corner trim the arc and edges of the rectangle.
2. Select the top horizontal line of the rectangle in the location shown in Figure 4−95.

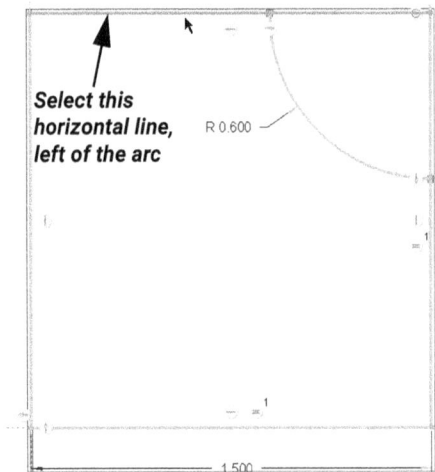

Select this horizontal line, left of the arc

R 0.600

Figure 4−95

Note: When trimming to a corner, select each entity on the portion you want to keep.

3. Select the arc. The entities are trimmed to a corner, as shown in Figure 4–96.

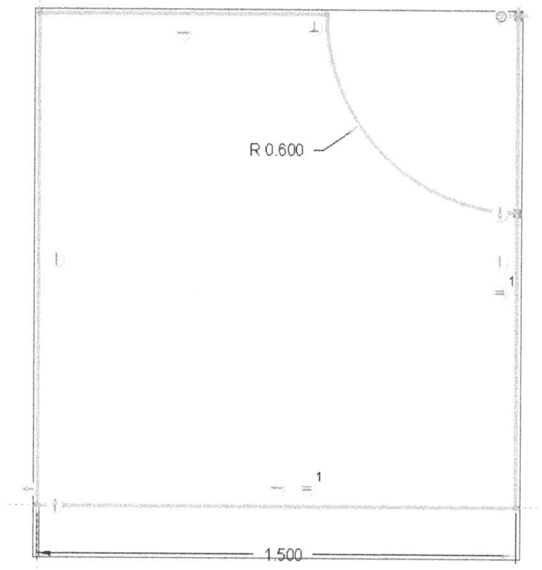

Figure 4–96

4. Corner trim the arc and the right vertical line of the rectangle in the same way. Remember to select the lines on the portions you want to keep. The sketch displays, as shown in Figure 4–97.

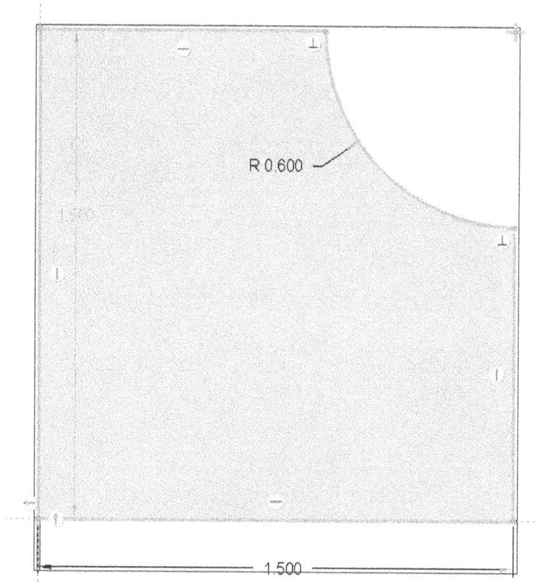

Figure 4–97

5. The sketch is now filled in because it is a closed loop. In the *Inspect* group of the *Sketch* tab, expand the arrow next to **Inspect**, and click ⬚ (Shade Closed Loops) to toggle the shading off.

6. Click ⬚ (Shade Closed Loops) again to toggle it back on.

Task 6: Apply the equal length constraint.

1. Note that two dimensions control the height and width of the remains of the rectangle. To apply the equal length constraint, click ═ (Equal) in the *Constrain* group.

   Note: The equal length constraint was removed when the top and right side of the rectangle were trimmed. The constraint can be re-applied to the bottom and left sides so that a single dimension controls these lengths.

2. Select the bottom line and the left line. The sketch displays, as shown in Figure 4−98. The extra weak dimension has been removed, and the ═ symbols display next to the lines.

Figure 4−98

Task 7: Complete the feature and rename it.

1. Click ✓ (**OK**) to complete the sketch.
2. Return the model to its default orientation by clicking <Ctrl>+<D>. The sketch displays, as shown in Figure 4–99.

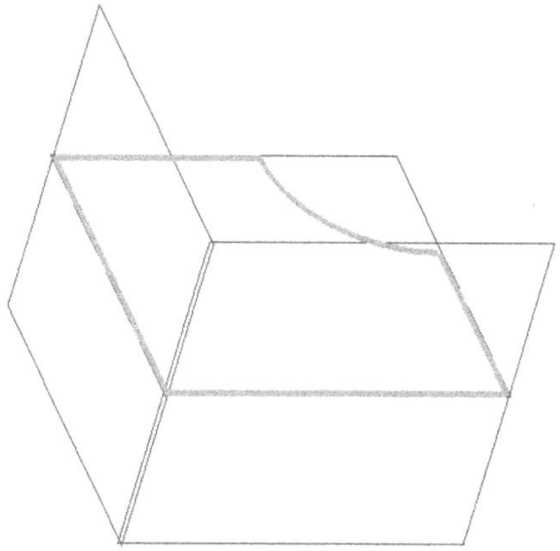

Figure 4–99

Note: The planes may display as shaded versions instead of just the boarders as shown

in Figure 4–99. This can be customized by toggling on/off 🔳 *(Plane Fill Display) found under the expanded* ᵡ⁄ᵗᵗ *(Datum Display Filters) icon in the In-graphics toolbar.*

3. In the Model Tree, select **Sketch 1**, right-click, and select **Rename**. You can also select the feature twice in the Model Tree.
4. Set the new *Name* of the sketch to **front_profile**. The Model Tree displays, as shown in Figure 4–100.

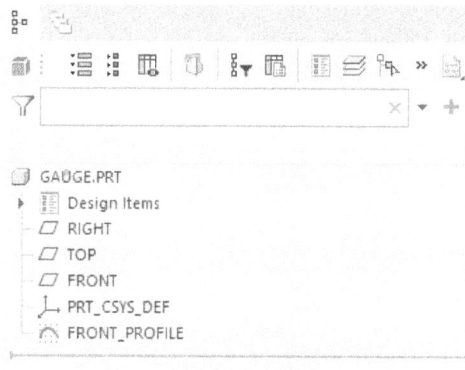

Figure 4–100

Task 8: Create the second sketch.

1. Select datum plane **TOP** from the Model Tree as the sketch plane for the second sketch.

2. Click ⬚ (Sketch) in the *mini* toolbar to begin creating the sketch. The *Sketch* tab becomes active and the system automatically selects a sketch orientation reference plane.

3. If necessary, click ⬚ (Sketch View) to orient the model.

Task 9: Sketch an obround section.

1. Click ⬚ (Circle) to sketch two circles as shown in Figure 4–101. Sketch the circles so that they have equal radii and their centers are aligned vertically, as indicated by the constraint symbols. The circles are sketched in the lower right quadrant of the intersection of datum planes.

   Note: The first sketch feature that was created cannot be seen because it is perpendicular to the current sketching plane.

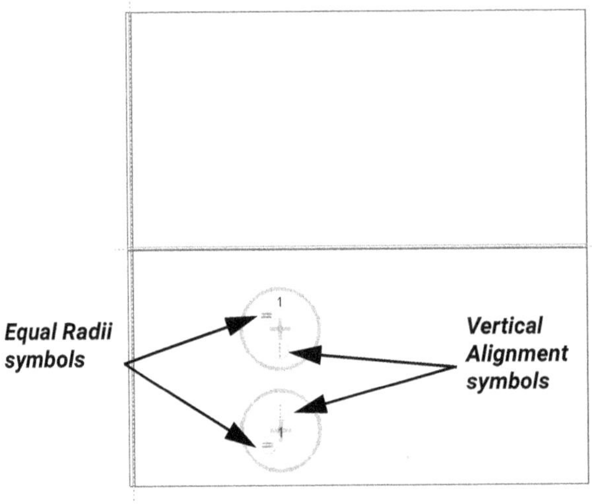

Figure 4–101

   Note: Sketcher dimensions are toggled off by clicking ⬚ (Sketcher Display Filters) and clearing the ⬚ (Disp Dims) option. The ⬚ (Shade Closed Loops) option is also disabled for clarity.

2. In the *Sketching* group, click ⌄ (Line).

3. Select the left side of the two circles, noting that the line snaps to the handle that displays on the circle. A line tangent to both circles is sketched, as shown in Figure 4-102.

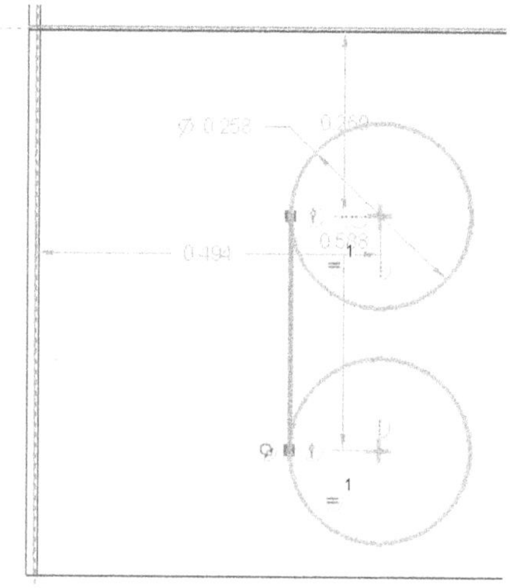

Figure 4-102

4. Sketch a second line tangent to the right sides of the circles, as shown in Figure 4-103.

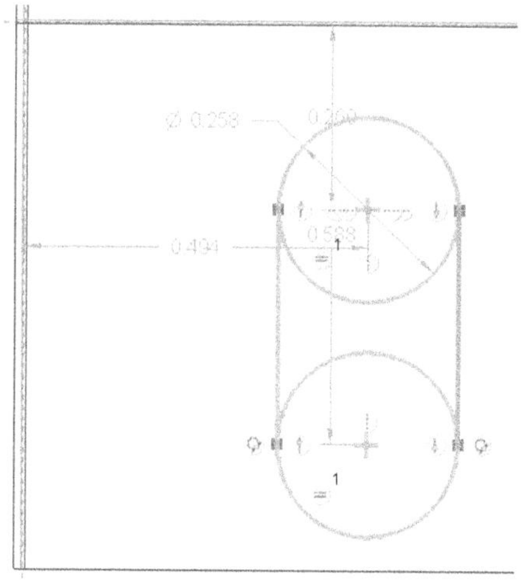

Figure 4-103

5. In the *Editing* group, click ⌇ (Delete Segment). When you select this option, all of the entities are temporarily divided where they intersect other entities.

6. Select the inner segments for trimming. Press and hold the left mouse button and drag a selection spline through the inner segments of the two circles, as shown in Figure 4–104.

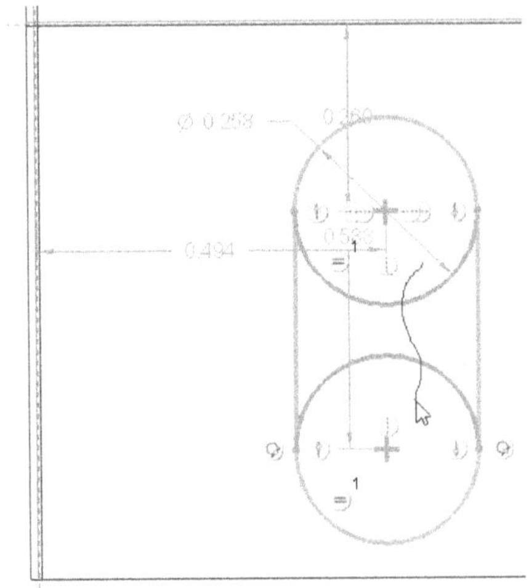

Figure 4–104

7. Release the left mouse button to delete the selected segments. The sketch displays, as shown in Figure 4–105.

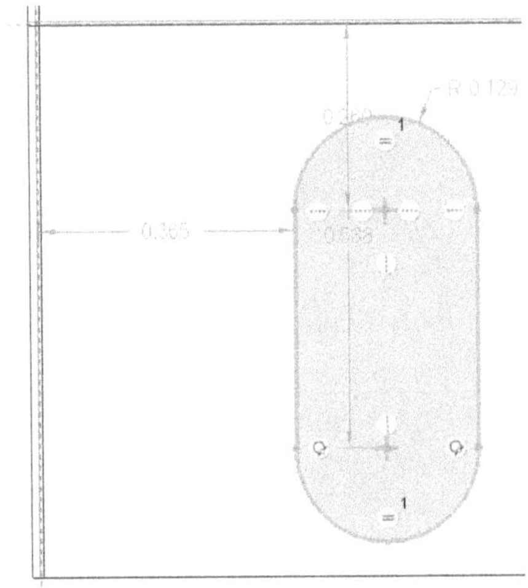

Figure 4–105

8. Click ⟷ (Dimension) to create dimensions. The current dimensions are the weak dimensions automatically created by the Creo Parametric software.

9. Create the dimension **0.15** shown in Figure 4–106. Select the two vertical lines and place the dimension with the middle mouse button.

Create this linear dimension

Figure 4–106

Note: You can move a dimension to a new position. Click ▷ (Select), select the dimension by holding the left mouse button, and drag the dimension to the required position.

10. Create the dimension **0.45** shown in Figure 4–107 by selecting the center of the lower arc and the vertical cyan reference entity. Place the dimension with the middle mouse button.

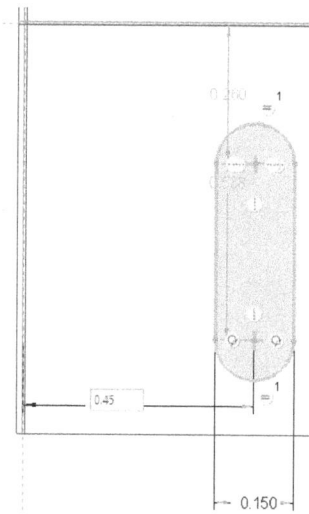

Figure 4–107

11. Create the dimension **0.45** shown in Figure 4–108 by selecting the two arcs. Select the arc entities, not their centers. Place the dimension with the middle mouse button.

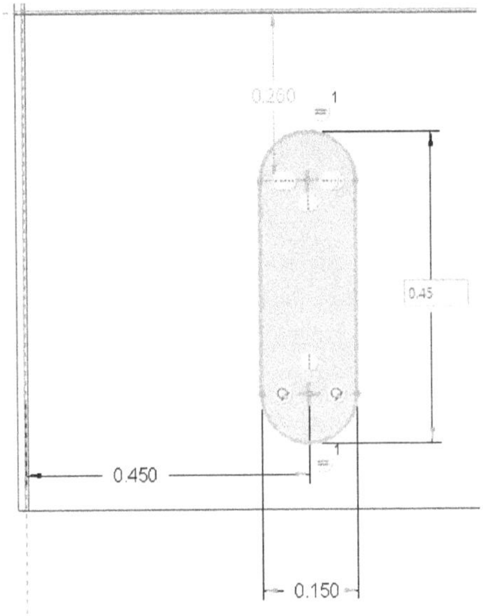

Figure 4–108

12. Finally, create the dimension **0.15** shown in Figure 4–109, by selecting the edge of the upper arc and the horizontal reference entity. Place the dimension with the middle mouse button.

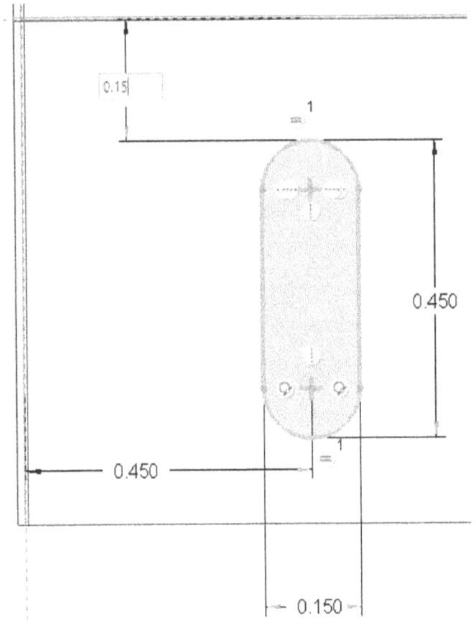

Figure 4–109

13. Move the dimensions to complete the sketch, as shown in Figure 4–110.

Figure 4–110

14. The sketch is now complete. Click ✓ (**OK**) to finish the sketch feature.

15. Press <Ctrl>+<D> to return to default orientation.

16. Click ⅍ (Datum Display Filters) and select ▱ (Plane Display) to toggle off the display of the datum planes.

17. The model displays in the default orientation, as shown in Figure 4–111.

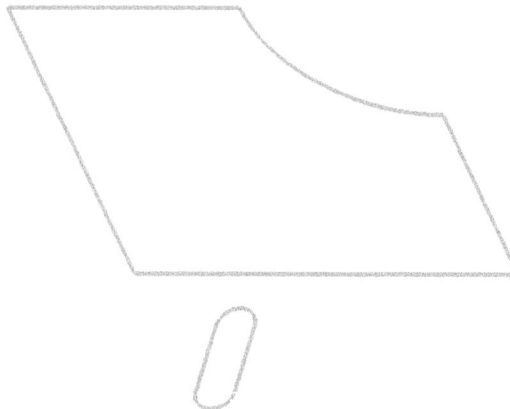

Figure 4–111

18. Save and erase the model.

End of practice

Practice 4c
Sketch on Existing Geometry

Practice Objectives

- Open an existing part model and add a 2D sketch on an existing surface in the model.
- Create the 2D sketch using the Centered Rectangle command.
- Modify the existing entities into a alternate sketch using the **Delete Segment** command.
- Modify and dimension sketched entities.
- Create an extrude feature using the 2D sketch.

In this practice, you will create a sketch in a part that already contains solid geometry. Instead of selecting a datum plane as the sketching plane, you will select a surface on the solid geometry. The sketch displays, as shown in Figure 4–112.

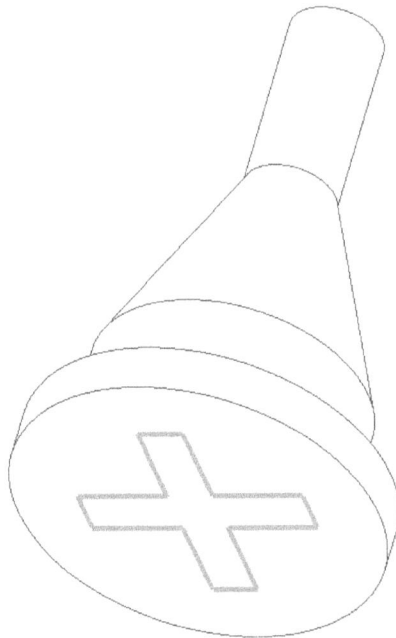

Figure 4–112

Task 1: Open a part file.

1.   Set the working directory to the *Sketch_On_Geometry* folder.

2.   Open **control_shaft.prt**.

3.   Set the model display as follows:

   - *⚡ (Datum Display Filters):* All Off

   - *⋟ (Spin Center):* Off

   - *▢ (Display Style):* ▢ (No Hidden)

Task 2: Start the creation of the sketch on the protrusion.

1.   For the sketching plane, select the surface of the solid, as shown in Figure 4−113.

Select this surface ─────────→

Figure 4−113

2.   In the *mini* toolbar, click ▦ (Sketch) to create a sketch.

3.   If required, click 📐 (Sketch View) to orient the model.

4. Click ⬚ (References) to open the *Reference* dialog box. Note that the Coordinate system and the **TOP** datum plane were automatically selected as references as shown in Figure 4–114.

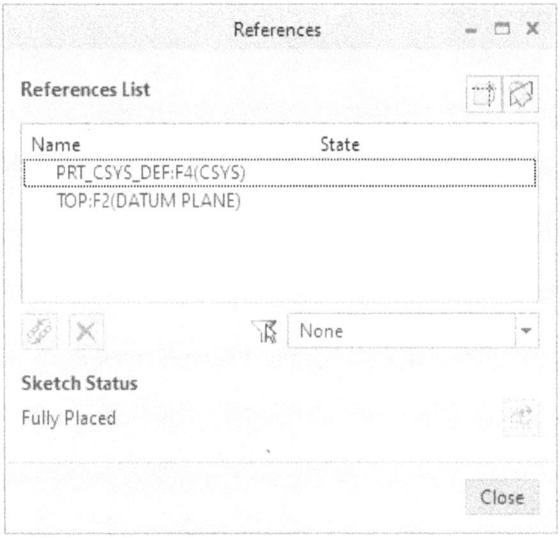

Figure 4–114

Note: You can sketch in 3D orientation, but it may be easier to sketch in 2D.

5. Select the **RIGHT** datum plane from the Model Tree as an additional sketcher reference. The model displays, as shown in Figure 4–115.

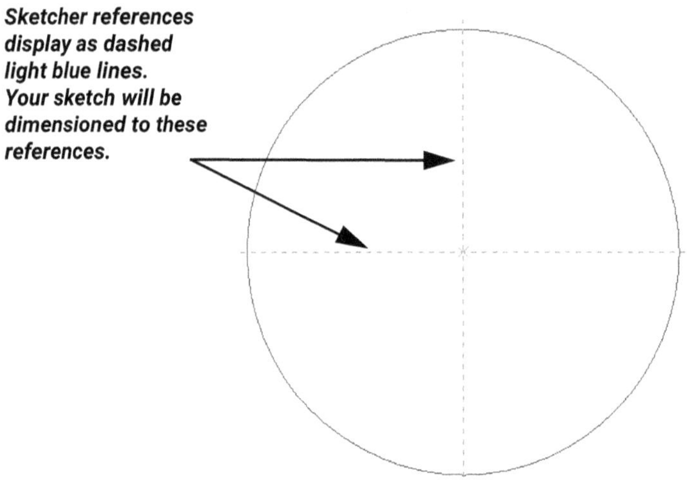

Sketcher references display as dashed light blue lines. Your sketch will be dimensioned to these references.

Figure 4–115

*Note: You can also right-click and select **References**.*

6. In the *References* dialog box, click **Close**.

7. Expand ⬚ (Rectangle) and click ⬚ (Center Rectangle). Begin the sketch by clicking on the intersection of the two sketcher references for the centerpoint of the rectangle, as shown in Figure 4−116.

Begin the sketch at the intersection of the two reference lines

Figure 4−116

8. Click the endpoint location of the rectangle, as shown in Figure 4−117. This creates a rectangle in the center of the geometry.

Click approximately this location for the second point

Figure 4−117

9. Click |↔| (Dimension) and dimension the rectangular sketch, as shown in Figure 4–118.

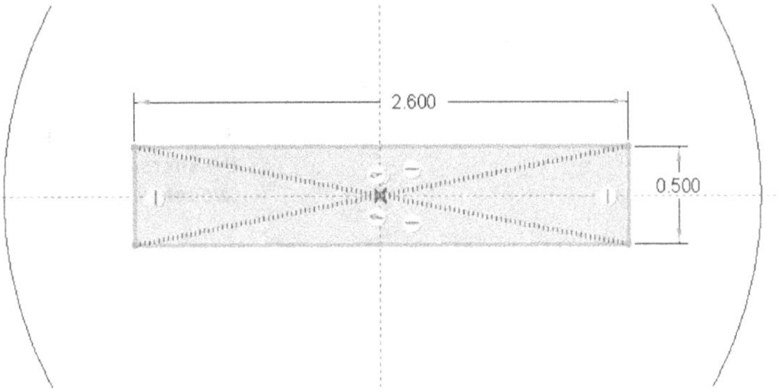

Figure 4–118

Note: *To dimension a line, click the line, then click the middle mouse button where you want to place the dimension.*

10. Sketch another centered rectangle vertically, as shown in Figure 4–119.

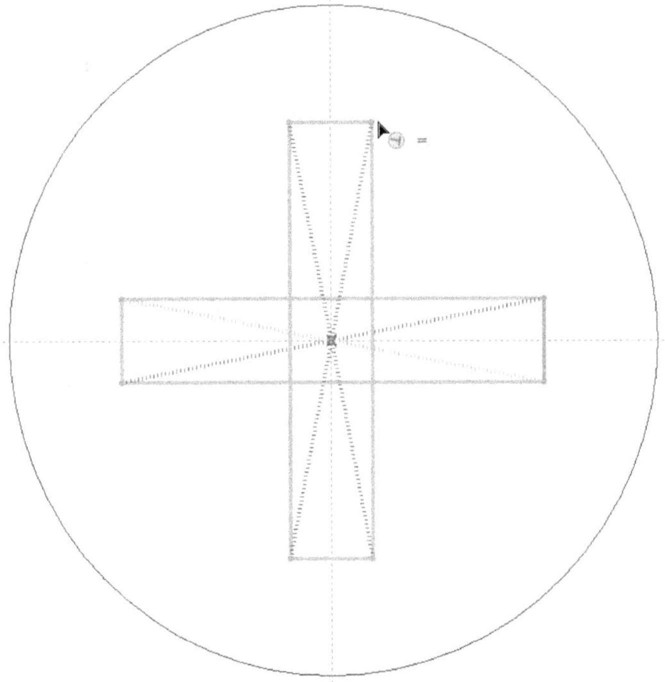

Figure 4–119

11. Click ✂ (Delete Segment) to trim away the segments shown in Figure 4–120.

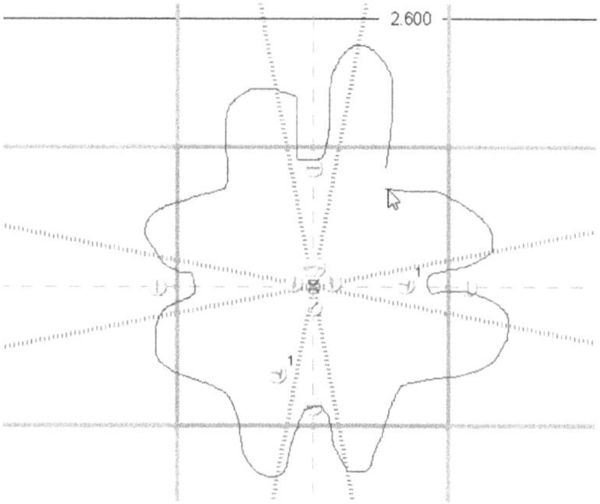

Figure 4–120

Note: You can drag a continuous line or select the individual segments. There are 16 individual segments.

12. Dimension the sketch shown in Figure 4–121. Apply constraints as required to create a fully constrained sketch that is only controlled by the two dimensions shown in Figure 4–121. Note that the dimensions can be on any appropriate line, not necessarily on the lines shown.

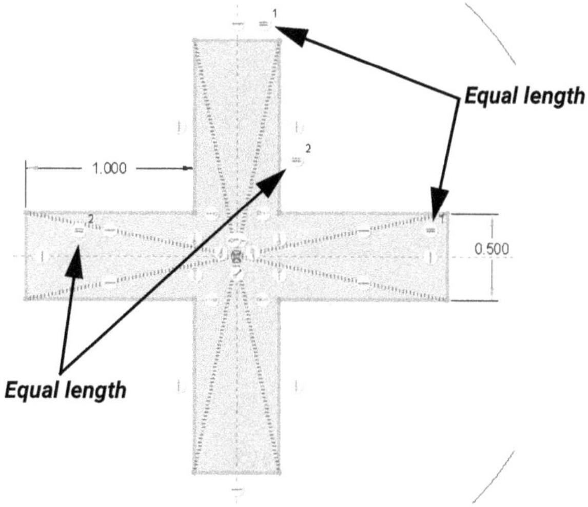

Figure 4–121

Note: Use the constraint icons or select the entities and use the contextual menu to apply the constraints. There are multiple ways in which this sketch can be constrained, so your sketch may not be exactly as shown.

13. Click ✓ (**OK**) to complete the sketch and exit Sketcher.

14. Press <Ctrl>+<D> to return to Standard Orientation. The completed sketch displays, as shown in Figure 4–122.

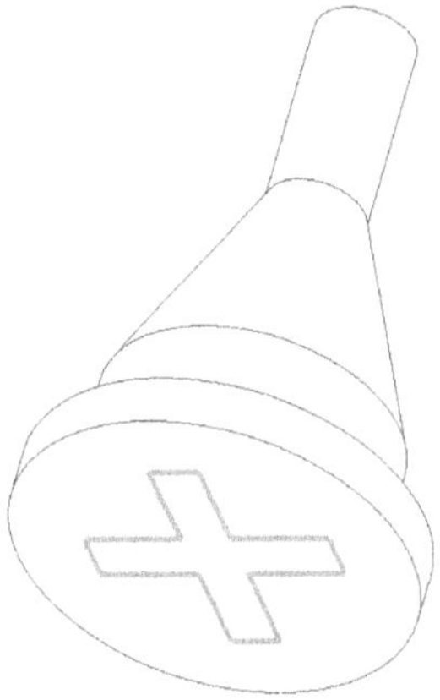

Figure 4–122

15. Select the **Sketch 1** feature in the Model Tree, if required.

16. In the *Shapes* group in the *Model* tab or the *mini* toolbar, click ▱ (Extrude).

17. Set the *Depth* to **1.0**, as shown in Figure 4–123.

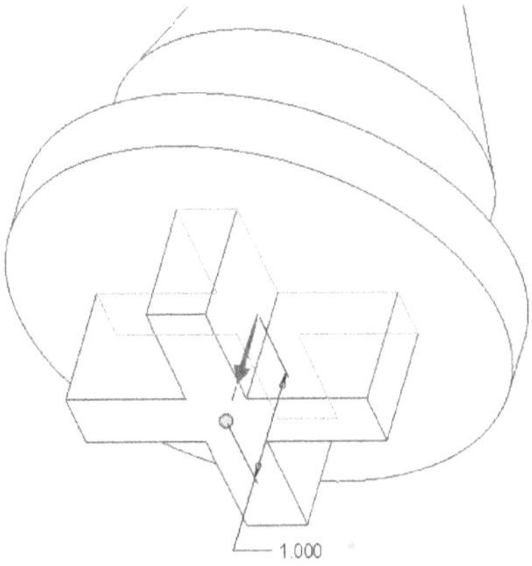

Figure 4–123

18. Click ✓ (**OK**).

19. Save the part and erase it from memory.

End of practice

Practice 4d
Complex Sketch

Practice Objectives

- Create a new sketch using the sketch and orientation planes.

- Create geometry using the mirror, trim, and fillet tools.

- Apply dimensions and constraints so that the sketch captures the design intent and is fully constrained.

In this practice, you will create a sketch in a new part. You will use many of the techniques used in previous practices. The sketch is shown in Figure 4-124.

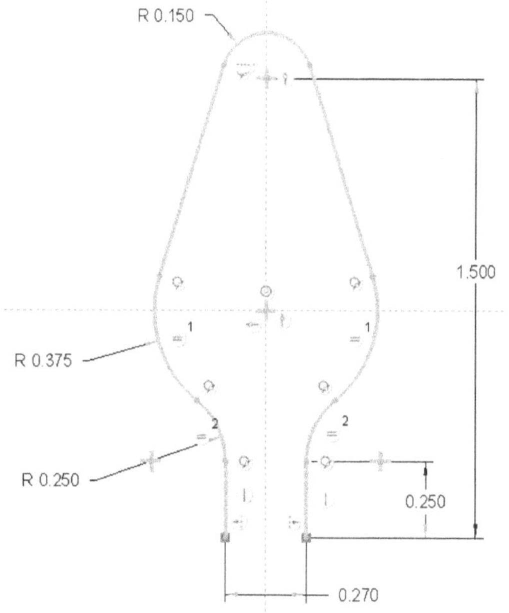

Figure 4-124

Task 1: Create a new part.

1. Set the working directory to the *Complex_Sketch* folder.

2. Click ☐ (New) to create a new part, and set the *Name* to **clip**.

3. Click **OK**.

4. Set the model display as follows:

- ⌗ *(Datum Display Filters):* All off

- ⟩⟩ *(Spin Center):* Off

- ▢ *(Display Style):* ▢ (No Hidden)

Task 2: Create the sketch.

1. Select datum plane **FRONT** from the Model Tree for the sketching plane.

2. In the *mini* toolbar, click ▨ (Sketch).

3. If required, click ▣ (Sketch View) to orient the model.

4. Sketch a circle at the intersection of the sketcher references as shown in Figure 4−125.

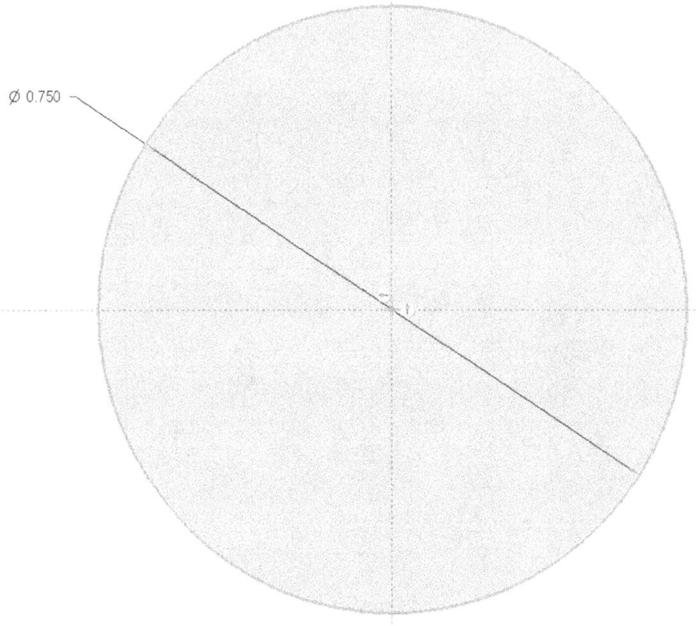

Ø 0.750

Figure 4−125

5. Select the **Diameter** dimension and click ⟳ (Radius) in the *mini* toolbar, as shown in Figure 4–126.

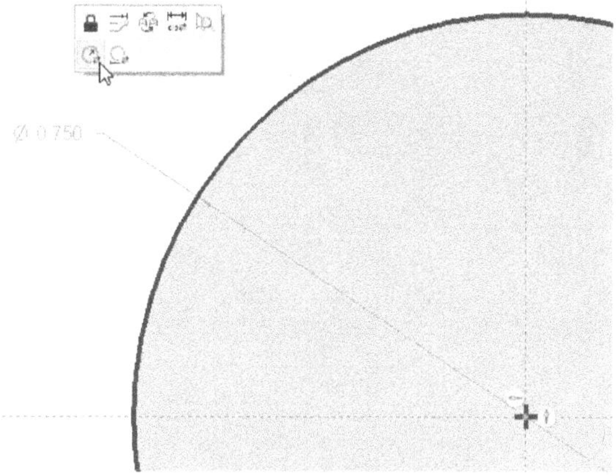

Figure 4–126

6. The *radius* updates to **0.375**, as shown in Figure 4–127.

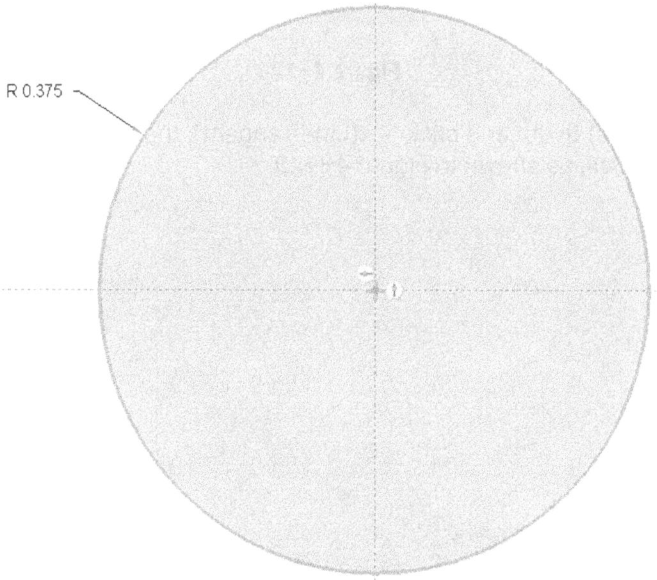

Figure 4–127

Note: Depending on your system setup, the dimension may only display two decimals. You will learn how to change that in a later chapter.

7. Sketch a second circle and dimension it with a *Radius* of **0.15**, as shown in Figure 4–128.

Figure 4–128

8. Expand the ⌄ (Line) flyout and click ＼ (Line Tangent), then sketch two lines that are tangent to the circles, as shown in Figure 4–129.

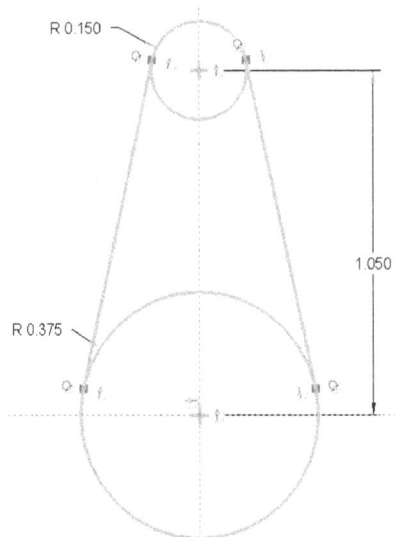

Figure 4–129

9. Expand the ╲ (Line) flyout and click ⌄ (Line Chain). Sketch the vertical line shown in Figure 4–130. Remember to click the two points, then click the middle mouse button to complete the line chain. Do not worry about the exact length.

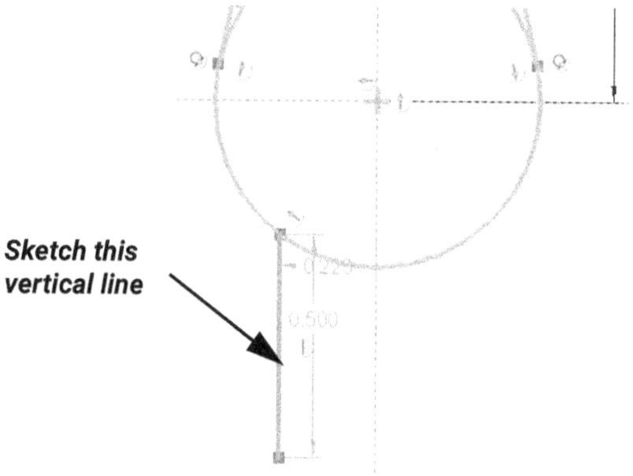

Sketch this vertical line

Figure 4–130

Task 3: Mirror a sketched entity.

1. Select the line you just created.

2. In the *Editing* group, click 🔁 (Mirror) to create a mirror copy of this line.

3. Select the vertical reference as the mirroring reference. The new line displays symmetric about the centerline with the original line, as shown in Figure 4–131.

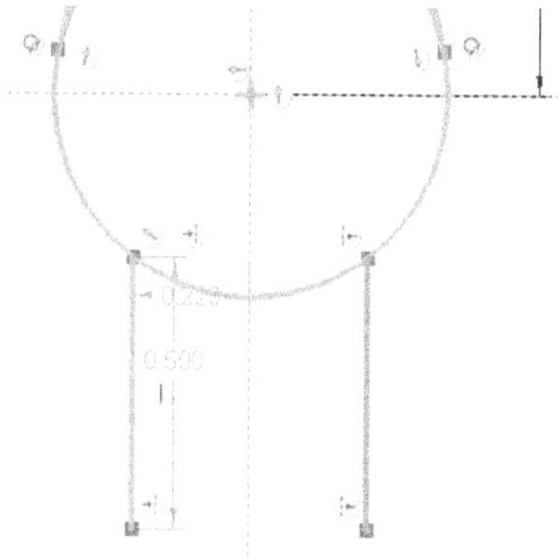

Figure 4–131

Note: You can also sketch a centerline by clicking ⋮ *(Centerline) in the Sketching group.*

4. Click ⌿ (Delete Segment) to trim the unnecessary segments of the circles. The sketch displays, as shown in Figure 4–132.

R 0.150

1.050

R 0.375

0.445

0.500

Figure 4–132

5. Click ⌌ (Fillet) to create a circular fillet between the arc segment and vertical line. Select a location on the arc for the first point and on the line for the second point as shown in Figure 4–133.

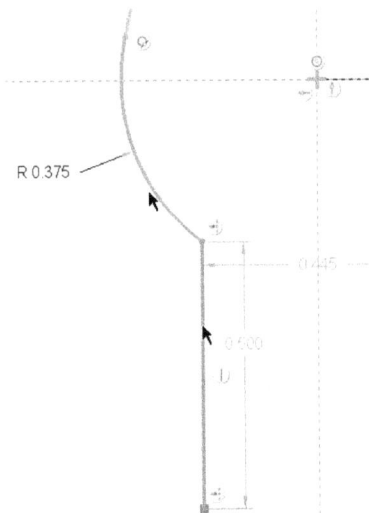

R 0.375

0.445

0.500

Figure 4–133

6. Create another circular fillet on the opposite side between the vertical line and arc segment. The sketch displays, as shown in Figure 4–134.

Create this circular fillet   **Create this circular fillet**

Figure 4–134

7. Note that the original entities have been trimmed.

8. Constrain the radii of the two fillet arcs to be equal.

9. Create the constraints and dimensions in Figure 4–135 and modify the values.

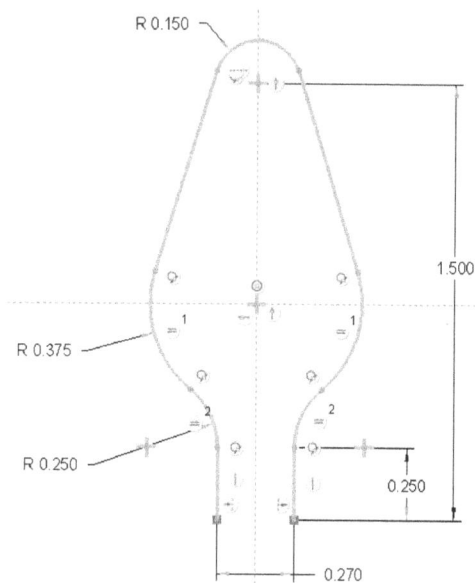

Figure 4–135

10. Complete the sketch. Press <Ctrl>+<D> to orient the model to the default orientation. It displays, as shown in Figure 4–136.

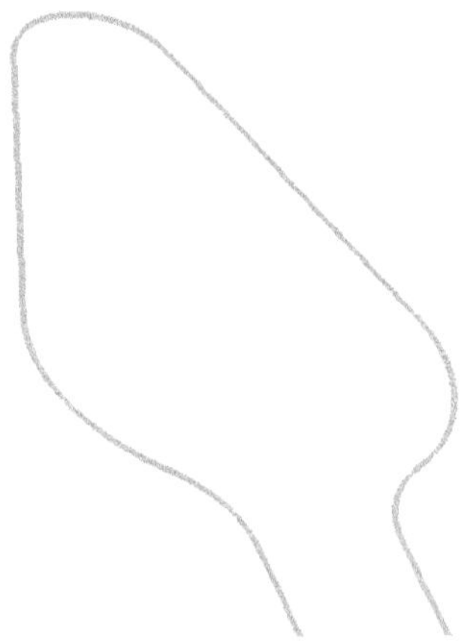

Figure 4–136

11. Save and erase the model.

End of practice

Chapter Review Questions

1. Which of the following should be defined before sketching geometry? (Select all that apply.)
   a. Sketch Plane
   b. Sketch Orientation
   c. Constraints
   d. Sketcher References

2. $=$ is used to apply the equal constraint to sketched geometry. Which of the following can be made equal with this constraint? (Select all that apply.)
   a. Angles
   b. Centerline Lengths
   c. Lengths
   d. Radii

3. Which of the following options enables you to create an arc between entities and automatically trim those entities?
   a.
   b.
   c.
   d.

4. Construction entities can be used directly to create solid geometry.
   a. True
   b. False

5. Which of the following icons enables you to divide an entity without trimming it?

   a.

   b.

   c.

   d.

6. Which of the following are true regarding the **Delete Segment** option? (Select all that apply.)

   a. Requires you to hold <Ctrl> while selecting multiple entities.

   b. Enables you to sketch a spline surrounding multiple entities, deleting all within the spline.

   c. Enables you to delete selected entities.

   d. Enables you to sketch a spline through the entities to be deleted.

7. All constraints must be manually assigned to the sketched geometry.

   a. True

   b. False

8. Which of the following can be used to remove a constraint that automatically displays as you are in the process of sketching an entity?

   a. <Tab>

   b. <Shift>

   c. <Ctrl>

   d. <Alt>

9. Which of the following can be used to disable the selection filter?

   a. <Tab>

   b. <Shift>

   c. <Ctrl>

   d. <Alt>

Answers: 1abd, 2acd, 3b, 4b, 5a, 6cd, 7b, 8b, 9d

Creating the Base Feature

The first solid feature created in Creo Parametric is the base feature, which serves as the foundation to which you add other features for building a model. The first feature adds solid material to the model. In this chapter, you will learn to use basic base feature forms and create extruded and revolved features by sketching cross-sections and applying depth or revolving them around an axis.

Learning Objectives

- Create a new part model based on predefined templates.
- Understand the three default datum plane features that exist in a default template and how to control their visibility.
- Learn about the different types of base features available in Creo Parametric and start the creation of the base feature.
- Start the creation of a sketch for the base feature by appropriately selecting the sketch and orientation planes.
- Create, dimension, and constrain 2D entities in a sketch so that they capture the design intent for the feature.
- Define the depth or angle and direction options to complete the base feature.
- Modify dimensional values using the **Edit** command.

5.1 Creating a New Part

The first solid feature in a new part is commonly referred to as the *base* feature, as shown in Figure 5-1. It is initially created by locating the new geometry using references, called *datum planes*. The base feature is a solid feature with a sketched cross-section. Once you create the initial geometry, the Creo Parametric software provides a variety of methods to edit and change it.

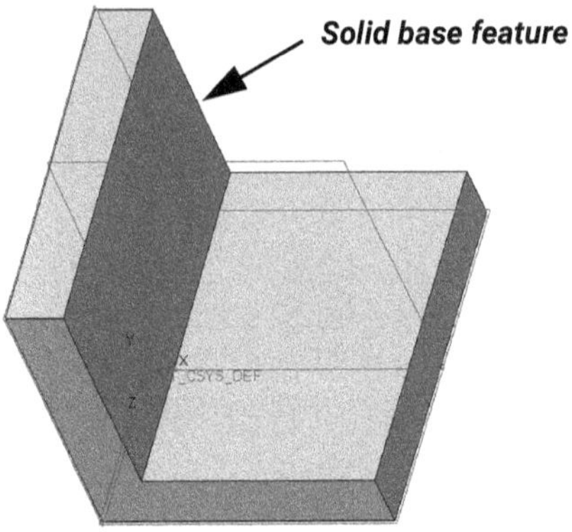

Figure 5-1

To create a new part, click ⬚ (New) in the *Quick Access* Toolbar or the *Home* tab. The New dialog box opens, as shown in Figure 5-2. Enter the *File name* and optional *Common name*.

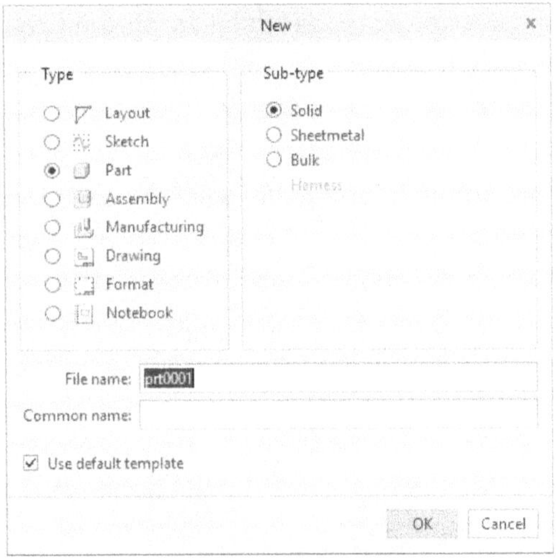

Figure 5-2

*Note: A common name is the more descriptive name of the model (e.g., 1/4-20 hex bolt). The software then creates the parameter **PTC_COMMON_NAME** and puts the Common Name string into it.*

Templates

When you create a new part, Creo Parametric provides you with the option to use a template. Templates enable you to create new parts that have standardized configurations and settings. This ensures that all models start with consistent and company-specific settings (if required). Templates contain useful features and settings, such as view orientations, reference datum plane features, and unit systems.

Select the type of object that you want to create from the list in the *Type* area in the *New* dialog box. For most object types, the **Use default template** option displays at the bottom of the dialog box. The default template for parts uses the Inch-Pound-Second system of units, but your company may set a default template that uses a different system of units. To use a different template, clear the **Use default template** option.

Once you have selected the type of model to create and have entered the filename, click **OK**. If you clear the **Use default template** option, the *New File Options* dialog box opens, as shown in Figure 5–3.

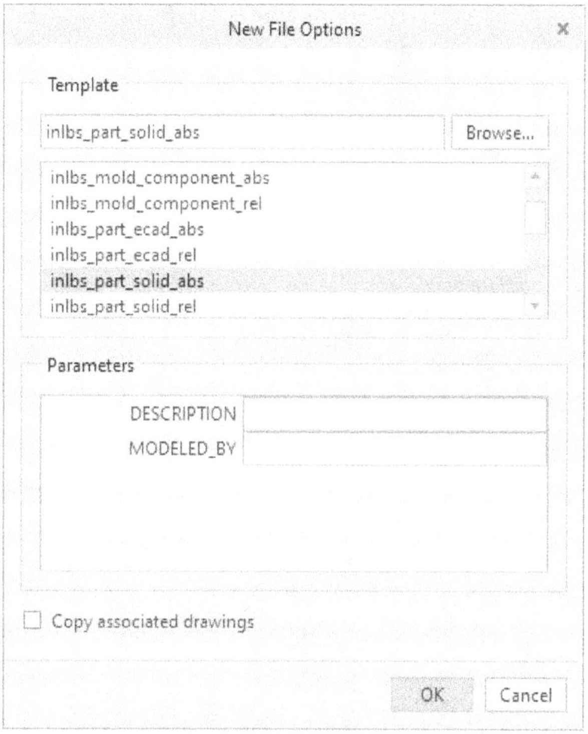

Figure 5–3

Note: You can create your own templates for creating new parts.

Note that you can select another template from the list in the dialog box. If you want to create a part with customized settings, select **Empty**.

Default Datum Planes

It is important to use the default datum planes when creating the base feature. Default datum planes are non-solid features that only exist in space; that is, they do not have thickness or mass. They are considered reference features because they are used as references when creating features. They also help you to orient the part. Every part template provided with Creo Parametric contains the following reference features, as shown in Figure 5–4.

- Three orthogonal datum planes named **RIGHT**, **TOP**, and **FRONT**. These are referred to as default datum planes.

- Default datum coordinate system labeled **PRT_CSYS_DEF**.

| **Standard Display** | **Datum Tags Toggled On** |

Figure 5–4

Note: *By default, the datum tags or names are toggled off. To display the tags, click*

 (Plane Tag Display) in the Show group in the View tab.

Most images in this course will not display datum tags. Datum tags will be mentioned in this chapter to help you familiarize yourself with them.

The datum planes extend to fit the part as its size increases. The datum planes are brown when viewed from one direction and gray when viewed from the opposite direction. The brown side is considered the *dominant* side. Actions to a selected datum plane, such as reorienting, are applied to the dominant side.

Reference features play an important role in the development of your model. While a part can be created without default datum planes, they are strongly recommended.

Note: *Default datum planes are very useful when your part has many non-planar surfaces. They can act as references for reorienting the part and creating features.*

Model Tree

When you create a new part using a template provided with Creo Parametric, the Model Tree lists a Design Items node, the three default datum planes, and the default datum coordinate system, as shown in Figure 5–5.

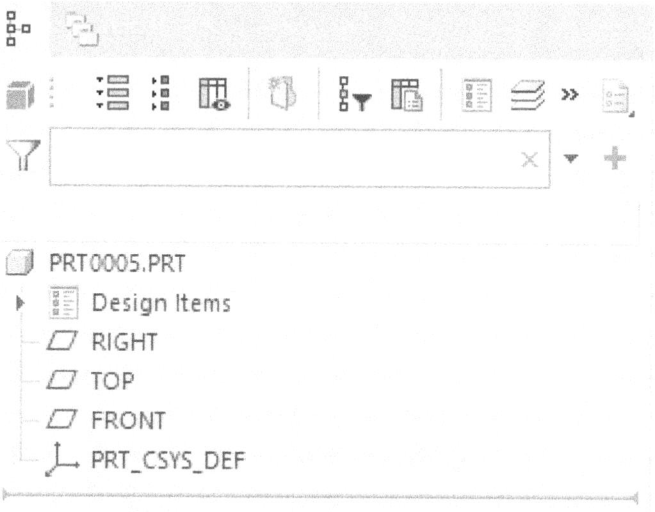

Figure 5–5

Bodies are discussed in detail in a later section. At this point, all solid geometry you create will belong to the main body.

Solid features with sketched cross-sections can add or remove material. Features that remove material are casually referred to as cuts. The first solid feature in a part must add material.

Feature Forms

You can use one of four basic feature forms to create the first solid protrusion. They are described as follows:

Feature Form	2D Cross-Section	3D Base Feature
Extrude		
Revolve		
Blend		
Sweep	Trajectory / Cross-section	

This chapter focuses on extruded and revolved solid features. Other feature forms are discussed later in this guide.

5.2 Extruded Form

To use the extrude form, ensure that the *Model* tab is selected and click ✎ (Extrude) in the *Shapes* group. Alternatively, select a reference plane or surface and select ✎ (Extrude) in the *mini* toolbar. The *Extrude* dashboard displays, as shown in Figure 5–6. You can use the message window, which displays at the bottom of the main window, or the on-screen prompts to guide you through the creation of an extruded feature.

Figure 5–6

The *Placement* panel heading initially displays in red, indicating that a feature section has not been fully defined. You can define the cross-section of the feature by sketching it or by selecting an existing sketch.

Selecting the Section

If you select an existing sketch to create the section, it is copied into the current sketch with an associative link. Changes made to the parent sketch update the extrusion and vice-versa. To break the associative link between the feature and the selected sketch, click **Unlink** in the *Placement* panel.

Sketching the Section

To sketch a section, select a plane on which to sketch, select ✎ (Extrude) in the *mini* toolbar, and begin sketching. This method does not open the *Sketch* dialog box, and is the most efficient method. Note that you can also click ✎ (Extrude) from the *Shapes* group in the ribbon and then select the plane, which achieves the same result.

If you require more control over the sketch orientation, click ✎ (Extrude) from the *Shapes* group in the ribbon before selecting the sketch plane, then use one of the following methods:

* Click **Placement** and click **Define** in the *Placement* panel.

* Click and select ✎ (Define Internal Sketch) from the *mini* toolbar.

Using either of the last two options, the *Sketch* dialog box opens, as shown in Figure 5–7. It enables you to select the **Sketch Plane** and **Sketch Orientation** references. Generally, the orientation references are already selected based on the selection of the sketch plane. However, they can be redefined, if required. Click **Sketch** to sketch the section.

Select this collector to define the sketch plane

Click Flip to flip the viewing direction

Select this collector to define the orientation reference plane

Expand this drop-down list and select an option to define the orientation direction

Figure 5–7

Sketch Plane

You must select a plane on which to sketch the section. The sketch plane can be any one of the three default datum planes. A 2D sketch is created on the selected datum plane and the protrusion is extruded in a direction normal to that plane. The default orientation of the model depends on the selected datum plane.

For example, consider the circular sketched section shown in Figure 5–8. The 2D section is sketched on datum plane **TOP** and extruded in a direction normal to the datum plane. The default orientation displays, as shown in Figure 5–9.

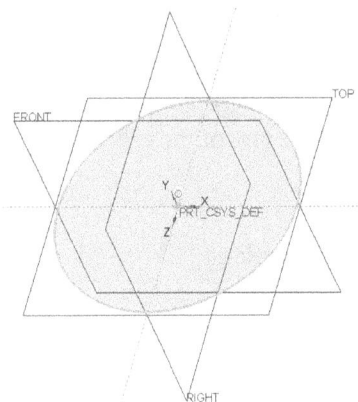

Figure 5–8

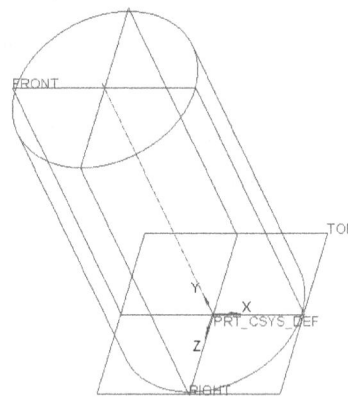

Figure 5–9

Similarly, the section could have been sketched on datum plane **FRONT**, as shown in Figure 5–10, or on datum plane **RIGHT**, as shown in Figure 5–11.

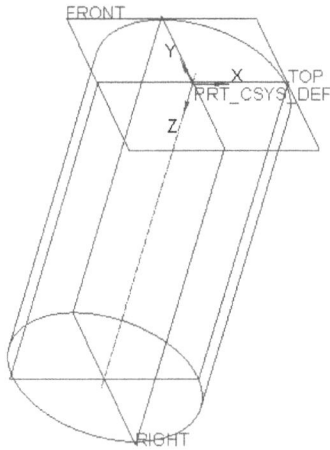

Figure 5–10

Figure 5–11

Note: The base feature becomes a child of the datum plane you select as a sketch plane.

An arrow displays next to the datum plane when you select the sketch plane. The arrow indicates the direction in which you are viewing the sketch plane, not the direction of extrusion. When selecting a datum plane as the sketch plane, the default viewing direction is always toward its dominant side.

For example, if you select datum plane **RIGHT** as a sketch plane, the brown side of the datum plane (the dominant side) displays while sketching. The protrusion is then extruded toward you, normal to the plane.

In Figure 5–12, datum plane **RIGHT** is selected as the sketch plane. The direction arrow indicates the direction in which you view the plane while sketching. The resulting protrusion is extruded in the opposite direction (i.e., toward you).

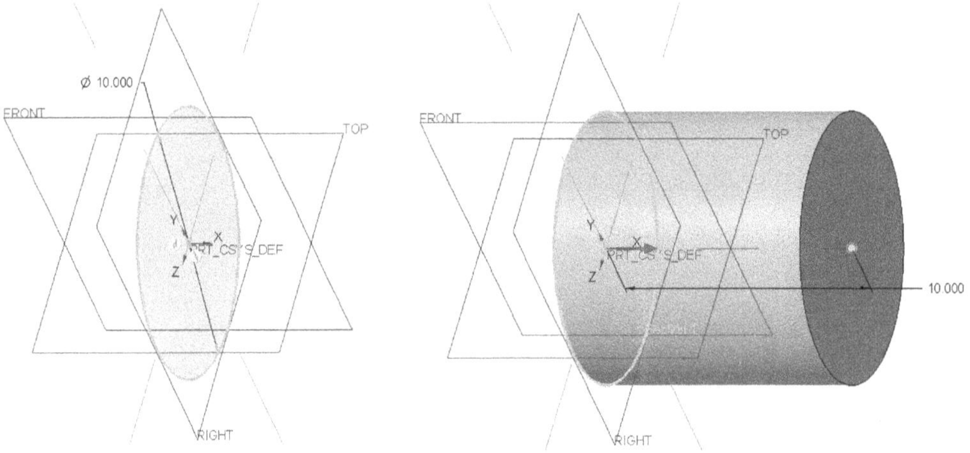

Figure 5–12

To change the viewing direction and extrude the protrusion in the opposite direction (i.e., away from the non-dominant side), click **Flip** in the *Sketch* dialog box or on the head of the arrow. The protrusion extrudes in the opposite direction, as shown in Figure 5–13.

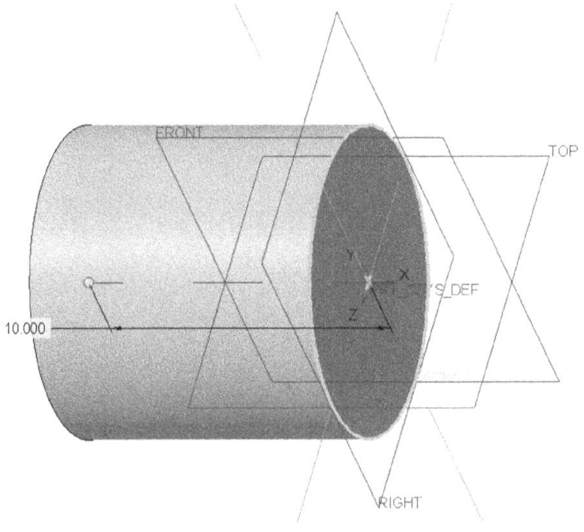

Figure 5–13

Sketch Orientation

The Creo Parametric software provides you with the option to select or change an orientation plane. The orientation plane is a horizontal or vertical reference plane that is normal to the sketch plane. It is used to orient the part while sketching. You can create your sketch entities while the model is in any orientation.

- To orient the part while sketching, if required, click ⌞ (Sketch View) in the *In-graphics* toolbar or in the *Setup* group in the *Sketch* tab.

- To make the sketching plane parallel to the screen automatically, select **File>Options> Sketcher** and select **Make the sketching plane parallel to the screen**. You can also change the **sketcher_starts_in_2d** to **yes** in the configuration editor.

  Note: The Creo Parametric software does not automatically reorient the part to make the sketch plane parallel to the screen when the Sketch tab becomes active.

When the model does not contain a planar surface perpendicular to sketching plane, the software uses a projection of the X-axis from the default coordinate system as the horizontal orientation for the sketch. If the model contains planar surfaces perpendicular to the sketching plane, then the software provides a default sketch orientation plane. You can accept the default plane or override it by selecting your own reference. Use the **Orientation** menu to select the direction for the datum plane to face.

Note: Always consider your design intent before accepting default selections.

For example, if you select datum plane **FRONT** as your sketch plane, you can select either datum plane **RIGHT** or **TOP** as your sketch orientation plane. The sketch orientation plane can be selected to face top, bottom, right, or left.

In the example shown in Figure 5–14, datum plane **RIGHT** is selected as the sketch plane. Datum plane **FRONT** could be selected to face bottom or datum plane **TOP** could be selected to face left to obtain the orientation shown in Figure 5–15.

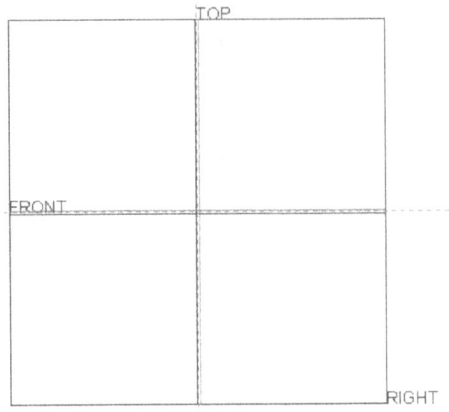

Figure 5–14

Figure 5–15

Note: The base feature becomes a child of the datum plane that you select as the sketch orientation plane.

Sketching

Once the sketch references have been established, the *Sketch* tab become active, as shown in Figure 5–16. The other tabs are still available for selection, but some of the icons in the tabs are dimmed, indicating they are not currently available.

Figure 5–16

Sketched geometry must always be located with respect to existing features in the part. Before the base feature is created, the only existing features in the part are the three default datum planes and the default datum coordinate system.

In this situation, the Creo Parametric software automatically selects the two datum planes that are normal to the sketch plane. Any geometry you sketch is aligned or dimensioned with respect to these references. To change sketcher or add additional references, click

⬚ (References), which opens the *References* dialog box, as shown in Figure 5–17.

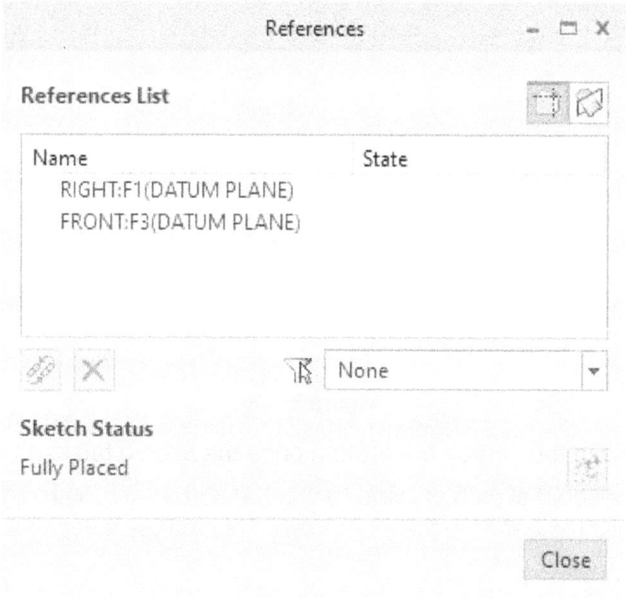

Figure 5–17

Note: References are represented by cyan dashed lines that are projected onto the sketch plane.

Setup

The *Setup* group in the sketch ribbon enables you to specify and change your sketcher options. References, orientation, and direction can all be changed using the icons or the **Setup** menu.

- To change the sketch plane, orientation plane, or direction of feature creation, click

  ▨ (Sketch Setup).

- The *Sketch* dialog box opens and enables you to change the references.

- You can also use the **Setup** menu to override the direction reference as shown Figure 5–18.

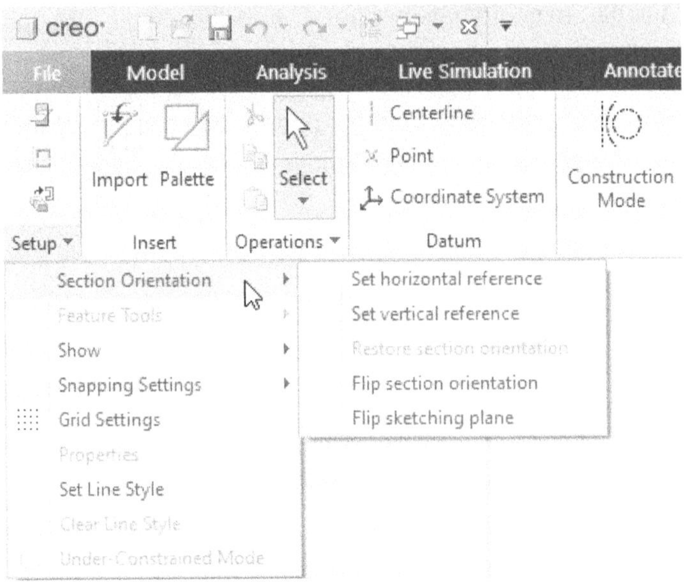

Figure 5–18

The geometry remains in the default orientation once the *Sketch* tab has been activated. To reorient so that the selected sketch plane is facing the screen, if required, click 🔲 (Sketch View) in the *In-graphics* toolbar or in the *Sketch* tab. This makes it easier to sketch your geometry.

Using all the mentioned tools, you can complete the sketch. When you have finished sketching, click ✓ (**OK**) to complete the section.

> *Note: You can also right-click and select* **OK** *to complete the section.*

The Creo Parametric software provides a number of options to define the depth of extruded features. Many of these options enable you to reference other geometry to control the depth. For an extruded base feature, the depth is commonly defined with a dimension that can be easily modified. The tab for the extruded protrusion contains an entry field in which you can enter a value for the depth, as shown in Figure 5–19.

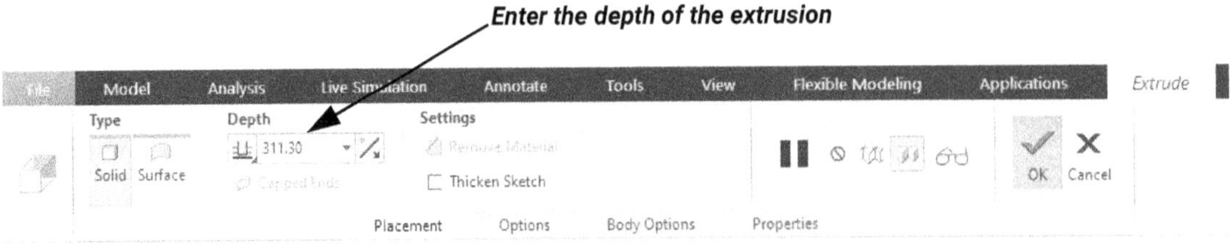

Figure 5–19

Alternatively, you can dynamically adjust the depth by dragging the handles that display on the model, as shown in Figure 5–20. You can also double-click the dimension and edit it directly.

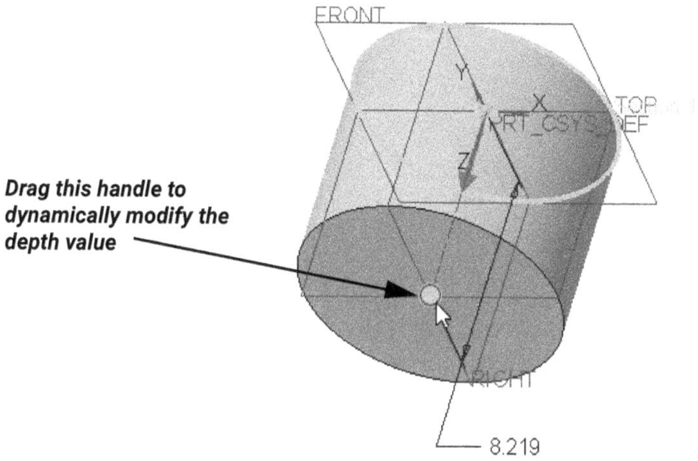

Drag this handle to dynamically modify the depth value

— 8.219

Figure 5–20

Several options are available for previewing the geometry before completing the feature and are described as follows:

Options	Description
(Verify Mode)	Displays the geometry as it is going to be when the feature is completed.
(Attached)	Displays the geometry as it is going to be when the feature is completed and enables you to dynamically change the geometry.
(Un-Attached)	Displays the outline of the geometry and enables you to dynamically change the geometry.
(No Preview)	Does not display the geometry.

The model is shaded differently depending on which icon is selected. If (Verify Mode) was enabled, click ▶ (Resume) to resume the feature after previewing.

Once the depth of the feature is defined, you can complete it by clicking ✔ (**OK**).

> *Note: Use* ✕ *(Cancel Feature) to cancel a feature.*

The Model Tree updates to list the base feature, as shown in Figure 5–21. The base feature displays in the Model Tree feature list after the default datum planes and the default datum coordinate system.

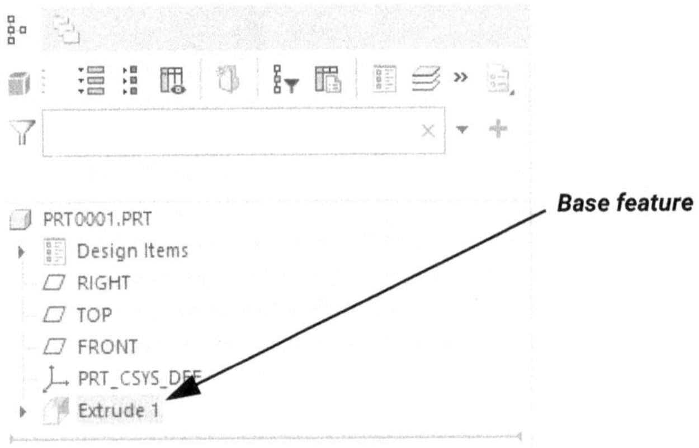

Figure 5–21

After you have created a feature, it is recommended to make changes, many of which can be initiated through the Model Tree. If you select the name of the feature in the model or Model Tree, the *mini* toolbar displays with options for making changes. The $\overleftrightarrow{\text{d1}}$ (Edit Dimensions) option accesses the dimensions for the feature. Any dimensions created for the sketch or depth of the feature become visible and you can modify them by double-clicking on a dimension and entering a new value in the field that displays, as shown in Figure 5–22. If the dimension has an open arrowhead, you can dynamically modify the dimension.

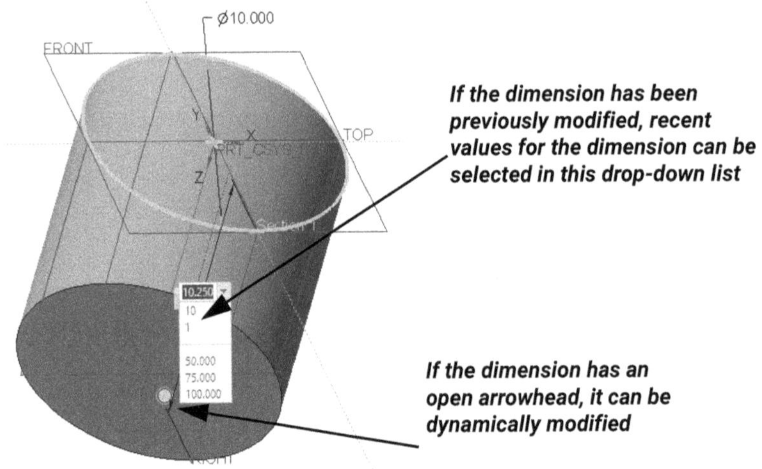

If the dimension has been previously modified, recent values for the dimension can be selected in this drop-down list

If the dimension has an open arrowhead, it can be dynamically modified

Figure 5–22

After you enter new values for dimensions, click ⬚ (Regenerate) in the *Quick Access* Toolbar or in the *Model* tab, or press <Ctrl>+<G> to incorporate the changes. Alternatively, you can click twice in the graphics window (do not double-click, but rather make two distinct clicks) to force a regeneration.

You can change the default feature name using either of the following methods:

* Select the feature name in the Model Tree, right-click, and select **Rename**. Enter the new name in the Model Tree.

* Select the feature name twice in the Model Tree (do not double-click). Enter the new name in the Model Tree.

Assigning your own names to features can help you locate and identify features in the Model Tree more easily, as shown in Figure 5–23.

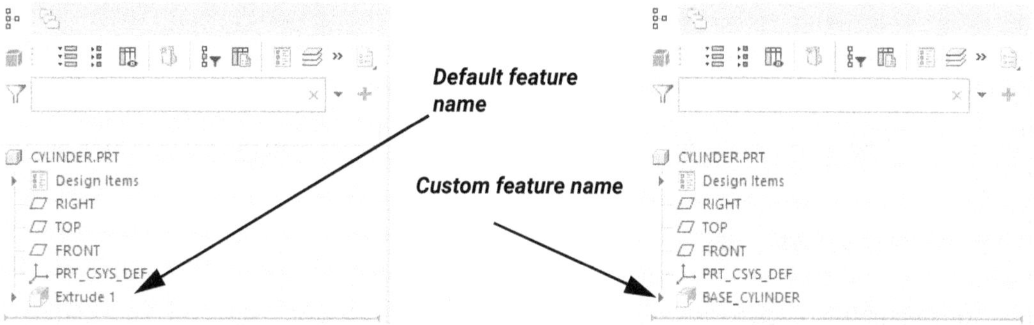

Figure 5–23

Note: Feature names cannot contain spaces and special characters, such as !, #, and *.

The 🖌 (Edit Definition) option in the *mini* toolbar opens the tab for the feature. From there you can make changes to the sketch for the feature (click and select 🖉 (Edit Internal Sketch) or click **Edit** in the Placement panel) and change the direction of extrusion by clicking 🗡 (Change Depth Direction).

5.3 Revolved Form

Revolved features are created in a similar manner to the extruded features. The main differences are that a revolve must contain reference an axis of revolution, which may be internal to the sketch, or an external axis, and an angle of revolution is defined instead of a depth.

To start the creation of the revolve, click 🔄 (Revolve) in the *Shapes* group in the *Model* tab. The dashboard for revolved features displays, as shown in Figure 5-24.

Figure 5-24

Alternatively, you can select the sketching reference, then select 🔄 (Revolve) in the *mini toolbar*. As with Extruded features, you can select an existing sketch to revolve or you can create a new sketch. Sketches are initiated in the same manner as extruded features, already discussed.

Axis of Revolution

When you create the revolve feature, you have to specify its axis of revolution. This can be included in the sketch, or you can assign it outside the sketch.

If the axis of revolution is included in the sketch, the *Axis collector* field indicates that an internal centerline exists (**InternalCL**), as shown in Figure 5-25.

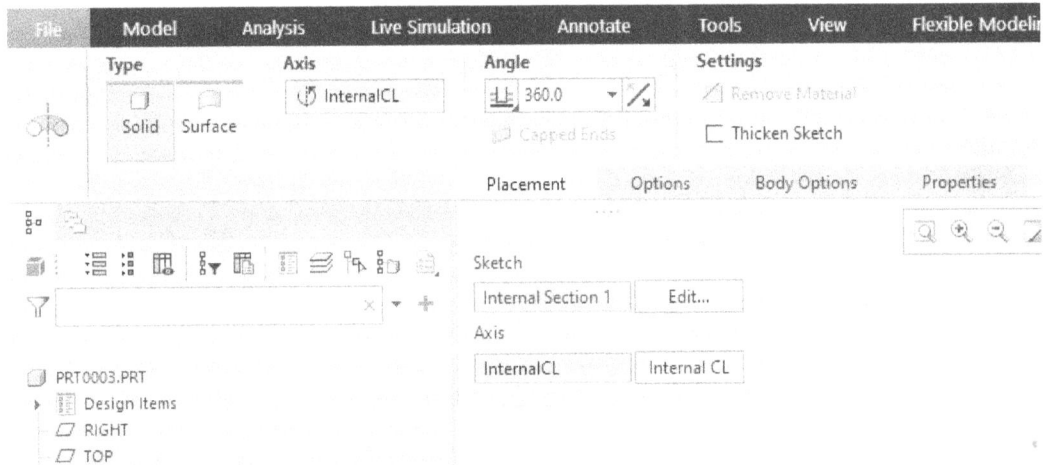

Figure 5-25

You can click ⋮ (Centerline) from the *Datum* group to create a geometry centerline, or

⋮ (Centerline) from the *Sketching* group to create a construction centerline.

If a sketch contains more than one centerline, the first geometry centerline created is used as the axis of revolution. If multiple centerlines exist in the sketch, select the appropriate centerline, right-click, and select **Designate Axis of Revolution**.

To clear the internal centerline, click **InternalCL** in the *Placement* panel, select the *Axis* collector, and select a new reference. The internal centerline in the sketch can be reused at any time by clicking **InternalCL** again.

If the axis of revolution is not included in the sketch, the *Axis collector* field indicates that you must select a reference: an existing straight curve, edge, axis, or the axis of a coordinate system that lies on the sketching plane.

The entities of the section must all lie on one side of the axis of revolution. The section cannot cross the centerline. These situations are described as follows:

Sketch	Shaft Geometry	Description
		Closed sketch with centerline aligned to one section edge.
		Closed sketch with centerline offset from section. The result is a hole in the revolve.
	Invalid	Closed sketch with centerline intersecting section. A revolve feature cannot have sketched geometry on both sides of the axis of rotation, since the geometry would overlap.

When creating a diameter dimension for a revolved section, three mouse selections are required. Two possibilities are shown in Figure 5–26.

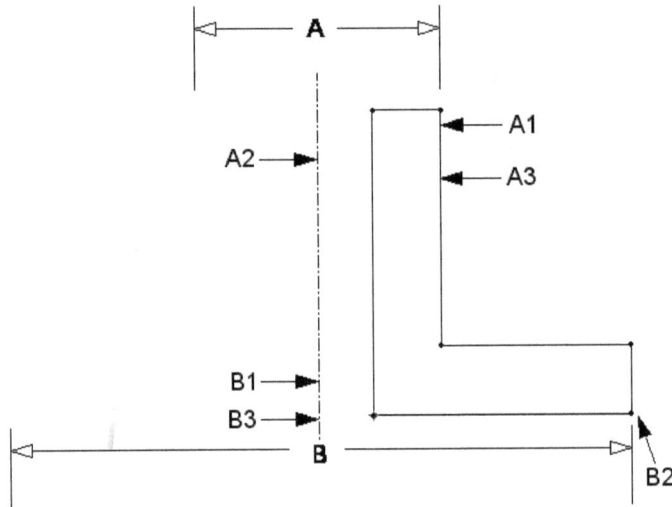

Figure 5–26

Note: To change the angle direction of the revolve to the other side of the sketch, click
✗₄ *(Change Angle Direction).*

A revolve feature is automatically revolved 360° in the direction of feature creation. You can enter or select a different value in the *Revolve* tab, as shown in Figure 5–27.

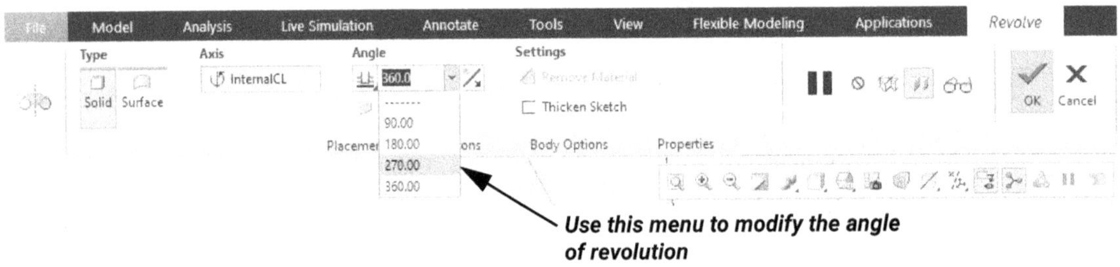

Figure 5–27

The angle value can also be defined by dragging the handles on the feature, as shown in Figure 5–28.

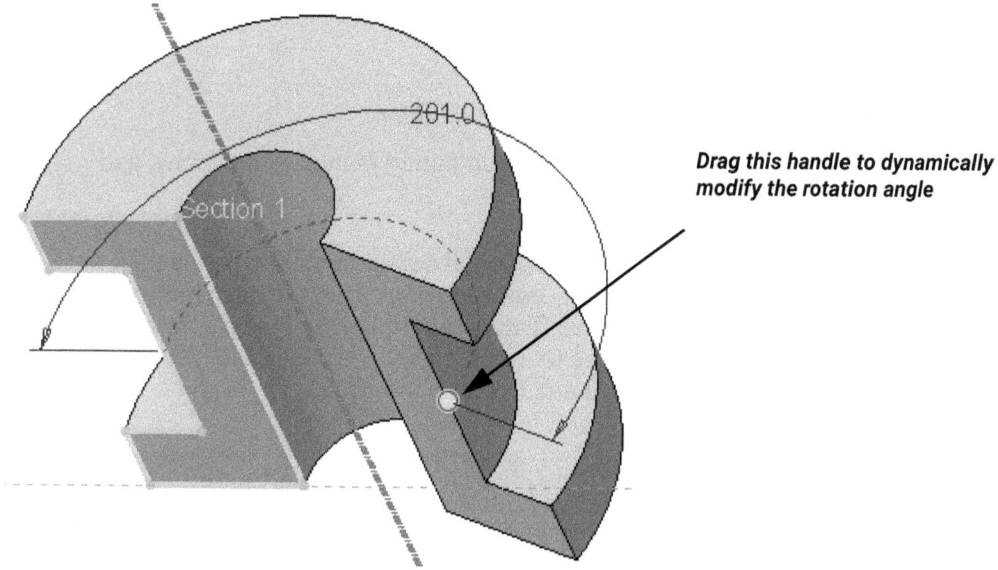
201.0
Section 1
Drag this handle to dynamically modify the rotation angle

Figure 5–28

When the feature is fully defined, click ✓ (**OK**) to complete the revolve.

Practice 5a
Extruded Base Features I

Practice Objectives

- Create two new part models using a predefined template.

- Create two extruded base features using default datum planes, dimensions, and constraints.

In this practice, you will create a new model using the default template provided in the Creo Parametric software. The first feature in any new model is called the base feature. The references selected when creating the base feature determine the model's default orientation. You will create extruded solids as the base features, as shown in Figure 5-29 and Figure 5-30. Sketch the extrusions using the rectangle and circle entities.

Figure 5-29

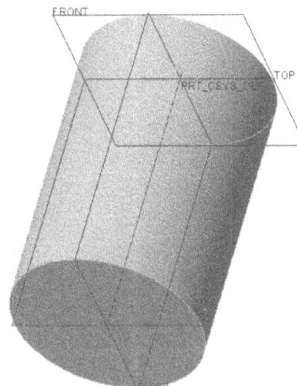

Figure 5-30

Task 1: Create a new part using the default part template.

1. Set your working directory to the *Extruded_Base_I* folder.

2. Click ⬜ (New).

3. In the *New* dialog box, select the **Part** option, if required.

4. Set the *File name* to **rectangle** and verify that the **Use default template** option is selected. The *New* dialog box displays, as shown in Figure 5–31.

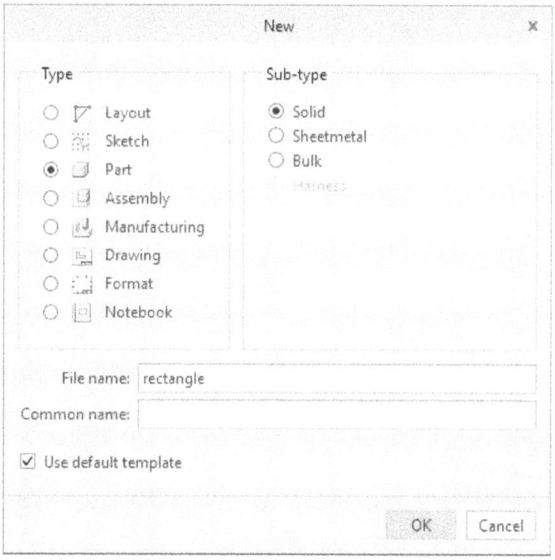

Figure 5–31

Note: When you create a new file or open an existing file in any mode, the software automatically knows the correct extension. You do not need to enter the extension with the filename.

5. Click **OK**. The Creo Parametric window displays the rectangle model as the active model. The model only contains the default datum planes and coordinate system from the default template, as displayed in the Model Tree and main window.

Task 2: Select the feature type of the first feature.

1. Set the model display as follows:

- ⁑ *(Datum Display Filters)*: All On

- ⋇ *(Spin Center)*: Off

- ⬜ *(Display Style)*: ▱ (Shading With Edges)

2. Select the *View* tab and click ⟳ (Plane Tag Display) in the *Show* group to toggle on the datum plane tags. This displays the names of the datum planes as shown in Figure 5–32.

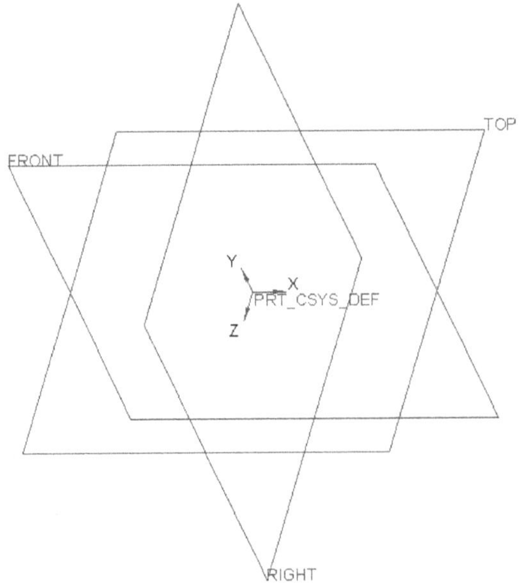

Figure 5–32

3. Select the *Model* tab, and in the *Shapes* group, click ⟳ (Extrude) to create an extruded base feature. The *Extrude* dashboard displays, as shown in Figure 5–33.

Figure 5–33

Task 3: Sketch the section for the extruded base feature.

1. Select datum plane **TOP** as the sketch plane. Creo Parametric automatically chooses datum plane **RIGHT** as the orientation reference, and opens the *Sketch* tab in the ribbon.

   Note: The system-defined reference or orientation can be changed if different references are required.

2. The software automatically selects the two datum planes that are normal to the sketch plane as sketcher references. These references are in light blue.

3. In the *In-graphics* toolbar, if required, click ⟳ (Sketch View) to reorient the model into 2D for sketching, as shown in Figure 5–34.

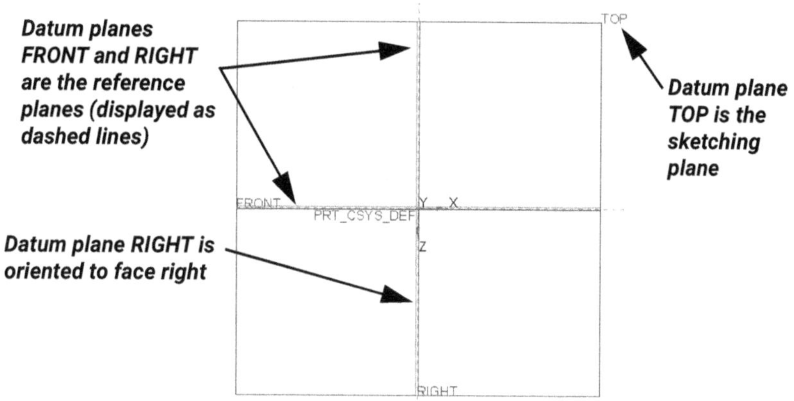

Datum planes FRONT and RIGHT are the reference planes (displayed as dashed lines)

Datum plane TOP is the sketching plane

Datum plane RIGHT is oriented to face right

Figure 5–34

Task 4: Sketch the rectangular section.

1. In the *Sketch* group, click ⬚ (Corner Rectangle) to sketch the base feature as a rectangular section.

2. Start the sketch by selecting the intersection of datum planes **FRONT** and **RIGHT**, as shown in Figure 5–35.

3. Drag the cursor upwards and to the right. Select the location shown in Figure 5–35 to define the rectangular shape.

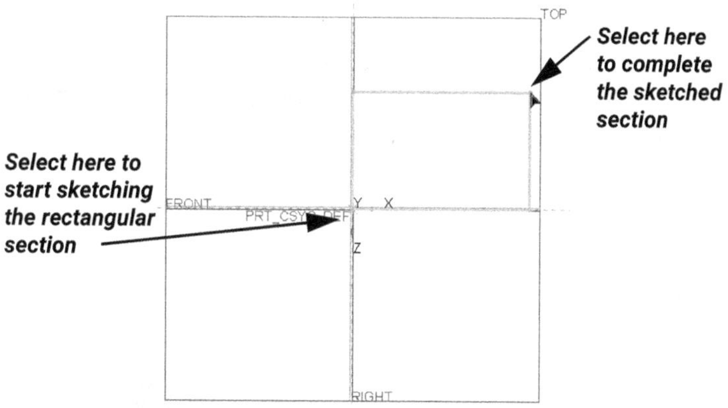

Select here to complete the sketched section

Select here to start sketching the rectangular section

Figure 5–35

Note: *To delete a sketcher entity, click* ⬚ *(Select), select the entity, and press <Delete> or right-click and select* **Delete***.*

4. Click the middle mouse button to complete the rectangle. The software automatically dimensions and constrains the sketch.

5. Double-click on the *Vertical Dimension* of the rectangle and set it to **15**. Press <Enter> to accept the new value.

6. Double-click on the *Horizontal Dimension* of the rectangle and set it to **25**. Press <Enter> to accept the new value.

7. In the *In-Graphics* toolbar, click ⌕ (Refit). The sketch displays, as shown in Figure 5–36.

Figure 5–36

8. Click ✓ (**OK**) to complete the sketch and exit the *Sketcher* tab.

Task 5: Define the depth of the extrusion.

1. The Creo Parametric software automatically applies a default depth value for the extrusion, as shown in Figure 5–37. This default value can be accepted or changed. Press <Ctrl>+<D> to orient the model to its default orientation.

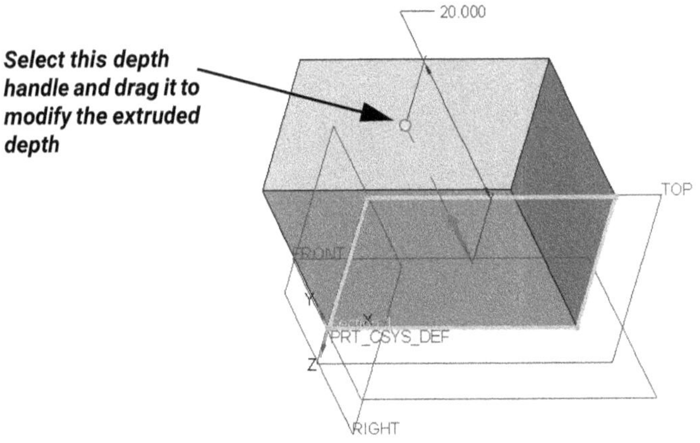

Figure 5–37

Note: You might have to pan (<Shift> + middle mouse button) and/or zoom out (<Ctrl> + middle mouse button) to display the entire model. Select and drag the depth handle on the model to change the depth dimension to approximately 7, as shown in Figure 5–37.

2. You can also modify the depth value in the *Extrude* dashboard (or by double-clicking it on the screen) to achieve an exact value. Set the *Depth* to **10**, as shown in Figure 5–38.

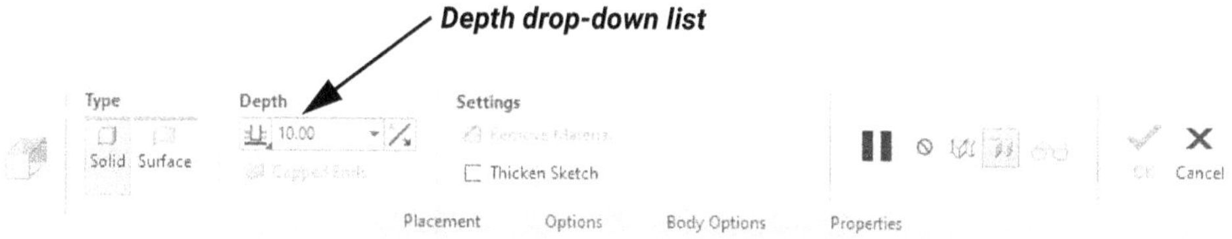

Figure 5–38

3. Complete the rectangular feature by clicking ✔ (**OK**) in the *Extrude* dashboard.

4. Orient the model to the default view by pressing <Ctrl>+<D>. The model and Model Tree display, as shown in Figure 5–39. The Model Tree identifies the first solid feature in the model as **Extrude 1**.

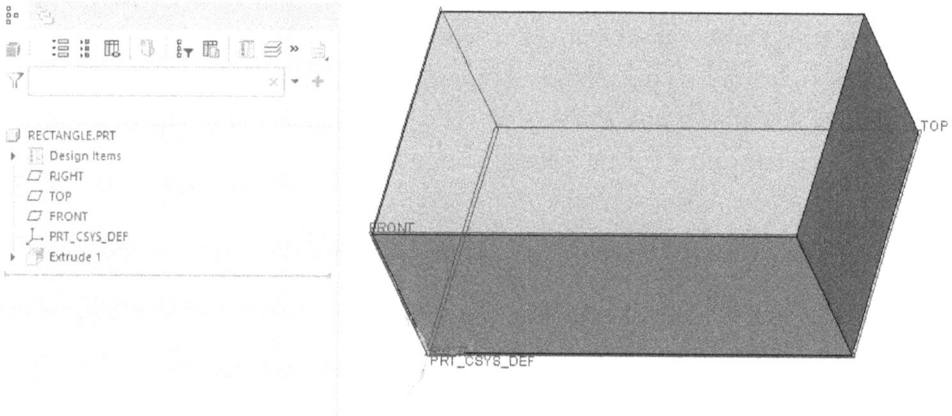

Figure 5–39

Task 6: Save the model and erase it from the session.

1. In the *Quick Access* Toolbar, click ⊟ (Save) to save the model.

2. Press <Enter> or click **OK** in the *Save Object* dialog box to save **rectangle.prt**.

3. Select **File>Manage Session>Erase Current** to erase **rectangle.prt** from the current session.

4. Click **Yes** in the *Erase Confirm* dialog box.

Task 7: Create a new part using the default part template.

1. Click ⬜ (New) to create a new file.
2. In the *New* dialog box, select the **Part** option. Set the *Name* to **cylinder**.
3. Verify that the **Use default template** option is selected.
4. Click **OK**. The Creo Parametric window now displays the cylinder model as the active model.

Task 8: Select the feature type and define all of the sketching references.

1. Select datum plane **FRONT**.

2. *In the mini toolbar, click* 🔲 *(Extrude) to create an extruded base feature.*

3. If required, click 🔲 (Sketch View) to orient the view.

Task 9: Sketch a circular section.

1. In *Sketching* group in the ribbon, click ⊙ (Center and Point).
2. Start the sketch by clicking the left mouse button at the intersection of datum planes **TOP** and **RIGHT**, as shown in Figure 5–40.
3. Drag the mouse outward. Click the mouse button to define the size.

   Note: To undo or redo sketching actions, you can click ↺ *(Undo) and* ↻ *(Redo) in the Quick Access Toolbar, respectively.*

4. Click the middle mouse button or press <Esc> to complete the sketch. Creo Parametric automatically dimensions and constrains the sketch, as shown in Figure 5–40.

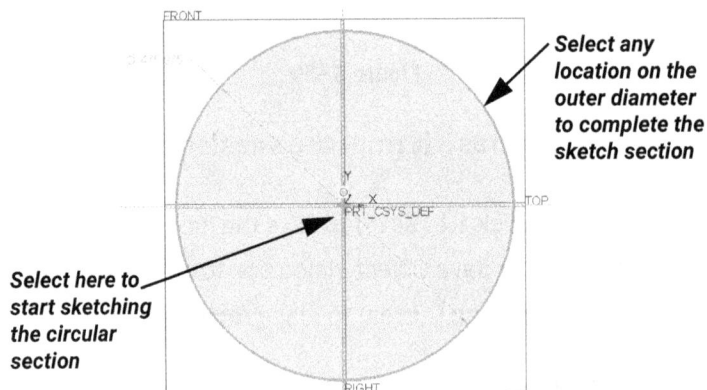

Figure 5–40

5. Double-click on the diameter dimension of the circle and set the new value to **10**. Press <Enter> to accept the new value.

6. In the *In-Graphics* toolbar, click ⌕ (Refit).

7. Click ✓ (**OK**) to complete the sketch and exit the *Sketcher* tab.

Task 10: Define the depth of the protrusion.

1. Press <Ctrl>+<D> to orient the model to its default orientation.

2. Double-click on the **Length** dimension and set it to **15**.

3. Complete the cylindrical feature by clicking ✓ (**OK**) in the *Extrude* tab. The model and Model Tree display, as shown in Figure 5–41. The Model Tree identifies the first solid feature in the model as **Extrude 1**.

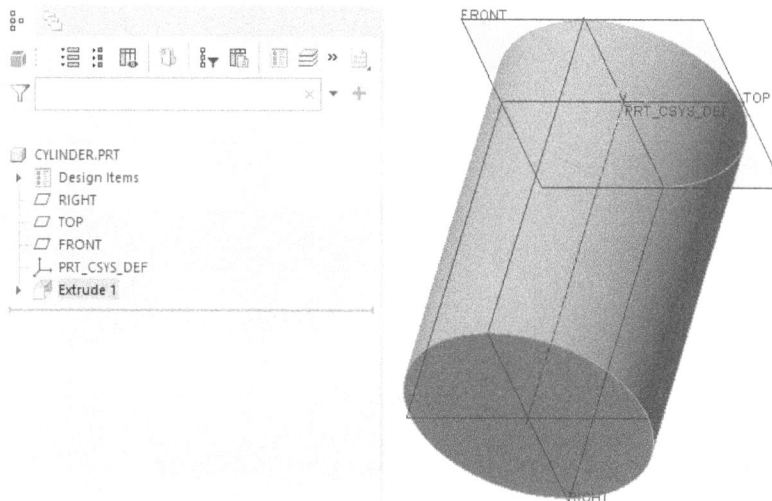

Figure 5–41

Task 11: Save the model and erase it from the session.

1. Click 💾 (Save).

2. Press <Enter> or click **OK** in the *Save Object* dialog box to save **cylinder.prt**.

3. Select **File>Manage Session>Erase Current** to erase **cylinder.prt** from the current session.

4. In the *Erase Confirm* dialog box, click **Yes**.

End of practice

Practice 5b
Extruded Base Features II

Practice Objectives

- Create a new part model using a predefined template.
- Create and rename an extruded base feature.
- Use **Edit Definition** to change the feature direction.

In this practice, you will create a new model using the default template provided in Creo Parametric. You will create an extruded solid as the base feature, as shown in Figure 5–42. Sketch the feature using line entities.

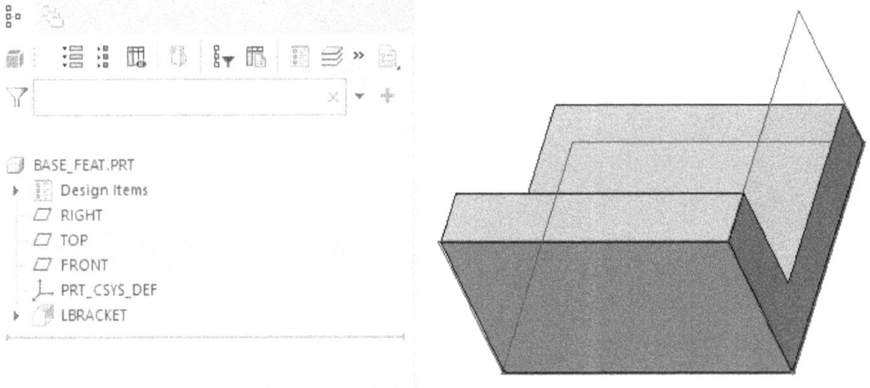

Figure 5–42

Task 1: Create a new part using the default part template.

1. Set your working directory to the *Extruded_Base_II* folder.
2. Click ☐ (New) to create a new file.
3. In the *New* dialog box, select the **Part** option. Set the *Name* to **base_feat**.
4. Click **OK** to create the new part model.
5. Set the model display as follows:

    - ⁙ *(Datum Display Filters)*: Only ◱ (Plane Display)
    - ⌁ *(Spin Center)*: Off
    - ▱ *(Display Style)*: ▱ (Shading With Edges)

6. Select the *View* tab in the ribbon and click ⬚ (Plane Tag Display) if required, to toggle on the datum plane labels.

7. Select the *Model* tab.

Task 2: Select the feature type and define all of the sketching references.

1. In the *Model* tab, click ⬚ (Extrude) to create an extruded base feature.

2. Left-click anywhere in the graphics area to bring up the feature *mini* toolbar.

   Note: In this practice, the default orientation references are not the required ones, so you will need to define the orientation manually.

3. Select ⬚ (Define Internal Sketch).

4. Select datum plane **RIGHT** as the sketch plane.

5. In the *Sketch* dialog box, select the *Reference* field and select datum plane **FRONT**. In the *Orientation* field, expand the drop-down list and select **Bottom**. The *Sketch* dialog box should display, as shown in Figure 5–43.

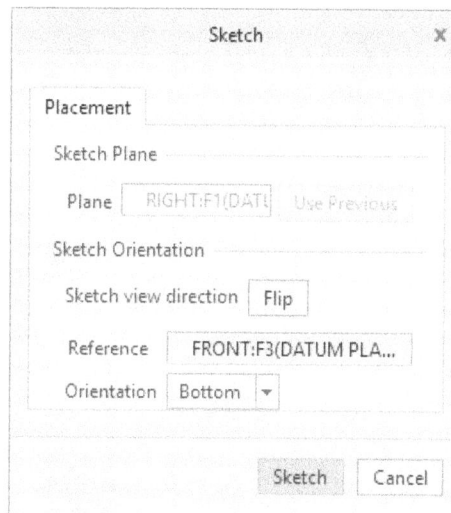

Figure 5–43

6. Click **Sketch** to begin sketching the section.

7. If required, click ⬚ (Sketch View).

Task 3: Sketch the section.

1. Click ⌄ (Line) to use the **Line** sketching tool.

2. Sketch the six line entities as shown in Figure 5–44. Use the left mouse button to start and end each line segment.

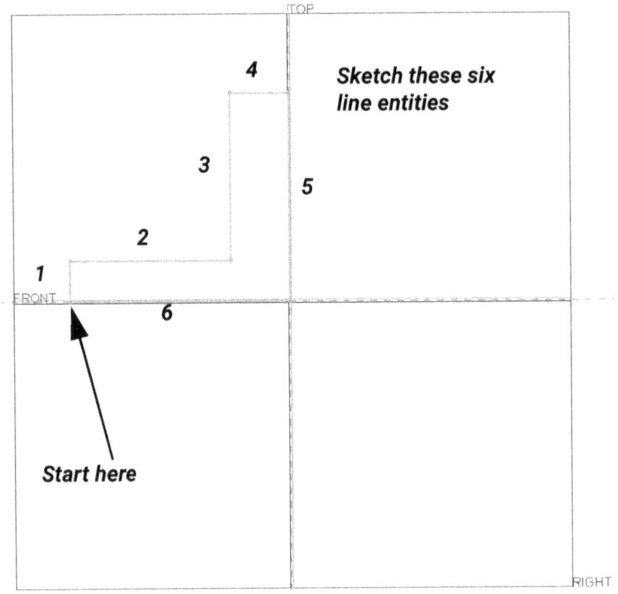

Figure 5–44

3. Click the middle mouse button to complete the line creation.

4. Click the middle mouse button a second time and the software automatically dimensions the sketch and applies constraints.

   Note: *These dimensions and constraints might not represent your required design intent.*

5. Click ↦↤ (Dimension) to create new dimensions on the sketch.

6. Zoom in on the sketch to make it easier to select the entities.

7. Using the left mouse button, select entity number **1** shown above in Figure 5–44.

8. Move the cursor to the location shown in Figure 5–45 and click the middle mouse button to locate the dimension.

9. Set the *Dimension* to **15.00**.

10. Continue to create the four linear dimensions and modify their values, as shown in Figure 5–45.

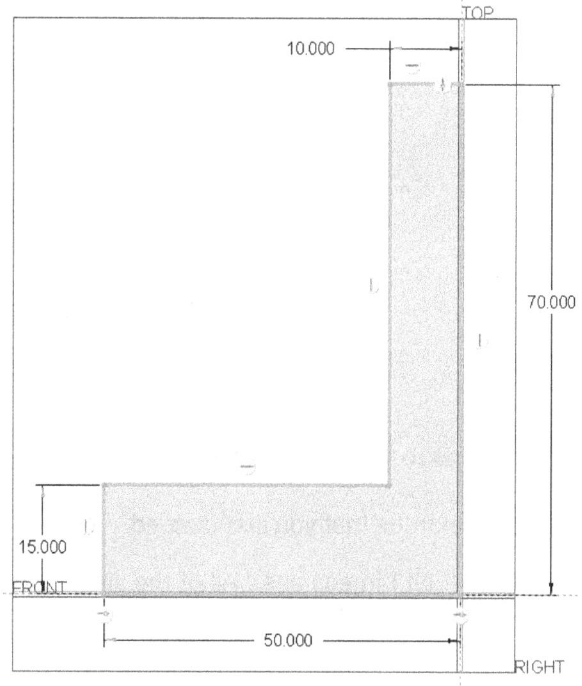

Figure 5–45

11. Click ✓ (**OK**) to complete the section.

Task 4: Define the depth of the protrusion.

1. Set the *Depth* field to **100**, as shown in Figure 5–46.

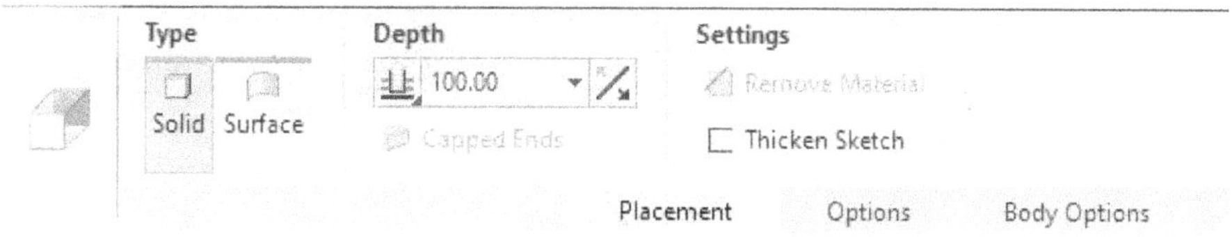

Figure 5–46

Note: *You can also drag the depth handle on the model.*

2. Click ✓ (**OK**) to complete the protrusion.

3. Press <Ctrl>+<D> to orient the model to the default view. The model and Model Tree display, as shown in Figure 5-47.

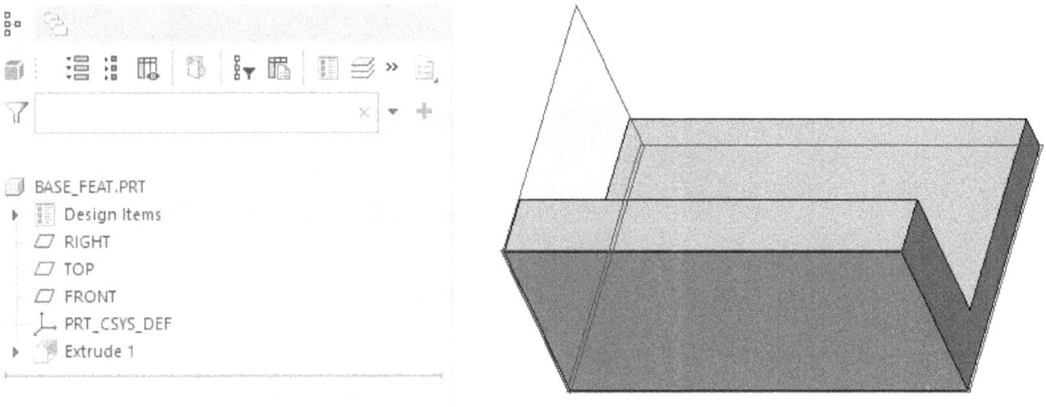

Figure 5-47

Task 5: Modify dimension values associated with protrusion.

1. In the Model Tree, select the extrude that you just created.

2. In the *mini* toolbar, select ⟶⟵ (Edit Dimensions). All of the dimensions associated with the extrusion display on the model, as shown in Figure 5-48.

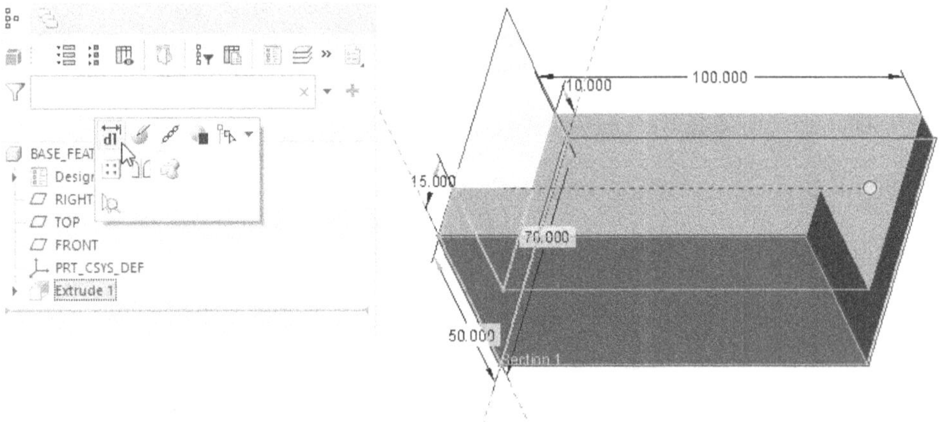

Figure 5-48

3. Double-click on the **10** dimension value.

4. Set the new dimension value to **15** and press <Enter>. The dimension displays in green when it has not been regenerated. The dimension will display in blue once it has been regenerated.

5. In the *Quick Access* Toolbar, click ⚏⃗ (Regenerate) to regenerate the model.

6. Alternatively, to edit the model you can double-click directly on the feature. Double-click anywhere on the extrude that you just created.

7. Double-click on the **100** *Depth* dimension.

8. Set the new *Depth* to **75** and press <Enter>.

9. Regenerate the model.

Task 6: Redefine the extrusion direction for the protrusion.

1. Select the **Extrude 1** protrusion that you just created. You can select it in the Model Tree or directly on the model.

2. In the *mini* toolbar, select 🖌 (Edit Definition). The *Extrude* dashboard displays again.

3. Click ⁄ₓ (Change Depth Direction) to switch the extrusion direction from one side of the sketch plane to the other as shown in Figure 5–49.

Figure 5–49

4. Click ✔ (**OK**) to complete the redefinition.

Task 7: Rename a feature.

1. In the Model Tree, right-click on **Extrude 1** and select **Rename**.

   *Note: You can also select **Extrude 1** in the Model Tree and click on the feature again to edit its name.*

2. For the new name, enter **Lbracket**. The model and Model Tree display, as shown in Figure 5–50.

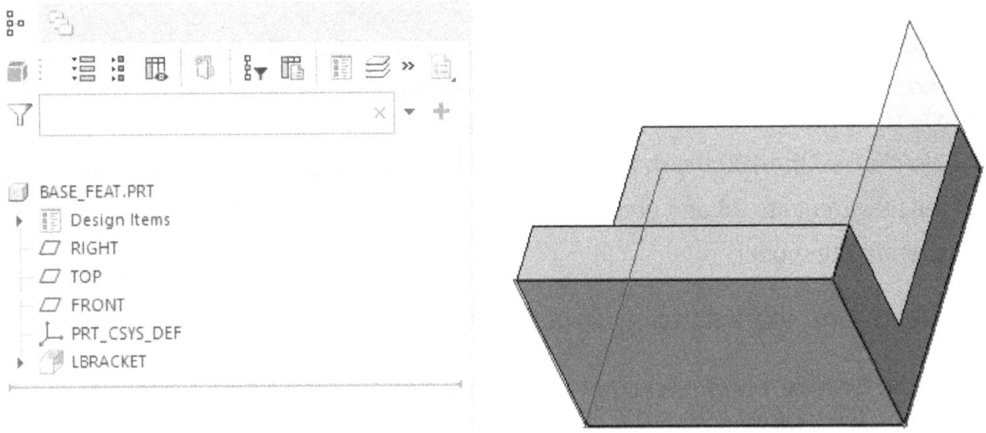

Figure 5–50

Task 8: Save the model and erase it from the session.

1. Click 💾 (Save) to save the model.

2. Press <Enter> or click **OK**.

3. Select **File>Manage Session>Erase Current** to erase **base_feat.prt** from the current session of Creo Parametric.

4. Click **Yes** in the *Erase Confirm* dialog box.

End of practice

Practice 5c
Revolved Base Features

Practice Objective

- Create a revolved base feature.

In this practice, you will create a revolve feature as the base feature for a part. The completed part displays, as shown in Figure 5–51.

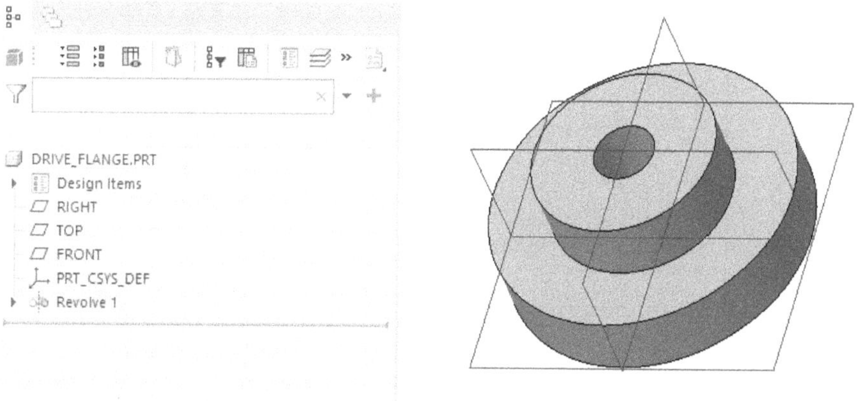

Figure 5–51

Task 1: Create a new part file.

1. Set the working directory to the *Revolved_Base* folder.

2. Click ⬜ (New) to create a new file.

3. In the *New* dialog box, select the **Part** option.

4. Set the part *Name* to **drive_flange**.

5. Click **OK** to create the new part model.

6. Set the model display as follows:

   - ⁀⁎, *(Datum Display Filters)*: Only ⬚ (Plane Display)

   - ⸾ *(Spin Center)*: Off

   - ⬛, *(Display Style)*: ⬜ (Shading With Edges)

7. Select the *View* tab in the ribbon and click ⬚ (Plane Tag Display) if required, to toggle off the datum plane labels.

8. Select the *Model* tab.

Task 2: Create a revolved feature.

1. In the Model Tree, select the datum plane **FRONT** as the sketch plane and click ✥ (Revolve) in the *mini* toolbar.

2. If required, click 🔲 (Sketch View).

3. In the *Sketching* group, create an axis by clicking ⋮ (Centerline), as shown in Figure 5–52). Then, click two points on the vertical reference.

Figure 5–52

Note: You could use ⋮ (Centerline) from the Datum group as well. To create the diameter dimension, select the vertical line, the centerline, then the vertical line a second time, and place the dimension with the middle mouse button

4. Create and dimension the sketch, as shown in Figure 5–53. Ensure that the section is driven with a *Diameter* dimension of **2**.

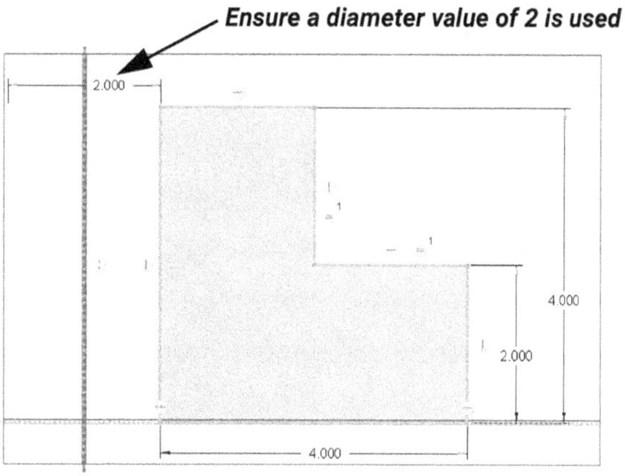

Figure 5–53

Note: To create the 2 diameter dimension, select the vertical line, the centerline, then the vertical line again and place the dimension with the middle mouse button.

5. Click ✓ (**OK**) to complete the sketch.

6. In the dashboard, set the *Angle of revolution* to **270** degrees and zoom in, as shown in Figure 5–54.

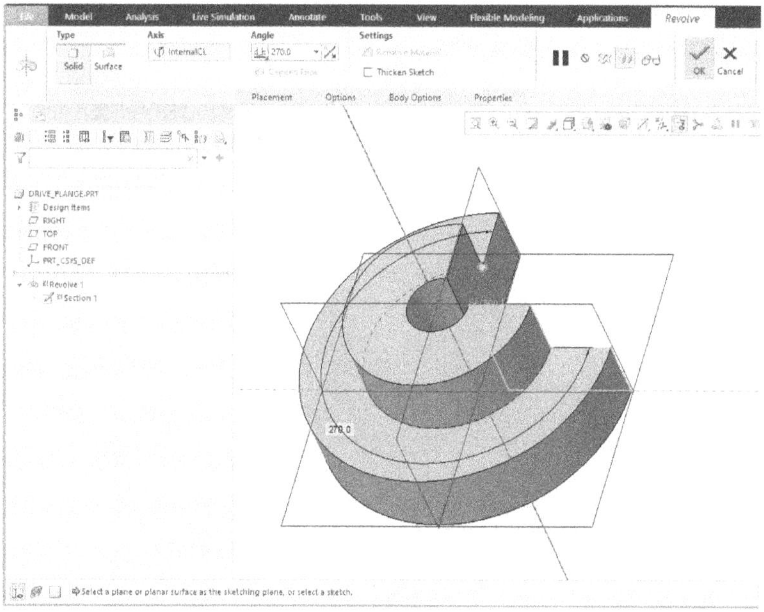

Figure 5–54

7. Set the *Angle of revolution* back to **360** degrees.

8. Click ✔ (**OK**).

9. Press <Ctrl>+<D>, if required, to return to default orientation. The model displays, as shown in Figure 5−55.

Figure 5−55

10. Click ⊟ (Save) to save the part.

11. Click ⊠ (Close).

12. Click ✂ (Erase Not Displayed) and **OK**.

End of practice

Practice 5d
Create Additional Parts

Practice Objectives

- Create new part models using a predefined template.

- Create base features in each part model using the correct default datums that represents the geometry provided.

In this practice, you will create base features as the first solid feature in a new part. Datum tags display to help you decide on sketcher orientation.

Task 1: Create a new part.

1. Set the working directory to the *Additional_Parts* folder.

2. Create a new part and set the *Name* to **channel**.

3. Set the model display as follows:

   - ⅍ *(Datum Display Filters)*: Only ⧄ (Plane Display)

   - ⧉ *(Spin Center)*: Off

   - ⧠ *(Display Style)*: ⧉ (Shading With Edges)

4. Select the *View* tab in the ribbon and click ⧄ (Plane Tag Display) if required, to toggle on the datum plane labels.

5. Use the extrude feature to create the base geometry shown in Figure 5–56. Select a sketch plane that will result in the default view shown.

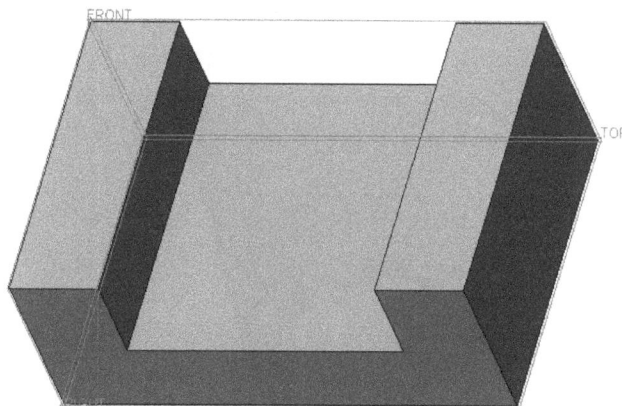

Figure 5–56

Task 2: Create an L-shaped part.

1. Create a new part and set the *Name* to **L_part**.

2. Use the extrude feature to create the base geometry shown in Figure 5–57. Select a sketch plane that will result in the default view shown.

Figure 5–57

Task 3: Create a pipe part using an extrude.

1. Create a new part and set the *Name* to **pipe**.

2. Use the extrude feature to create the base geometry shown in Figure 5–58. Select a sketch plane that will result in the default view shown.

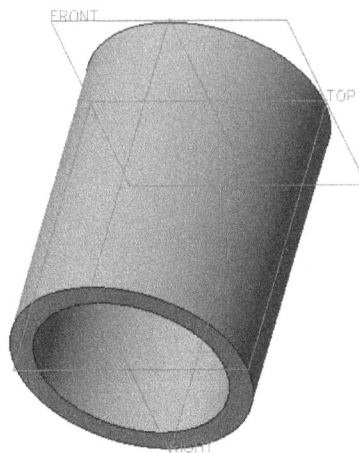

Figure 5–58

Task 4: Undo the previous feature and create the pipe as a revolve.

1. In the *Quick Access* Toolbar, click ↶ (Undo).
2. Create the base feature shown in Figure 5–58 using a **Revolve**.

Task 5: Create a wedge part.

1. Create a new part and set the *Name* to **wedge**.
2. Use the extrude feature to create the base geometry shown in Figure 5–59. Select a sketch plane that will result in the default view shown.

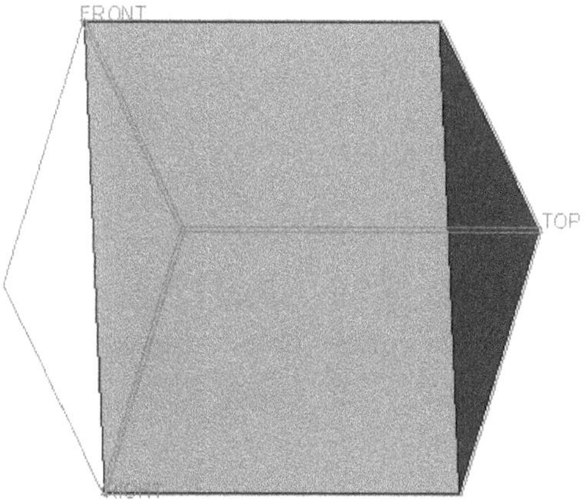

Figure 5–59

End of practice

Chapter Review Questions

1. Identify the base feature form shown in Figure 5–60, if the geometry were created by a single sketch.

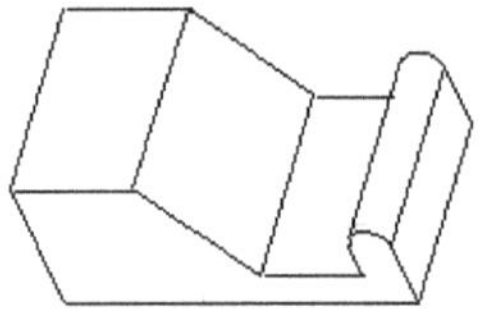

Figure 5–60

   a. Extrude

   b. Revolve

   c. Sweep

   d. Blend

2. Identify the base feature form that should be used to create the feature shown in Figure 5–61, if the geometry were created by a single sketch.

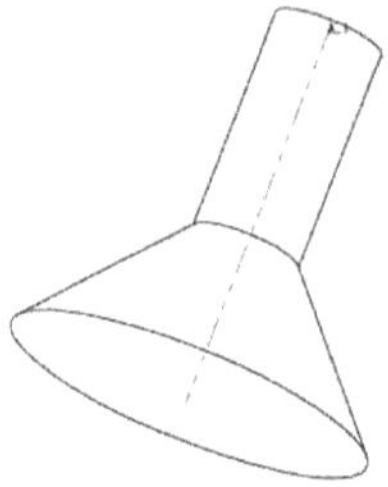

Figure 5–61

   a. Extrude

   b. Revolve

   c. Sweep

   d. Blend

3. Which of the following statements describes default datum planes? (Select all that apply.)
   a. First solid features
   b. Reference features
   c. Have mass
   d. Foundation for part

4. Which of the following can be selected as the sketching plane for the first solid feature? (Select all that apply.)
   a. Datum plane **RIGHT**
   b. Datum plane **FRONT**
   c. Datum plane **TOP**

5. What was the sketching plane for the extruded protrusion shown in Figure 5–62?

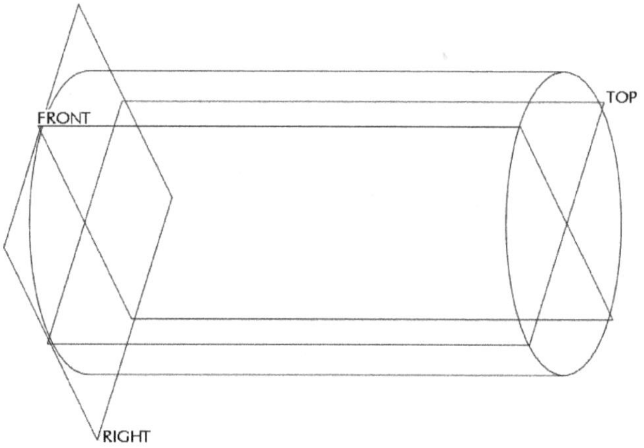

Figure 5–62

   a. Datum plane **RIGHT**
   b. Datum plane **FRONT**
   c. Datum plane **TOP**

6. The sketch orientation plane that is automatically selected by Creo Parametric must be used to orient the model while sketching the section for the base feature.

   a. True

   b. False

7. When locating sketched geometry with respect to existing features in the part, what must first be established?

   a. References

   b. Sketch plane

   c. Rectangle command

   d. Circle command

8. Dimensions that you create are referred to as weak dimensions and can be automatically removed by the system as constraints are added.

   a. True

   b. False

9. Which option is used to access the dashboard for an existing feature to make changes to it, such as flipping the extrusion direction?

   a. Edit

   b. Dynamic Edit

   c. Modify

   d. Edit Definition

10. Where could you click and drag to change the depth of the extrusion shown in Figure 5–63? (Select all that apply.)

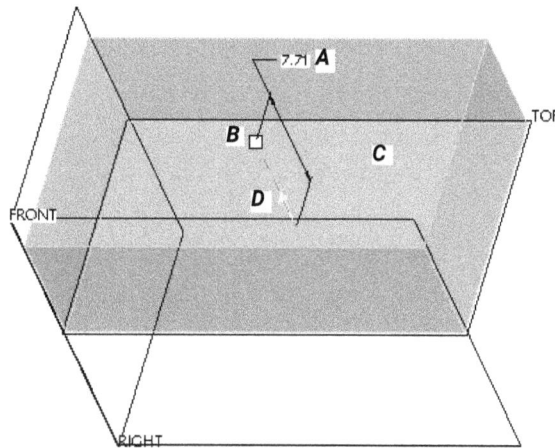

Figure 5–63

a. A

b. B

c. C

d. D

Datum Features

Datum features are non-solid features that are used when creating or sketching geometry. In cast models, they can be used to define location points to aid in assembly and to mark interfacing areas between components. Datum features simplify designs by regenerating quickly and displaying easily. Even models composed entirely of datum features can effectively convey the intended design.

Learning Objectives

- Use datum planes to create geometry that cannot be created using the existing planes or faces in the model.
- Explore internal versus external datum plane creation methods.
- Use datum axes, points, and coordinate systems to create geometry and datum features without using existing references in the model.
- Select references and constraint options using various methods.

6.1 Datum Features

Additional datum features, such as planes, axes, points and coordinate systems, are often required to complete a model. For example, a datum plane might be required if a feature's sketching plane or orientation plane are not satisfied by any of the three default datum planes or by selecting existing geometry. In these situations, datum planes can be created in a model.

*   For example, to create the cut shown in Figure 6-1, the cylindrical surface does not fulfill the planar requirement for a sketching plane. Therefore, an additional sketching plane is required.

*   To create the protrusion shown in Figure 6-2, an additional sketching plane is required.

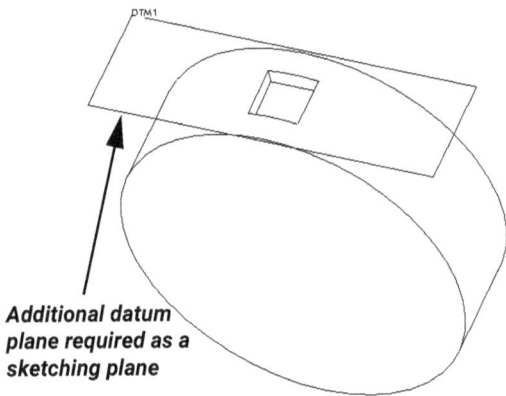

Additional datum plane required as a sketching plane

Figure 6-1

Figure 6-2

A datum feature can be created as a stand-alone feature, and can then be used as a reference for other features. For example, when a datum plane is created as a separate feature, the Model Tree displays, as shown in Figure 6-3.

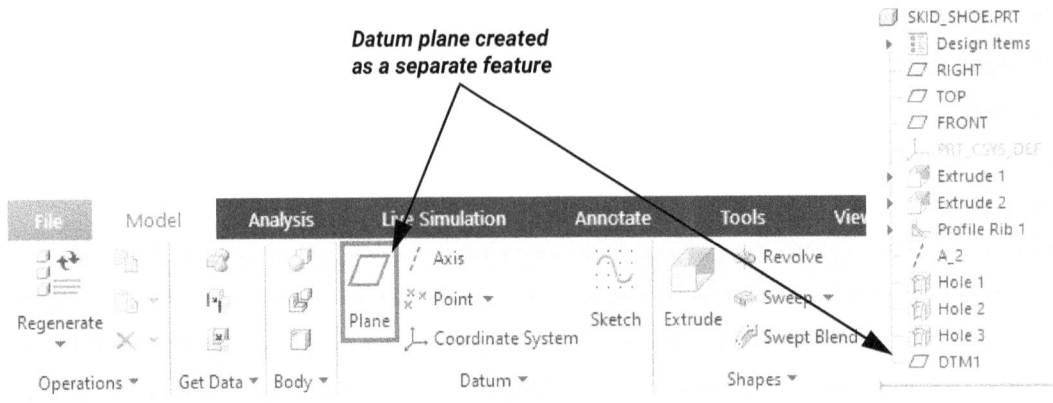

Datum plane created as a separate feature

Figure 6-3

Note: Datums that are referenced by more than one feature should be created as separate features in the model.

Datums that are referenced by only a single feature should be created during that feature's creation, to simplify the appearance of the model.

To create a datum during feature creation, expand ⬚ (Datum) in the feature dashboard and click the appropriate icon to create the required datum feature. The main feature is paused, as indicated by **‖** (Pause) in its dashboard. Once you have completed the datum feature creation, you can resume the main feature by clicking ▶ (Resume). The created datum feature can be referenced as a sketch, orientation, dimension or depth reference.

When you finish the main feature creation, the datum feature is embedded inside the main feature in the Model Tree, such as the datum plane shown in Figure 6−4. By default, a datum feature created in another feature is hidden. To show it, select it in the Model Tree, right-click, and select **Unhide**.

Datum plane created in the feature

Extrude 3

Section 1

DTM2

Applications   Extrude

✓ ✗
OK Cancel

Create 3D geometry by translating a 2D section normal to the sketching plane as a solid or a surface, adding or removing ma...

Read more...

Datum

Datum

Figure 6−4

6.2 Creating Datum Planes

To start the creation of a datum plane, expand ⬚ (Datum) in the dashboard of the current feature, and click ▱ (Plane). You can also click ▱ (Plane) in the *Model* tab. The *Datum Plane* dialog box opens, as shown in Figure 6−5.

Figure 6−5

Once you have started the creation of a datum plane, you must select constraints and references to locate it. When creating a datum plane, its location is defined by constraining it to existing features. Constraints are required to fully locate the datum plane. To constrain a datum plane, select references from existing features in the model. You can select any of the following types of features as references:

> **Note:** *Alternatively, you can select the reference before clicking* ▱ *(Plane).*

- Axis
- Edge
- Curve
- Point/Vertex
- Plane
- Cylinder
- Coordinate System

> **Note:** *To select multiple references at the same time, press and hold <Ctrl>.*

After selecting the appropriate placement references, select a constraint type for each of them. By selecting the column to the right of the reference, you can select the required constraint in the drop-down list. Only constraints that work in combination with the previously selected references display. Figure 6−6 shows an example of a datum **Tangent** to the smaller cylinder and **Parallel** to the flat surface.

Figure 6−6

The following constraints can be used to create a datum plane:

* Through

* Normal

* Parallel

* Offset

* Midplane

* Tangent

* Blend Section

Only constraints that work in combination with the previously selected references display.

For example, if you select a Normal constraint for a planar reference and a Tangent constraint for a cylindrical surface, a datum plane would be successfully created.

Figure 6-7 and Figure 6-8 shows examples of datum planes that pass through the axial reference but have different secondary constraints. In Figure 6-7, the datum plane has a parallel constraint with the vertical planar surface, whereas in Figure 6-8, the datum plane has a rotational offset constraint with the vertical planar surface.

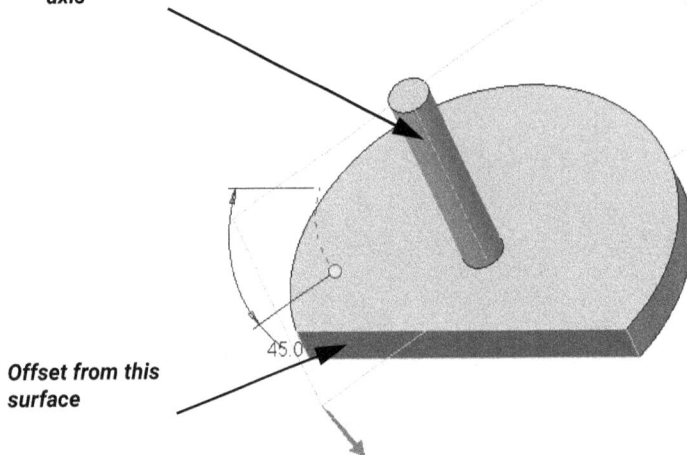

Figure 6-7

Figure 6-8

*Note: References can be removed from the Datum Plane dialog box. Select the reference, right-click, and select **Remove**.*

As an alternative to starting the creation of a datum plane and then selecting references, you can preselect the references required to place the datum plane before clicking ▱ (Plane). For example, the top surface shown in Figure 6−9 was preselected. The dialog box that opens when you click ▱ (Plane) contains the preselected reference as one of the current references.

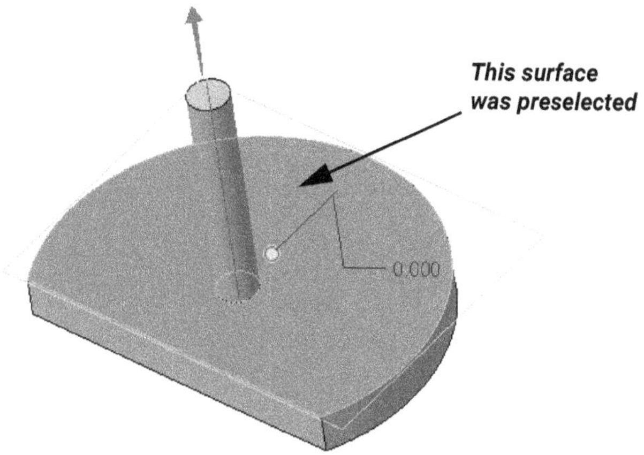

This surface was preselected

0.000

Figure 6−9

You can create a midplane between two references, as shown in Figure 6−10.

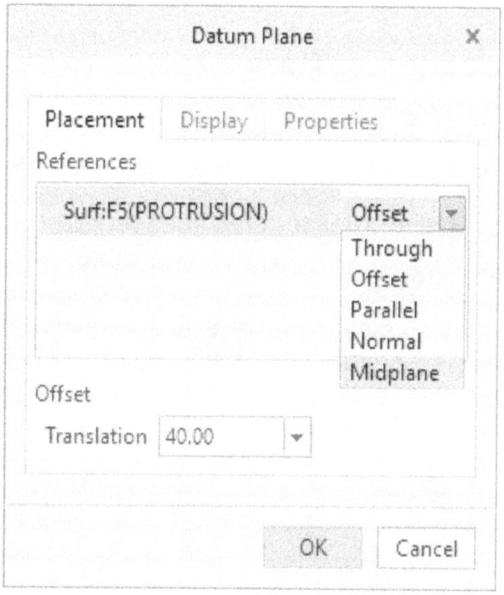

Figure 6−10

If a pair of planar references are selected, **Midplane** is automatically selected as the default option.

Depending on the selected references, the midplane is created parallel to the references or in the direction of one of the bisectors, as shown in Figure 6−11.

Bisector 1   Bisector 2

Figure 6−11

The reference pairs can include the following:

- Planar surfaces or datum planes.

- A datum, cylinder or cone axis, and linear curve or edge.

- Datum points, coordinate systems, or vertices.

You can change the appearance, direction, or name of the datum plane using the *Display* and *Properties* tabs in the *Datum Plane* dialog box.By default, datum planes are sized to fit the overall geometry; when working on small features, the default datum plane size might be too large.

- The *Display* tab enables you to modify the size of the datum plane to fit the feature and flip the normal direction of the datum plane, as shown in Figure 6–12.

- The *Properties* tab shown in Figure 6–13, enables you to change the name of the datum plane.

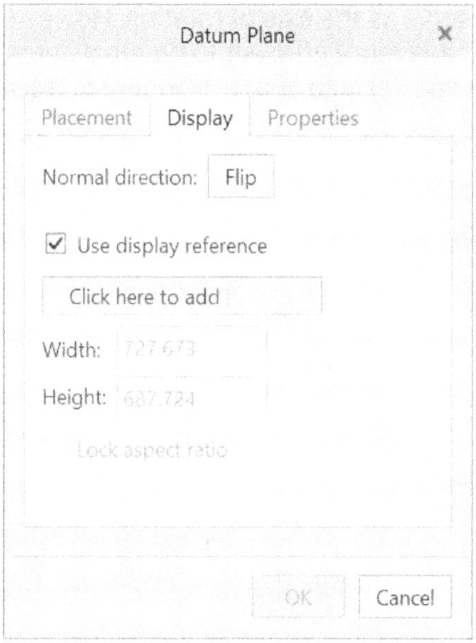

Figure 6–12

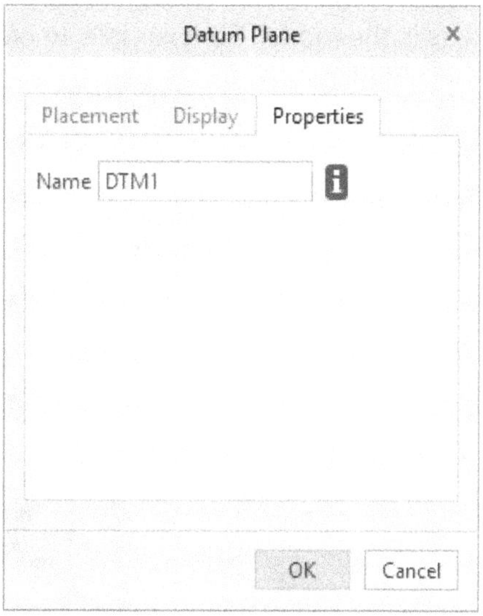

Figure 6–13

Once the datum plane has been constrained, click **OK** to place it. If the datum plane was created in another feature, proceed with its feature creation by clicking ▶ (Resume) in the dashboard.

6.3 Creating Datum Axes

Cylindrical, rotational features, and holes are the only features that automatically generate their own datum axes on creation. Because datum axes can be used as placement references for coaxial holes and rotational features, additional datum axes might be required. In the case of rotational features, a centerline can be sketched to serve as the axis of rotation. However, if this axial location is referenced by subsequent features, it is more efficient to create a permanent datum axis in the model. For example, to create the coaxial hole shown in Figure 6–14, an axial reference is required.

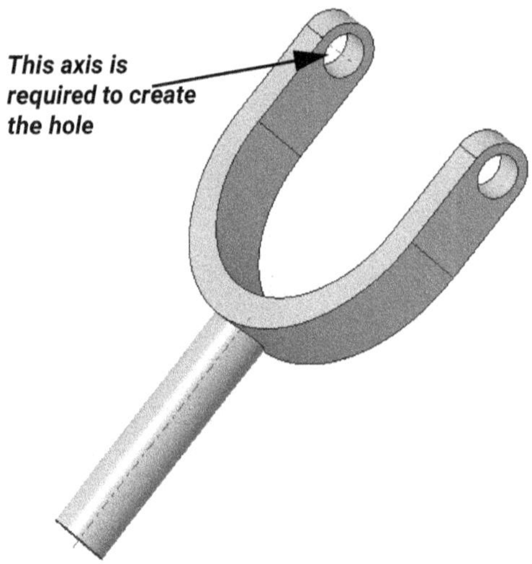

This axis is required to create the hole

Figure 6–14

Datum axes can be created before or during feature creation. The process during feature creation is the same as with datum planes.

To create a datum axis, click ⁄ (Axis) in the *Model* tab if standalone, or expand ⁝ (Datum) in the dashboard of the current feature, and click ⁄ (Axis). The *Datum Axis* dialog box opens, as shown in Figure 6–15. Similar to datum planes, placement references and constraints must be selected to fully locate the datum axis.

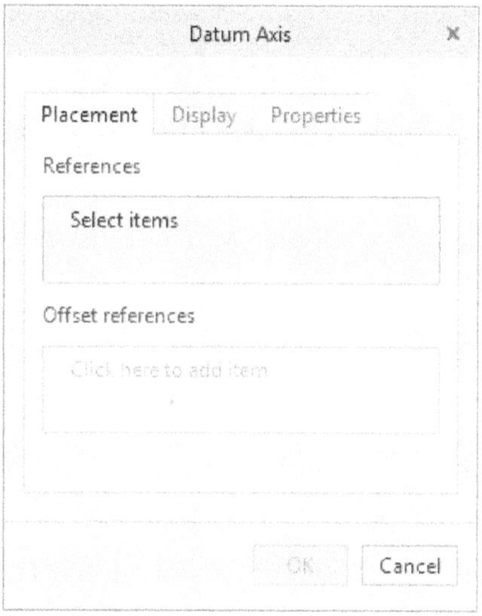

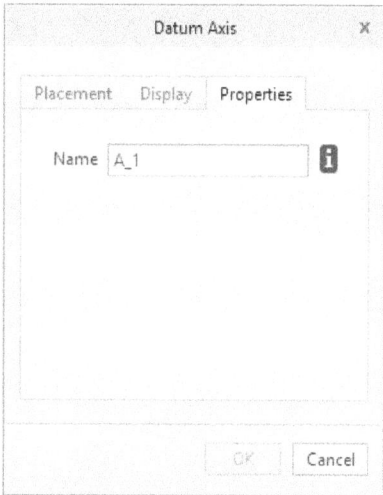

Figure 6-15

- The *Display* tab enables you to modify the size of the datum axis, as shown in Figure 6-16.

- The name of the axis can also be changed from the default name to a custom name in the *Properties* tab, as shown in Figure 6-17.

Figure 6-16   **Figure 6-17**

Once you have started the creation of a datum axis, you must select constraints and references. Some constraints only require one reference, while others must be used in combination with other references to fully locate the datum axis.

Note: Alternatively, you can select the reference before clicking ⌗ (Axis).

To constrain a datum axis, select references from existing features in the model. References can be any of the following types:

- Edge/Curve
- Planar surfaces
- Cylindrical surfaces
- Coordinate systems
- Points/Vertices

After selecting the appropriate placement references, a default constraint type displays next to the reference in the dialog box. If multiple constraints are available, you can access a drop-down list by selecting the constraint column. Only constraints that work in combination with the previously selected references display.

Figure 6−18 shows an example where the created datum axis references the existing cylindrical surface that was generated by the rounds. This is the only reference required to fully constrain the datum axis.

Figure 6−18

Note: This axis can also be created without having to use the dialog box, by preselecting the cylindrical surface formed by the round and then clicking ⸝ (Axis).

In the example shown in Figure 6–19, the top planar surface is selected as a placement reference with a Normal constraint. When a planar surface is selected as a reference, two linear placement handles display. They can be dynamically dragged to fully locate the datum axis. By dragging the handle to adjacent edges or surfaces, offset references are added to the dialog box that can be modified to locate the datum axis as required.

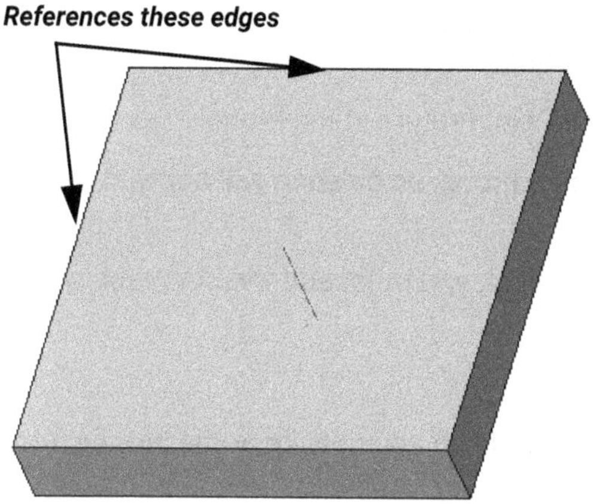

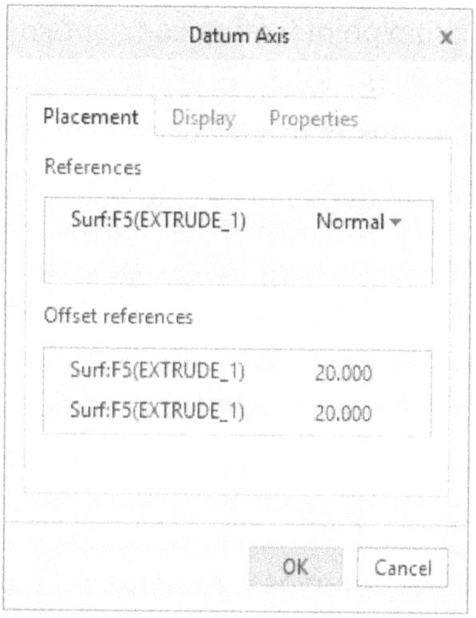

Figure 6–19

Note: *References can be removed using the Datum Plane dialog box. Select the reference, right-click, and select* **Remove**.

6.4 Creating Datum Points

Datum points can be used as construction elements for modeling or as known points for analyses. Similar to planes and axes, you can add points at any time, including during the creation of other features.

A single datum point feature can contain multiple individual points. When multiple points are created in a single point feature, the following apply:

- All datum points display under one Datum Point feature in the Model Tree.

- All points in the Datum Point feature act as a group, so deleting will apply to all points in the feature.

- To delete an individual point in the Point feature, you must edit the definition of the Datum feature.

There are three types of datum points:

- $\overset{\times\times}{\times}$ (Point): A datum point created on or offset from an entity, or at the intersection of entities.

- $\overset{\times}{\lrcorner}$ (Offset Coordinate System): A datum point created by offsetting from a selected datum coordinate system.

  Note: Offset Coordinate System points are covered in the Creo Parametric 11.0: Advanced Part Modeling guide.

- $\overset{\times}{\ldots}$ (Field): A field point identifies a geometric domain, and is used in Behavioral Modeling analyses. Field points will not be covered in this guide.

To create a datum point, expand the $\overset{\times\times}{\times}$ (Point) fly-out in the *Model* tab if standalone, or expand $\vdots$ (Datum) in the dashboard of the current feature, and expand the $\overset{\times\times}{\times}$ (Point) fly-out. Select either $\overset{\times\times}{\times}$ (Point) or $\overset{\times}{\lrcorner}$ (Offset Coordinate System), as required.

To create a general point, click $\overset{x\,x}{x}$ (Point). The *Datum Point* dialog box opens, as shown in Figure 6–20. Placement references and constraints need to be selected to fully locate the datum points.

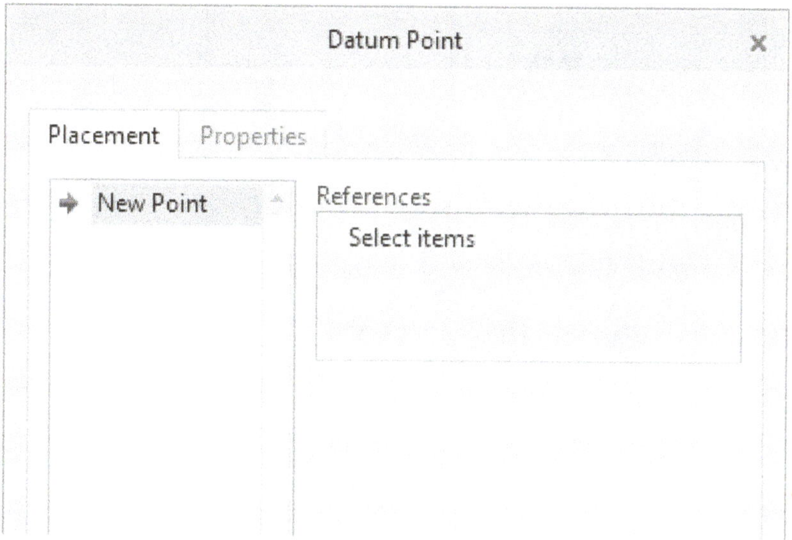

Figure 6–20

Note: References can be selected first, then click $\overset{x\,x}{x}$ (Point) in the mini toolbar.

Datum points can be created in the following locations:

- On a curve, edge, or axis.
- At the center of a circular or elliptical entity.
- On a surface or quilt, or offset from a surface or quilt.
- On a vertex or offset from a vertex.
- Offset from an existing datum point.
- Projected from a vertex, curve endpoint, or another datum point.
- Offset from a coordinate system.
- At the intersection of entities.

Figure 6–21 shows a point labeled **PNT0** created at the edge formed between the cylinder and the block.

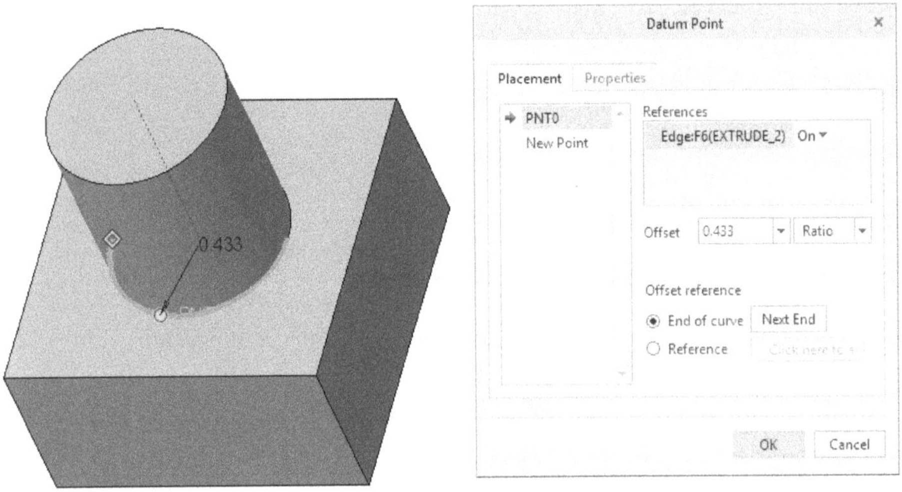

Figure 6–21

When you create a point on an edge, you must locate the point. The most common option is to offset the point by a ratio between 0 (the start) and 1 (the end). In this example, the point was created half way around the curve, or at a ratio of 0.50.

In a single datum point feature, you can create multiple individual points by creating a point, clicking **New Point**, and adding an additional point with new references, as shown in Figure 6–22. This can be repeated as many times as required. In Figure 6–22, the surface and axis were selected as references to create **PNT1**.

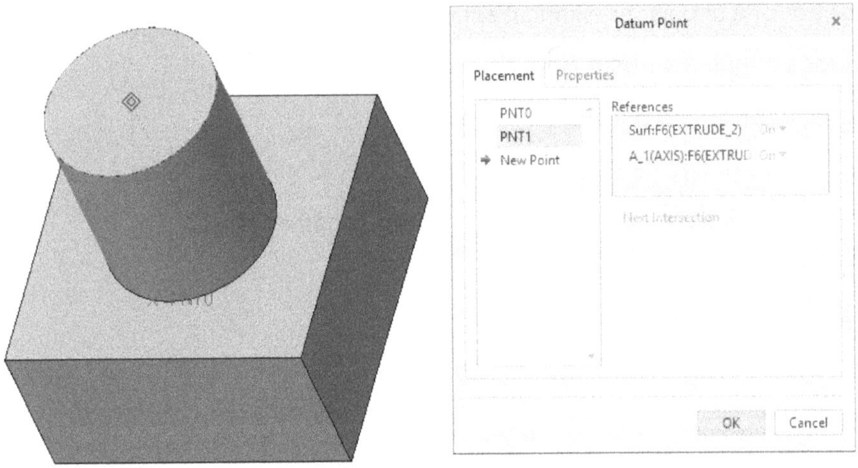

Figure 6–22

In Figure 6–23, the point **PNT2** is created on the surface shown, and offset from the two perpendicular surfaces, in a similar fashion to how a linear hole is located.

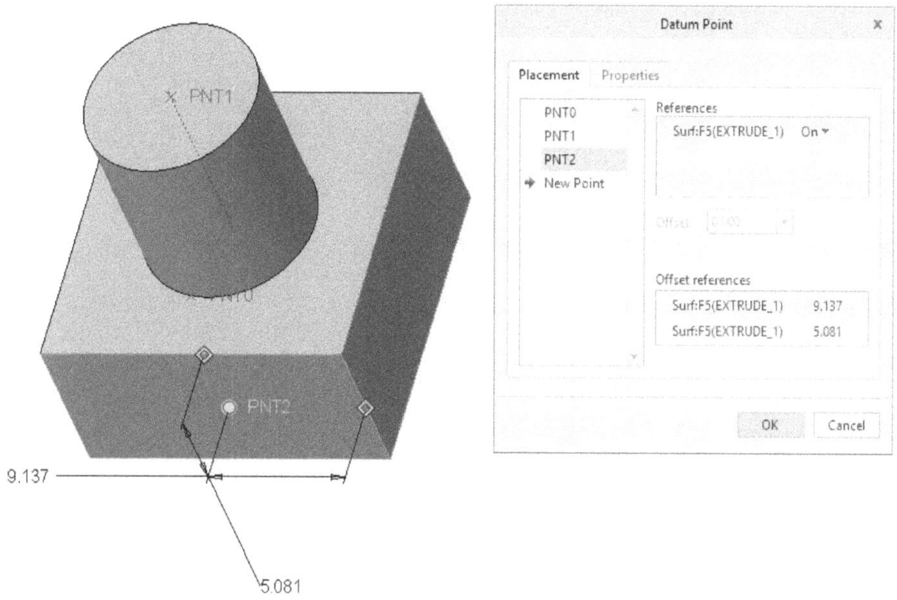

Figure 6–23

In the final example, the point **PNT3** is created at the selected vertex, as shown in Figure 6–24.

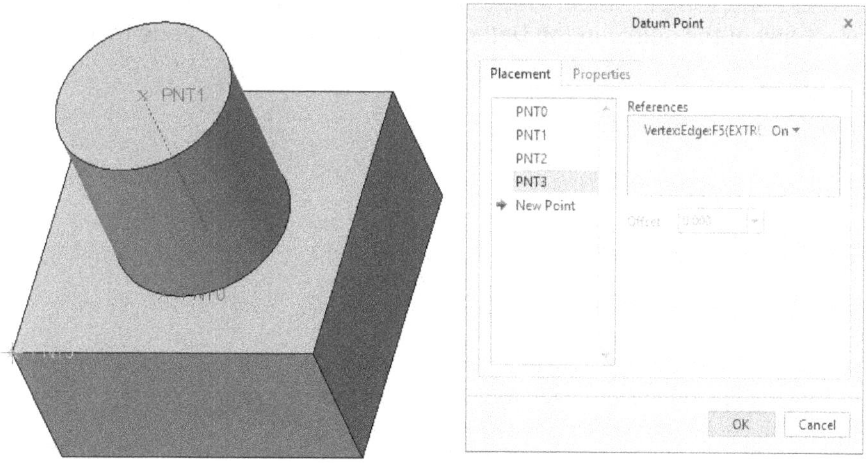

Figure 6–24

Once the points are complete, click **OK** to create the datum point feature. The grouped points display as a single feature in the Model Tree, as shown in Figure 6–25.

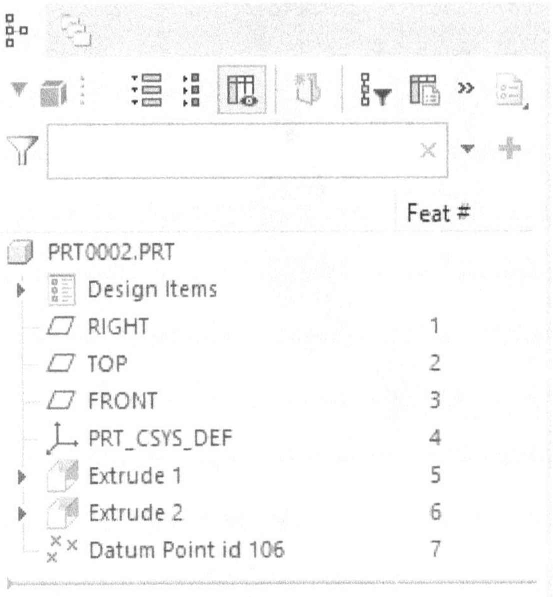

	Feat #
PRT0002.PRT	
▶ Design Items	
RIGHT	1
TOP	2
FRONT	3
PRT_CSYS_DEF	4
▶ Extrude 1	5
▶ Extrude 2	6
Datum Point id 106	7

Figure 6–25

To change any of the individual points in the feature, select any of the points on screen or select the Datum Point feature in the Model Tree and click (Edit Definition) in the *mini* toolbar. You can then select any of the points in the *Datum Point* dialog box to change them.

6.5 Creating Datum Coordinate Systems

Coordinate systems are used as reference features in parts and assemblies for the following scenarios:

* Serving as a reference for positioning other features.

* Direction references for most modeling tasks.

* Conducting mass property calculations.

* Assembling components.

* Placing constraints for Finite Element Analysis (FEA).

* Providing manufacturing operation references for tool paths.

Coordinate systems can be created by:

* Clicking ⊥ (Coordinate System) in the *Model* tab.

* Clicking ☼ (Datum) and then ⊥ (Coordinate System) while in a feature's dashboard

* Sketching a coordinate system while in Sketcher.

In any case, the *Coordinate System* dialog box opens, as shown in Figure 6–26.

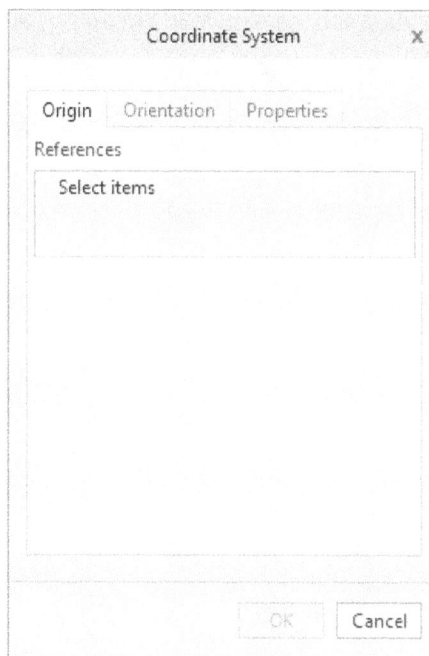

Figure 6–26

You can select placement references, such as surfaces, edges, vertices, or other coordinate systems, and then define the orientation of the coordinate system axes. Figure 6–27 shows a coordinate system created in a surface, using a Linear dimensioning scheme. The two perpendicular surfaces are used as dimensioning references.

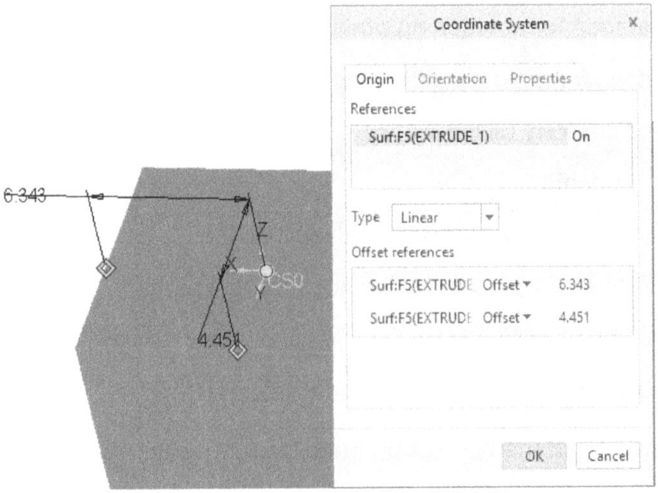

Figure 6–27

The system automatically determines the orientation for the X-, Y-, and Z-axis. You can control the orientation using the *Orientation* tab, as shown in Figure 6–28. You can use references to determine the direction in which any two of the coordinate system axes face. The third is then automatically set.

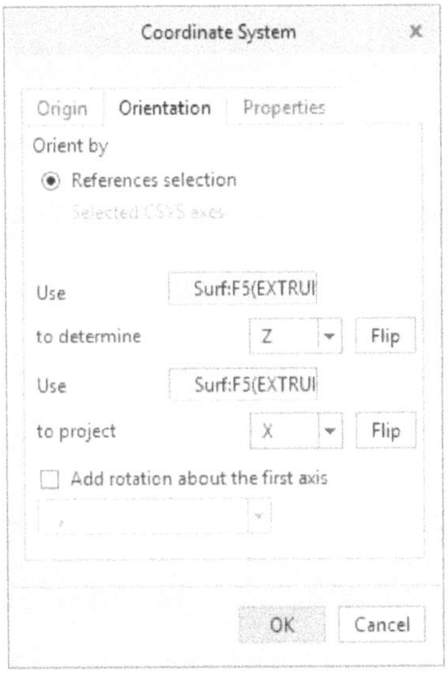

Figure 6–28

6.6 Sketched Datum Features

You have seen previously that in Sketcher, you can sketch points, centerlines, and coordinate systems using the applicable option in the *Sketching* group, as shown in Figure 6–29.

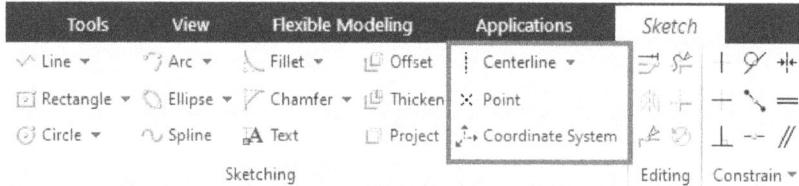

Figure 6–29

Points, centerlines, and coordinate systems sketched this way are only available as sketching references for constructing your sketches. They can only be referenced while in Sketcher.

You can, however, create datum centerlines, points, and coordinate systems within Sketcher that are available outside it. To create Sketcher datum entities, use the options found in the *Datum* group, as shown in Figure 6–30.

Figure 6–30

Sketched datum entities have to be located relative to existing geometry in the same way as any other sketched entities, as shown in Figure 6–31.

Figure 6–31

These sketched datum features display on the model as shown in Figure 6-32 and can be used as references for creating other features.

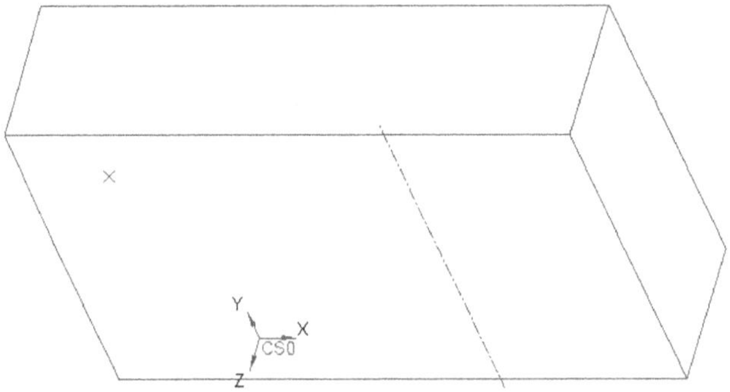

Figure 6-32

The datum entities are shown in the Model Tree as a single Sketch feature, as shown in Figure 6-33.

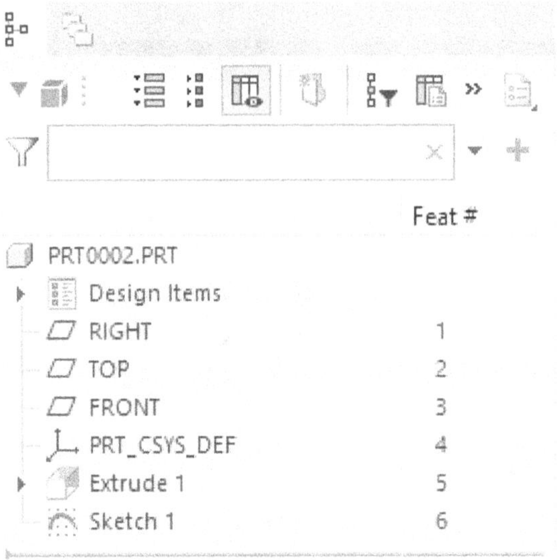

Figure 6-33

If the sketch contains multiple datums and you want to delete one or more, you must redefine the sketch feature and delete them from the sketch.

6.7 Datum Display

The display of datum features can be toggled on and off by selecting or clearing the appropriate option in the *In-graphics* toolbar, as shown in Figure 6–34.

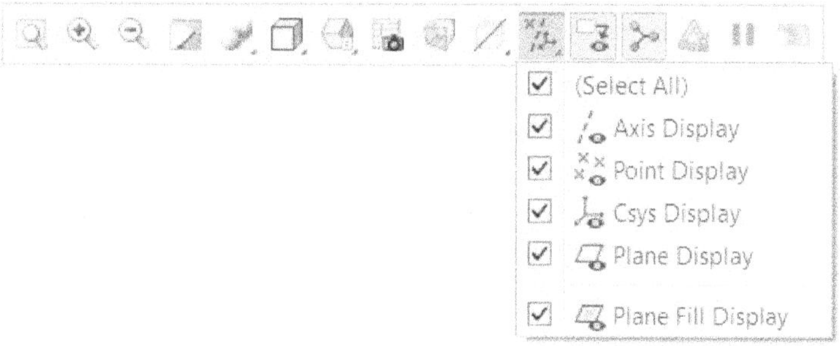

Figure 6–34

By default, the datum names are not displayed for datum entities other than coordinate systems. To display datum tags, select the *View* tab, and select the appropriate option from the *Show* group, as shown in Figure 6–35.

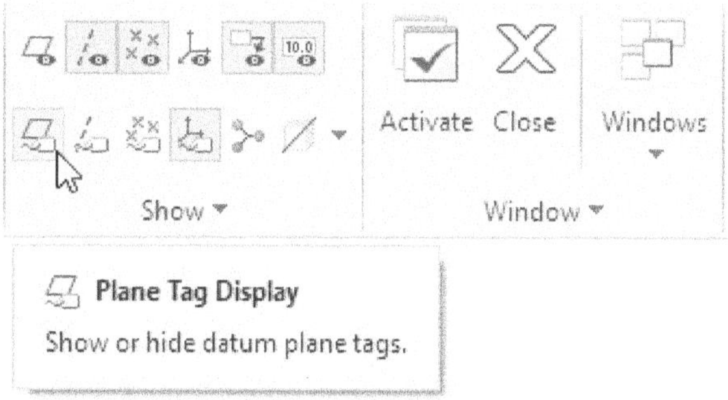

Figure 6–35

The datum display can be controlled from the *Show* group as well.

Hiding Datum Features

The options in the *In-graphics* toolbar enable you to control the display of all the features of the same type.

The ✎ (Hide) option enables you to control the display of individual datum features. For example, you can select the datum plane **FRONT** and hide it, which only removes that datum from the display.

To hide a datum feature, select it in the model or from the Model Tree and click ✎ (Hide) in the *mini* toolbar. To show it again, select it and click ◉ (Show) in the *mini* toolbar.

Additionally, you can select a datum in the Model Tree or graphics area and in the *mini* toolbar, select ⬤ (Show Only) or ⬤ (Show All Except). Alternatively, you can select the *View* tab and select the options in the *Visibility* group, as required.

- ⬤ (Show Only): Shows the selected object while hiding all other objects of the same type.

- ⬤ (Show All Except): Hides the selected object, and all other objects of the same type display, as shown in Figure 6-36.

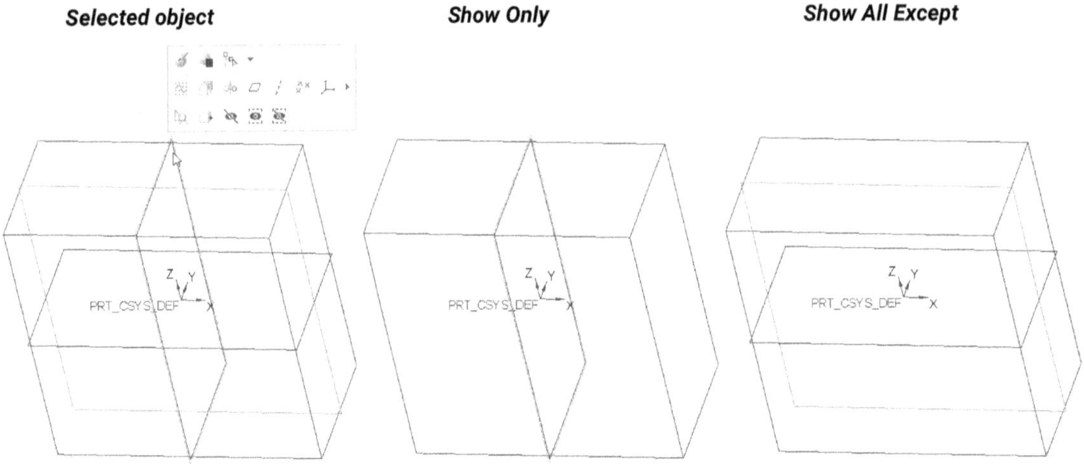

Figure 6-36

Practice 6a
Reference Elements

Practice Objectives

- Create reference elements.
- Create solid features using reference elements.

In this practice, you will create the part shown in Figure 6–37. You will create reference elements to use as sketch planes. From these, you will create the features.

Figure 6–37

Task 1: Open a model with an initial pad feature.

1. Set your working directory to the *Reference_Elements* folder.
2. Open the **datum_refs.prt**.
3. Set the model display as follows:

   - ⅍ *(Datum Display Filters)*: All On
   - ⅀ *(Spin Center)*: Off
   - ▢ *(Display Style)*: ▢ (Shading With Edges)

Task 2: Create a point at the center of the part.

Design Considerations

The point you create here is used later to constrain the sketch of an extrude feature. It is also used as a starting point for an axis, which will serve as a reference for datum planes.

1. Select the top surface of the part, as shown in Figure 6–38, and click $\times^\times_\times$ (Point) in the *mini* toolbar.

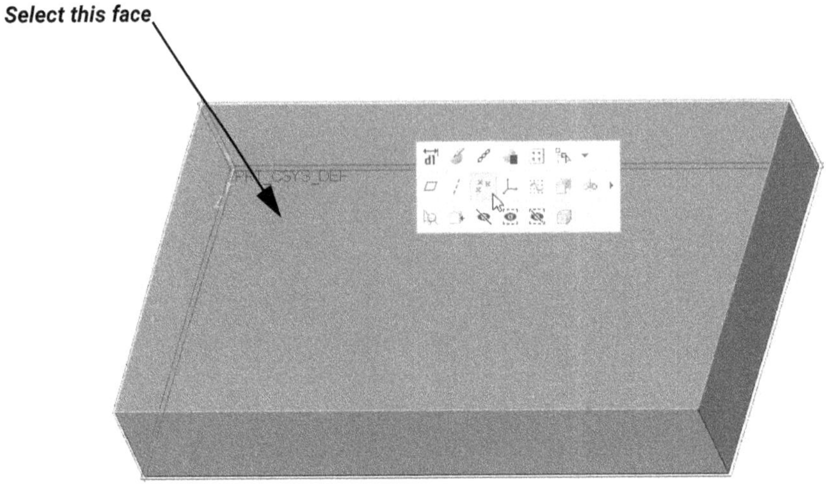

Select this face

Figure 6–38

2. The *Datum Point* dialog box opens, as shown in Figure 6–39.

Figure 6–39

3. Note the two drag handles on the model.

4. Move the drag handles to the two surfaces shown in Figure 6–40.

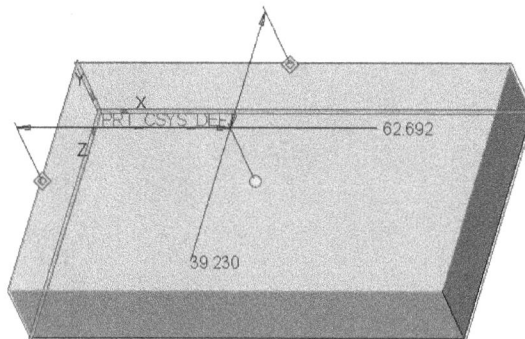

Figure 6–40

5. Set the *dimensions* to **38** and **63.5**, as shown in Figure 6–41.

Figure 6–41

6. Click **OK** to complete the point.

Task 3: Create an axis.

Design Considerations

This axis will reference the point you previously created. It is used as a pivot axis for an angled plane.

1. Select the datum point and click (Axis) in the *mini* toolbar.

2. Press and hold <Ctrl> and select datum plane **FRONT** from the Model Tree.

3. The *Datum Axis* dialog box should display, as shown in Figure 6-42.

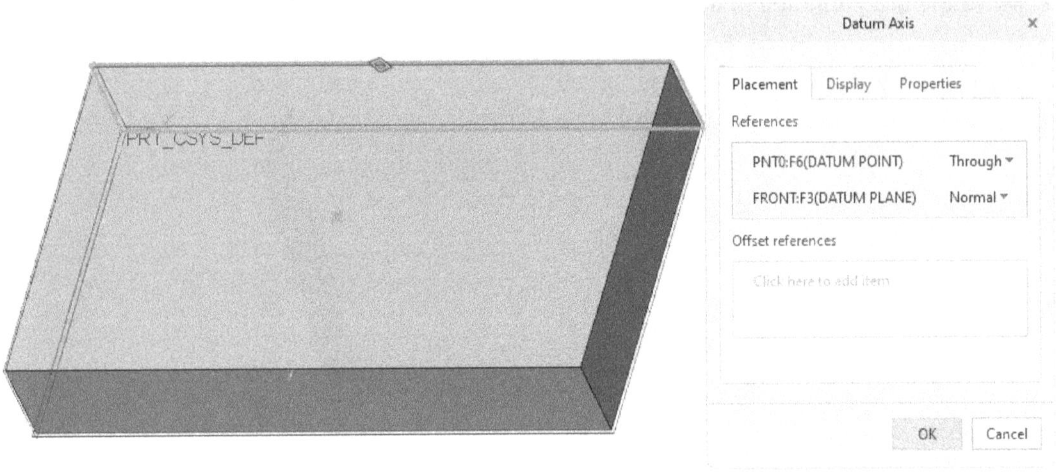

Figure 6-42

4. Click **OK** to complete the axis. The resulting part displays as shown in Figure 6-43.

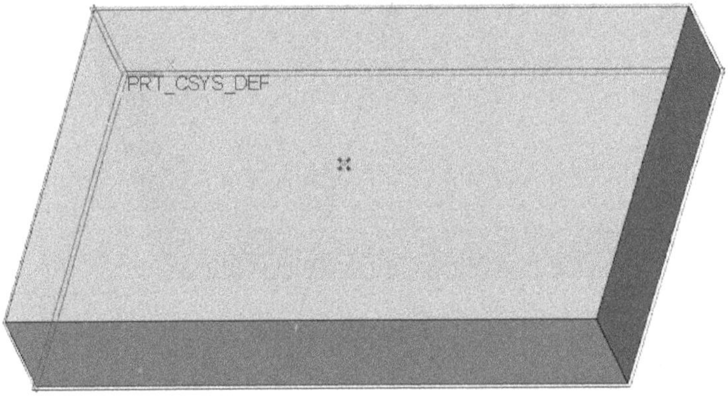

Figure 6-43

Task 4: Create planes to locate a sketch.

Design Considerations

Using the previously created axis and one of the datum planes, you will create an angled plane. This plane will be used as a reference for the next plane that you will create.

1. Select the datum axis previously created and click ▱ (Plane) from the *mini* toolbar.

2. Press and hold <Ctrl> and select datum plane **TOP** from the Model Tree as the plane to measure the angle from.

3. Set the *Angle* to **60**.

4. The *Datum Plane* dialog box displays, as shown in Figure 6−44.

Figure 6−44

5. Click **OK** to complete the datum plane.

Design Considerations

The following plane will be used as a sketching plane for the profile sketch of a pad feature. The plane will be offset from the angle plane.

6. Select the plane you just created and click ⬜ (Plane) in the *mini* toolbar.

7. Set the *Translation* to **50.00**.

8. Click **OK** to complete the creation of this plane. The resulting part displays as shown in Figure 6−45.

Figure 6−45

Task 5: Create an extrusion on the offset plane.

Design Considerations

This sketch will be used as a profile for an extruded feature. It is created on the offset plane and will be constrained to the point that you created earlier.

1. Select the offset plane and click ⬜ (Extrude) in the *mini* toolbar.

2. If required, click ⬚ (Sketch View).

3. Sketch a circle that is centered on the datum point, as shown in Figure 6−46.

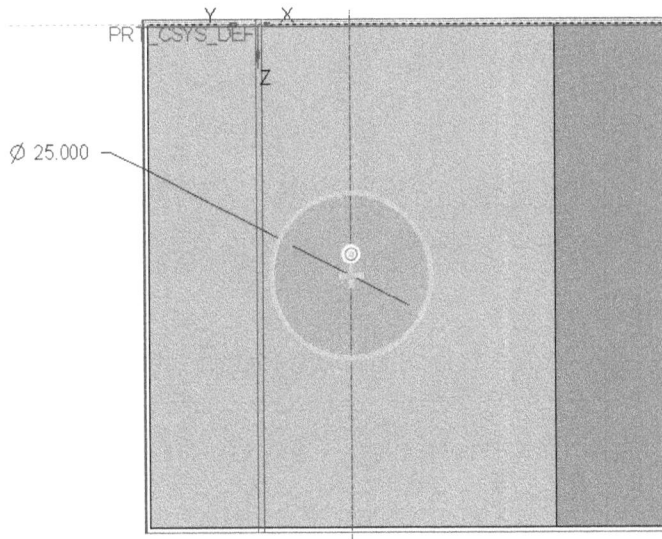

Figure 6−46

4. Click ✓ (**OK**) to complete the sketch.

5. Press <Ctrl>+<D> to return to the default orientation.

6. Select the depth drag handle.

7. Press and hold <Shift> and drag the handle until the top surface of the model highlights.

8. Click ✔ (**OK**) to complete the extrusion. The resulting part displays as shown in Figure 6−47.

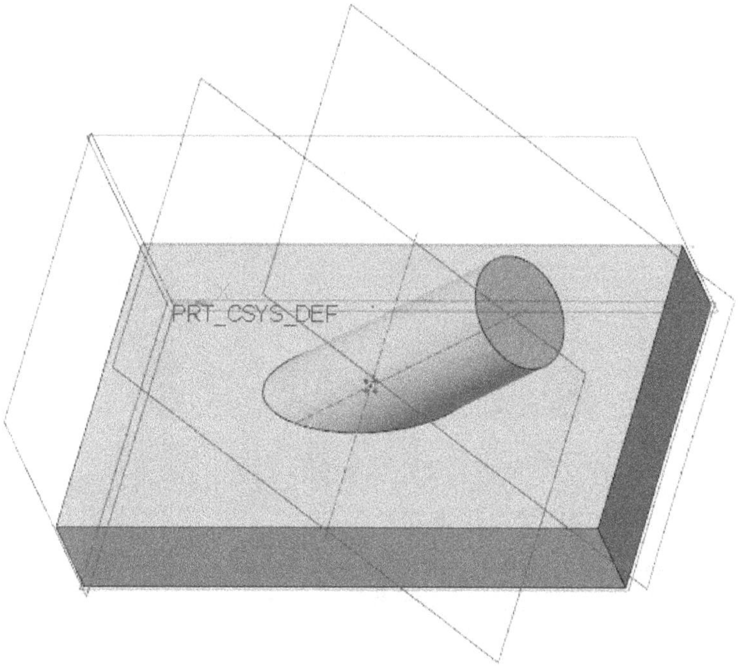

Figure 6−47

Task 6: Modify the angle, offset distance, and location of the extrusion.

1. Double-click on the offset datum (**DTM2**), and change the *50 Translation* to **100.00.**

2. Double-click on the angle datum plane (**DTM1**) and set the *Angle* to **30.00**.

3. Double-click on **PNT0** and change the *63.5* value to **100.00**.

4. Click ⬚ (Regenerate).

5. Toggle off the display of all datum entities. The model displays as shown in Figure 6–48.

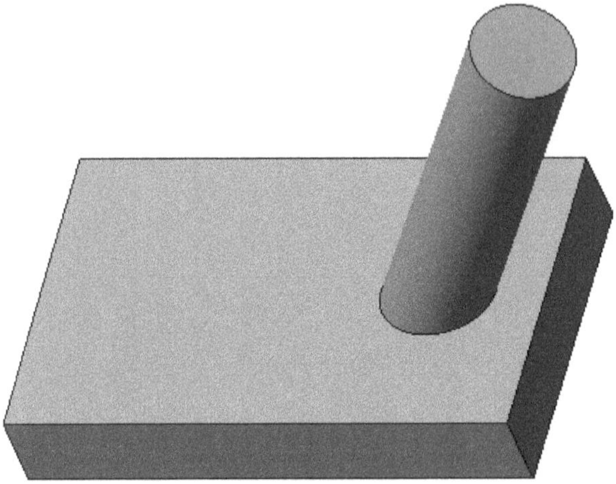

Figure 6–48

6. Save the model and erase it from memory.

End of practice

Practice 6b
Create Datum Features

Practice Objective

- Create internal datum planes and datum axes that can be used as references in the creation of a solid feature.

In this practice, you will create the model shown in Figure 6–49. To create the geometry for this model, you must create an additional datum plane and axis.

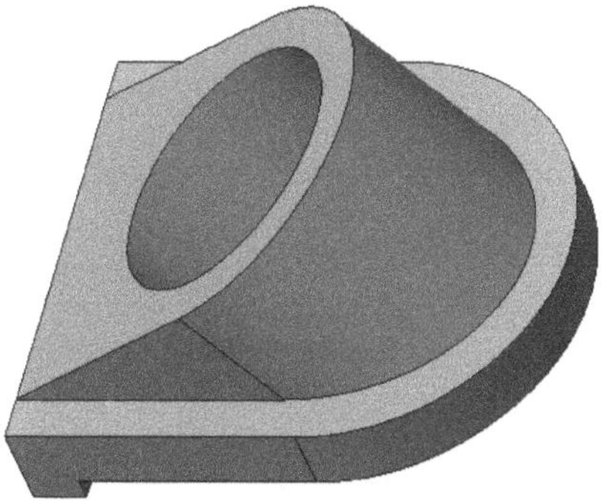

Figure 6–49

Task 1: Create a new part.

1. Set the working directory to the *Datum_Features* folder.
2. Create a new part using the default template and set the *Name* to **bevel_washer**.
3. Set the model display as follows:

    - ˣᵎ. *(Datum Display Filters)*: Only ⬡ (Plane Display) and ⚬ (Axis Display)
    - ⤳ *(Spin Center)*: Off
    - ▫. *(Display Style)*: ▱ (Shading With Edges)

Task 2: Create the base feature.

1. Select datum plane **TOP** and click ◶ (Extrude) in the *mini* toolbar.
2. If required, click ⬚ (Sketch View).

3. Sketch the section shown in Figure 6–50, using the default references.

Figure 6–50

Note: The centerline is coincident with the horizontal reference, and the section is made symmetric about the centerline.

4. Click ✓ (**OK**) to complete the sketch.
5. Pres <Ctrl>+<D> to return to the default orientation.
6. Set the *Depth* to **0.75**.

7. Click ✔ (**OK**) to complete the extrusion. The model displays as shown in Figure 6–51.

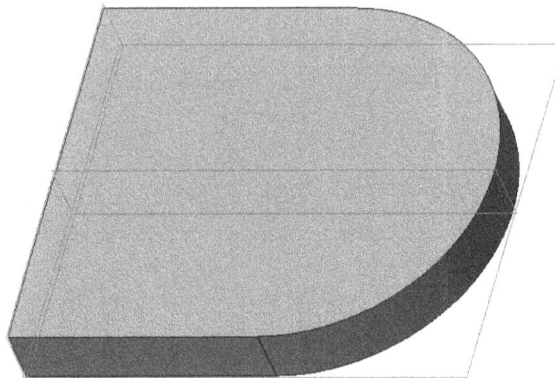

Figure 6–51

Task 3: Create the angled protrusion.

1. In the *Shapes* group in the ribbon, click (Extrude) to create the angled extrusion.

2. An additional datum plane is required as a sketching plane. In the *Extrude* dashboard, expand (Datum) and click (Plane), as shown in Figure 6–52.

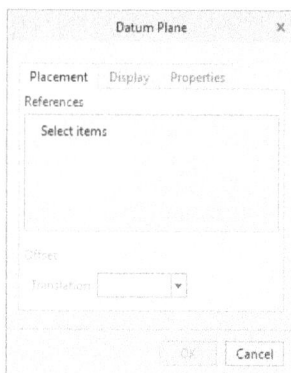

Figure 6–52

Note: Creation of the extrusion is paused automatically.

3. The *Datum Plane* dialog box opens, as shown in Figure 6–53.

4. Press and hold <Ctrl>, and select the edge and surface shown in Figure 6–54. The datum plane displays once the references have been selected.

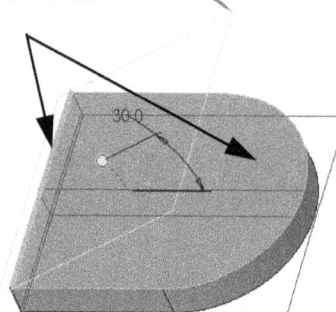

Figure 6–53

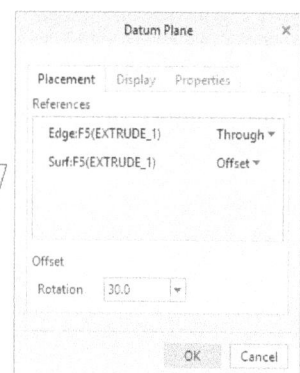

Figure 6–54

5. In the *Datum Plane* dialog box, note that the **Through** constraint is selected for the edge, and the **Offset** constraint is selected for the surface.

   *Note: The constraint types (e.g., **Through** or **Offset**) are dependent on the reference type (e.g., edge or surface). A default constraint type is assigned for each reference. However, it can be changed by selecting the constraint and using the drop-down list to select from the list of available constraints.*

6. Set the *Rotation* to **30**, if required. If you need to flip the datum plane to the opposite side of the selected surface, set the *Rotation* to **-30**. In the *Datum Plane* dialog box, select the *Properties* tab. Change the *Name* of the datum plane to **angled_datum**, as shown in Figure 6−55.

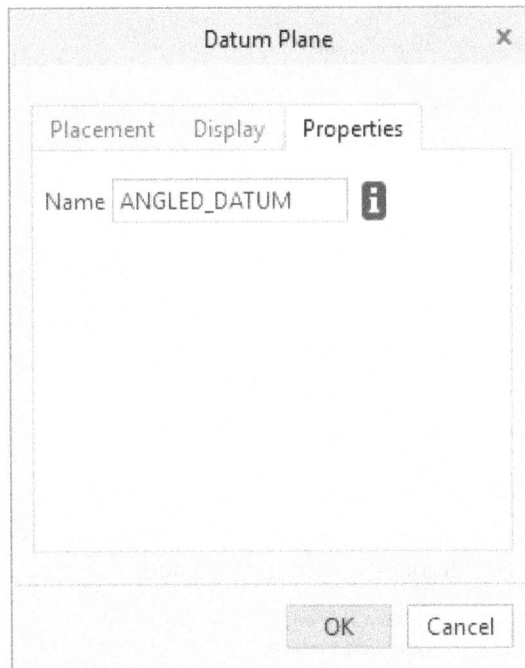

Figure 6−55

7. Click **OK** to complete the creation of the datum plane.

8. Click ▶ (Resume) to continue creating the protrusion. The *Sketch* tab is now active. The system automatically uses the new plane as the sketching plane and the **FRONT** plane to face the bottom direction.

9. Sketch the section shown in Figure 6–56. Note that the vertical line is sketched so that it snaps to the underlying edge.

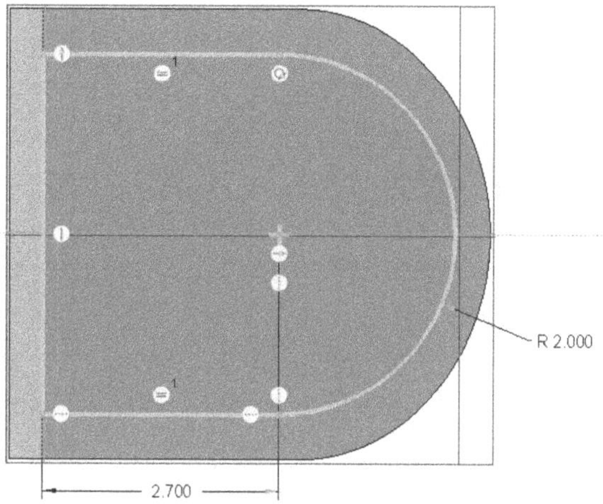

Figure 6–56

10. Click ✓ (**OK**) to complete the sketch.

11. If required, click the arrow head so the feature extrudes toward the existing geometry.

12. Right-click on the depth drag handle and select **To Next**. The preview displays, as shown in Figure 6–57.

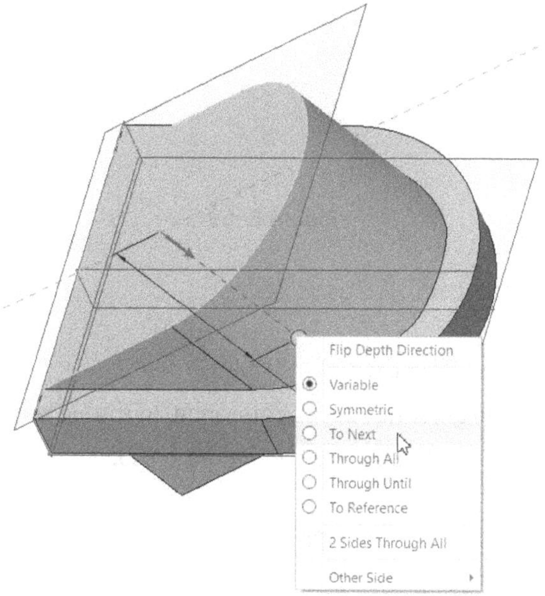

Figure 6–57

13. Click ✔️ (**OK**) to complete the feature. The model displays, as shown in Figure 6–58.

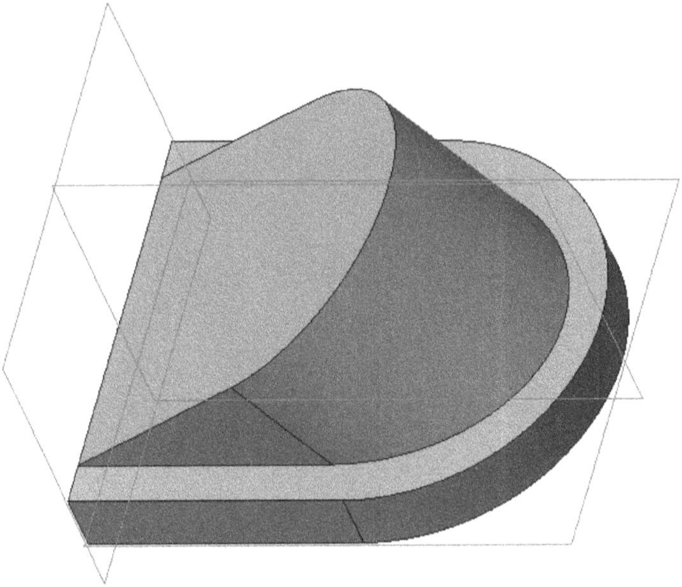

Figure 6–58

The feature that has been added to the Model Tree is an extrude feature. If you expand the feature it consists of the section and the datum plane, as shown in Figure 6–59.

▼ 🗂 Extrude 2
    📝 Section 1
    ▱ ANGLED_DATUM

Figure 6–59

Task 4: Create a coaxial hole.

1. In the *Shapes* group in the ribbon, click 🔲 (Hole).
2. To create the hole, an axis is required as a reference. In the *Hole* dashboard, expand ▦ (Datum) and click ⁄ (Axis), as shown in Figure 6–60.

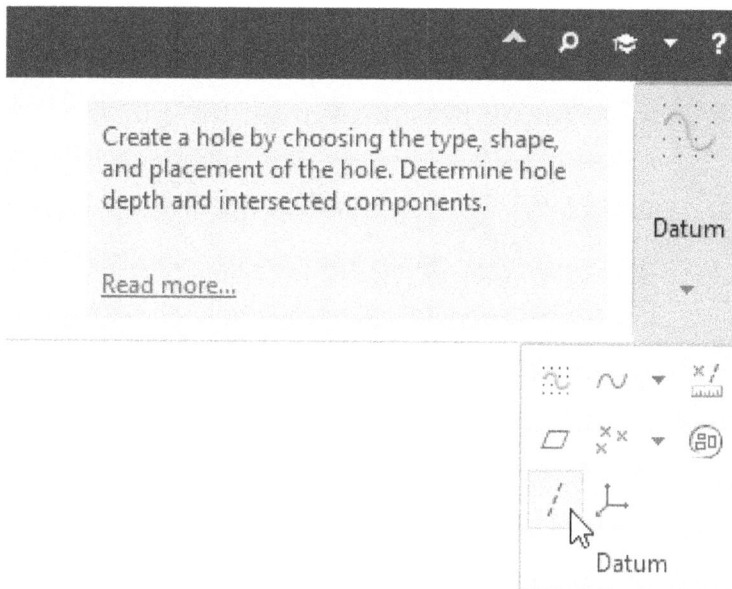

Figure 6-60

Note: Creation of the hole is paused automatically.

3. Select the surface shown in Figure 6-61 as a reference. The constraint type should automatically be set to **Through**.

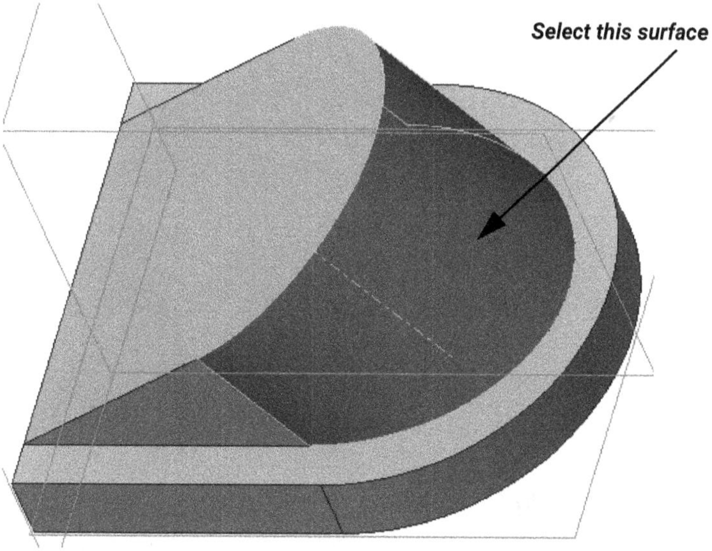

Select this surface

Figure 6-61

4. The *Datum Axis* dialog box updates, as shown in Figure 6−62. Click **OK** to complete the datum axis.

Figure 6−62

5. Click ▶ (Resume) to continue creating the hole. The *Hole* dashboard is now active.

6. The newly created axis is automatically selected as a primary placement reference. This establishes a coaxial constraint.

Note: The Placement panel can be selected to review or change the references.

7. Move the cursor into the Creo Parametric window, hold <Ctrl>, and select the top surface of the angled protrusion, as shown in Figure 6−63.

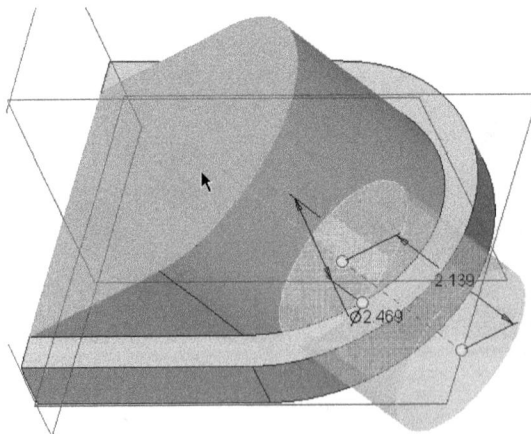

Figure 6−63

8. Right-click the depth handle and select **Through All** to intersect with the through all surfaces.

9. Double-click on the *Diameter* of the hole and set it to **3.00**.

10. Click ✔ (**OK**) to complete the feature. The model displays, as shown in Figure 6–64.

Figure 6–64

Task 5: Create an extruded lip.

1. Create an extrusion on the underside of the model with the dimensions shown in Figure 6–65.

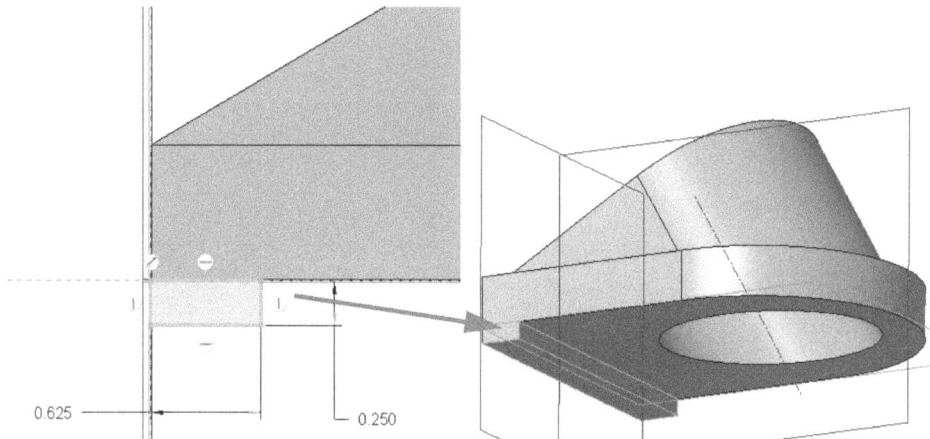

0.625   0.250

Figure 6–65

2. In the *In-graphics* toolbar, click ⁺⁄✳. (Datum Display Filters) and toggle off ⁄◦ (Axis Display) and ⊿ (Plane Display).

3. The completed model displays, as shown in Figure 6-66.

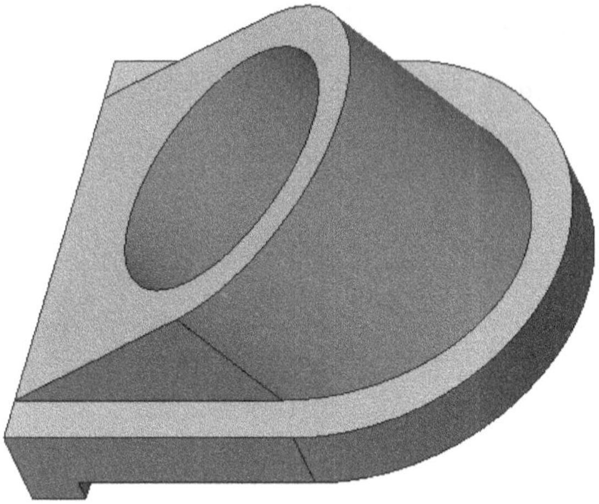

Figure 6-66

4. Save the model and erase it from memory.

End of practice

Practice 6c
Additional References

Practice Objective

- Create datum planes and axis that can be used as references in the creation of a solid feature.

In this practice, you will create the model shown in Figure 6–67. To create the geometry for this model, you must create an additional datum plane and axis.

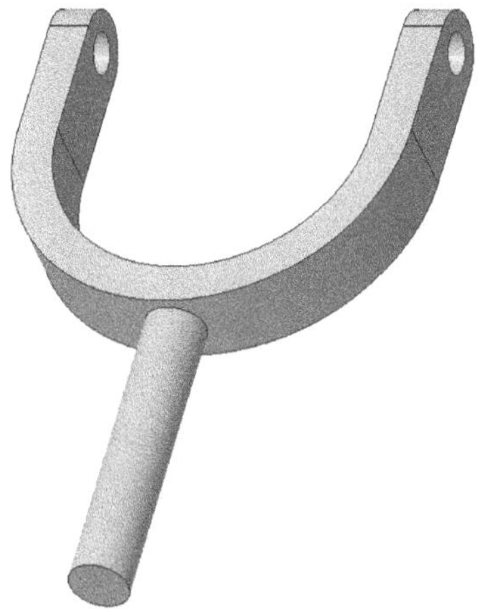

Figure 6–67

Task 1: Create a new part.

1. Ensure that the working directory is set to the *Additional_References* folder.
2. Use the default template to create a new part and set the *Name* to **fork**.
3. Set the model display as follows:

    - *(Datum Display Filters)*: Only (Plane Display) and (Axis Display)
    - *(Spin Center)*: Off
    - *(Display Style)*: (Shading With Edges)

Task 2: Create the base feature.

1. Select datum plane **TOP** and click (Extrude) in the *mini* toolbar to create the base feature.

2. If required, click ⌖ (Sketch View) then sketch the section shown in Figure 6-68.

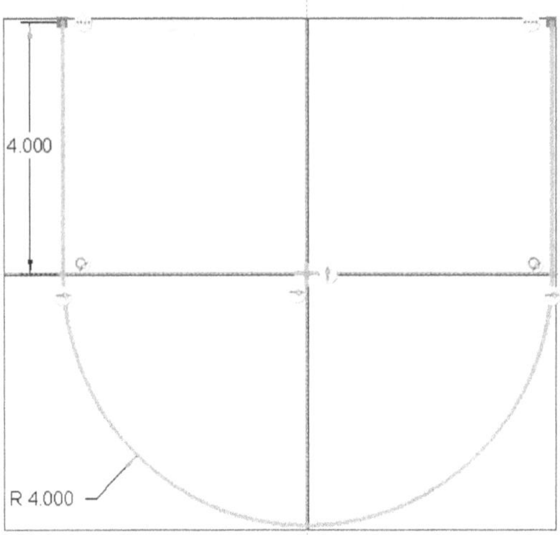

4.000

R 4.000

Figure 6-68

3. Click ✓ (**OK**).

4. A warning dialog box opens, indicating that the sketch is not closed. Click **OK**.

5. Click ▢ (Solid) and note that ▢ (Thicken Sketch) is automatically enabled.

6. Set the *Thickness* to **1.00**.

7. If required, click ⌖ (Change Material Direction) in the dashboard until the thickness is created on the inside of the sketch.

8. Click ⊟ (Symmetric) to extrude the feature on both sides of the sketching plane. Set the *Depth* to **2.00**.

9. Click ✓ (**OK**) to complete the feature. Return to default orientation and the model displays, as shown in Figure 6-69.

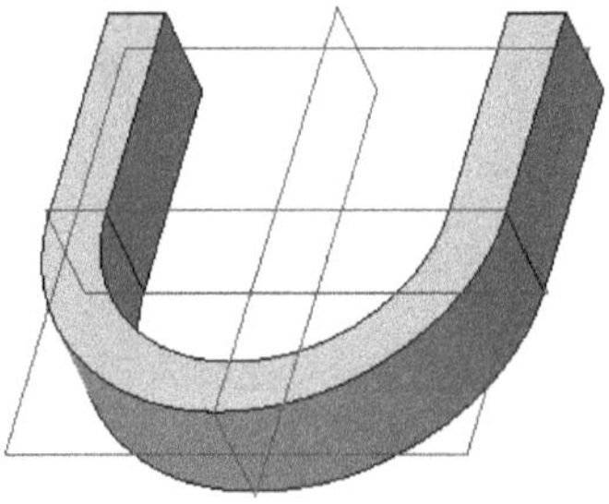

Figure 6-69

Task 3: Create two full rounds.

1. Click ⁺⁄ᵪ (Datum Display Filters) and toggle 🔲 (Plane Display) off.

2. Select one of the edges shown in Figure 6−70. Press and hold <Ctrl> and select the other edge, then release <Ctrl>.

3. In the *mini* toolbar, select ⌐ (Round). Then, click again and select ⌐ (Full Round).

4. Click ✔ (**OK**) and the model displays, as shown in Figure 6−71.

Figure 6−70   **Figure 6−71**

5. Repeat the previous steps to create the full round on the other side.

Task 4: Create a coaxial hole.

An axis is required to create a coaxial hole through the ends of the base feature. Because this axis might be referenced by other features, create the axis before the hole so that it is not embedded with the hole feature.

1. In the *Model* tab, click ∕ (Axis) to create the datum axis.

2. Select either of the surfaces formed by the full rounds as the placement reference. Ensure that the constraint type is set to **Through**.

3. Click **OK** in the *Datum Axis* dialog box.

4. With the axis still selected, in the *Model* tab, click 🕳 (Hole) to create a hole through the ends of the base feature so that it is coaxial with the full rounds.

   Note: *The axis should still be active after creation.*

5. Press <Ctrl> and select the surface shown in Figure 6–72.

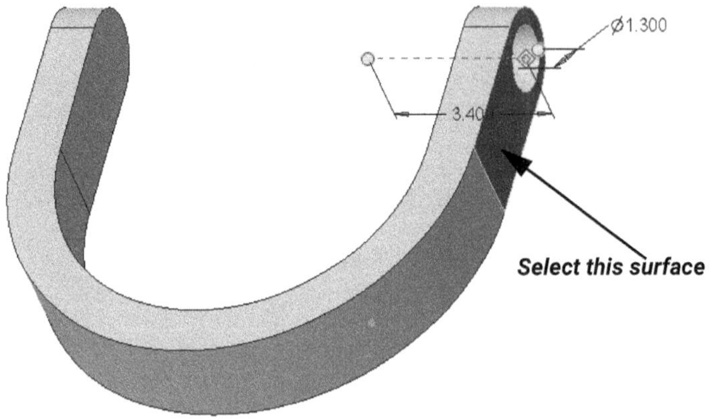

Figure 6–72

Note: If the default hole diameter, which is set from the last hole you created, is too large, it might cut off the end of the model. Simply drag the diameter handle to make it fit.

6. Set the hole *Diameter* to **1.00**.

7. Right-click on the depth drag handle and select **Through All**.

8. Click ✔ (**OK**) to complete the feature.

Task 5: Create the post.

1. Click 🗲 (Extrude) to create an extruded feature.

2. Click ⤬ (Datum Display Filters) and toggle 🗔 (Plane Display) on.

3. A sketching plane is required that does not currently exist in the model. In the *Extrude* dashboard, expand ⬚ (Datum), and click ▱ (Plane). Press and hold <Ctrl> and multi-select the surface and datum plane **FRONT** as references, as shown in Figure 6−73. Constrain the datum plane to be **Tangent** to the cylindrical surface and **Parallel** to datum plane **FRONT**. The resulting datum plane displays, as shown in Figure 6−73.

Figure 6−73

Note: Creation of the protrusion is paused automatically.

4. Click **OK** to complete the datum plane.

5. Click ▶ (Resume) to continue creating the extruded feature.

6. If required, click 🔁 (Sketch View).

7. Sketch the section shown in Figure 6−74 on the newly created datum plane.

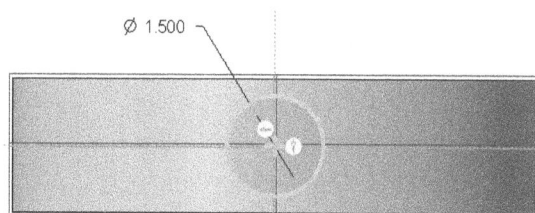

Figure 6−74

8. Click ✓ (**OK**) to complete the sketch.

9. In the *Options* tab, in the *Side 1* field, set the *Depth* to **Variable** and enter a value of **7.50**. In the *Side 2* field, set the *Depth* to **To Next**. The panel is shown in Figure 6–75.

Options	Body Options	Properties

Depth

| Side 1 | ⊥⊢ Blind | ▼ | 7.500 | ▼ |
| Side 2 | ≛ To Next | ▼ | | |

☐ Capped ends

☐ Add taper

| | ▼ |

Figure 6–75

Note: The Options panel must be used to set options for Side 2. Alternatively, the Extrude tab can be used for Side 1.

10. Click ✔ (**OK**) to complete the cylindrical protrusion. Toggle off the display of datum features. The model displays, as shown in Figure 6–76.

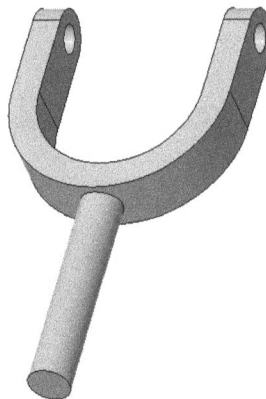

Figure 6–76

Note: What would have happened if the Side 2 depth was not set?

11. Save the model and erase it from memory.

End of practice

Chapter Review Questions

1. By default, datum axes are automatically generated with cylindrical features.

   a. True

   b. False

2. Both datum planes and datum axes can be renamed using the *Properties* tab in their associated dialog boxes.

   a. True

   b. False

3. Which combination of constraints enables you to create **DTM2**, as shown in Figure 6−77? (Select all that apply.)

Figure 6−77

   a. Tangent to the Round at an Angle to **TOP**.

   b. Through **A_6** at an Angle to **TOP**.

   c. Through **A_6** at an Angle to **FRONT**.

   d. Through **TOP** at an Angle to **FRONT**.

4. Which of the following are valid constraint combinations to create a datum plane? (Select all that apply.)

   a. Through a plane and parallel to an axis.

   b. Through a plane and offset from a surface.

   c. Tangent to a surface and parallel to a surface.

   d. Through an axis and Normal to a surface.

5. Which of the following statements is true regarding the Model Tree shown in Figure 6−78?

   ▼ ⬛ Extrude 2
       ▨ Section 1
       ⬠ ANGLED_DATUM

   Figure 6−78

   a. The datum plane was created as a separate feature.

   b. The datum plane was created in the extrusion.

   c. The datum axis is created with the feature.

   d. **Section 1** is suppressed.

6. A datum axis can be fully constrained by selecting the surface of a round.

   a. True

   b. False

Display Control and Feature Order

As models become more complex, the number of features and components increases. It may be useful to display only relevant features and components, rather than everything simultaneously, when working with the model. Simplifying the process will make it easier to manage and visualize specific parts. Tools such as Hide, Suppress, and Layers can be used to simplify the model.

Learning Objectives

- Temporarily remove a non-solid feature to exclude it from the model geometry.
- Temporarily remove a feature to exclude it from the model geometry and regeneration sequence.
- Create a new layer, add features or components to that layer, and specify the display option (i.e., Hide, Show, or Isolate).
- Learn how to use default layers.
- Use layers as a selection tool to perform additional tasks.
- Understand how the feature creation sequence affects the resulting model geometry.
- Change the order of features in the Model Tree by dragging and dropping them.
- Change the location of the new features that are added to a model using the Insert Here arrow.

7.1 Hiding Features

The ✎ (Hide) option enables you to quickly simplify the model. When you hide a feature or component, it remains in the Model Tree and in the regeneration sequence. When hiding features in a part, the solid geometry remains visible and only the datum features associated them are removed from the display. When hiding components in an assembly, the selected components are entirely removed from the display. The ✎ (Hide) setting can be saved with the model using the ⚙ *(Status)>* ⚙ (Save Status) option in the *View* tab of the ribbon. Once something is hidden, it is not shown again until it is unhidden.

> **Note:** *Select the View tab and click* ⚙ *(Status), in the Visibility group to ensure that all hidden settings are saved when the model is saved. You can also click* ⚙ *(Reset Status) in the flyout menu, to reset your settings.*

- Note that, although the default behavior of the software is to have the datum tags toggled off for points, planes and axes, the examples in this chapter may show the tags enabled to make it easier to refer to specific entities.

- Select the feature or component to be hidden, from the Model Tree or directly in the model. Parent/child relationships do not affect children of hidden parents because they remain in the regeneration sequence.

- To hide a feature or component, select it and click ✎ (Hide) in the *mini* toolbar, or select the *View* tab and click ✎ (Hide) in the *Visibility* group. Hidden features are identified in the Model Tree with a gray box that surrounds the feature or component symbol, as shown in Figure 7−1.

Axis A_1, used to create the coaxial hole (Hole 1), is hidden. This feature was hidden by default when it was created on the fly with the hole.

Hole 2 is Hidden. Although the feature still displays, the axis is hidden.

Coaxial hole

Figure 7−1

- To display the selected feature or component while hiding all other objects of the same type, click. 👁 (Show Only).

- To hide the selected feature or component but display all other objects of the same type, click ⬚ (Show All Except).

- To unhide a feature (or component), select it and click ● (Show) in the *mini* toolbar. You can also select the *View* tab and click ● (Show) in the *Visibility* group. The Show flyout icon also enables you to unhide all hidden features at once by clicking ● (Unhide All).

- You can obtain a list of hidden features in the Layer Tree. To access the Layer Tree, select ≡ (Layer Tree) in the Model Tree. Figure 7–2 shows the same model and its associated Layer Tree. Select the **Hidden Items** row to highlight the hidden items.

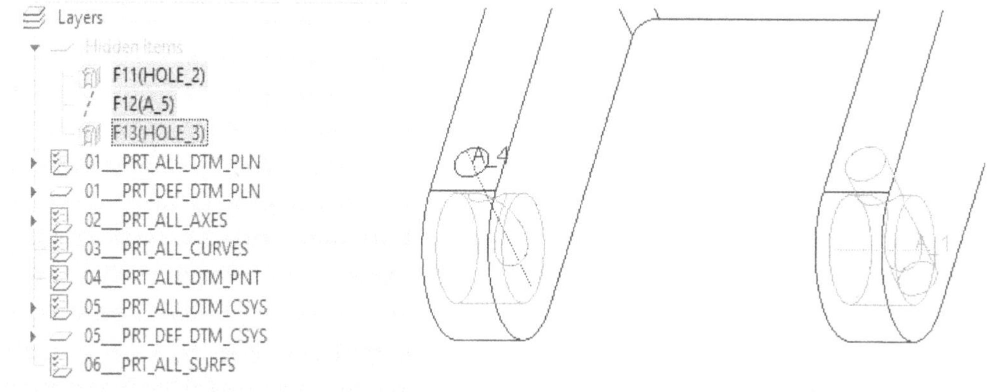

Figure 7–2

Note: You can also access the Layer Tree by selecting the View tab and click ≡ (Layers Tree) in the Visibility group.

7.2 Suppressing Features

Suppressed features and/or components are temporarily removed from the display and the regeneration sequence. This simplifies the appearance of the model and decreases the amount of time it takes to regenerate. In Figure 7-3 the cut is suppressed and is therefore removed from the Model Tree and regeneration sequence.

The extruded feature is suppressed.

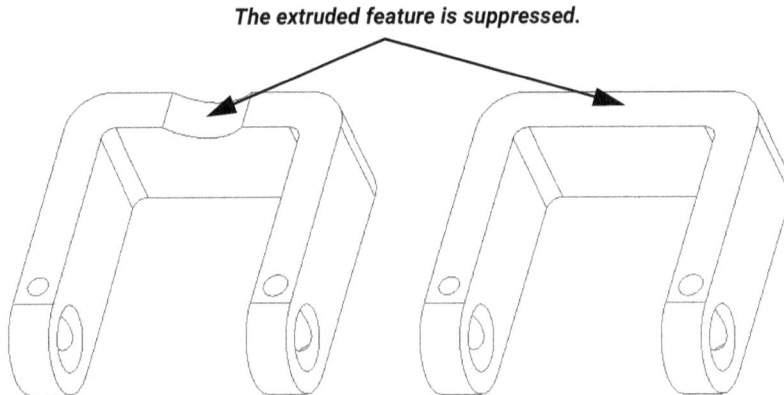

Figure 7-3

Select the feature or component to be suppressed from the Model Tree or directly on the model. Careful consideration must be taken with regard to parent/child relationships. By default, all children are suppressed with their parents.

To suppress the selected feature, click ◢ (Suppress) in the *mini* toolbar. You can also select **Operation>Suppress>Suppress** in the *Model* tab, as shown in Figure 7-4. The two options are available in the **Operations** menu are as follows:

- **Suppress to End of Model:** suppresses the selected feature and any feature that is created after it

- **Suppress Unrelated Items:** suppresses the selected feature and any feature that is not related

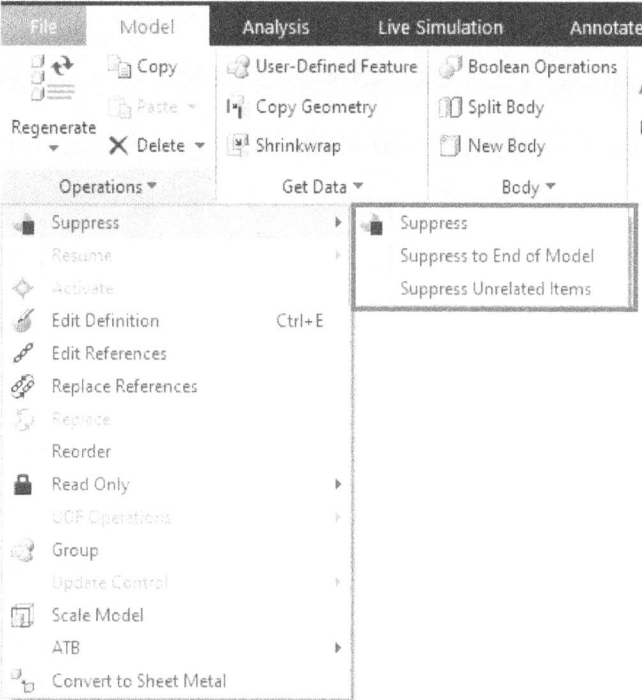

Figure 7−4

Note: *All suppressed settings are saved when the model is saved.*

When suppressing a feature with children, all children are subsequently selected and the *Suppress* dialog box opens, as shown in Figure 7−5.

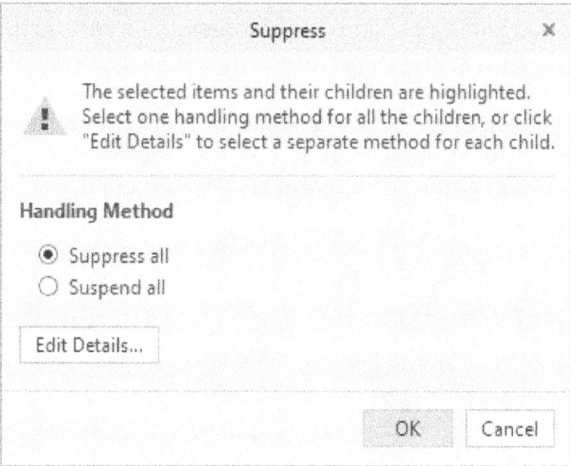

Figure 7−5

You can click **OK** to confirm suppression of the feature and all of its children or you can click **Cancel** to cancel the operation. For advanced options for controlling children, click **Edit Details**. The *Children Handling* dialog box opens, as shown in Figure 7−6.

Figure 7−6

You can set the status of any of the children to **Suppress** (suppresses the child with the parent) or to **Suspend** (does not suppress the child). By default, the status is set to **Suppress**. However, the feature cannot be regenerated with its parent missing. If you attempt to regenerate the model, it fails and an Information window opens indicating that the parents of the feature are missing. Suspending the feature enables you to edit it so that you can remove the parent/child relationship between the suppressed parent and suspended child.

> *Note: In the Assembly mode,* **Freeze** *can also be assigned when suppressing a parent component or feature. Freezing enables you to lock the item in its current location.*

Suppressed features can be restored to the display by selecting **Operations>Resume>Resume** in the *Model* tab. The following options are available to resume previously suppressed features:

* Resume

* Resume Last Set

* Resume All

If the suppressed feature is displayed in the Model Tree you can resume it by selecting it and selecting **Resume**. A selected item can also be resumed by selecting **Operations>Resume> Resume** in the *Model* tab. By default, all suppressed features are removed from the Model Tree display when they are suppressed.

> Note: *The* **Resume** *option is only available if a suppressed feature is selected in the Model Tree before you select* **Operations>Resume>Resume**.

To display the suppressed features, click ⦂▾ (Tree Filters) and select **General>Suppressed** in the *Items by State* area in the *Tree Filters* dialog box. Suppressed features are displayed in the Model Tree with a black dot, as shown in Figure 7−7.

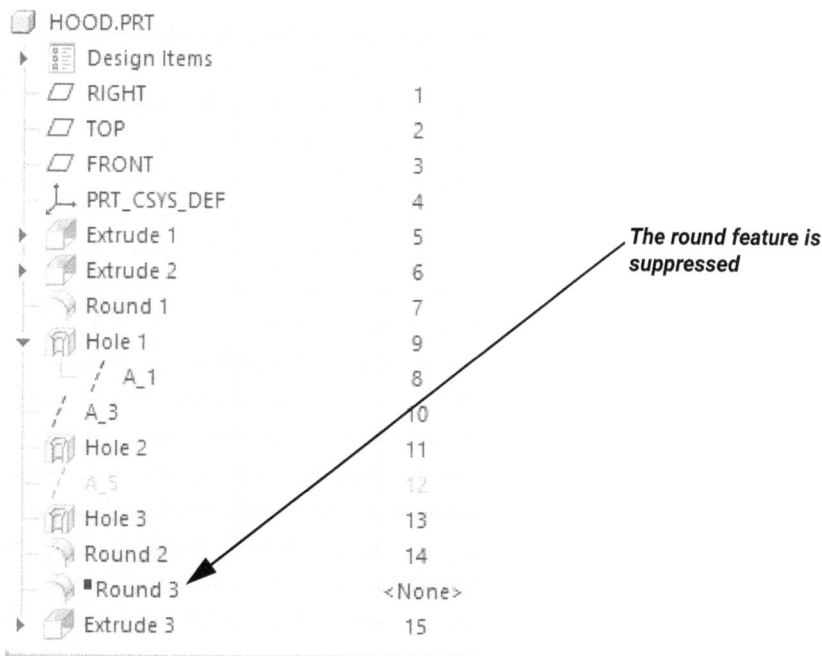

Figure 7−7

> Note: *Resuming individual features using the* **Resume** *option can cause failures if the resumed feature references a feature that is still suppressed. Consider this when resuming individual features.*

The **Resume Last Set** option restores the last set of suppressed features, while the **Resume All** option restores all of the features that are currently suppressed in the model. If suppressed features are displayed in the Model Tree, they can be resumed by selecting them and clicking

⦂ (Resume).

7.3 Adding Layers

Layers enable you to organize model items (e.g., solid features, datum features, and components) in a model so that you can perform operations, such as displaying or hiding them collectively. A layer can contain any number of features and components, and any one item can exist on more than one layer. For example, several datum features could be placed together on a layer, and then be hidden. All other datum features would still be visible.

- Similar to hiding features, only the datum feature associated with a solid feature is removed from the display and the solid geometry remains.

- All Layer information can be found in the Layer Tree. To access the Layer Tree, click ⬚ (Layer Tree) in the *View* tab or click ⬚ (Layer Tree) in the Model Tree. Depending on the size of the Navigator window the ″ (Expand) arrows may need to be selected to show the Layer Tree icon. The Layer Tree will be added under the Model Tree, as shown in Figure 7−8.

Figure 7−8

Note: The Layer Tree can be moved from its default position under the Model Tree by selecting the Layer Tree icon ▦ (Layer Tree) at the header, and dragging it to a new screen position. It can be left floating on the screen or can be docked to one of the sides of the Creo interface.

- By default, all models created using the default template contain default layers. These are set up to include the datum features (planes, axes, curves, points, and coordinate systems) and surfaces that are added to the model.

Creating Layers

To create a new layer, click ▤ (Layer Options) and select **New Layer** in the drop-down list. The *Layer Properties* dialog box opens, as shown in Figure 7–9.

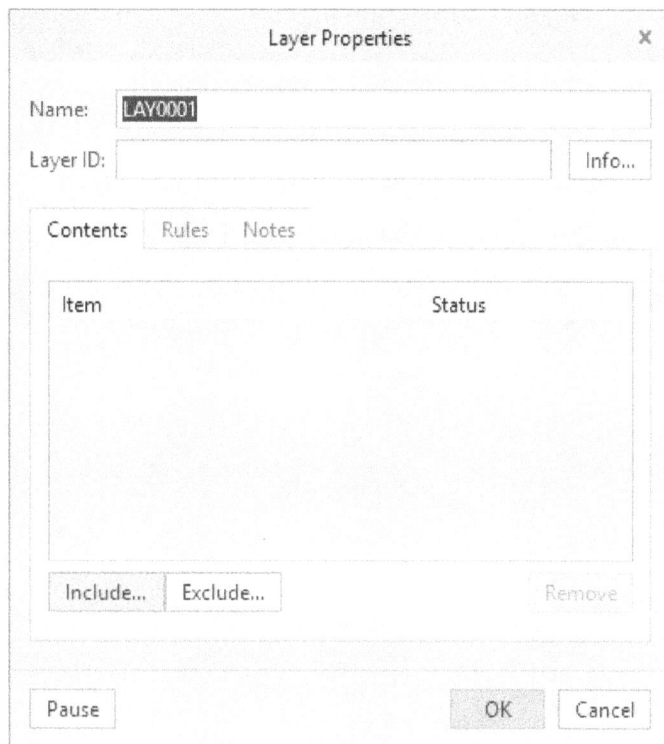

Layer Properties	×
Name: `LAY0001`	
Layer ID:	Info...
Contents Rules Notes	
Item	Status
Include... Exclude...	Remove
Pause	OK Cancel

Figure 7–9

The default name of a new layer is LAY#, where # represents the number of layers that are created in the model. For example, the first layer that is created in the model is by default called LAY0001. It is recommended that you replace this name with one that describes the contents of the layer. Layer names can be numeric or alphanumeric, with a maximum of 31 characters. Names cannot consist of special characters (i.e., !, %, or &) or spaces. If a space is required, consider using an underscore (_).

Select features or components in the Model Tree or directly on the model to populate the layer. The *Layer Properties* dialog box opens, as shown in Figure 7-10, with all of the items listed in the *Contents* tab. Click **Include** to add items to the layer. Once added, the status updates to display ✛. Click **Exclude** to exclude an item from the layer without actually removing it. Once removed, the status updates to ▬.

> *Note: You can use the selection filter at the bottom of the main window to help select the correct item on the model.*

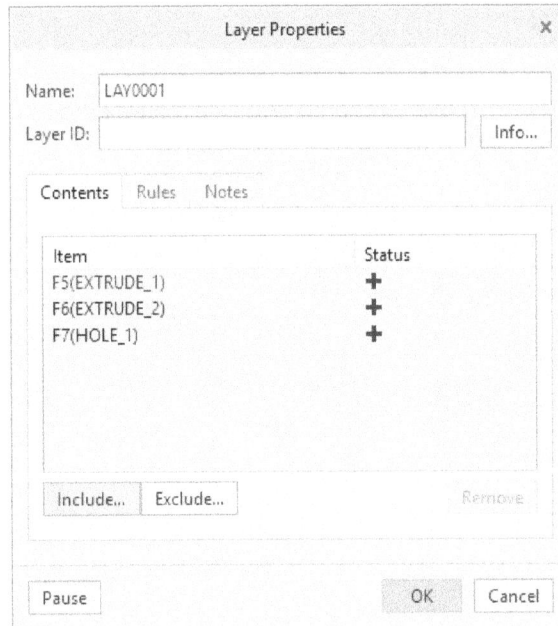

Figure 7-10

> *Note: Clicking **Pause** enables you to pause the selection of items without closing the Layer Properties dialog box. This button is useful if you want to review features before adding them to the layer.*

To remove an item from the layer, select it in the *Contents* tab in the dialog box and click **Remove**. To complete adding items to the layer, click **OK**.

Setting Layer Display

The display status of a layer can include the following settings:

* Hide

* Show

* Isolate

Hide

The Hide status removes items in the layer from the display. To set the Hide status, select a layer in the Layer Tree, right-click, and select **Hide**. Another method is to select the layer, click

⊟ (Layer Options) in the Layer Tree and select **Hide**.

When hiding layers in a part, only the datum items in the layer are hidden. If you must remove a solid feature from the display, consider using the **Suppress** option. When hiding layers in an assembly, the solid components placed on a layer are hidden.

Show

The **Show** status sets all items on the layer to be visible. This is the default display status for all new layers.

Isolate

The Isolate status enables you to show the items on the isolated layers, while all other layers

are hidden. To set the display status of a layer to **Isolate**, click ⊟ (Layer Options) and select **Isolate** in the drop-down list.

To display the current display status of a layer, right-click and select **Layer Info**. The *Information* window for the selected layer opens, as shown in Figure 7−11.

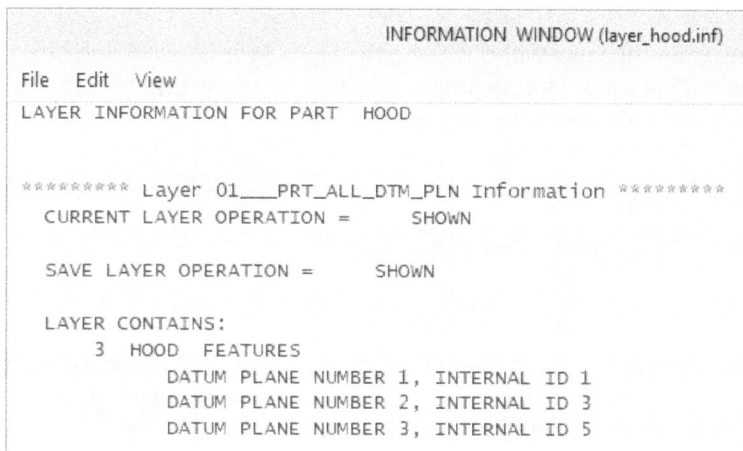

```
                          INFORMATION  WINDOW (layer_hood.inf)

File   Edit   View
LAYER INFORMATION FOR PART   HOOD


********* Layer 01___PRT_ALL_DTM_PLN Information *********
   CURRENT LAYER OPERATION =      SHOWN

   SAVE LAYER OPERATION =      SHOWN

   LAYER CONTAINS:
       3   HOOD   FEATURES
              DATUM PLANE NUMBER 1, INTERNAL ID 1
              DATUM PLANE NUMBER 2, INTERNAL ID 3
              DATUM PLANE NUMBER 3, INTERNAL ID 5
```

Figure 7−11

The following two lines in the Information window identify the layer's display status:

* Current Layer Operation

* Save Layer Operation

The *Current Layer Operation* line identifies the display status of the layer in the current session of Creo Parametric. The *Save Layer Operation* line identifies the saved status of the layer. The model always opens using the saved display status for each layer. To save the display status for all layers in the model, right-click and select **Save Status**. To reset the layer display status to that which was previously saved, right-click and select **Reset Status**. You can also click
 (Save Status) and (Reset Status) in the *Visibility* group in the *View* tab.

Modifying Layers

The following actions can be performed on a layer using the Layer Tree:

- Add items to a layer

- Remove items from a layer

- Delete a layer

- Copy and paste items between layers

To perform actions on a layer, the Layer Tree must be displayed. You can add and remove items by right-clicking in the Layer Tree. You can also use the original *Layer Properties* dialog box by right-clicking and selecting **Layer Properties**.

> *Note: To display the Layer Tree, click (Layer Tree) in the Visibility group in the View tab.*

To delete all items from the layer without using the *Layer Properties* dialog box, select the layer, right-click, and select the **Select Items** option to select all of the layer items. Right-click again and select **Remove Item**. All items on the layer are removed. However, the layer remains in the model. To delete an entire layer, select the layer, right-click, and select **Delete Layer**.

> *Note: To select multiple items in the Layer Tree, press and hold <Ctrl> while selecting the items. To select all items between two selected items, press and hold <Shift> while selecting the first and last items in the selection.*

Items from one layer can be copied and pasted to another layer using the options in the
 (Layer Operations) flyout or in the contextual menu. To copy an item, select it in the Layer Tree and select the **Copy** option. To paste an item, select the new layer and select the **Paste** option. The **Cut** option is also available.

Activate/Deactivate Layers

You can activate a layer by selecting it, right-clicking and selecting **Activate**. When you activate a layer, any newly created 3D elements are added to it. This can be a tremendous time saver over creating features and manually adding them to layers.

Remember to deactivate layers when you no longer want items automatically added to them. An active layer remains active for the duration of your session, unless you select it, right-click and select **Deactivate**.

Default Layers

Default layers, each containing a different type of feature, are created when you use the default template. A default layer automatically associates features of the same type to itself. Using default layers prevents you from having to manually add items to the layer once the feature has been created.

Figure 7–12 shows the default datum plane and default coordinate system layers as hidden, so the items that were automatically placed on those layers are removed from display.

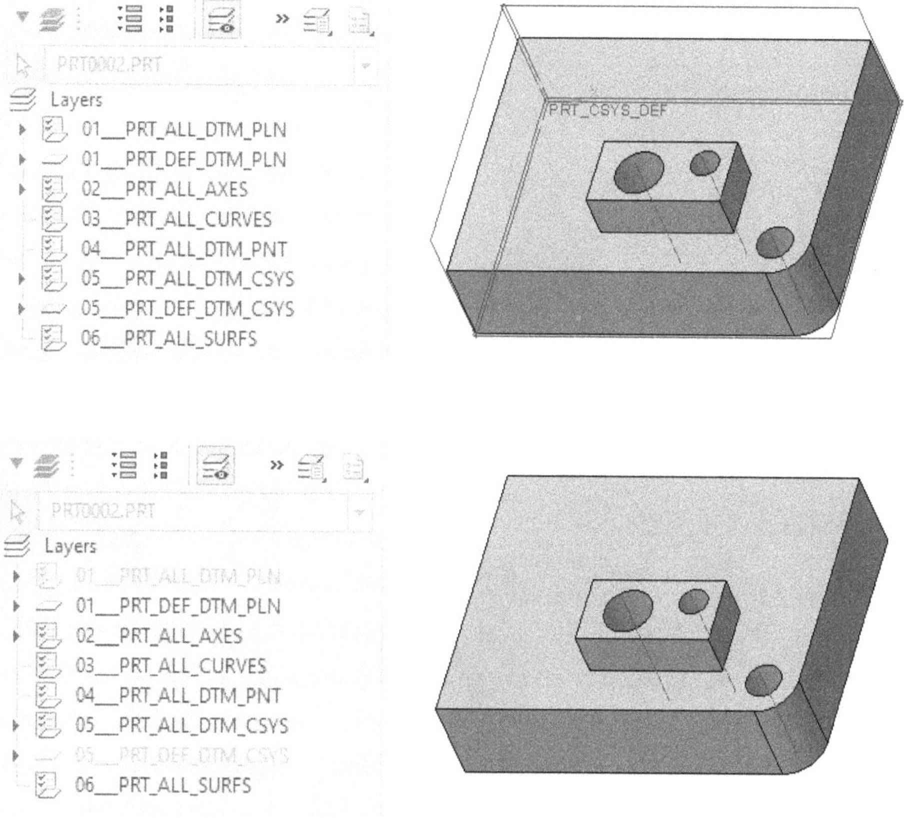

Figure 7–12

Layers as a Selection Tool

Layers can be used as a selection tool for feature operations. To select features, open the Layer Tree, select the layer(s), right-click, and select **Select Items**. You can then apply feature operations as you would had you selected the features directly.

7.4 Reordering Features

Models are regenerated in the order in which the features display in the Model Tree. In certain situations, the resulting geometry can vary greatly depending on the order of feature creation. The **Reorder** option can be used to rearrange the creation sequence of the features to achieve the required geometry.

To reorder features on your model, select the feature and drag and drop it directly in the Model Tree. Note that features cannot be reordered before their parent features. The examples in Figure 7−13 and Figure 7−14 show the use of the reorder tool.

A Shell feature leaves a wall thickness on all surfaces. Therefore, a hole becomes a pipe when a shell is applied to it.

Shell surfaces to remove

A wall thickness is applied to the remaining surfaces, including surfaces on the hole.

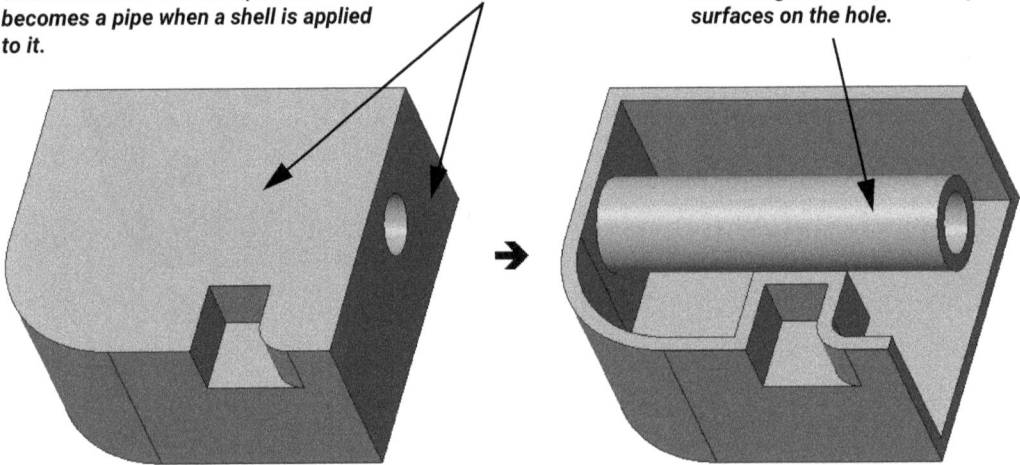

Figure 7−13

The shell is not applied to features that display after it in the feature list.

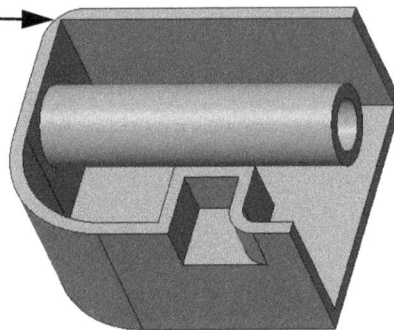

Figure 7−14

Note: A Round placed after a shell might not have the required results.

The reorder function can be used to rearrange the order in which features are regenerated. Figure 7–15 shows a part created with the feature sequence displayed in the Model Tree. Note that **Hole 1** displays before **Shell 1** in the Model Tree, because **Hole 1** is regenerated before **Shell 1**. The surfaces of the hole exist when the shell is created, so a thickness is applied to the hole surface.

The opposite is true for **Round 3**. It regenerates after the shell, so the shell does not apply a thickness to it.

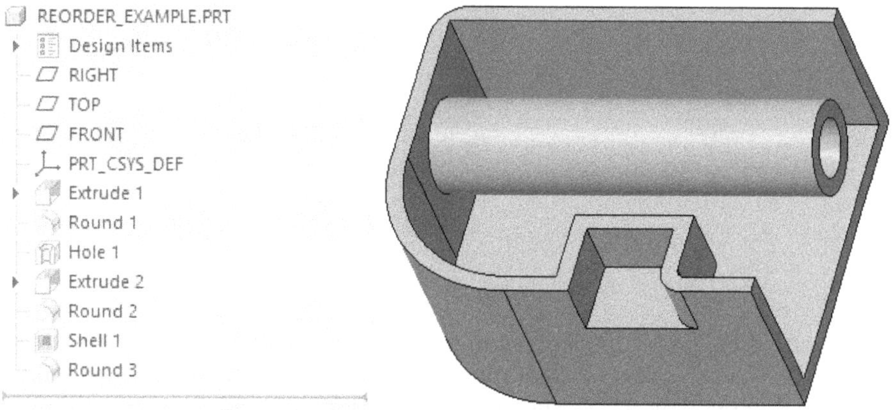

Figure 7–15

Reordering **Hole 1** after the shell, and **Round 3** before the shell, results in the part shown in Figure 7–16.

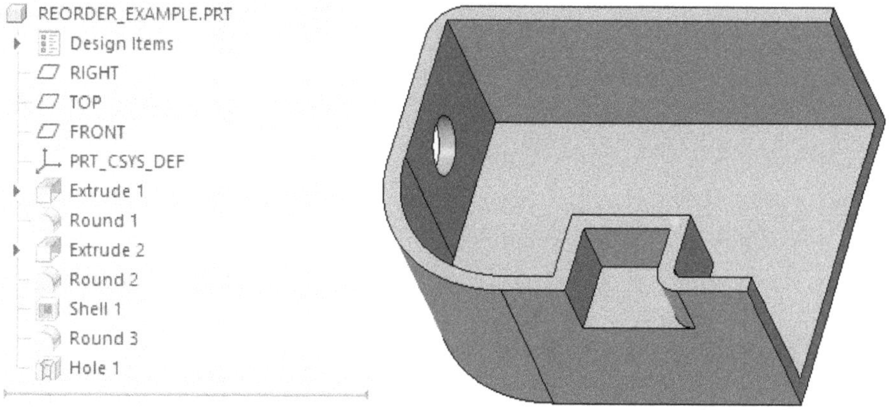

Figure 7–16

Complicated models might result in difficult parent/child relationships. If a feature depends on another feature for regeneration, a parent/child relationship exists. For example, if you create an extrusion and use an edge of the extrusion to create a round, the extrusion is a parent of the round. You cannot reorder the round to come before the extrusion.

In addition, although you may want to reorder a single feature, it is sometimes required to also reorder children of that feature. In Figure 7-17, **Round 2** is created on the edge of **Extrude 2**. To reorder **Extrude 2** and make it come later in the regeneration sequence, you would have to move the round as well.

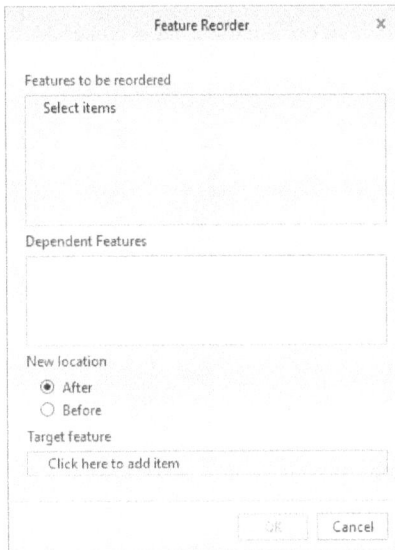

Figure 7-17

When you drag and drop to reorder, it can sometime not be obvious that additional features are also being moved. You can click the **Operations** option in the *Model* tab and select **Reorder** to open the *Feature Reorder* dialog box, shown in Figure 7-18.

Select the feature you want to reorder, select the new location as **After** or **Before**, and select the *Target feature*. Any dependent features that have to be moved will be listed in the *Dependent Features* area, as shown in Figure 7-19.

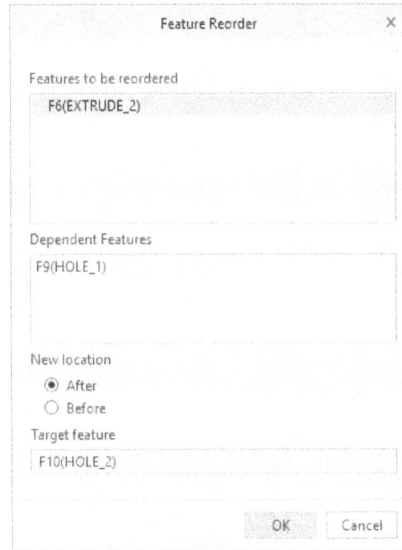

Figure 7-18   Figure 7-19

7.5 Inserting Features

When features are added to a model, they are added by default at the end of the feature list. Insert Mode is used to insert new features between existing features.

Insert Mode can be used in situations in which a design change occurs and you would like to create a feature earlier in the design process. It *rolls back* the model to the location in which you want to place the feature. This ensures that you only use references that exist at that point in the model. On occasion, features might abort during creation due to existing features on the part. In these cases, Insert Mode might enable the feature to be created.

To activate Insert Mode, click and drag the green line at the bottom of the Model Tree to the location at which you want to insert a feature(s). Figure 7–20 shows a model and its Model Tree before inserting a feature.

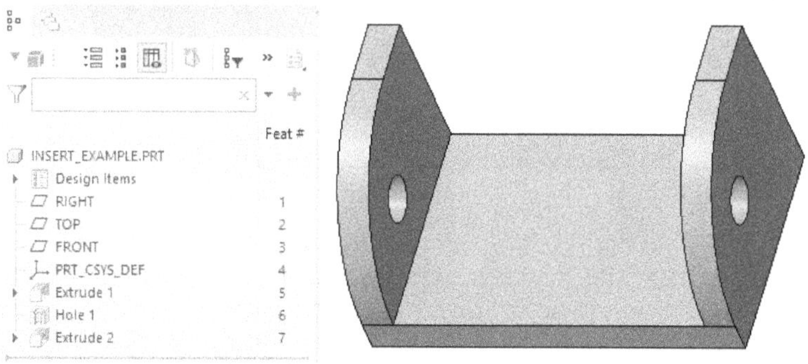

Figure 7–20

Figure 7–21 shows the model and its Model Tree once the green line has been moved. Note that the system temporarily suppresses any features that regenerate after the insertion point.

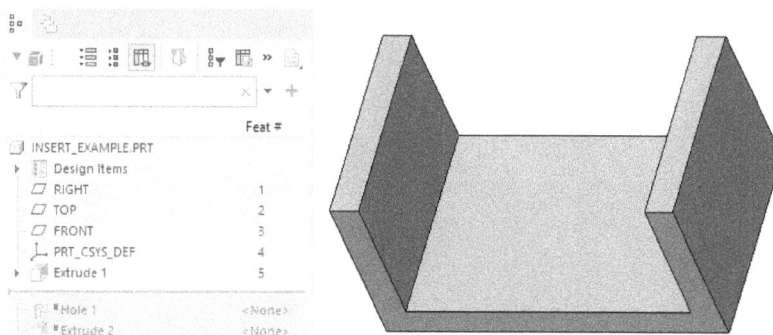

Figure 7–21

Note: Once the green line has been moved, the part is rolled back to the point at which you are inserting a feature.

Once the green line has been moved to the required location in the Model Tree, you can start using the standard feature creation tools to insert one or more features. An extruded protrusion has been added to the model, as shown in Figure 7-22.

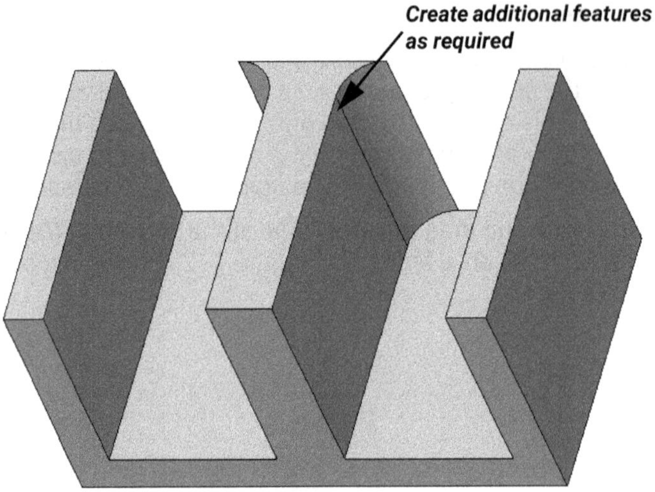

Create additional features as required

Figure 7-22

When you have finished inserting features, select and drag the green line back to the bottom of the feature list, or right-click it and select **Exit Insert Mode**. Click **Yes** when prompted to resume suppressed features. All of the features are then regenerated, as shown in Figure 7-23.

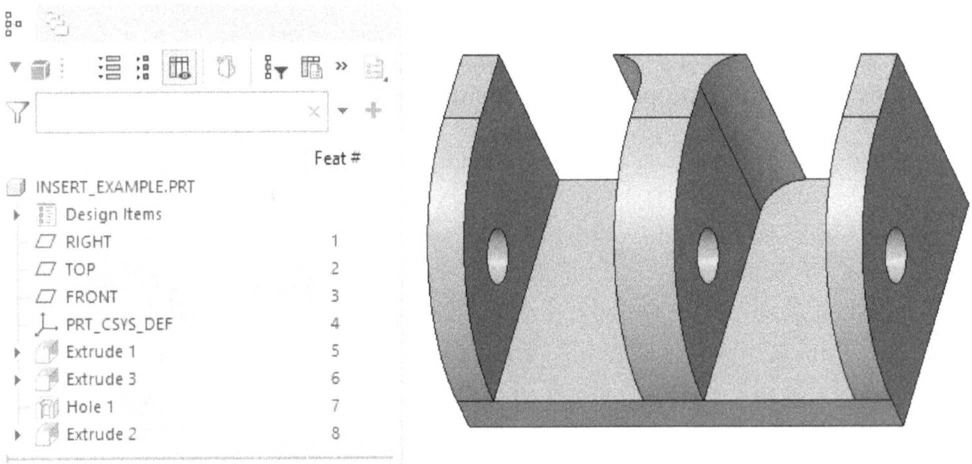

Figure 7-23

*Note: The same result could be accomplished by creating the extrude and then reordering it, but using **Insert Mode** can help reduce inadvertent parent/child relationships by temporarily removing features you might accidentally reference.*

Practice 7a
Feature Order

Practice Objective

- Change the order of features in the Model Tree to obtain required geometry.

In this practice, you will explore the impact of the feature order on part geometry. You will create the switch plate part shown in Figure 7–24 with limited instructions. Once complete, you will reorder two holes, an extrude, and a shell feature.

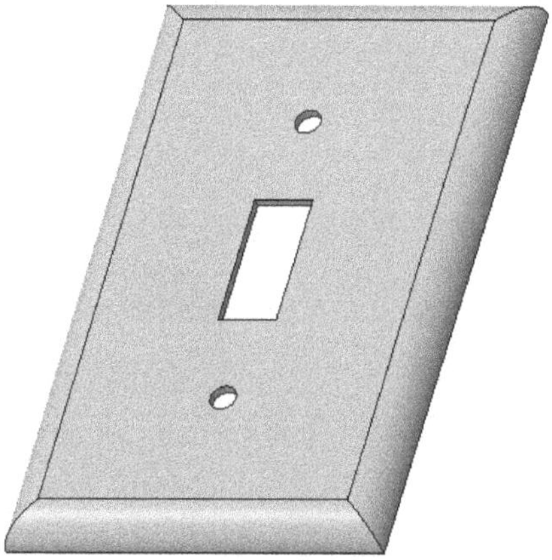

Figure 7–24

Task 1: Create a new part.

1. Set the working directory to the *Feature_Order* folder.
2. Create a new part and set the *Name* to **switch_plate**.
3. Set the model display as follows:

   - *(Datum Display Filters)*: All Off
   - *(Spin Center)*: Off
   - *(Display Style)*: ☐ (Shading With Edges)

4. Create an extruded feature using the sketch shown in Figure 7−25 using datum **TOP** as the sketch plane.

5. Edit the depth to **0.25**, as shown in Figure 7−26.

Figure 7−25

Figure 7−26

Task 2: Create a hole.

1. In the *In-graphics* toolbar, click ⁺⁄ₓ (Datum Display Filters) and enable ◿ (Plane Display).

2. Create a hole in the location shown in Figure 7−27 and set the following:

- *Diameter:* **0.188**
- *Offset* from datum **FRONT: 1.150**
- Align to datum **RIGHT**
- *Depth:* ⌐ ⌐ (Through All)

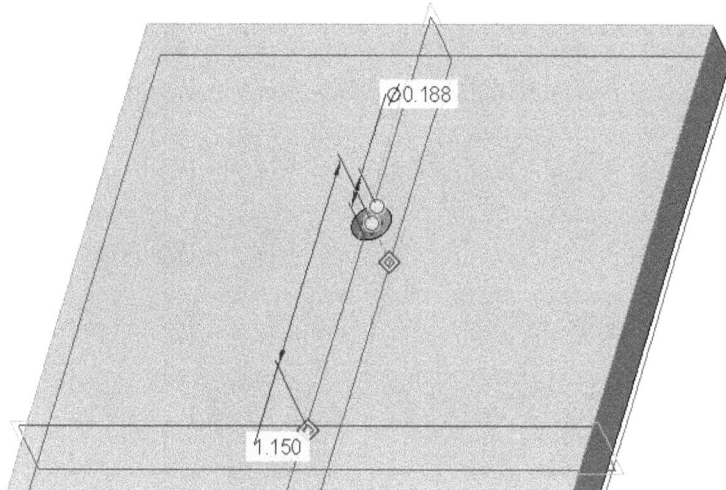

Figure 7–27

Task 3: Create a second hole.

1. Create a second hole as shown in Figure 7–28, using the same references and dimensional values as the previous hole.

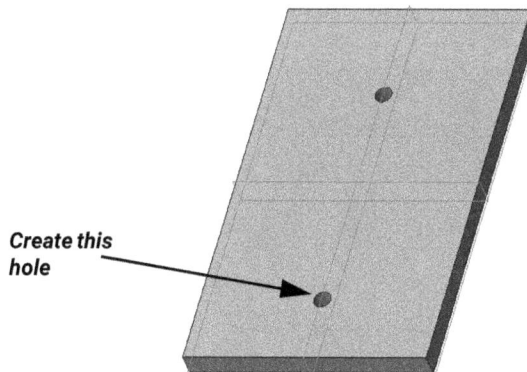

Create this hole

Figure 7–28

2. Click ⚝ (Datum Display Filters) and disable ⬜ (Plane Display).

Task 4: Create a round.

1. Create a round with a *Radius* of **0.25**, on the four edges shown in Figure 7–29.

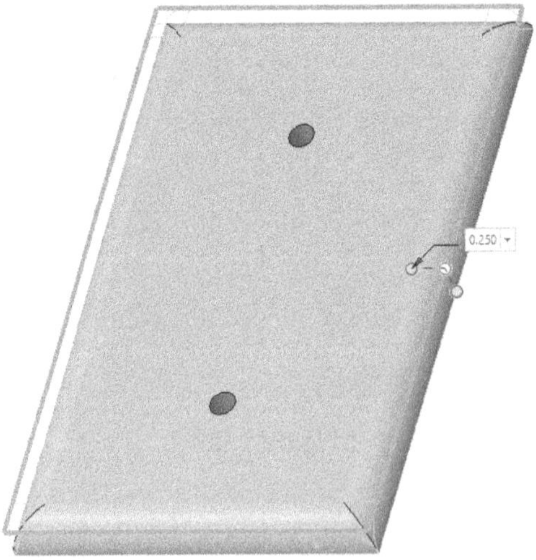

Figure 7–29

Task 5: Shell the part.

1. Shell the part by selecting the surface shown in Figure 7–30 and then clicking ▦ (Shell).

2. Edit the thickness to **0.063**, and then click ✔ (**OK**).

3. Once the shell is complete, the part displays, as shown in Figure 7–31.

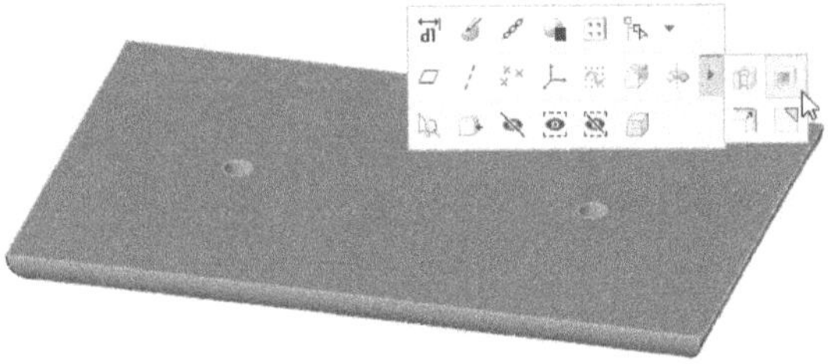

Figure 7–30

Figure 7–31

Task 6: Create an extruded cut.

1. Create an extrude using the surface shown in Figure 7−32 as the sketch plane.

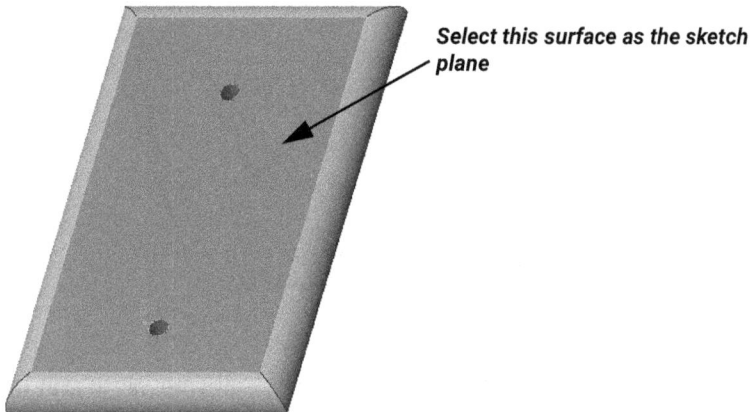

Select this surface as the sketch plane

Figure 7−32

2. Sketch and dimension the section shown in Figure 7−33.

3. Extrude the sketch to cut through the part. The part should display, as shown in Figure 7−34.

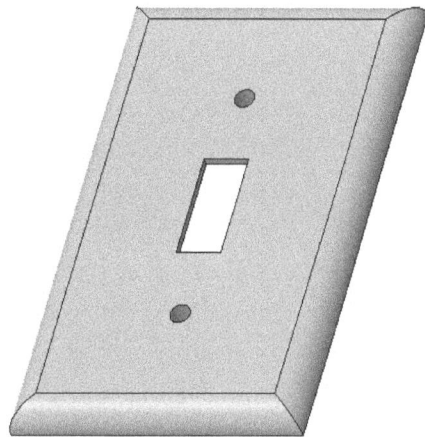

Figure 7−33   **Figure 7−34**

Task 7: Reorder features.

1. Ensure that the part is oriented as shown in Figure 7–35.

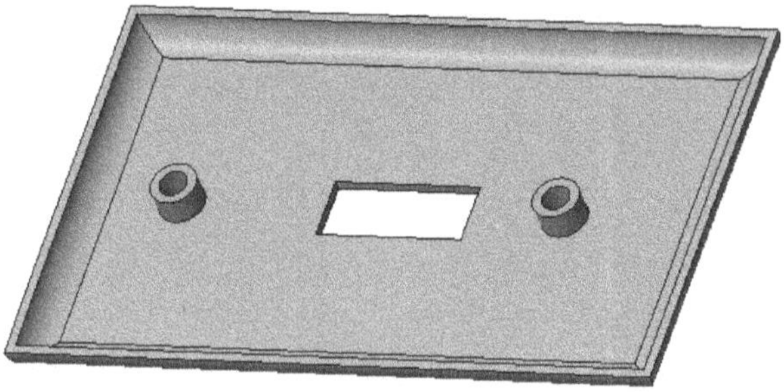

Figure 7–35

2. Note the order in which the features are listed in the Model Tree. Note that the **Shell 1** feature comes before the **Extrude 2** feature, as shown in Figure 7–36.

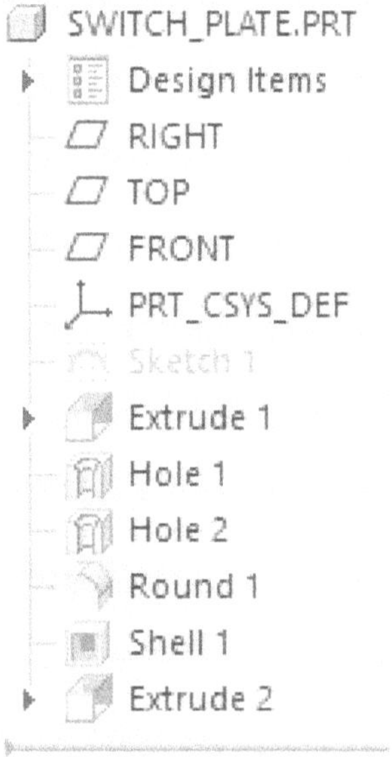

Figure 7–36

3. Select **Shell 1** from the Model Tree and drag it below **Extrude 2,** as shown in Figure 7–37.

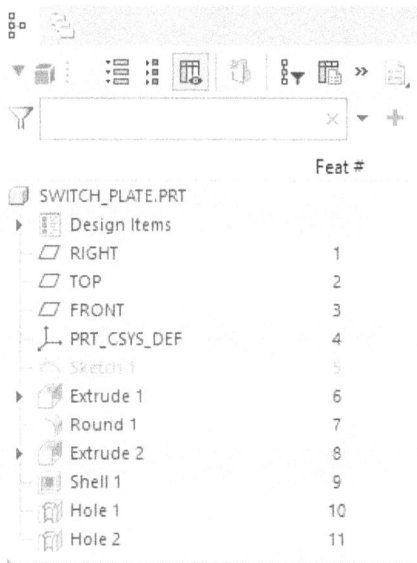

Drag the shell to bottom of the
feature list

Figure 7–37

4. Hold <Ctrl>, select the two holes, and drag them to after the shell to obtain the geometry shown in Figure 7–38.

Figure 7–38

5. Make the appropriate changes to obtain the geometry shown in Figure 7–39.

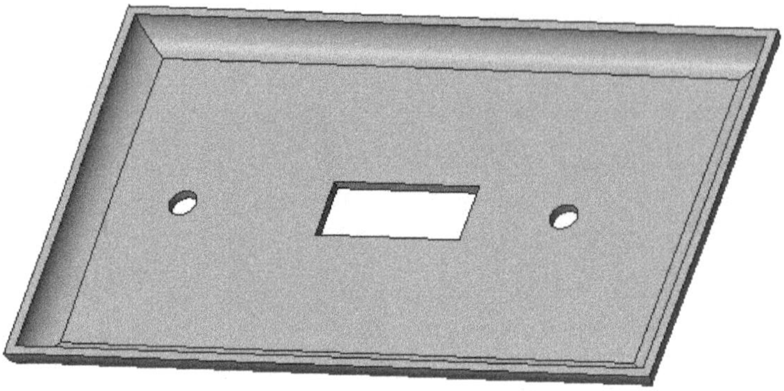

Figure 7–39

6. Save the part and erase it from memory.

End of practice

Practice 7b
Insert Mode

Practice Objective

*   Insert a new feature at a point other than the end of the feature list using the **Insert Here** arrow.

In this practice, you will use Insert Mode to insert an auto round into the feature list. When an auto round is created, a round is created on all edges of a part, except for the ones that are excluded by user input. The design intent of this part includes adding rounds to all edges (except excluded edges) that are on the outside of the part. Rounds are not required on any of the edges of the internal geometry. Insert Mode will be used to achieve this design intent.

Task 1: Open a part file.

1. Set the working directory to the *Insert_Mode* folder.
2. Open **hydrant.prt**.
3. Set the model display as follows:

    *   *(Datum Display Filters)*: All Off

    *   *(Spin Center)*: Off

    *   *(Display Style)*: (Shading With Edges)

Task 2: Investigate the part.

1. Orient the part to display the internal geometry, as shown in Figure 7-40.

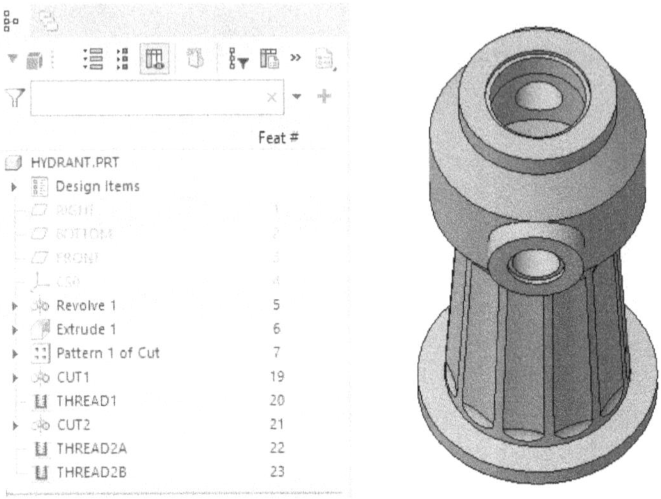

Figure 7-40

Task 3: Activate Insert Mode.

1. In the Model Tree, click the green line and drag and drop it after **Pattern 1 of Cut**, as shown in Figure 7-41.

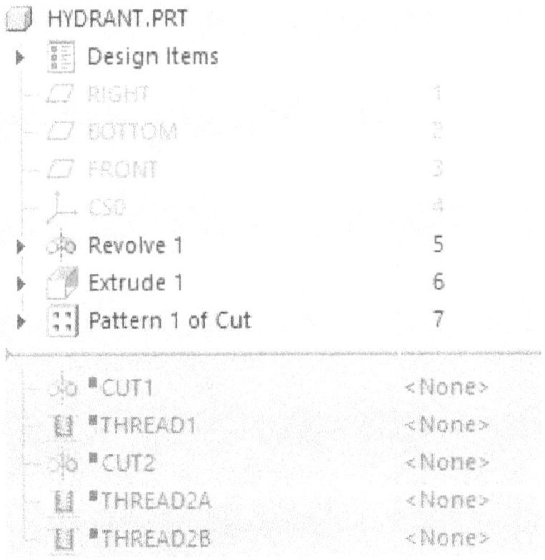

Figure 7-41

Task 4: Create an auto round feature.

1. In the *Engineering* group, click the (Round) fly-out and select (Auto Round).

2. In the *Auto Round* tab, for the convex edges, set the *Radius* to **20.0**. For the concave edges, select **Same**.

3. Exclude the four edges shown in Figure 7−42.

Figure 7−42

4. Click (**OK**) to complete the feature. The completed model displays, as shown in Figure 7−43.

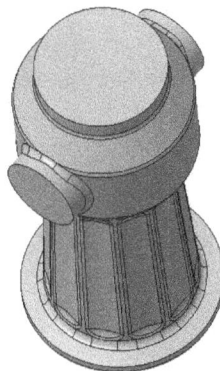

Figure 7−43

Note: It may take some time to regenerate.

Task 5: Deactivate Insert Mode.

1. In the Model Tree, click the green **Insert Here** line and drag and drop it at the bottom of the feature list, as shown in Figure 7–44.

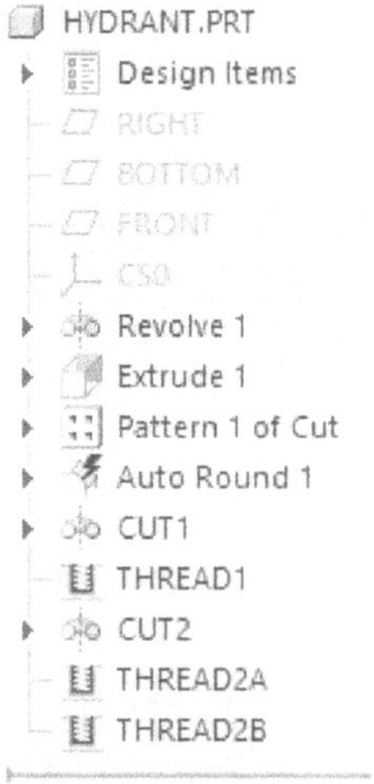

Figure 7–44

The completed model displays, as shown in Figure 7–45. Note that the internal geometry has not been affected by the auto round.

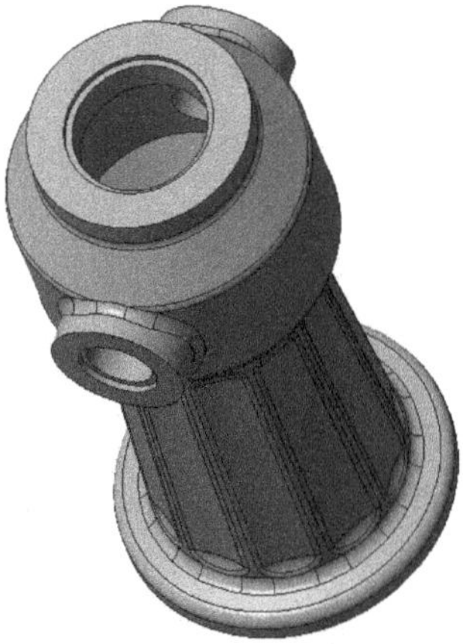

Figure 7–45

2. Save the model and erase it from memory.

End of practice

Practice 7c
Feature Management

Practice Objectives

- Temporarily hide a datum plane and a hole from being included as part of the model geometry.
- Temporarily remove features and their children from being included as part of the model geometry and regeneration sequence.

In this practice, you will open an existing model and use the **Hide**, **Suppress**, and **Layers** tools to control the display of features in the model. You will learn how to switch between the Model Tree and Layer Tree by hiding and unhiding geometry using layers. You will also, specify the display options to a newly created layer. The complete model is shown in Figure 7–46.

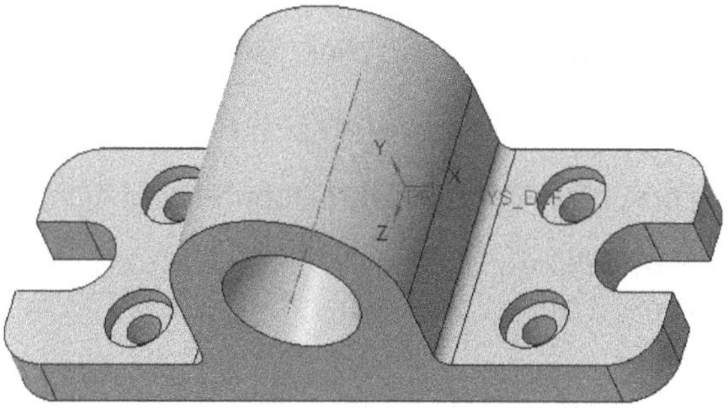

Figure 7–46

Task 1: Open a part file.

1. Set the working directory to the *Feature_Management* folder.
2. Open **chamber.prt**.
3. Set the model display as follows:

- *(Datum Display Filters)*: All On
- *(Spin Center)*: Off
- *(Display Style)*: (Shading With Edges)

Task 2: Hide DTM1 from the display.

1. Select **DTM1** from the Model Tree or directly on the model.
2. Select (Hide) in the *mini* toolbar. The datum plane is removed from the display.

Note: You can also select the View tab and click ✎ (Hide) in the Visibility group.

3. Select **HOLE** in the Model Tree and click ✎ (Hide) in the *mini* toolbar. The datum axis in that hole is removed from the display. However, the solid feature remains displayed.

4. Select **HOLE** from the Model Tree and click ◉ (Show) in the *mini* toolbar. Its axis displays on the model again.

The ✎ (Hide) option enables you to remove datum features from the display without using the datum feature display icons that affect all like features. The ✎ (Hide) option cannot be used to control the display of solid geometry in parts.

Note: You can also select the View tab to access the **Show** and **Unhide All** icons.

Task 3: Suppress all features except for the base feature and rounds.

1. Select **NOTCH** (shown in Figure 7–47) and click ◼ (Suppress) in the *mini* toolbar.

   Note: You can also select **Operations>Suppress>Suppress** in the Model tab.

2. In the *Suppress* dialog box, click **OK** to confirm suppressing the cut.

   Note: You can click **Edit Details>>** and suspend children. Suspending enables you to retain the feature. However, it cannot be regenerated because its parent is missing. You can edit the feature to remove parent/child relationships.

3. Select **HOLE** (shown in Figure 7–47) and click ◼ (Suppress) in the *mini* toolbar. A *Suppress* dialog box opens prompting you to confirm suppression of all highlighted features. The highlighted features are all children of **HOLE**. To suppress this feature you must deal with the children.

4. Click **OK** to suppress the hole and its children.

5. Suppress **SLOT**, shown in Figure 7–47, and all of its children. The model, with its non-hidden datum features, displays, as shown in Figure 7–48.

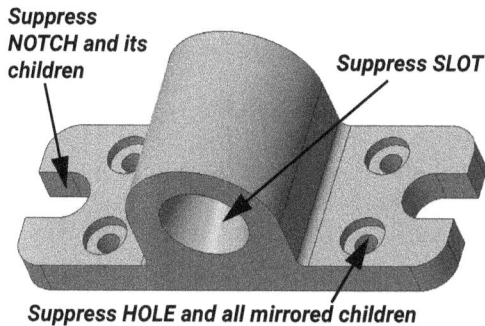

Suppress NOTCH and its children

Suppress SLOT

Suppress HOLE and all mirrored children

Figure 7–47

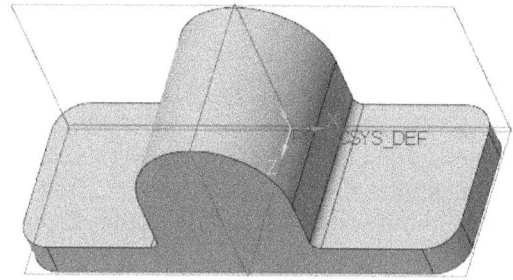

Figure 7–48

Task 4: Review the feature list of the part.

1. Select the *Tools* tab in the *Investigate* group and click ⬛ (Feature List). The *Feature List* displays in the Creo Parametric Browser window listing all of the features in the model, including those that have been suppressed, as shown in Figure 7–49.

   Note: Suppressed features are easily identified in the Status column in the Browser, which lists the features as Suppressed rather than Regenerated. Suppressed features do not have a feature number because they have been removed from the regeneration list.

Click ✕ to close the Browser window

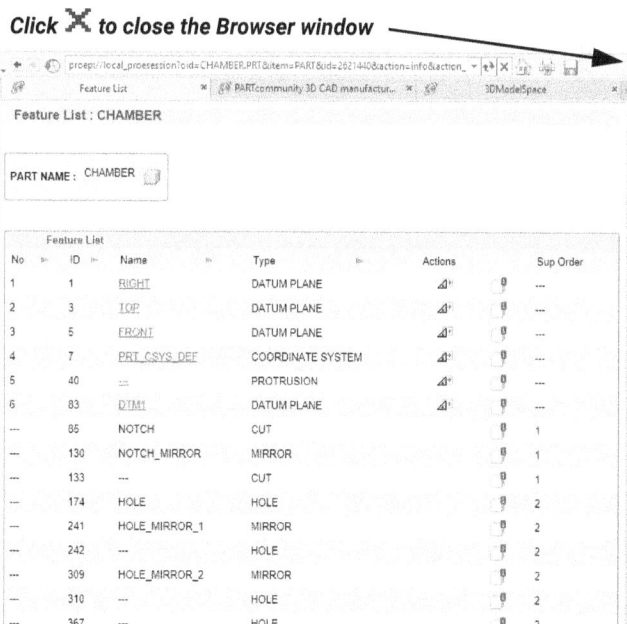

Figure 7–49

2. Close the Browser window.

Task 5: Attempt to suppress datum plane FRONT.

1. Select datum plane **FRONT** and click ⬛ (Suppress) in the *mini* toolbar. The base feature and all subsequent features highlight on the model and in the Model Tree because they are children of datum plane **FRONT**. If you suppress this datum you also have to suppress or suspend all of the additional features. Suspending these features would not be recommended because it would require extensive work to reroute the parent/child references.

2. In the *Suppress* dialog box, click **Cancel**.

    If datum plane **FRONT** must be removed from the display, consider using the ⬚ (Hide) option or adding the datum plane to a layer and hiding the layer.

Task 6: Show all of the suppressed features in the Model Tree.

1. Select ⬚▼ (Tree Filters) in the Model tree, and the *Tree Filters* dialog box opens.

    Note: By default, all suppressed features are removed from the Model Tree display.

2. Within the **General** category, select **Suppressed**. To ensure that they are enabled, then click **OK**. The Model Tree updates and displays all of the suppressed features. The suppressed features are identified by ⬛ next to their names.

Task 7: Resume all the features.

1. In the Model Tree, select **HOLE** and click ⬗ (Resume) in the *mini* toolbar to resume the suppressed feature.

2. Resume the **HOLE_MIRROR_#** features.

3. Select the *Model* tab. Select **Operations>Resume>Resume Last Set**. This resumes the last feature or group of features that were suppressed. In this case it resumes **SLOT**.

4. Select **Operations>Resume>Resume All** to resume the remaining suppressed features.

    Note: You must select the suppressed features in the Model Tree to access the Operations>Resume>Resume option.

Task 8: Hide a layer.

1. In the Model Tree, click ⬚ (Layer Tree). Depending on the width of the navigator window, you may need to drag the side of the navigator window to make it larger or select

   " (Expand) in the model tree to be able to see the **Layer Tree** option.

2. In the Layer Tree, select **01_PRT_DEF_DTM_PLN**.

3. Right-click and select **Hide**. All of the default datum planes (**RIGHT**, **TOP**, and **FRONT**) are hidden. Click anywhere in the main window to repaint the screen.

4. Note that the **RIGHT**, **TOP**, and **FRONT** datum planes are grayed out, indicating that they are hidden, as shown in Figure 7–50.

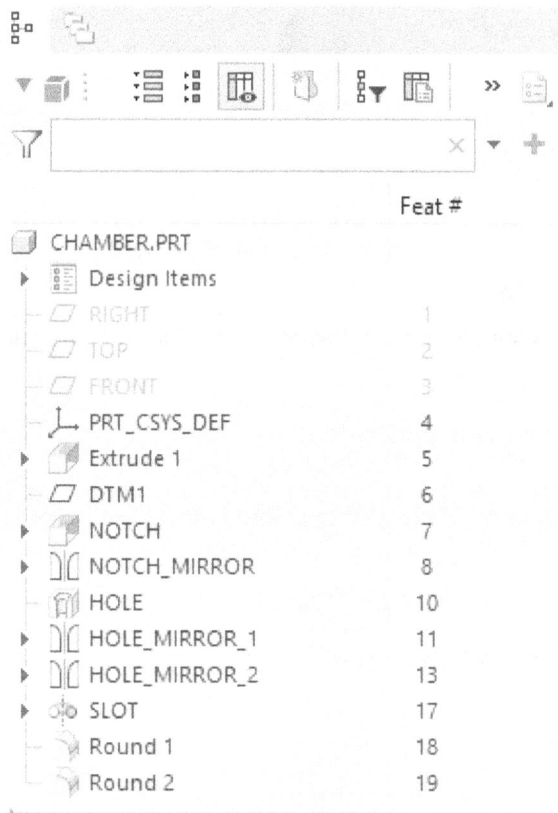

Figure 7–50

Note: The Hide/Show status of objects is reflected consistently between Layer Tree and Model Tree.

5. Show **DTM1**. This datum plane is not a default datum plane and was therefore not hidden from the display when you hid the default datum plane layer. The model displays, as shown in Figure 7−51.

Figure 7−51

Task 9: Show a layer.

1. In the Layer Tree, select the **01_PRT_DEF_DTM_PLN** layer.

2. Right-click and select **Show**.

3. Click on the screen to update the display. All of the datum planes are now displayed on the model.

Task 10: Create a new layer and hide it.

1. In the layer tree, Expand ▤ (Layer Options) and select **New Layer**. The *Layer Properties* dialog box opens.

   *Note: You can also right-click and select **New Layer**.*

2. Set the *Name* to **mounting_holes**. DO NOT press <Enter>.

3. Set the selection filter to **Feature** to select the hole features. The selection filter is located at the bottom right of the window as shown in Figure 7–52.

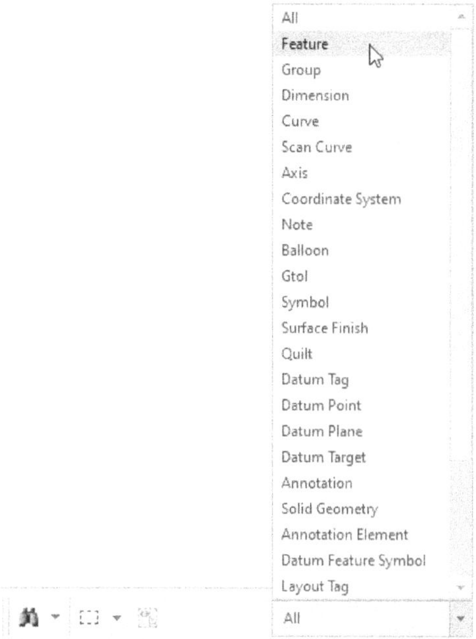

All
Feature
Group
Dimension
Curve
Scan Curve
Axis
Coordinate System
Note
Balloon
Gtol
Symbol
Surface Finish
Quilt
Datum Tag
Datum Point
Datum Plane
Datum Target
Annotation
Solid Geometry
Annotation Element
Datum Feature Symbol
Layout Tag
All

Figure 7–52

4. Select the four countersunk holes. The contents of the layer update in the *Layer Properties* dialog box, as shown in Figure 7–53.

Layer Properties
Name: mounting_holes
Layer ID:
Info...
Contents
Rules
Notes
Item
Status
F10(HOLE)
F12(HOLE_1)
F14(HOLE_2)
F15(HOLE_3)
Include...
Exclude...
Remove
Pause
OK
Cancel

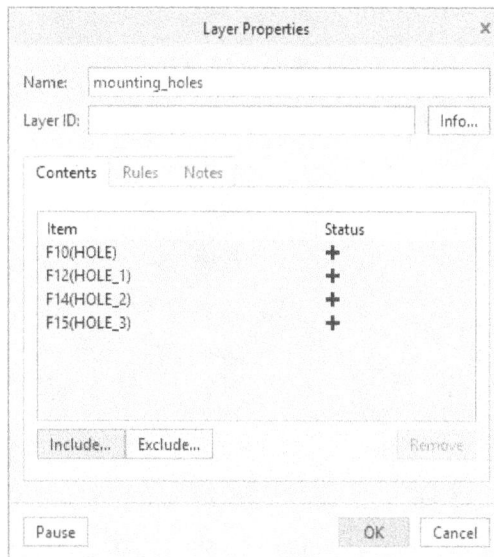

Figure 7–53

5. Click **OK** to close the *Layer Properties* dialog box.

6. In the Layer Tree, select the **MOUNTING_HOLES** layer. Right-click and select **Hide**.

   Note: The axes are removed from display, but the features are not. Hiding features does not hide solid geometry.

7. Click on the screen to update the display. The axes of the four countersunk sketched holes are hidden, as shown in Figure 7–54.

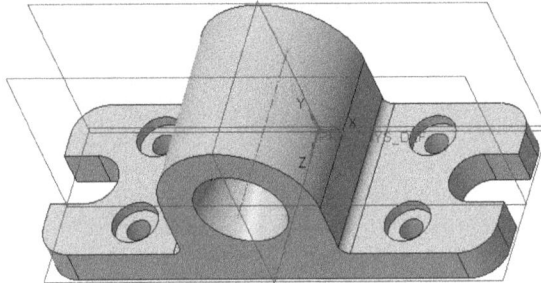

Figure 7–54

Task 11: Isolate the MOUNTING_HOLES layer.

Note: The Isolate option is helpful when you are using several layers and you only need a few of them to be visible. The isolated layers are shown and all others are automatically hidden.

1. Select the **MOUNTING_HOLES** layer.

2. Expand ⬚ (Layer Options) and select **Isolate** to change the layer status to isolate. The part displays, as shown in Figure 7–55. Note that the only datum entities now visible are the axes in the counterbore holes.

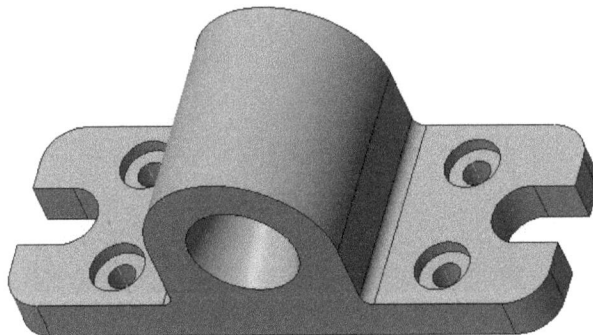

Figure 7–55

Task 12: Create a layer for defeaturing the model.

Design Considerations

When conducting a finite element analysis, it is common practice to simplify the model by temporarily removing machined features such as rounds and holes. Create a layer for defeaturing the model.

1. Right-click in the Layer Tree and select **Reset Status**.
2. Right-click in the Layer Tree and select **New Layer**.
3. Set the layer *Name* to **Defeature** but do not press <Enter>.
4. Set the *Selection Feature* to **Feature**.
5. Select the four counterbore holes and the two round features, as shown in Figure 7–56.

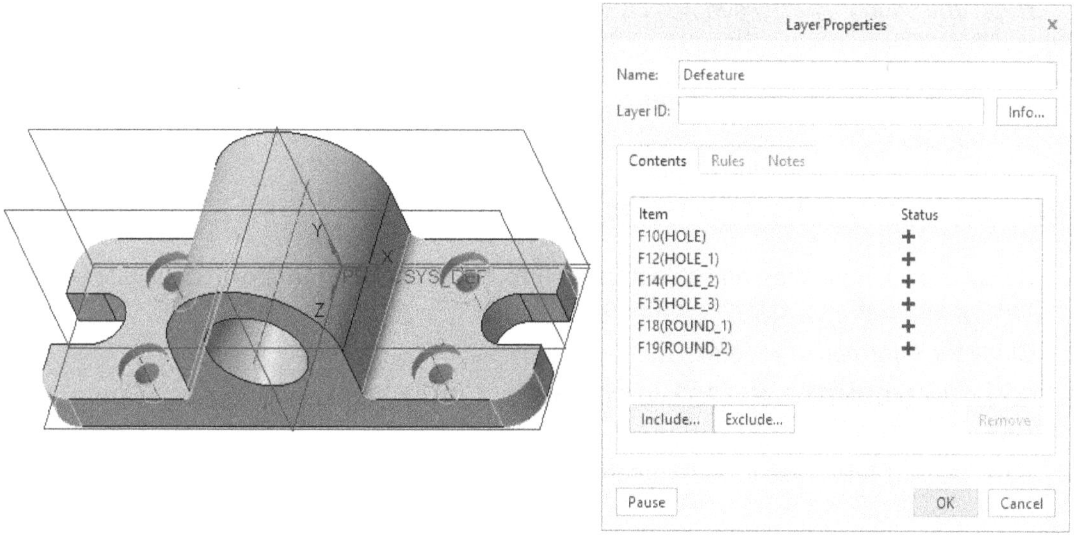

Figure 7–56

6. Click **OK**.
7. Right-click on the **DEFEATURE** layer and select **Select Items**.

8. Right-click in the main window, select ▪ (Suppress), and click **OK** in the *Suppress* dialog box. The model displays as shown in Figure 7–57.

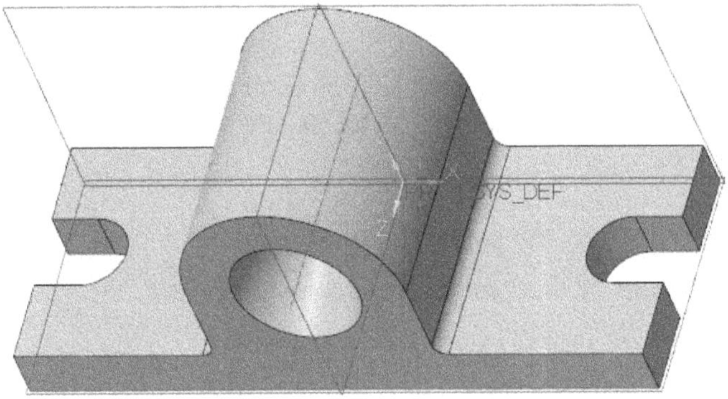

Figure 7–57

Note: You cannot directly suppress a layer, but it can be used to quickly select features which can then be suppressed.

9. Use the layer to select the features again, right-click in the main window, and select ◈ (Resume).

Task 13: Obtain information on the layers.

1. Select a layer, right-click, and select **Layer Info**. An Information window opens displaying the layer operation and layer contents.

2. Close the *Information* window.

3. Select the **MOUNTING_HOLES** and **01_PRT_ALL_DTM_PLN** layers, right-click, and select **Hide**.

4. Save the part and erase it from memory.

Task 14: Open and investigate the model display status.

1. Open **chamber.prt**. Note that the layer settings that were set before saving the part have been lost.

   *Note: Layer information is saved with the part, but the layer display status is only saved if the **Save Status** option is selected.*

2. If needed click ≡ (Layer Tree) to display the Layer Tree.

3. Select the **MOUNTING_HOLES** and **01__PRT_ALL_DTM_PLN** layers, right-click, and select **Hide**.

4. Right-click and select **Save Status** to save the display status of the layer with the part.

5. Save the part and erase it from memory.

6. Open **chamber.prt**. Note that the layer settings that were set before saving the part have been retained in the model, as shown in Figure 7–58.

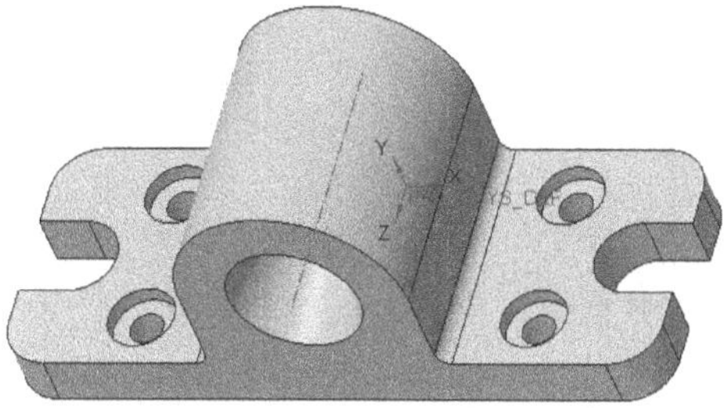

Figure 7–58

7. Close the part and erase it from memory.

End of practice

Chapter Review Questions

1. Parent/child relationships do not affect the children of hidden parents.

   a. True

   b. False

2. The easiest technique for simplifying a model's display is to use the ✎ (Hide) option. Which of the following statements are true regarding hiding a feature in a model? (Select all that apply.)

   a. When you hide a feature, it remains in the Model Tree.

   b. When you hide a feature, it continues to regenerate.

   c. When you hide a feature, solid geometry remains visible.

   d. When you hide a feature, datum features associated with it are hidden.

3. Which of the following statements are true regarding Figure 7–59? (Select all that apply.)

```
    HOOD.PRT
    ▶  ⚏ Design Items
        ▱ RIGHT
        ▱ TOP
        ▱ FRONT
        ⌙ PRT_CSYS_DEF
    ▶  ⬛ Extrude 1
    ▶  ⬛ Extrude 2
        ⬝ Round 1
    ▼  ⬛ Hole 1
           ⁄ A_1
        ⬛ ▪Hole 2
        ⬛ Hole 3
        ⬝ Round 2
        ⬝ Round 3
    ▶  ⬛ Extrude 3
```

Figure 7–59

   a. The **Hole 2** geometry is removed from the display.

   b. The internal axis used to create **Hole 1** will be removed from display.

   c. The axis created with **Hole 2** remains displayed.

   d. Datum planes **RIGHT**, **TOP**, and **FRONT** are hidden.

4. Which of the following statements are true regarding suppressing a feature in a model?

    a. When you suppress a feature, it is displayed in the Model Tree with ■ next to its name.

    b. When you suppress a feature, it continues to regenerate.

    c. When you suppress a feature, solid geometry remains visible.

    d. When you suppress a feature, only datum features associated with it are suppressed.

5. Which feature(s) in Figure 7–60 are suppressed?

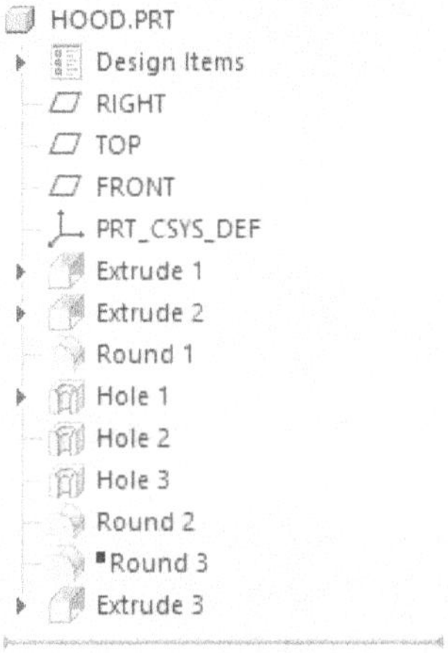

Figure 7–60

    a. Datum planes RIGHT, TOP and FRONT

    b. Hole 3

    c. A_1

    d. Round 3

6. How do you display suppressed features in the Model Tree?

    a. Select ⸜ (Tree Filter) and select **General>Suppressed.**

    b. Select ⸜ (Tree Filter) and select **Core Features>Suppressed.**

    c. Expand ⸜ (Model Tree Settings) and select **Settings>Suppressed**.

    d. Expand ⸜ (Model Tree Settings) and select **Tree Columns>Suppressed objects**.

7. Which of the following statements are true regarding adding a feature to a layer and hiding it? (Select all that apply.)

   a. When you add a feature to a layer and hide it, it is removed from the Model Tree.

   b. When you add a feature to a layer and hide it, it continues to regenerate.

   c. When you add a feature to a layer and hide it, solid geometry remains visible.

   d. When you add a feature to a layer and hide it, only datum features associated with it are hidden.

8. Which of the following settings are valid display statuses for a layer?

   a. Hide

   b. Show

   c. Suppress

   d. Isolate

9. Which of the following statements is true regarding reordering and inserting features in a model? (Select all that apply.)

   a. Reordering enables you to drag and drop features so that you can rearrange the feature creation order.

   b. When reordering, features can be moved anywhere in the model.

   c. Insert Mode enables you to rearrange features to change their order.

   d. Insert Mode is activated by selecting and dragging **the** green line in the Model Tree and moving it to where you want to insert a new feature.

Answers: 1b, 2abcd, 3bc, 4a, 5d, 6a, 7bcd, 8abd, 9ad

Model Information

Creo Parametric provides you with several tools that can be used to obtain information about a part's measurements and mass properties. Cross-sections can also be created to further analyze a model.

Learning Objectives

- Learn how to efficiently access the measurement tools using the ribbon.
- Measure the distance between geometry using the **Distance** command.
- Learn how to save or create a feature for the measurement.
- Learn how to efficiently access the mass properties tool using the ribbon.
- Set the type and run the analysis.
- Create a cross-section using one of the two methods.
- Create the cross-section using options in the *Section* tab.
- Activate, deactivate, or show the cross-section using the Model Tree or the *View Manager* dialog box.
- Set, create, and change the model units using the *Model Properties* dialog box.
- Assign material to the model.

8.1 Measure Analysis

Select the *Analysis* tab to access options to measure specific parameters in your model, as shown in Figure 8-1.

Measure options

Figure 8-1

To perform a distance analysis, in the *Analysis* tab, expand ✎ (Measure) and select ⌐ (Distance). The *Distance* dialog box opens, as shown in Figure 8-2.

Figure 8-2

Note: The process to perform each of the measurement options is similar.

The dialog box can be expanded to display additional options by clicking ⊕ (Expand The Dialog) as shown in Figure 8-3.

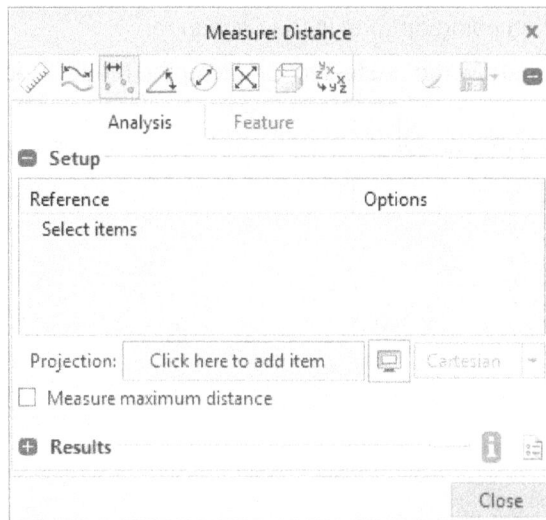

Figure 8-3

Note: You can toggle and select a different type of measurement command in the Measure dialog box.

Select the required references to measure the distance between the entities. The distance is calculated and displayed in the view window and in the *Results* area in the *Measure dialog box*, as shown in Figure 8−4. The measurement can be expanded or collapsed in the View window.

Use the *Measure* dialog box to review or change the references, as shown in Figure 8−4.

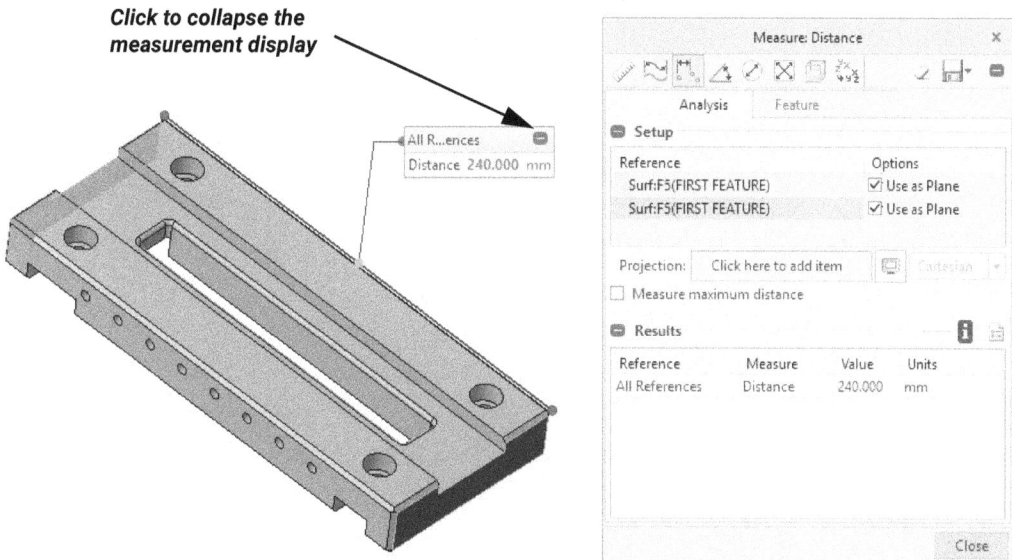

Click to collapse the measurement display

Figure 8−4

In the *Setup* area, the selected references are listed in the *Reference* column of the dialog box. Depending on the selected reference, there are several options available in the *Options* column.

- **Use as Plane** - Extends the selected surface or plane infinitely in both directions so you can measure normal to that reference entity. The extension does not physically extend the entity, as it is only for the measurement you are making.

- **Use as Line** - Extends the selected straight edge or curve infinitely in both directions so you can measure normal to that reference entity. The extension does not physically extend the entity, as it is only for the measurement you are making.

- **Use as Center** - Measures the distance from the center of a circle or an arc-shaped curve or edge. Clear this option to measure from the edge instead of the center.

- **Use as Axis** - Measures the distance from the central axis of the cylindrical surface. Clear this option to measure from the surface instead of the axis.

You can select the **Measure maximum distance** check box to determine the maximum distance between the two selected entities. For entities that are parallel, this option has no impact on the result.

Once the measurement has been created, click 🖫▾ (Save Analysis) to save, name, or create the measurement as a feature, as shown in Figure 8−5.

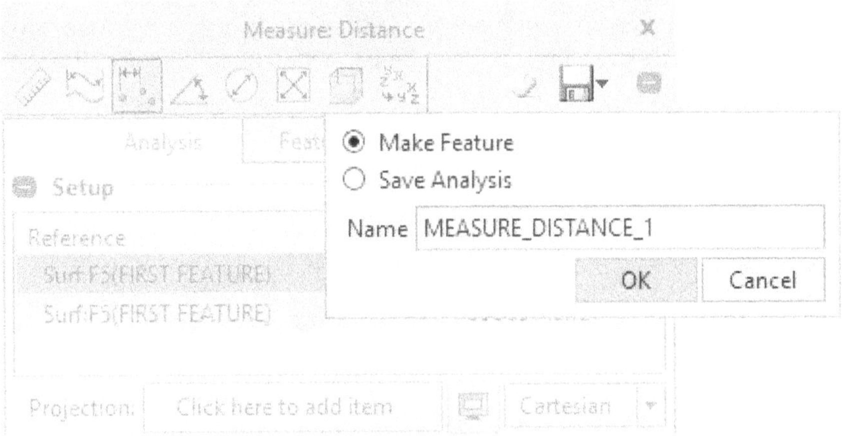

Figure 8−5

8.2 Mass Properties

To calculate a model's mass properties, in the *Model Report* group in the *Analysis* tab, click ☂ (Mass Properties). The *Mass Properties* dialog box opens, as shown in Figure 8–6.

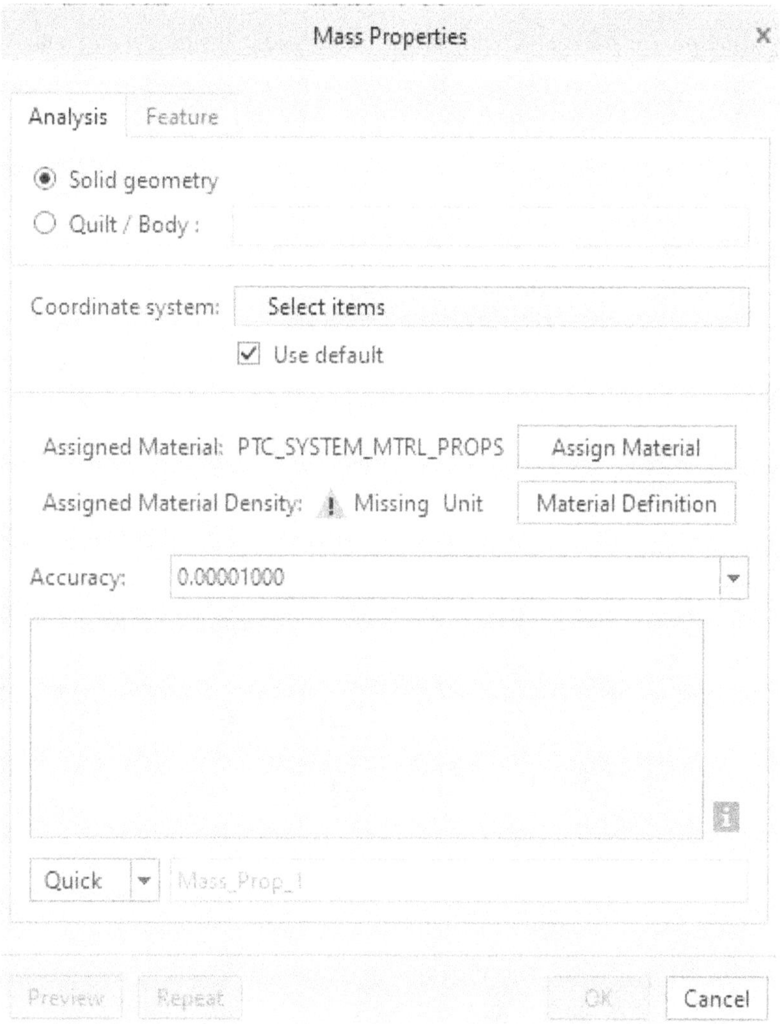

Figure 8–6

Note: If the model does not have an assigned density, Creo Parametric prompts you to set it before the calculation starts.

By default, the analysis type is set to **Quick**. You can change the type of analysis using the *Analysis* tab.

The three types of analysis are described as follows. In this example, a Quick analysis is performed.

Type	Description
Quick	The analysis is calculated and the result displayed in the dialog box.
Saved	The analysis is calculated and the result displayed in the dialog box and graphics window. The definition of the analysis is saved in the model and automatically recalculated when the model changes. To access a saved analysis, click ⊞ (Saved Analysis) in the *Manage* group in the *Analysis* tab.
Feature	The analysis is calculated and the result displayed in the dialog box. Additionally, an analysis feature is created and shown in the Model Tree. This option enables you to create feature parameters and datum features based on the analysis.

Keep **Use default** enabled, or select a coordinate system on the model.

The mass properties of the model are calculated and displayed in the *Results* area in the *Analysis* tab, as shown in Figure 8–7. It is important to note that the calculation does not include information on suppressed features or components.

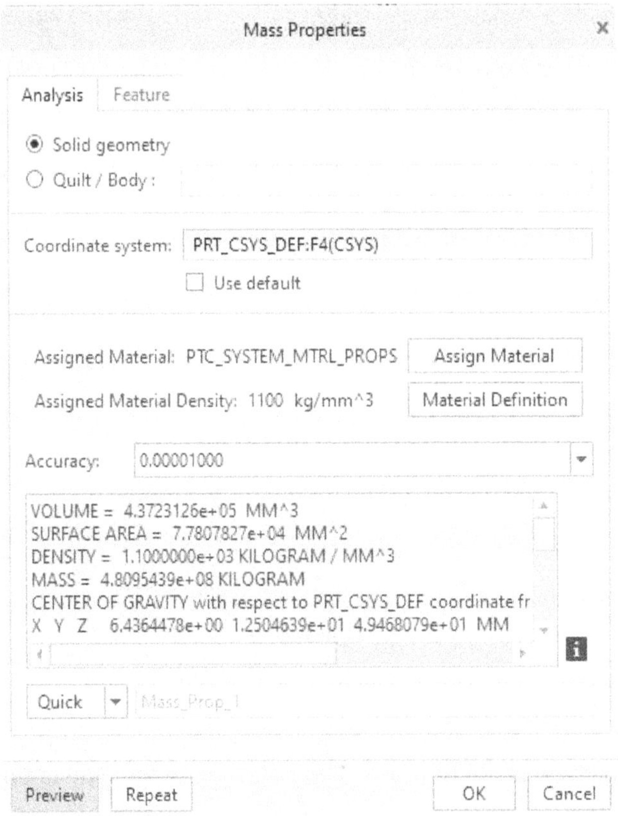

Figure 8–7

8.3 Creating Cross-Sections

A cross-section defines a slice through a model as shown in Figure 8−8. Cross-sections can be created in parts and assemblies. Two methods can be used to create cross-sections.

X Directional cross-section   *Planar cross-section*   *Offset cross-section*

Figure 8−8

- The first method requires you to expand ▢ (Section) in the *View* tab and select the type of cross-section you want to create.

- The second method uses the *View Manager* dialog box to create a cross-section by selecting the *Section* tab. The types of cross-sections that can be created using either method are described as follows:

Option	Description
Planar	A planar cross-section is created using a datum plane in the location of the required slice, as shown on the left in image above.
X Direction	A X Direction cross-section is created in the X direction. The location can be changed by entering a value or by dragging the arrow.
Y Direction	A Y Direction cross-section is created in the Y direction. The location can be changed by entering a value or by dragging the arrow.
Z Direction	A Z Direction cross-section is created in the Z direction. The location can be changed by entering a value or by dragging the arrow.
Offset Section	An offset cross-section is created by sketching a *cut line* to define the required cross-section, as shown on the right in the image above.
Zone	Zones enable you to divide a component into geometric work regions that can be used to define a condition for rule-driven simplified representations.

To start the creation of a cross section, use one of the following methods:

Method 1

To start the creation of a cross-section, expand ⬚ (Section) and select the type of section in the *View* tab, as shown in Figure 8−9.

Figure 8−9

Method 2

1. To start the creation of a cross-section, click ▦ (View Manager) in the *In-graphics* toolbar, and the *View Manager* dialog box opens. Select the *Sections* tab, as shown in Figure 8−10.

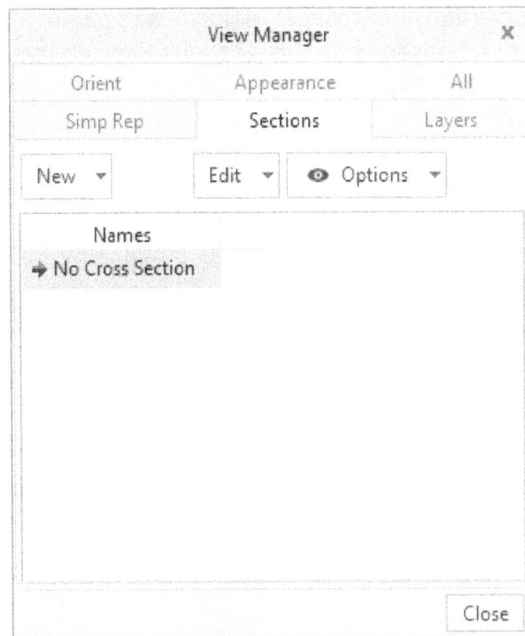

Figure 8−10

Note: You can also click 🔲 *(Manage Views) in the View tab to open the View Manager, then select the Section tab.*

2. Click **New** and select a type of cross-section, as shown in Figure 8–11. Enter a name for the cross-section and press <Enter>.

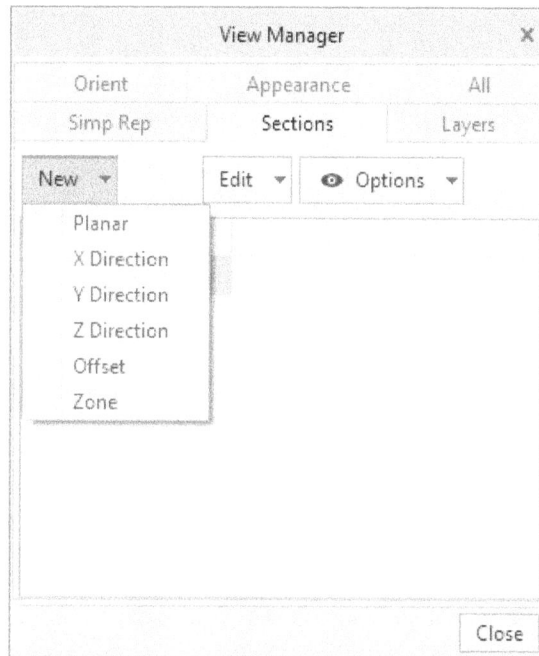

Figure 8–11

Note: The View Manager tabs vary depending on the current mode in which you are working. In Part mode, there are four tabs, and in Assembly mode, there are six.

The cross-section definition varies depending on its type.

Planar Cross-Section

Select a datum plane or planar surface that defines the location of the cross-section. The *Section* dashboard activates as shown in Figure 8–12.

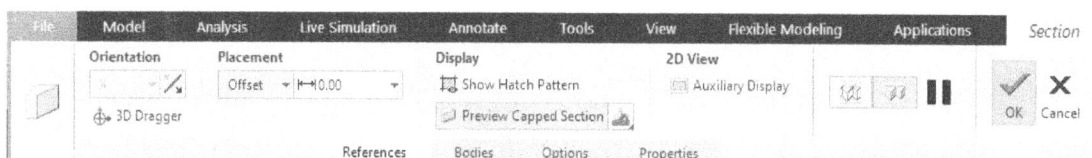

Figure 8–12

Once the *Section* dashboard is active, you can dynamically change the offset plane by using the mouse to drag the arrow, as shown in Figure 8–13. You can also toggle on the 3D dragger to dynamically translate and rotate the section.

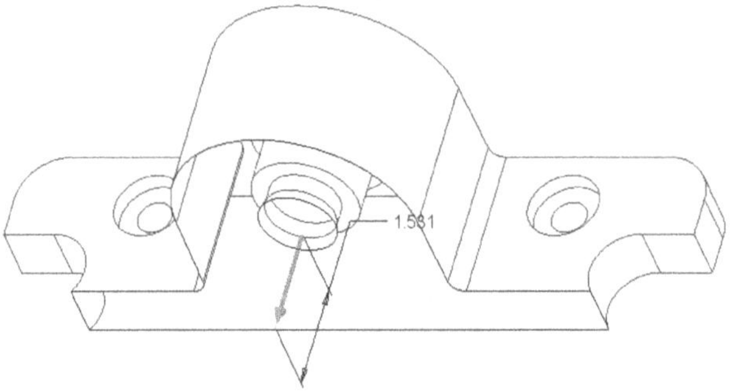

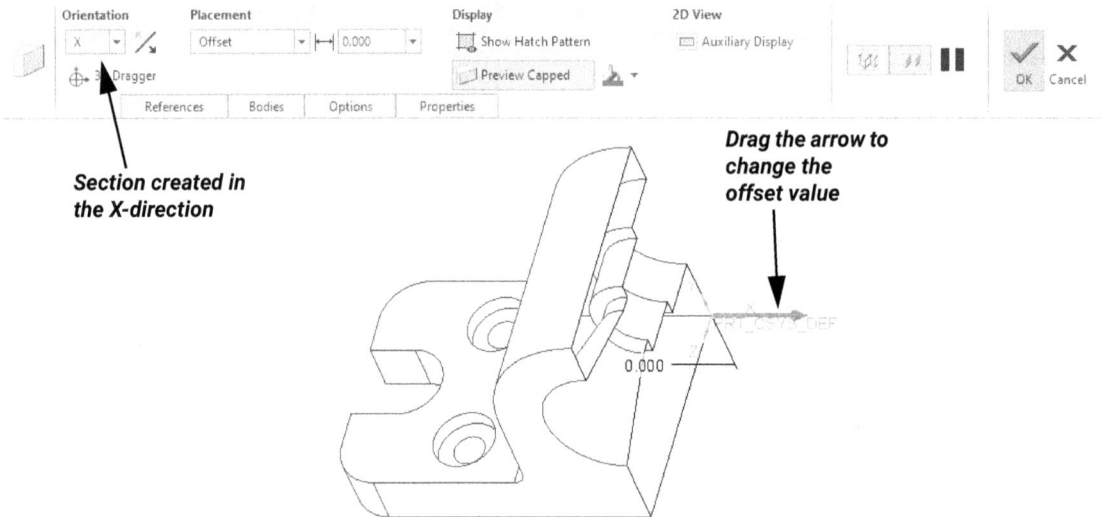

Drag the arrow to change the offset value

Figure 8–13

Note: You can also change the offset value in the Section tab.

Directional Cross-Section

The directional cross-section does not require a selection. The location of the cross-section is dependent on the type, default coordinate system, and offset value in the *Section* dashboard. Once the *Section* dashboard is active, you can dynamically change the offset plane by using the mouse to drag the arrow, as shown in Figure 8–14. You can also toggle on the 3D dragger to dynamically translate and rotate the section.

Section created in the X-direction

Drag the arrow to change the offset value

Figure 8–14

Offset Cross-Section

The Offset cross-section option enables you to sketch the section using the tools in the *Sketch* tab. The *Section* dashboard activates once the Offset type has been selected, as shown in Figure 8-15.

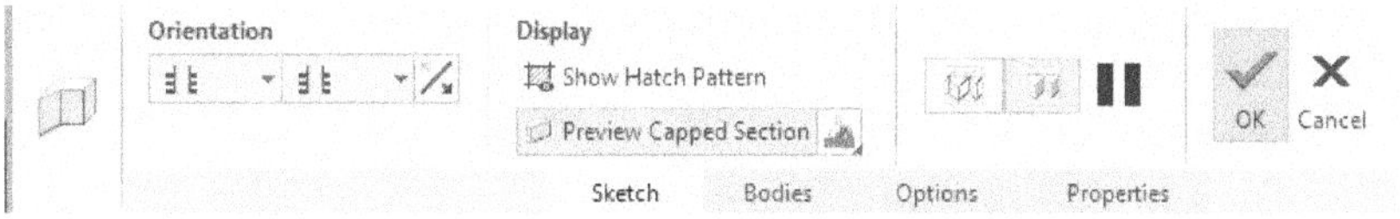

Figure 8-15

Select a sketching plane on which you can sketch the cut line for the offset cross-section. Sketch the required cut line as shown in Figure 8-16.

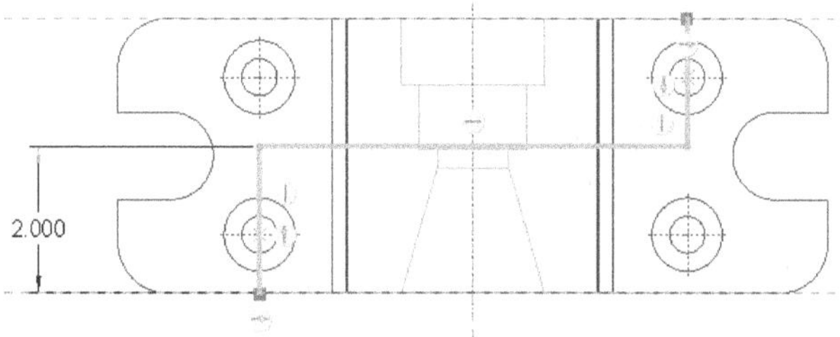

Figure 8-16

The commands and options in the *Section* tab are described as follows:

Option	Description
	Flips the clipping direction.
	Caps the surface of the cross-section.
	Opens the section color palette.
	Displays the hatching pattern.
	Extend the cross section to the first/second side of the sketch and normal to the sketch reference.
	Toggles on the 3D dragger to dynamically rotate or translate the cross-section.
	Displays a separate window of the 2D view.
	Previews the cross-section without clipping.
	Previews the cross-section with clipping.

You can also dynamically detect any component interference using the **Show Interference** option in the *Options* panel, as shown in Figure 8–17.

Figure 8–17

Components can be excluded from the section by selecting the *Bodies* panel, as shown in Figure 8–18.

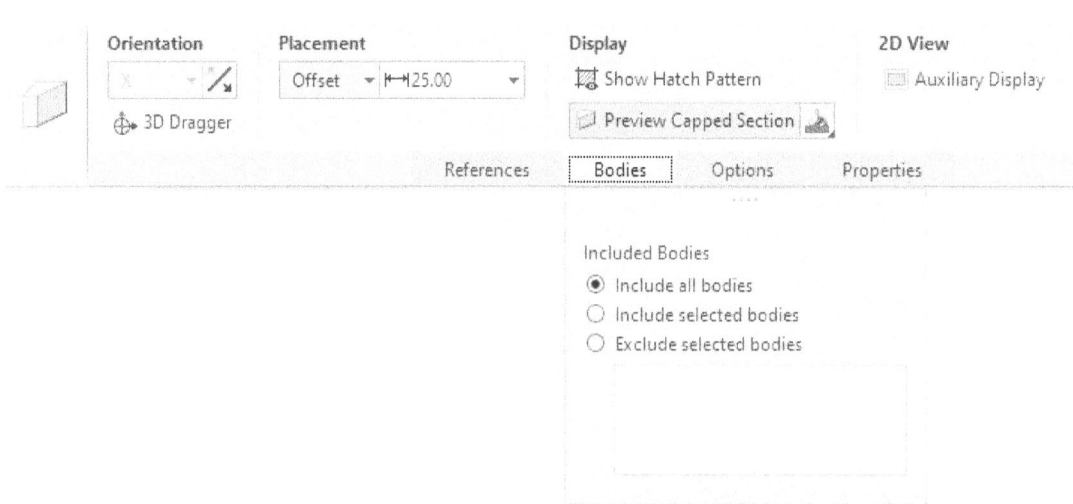

Figure 8–18

Click ✔ (**OK**) to complete the cross-section. Cross-sections display in the Model Tree, as shown in Figure 8–19.

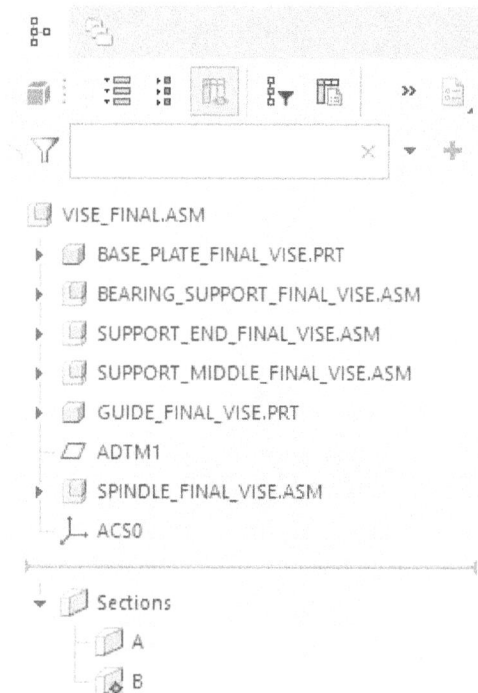

Figure 8–19

When you show a cross-section, it displays with the default line spacing and line angle for the cross-hatching, as shown in Figure 8–20.

Figure 8–20

To modify the default cross-hatching, select the cross-section in the Model Tree, right-click, and select ▨ (Edit Hatching). The *Edit Hatching* dialog box opens, as shown in Figure 8−21.

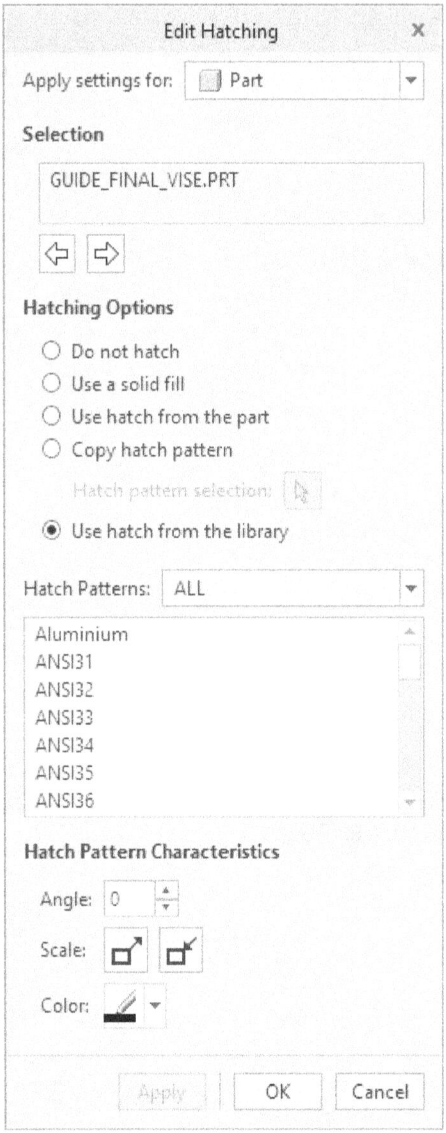

Figure 8−21

*Note: You can also expand **Edit** and select the **Edit Hatching** option in the View Manager.*

You can select from the hatch library or create your own by setting the angle and scale values. You can also click ⊓⃗ (Double Spacing) or click ⊓⃖ (Halve Spacing) to change the spacing between the hatching lines. Expand ✎ (Set Color) to specify the hatching color.

When you finalize the cross-section, it is automatically active and cuts the model. The active cross-section displays, as shown in Figure 8–22.

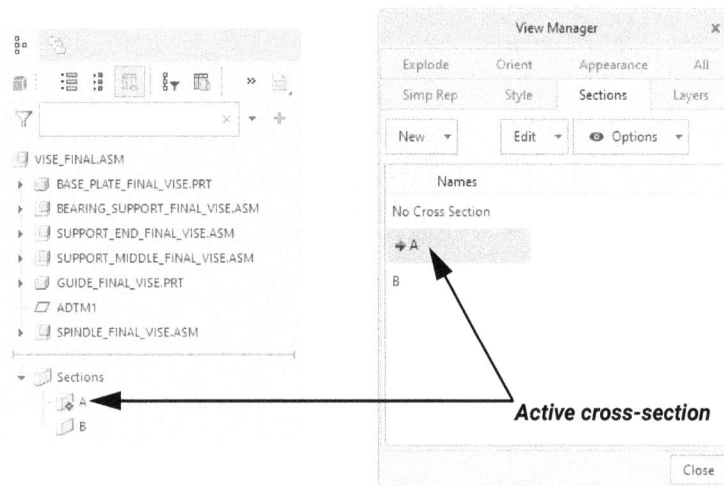

Figure 8–22

Note: The tool does not actually cut the geometry, it is for visualization purposes only.

Select a cross-section in the Model Tree, and then select ✲ (Deactivate) in the *mini* toolbar to disable the cross-section. You can enable a different cross-section by selecting the section in the Model Tree or View Manager, and selecting **Activate**, as shown in Figure 8–23. Only one cross-section can be set as active.

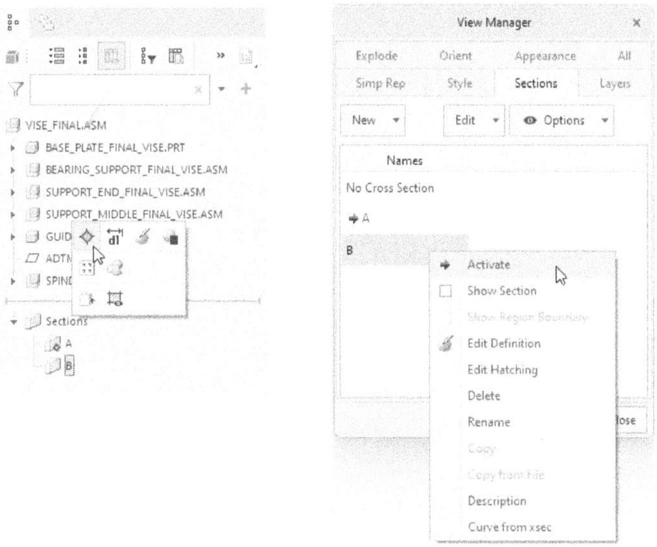

Figure 8–23

You can display the cross-hatching lines, as shown in Figure 8–24, by right-clicking on the section and selecting **Show Section** in the Model Tree or in the *View Manager* dialog box. Note that the symbol in the Model Tree changes, as shown in Figure 8–24.

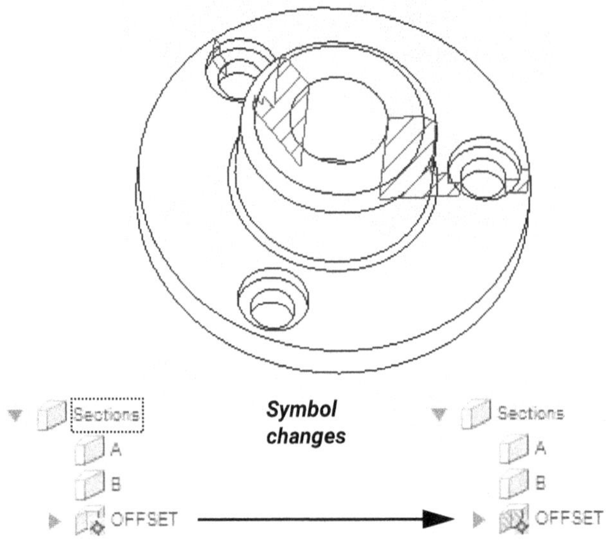

Figure 8–24

8.4 Changing Model Units and Material

Occasionally, the part units in your models might need to be modified. When modifying the part units, you can convert the existing units to the new system of units or you can maintain the current values in the new system.

How To: Change Part Units

1. To change the units of your model, select **File>Prepare>Model Properties** to open the *Model Properties* dialog box as shown in Figure 8-25.

Model Properties			− ☐ ✕
3] **Materials**			
Material	Not assigned		change
Units	Inch lbm Second (Creo Parametric Default)		change
Accuracy	Relative 0.0012		change
Mass Properties		ⓘ	change ⌄

Figure 8-25

2. Click **change** beside Units in the *Materials* area in the dialog box. The *Units Manager* dialog box opens, as shown in Figure 8-26.

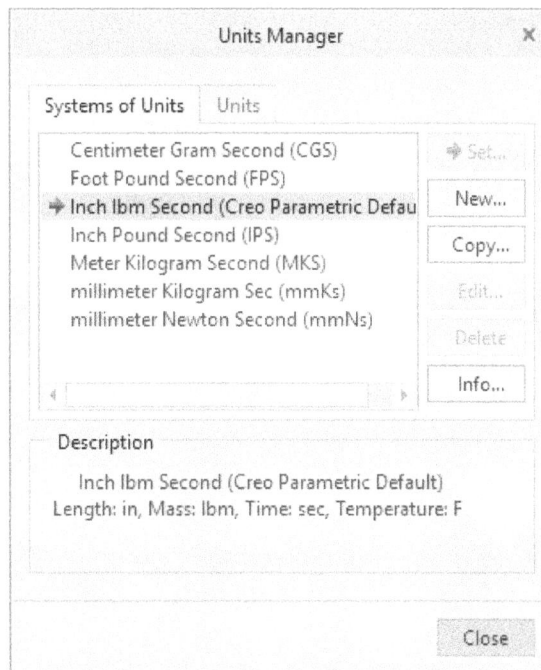

Units Manager ✕

Systems of Units | Units

Centimeter Gram Second (CGS)
Foot Pound Second (FPS)
➜ Inch lbm Second (Creo Parametric Defau
Inch Pound Second (IPS)
Meter Kilogram Second (MKS)
millimeter Kilogram Sec (mmKs)
millimeter Newton Second (mmNs)

➜ Set...
New...
Copy...
Edit...
Delete
Info...

Description

Inch lbm Second (Creo Parametric Default)
Length: in, Mass: lbm, Time: sec, Temperature: F

Close

Figure 8-26

3. To define a new system of units, you can select from the list of predefined systems or create a new one. A description of the predefined units is listed at the bottom of the *Units Manager* dialog box. To create a new system of units, click **New**. The *System of Units Definition* dialog box opens, as shown in Figure 8−27.

Figure 8−27

To define the new system of units, assign a name and type, and select the required type of units. Click **OK** to complete the definition.

4. Select the new system of units and click **Set** to finalize the change of units. The *Changing Model Units* dialog box opens, as shown in Figure 8−28.

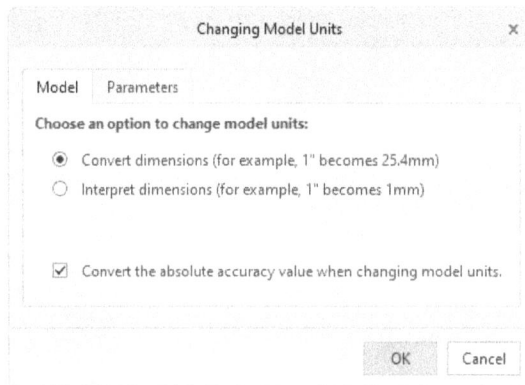

Figure 8−28

- In the *Model* tab, select how the current dimension values are going to change in the model. You must select one of the following:

  - The **Convert Dimensions** option converts the existing dimensions to the new system of units, while maintaining the same size in the resulting model (i.e., 1" becomes 25.4 mm).
  - The **Interpret Dimensions** option keeps the same numeric values in dimensions when changing the system of units (i.e., 1" becomes 1 mm).

  *Note: The **Interpret Dimensions** option can be useful if you accidentally design the model using the wrong units.*

- In the *Parameters* tab, select how the parameters change in the model, as shown in Figure 8–29. The *Parameters* tab lists Real number parameters that only have units assigned to them.

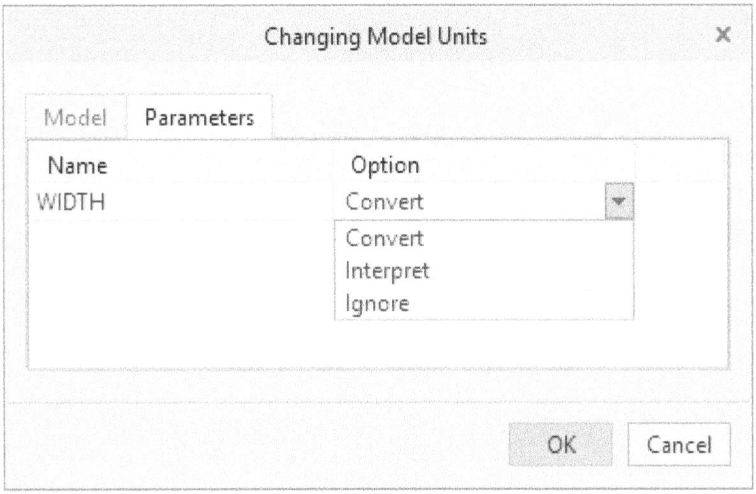

Figure 8–29

5. Click **OK** to complete the change of units and close the *Units Manager* dialog box.

You can also assign a material to the model using the *Model Properties* dialog box. Click change next to Material in the *Model Properties* dialog box, and the *Materials* dialog box is displayed as shown in Figure 8–30.

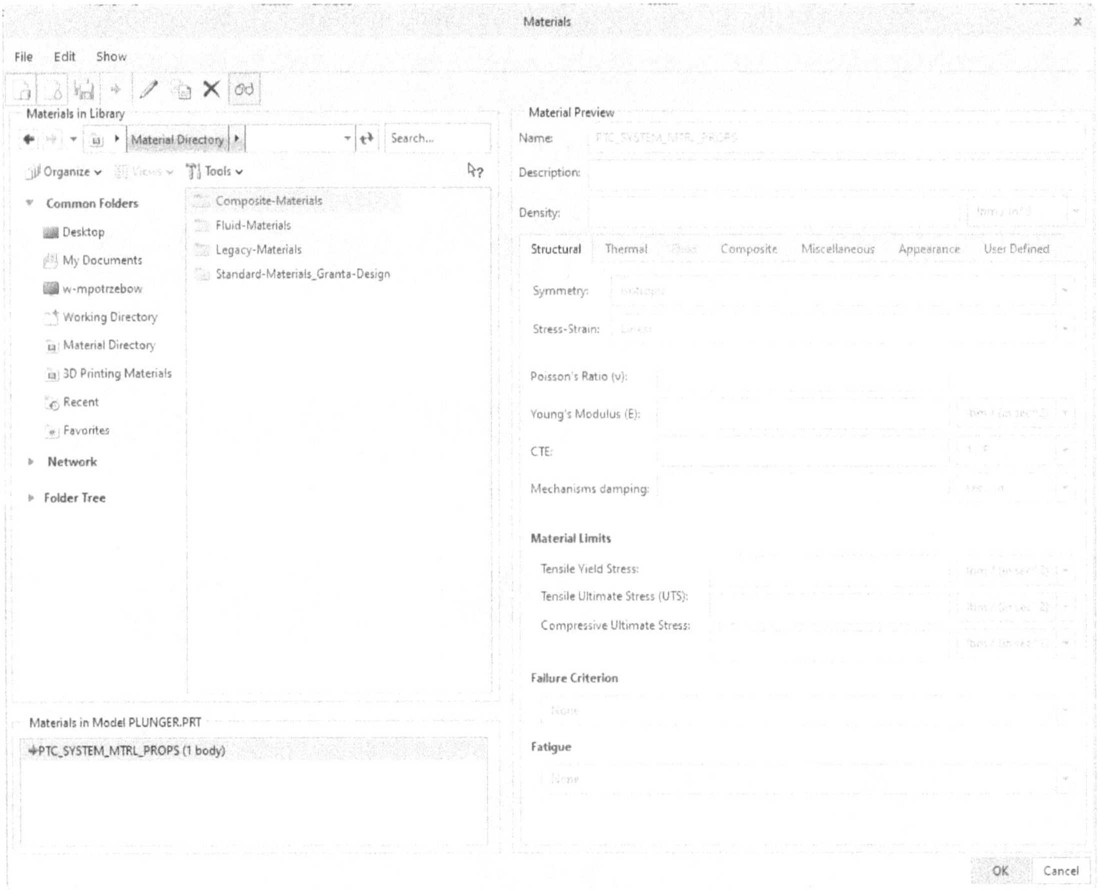

Figure 8–30

6. Navigate to the material folder and double-click on a material from the list to add it to the model. If more than one material is assigned, the first one assigned will be the active material.

7. Right-click on any other materials added to make them active, as shown in Figure 8–31.

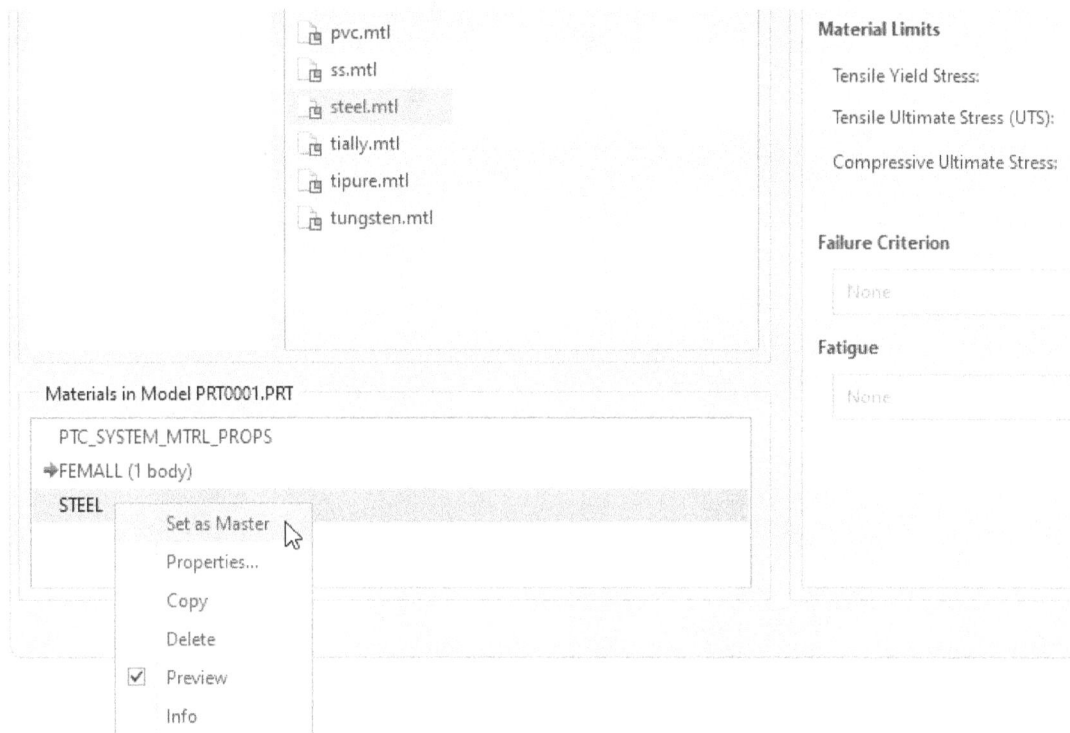

Figure 8–31

Practice 8a
Cross-Sections

Practice Objective

- Create a planar and an offset cross-section using the **Section** command.

In this practice, you will use the *View Manager* dialog box to create two types of cross-sections, as shown in Figure 8–32. Note that assemblies are covered in detail in upcoming chapters.

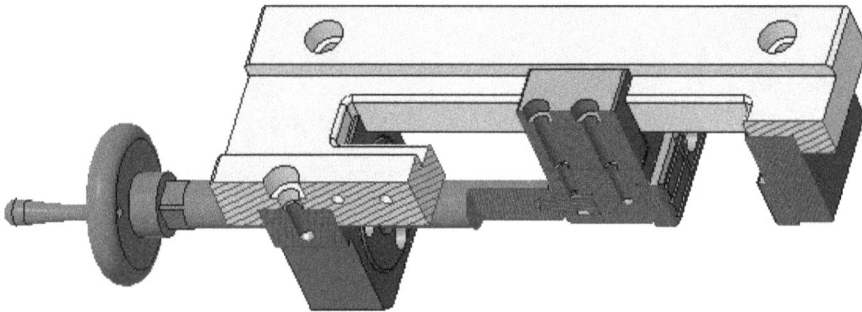

Figure 8–32

Task 1: Open an assembly file.

1. Set the working directory to the *Cross-Sections* folder.
2. Open **vise_final.asm**.
3. Set the model display as follows:

  - *(Datum Display Filters)*: *(Axis Display) only
  - *(Spin Center)*: Off
  - *(Display Style)*: (Shading With Edges)

Task 2: Create an assembly datum plane.

1. While holding <Ctrl> select the two axes shown in Figure 8–33. Release <Ctrl> and click
    ⬜ (Plane) in the *mini* toolbar.

**Select these two axes as
datum references**

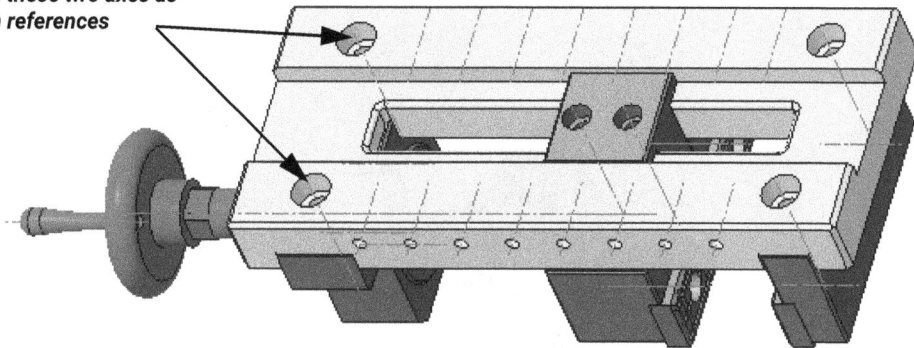

Figure 8–33

2. In the *Datum Plane* dialog box, select the *Properties* tab and rename the plane to
    SECTION-B.

3. Click **OK**.

4. Click on the screen to clear any selections.

Task 3: Create a planar cross-section.

1. Select the *View* tab. Expand ⬜ (Section) and select **Planar**. The *Section* tab activates as
    shown in Figure 8–34.

Figure 8–34

Note: You can also select the View tab to create a section.

2. Select **SECTION-B** from the Model Tree.

3. Select the *Properties* panel and set the *Name* to **B**.

4. Click ✓ (**OK**) to complete the cross-section.

5. In the *In-graphics* toolbar, click ⁺ˣ⸝ (Datum Display Filters) and disable ⸝ₒ (Axis Display).

6. The cross-section displays, as shown in Figure 8–35. One side of the cross-section is removed from the display.

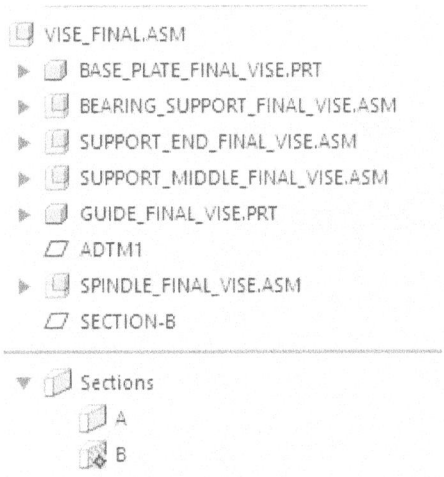

Figure 8–35

7. In the Model Tree, select section **B** and click ▭ (Show Section) in the *mini* toolbar, to display the cross-hatching for the section. The section displays, as shown in Figure 8–36.

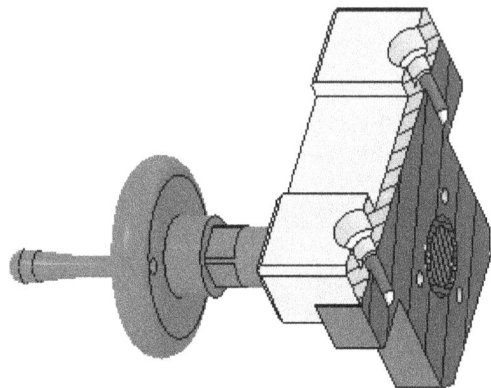

VISE_FINAL.ASM
▶ BASE_PLATE_FINAL_VISE.PRT
▶ BEARING_SUPPORT_FINAL_VISE.ASM
▶ SUPPORT_END_FINAL_VISE.ASM
▶ SUPPORT_MIDDLE_FINAL_VISE.ASM
▶ GUIDE_FINAL_VISE.PRT
  ▱ ADTM1
▶ SPINDLE_FINAL_VISE.ASM
  ▱ SECTION-B

▼ Sections
    A
    B

Clipping State:B

Figure 8–36

8. Toggle off cross-hatching for the section.

9. Select the section and click ⸝ (Deactivate) to return the display to normal.

Task 4: Create an offset cross-section.

1. In the *Model* tab, expand ▱ (Section) and select **Offset Section**. The *Section* tab activates.
2. In the *Properties* panel, name the cross-section **C**.
3. Select the top-most surface of the assembly as a sketching plane as shown in Figure 8–37.

Select this surface for the sketch plane

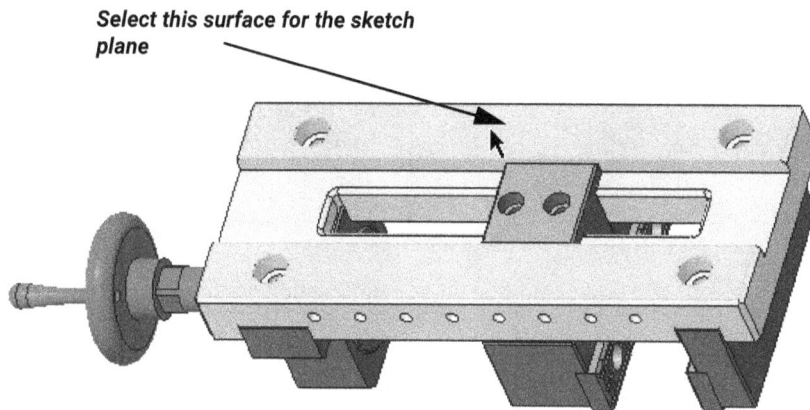

Figure 8–37

4. In the *Setup* group, if required, click ⬚ (Sketch View).
5. Select the left and right sides of **base_plate_final_vise.prt** as the sketching references. Two vertical dashed lines display. Do not close the *Reference* dialog box.
6. In the *In-graphics* toolbar, click ⌖ (Datum Display Filters) and enable ⊙ (Axis Display).
7. In the lower-right corner of the Creo Parametric window, change the *Selection Filter* to **Axis** and select the two axes shown in Figure 8–38.

Select these axes

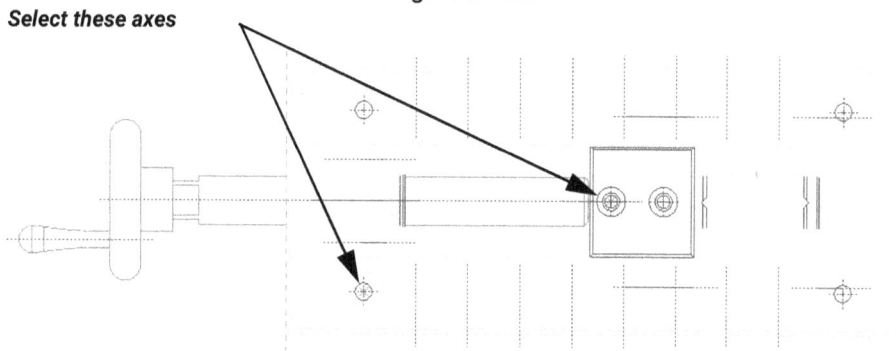

Figure 8–38

Note: *Shading is toggled off for clarity.*

8. Close the *References* dialog box.

9. Disable axis display.

10. Create the sketch shown in Figure 8–39.

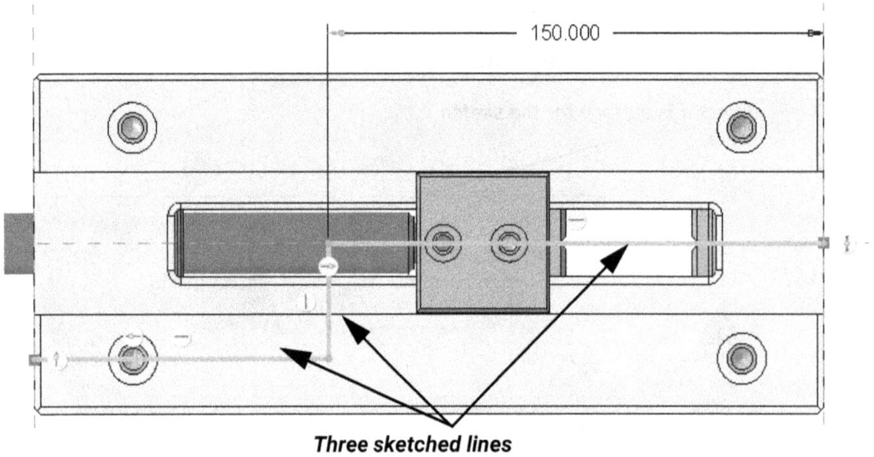

Three sketched lines

Figure 8–39

11. Complete the sketch.

12. If necessary, click ✏ (Flip Clipping Direction) so the result appears as shown in Figure 8–40.

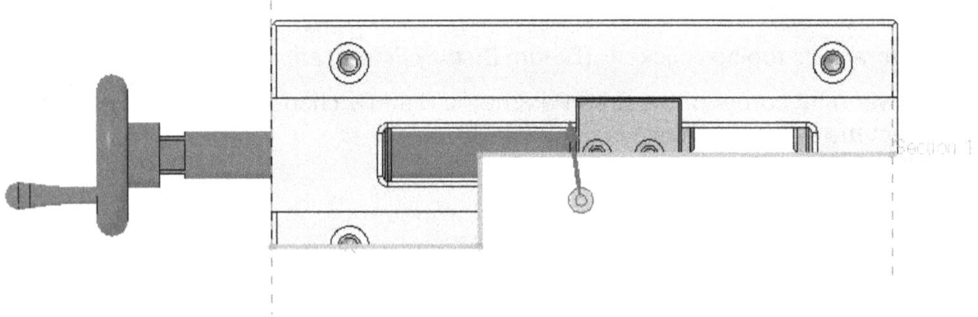

Figure 8–40

13. Click ✔ (**OK**).

14. Select section **C** in the Model Tree and click ⊞ (Show Section) in the *mini* toolbar to display the cross-hatching. The model should look similar to the one shown in Figure 8−41.

Figure 8−41

15. Save the assembly and erase it from memory.

End of practice

Practice 8b
Model Measurements

Practice Objective

- Find the length, height, angle, and the distance between entities using the measurement tools.

In this practice, you will use the measurement tools to investigate a model. You will use the measurement tools to verify the distance, area, angle, and diameter of various features in the model.

Task 1: Open a part file.

1. Set the working directory to the *Model_Measurements* folder.
2. Open **pillow_block.prt**.
3. Set the model display as follows:
   - $\overset{x'}{\underset{\Rightarrow}{}}$ *(Datum Display Filters)*: All Off
   - $\overset{\rightarrow}{\sim}$ *(Spin Center)*: Off
   - $\square$ *(Display Style)*: $\square$ (Shading With Edges)

Task 2: Measure the overall length.

1. Select the *Analysis* tab, expand the $\mathscr{P}$ (Measure) drop-down and select $\overset{\square}{\square}$ (Distance).
2. If required, click $\oplus$ (Expand The Dialog) to expand the *Measure: Distance* dialog box as shown in Figure 8–42.

Click to expand the dialog box

Figure 8–42

3. If required, click ⊕ (Expand The Dialog) next to *Setup* and *Results* to expand the *Measure* dialog box as shown in Figure 8–43.

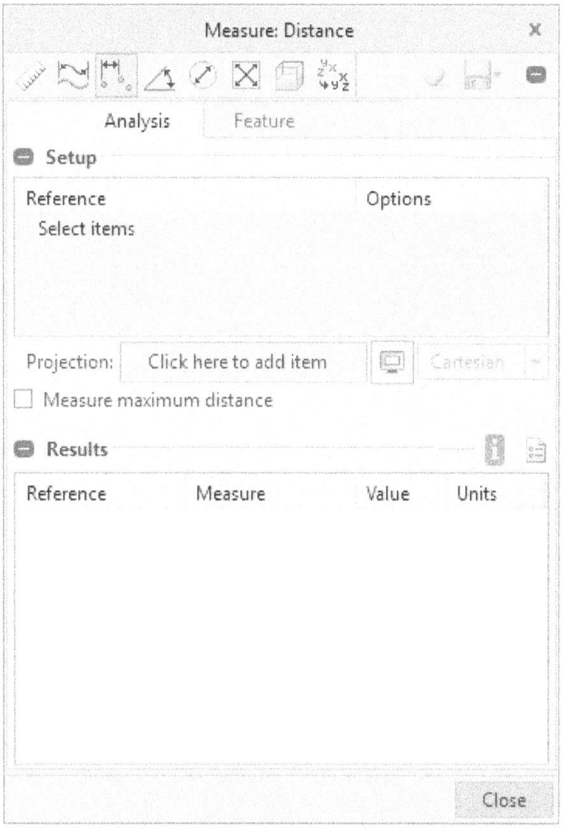

Figure 8–43

4. Select the vertical planar surface on the right side of the model, as shown in Figure 8–44.

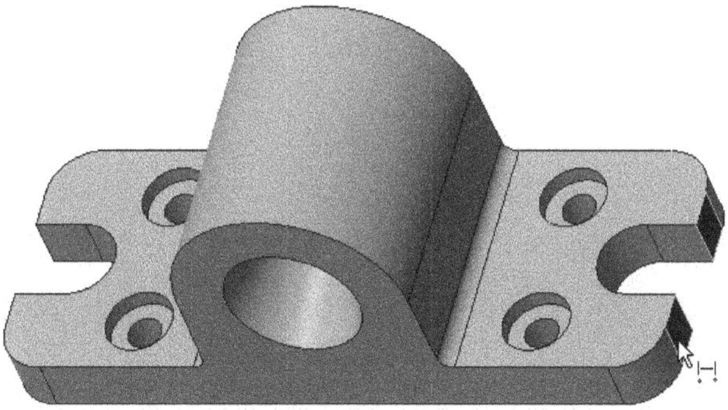

Figure 8–44

5. Hold <Ctrl> and select a similar vertical planar surface on the left side of the model.

6. The information displayed in the *Graphics* window and in the *Distance* dialog box indicates that the *Distance* = **10.0000** as shown in Figure 8−45.

Figure 8−45

7. Do not close the *Distance* dialog box.

Task 3: Measure the overall height.

---

1. Click ⟋ (Clear All Selections) in the *Measure* dialog box to clear the selected references.

*Note: You can also right-click and select **Remove** to clear the selected references or to select new references.*

2. Select the bottom surface of the part as shown in Figure 8−46.

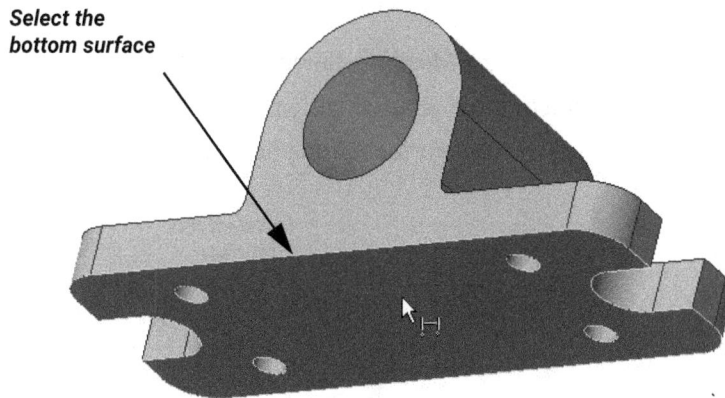

Select the bottom surface

Figure 8−46

3. Hold <Ctrl> and select **DTM2** from the Model Tree to measure the overall height as shown in Figure 8−47.

All R...ences
Distance 3.95000 in

Figure 8−47

4. The information displayed in the Graphics window and in the *Distance* dialog box indicates that the *Distance* = **3.95000**.

5. Do not close the *Distance* dialog box.

Task 4: Measure a distance between the U-shaped cut and the hole.

1. Click ✐ (Clear All Selections) in the *Measure* dialog box to clear the selected references.
2. Select the cylindrical surface of the U-shaped cut, as shown in Figure 8–48.
3. Hold <Ctrl> and select the cylindrical surface of the hole, as shown in Figure 8–48.

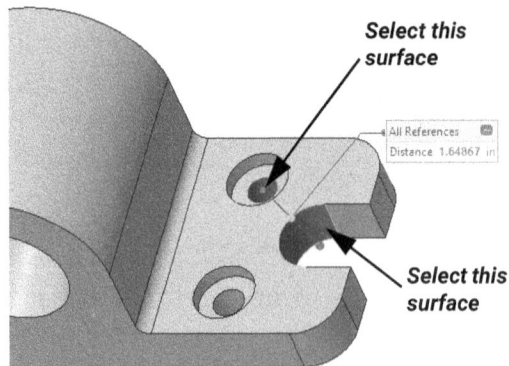

Figure 8–48

4. The information displayed in the Graphics window and in the *Distance* dialog box indicates that the *Distance* = **1.64867**.
5. Clear **Use as Axis** for both references in the *References* area of the dialog box. The information displayed in the Graphics window and in the *Distance* dialog box indicates that the *Distance* = **0.798678**.
6. Enable **Use as Axis** for both references in the *Options* area of the dialog box.
7. Enable **Measure maximum distance** and the information displayed in the Graphics window and in the *Distance* dialog box indicates that the *Maximum Distance* = **2.49867**, as shown in Figure 8–49.

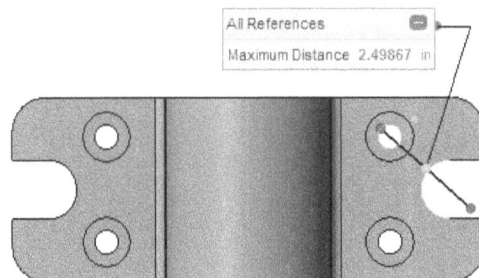

Figure 8–49

Note: As shown in Figure 8–49, the Maximum Distance option measures the distance between the opposing surfaces.

Task 5: Measure the length of an edge.

1. Click ✐ (Clear All Selections) in the *Measure* dialog box to clear the selected references.

2. Click ⌇ (Length) in the dialog box.

    *Note: You can also right-click and select **Measure>Length**.*

3. Select the edge as shown in Figure 8–50.

Figure 8–50

4. Right-click in the *References* collector and select **Use as Chain** as shown in Figure 8–51.

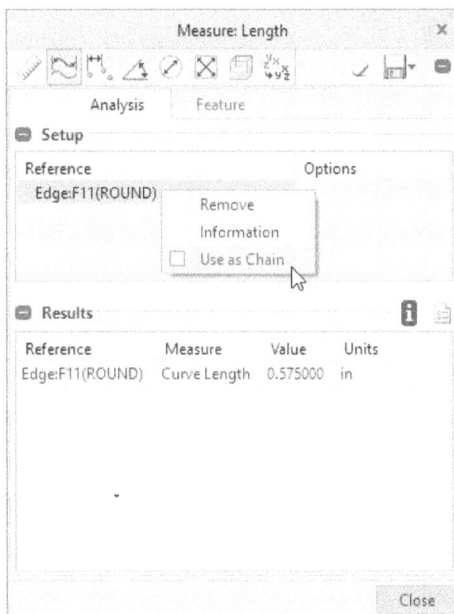

Figure 8–51

5. Select **Rule-based** and ensure that **Tangent** is selected. All of the tangent edges are selected as shown in Figure 8–52.

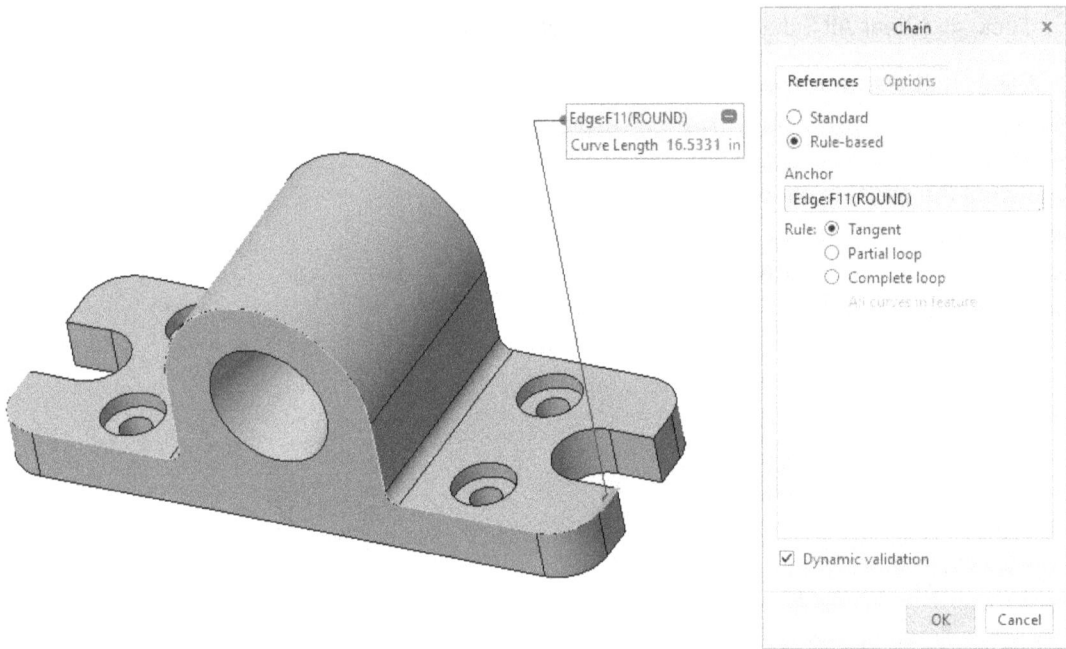

Figure 8–52

6. Click **OK** in the *Chain* dialog box.

7. The information displayed in the Graphics window and in the *Length* dialog box indicates that the *Length* = **16.5331**.

Task 6: Measure point to point with a distance measurement.

1. Click ✓ (Clear All Selections) in the *Measure* dialog box to clear the selected references.

2. Click 🖳 (Distance) in the *Measure* dialog box.

3. Select the vertex shown in Figure 8-53.

4. Hold <Ctrl> and select the cylindrical edge shown in Figure 8-54. The centerpoint of the arc is selected by default.

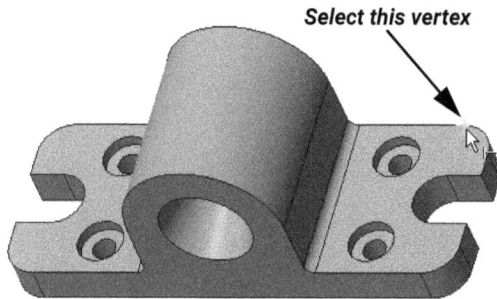

Select this vertex   **Select this edge**

Figure 8-53

Figure 8-54

5. Select the **Projection** reference collector in the *Measure: Distance* dialog box as shown in Figure 8-55.

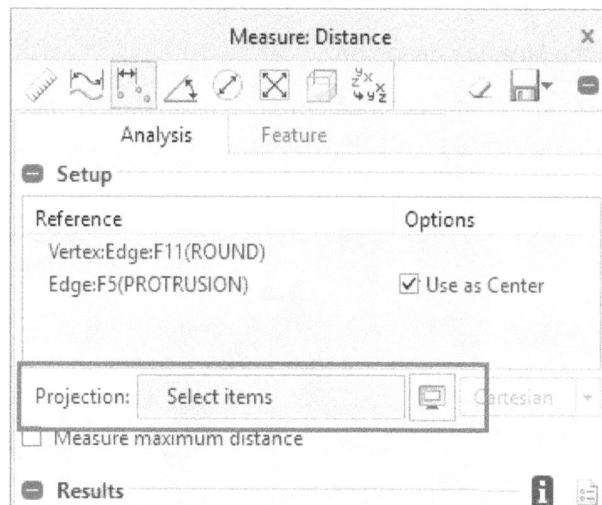

Figure 8-55

6. Select the **PRT_CSYS_DEF** coordinate system from the Model Tree. This projects the measurement to the coordinate system. The measurement displays, as shown in Figure 8–56.

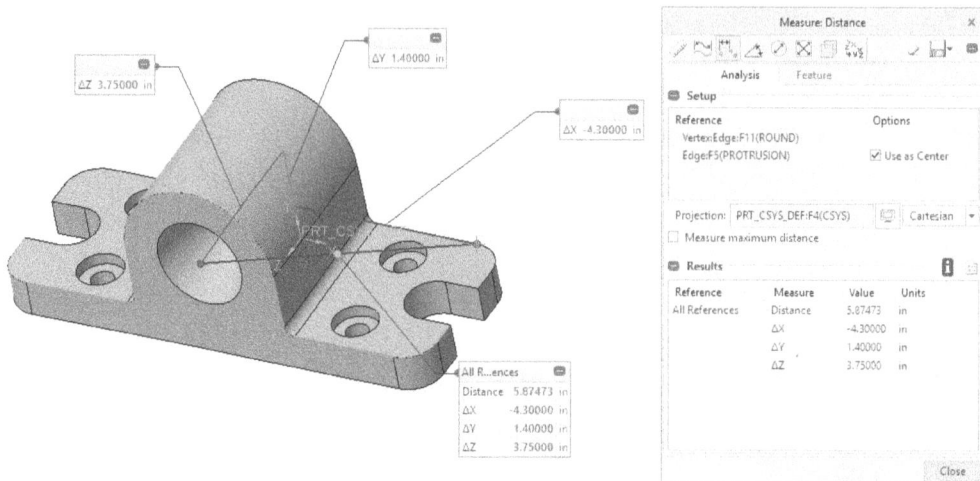

Figure 8–56

Task 7: Measure an angle between surfaces.

1. Click ⟋ (Clear All Selections) in the *Measure* dialog box to clear the selected references.

2. Click △ (Angle) in the *Measure* dialog box.

   *Note: You can also right-click and select **Angle**.*

3. Hold <Ctrl> and select the two planar surfaces shown in Figure 8–57.

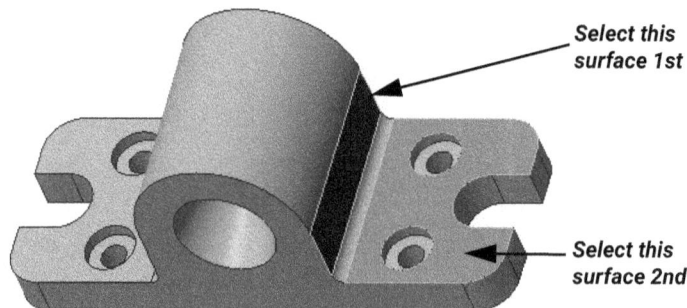

Select this surface 1st

Select this surface 2nd

Figure 8–57

4. The information displayed in the Graphics window and in the *Angle* dialog box indicates that the *Angle* = **89.0000**.

5. Expand the *Angle* drop-down list and select **Supplement** in the *Angle* field as shown in Figure 8−58. This changes the angle direction with an *Angle* of **91.0000** degrees.

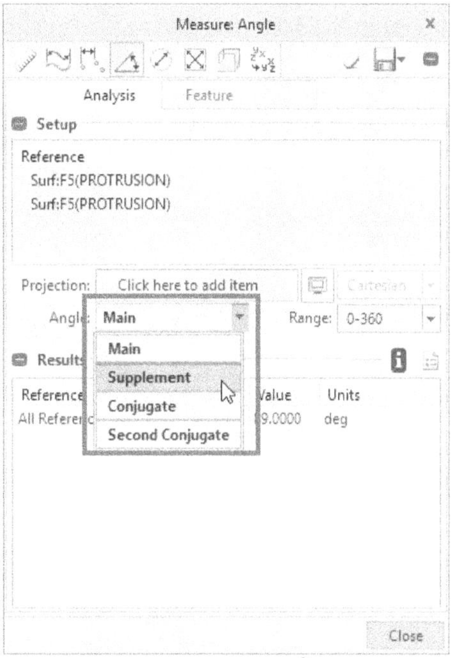

Figure 8−58

6. The information displayed in the Graphics window and in the *Angle* dialog box indicates that the *Angle* = **91.0000**, as shown in Figure 8−59. This is the correct value.

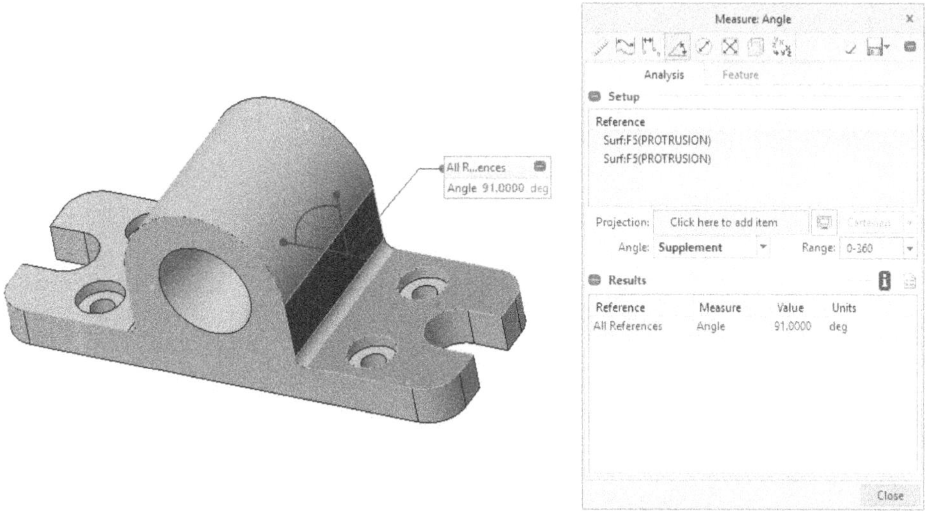

Figure 8−59

Task 8: Measure the area of a surface.

1. Click ✓ (Clear All Selections) in the *Measure* dialog box to clear the selected references.

2. Click ⊠ (Area) in the *Measure* dialog box.

3. Select a planar surface as shown in Figure 8–60.

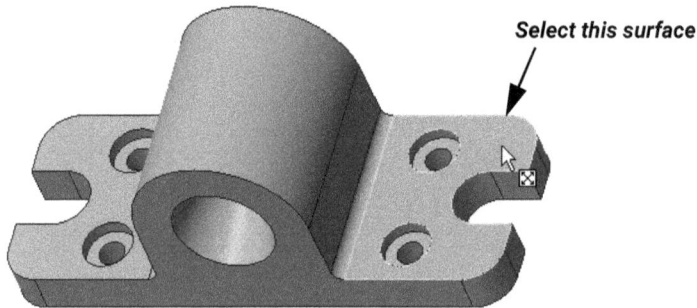

Select this surface

Figure 8–60

4. The information displayed in the Graphics window and in the *Area* dialog box indicates that the *Area* = **8.1125**.

Task 9: Measure the diameter of a surface.

1. Click ✓ (Clear All Selections) in the *Measure* dialog box to clear the selected references.

2. Click ⌀ (Diameter) in the *Measure* dialog box.

3. Select a cylindrical surface as shown in Figure 8–61.

Select this surface

Figure 8–61

4. The information displayed in the Graphics window and in the *Diameter* dialog box indicates that the *Diameter* = **3.5000** and *Radius* = **1.7500**.

5. Click ✐ (Summary) in the *Measure* dialog box. Note that the summary displays the area, perimeter, and diameter, as shown in Figure 8–62.

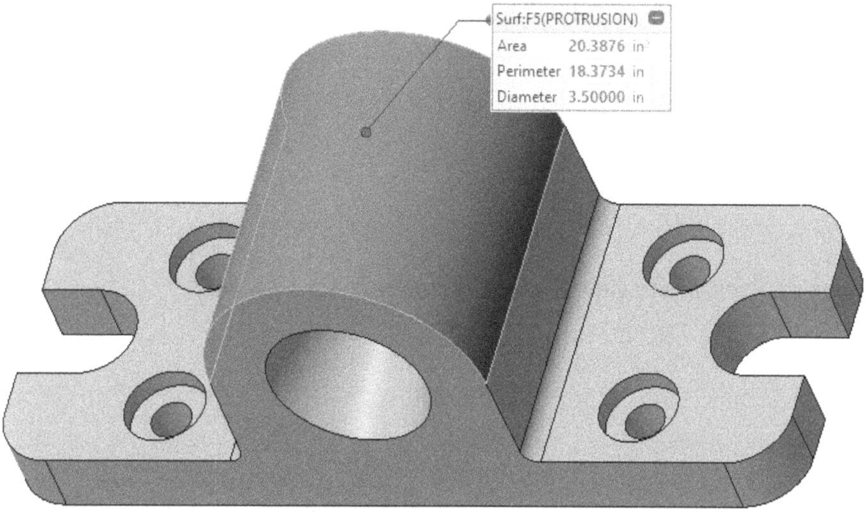

Figure 8–62

6. Click 💾▾ (Save Analysis) and select **Save Analysis**.

7. Click **OK**.

8. Close the *Measure* dialog box.

9. Click 📊 (Saved Analysis) in the *Analysis* tab.

10. Expand the **All** drop-down list in the lower right of the *Saved Analysis* dialog box and select **Hide All** to remove the analysis from the View window.

    Note: You can also collapse the measurement in the View window by clicking ⊖ next to the measurement.

11. Close the *Saved Analysis* dialog box.

12. Erase the model from memory.

End of practice

Chapter Review Questions

1. Which of the following options places your analysis in the Model Tree?
   a. Quick
   b. Saved
   c. Feature
   d. You cannot save an analysis.

2. Which icon enables you to view a saved distance measurement?

   a. ⌷

   b. ↦⊣

   c. ◿

   d. ⌷

3. Mass Property calculations include information on suppressed features or components.
   a. True
   b. False

4. A _____ cross-section is created using a datum plane in the location of the required slice.
   a. Offset Cross-section
   b. Planar Cross-section
   c. Directional Cross-section

5. Cross-sections only remove material visually from the model.
   a. True
   b. False

6. The _____ option changes existing dimensions to the new system of units (i.e., 1" becomes 25.4 mm).

   a. Convert

   b. Interpret

7. If a model has been created using the wrong units, but the numerical values of the dimensions are correct, what is the best conversion method to use?

   a. Convert Dimensions

   b. Interpret Dimensions

   c. You must scale the model.

View Manager

Creo Parametric offers tools that can be used to make large assemblies more manageable. You can simplify an assembly to ease display resources and regeneration times by using simplified representations. Component styles can also be defined to simplify the display of an assembly.

Learning Objectives

- Learn how to create and use the display styles for components in an assembly for multiple purposes.
- Use simplified representations to control how components are displayed and when they are opened to improve efficiency.
- Learn the advantages and disadvantages of the different types of system-defined simplified representations available in an assembly.
- Learn to create user-defined simplified representations to help reduce regeneration times for large assemblies.
- Learn to open a simplified representation without having to open the top-level assembly.

9.1 Component Display Styles

By default, all of the components in an assembly are displayed according to the global display setting. The choice of setting can affect the display refresh rates for large assemblies. The six display types and how they affect the display are described as follows:

Option	Icon	Description
Shading With Edges		Shades all of the model surfaces with highlighted edges. Performance depends on the hardware's graphics capabilities.
Shading With Reflections		Shades all of the model surfaces and adds reflections. Performance depends on the hardware's graphics capabilities.
Wireframe		Reduces the display refresh rates in situations, such as when the model is reoriented or regenerated.
Shading		Shades all of the model surfaces. Performance highly depends on the hardware's graphics capabilities.
Hidden Line		Facilitates better visualization of the model by displaying hidden lines in a different color. This option can take more time to refresh large, detailed models.
No Hidden		Facilitates better visualization of the model by not displaying hidden lines. This option can take even more time to refresh large, detailed models.

*Note: The global display settings can be set using the tools in the In-graphics toolbar, the Display Style icons in the View tab, or the configuration option **entity_display** in the Creo Parametric dialog box.*

Instead of using the same display setting for all of the components in an assembly, you can specify display styles for individual components as shown in Figure 9–1.

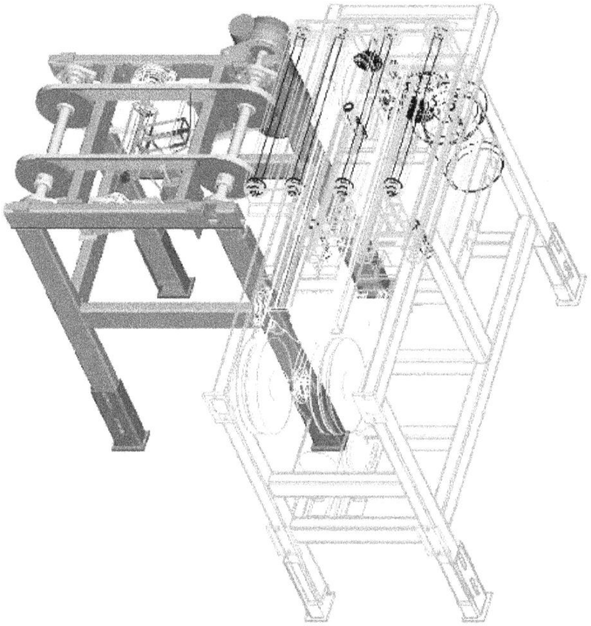

Figure 9–1

Display styles are defined using the *View Manager*. To open the *View Manager*, click ▣ (View Manager) in the *In-graphics* toolbar or click ▣ (Manage Views) in the *View* tab. In the *View Manager* dialog box, select the *Style* tab, as shown in Figure 9–2.

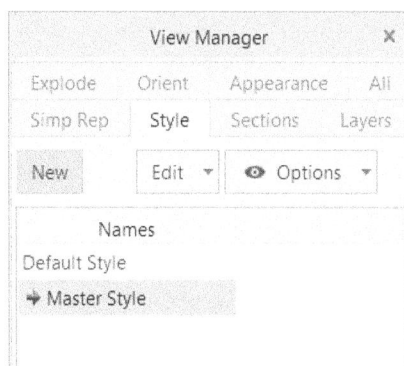

Figure 9–2

Note: You do not have to make any selections in the EDIT dialog box to continue.

➔ *indicates the active display setting.*

To create a display style, click **New**. Enter a name for the style and press <Enter>. The *EDIT* dialog box opens, as shown in Figure 9–3. You can select the components to blank, or select the *Show* tab and select the display method, as shown in Figure 9–4.

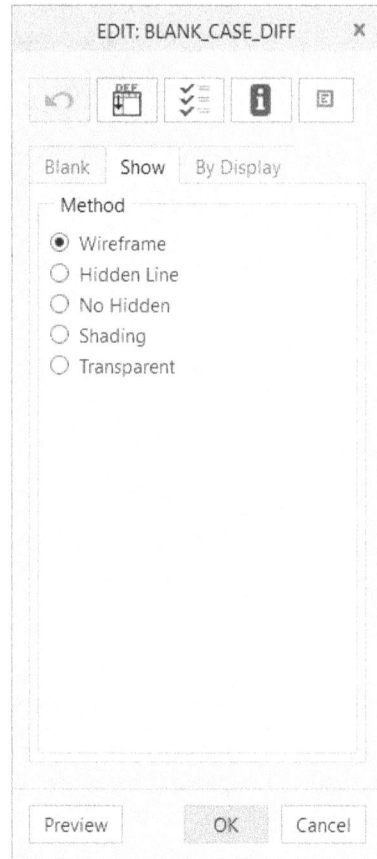

Figure 9–3   Figure 9–4

Once finished in the *EDIT* dialog box, click **OK**. The *View Manager* displays as shown in Figure 9–5.

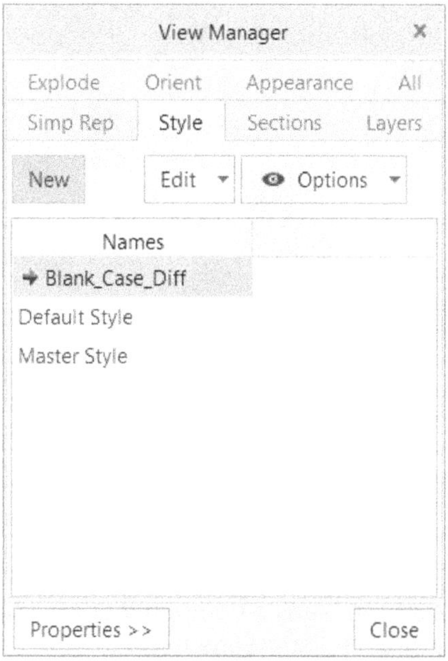

Figure 9–5

To define the display setting for selected components, click **Properties**. Select a component in the *Model Tree* and select the required display setting in the top row of icons in the *Style* tab. Similar to the global display settings, you can assign the following display settings to a component:

(Shaded With Edges)

(Shading With Reflections)

(Wireframe)

(Shading)

(Transparent)

(Hidden line)

(No Hidden)

Components can be set as transparent in assemblies so that you can display the interior components more clearly, as shown in Figure 9–6. The **style_state_transparency** configuration option sets the level of transparency for components. The value can range from 0 to 100.

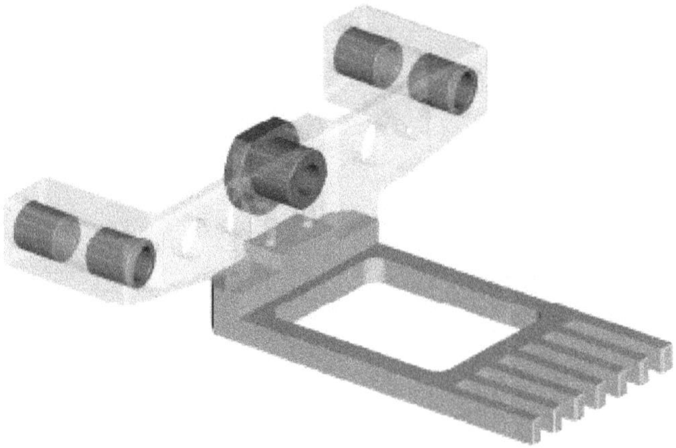

Figure 9–6

In addition, you can use ✎ (Blank) to blank a component or 🔒 (Activate From Selected) to assign the display style from a selected component.

For example, when a component with a defined style is assembled into a top-level assembly, you can use its user-defined style in the top-level assembly. The component and its display setting status are displayed in the View Manager, as shown in Figure 9–7.

Figure 9–7

Continue selecting components and assigning display settings as required.

Once you have defined the display settings for the components, click **List** to return to the list of display styles. The current style that was defined has a plus (+) symbol next to its name, as shown in Figure 9−8.

Figure 9−8

*Note: To display a component's style in the Model Tree, click **Tree Columns**. Select **Display Styles** in the Type pull-down list, and move the Display Style column to the list of the displayed columns.*

*To remove the column, select **Tree Columns**, select **Display Styles** in the Type pull-down list, and remove the Display Style column from the list of displayed columns.*

The plus (+) symbol indicates that the style has been modified. Click **Edit>Save** and click **OK** to save the style. Click **Close** to complete the display style. The assembly shown in Figure 9−9 displays the **Wireframe_Housing** style where the **grip_housing** component has been set to wireframe and all of the other components in the assembly maintain the current display style (i.e., shaded). You can easily identify that a style state is displayed because its name is listed in the main working window next to the model.

Style State:WIREFRAME_HOUSING

Figure 9−9

To make changes to an existing display style, open the *View Manager*, select the display style, and click **Properties** to redefine the style's display settings. You can also set the temporary display styles of selected components by selecting **Display Style** in the *Model* tab or in the In-graphics toolbar.

Temporary display styles can be used to quickly control the display of components without having to use the *View Manager*. A temporary display style is not saved with the model unless you open the *View Manager* and create a new style.

Appearance States

You can define different appearance states for your model using the *Appearance* tab in the *View Manager* dialog box, as shown in Figure 9–10. You can define and switch between different color combinations for your designs.

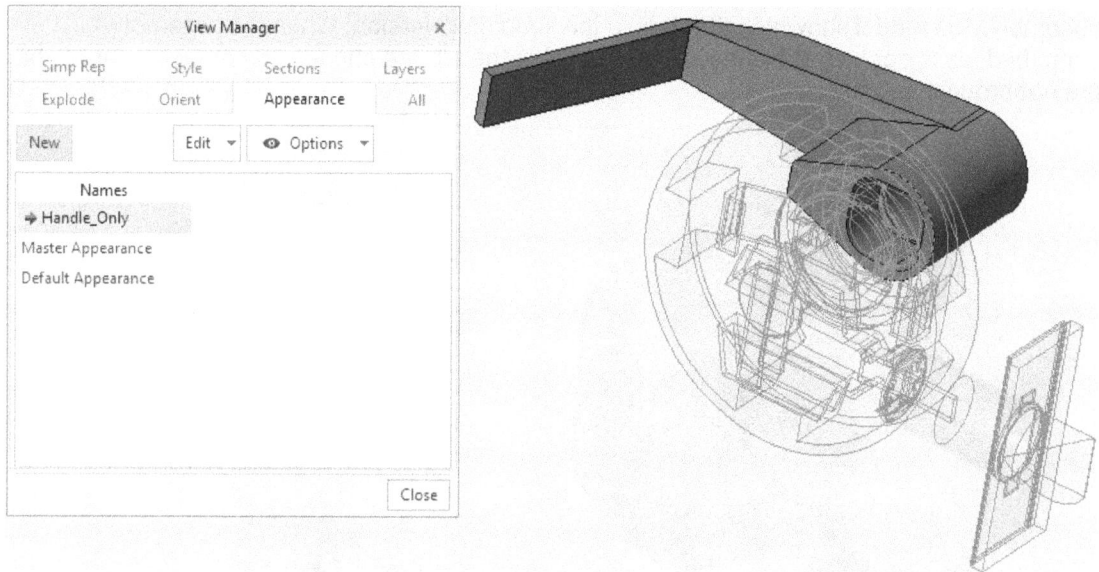

Figure 9–10

Apply appearances to surface, features, or components in your model. In the *Appearance* tab of the *View Manager*, click **New** and enter a name. You can repeat this for as many different combinations of colors, textures, etc. that you require. This enables you to quickly change the appearance for various use cases.

9.2 Simplified Representations

Simplified representations (simplified reps) are used to improve retrieval, display, and regeneration times, which significantly increases efficiency while working with assemblies. They are used to control which components (parts or subassemblies) of an assembly are opened and how they are displayed. The model shown on the left in Figure 9–11 is a complete assembly. The model shown on the right is the simplified version. When the assembly simplified rep is opened, only those components in the rep are opened, the other components are not brought into the session.

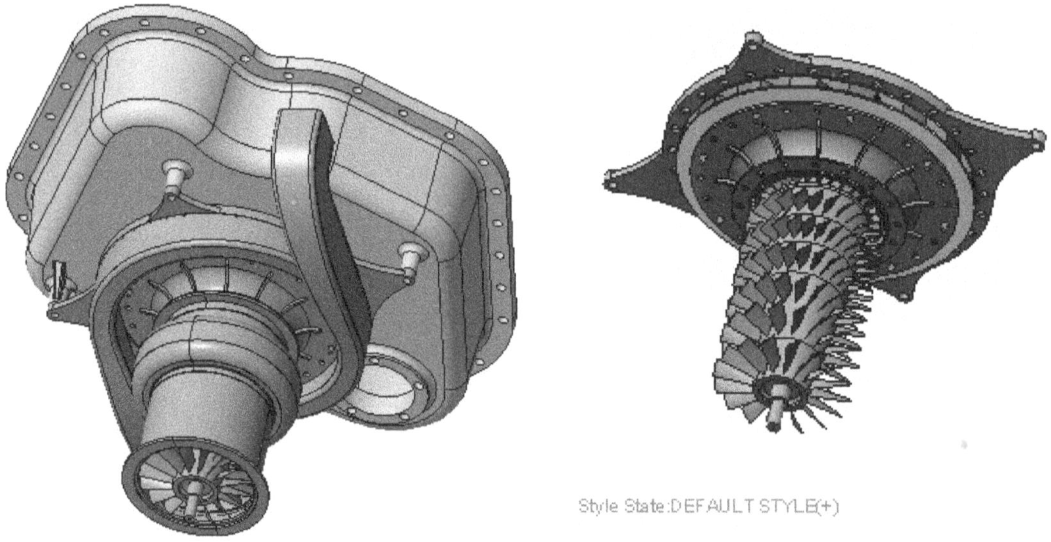

Style State:DEFAULT STYLE(+)

The top-level assembly has been simplified to remove components.

Figure 9–11

You can represent your model using system-defined simplified representations or a user-defined simplified representation.

9.3 Automatic Representations

Previous releases of Creo Parametric enabled you to create several different types of Simplified representations, such as Graphics representations, Geometry representations, Boundary Box representations, etc. As of Creo Parametric 4.0, all of the representation types are obsolete and are replaced with a single Automatic representation, as shown in Figure 9–12.

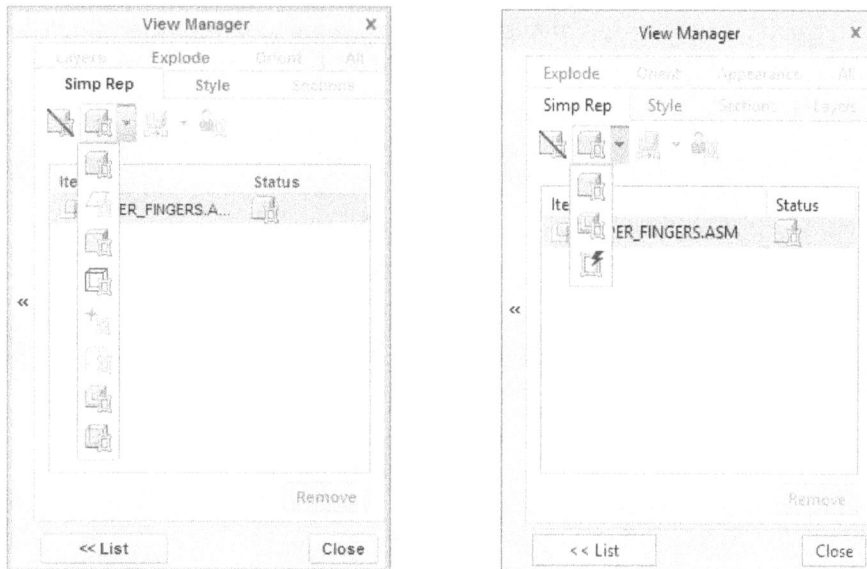

Previous releases   Creo 4.0+

Figure 9–12

The Automatic representation retrieves the assembly geometry as light-weight surfaces to retrieve your assembly as fast as possible. Some operations such as taking measurements can be conducted on the light-weight geometry, or you can bring the full models into session to conduct more extensive operations such as adding assembly features.

Note that only assembly components included in the representation are retrieved in an Automatic representation, whereas all other components remain excluded.

You can control the handling of simplified representations from previous releases using the configuration option *hide_pre_creo4_reps*:

* **yes:** Hides all simplified representations created in Creo Parametric 3.0 and earlier, except for **Exclude** simplified representations. By default, when opening an assembly, it opens as an Automatic representation.

* **no:** Maintains all simplified representations for Creo 3.0 and earlier.

* **maintain_master:** (Default) Hides all simplified representations for Creo 3.0 and earlier, except for **Master** and **Exclude** simplified representations.

9.4 Additional System-Defined Simplified Representations

In addition to the Automatic representation, assemblies have other system-defined simplified representations that are created automatically. These can be used to simplify the display and speed up the retrieval process of large assemblies.

System-defined simplified representations are enabled in the *View Manager*. Open the *View Manager* and select the *Simp Rep* tab. The *View Manager* displays as shown in Figure 9–13.

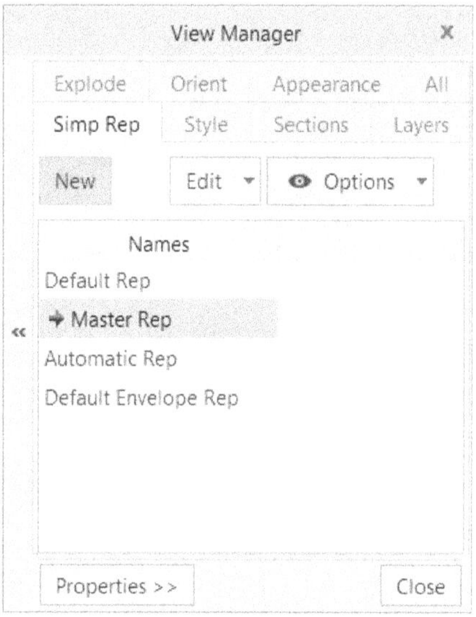

Figure 9–13

Double-click on a system-defined representation in the *View Manager* to enable it.

- **Default Representation:** Enables you to set a representation that automatically opens when the model is opened. By default, this representation is identical to the **Master Representation**. You do not actually see any difference in the model display until you redefine the **Default Representation** and manipulate the components.

- **Master Representation:** The representation that is used by default if customized simplified representations are not created. It opens the full assembly into session, including all of the components. All of the simplified representations are based on the master representation. Any assembly actions or modifications applied to a simplified representation are also applied to the master representation.

- **Default Envelope Representation:** Substitutes selected components with the default envelope representation. An envelope is a part that represents the geometry of any number of components in an assembly. It enables you to simplify the model by substituting complex geometry with a simple envelope feature (i.e., extrude or revolve). If there is no default envelope, the system opens the dialog box to create one.

9.5 User-Defined Simplified Representations

You can create user-defined simplified representations in an assembly to simplify the display and help ease the regeneration times of working with large assemblies.

User-defined simplified representations are created using the *View Manager*. Open the View Manager and select the *Simp Rep* tab. Click **New** in the *Simp Rep* area in the *View Manager*. Enter a name for the simplified rep and press <Enter>. The *Edit* dialog box opens, which enables you to quickly exclude components. Click **OK** to close the dialog box. The new representation is now active, as indicated by ⭢ .

You can select components for a simplified representation manually using the *Model Tree*, selecting directly on the model, or using defined rules.

> *Note: To delete a simplified representation, click **Edit>Remove** or right-click and select **Remove**.*

Manual Selection

Use one of the following two methods to modify the representation settings by manually selecting components.

Method 1

Use the *Edit* dialog box by clicking **Edit** and selecting **Edit Definition**. The dialog box opens as shown in Figure 9–14.

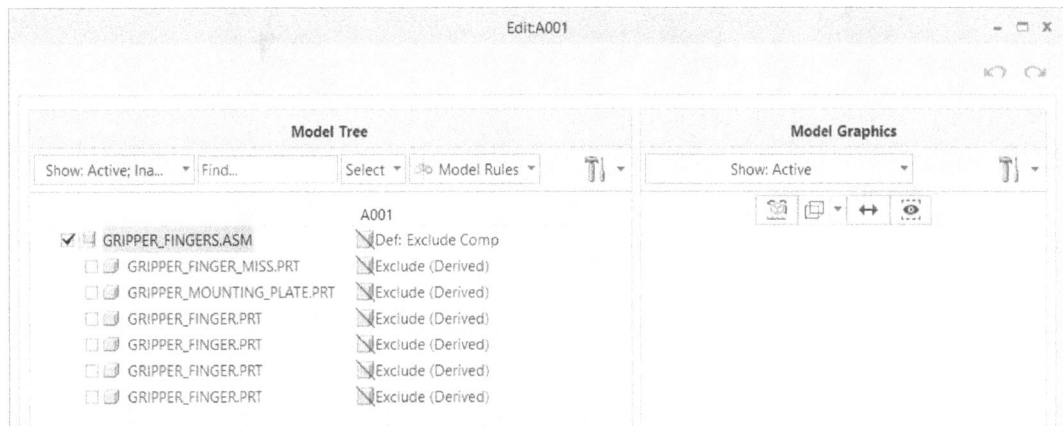

Figure 9–14

When creating a new simplified representation, components are excluded by default and the Default Simp Rep rule changes from *Master Rep* to **Exclude**. This eliminates the unnecessary retrieval of large data into the Creo Parametric session. This is useful when you are managing large assemblies. You can change the status of the top-level assembly using the flyout menu, as shown in Figure 9–15.

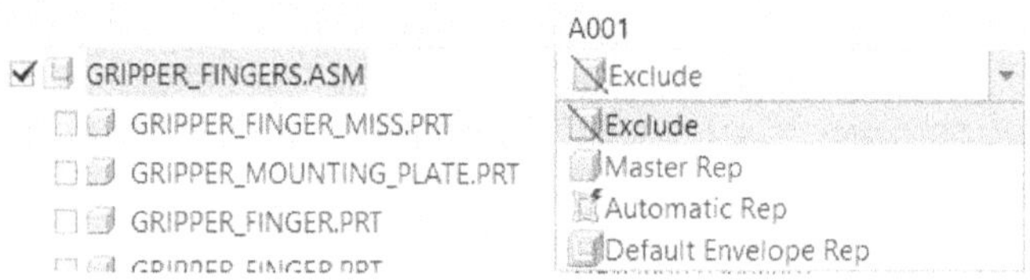

Figure 9–15

Assign representation settings using the options in the drop-down list as shown in Figure 9–16, or select the check box to switch between **Master Rep** and **Exclude**. The view window updates to reflect the changes.

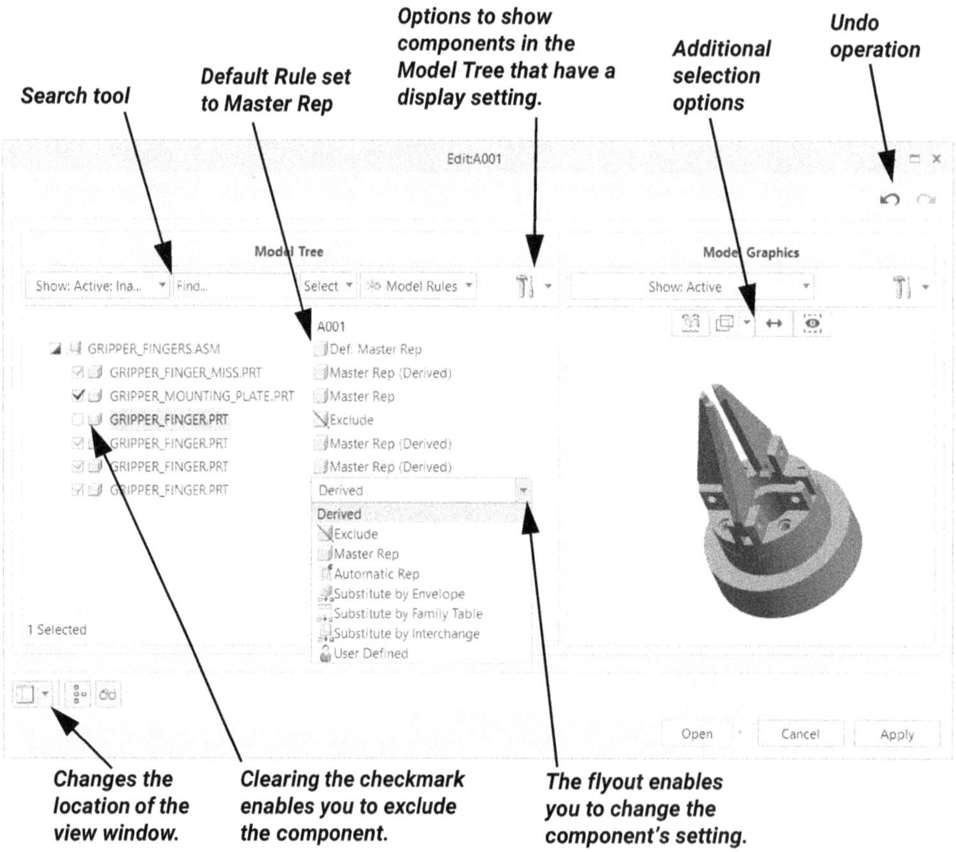

Figure 9–16

The *Show: Active, Inactive* drop-down list enables you to specify what is displayed. For example, you can remove the components that are inactive to simplify the amount of components listed in the column. The two components that were excluded from the simplified representation have been removed from the column as shown in Figure 9–17.

Clear the Inactive option and the two excluded components are removed from the column.

Figure 9–17

Additional options in the *View* window in the *Edit* dialog box are described as follows:

Icon	Description
	Removes components from the selection by geometric size.
	Removes internal components from the selection.
	Removes external components from the selection.
	Inverts the selection of displayed objects.
	Includes only the selected components and excludes all of the others.

*Note: A component's representation setting can also be assigned by selecting the component, right-clicking, and selecting **Representation**.*

Click **OK** to close the dialog box. The *Model Tree* adds a column to indicate the representation of the components.

Method 2

Select the simplified rep in the *View Manger* dialog box and click **Properties**. The *View Manager* opens. The default rule when creating a new simplified representation is **Master Representation**, as shown in Figure 9–18.

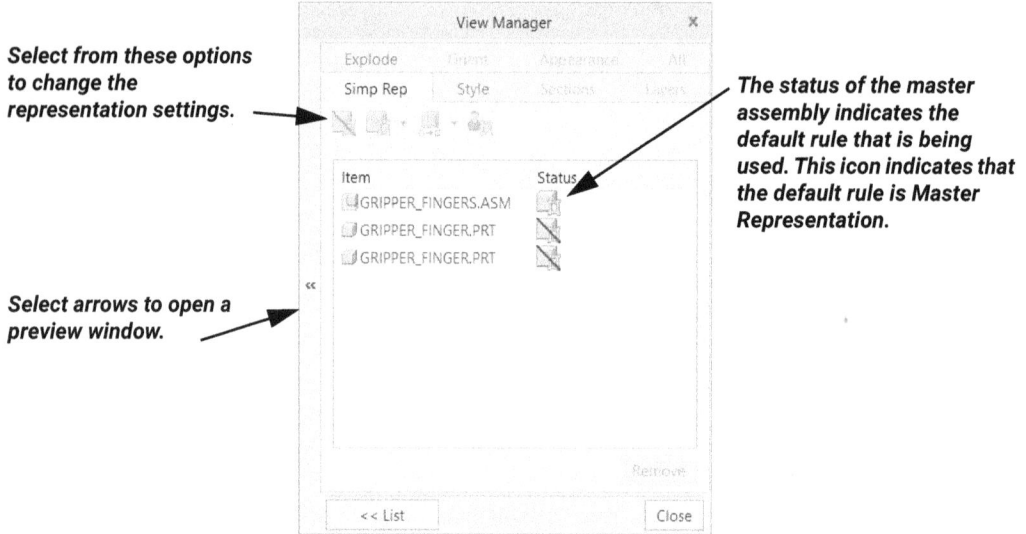

Select from these options to change the representation settings.

Select arrows to open a preview window.

The status of the master assembly indicates the default rule that is being used. This icon indicates that the default rule is Master Representation.

Figure 9–18

Select components in the model or *Model Tree* and assign representation settings using the options in the drop-down list as shown in Figure 9–19.

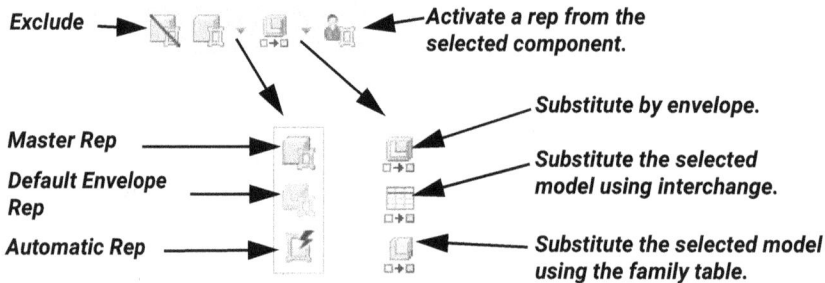

Exclude

Activate a rep from the selected component.

Master Rep

Default Envelope Rep

Automatic Rep

Substitute by envelope.

Substitute the selected model using interchange.

Substitute the selected model using the family table.

Figure 9–19

Click **List** to return to the listing of the simplified reps.

> *Note:* To display the simp rep settings in the Model Tree, click **Options** and select **Add Column**.

The settings and their icons for each method are described as follows:

Option	Icon	Description
Exclude		Selected components of the master representation are excluded as members of the simplified representation.
Master Rep		Selected components of the master representation are included as members of the simplified representation.
User Defined		Substitutes a user-defined simplified representation from a selected component.
Automatic Rep		Selected components of the master representation are included as Automatic.
Default Envelope Representation		Substitutes the selected components with the default envelope representation.

The current representation (➔) is temporarily modified with the new settings and displayed with a plus (+) symbol appended to the end of its name. For example, **No_Engine** (+) indicates that the **No_Engine** representation was displayed and that is has been modified.

To save the changes to the simplified rep, click **Edit>Save** and click **OK**.

You might need to make changes to the simplified representation once it has been created. Use either of the following techniques to redefine the representation settings:

- Click **Properties** and use the technique that was used in Method 2.
- Click **Edit>Edit Definition** and use the technique that was used in Method 1.
- Right-click on a simplified representation, click **Edit Definition**, and use the techniques that was used in Method 1.

9.6 Opening Simplified Representations

One of the main purposes of a simplified representation is to improve retrieval times when working with large assemblies. By directly opening a simplified rep instead of the master rep, only the required components are opened into session. To open a simplified rep you can select the **Open Representation**, **Open Automatic**, or **Open Subset options** in the *File Open* dialog box. You can also set the **open_simplified_rep_by_default** configuration option to determine how the model is opened. **No** is the default option and opens the **Master Rep**. If set to **Yes**, the *Open Representation* dialog box opens, enabling you to select a representation.

Use the Default Rep to eliminate the use of selecting **Open Representation**, **Open Subset**, or using the **open_simplified_rep_by_default** configuration file option.

Open Representation

Click 📂 (Open), select the assembly in the *File Open* dialog box, expand **Open**, and select **Open Representation**. The *Open Representation* dialog box opens as shown in Figure 9–20, enabling you to select the representation that you want to open.

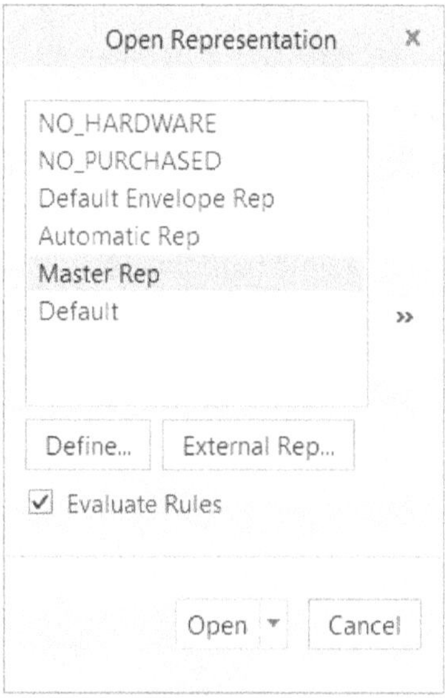

Figure 9–20

You can easily define and edit simplified representations without loading models into memory. Using the dynamic preview, you can display the preview and add or remove the components easily from a simplified representation, as shown in Figure 9–21.

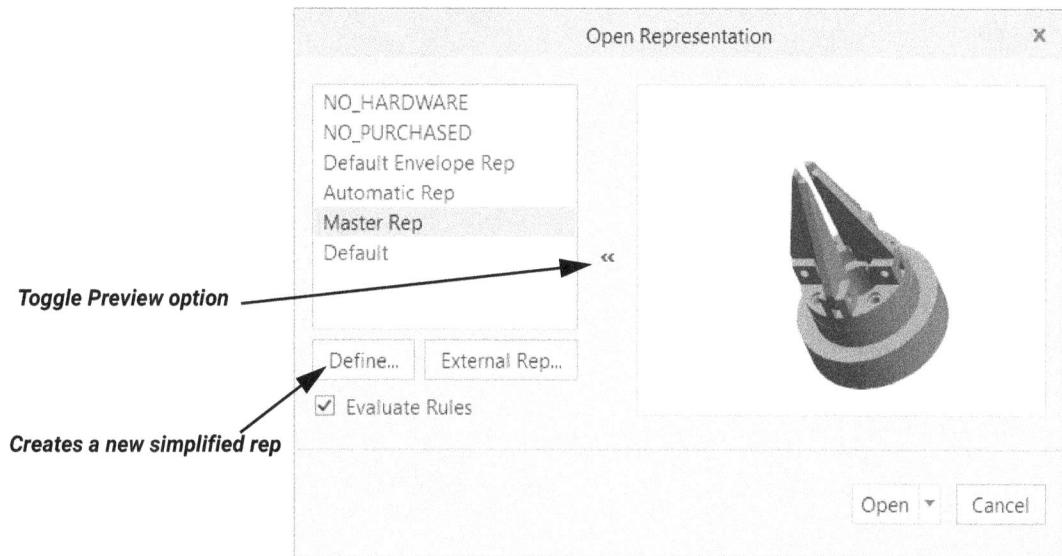

Figure 9–21

Open Automatic

Click (Open), select the assembly in the *File Open* dialog box, expand **Open**, and then select **Open Automatic**. The Automatic representation of the assembly will open.

Open Subset

Click 📂 (Open), select the assembly in the *File Open* dialog box, and click **Open Subset**. The *Retrieval Customization* dialog box opens as shown in Figure 9–22. It is similar to the *Edit* dialog box.

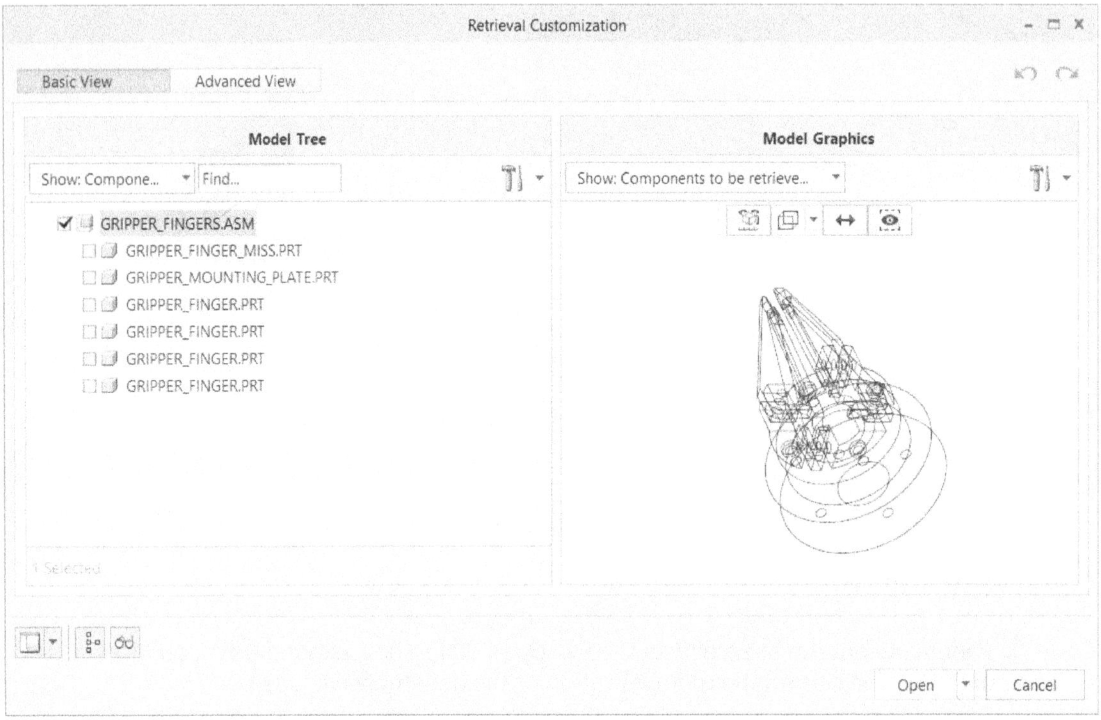

Figure 9–22

Practice 9a
Use Component Display Styles

Practice Objectives

- Set the display style of an assembly and of a subassembly.
- Set the default display style.

In this practice, you will create display styles to customize how the model is displayed. You will create styles in the top-level assembly and in subassemblies so that their styles are passed back to the top-level assembly. In addition, you will customize the default style to control the style that is used when the model is opened. The model shown on the left in Figure 9–23 is the complete top-level assembly and the model on the right is one of the display styles that you will create.

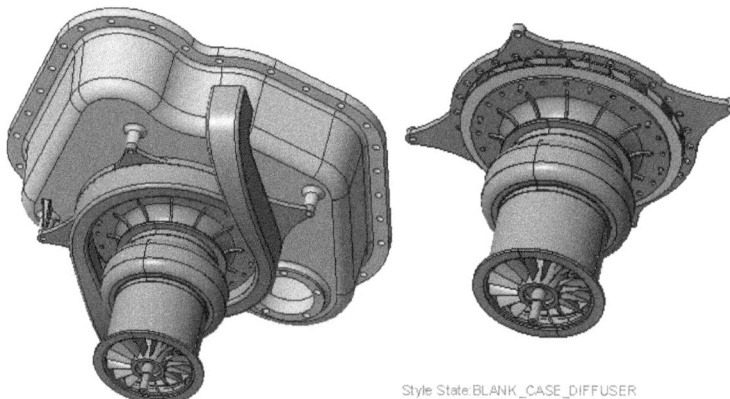

Style State:BLANK_CASE_DIFFUSER

Figure 9–23

Task 1: Open an assembly file.

1. Change your working directory to the **Component_Display_Styles** folder.
2. Open **turbine.asm**.
3. Set the model display as follows:

   - *(Datum Display Filters)*: All Off
   - *(Spin Center)*: Off
   - *(Display Style)*: (Shading With Edges)

4. In the *In-graphics* toolbar, click (View Manager) to open the *View Manager*.

   Note: *You can also click (Manage Views) in the Model tab.*

5. Select the *Style* tab, as shown in Figure 9-24.

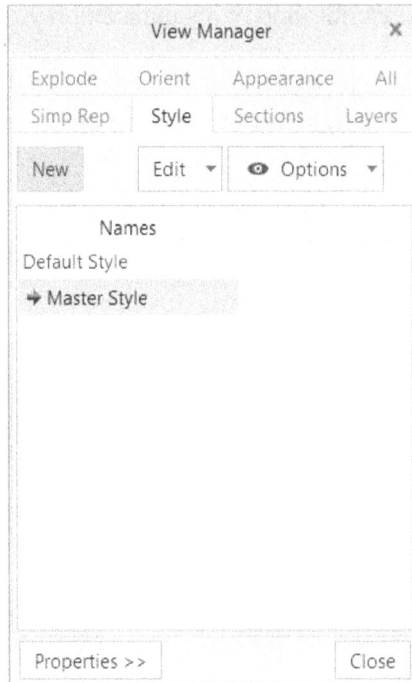

Figure 9-24

Task 2: Create a user-defined view style.

1. Click **New**.
2. Enter **Blank_Case_Diffuser**, as shown in Figure 9-25.

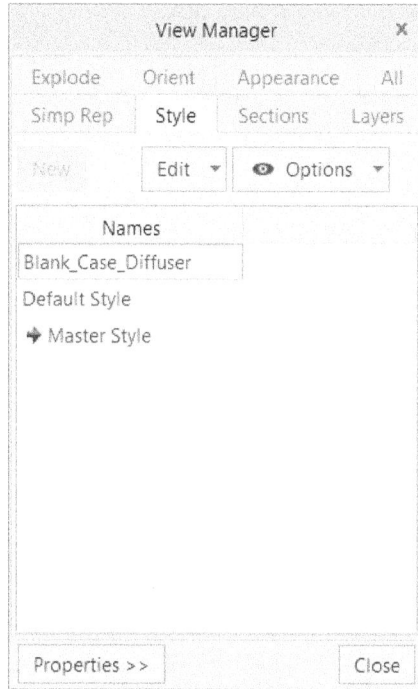

Figure 9–25

3. Press <Enter>.

4. Hold <Ctrl> and select **GEAR_CASE.PRT** and **DIFFUSER.PRT** in the *Model Tree,* as shown in Figure 9–26.

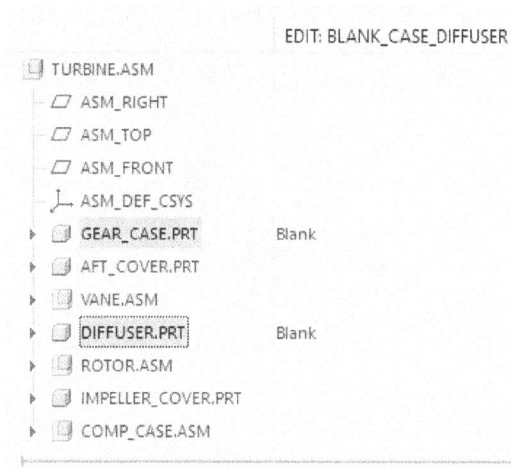

Figure 9–26

5. Click **OK** in the *EDIT* dialog box.

6. Click **Properties** in the *View Manager* dialog box.

7. The *Item* and *Status* columns display in the *View Manager* dialog box, as shown in Figure 9-27.

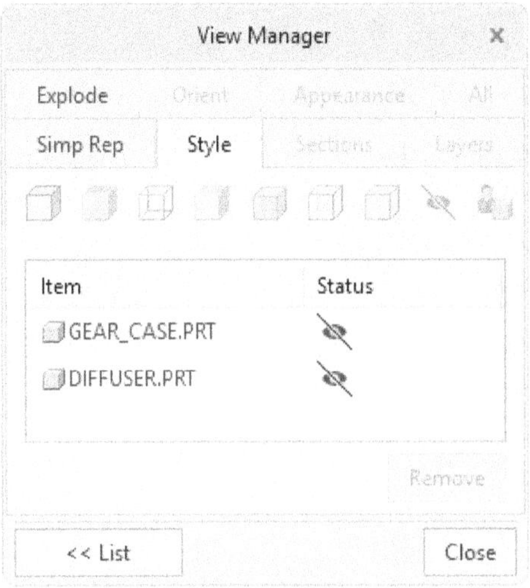

Figure 9-27

8. Click **List**.

9. Click **Close**. The assembly view style displays as shown in Figure 9-28.

Style State:BLANK_CASE_DIFFUSER

Figure 9-28

*Note: The model continues to display the **BLANK_ CASE_DIFFUSER** display style. This is because it is the active style, as indicated by ➔ .*

Task 3: Activate the Default Style and modify its settings.

Design Considerations

The Default Style is the view style that is displayed when the assembly is opened. By default, it includes all of the components and uses the global display setting for the current session for all of the components. In this task, you will edit the default style so that when the model is opened, it automatically displays a custom style.

1. Open the *View Manager*. The **Blank_Case_Diffuser** is still the active style. Double-click on **Default Style** to activate it. This style contains all of the components, and they all use the global display setting for the current session, as shown in Figure 9–29.

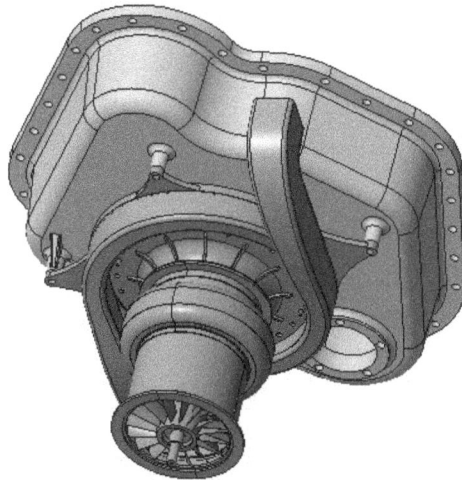

Style State:DEFAULT STYLE

Figure 9–29

2. Click **Properties**.

3. Select the three components shown in Figure 9–30 and remove them from the display by clicking ✎ (Blank). The model displays as shown in Figure 9–30.

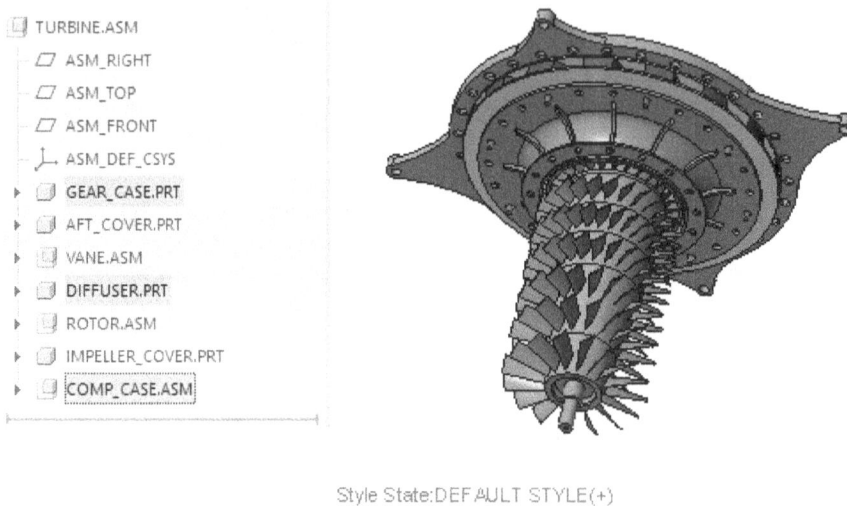

Style State:DEFAULT STYLE(+)

Figure 9–30

4. Click **List**.
5. Click **Edit>Save** and click **OK** to save the style. The warning shown in Figure 9–31 displays.

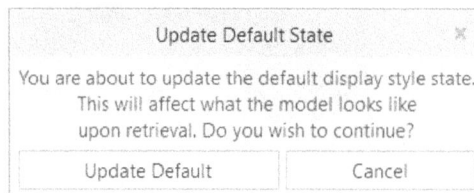

Update Default State   ✕

You are about to update the default display style state.
This will affect what the model looks like
upon retrieval. Do you wish to continue?

Update Default	Cancel

Figure 9–31

6. Click **Update Default**.
7. Close the *View Manager*.
8. Regenerate the assembly.
9. Save the assembly.
10. Close the window and erase it from memory.

Task 4: Open the assembly.

1. Open **turbine.asm**. The model displays as shown in Figure 9–32.

Design Considerations

The assembly opens and is displayed in the default style that you just customized, as shown in Figure 9–32. Now that you have changed the default state, the state is displayed each time this assembly is opened. However, the file retrieval time has not been reduced. Setting a view state only simplifies the visual display of an assembly. File retrieval and regeneration time are not affected.

Style State:DEFAULT STYLE

Figure 9–32

Task 5: Use a display style of a subassembly in the top-level assembly.

1. Open **comp_case.asm** using the *Model Tree*. The assembly displays as shown in Figure 9–33.

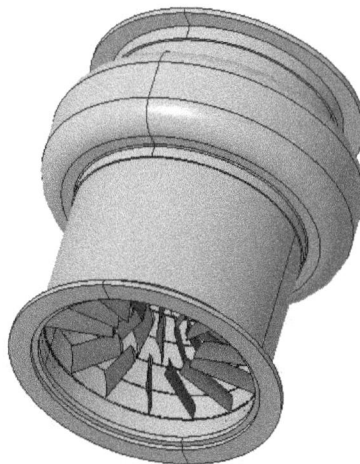

Figure 9–33

2. Use the *View Manager* to create a display style called **NO_HIDDEN**.

3. In the *EDIT* dialog box, click the *Show* tab.

4. Select **No Hidden** in the Method area as shown in Figure 9-34.

Figure 9-34

5. In the *Model Tree*, select all of the components in the assembly, then click **OK** in the *EDIT* dialog box.

6. If necessary, save the display style and close the *View Manager*. The assembly displays as shown in Figure 9-35.

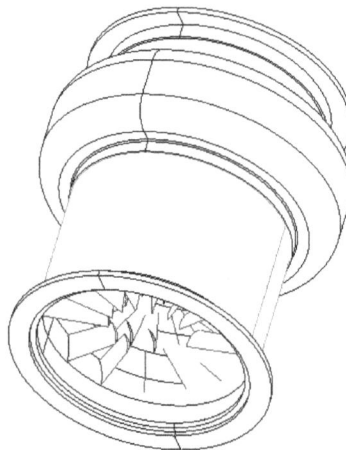

Style State:NO_HIDDEN

Figure 9-35

7. Save the assembly and close the window. The **TURBINE** window should now be active.

Task 6: Create a view state by copying an existing state.

1. Open the *View Manager*.
2. Select the **Blank_Case_Diffuser** state, right-click, and select **Copy**, as shown in Figure 9–36.

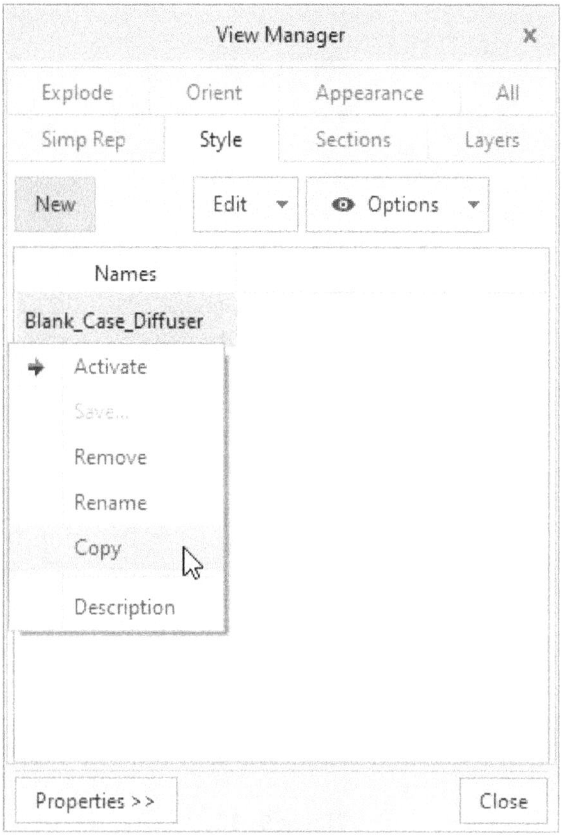

Figure 9–36

3. Enter **Comp_Case_No_Hidden** in the *Copy to* field, as shown in Figure 9–37.

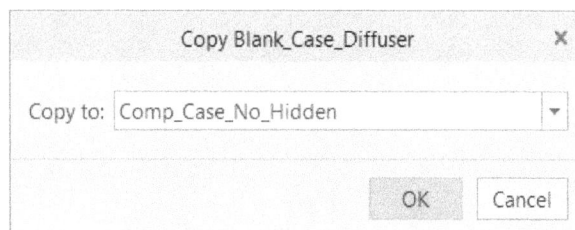

Figure 9–37

4. Click **OK**.

5. Activate **Blank_Case_Diffuser** and click **Properties**.

6. Select **COMP_CASE.ASM** in the *Model Tree* and click 🔓 (Activate From Selected) to assign a style from the subassembly level.

7. In the *SELECT DISPLAY STYLE* dialog box, select **NO_HIDDEN** and click **OK**. The *View Manager* updates as shown in Figure 9–38.

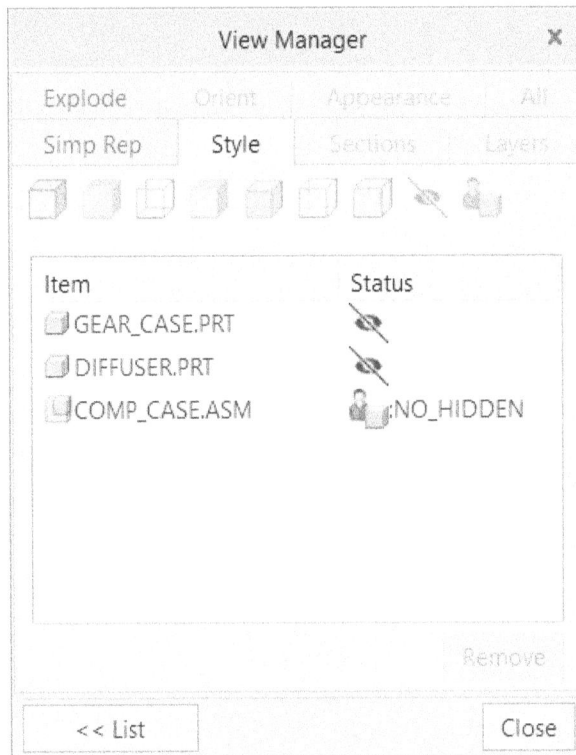

Figure 9–38

8. Click **List** and save the **Blank_Case_Diffuser**.

9. Close the *View Manager*. The assembly displays as shown in Figure 9–39.

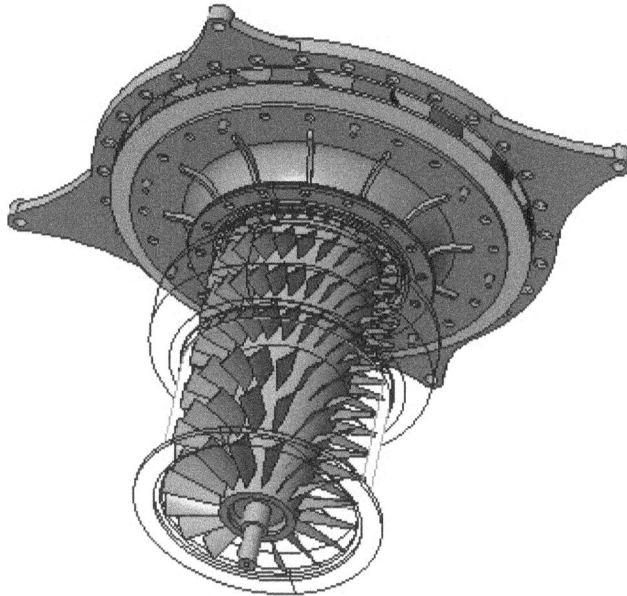

Style State:BLANK_CASE_DIFFUSER

Figure 9–39

Task 7: Edit the default style.

1. Open the *View Manager*.

Design Considerations

By customizing the default style, each time you open the assembly it displays with this display style. This might only be required while you are working on a specific aspect of the assembly. To return the style to display all of the components, such as the master style when opened, you must remove all of the customization from this style. It can be further customized at a later date, if required.

2. Double-click on **Default Style** and click **Properties**.

3. Select all three items as shown in Figure 9–40, and click **Remove**.

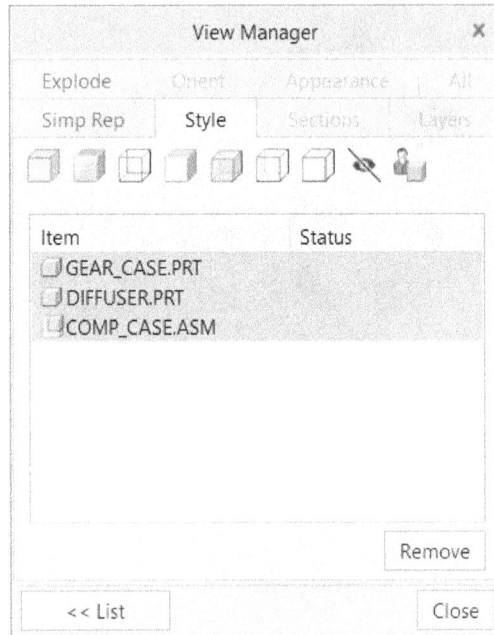

Figure 9–40

4. Save the default style. Click **Update Default** to complete the save.

5. Set **Master Style** to be the active view style and close the *View Manager*.

6. Save the assembly and erase all files from memory.

End of practice

Practice 9b
Simplified Representations

Practice Objectives

- Create and open simplified representations.
- Set the default simplified representation.

In this practice, you will create simplified representations that remove components from the display. In addition, you will learn how to open these user-defined representations so that the removed components are not brought into session. The model shown on the left in Figure 9–41 is the complete top-level assembly and the model shown on the right is one of the simplified representations that you will create.

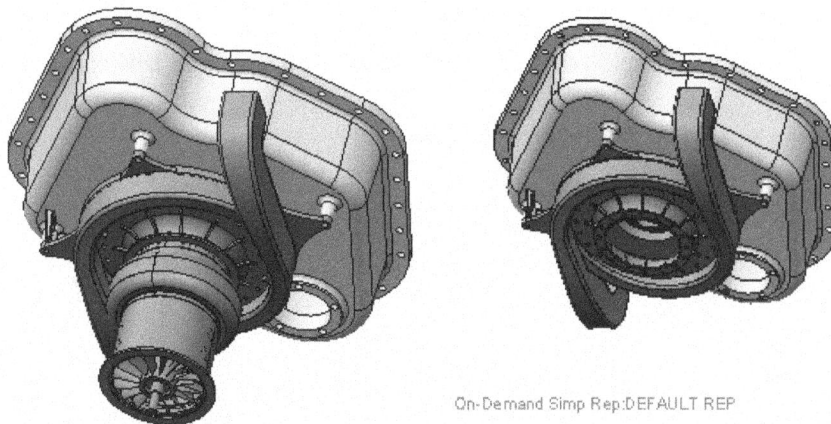

On-Demand Simp Rep:DEFAULT REP

Figure 9–41

Task 1: Open the View Manager.

1. Change your working directory to the **Simplified_Representations** folder.
2. Open **turbine.asm**.
3. Set the model display as follows:

   - ⅍ *(Datum Display Filters)*: All Off
   - ⌖ *(Spin Center)*: Off
   - ▢ *(Display Style)*: ▢ (Shading With Edges)

4. In the In-graphics toolbar, click ▣ (View Manager) to open the *View Manager*.

5. Select the *Simp Rep* tab. The *View Manager* updates as shown in Figure 9–42.

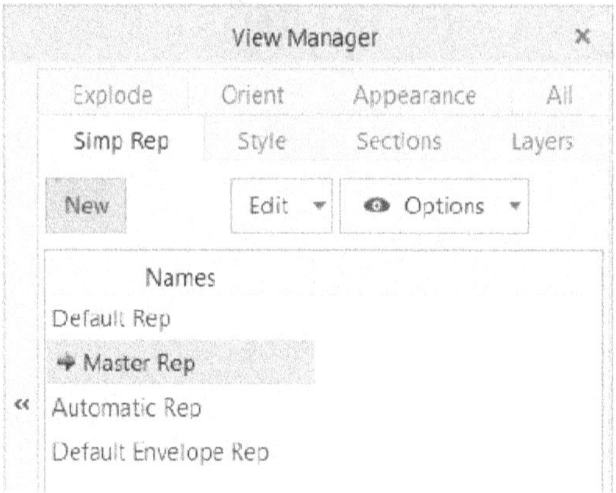

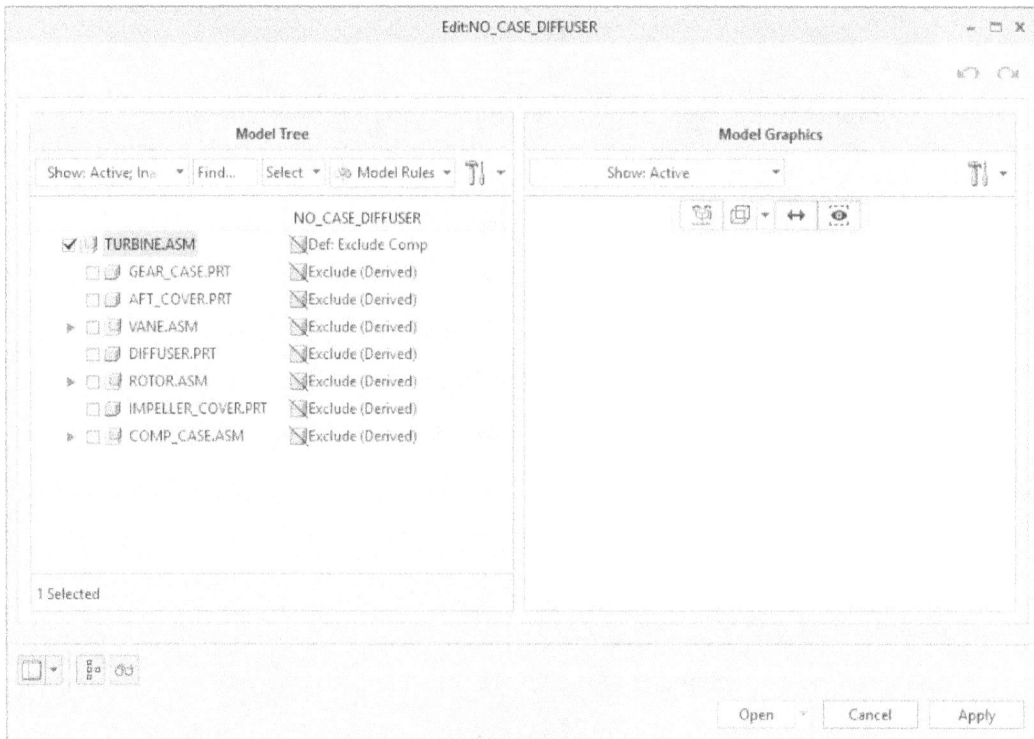

Figure 9–42

6. Click **New**, set the new simplified representation *Name* to **No_Case_Diffuser**, and press <Enter>.

7. The *Edit* dialog box opens as shown in Figure 9–43.

Figure 9–43

8. Select **Def: Exclude Comp** next to **TURBINE.ASM** and select **Master Rep** in the drop-down list, as shown in Figure 9−44. This changes the default rule to *Master Representation*.

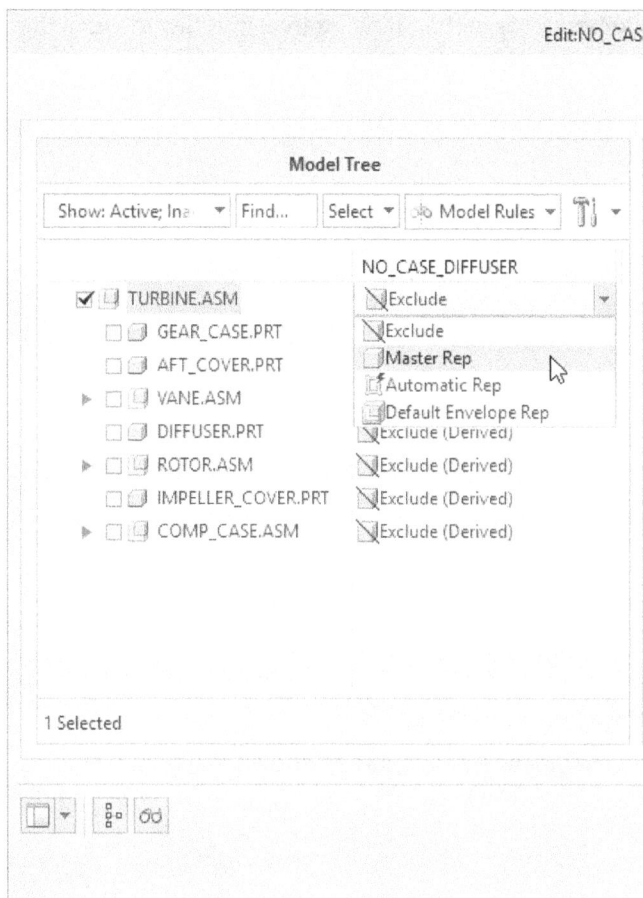

Figure 9−44

9. Click twice on the check box next to **GEAR_CASE.PRT** and **DIFFUSER.PRT** to clear the selection and change *Master Rep (Derived)* to **Exclude** as shown Figure 9-45. The column indicates the components that have been excluded in this representation (you may need to include **Inactive Components** in the **Show: Active; Inactive** menu in the upper left to display the rows for the excluded components).

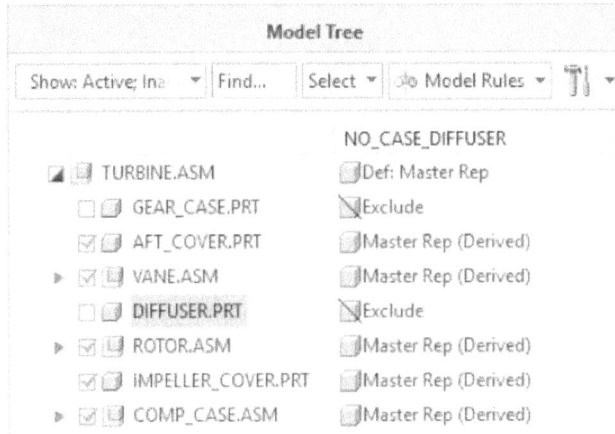

Figure 9-45

10. Click **Open**.

11. If required, use (Tree Columns) to turn on the **Current Rep** column in the *Simplified Reps* type so they display in the *Model Tree*.

12. The assembly and the *Model Tree* display as shown in Figure 9-46.

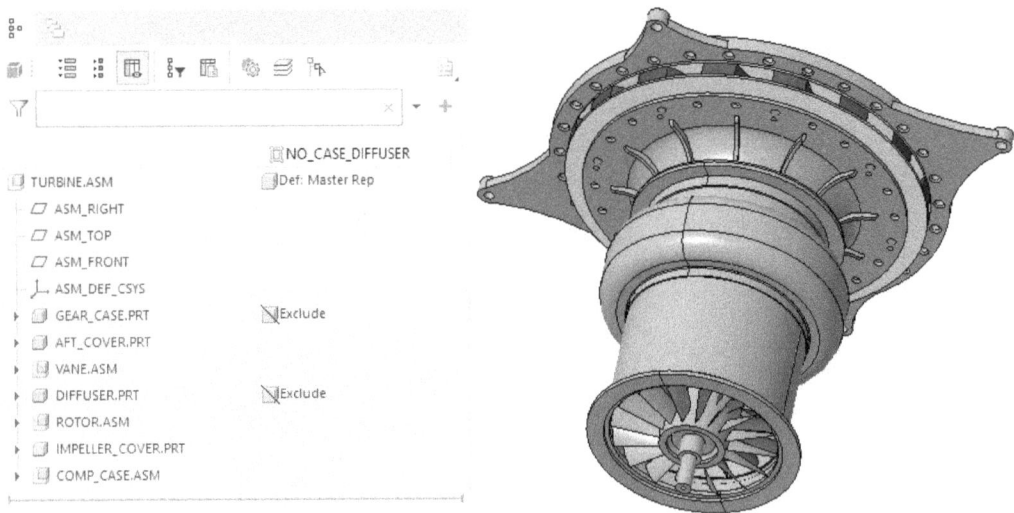

Figure 9-46

Design Considerations

When you create a simplified rep that excludes components or a display style that excludes components, the display of the model displays in the same way. However, using a simplified rep reduces system resources and retrieval and regeneration times. A view state does not reduce system resources.

Task 2: Edit an existing simplified representation.

1. Select **No_Case_Diffuser**, and click **Edit>Edit Definition**. The *Edit* dialog box opens as shown in Figure 9–47.

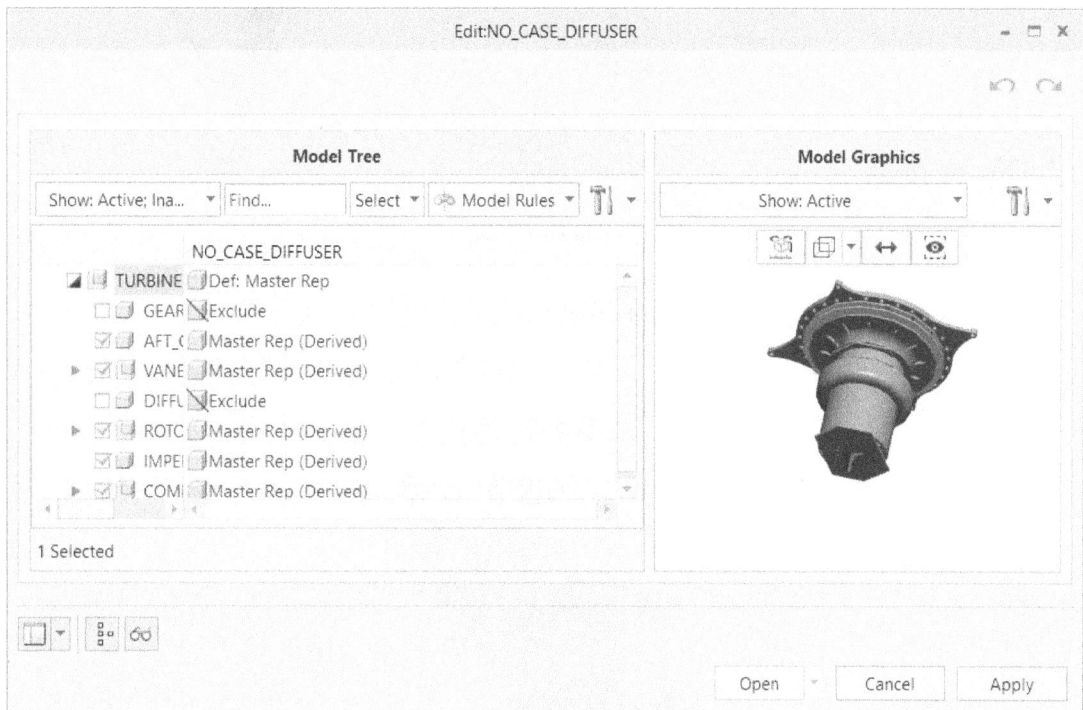

Figure 9–47

2. Clear the checkmarks next to **VANE.ASM** and **ROTOR.ASM**, as shown in Figure 9–48. The column indicates that the components have been excluded in this representation.

Figure 9–48

3. Click **Open** to complete the redefinition of the **No_Case_Diffuser** representation. The assembly displays as shown in Figure 9–49.

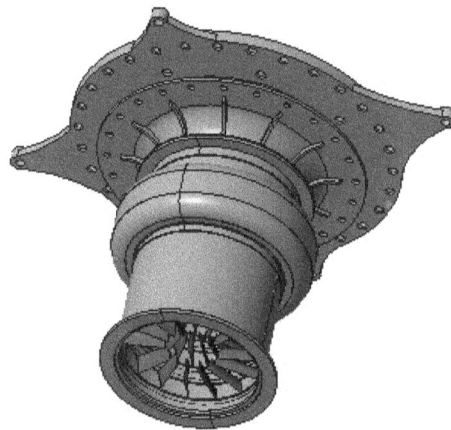

On-Demand Simp Rep:NO_CASE_DIFFUSER

Figure 9–49

4. Close the *View Manager*.

5. Save the assembly.

6. Close the window and erase all of the files from memory.

Task 3: Open a simplified representations of an assembly.

1. In the *Home* tab, click 📂 (Open).

2. Select **turbine.asm**, expand **Open**, and select **Open Representation,** as shown in Figure 9–50.

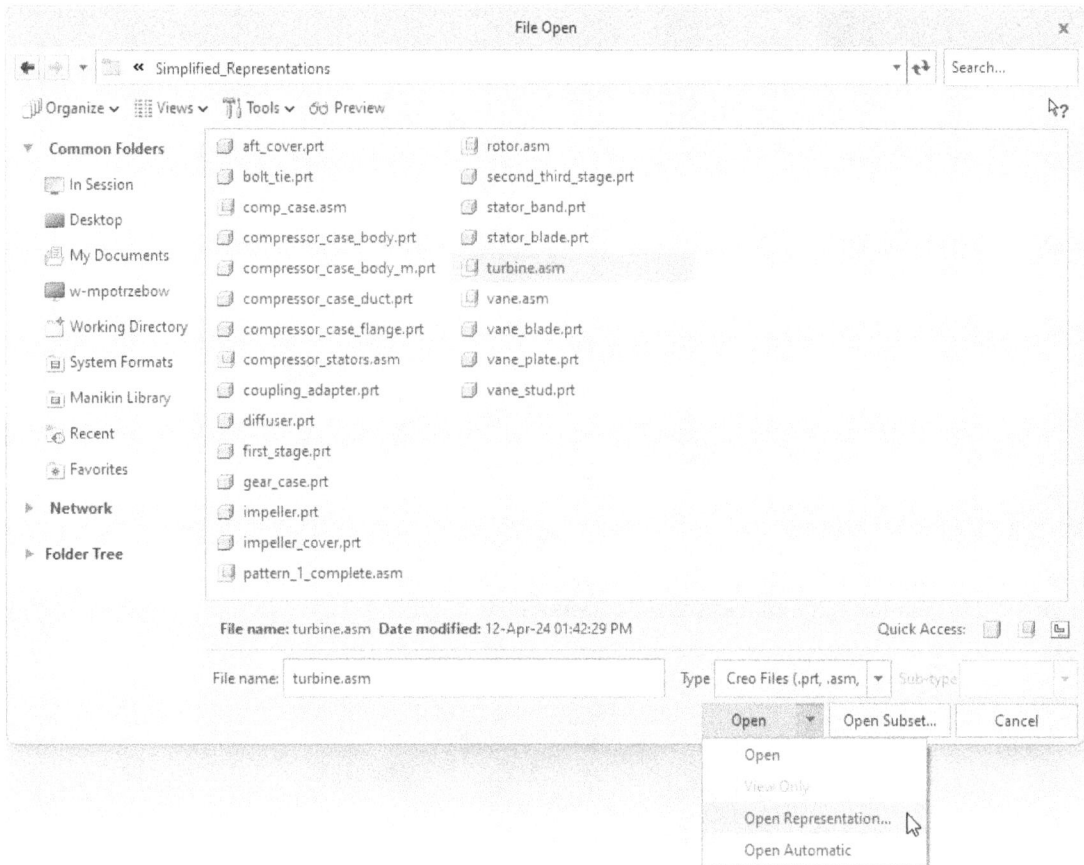

Figure 9–50

3. Select **NO_CASE_DIFFUSER** in the *Open Representation* dialog box, as shown in Figure 9–51.

Figure 9–51

4. Click **Open**.

Design Considerations

The assembly opens according to the selected simplified representation, as shown in Figure 9–52. The file retrieval time has decreased.

On-Demand Simp Rep:NO_CASE_DIFFUSER

Figure 9–52

Task 4: Review the files that are in memory.

1. Select **File>Manage Session>Object List**.

Design Considerations

The information window lists all of the components that have been loaded into memory, as shown in Figure 9–53. The excluded components, such as **gear_case.prt**, **diffuser.prt**, and **vane.asm** are not listed, but are listed in the *Model Tree*. A simplified representation only loads the required data, which reduces the file retrieval and regeneration time.

```
INFORMATION  WINDOW (names.inf.1)        –  ☐  ×

File    Edit    View


Parts
-----
  AFT_COVER
  IMPELLER_COVER
  COMPRESSOR_CASE_BODY_M
  COMPRESSOR_CASE_BODY
  STATOR_BAND
  STATOR_BLADE
  STATOR_25
  STATOR_BLADE_18
  STATOR_30
  STATOR_BLADE_15
  STATOR_35
  STATOR_BLADE_11
  STATOR_40
  STATOR_BLADE_7
  STATOR_45
  STATOR_BLADE_2
  COMPRESSOR_CASE_FLANGE
  COMPRESSOR_CASE_DUCT


                     Close
```

Figure 9–53

Task 5: Erase memory and open without representation.

1. Close the *Information Window*.
2. Close the window and erase all of the files from memory.
3. Open the Master Rep for **turbine.asm** (do not use Open Rep).
4. Select **File>Manage Session>Object List** and view all of the files that have been loaded into memory. **Gear_case.prt**, **diffuser.prt**, and **vane.asm** are now listed.

Task 6: Set the default representation.

1. Open the *View Manager*.

Design Considerations

Customizing the Default Rep is good practice when working with large resource-intensive assemblies. By starting work using a customized Default Representation, only the required components are brought into session each time the assembly is opened. If at any time you need to work with another rep or the Master Rep, you can use the View Manager to activate another rep. Any missing components are automatically brought into session.

2. Double-click on **Default Rep** to make it the active representation.

3. Use **Edit>Edit Definition** to customize the Default Rep to exclude the three memory intensive assemblies:

   - vane.asm
   - rotor.asm
   - comp_case.asm

   The *Edit* dialog box displays as shown in Figure 9−54.

TURBINE.ASM		Def: Master Rep
GEAR_CASE.PRT		Master Rep (Derived)
AFT_COVER.PRT		Master Rep (Derived)
VANE.ASM		Exclude
DIFFUSER.PRT		Master Rep (Derived)
ROTOR.ASM		Exclude
IMPELLER_COVER.PRT		Master Rep (Derived)
COMP_CASE.ASM		Exclude

Figure 9−54

4. If necessary, save the changes that you have made to the Default Rep. The model displays as shown in Figure 9–55.

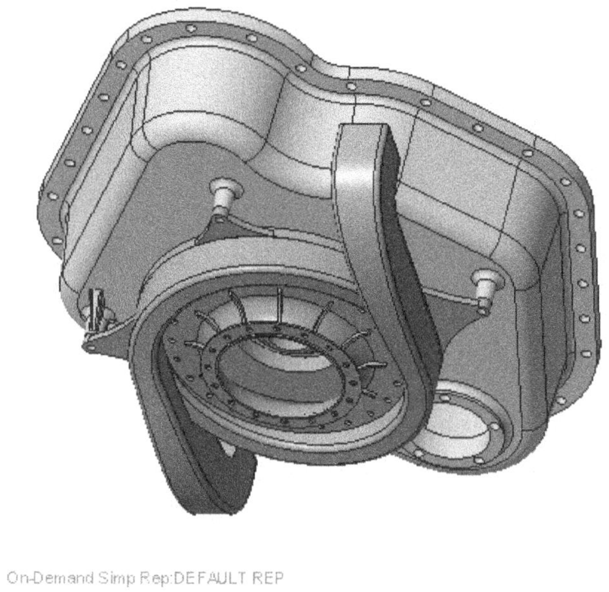

On-Demand Simp Rep:DEFAULT REP

Figure 9–55

5. Close the *View Manager*.

6. Save the assembly.

7. Close the window and erase all of the files from memory.

8. Open the Default Rep for **turbine.asm** (without using Open Rep).

9. The model loads very quickly and is displayed in the **DEFAULT REP** state.

10. Close the assembly and erase it from memory.

End of practice

Practice 9c
Automatic Simplified Representations

Practice Objectives

- Apply materials to components in the assembly.
- Review the simplified representations in the assembly.
- Review the Automatic Rep.

In this practice, you will work with a motor assembly and investigate some of the assembly updates, including applying materials and simplified representations.

Task 1: Open the aft_engine_section model.

1. Set the working directory to **Automatic_Simplified_Rep**.
2. Open **aft_engine_section.asm**.
3. Set the model display as follows:

    - *(Datum Display Filters)*: None
    - *(Spin Center)*: Off
    - *(Display Style)*: (Shading With Edges)

    The model displays as shown in Figure 9–56.

Figure 9–56

Task 2: Apply an aluminum material to the block part.

1. In the *Model Tree*, select **BLOCK.PRT** and click ☺ (Open) from the mini toolbar.
2. Click **File>Prepare>Model Properties**.
3. In the *Model Properties* dialog box, click **change** in the *Material* field, as shown in Figure 9–57.

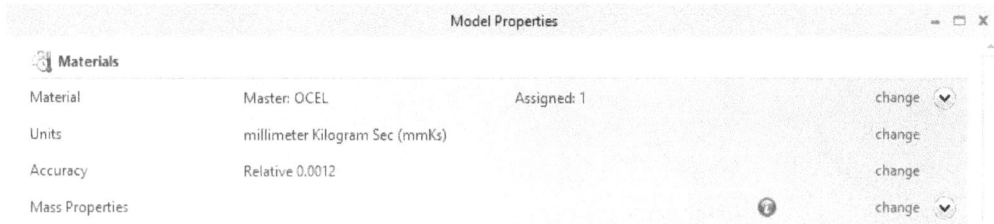

Figure 9–57

4. The *Materials* dialog box displays, as shown in Figure 9–58.

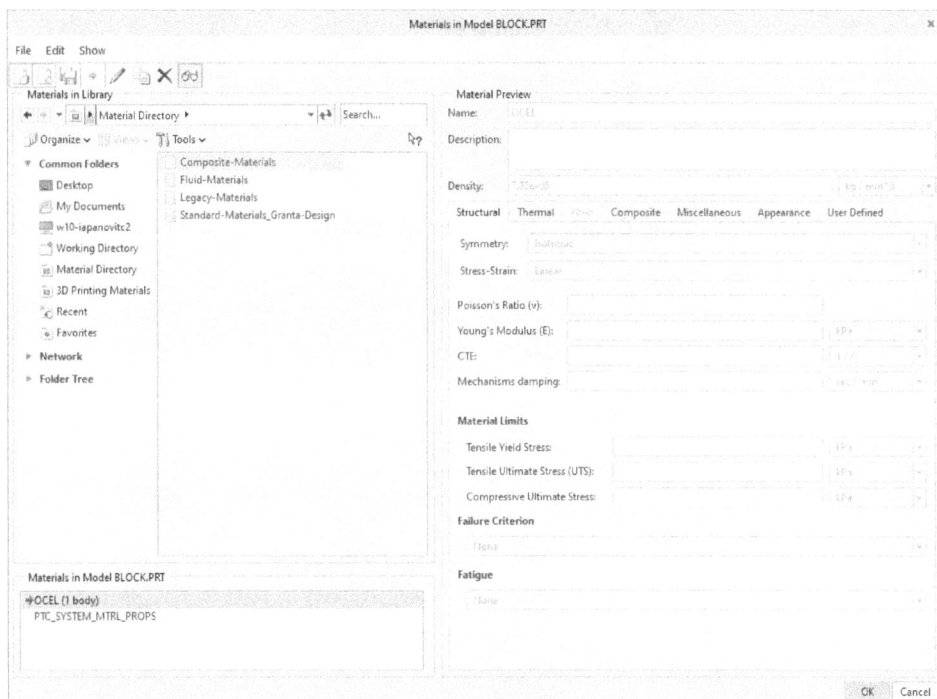

Figure 9–58

Note: A Material Preview displays in the Materials dialog box, listing the material properties. You can toggle the preview on and off using ᎧᎧ (Show/Hide Material Preview).

5. Double-click on **Legacy-Materials** to open the folder.

6. Double-click on **al2014.mtl**. Note that it is not assigned to the model but rather it is added to the list of materials available in the model, as shown in Figure 9–59.

Figure 9–59

Note: The custom material OCEL is the still assigned to the model.

7. Click **OK**.

8. In the *Model Properties* dialog box, click **Close**.

9. In the *Model Tree*, expand the **Design Items** and **Materials** nodes, as shown in Figure 9–60.

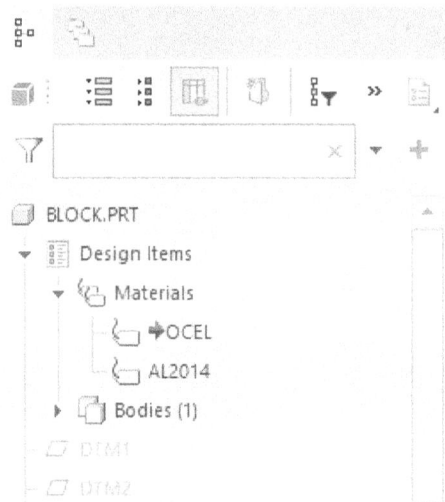

Figure 9–60

10. Right-click on **AL2014** and select **Set as Master**. Note the warning that displays, as shown in Figure 9–61.

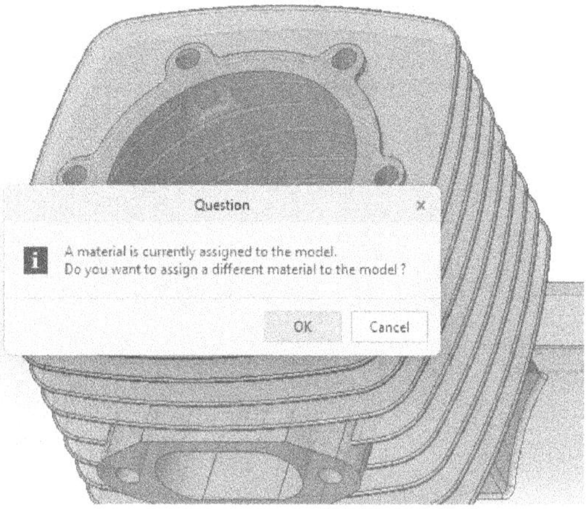

Figure 9–61

11. Click **OK**.

12. Right-click on **AL2014** and select **Info**. The browser window displays the material parameters, as shown in Figure 9–62.

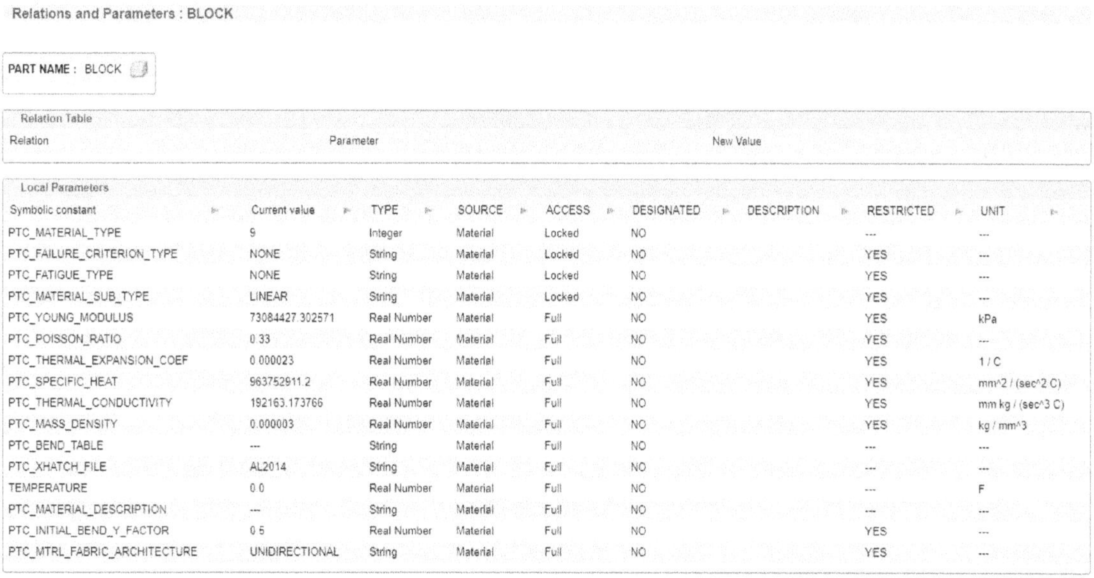

Relations and Parameters : BLOCK

PART NAME : BLOCK

Relation Table

Relation	Parameter	New Value

Local Parameters

Symbolic constant	Current value	TYPE	SOURCE	ACCESS	DESIGNATED	DESCRIPTION	RESTRICTED	UNIT
PTC_MATERIAL_TYPE	9	Integer	Material	Locked	NO		---	---
PTC_FAILURE_CRITERION_TYPE	NONE	String	Material	Locked	NO		YES	---
PTC_FATIGUE_TYPE	NONE	String	Material	Locked	NO		YES	---
PTC_MATERIAL_SUB_TYPE	LINEAR	String	Material	Locked	NO		YES	---
PTC_YOUNG_MODULUS	73084427.302571	Real Number	Material	Full	NO		YES	kPa
PTC_POISSON_RATIO	0.33	Real Number	Material	Full	NO		YES	---
PTC_THERMAL_EXPANSION_COEF	0.000023	Real Number	Material	Full	NO		YES	1 / C
PTC_SPECIFIC_HEAT	963752911.2	Real Number	Material	Full	NO		YES	mm^2 / (sec^2 C)
PTC_THERMAL_CONDUCTIVITY	192163.173766	Real Number	Material	Full	NO		YES	mm kg / (sec^3 C)
PTC_MASS_DENSITY	0.000003	Real Number	Material	Full	NO		YES	kg / mm^3
PTC_BEND_TABLE	---	String	Material	Full	NO		---	---
PTC_XHATCH_FILE	AL2014	String	Material	Full	NO		---	---
TEMPERATURE	0 0	Real Number	Material	Full	NO		---	F
PTC_MATERIAL_DESCRIPTION	---	String	Material	Full	NO		---	---
PTC_INITIAL_BEND_Y_FACTOR	0 5	Real Number	Material	Full	NO		YES	---
PTC_MTRL_FABRIC_ARCHITECTURE	UNIDIRECTIONAL	String	Material	Full	NO		YES	---

Figure 9–62

13. Close the browser window.

14. Right-click on **AL2014** and click **Delete**.

15. In the *Warning* dialog box, click **OK**.

16. Right-click on the **Materials** node and select **Edit Materials**, as shown in Figure 9–63.

Figure 9–63

17. In the *Materials* dialog box, double-click on **Legacy-Materials** to open the folder.

18. Double-click on **al6061.mtl**.

19. In the *Materials in Model BLOCK.PRT* area, right-click on **AL6061** and select **Set as Master**, as shown in Figure 9–64.

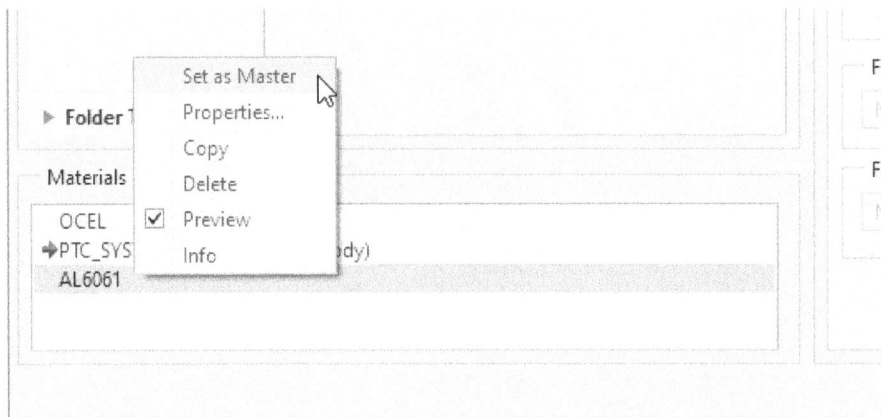

Figure 9–64

20. Click **OK** in the *Materials* dialog box. Note that the material is assigned, as shown in Figure 9−65.

Figure 9−65

21. Close the part window and return to the assembly.

Task 3: Investigate the simplified representations in the assembly.

Design Consideration

The assembly was created in a previous release of Creo Parametric. In this task, you will investigate how legacy simplified representations are handled.

1. In the In-graphics toolbar, select (View Manager).

2. In *View Manager*, select the *Simp Rep* tab, as shown in Figure 9–66.

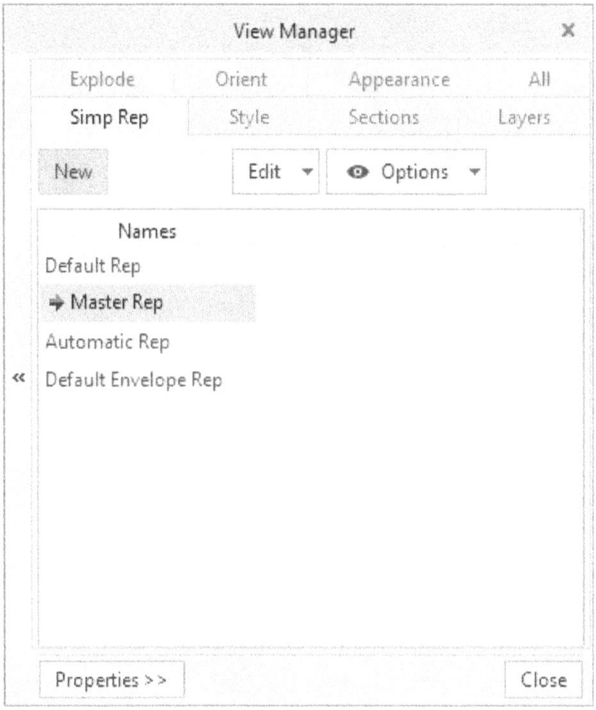

Figure 9–66

Note: *Note that only four representations are visible in the View Manager.*

3. Close *View Manager*.

4. Click **File>Options**.

5. In the *Creo Parametric Options* dialog box, select **Configuration Editor**. Click **Add** and type **hide**. Note that the *Option name* automatically fills in with **hide_pre_creo4_reps** and the default *Option value* is **maintain_master**, as shown in Figure 9–67.

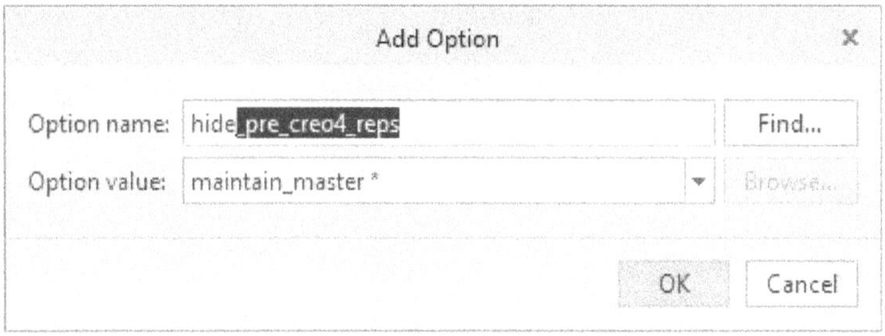

Figure 9–67

6. In the *Option value* drop-down list, select **no**.

7. Click **OK**.

8. Click **OK** in the *Creo Parametric Options* dialog box.

9. When prompted to save the settings in the configuration file, click **No**.

10. In the In-graphics toolbar, select 📷 (View Manager). Note that the list updates to include the representations made before the release of Creo Parametric 4.0, as shown in Figure 9–68.

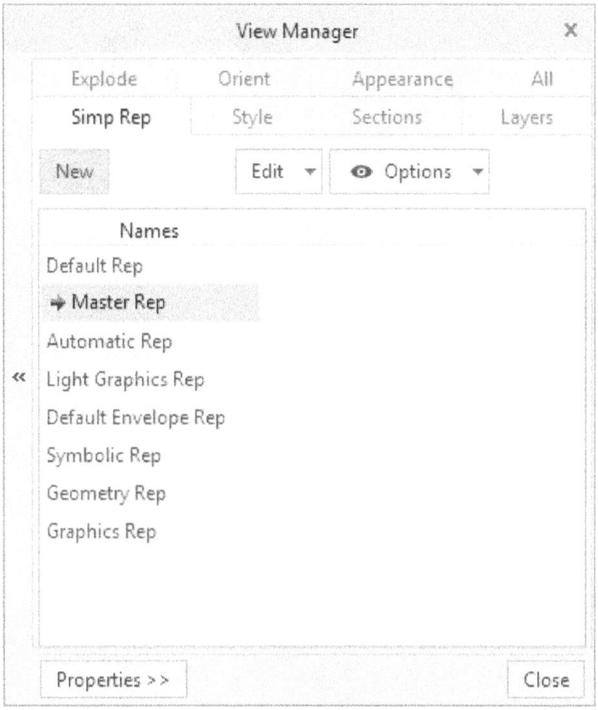

Figure 9–68

11. Close *View Manager*.

12. Click **File>Options**.

13. In the *Creo Parametric Options* dialog box, select **Configuration Editor** then in the *Show* drop-down list, select **Current Session**.

14. Beside **hide_pre_creo4_reps**, click in the *Value* field and select **maintain_master***, as shown in Figure 9–69.

View and manage Creo Parametric options.

Options

Sort: Alphabetical ▼   Show: Current Session

Name	Value	Status	Description
default_dec_places	3	●	Sets the default number of de
default_gtol_owned_by_model	yes	●	Defines the default destination
drawing_setup_file	$PRO_DIRECTORY\tex	●	Sets the default drawing setup
edge_display_quality	very_high	●	Controls display quality of an
format_setup_file	$PRO_DIRECTORY\tex	●	Assigns a specified setup file t
hide_pre_creo4_reps	no ▼	●	yes - Hides all pre Creo 4.0 sim
highlight_erased_dwg_views	maintain_master *	●	Controls the display of erased
hlr_for_quilts	no	●	In Drawing, controls quilt disp
parenthesize_ref_dim	yes	●	Encloses reference dimension:
pro_unit_length	unit_inch *	●	Sets the default units for new
pro_unit_mass	unit_pound *	●	Sets the default units for mass

Figure 9–69

15. Click **OK**, then click **No** when prompted to save the configuration file.

16. In the *Quick Access toolbar*, click ✕ (Close) to close the window.

17. In the *Home* tab, click ✎ (Erase Not Displayed).

18. Click **OK**.

Task 4: Investigate the Automatic Representation.

1. In the *Home* tab, click 📂 (Open).
2. Select **aft_engine_section.asm** and select **Open Automatic,** as shown in Figure 9−70.

Figure 9−70

3. The assembly opens, as shown in Figure 9−71.

Figure 9−71

4. Hover the cursor over several surfaces of the assembly and note that the surfaces are indicated as Light Surfaces, as shown in Figure 9−72.

Figure 9−72

Note: The light surfaces allow certain surface-based actions such as measuring. The light surfaces allow the full assembly to be visible, without having to retrieve the full solid geometry into session.

5. In the In-graphics toolbar, select ⬓ (View Manager).

6. In the *View Manager*, click **Properties**, and the dialog box displays as shown in Figure 9−73.

Figure 9−73

7. Hold <Ctrl>, and in the model or *Model Tree*, select both instances of **HEAD.PRT**.

8. In the *View Manager*, click ✎ (Exclude) to remove the components from the representation.

9. Hold <Ctrl>, and in the model or *Model Tree*, select both instances of **BLOCK.PRT**.

10. In the *View Manager*, click ⊞ (Master Representation).

11. Click **Close** in the *View Manager* dialog box. The *Model Tree* updates to indicate the representation status, as shown in Figure 9–74.

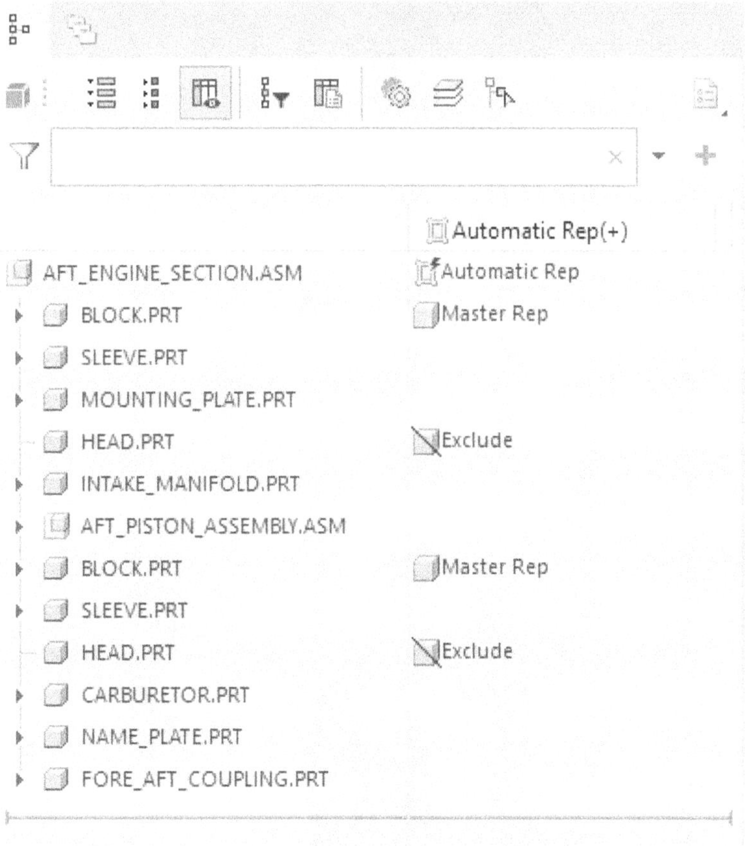

Automatic Rep(+)

AFT_ENGINE_SECTION.ASM	Automatic Rep
▸ BLOCK.PRT	Master Rep
▸ SLEEVE.PRT	
▸ MOUNTING_PLATE.PRT	
HEAD.PRT	Exclude
▸ INTAKE_MANIFOLD.PRT	
▸ AFT_PISTON_ASSEMBLY.ASM	
▸ BLOCK.PRT	Master Rep
▸ SLEEVE.PRT	
HEAD.PRT	Exclude
▸ CARBURETOR.PRT	
▸ NAME_PLATE.PRT	
▸ FORE_AFT_COUPLING.PRT	

Figure 9–74

12. Hover the cursor over the surface of the block part shown in Figure 9–75.

Figure 9–75

Note: The surface is no longer a light surface due to the representation being set to Master Rep. This results in the object being fully retrieved into session.

13. Select the surface shown in Figure 9–76 and select ⬚ (Retrieve) from the mini toolbar.

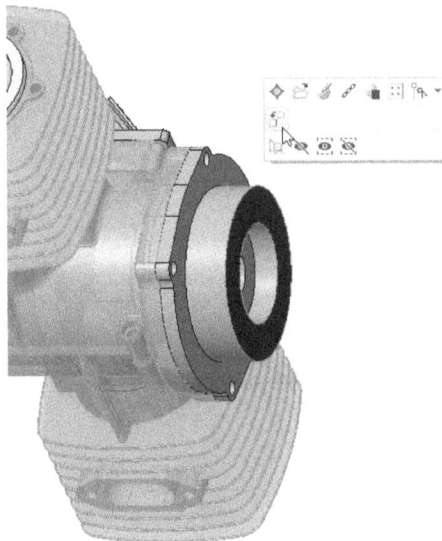

Figure 9–76

14. Hover the cursor over the surface of **for_aft_coupling.prt** shown in Figure 9–77 and note that it is no longer a light surface.

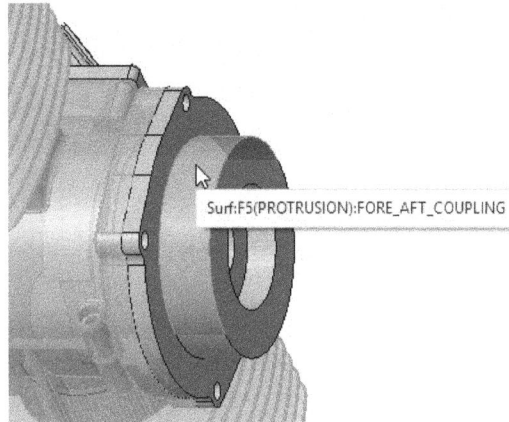

Figure 9−77

Note: The component was retrieved into session, so it is now the solid model.

- Note that manually retrieving the component into session does not impact the simplified representation, as shown in Figure 9−78.

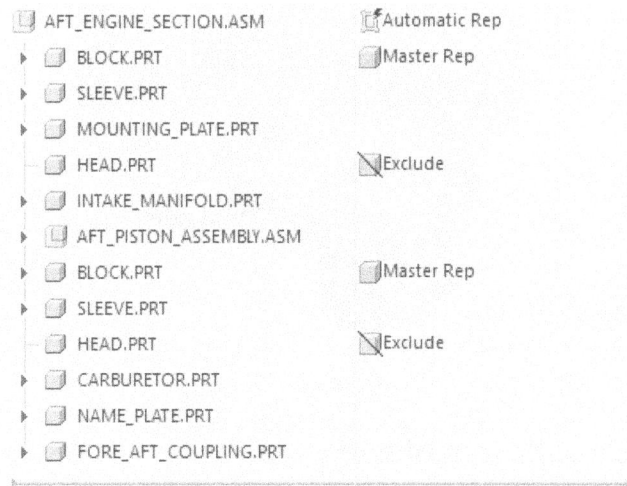

Figure 9−78

Note: The automatic representation retrieves the components with no solid geometry, allowing the assembly to be retrieved quickly. When you manually retrieve a component, the retrieval applies only to the current session.

15. Close and erase all files.

End of practice

Practice 9d
(Optional) Define a Simplified Rep Without Loading the Model

Practice Objective

*   Create a simplified rep before loading the assembly.

In this practice, you will create a simplified representation without opening the assembly and load a part that needs to be viewed. The model shown in Figure 9–79 is the complete top-level assembly.

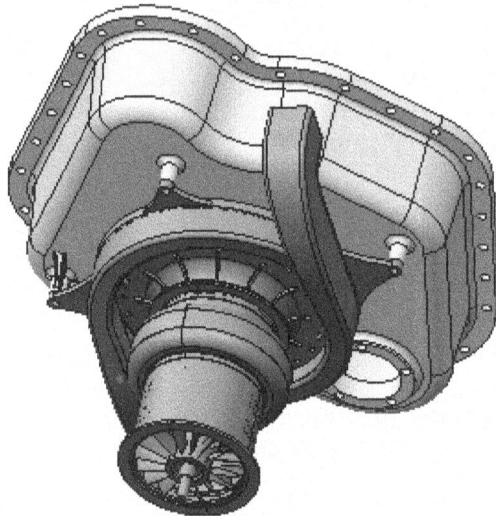

Figure 9–79

Task 1: Create a simplified rep with no parts.

1. Change your working directory to the **Rep_Without_Loading** folder.

2. Click 📂 (Open) in the *Home* tab.

3. Select **turbine.asm**, expand **Open**, and select **Open Representation**. The *Open Representation* dialog box opens, as shown in Figure 9−80.

Figure 9−80

4. Click **Define**, edit the new simplified rep *Name* to **No_Parts**, and press <Enter>.

5. If necessary, in the *Edit* dialog box, leave the default rule as **Exclude Comp**, as shown in Figure 9−81.

Figure 9−81

Note: This excludes all of the parts from the assembly, which enables you to open the assembly more quickly. Use this simplified rep when you only need to work with a small number of components in a large assembly.

6. Click **Open** to close the *Edit* dialog box.

7. Set the model display as follows:

- ⁛⁘. *(Datum Display Filters)*: All Off

- ⤳ *(Spin Center)*: Off

- ⬚. *(Display Style)*: ⬚ (Shading With Edges)

- *Model Tree*: Show Features

Task 2: Open two parts in automatic rep to view.

1. Hold <Ctrl> and select **AFT_COVER.PRT** and **VANE.ASM** in the *Model Tree*.

2. Right-click and select **Representation>Automatic,** as shown in Figure 9–82. **AFT_COVER.PRT** and **VANE.ASM** open in the assembly.

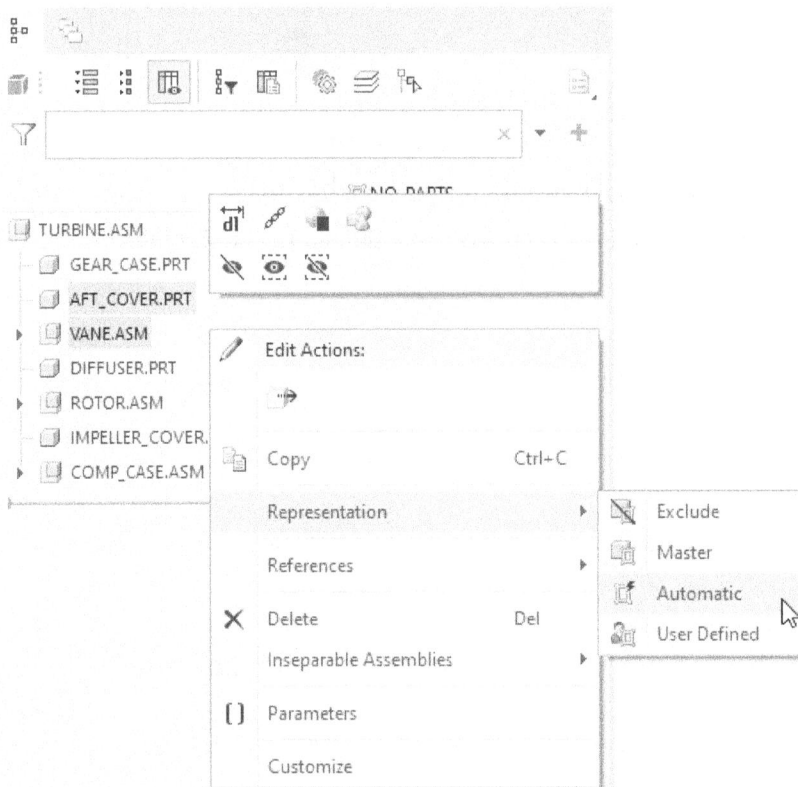

Figure 9–82

*Note: You can also select **Automatic Rep** in the drop-down list in the NO_PARTS column in the Model Tree.*

- The model displays as shown in Figure 9–83.

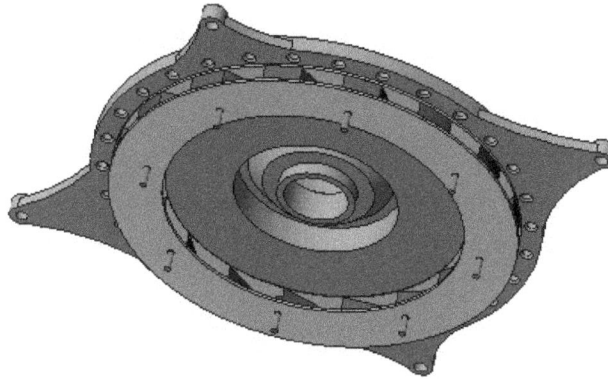

On-Demand Simp Rep:NO_PARTS(+)

Figure 9–83

3. Erase the assembly without saving.

End of practice

Chapter Review Questions

1. Which of the following statements are true regarding simplified representations? (Select all that apply.)

   a. Improve retrieval time.

   b. Improve regeneration times.

   c. Increase efficiency while working with large assemblies.

   d. They control which components of an assembly are opened and how they are displayed.

2. The **Open Subset** option can only be used to open existing simplified representations.

   a. True

   b. False

3. The Automatic representation retrieves the minimum required data and is used to retrieve your assembly as fast as possible.

   a. True

   b. False

4. Which option enables you to create a simplified representation without opening the assembly? (Select all that apply.)

   a. Select **Open Representation** in the *File* dialog box.

   b. Click **Open Subset...** in the *File* dialog box.

   c. Click **Open** in the *File* dialog box.

   d. Click ▦ in the Quick Access toolbar.

5. In the *Style* tab, components can be set as **Transparent** in assemblies so you can display the interior components more clearly.

   a. True

   b. False

Answers: 1. abcd, 2. b, 3. a, 4. ab 5. a

Drawing Basics: View Creation and Detailing

Drawings can be created from Part or Assembly models. These drawings are associative, meaning that any modifications made to the model will be reflected in the drawing, and conversely, changes made in the drawing will be mirrored in the model.

Learning Objectives

- Create a new drawing.
- Add General, Projected, Auxiliary, Detailed, and Section views to create the required documentation of a model.
- Show dimensions on a drawing using the *Show Model Annotations* dialog box.
- Create additional dimensions and notes in the drawing.
- Manipulate detail items using the contextual menu or the *Properties* dialog box.
- Add a custom symbol to a drawing.
- Add additional sheets to a drawing, and move objects to it.

10.1 Creating a New Drawing

This section covers the process of creating a basic drawing of your model.

General Steps

Use the following general steps to create a drawing:

1. Create a new drawing.
2. Place the first drawing view.
3. Add views.
4. Modify view properties.
5. Manipulate drawing views, as required.
6. Detail the drawing (e.g., dimensions, notes, tolerances, etc.).
7. Manipulate detail items, as required.
8. Print (or Plot) the drawing.

Step 1 - Create a new drawing.

To create a new drawing, click ⬚ (New) in the *Quick Access* Toolbar. Select the **Drawing** option in the *New* dialog box and you are presented with several options, as shown in Figure 10-1.

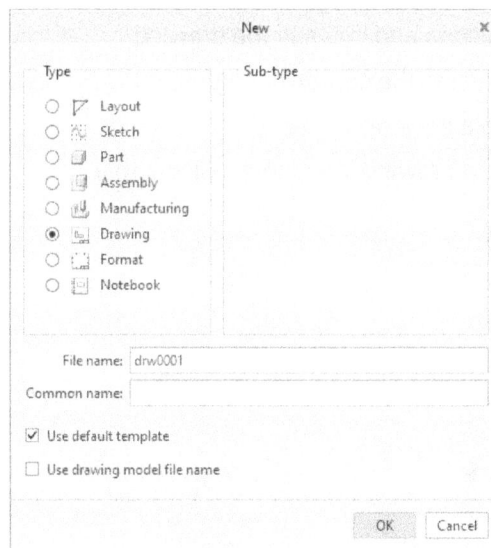

Figure 10-1

The **Use default template** option will create a set of predefined views in the drawing. In this course, we will disable this option.

You can enter a name or enable the **Use drawing model file name**. The later will automatically name the drawing with the same name as the model used. When using this option, the File name field changes to **<Generated>**, as shown in Figure 10−2.

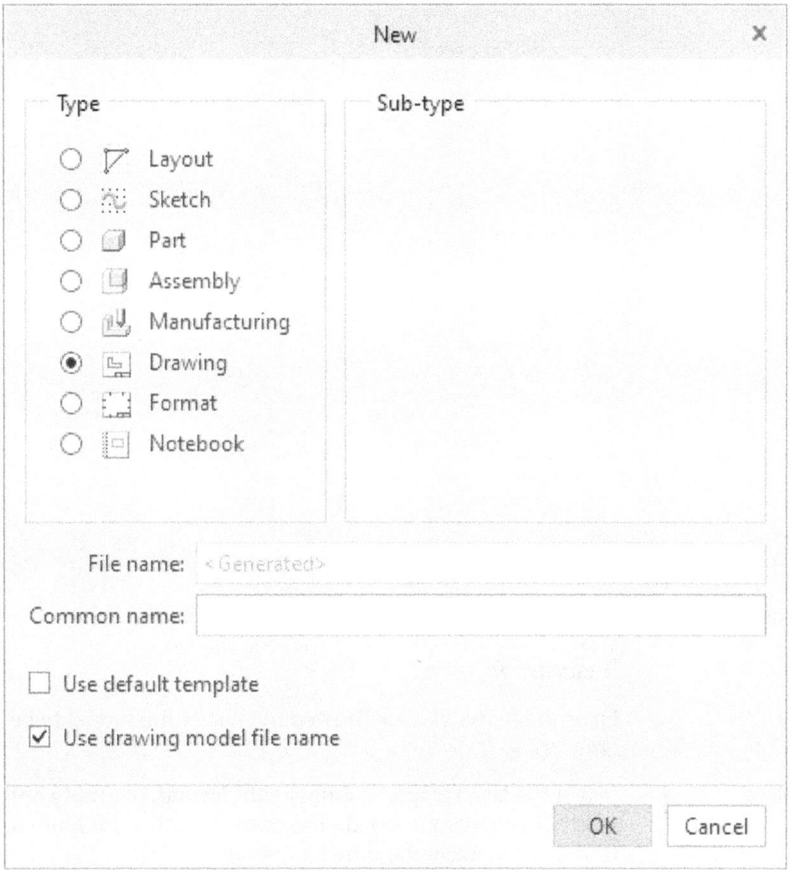

Figure 10−2

Click **OK** and the *New Drawing* dialog box opens, as shown in Figure 10−3.

Figure 10−3

The areas in the *New Drawing* dialog box are described in the following table.

Area	Description
Default Model	Enter the name or click **Browse** to specify the model to be used in the drawing.
Specify Template	Select the **Use template**, **Empty with format**, or **Empty** option to specify whether you want to create the drawing with a predefined template, a format, or to leave the drawing empty.
Template	Enter the name or click **Browse** to specify the template that is to be used in the drawing. Only available when the **Use template** option is selected.
Format	Enter the name or click **Browse** to specify the format that is to be used in the drawing. Only available when the **Empty with format** option is selected.
Orientation and Size	Select the appropriate icon to define the orientation of the drawing sheet (portrait, landscape, or variable) and set the sheet size for the drawing. Only available when the **Empty** option is selected.

Note: If a model is in session, Creo Parametric assigns that model as the default.

Templates

A drawing template contains predefined views, sets the view display, creates snap lines, and displays preassigned model dimensions based on the information specified when the template was created. Templates are discussed further in *Creo Parametric: Design Documentation & Detailing*.

Formats

A drawing format can contain standard information that is present in all drawings, such as the title block, company logo, BOM tables, etc. Drawing formats can be used in conjunction with drawing templates.

When you have finished making selections in the *New Drawing* dialog box, click **OK** to create the drawing.

Step 2 - Place the first drawing view.

The first view placed on the drawing is always a General view. This kind of view is independent of other views. To place the first (General) view, right-click and select **General View** or click

🖨 (General View), in the *Model Views* group, in the *Layout* tab.

> *Note: Drawings created using a template already contain certain views. Additional views can be added at any time.*

Select **OK** if the *Select Combined State* dialog box displays. Select a location on the drawing to place the view. The General view is initially placed on the drawing sheet in its default orientation and the *Drawing View* dialog box opens, as shown in Figure 10-4.

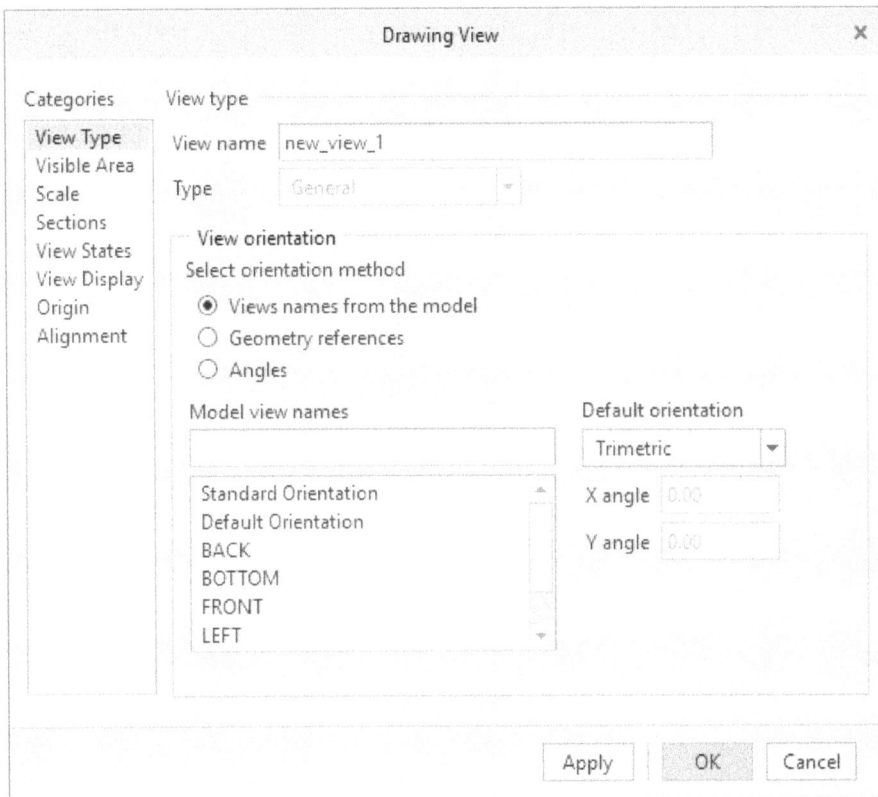

Figure 10-4

By default, the *View Type* category settings are displayed in the *Drawing View* dialog box. You can enter the View name and change the default view orientation using the options in the *View orientation* area.

To modify the view orientation, you can select one the following methods in the *View orientation* area:

*   View names from the model

*   Geometry references

*   Angles

To apply the new view orientation, click **Apply**.

View Names From the Model

The **View names from the model** option enables you to orient the General view on the drawing, using a predefined view saved from the model. The list of predefined views displays in the *Drawing View* dialog box, as shown in Figure 10-5.

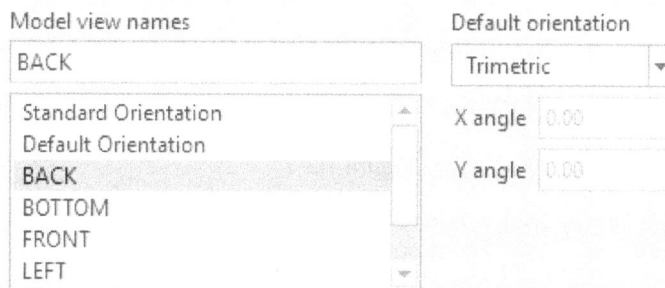

Model view names

BACK

Standard Orientation
Default Orientation
BACK
BOTTOM
FRONT
LEFT

Default orientation

Trimetric

X angle 0.00

Y angle 0.00

Figure 10-5

Geometry References

The **Geometry references** option enables you to orient the General view using the orientation tools that are used in other 3D models. You must select an orientation (e.g., Front, Top, Right, etc.), and then select a planar surface, datum plane or coordinate system axis as its reference, as shown in Figure 10-6. The two references must be perpendicular to one another to orient the view into 2D.

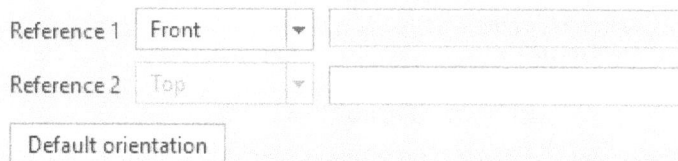

Reference 1   Front

Reference 2   Top

Default orientation

Figure 10-6

Note: Using default datum planes to orient the model is recommended. Orientation references can be lost if the selected planar surface references are later deleted.

You can click **Default orientation** to return the view to the default orientation.

Angles

The **Angles** option enables you to orient the General view by selecting a direction and entering angular values to place the view. The available directions are: **Normal, Vertical, Horizontal**, and **Edge/Axis**. The **Normal, Vertical**, and **Horizontal** directions are relative to the drawing sheet (monitor) and the **Edge/Axis** direction enables you to select a reference on the model from which to orient. Figure 10−7 shows the *Angles* area. You can add and remove orientation angles as required, using ✚ and ▬.

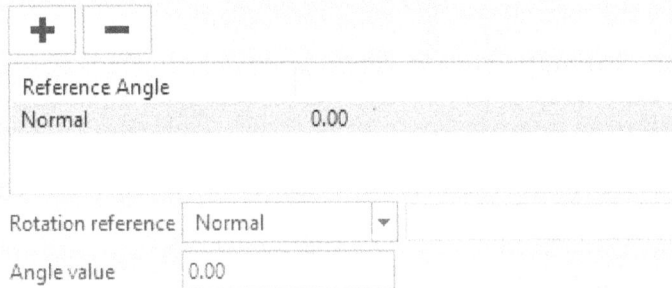

Figure 10−7

For example, the model in Figure 10−8 is oriented to 2D using the **Geometry references** option and by selecting references for the **Front** and **Top** reference options.

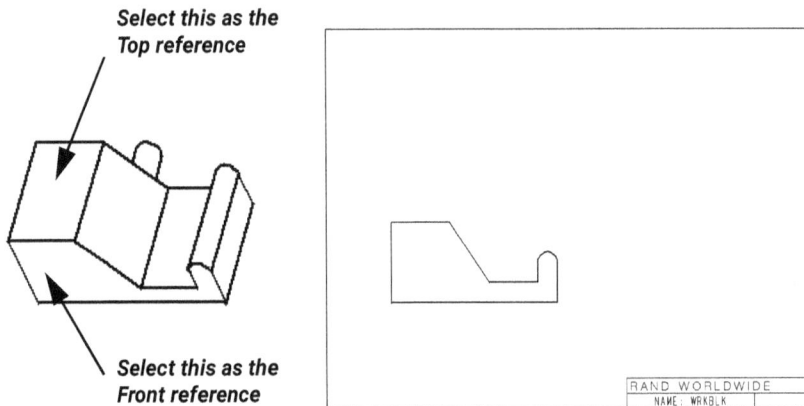

Figure 10−8

Once the orientation has been defined, click **OK** in the *Drawing View* dialog box to continue the drawing creation.

Step 3 - Add views.

Additional view types are available after the first general view has been added. To place an additional view, click the icon representing the view you want use in the *Layout* tab, as shown in Figure 10-9.

Figure 10-9

Additional views and options for views can be found in the *Layout* tab.

The available view types are described as follows:

Option	Description
General	A view that is originally displayed in 3D and can be oriented into 2D.
Projection	An orthographic projection of an existing view.
Detailed	A selected portion of an existing view.
Auxiliary	A view projected 90° to a surface, datum, or axis.
Revolved	A cross-section revolved 90° about a cut line.
Copy and Align	A copy of an existing Detailed view with a different boundary defined.

The available view types are dependent on the views that currently exist in the drawing, and whether a view is preselected before you select a view in the View toolbar. If a view is not selected, the system provides a more detailed list that enables you to create new parent views. If a view is preselected, the system assumes that you are creating a child view to the selected view and provides the appropriate view types.

Figure 10–10 shows examples of different view types.

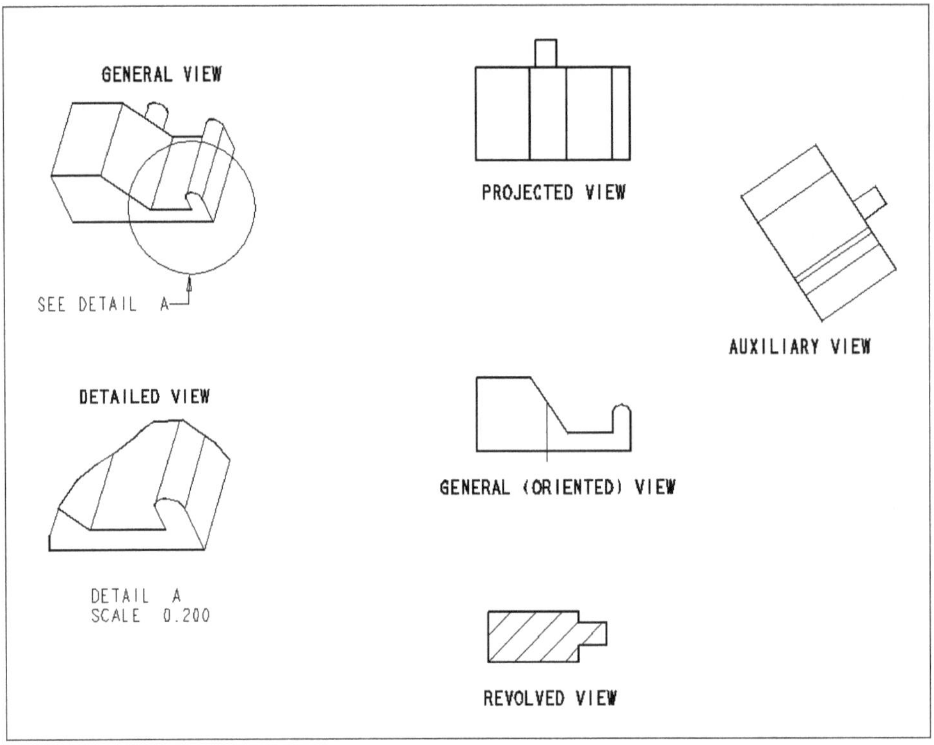

Figure 10–10

Shortcuts for General and Projected Views

To quickly create General, Projection, and Auxiliary views, you can right-click and select an option in the contextual menu. To create a General view, right-click and select **General View** and place the view. To create a Projected or Auxiliary view, select the parent view, right-click, and select **Projection View** or **Auxiliary View.** Place the view relative to the parent view. Projected views can also be created by clicking (Projection View) in the *mini* toolbar.

Step 4 - Modify view properties.

To change the view properties, double click on the view or select the view and click
🖌 (Properties) in the *mini* toolbar. The *Drawing View* dialog box opens. You can now change the properties in individual categories.

View Type

The *View Type* category enables you to change the view type in the *Type* drop-down list, as shown in Figure 10–11. For example, you can change the General view to a Projection view. Note that the view type modification can be restricted. Some view types might display in gray, indicating that they are not available for selection.

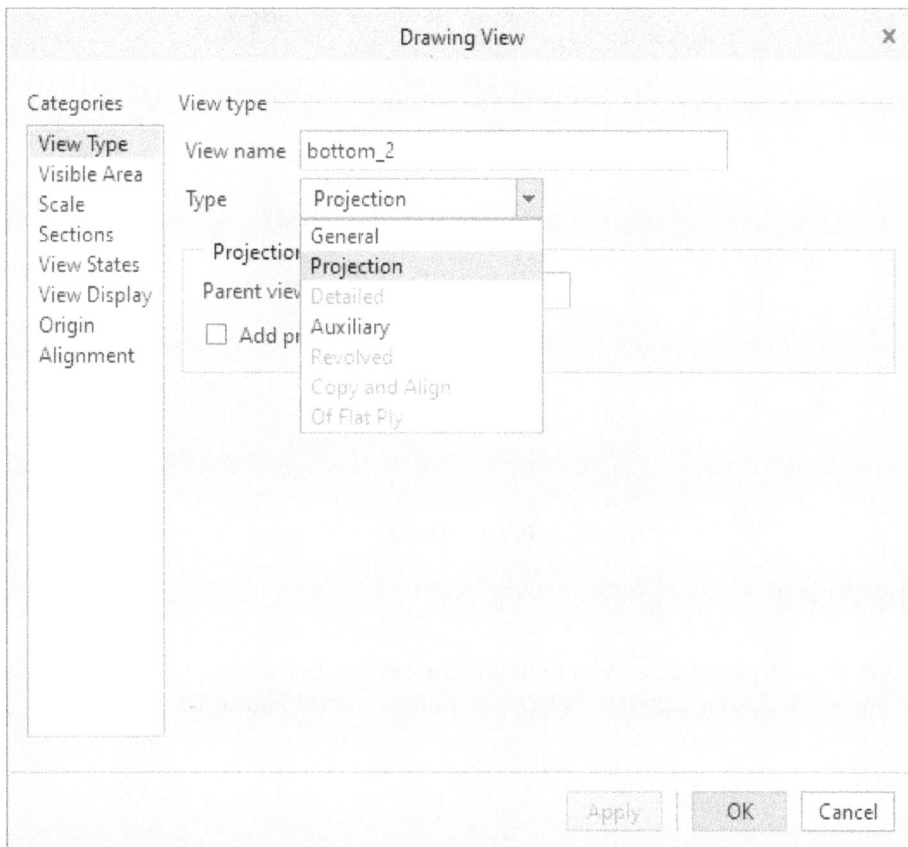

Figure 10–11

The *View Type* category enables you to change the view orientation, using the options in the *View orientation* area. See Step 1 for more detailed information.

When modifying a Detailed view, the *View Type* category enables you to re-sketch the view boundary. Select the *Reference point on parent view* collector and select the new reference point. Select the *Spline boundary on the parent view* collector and sketch the spline representing the view boundary. The options for the *View Type* category are shown in Figure 10–12.

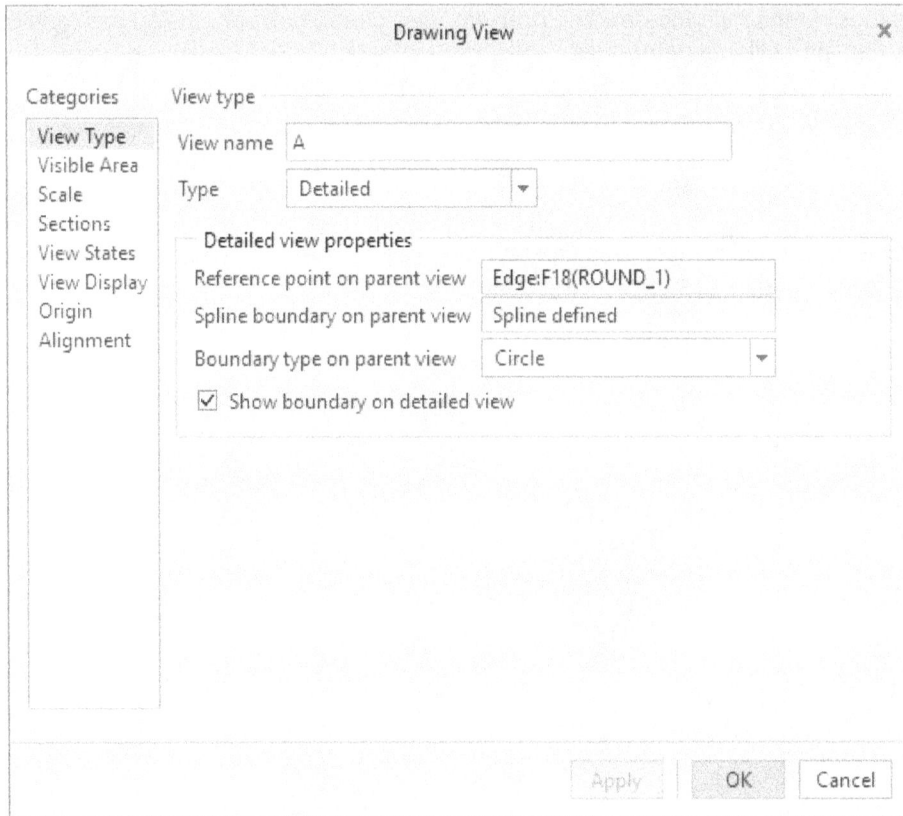

Figure 10–12

Visible Area

The *Visible Area* category enables you to define the portion of the view (visibility) that is displayed and view clipping options. The options are shown in Figure 10–13.

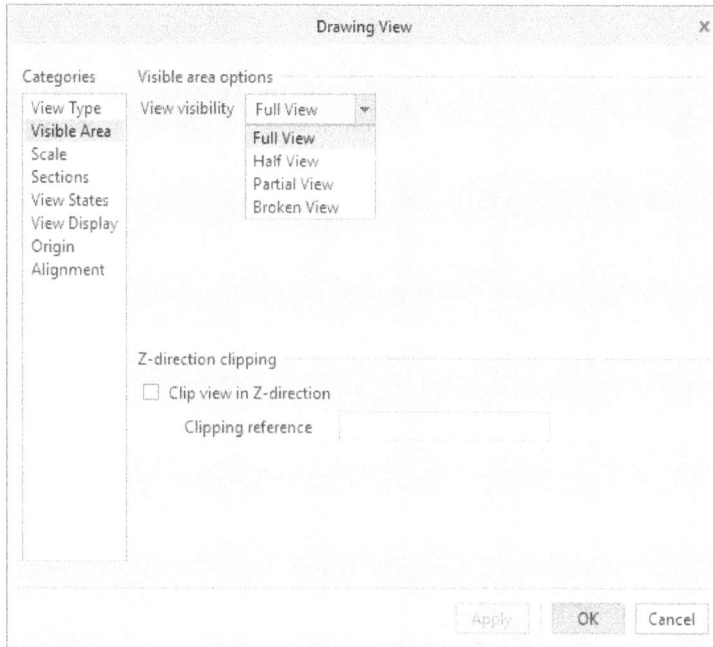

Figure 10–13

The visibility of a view can be defined as Full, Half, Partial, or Broken, as shown in Figure 10–14. Depending on the view type, some visibility options might not be available.

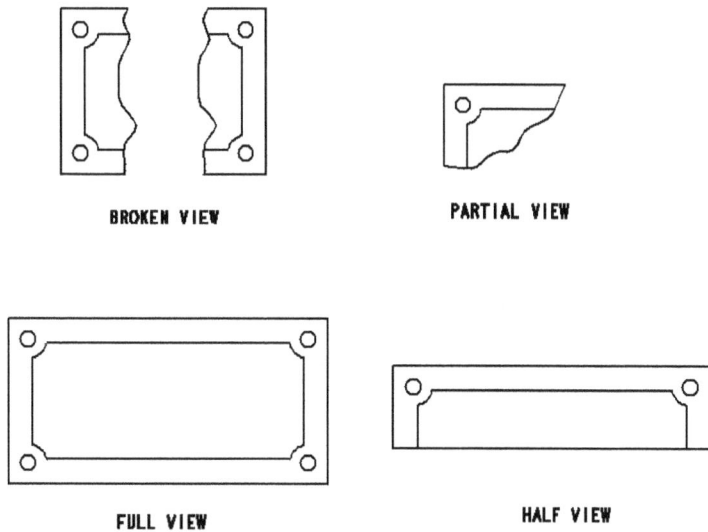

BROKEN VIEW

PARTIAL VIEW

FULL VIEW

HALF VIEW

Figure 10–14

*Note: The **Visible Area** options enable you to highlight key areas of a drawing view.*

Scale

The *Scale* category enables you to define whether the view uses the default sheet scale (**Default scale for sheet**) or whether an independent scale is applied (**Custom scale**), as shown in Figure 10−15.

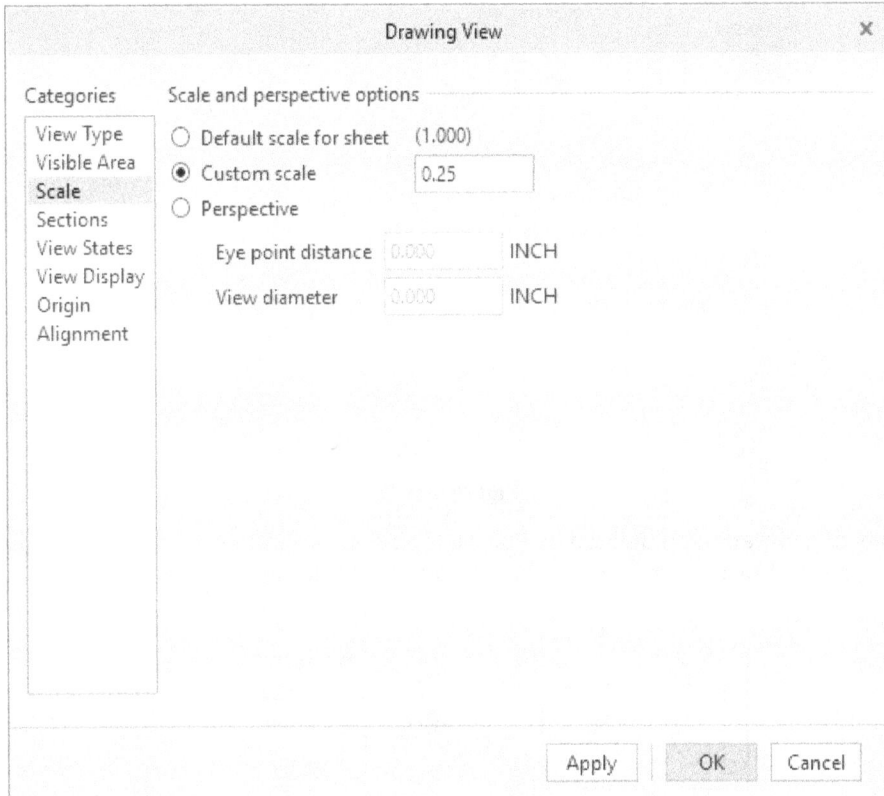

Figure 10−15

Default Scale for Sheet

Select the **Default scale for sheet** option in the *Drawing View* dialog box to set the default scale for a view. The default drawing scale displays in the lower left corner of the drawing, as shown in Figure 10−16. The scale value is based on sheet and model size, and affects all views in the drawing that are not independently scaled.

Figure 10−16

Custom Scale

Select the **Custom scale** option in the *Drawing View* dialog box to add an independent view scale. The scale value is displayed directly below the view, as shown in Figure 10–17. Customized scaling is useful when you want views to appear smaller or larger than the default scale permits.

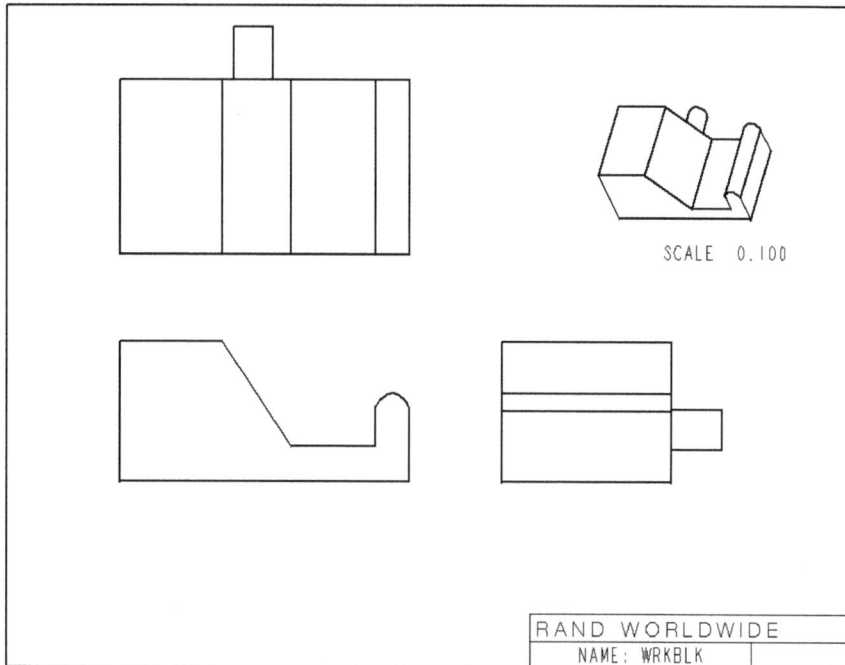

Figure 10–17

*Note: The scale values associated with individual views can be moved using the standard **Move** tools.*

Sections

The *Sections* category enables you to define whether or not the view contains a cross-section.

To add a 2D section created in the model while in Part mode, click ✚, select the cross-section name in the *Name* column, and select an area type in the *Sectioned Area* column, as shown in Figure 10−18. Click ▬ to remove a section from the view. Click ⁄ to flip the material side.

Figure 10−18

Figure 10−19 shows two of the basic cross-section types that can be used. These types are set using the **Model edge visibility** options.

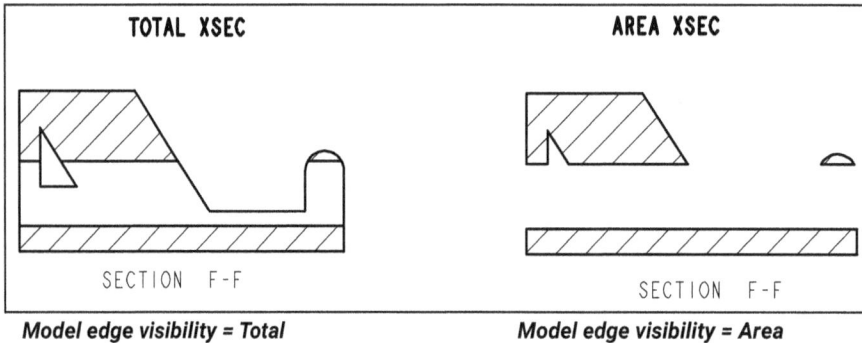

Figure 10−19

View Display

By default, all views are displayed according to the view display icon that is selected in the In-graphics toolbar (⬚ (Wireframe), ⬚ (No Hidden), ⬚ (Hidden Line), ⬚ (Shading) or ⬚ (Shading With Edges)). This setting affects all views in the drawing. The *View Display* category enables you to set the display for each view using the Display style drop-down list as shown in Figure 10–20. Once set, the display for the view is independent of the settings made in the Creo Parametric session.

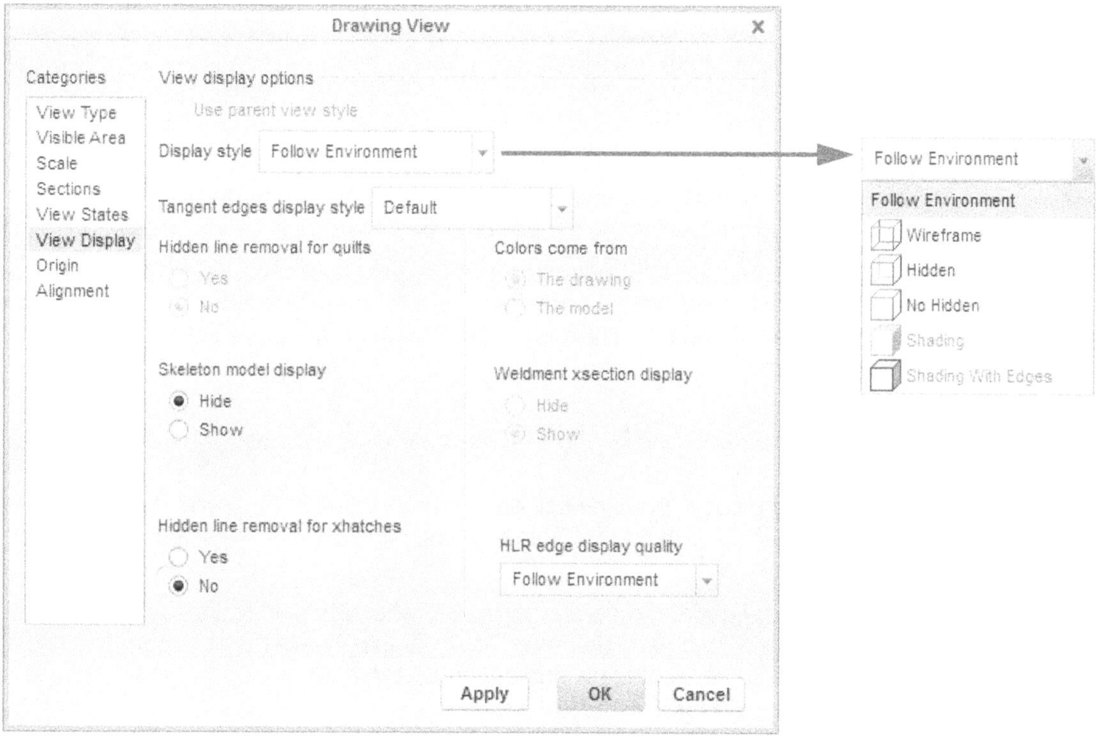

Figure 10–20

Step 5 - Manipulate drawing views, as required.

Once views have been added and modified, some common changes can be made to them including: deleting views, moving views, changing scale, and view display.

Delete Views

Views can be deleted from a drawing using any of the following methods.

- Select the view and click ✕ (Delete) in the *mini* toolbar.

- Select the view and press <Delete>.

- Select the view and click ✕ (Delete) in the *Annotate* tab.

- Select the view name in the Drawing Tree and click ✕ (Delete) in the *mini* toolbar.

    Note: *Deleted views are permanently removed from the drawing.*

Move Views

Views are automatically locked to the original location at which they were placed. To enable movement of views, right-click on a view and click **Lock View Movement** in the contextual menu or click ⬚ (Lock View Movement) in the *Document* group in the *Layout* tab. Once unlocked, you can select the view and drag it as required on the drawing. All dependent views move relative to their parents. Once you finish moving a view, it is recommended that you relock the view movement using the same tool.

Change Scale

To modify the default drawing scale, double-click on the scale value in the lower left corner of the drawing and enter a value at the prompt. Changing this value affects the scale of all but the independently scaled views.

To modify the scale of an independently scaled view, select the note containing the scale value, and double-click on the scale value inside the note. You can also select the note containing the scale value. Select the scale value, right-click, and select **Edit Value**.

Step 6 - Detail the drawing (e.g., dimensions, notes, tolerances, etc.).

When drawing views have been placed on a drawing, you can add dimensions and notes to communicate information to manufacturing. These items are associative and update with changes to other views and modifications to the model. Detail items display in the drawing tree as shown in Figure 10–21.

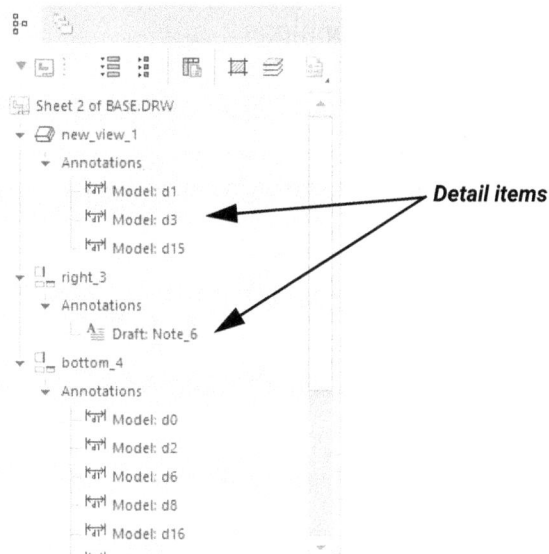

Figure 10–21

Dimensions

Dimensions can be shown or created to provide the required dimensional information for manufacturing the model, as shown in Figure 10–22.

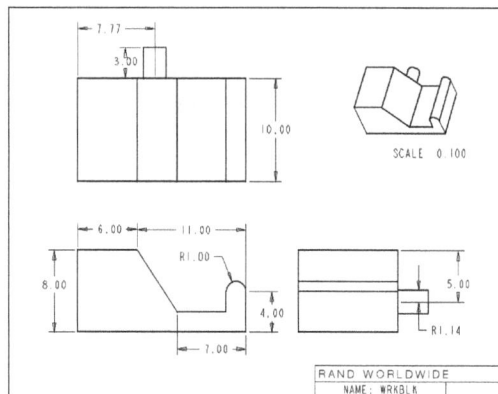

Figure 10–22

Note: Dimensions can be created in Drawing mode, but these dimensions do not drive the geometry. Only those displayed directly from the model can drive the geometry.

Showing Model Annotations

Model dimensions refer to dimensions that are used to create the part model.

How To: Display or Erase Model Dimensions

1. Select the *Annotate* tab.

2. Click 📝 (Show Model Annotations) in the *Annotations* group or *mini* toolbar. The *Show Model Annotations* dialog box opens, as shown in Figure 10–23.

Figure 10–23

*Note: Dimensions can also be added by selecting a feature in the Model Tree, right-clicking and selecting **Show Model Annotation**.*

3. The *Dimension* tab (⊢⊣) displays by default and the *Type* drop-down is set to **All**. You can filter your selections as shown in Figure 10–24.

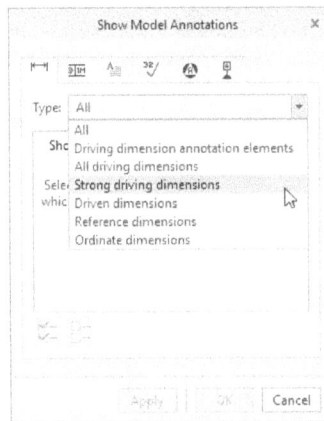

Figure 10–24

4. Select a feature in the view in which you want the dimensions to display in the drawing window. The dimensions display on the view in red and in the dialog box. Select the dimensions that you want to keep for that view as shown in Figure 10–25. They display in black. Use <Ctrl> to select multiple features or views.

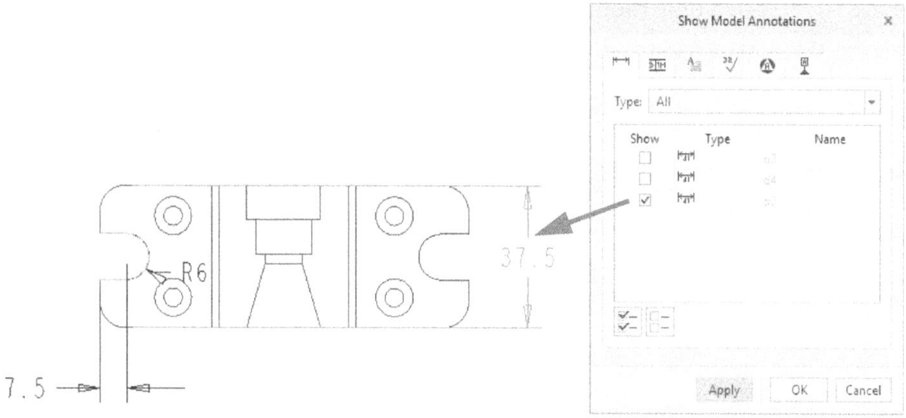

Figure 10–25

5. Click **Apply**.

6. Repeat the procedure to add dimensions to other features in the drawing.

Additional detail items that can be added to a drawing are described as follows:

Icon	Description	Icon	Description
⊢⊣	Dimension	³²√	Surface Finish
⫛ᵀᴴ	Geometric Tolerance	Ⓐ	Model Symbols
A≡	Note	⫫	Datum Feature Symbols

Creating Dimensions

When showing dimensions, only those that were created in the model are displayed. If a required dimension does not exist in the model (and therefore is not shown), it can be created. Since created dimensions are driven by the model geometry, their values cannot be modified. However, these values automatically update if the geometry changes in the part. Only displayed dimension values can be modified to change the model.

To create a dimension, click ⊢⊣ (Dimension) in the *Annotate* tab. Select the references on the drawing view and place the dimension with the middle mouse button. Dimensions created in Drawing mode use the same creation methods as in Sketcher mode.

The following sections describe how to create the various dimension types in your drawing.

Linear Dimensions

To place linear dimensions in sketcher, select the entities with the left mouse button and place the dimension with the middle mouse button. The following information describes different methods of dimensioning the linear entities shown in Figure 10–26.

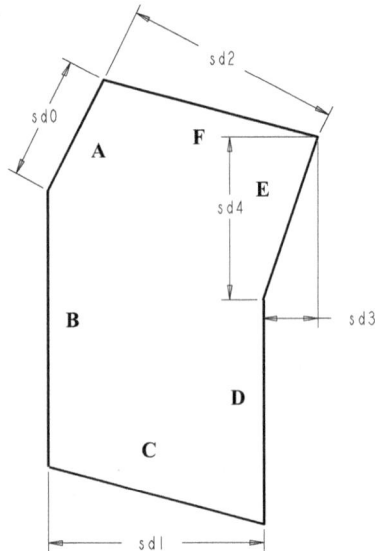

Figure 10–26

Note: *Keep the design intent in mind when considering the dimensioning scheme.*

How To: Place Dimension sd0

1. Select line **A**.

2. Position the cursor at the location you want to place the dimension, and click the middle mouse button.

How To: Place Dimension sd1

1. Select line **B** and line **D**.

2. Position the cursor at the location you want to place the dimension, and click the middle mouse button.

   Note: *The placement of the dimension dictates whether it is a horizontal or vertical dimension. In some cases, Creo Parametric prompts to show either horizontal or vertical.*

How To: Place Dimension sd2

1. Select line A and the vertex between lines **E** and **F**.

2. Position the cursor at the location you want to place the dimension, and click the middle mouse button.

How To: Place Dimensions sd3 and sd4

1. Select the two vertices at the ends of line **E**.

2. Position the cursor at the location you want to place the dimension, and click the middle mouse button.

Center/Tangential Dimensions

To dimension the distance between circles and arcs, select the two entities and place the dimension using the middle mouse button. You can right-click and select one of the options shown in Figure 10–27 for the dimension orientation.

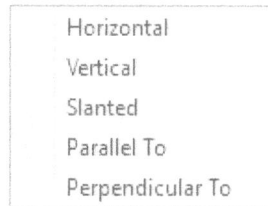

Figure 10–27

These options can be used to create the dimensions shown in Figure 10–28.

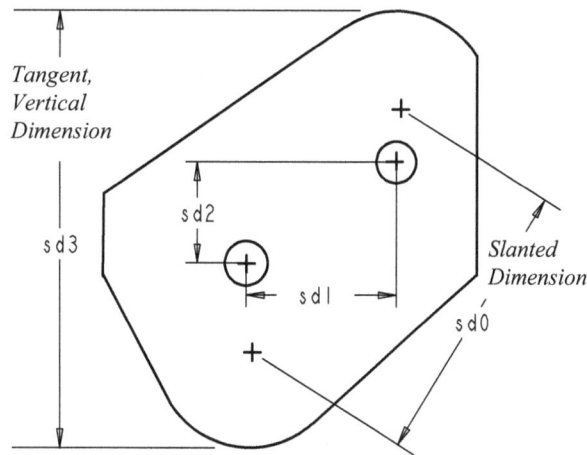

Figure 10–28

Radial/Diameter Dimensions

To create a radius dimension, select on an arc or a circle once and place the dimension using the middle mouse button. To create diameter dimensions, select an arc or circle twice and then place the dimension using the middle mouse button. Examples of radius and diameter dimensions are shown below in Figure 10-29.

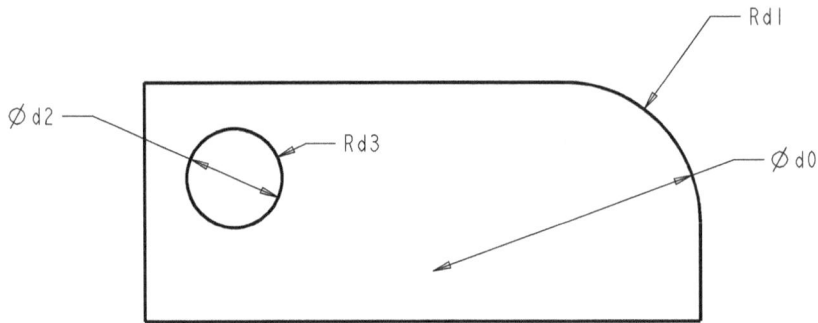

Figure 10-29

Angular Dimensions

For an angular dimension, select lines **A** and **B** (shown in Figure 10-30) and place the dimension using the middle mouse button. The angle is dependent on the placement of the dimension.

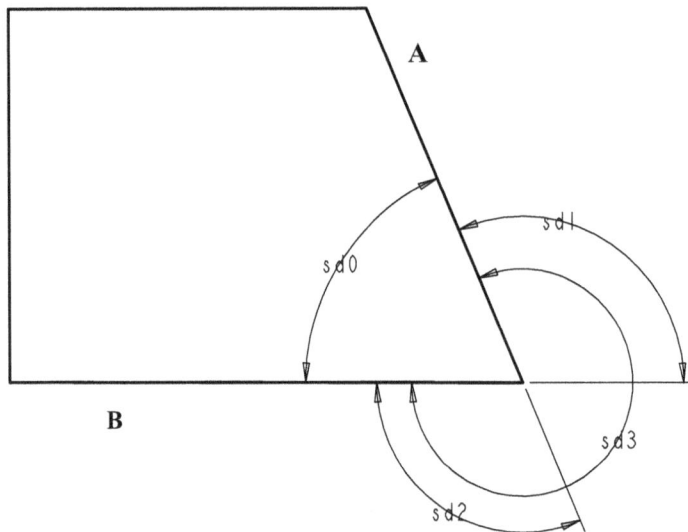

Figure 10-30

Dimensioning arc angles requires three selections. Select the arc (it turns red), then select the two end points, and place the dimension using the middle mouse button, as shown in Figure 10-31.

Figure 10-31

Notes

Notes can be added to detail the drawing, as shown in Figure 10-32.

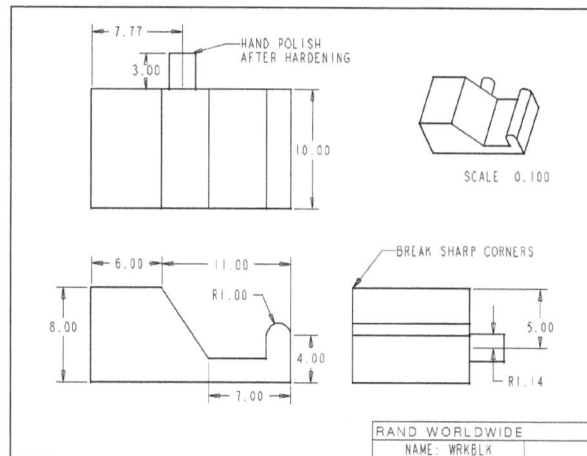

Figure 10-32

Several note types exist, but this course will focus only on unattached and leader notes.

- Unattached notes do not have a leader line, and can be placed freely on the sheet.

- Leader lines are placed with a leader pointing to some aspect of the geometry.

- The other note types are covered in the *Creo Parametric Design Detailing and Drafting* course.

Unattached Note

To create an unattached note, click $^{A\equiv}$ (Unattached Note) in the *Annotate* tab. The *Select Point* dialog box opens, as shown in Figure 10–33.

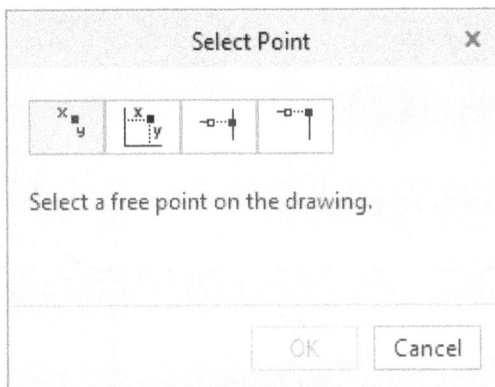

Figure 10–33

Select from the following point options:

- $^{x}\!_{y}$ (Free Point)

- $\vdots^{x}\!_{y}$ (Absolute Coordinates)

- $\neg\!\!\circ\cdots\vdots$ (On Object)

- $\neg\!\!\circ\cdots\mathsf{I}$ (On Vertex)

Select the appropriate location to begin creating the note.

Leader Note

To Create a Leader Note, expand the $^{A\equiv}$ (Note) fly-out in the *Annotate* tab and select $\swarrow^{A}$ (Leader Note). The *Select Reference* dialog box opens, as shown in Figure 10–34.

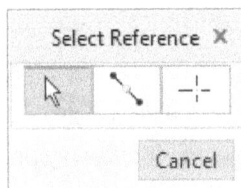

Figure 10–34

Select from the following reference options:

- ⮡ (Reference)

- ⬉ (Midpoint)

- ⊣⊢ (Intersection)

Select the appropriate reference then click the middle mouse button to place the note.

Regardless of the note type, the *Format* dashboard displays, as shown in Figure 10–35, enabling you to define the note details.

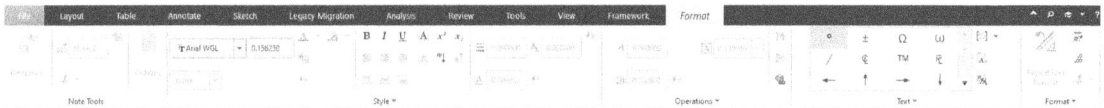

Figure 10–35

Once you select the location for the note, the system creates a text entry area for you to enter the note.

You can apply the following:

- The text style (e.g., Bold, Italic, Color, Height, and so on).

- Special symbols.

- Import a note from a file.

- Arrow Style.

Once the options in the *Format* dashboard are defined, click on the screen to complete the note placement.

Notes can incorporate parametric information that updates as the model changes. An ampersand (&) symbol is used to incorporate parametric information. For example, the parametric note shown in Figure 10−36 is entered as **&d23 DRILL- &P0 HOLES**, where the **&d23** and **&P0** reference dimension values are from the model. When you include parametric information, modifications to the size or number of holes in the pattern automatically update in the note.

Figure 10−36

Note: During note creation, click ⬚ (Switch Dimensions) in the Text group to display dimensions in their symbolic form.

Step 7 - Manipulate detail items, as required.

Once detail items have been added to a drawing, changes might be required. Some common changes that can be made to detail items include moving detail items, erasing, editing values, flipping arrows, moving an item to a view, and adding dimensional tolerances.

Move

Select and drag detail items to move them, as required. Detail items can be rotated by selecting the green rotate handle and rotating as shown in Figure 10−37.

Use this handle to rotate

Remove Sharp Edges

Figure 10–37

Erase

You can erase detail items by selecting the item in the drawing **and clicking** ✐ (Erase) **in the mini toolbar**. The erased annotations still display in the drawing tree as shown in Figure 10–38.

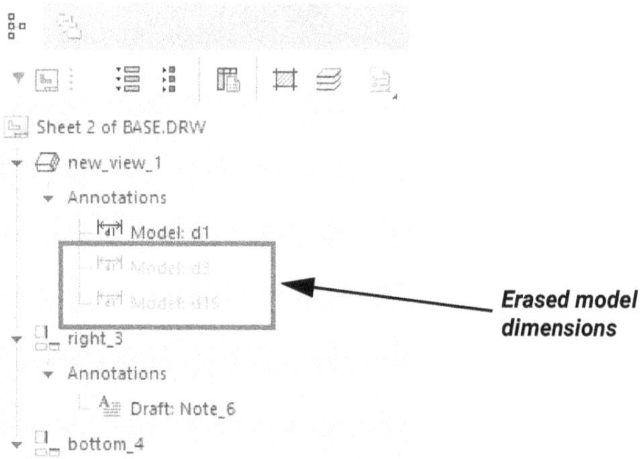

Sheet 2 of BASE.DRW
new_view_1
  Annotations
    Model: d1
    Model: d3
    Model: d15 ← *Erased model dimensions*
right_3
  Annotations
    Draft: Note_6
bottom_4

Figure 10–38

Edit Values

The value for a model dimension can be modified directly in Drawing mode by double-clicking it. The change is reflected in the model. You can also modify a dimension value by selecting the dimension **and editing the value in the *Dimension* tab in the ribbon**. Created dimensions cannot be modified. However, changes to the model geometry are reflected in the updated dimension value.

Flip Arrows

Select a dimension and click ↦↤ (Flip Arrows) **in the mini toolbar** to change the direction of the dimension arrows.

Move Item to View

When detail items, such as dimensions, are displayed on the drawing, they are not necessarily displayed on the required view. To switch detail items between views, select the dimension(s) and select ⊥ (Move to View). Select the new view on which you want the dimension to be displayed. You can select multiple items to be moved by holding <Ctrl> as you are selecting them.

Dimensional Tolerances

To enable dimension tolerances in Drawing mode, the Drawing Options file must have the **tol_display** option set to **yes**. To open the *Options* dialog box and set the value, select **File> Prepare>Drawing Properties**. The *Drawing Properties* dialog box opens, as shown in Figure 10–39. Select **change** in the *Detail Options* area.

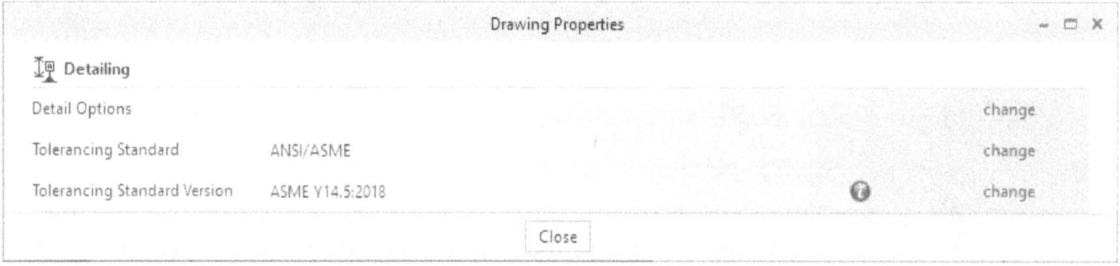

Drawing Properties		— ☐ ✕
⊥ Detailing		
Detail Options		change
Tolerancing Standard	ANSI/ASME	change
Tolerancing Standard Version	ASME Y14.5:2018	change
	Close	

Figure 10–39

To set dimension tolerances, select the dimension(s) and the *Dimension* tab displays, as shown in Figure 10–40.

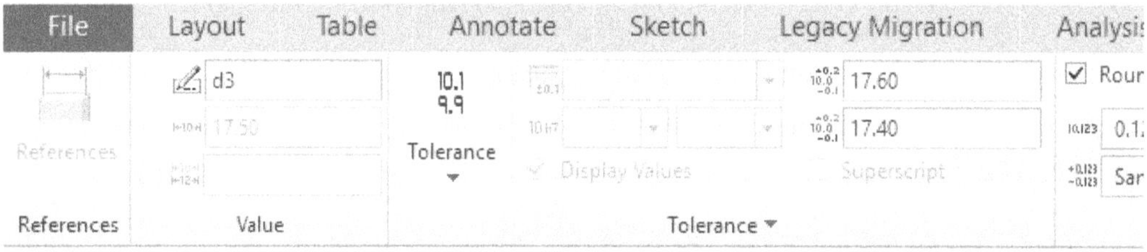

Figure 10–40

The available tolerance modes are listed as follows:

Option	Example
Nominal	1.25
+/- Symmetric	1.25 ± 0.05

Option	Example
Plus-Minus	$1.25 \ {}^{+0.05}_{-0.01}$
Limits	1.30
	1.20

Step 8 - Print (or Plot) the drawing.

To print or plot the drawing, select **File>Print>Print**. The *Printer's* dialog box displays, which enables you to print.

Click **Settings** in the *Print* tab to display the *Printer Configuration* dialog box and all of the plotting options, as shown in Figure 10–41.

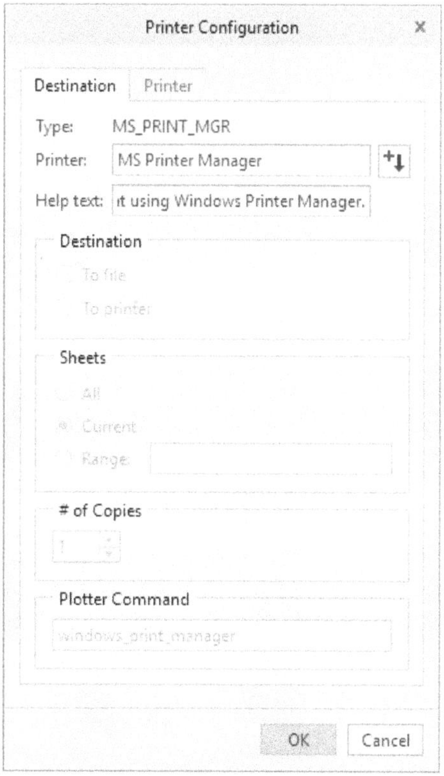

Figure 10–41

To print the file, you must define the destination printer in the drop-down list and configure it, as required. You must also select whether the file is printed to the printer or to a file and the number of copies.

10.2 Placing a Custom Symbol

Your organization will have both standard and custom symbols available for annotating your drawings.

To place a symbol in a drawing, click 🅐 (Symbol) in the *Annotations* group. Select the symbol from the Gallery, Symbol Palette, or browse to the required location on your system using Browse Symbols. If you select Browse Symbols, the *Open* dialog box displays, as shown in Figure 10–42. Double-click on the required file. The *Select Reference* dialog box displays.

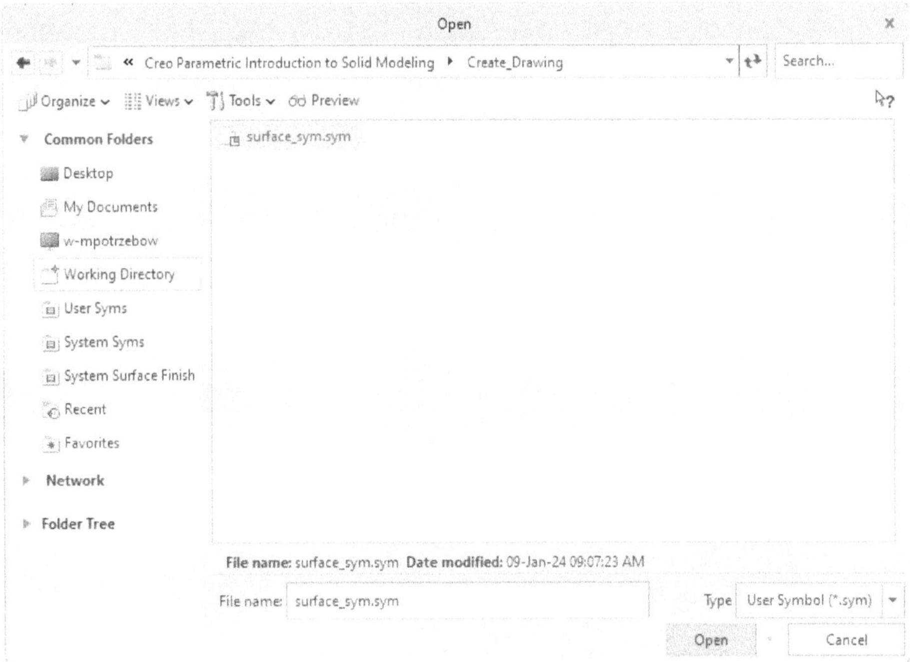

Figure 10–42

To select a placement type, right-click in the drawing area. The options for placement are shown in Figure 10–43. Move the cursor to the location where you want to attach the symbol and click there. Press the middle mouse button to place the symbol in the drawing.

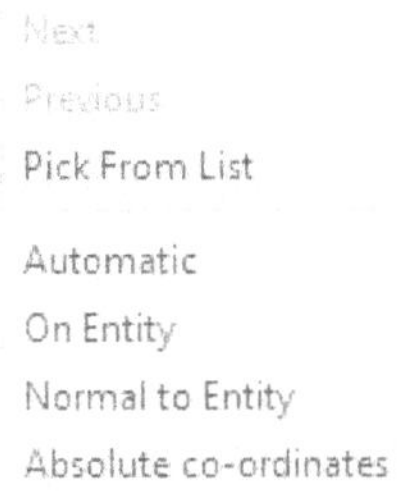

Figure 10–43

To customize the selected symbol using *Grouping* and *Variable Text*, click on **Symbol Customization**. The *Symbol Customization* dialog box is displayed as shown in Figure 10–44. To define the symbol, you must select the groups that you want to include from the *Grouping* area.

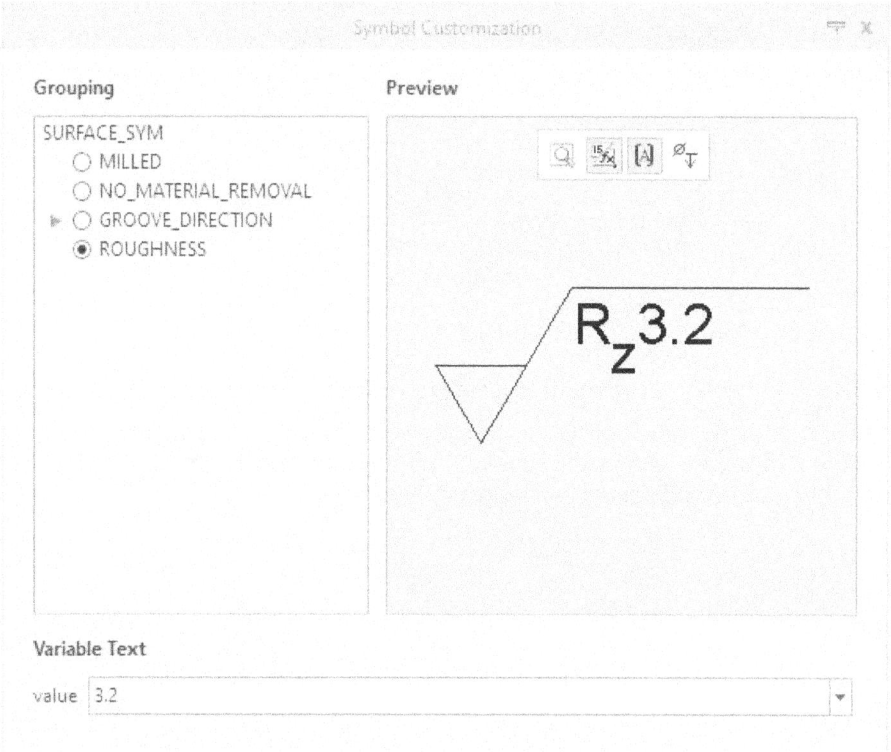

Figure 10–44

The *Variable Text* area, in the *Symbol Customization* dialog box is used to set the variable text values, as shown in Figure 10–45. If options are available for selection, they display in the **value** field.

Figure 10–45

To complete symbol placement, click in the drawing area where you want to place the symbol and the press the middle mouse button. The symbol is placed at that location. Click in the drawing area to exit from the *Symbol* tab.

10.3 Multiple Sheets

Additional sheets can be added to your drawings. You can add a sheet by clicking ⬚ (New Sheet) in the *Document* group, in the *Layout* tab in the ribbon. Alternatively, you can click

   ✦ (New Sheet) at the bottom of the Creo Parametric window.

As you add sheets, they are listed as tabs at the bottom of the window, as shown in Figure 10−46.

Figure 10−46

Note: To move between sheets, simply select the applicable tab.

Views and detail items can be moved from view to view by selecting the object and clicking

   ⇥ (Move to Sheet) in the *mini* toolbar. If there is only one sheet, the system automatically creates a second sheet and moves the objects.If more than one sheet is already in the drawing, the *Select Sheet* dialog box displays, as shown in Figure 10−47.

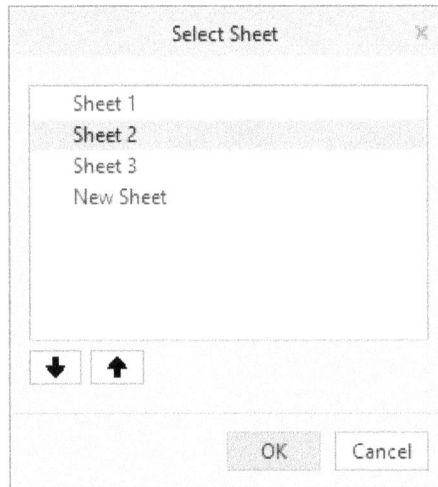

Figure 10−47

In this dialog box, you can select one of the existing sheets or add a New Sheet.

Practice 10a
Create a Drawing

Practice Objectives

- Create a new drawing based on a drawing template.
- Add General, Projected, Section, and Detail views to create a drawing.
- Change the orientation, display style, scale, and add a section using the *View* dialog box.
- Show dimensions on the drawing using the *Show Model Annotations* dialog box.
- Create and edit notes in the drawing.
- Add a custom symbol.
- Add a second sheet to the drawing and move a view to it.

In this practice, you will create the two-sheet drawing shown in Figure 10–48, using a predefined format. To complete the drawing, add all of the required views, dimensions, notes and symbols. Manipulate them as required to match the detail shown in Figure 10–48.

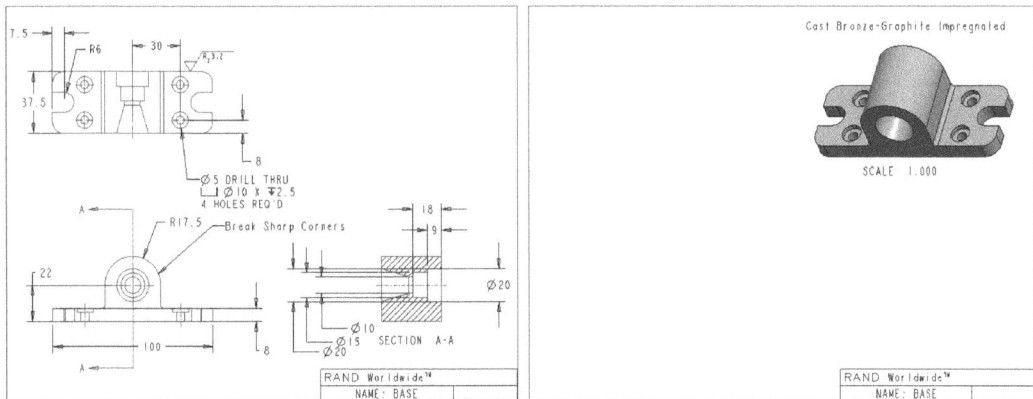

Figure 10–48

Task 1: Create a drawing and open a format.

1. Set the working directory to the *Create_Drawing* folder.
2. Click ⬜ (New).
3. In the *Type* area in the *New* dialog box, select the **Drawing** option.
4. Clear the **Use default template** option to create the drawing without a template.
5. Enable the **Use drawing model file name** option if necessary.
6. Click **OK**.

7. Click **Browse** then browse to and double-click **base.prt**.

8. In the *Specify Template* area in the *New Drawing* dialog box, select the **Empty with format** option.

9. In the *Format* area, click **Browse**, click ☐ (Working Directory) in the *Common Folders* area, and select the **rand.frm** format file. The *New Drawing* dialog box displays, as shown in Figure 10−49.

Figure 10−49

10. Click **OK** to finish creating the drawing. A drawing sheet is displayed in the main window, and note that the name of the drawing is BASE, as shown in Figure 10−50, matching the part file name.

Figure 10−50

11. Select **File>Prepare>Drawing Properties**. Select **change** in the *Detail Options* area as shown in Figure 10−51.

Figure 10−51

12. In the *Option* text field, type **tol_display**. In the value field, ensure that the *Value* is set to **no**. Click **Add/Change** and close the dialog box.

13. Click **OK** in the *Drawing Properties* dialog box.

14. Close the *Drawing Properties* dialog box.

Task 2: Add four views to the drawing.

In this task, you will create the views shown in Figure 10–52.

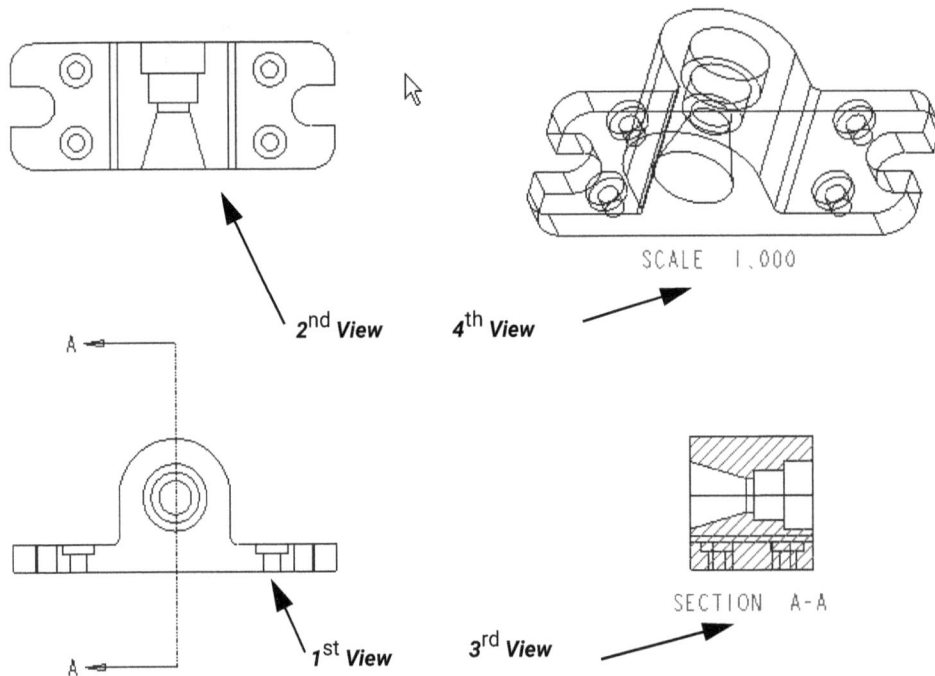

SCALE 1.000

2nd View   4th View

SECTION   A-A

1st View   3rd View

Figure 10–52

1. Set the model display as follows:

    * $\overset{x'}{\gamma_{+}}$ *(Datum Display Filters)*: All Off

    * $\square$ *(Display Style)*: $\boxplus$ (Wireframe)

2. Verify that the *Layout* tab is selected. Click $\overset{\ominus}{}$ (General View) to add the first view. You can also right-click and select **General View**.

3. If the *Select Combined State* dialog box opens, select **Do not prompt for combined state** and click **OK**. Select a location on the screen to place the first General view, as shown in Figure 10–53.

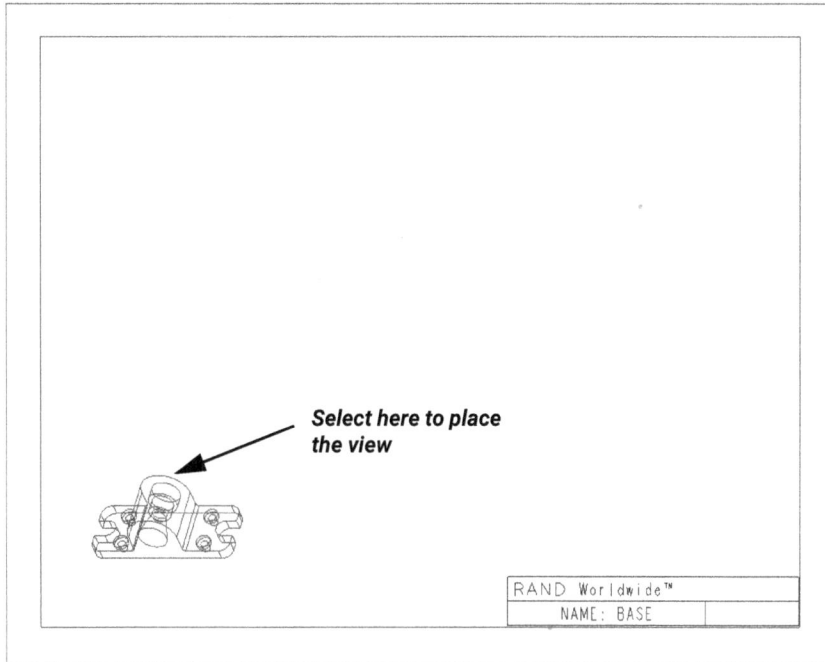

Figure 10–53

4.   In the *Drawing View* dialog box, the **View names from the model** option is selected, enabling you to select a predefined model view to orient the model. In the *Model view names* area, double-click on the **FRONT** view to reorient the model, as shown in Figure 10–54.

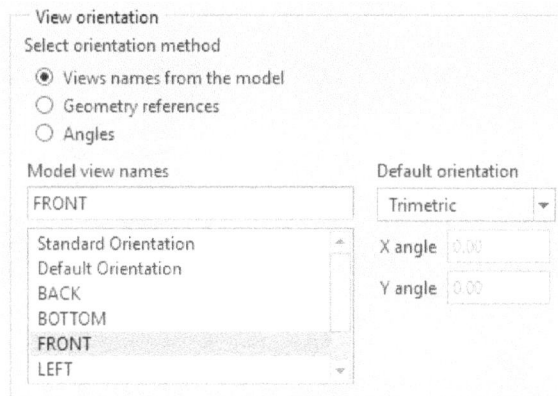

Figure 10–54

Note: To reorient the model, you can also select the **Geometry references** option and select two orthogonal planar references. Use the default datum planes for the orientation references.

5. Click **OK** to complete the view placement. The view displays, as shown in Figure 10–55.

Figure 10–55

6. Select the first view and click ⬚ (Projection View) in the *mini* toolbar.

   Note: *You can also click* ⬚ *(Projection View).*

7. Place the second view at the location shown in Figure 10–56.

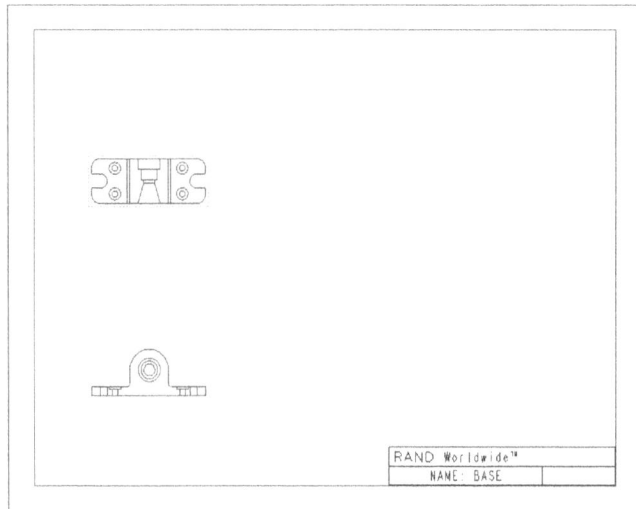

Figure 10–56

Note: A Projected view cannot have an independent scale. It must have the same scale as its parent General view.

8. Select the first view and click ⬚ (Projection View) in the *mini* toolbar.

9. Place the third view in the location shown in Figure 10−57.

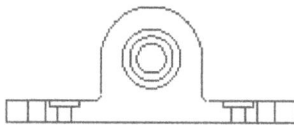

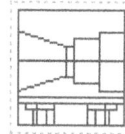

Figure 10−57

10. Select the third view and click ✎ (Properties) in the *mini* toolbar.

   Note: You can also open the Drawing View dialog box by double-clicking on the view.

11. In the *Drawing View* dialog box, select the *Sections* category.

12. In the *Section options* area, select the **2D cross-section** option.

13. Click ✚.

14. In the *Name* column, select cross-section **A**.

15. In the *Sectioned Area* column, select **Full**, as shown in Figure 10-58.

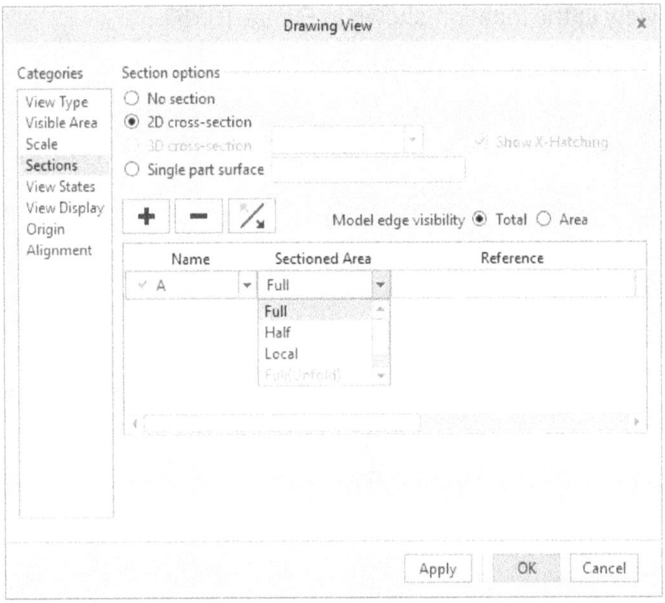

Figure 10-58

16. Click **OK** to complete the view modification.

17. Select the third view, then right-click and select **Add Arrows**.

18. Select the first view in which to place cross-section arrows. The drawing displays, as shown in Figure 10-59.

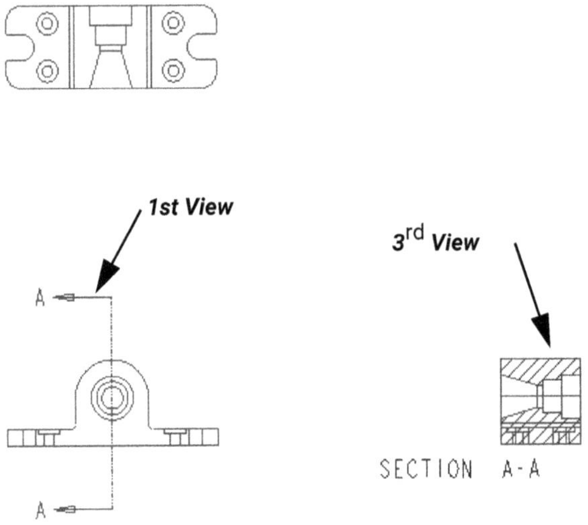

Figure 10-59

19. Right-click and select **General View**, and add the fourth view, as shown in Figure 10−60. Keep the *View* dialog box open.

4th View

SECTION A-A

Figure 10−60

20. In the *Drawing View* dialog box, select the *Scale* category.

21. In the *Scale and perspective options* area, select the **Custom scale** option. Set the *Scale* to **1.0**.

22. Click **Apply** to apply the changes.

23. Click **OK** to close the *Drawing View* dialog box. The fourth view displays, as shown in Figure 10−61.

SCALE 1.000

SECTION A-A

Figure 10−61

Task 3: Modify the scale of the drawing and move the views.

1. Double-click on the scale value in the lower left corner of the drawing and enter a scale value of **0.8** in the field that opens at the top of the window, as shown in Figure 10−62.

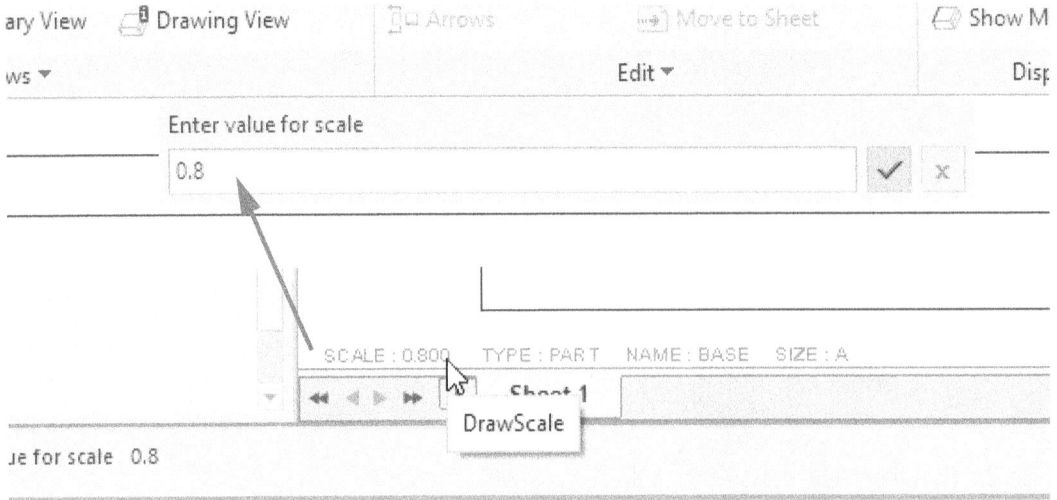

Figure 10−62

Note: The scale of the fourth view remains set at **1.0** because this view has a scale that is independent to the rest of the drawing.

2. You can lock or unlock views to prevent them being moved by the mouse. To unlock them, ensure the ⌖ (Lock View Movement) is not selected in the *Layout* tab or in the shortcut menu.

Note: You can also click ⌖ (Lock View Movement) in the Document group in the Layout tab to lock and unlock all of the views.

3. Select the views individually and move them, as shown in Figure 10–63. Note how moving a parent view reflects in the placement of dependent views. Click and drag to move the scale and section notes to the positions shown.

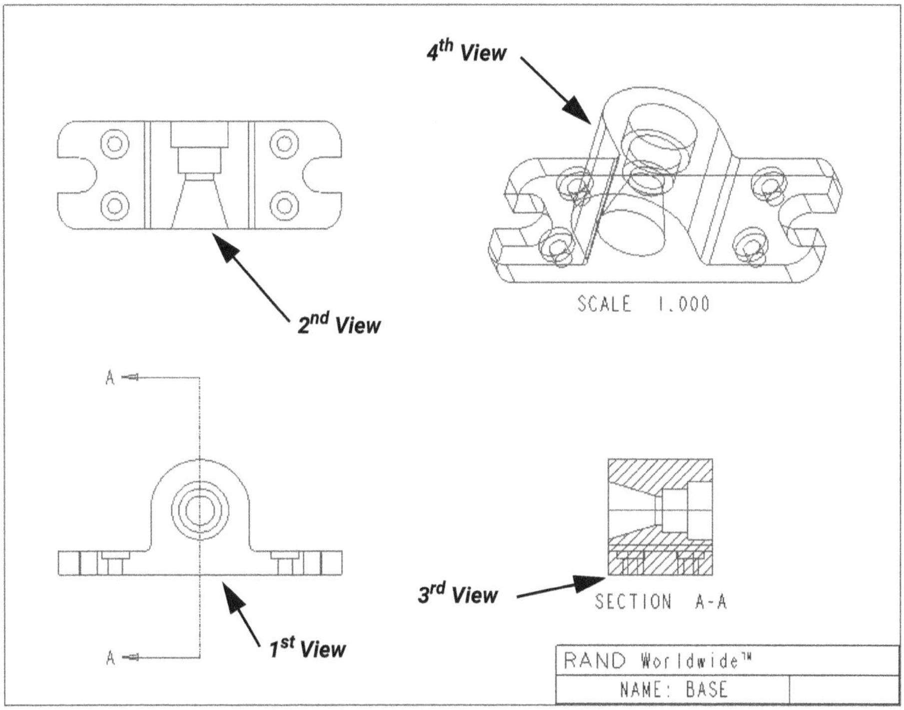

Figure 10–63

Task 4: Change the view display of the third and fourth views.

1. Double-click on the third view.

   Note: You can modify the view display for multiple views at the same time. Press and hold <Ctrl> while selecting the views and click 🖌 *(Properties) to open the Drawing View dialog box.*

2. In the *Drawing View* dialog box, select the *View Display* category.

3. In the *Display Style* drop-down list, select **No Hidden**.

4. Click **OK** to complete the view modification.

Task 5: Change the view display of the fourth view.

1. Double-click on the isometric view.

2. In the *Drawing View* dialog box, select the *View Display* category.

3. In the *Display Style* drop-down list, select **Shading With Edges**.

4. Click **OK** to complete the view modification. The drawing displays, as shown in Figure 10-64.

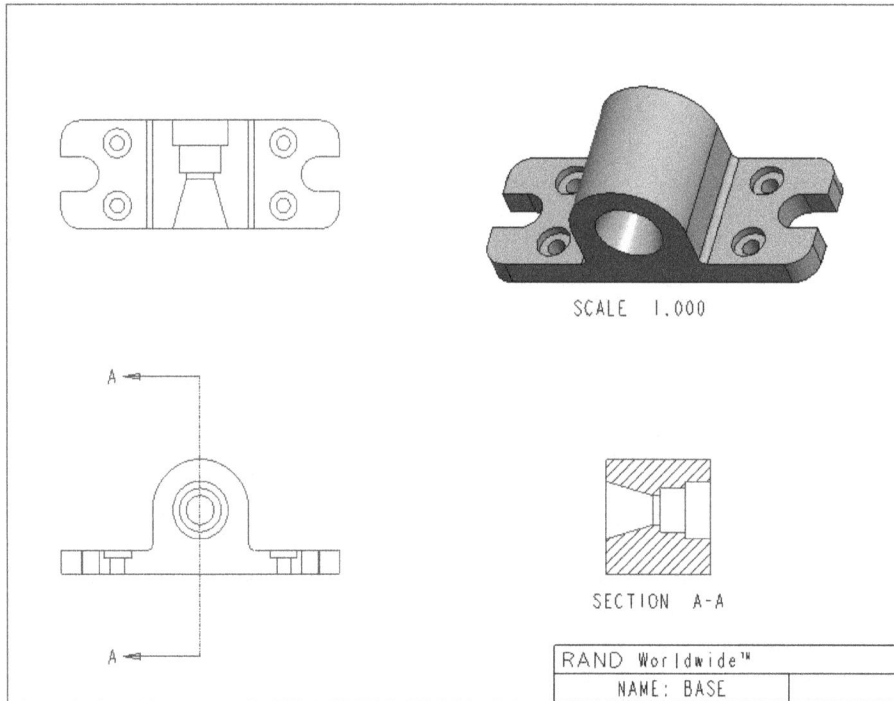

Figure 10-64

Task 6: Display the dimensions of the base feature.

1. Select the *Annotate* tab. Click 📑 (Show Model Annotations) to open the *Show Model Annotations* dialog box.

   Note: You can also use the Model Tree to display dimensions for each feature.

2. In the *Show Model Annotations* dialog box, select the *Dimensions* tab (⊢→), if required. Verify that the **All** type is selected.

3. In the Top view, select the base feature **(EXTRUDE_1)**.

4. Three dimensions display. In the *Show* column, place a check next to the **37.5** dimension (d0), and click **Apply**, as shown in Figure 10–65.

Figure 10–65

5. In the Front view, select the base feature (**EXTRUDE_1**). Keep the dimensions shown in Figure 10–66. Click **Apply**.

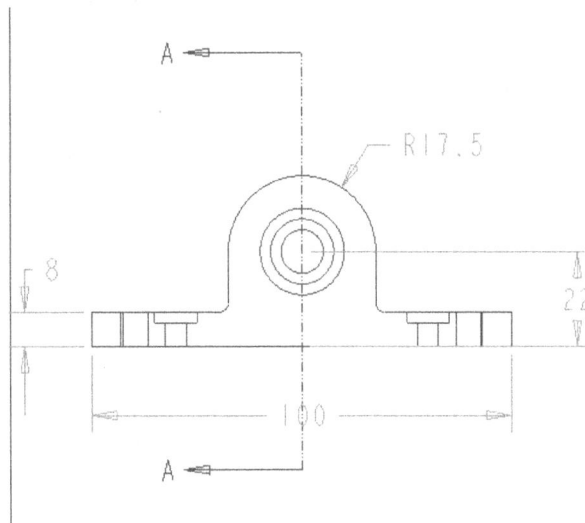

Figure 10–66

Note: You can select the dimension you want to keep directly on the drawing.

Task 7: Display the dimensions of the U-shaped cut and the hole in the boss.

1. Display and select the dimensions of the U-shaped cut (**NOTCH**), as shown in Figure 10−67. If the cut was copied, you must select the original cut, which is on the left side of the view.

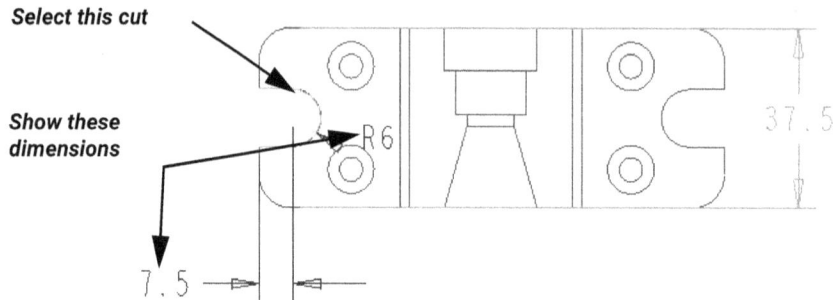

Figure 10−67

2. Click **Apply** in the *Show Model Annotations* dialog box to keep the dimensions.

Note: Click ☑− *to select all the dimensions. If selecting the hole in the first or third view, right-click and select* **Pick From List**.

3. Display the dimensions for the hole in **SLOT** by selecting the feature on the Right (cross-section) view, as shown in Figure 10−68.

4. Click ☑− (Select All) and **Apply** in the *Show Model Annotations* dialog box to keep the dimensions.

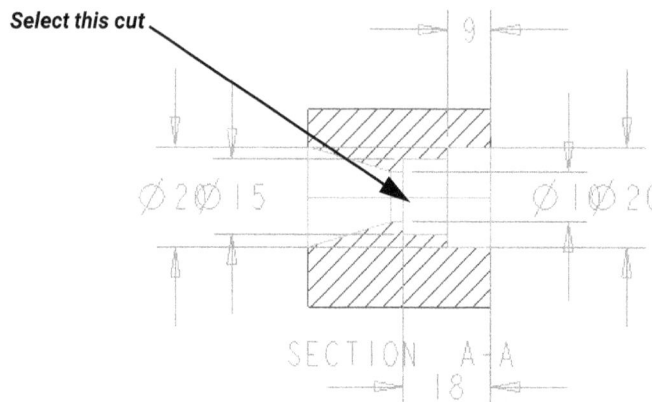

Figure 10−68

Note: Model dimensions can only be shown once on a drawing.

Task 8: Continue selecting features to show dimensions.

1. Show dimensions for the remaining features.

2. When all of the dimensions are displayed, close the *Show Model Annotations* dialog box.

Task 9: Delete dimensions.

1. Select any unwanted dimensions and click ✕ (Delete) to remove them. Repaint the screen if required.

Task 10: Arrange the dimensions.

1. Select one of the hole dimensions in the Top view and move the dimension to the location shown in Figure 10−69.

Figure 10−69

2. Move the other hole dimension in the Top view.

3. Select each hole dimension and click ⊬⊬ (Flip Arrows) in the *mini* toolbar.

4. Rearrange the dimensions, as shown in Figure 10−70.

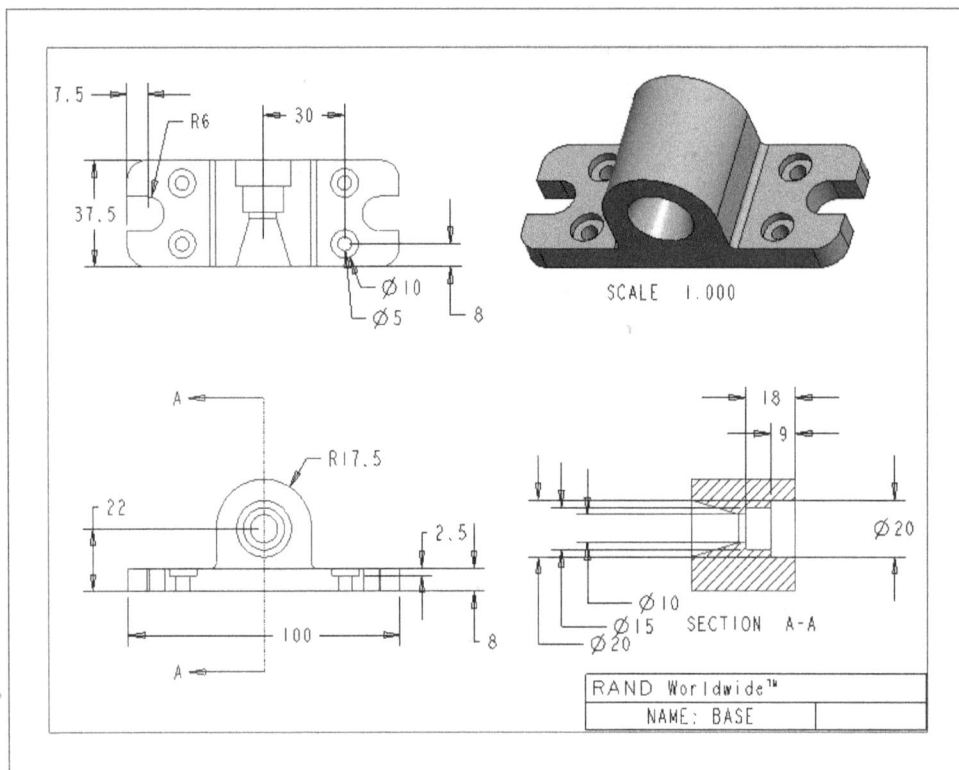

Figure 10−70

Task 11: Create additional dimensions.

Created dimensions update with any part changes. However, they cannot be modified to drive part geometry.

1. Click ⊢⊣ (Dimension). The *Select Reference* dialog box opens. Leave the default selection option selected.

2. Select the edge of the round shown in Figure 10–71, move to the appropriate location, then middle-click to place the dimension.

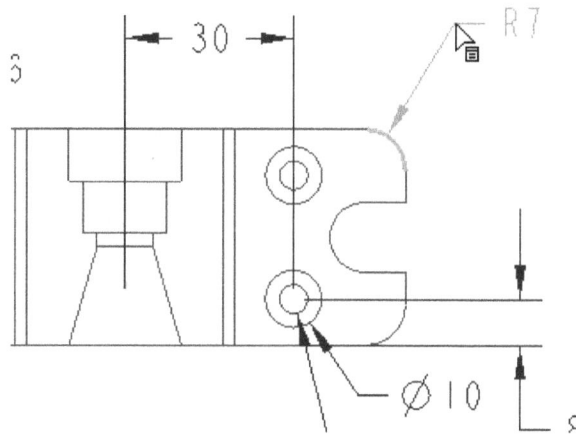

Figure 10–71

3. Select the left edge shown in Figure 10–72, press and hold <Ctrl> and select the right edge, then move the dimension to the correct location and middle-click to place it.

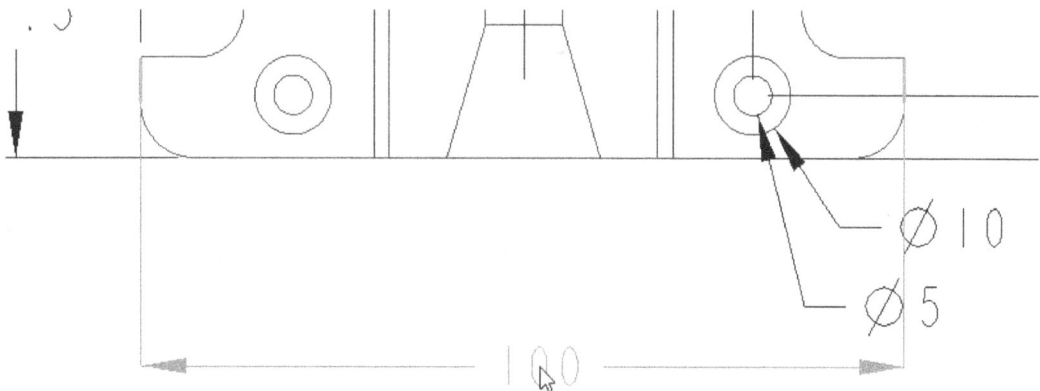

Figure 10–72

Task 12: Delete some dimensions.

1. Press and hold <Ctrl>, select each of the of the dimension you just created, right-click and select **Delete**.

Design Considerations

In the following tasks, you will create the three notes shown in Figure 10–73.

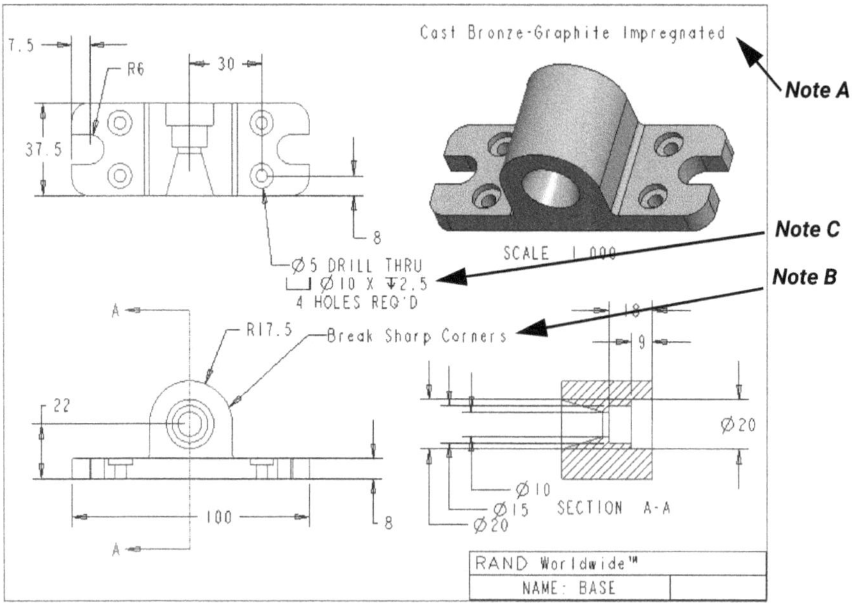

Figure 10–73

Task 13: Create Note A.

1. Select the *Annotate* tab and click ᴬ≣ (Note) to create the first note.
2. Select a location at which to place the note.
3. Enter **Cast Bronze-Graphite Impregnated**.
4. Click on the screen to complete the note. Move it to the appropriate location.

Task 14: Create Note B.

1. Expand the ᴬ≣ (Note) flyout and select ⌐ᴬ (Leader Note). Read the message window and select the boss edge, as shown in Figure 10–73.
2. Click the middle mouse button in a location to place the note.

3. For the note, enter **Break Sharp Corners**.

4. Click the screen twice to finish creating the note.

Task 15: Create Note C and move Note A.

1. Click ✓ᴬ (Leader Note).

2. Select the counterbore hole shown in Figure 10−73.

3. Click the middle mouse button in a location at which to place the note.

4. Enter the note shown in Figure 10−74. In the *Format* tab, select all of the special symbols from the palette in the *Text* group, except the ampersand (&) symbol. Use the keyboard to enter the ampersand symbol. Press <Enter> once after you complete each of the first two lines.

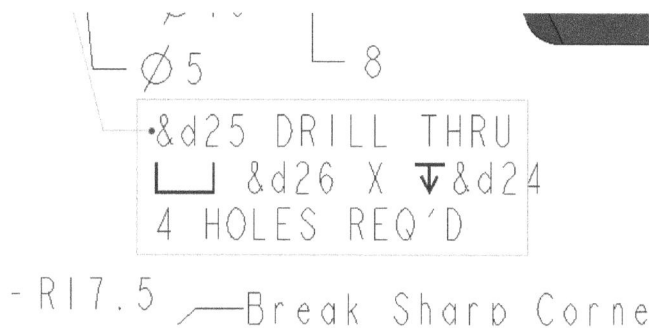

Figure 10−74

Note: As symbols are selected in the palette, they display in the message window.

5. Click twice on the screen to complete the note.

6. Select **Note A**.

7. Move the note to be centered above the isometric view.

Task 16: Place the symbol in the model.

1. In the *Annotate* group in the ribbon, click ⓐ (Symbol). Expand the *Symbols* panel from the *Symbol* tab and click **Browse Symbols**.

2. In the *Common Folders* area of the *Open* dialog box, click **Working Directory**.

3. Double-click on **surface_sym.sym** to open it.

4. Click **Symbol Customization** from the *Symbol* tab. In the *Symbol Customization* dialog box, in the *Grouping* area, click the **Roughness** radio button.

5. Select the edge shown in Figure 10–75.

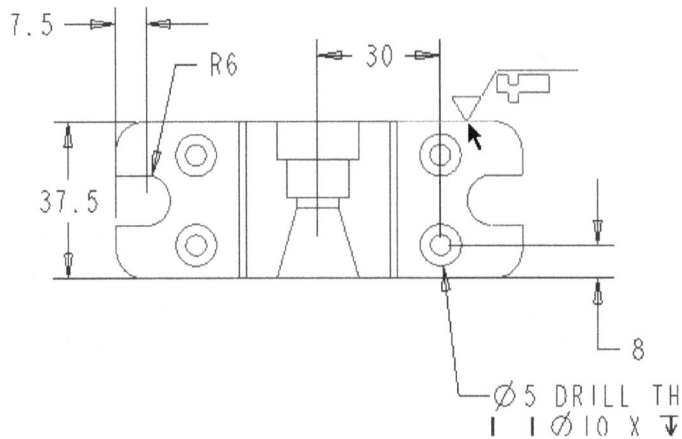

Figure 10–75

6. Click the middle mouse button to complete the symbol placement, as shown in Figure 10–76.

Figure 10–76

7. Click in the drawing area to complete the process.

Task 17: Move the isometric view to another sheet.

1. Select the isometric view and click ⇥ (Move to Sheet).

2. Creo Parametric automatically creates a second sheet, and moves the view as shown in Figure 10−77.

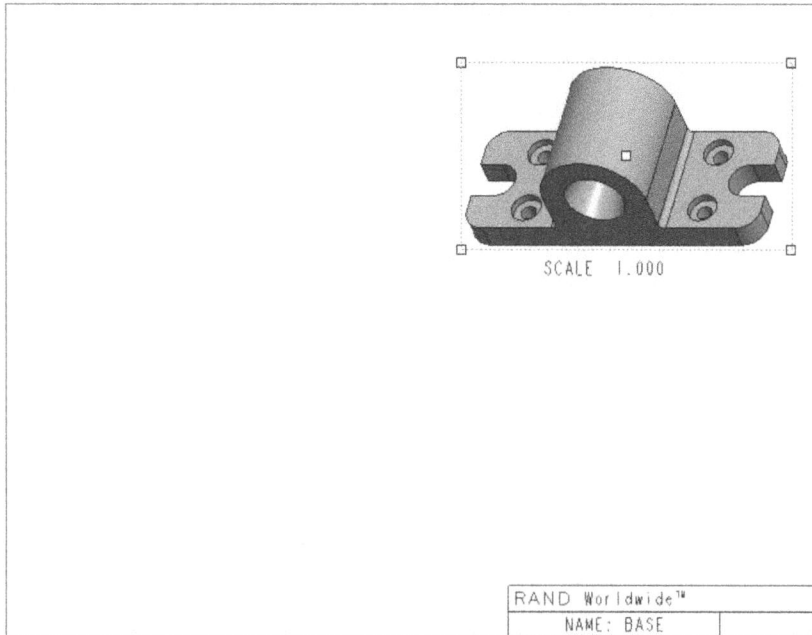

SCALE 1.000

RAND Worldwide™
NAME: BASE

Figure 10−77

3. Place your cursor over the view to see the view information tool-tip, as shown in Figure 10−78.

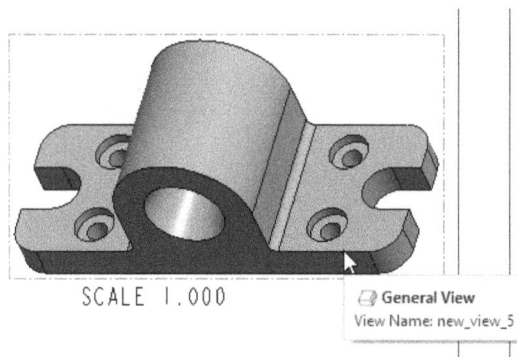

SCALE 1.000

General View
View Name: new_view_5

Figure 10−78

4. Select the *Sheet 1* tab in the lower left of the Creo Parametric window to return to the first sheet.

5. Select the **Cast Bronze-Graphite Impregnated** note and click ➞ (Move to Sheet).

---

6. In the *Select Sheet* dialog box, select **Sheet 2**, as shown in Figure 10-79.

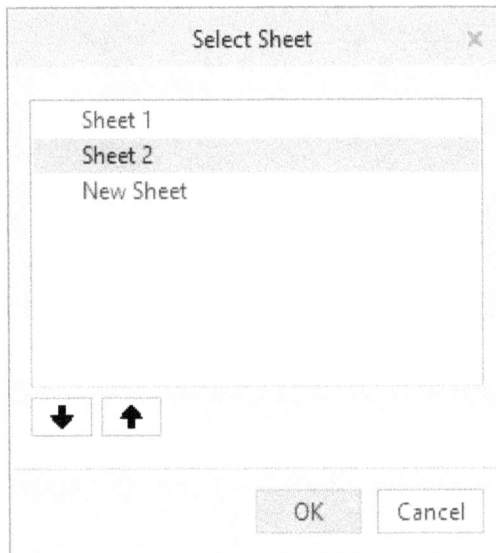

Figure 10-79

7. Click **OK**.

8. **Sheet 2** updates, as shown in Figure 10-80.

Figure 10-80

Task 18: Display axes in the views on the first sheet.

1. Select the *Sheet 1* tab at the bottom of the Creo Parametric window.

2. Select the *Annotate* tab in the ribbon.

3. In the *Annotations* group, click 🔲 (Show Model Annotations).

4. Select the 🔲 (Show Model Datums) tab in *Show Model Annotations* dialog box.

5. Press and hold <Ctrl> and select the holes shown in Figure 10–81.

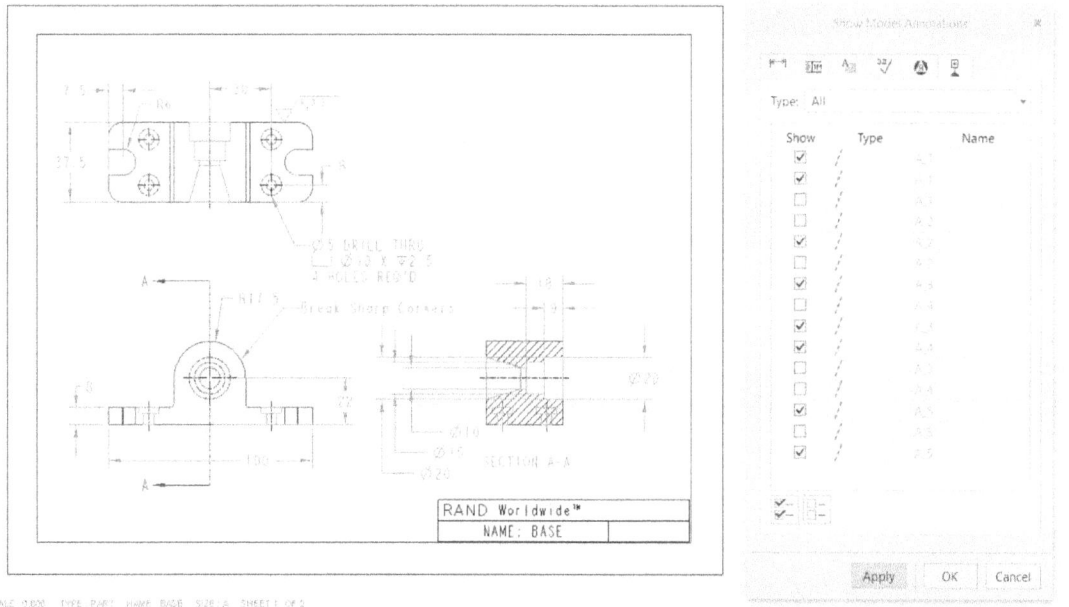

Figure 10–81

6. Click 🔲 (Select All) and click **OK**.

7. Click on the screen to clear any selected entities and the drawing displays, as shown in Figure 10−82.

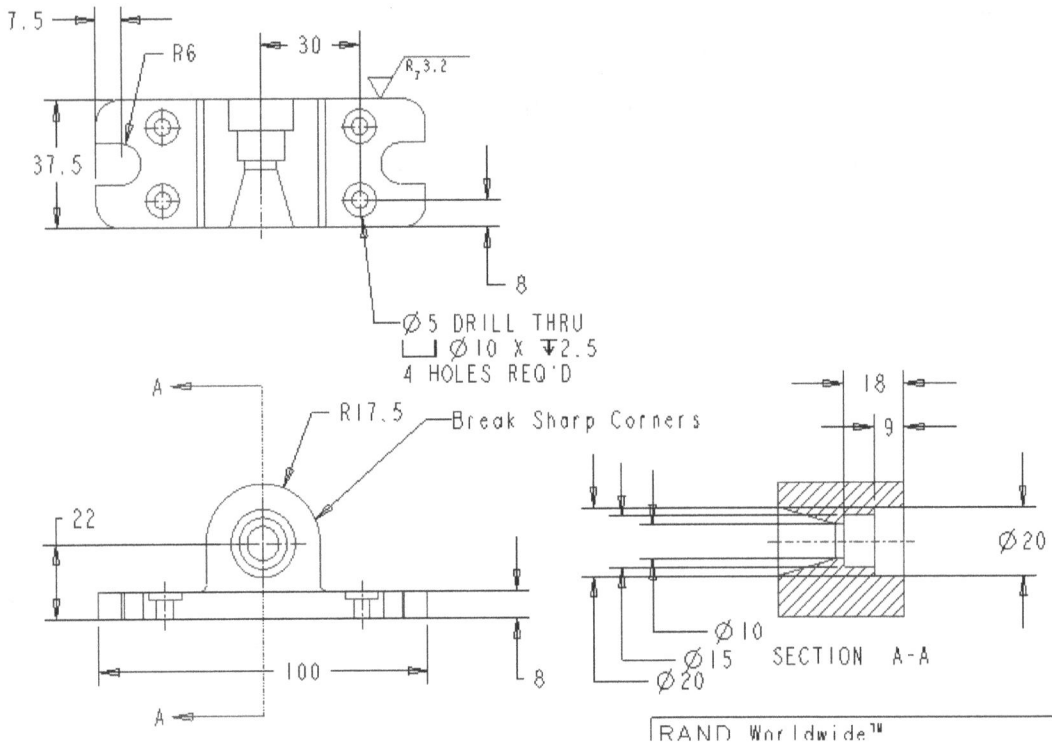

Figure 10−82

Task 19: Arrange any remaining detail items and save the drawing.

1. Arrange any detail items or views that need to be organized.

2. Save the drawing and erase all of the files from memory.

End of practice

Practice 10b
Create a Drawing Using Additional Tools

Practice Objective

* Create a new drawing, add views, and show dimensions.

In this practice, you will use drawing tools to create the drawing shown in Figure 10–84. Tips are provided for you to create the radial circle of dimensions for the pattern of holes.

Task 1: Open a part file.

1. Set the working directory to the *Drawing_Tools* folder.

2. Open **end_cap.prt**.

3. Set the model display as follows:

   * ⅔ *(Datum Display Filters)*: All Off

   * ⅓ *(Spin Center)*: Off

   * ⬜ *(Display Style)*: ⬜ (Hidden Line)

   The part displays, as shown in Figure 10–83.

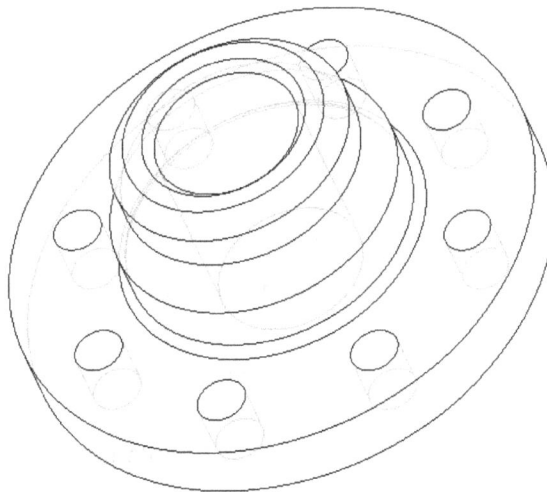

Figure 10–83

4. Review the part and its features.

Task 2: Create a drawing with limited instruction.

1. Create the drawing shown in Figure 10–84. Set the drawing scale to **0.050**.

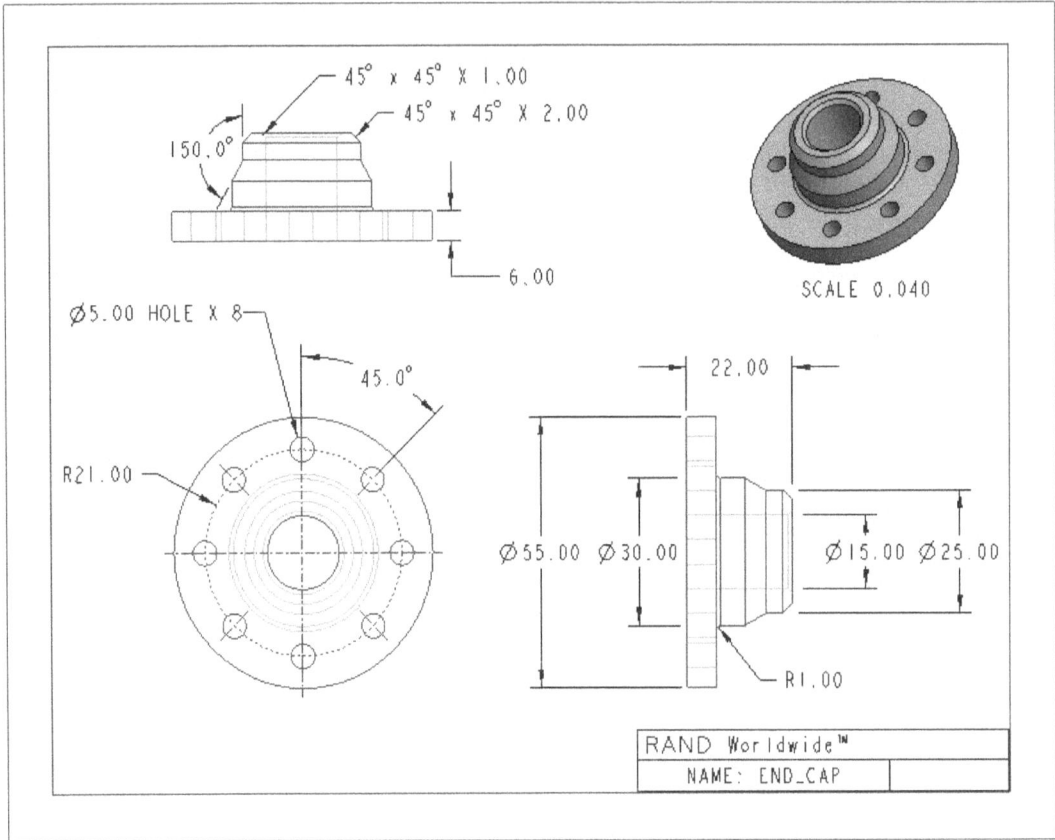

Figure 10–84

Use the following information to help you create the radial circle for the pattern:

- In the drawing setup file, edit an option. Select **File>Prepare>Drawing Properties** and select **change** in the *Detail Options* dialog box. Edit the **radial_pattern_axis_circle** option, and set it to **Yes**.

- Select the view, right-click and select **Show Model Annotation**.

2. Save the drawing and erase the files from memory.

End of practice

Chapter Review Questions

1. Which of the following **Specify Template** options enables you to define the orientation of the drawing sheet and set the sheet size for the drawing?

   a. Use template

   b. Empty with format

   c. Empty

2. Which of the following view types must be the first view in a drawing?

   a. Projection

   b. Auxiliary

   c. General

   d. Detailed

3. Which of the following view types enables you to create an isometric view in its default orientation?

   a. Projection

   b. Auxiliary

   c. General

   d. Detailed

4. Which of the following references can be selected when orienting a drawing view? (Select all that apply.)

   a. Datum planes

   b. Datum axis

   c. Planar surfaces

   d. Cylindrical surfaces

   e. Coordinate system axis

5. Views are automatically locked to the original location at which they were placed. Which of the following options or icons enables you to unlock the view movement?

   a. Click ⊢⊣ in the toolbar.

   b. Click ⁄ in the toolbar.

   c. Right-click and select **Unlock**.

   d. Right-click and ensure that **Lock View Movement** is not selected.

6. Which of the following categories in the *Drawing View* dialog box enables you to redefine a Projected view as a General view?

   a. View Type

   b. Visible Area

   c. Sections

   d. View Display

Annotation Features

Creo Parametric provides functionality for annotating your models, enabling you to display information directly on the 3D model.

Learning Objectives

- Learn to create various types of annotation features and display them on the solid model to communicate your design without using a 2D drawing.
- Set or create an annotation plane for the orientation reference.
- Use the various tools in the Annotation Feature dialog box to define the annotation element and select references for the placement.
- Learn to add parameters, rename, and pattern the annotation feature once it has been created.
- Learn to automatically display a drawing view that has the same orientation and direction as the annotation plane.
- Learn the various techniques used to select, display, and manipulate the annotation feature.

11.1 Creating Annotation Features

Annotations communicate design information. You can create various types of annotations, such as notes, symbols, and geometric tolerances. Annotations can be created in solid models or in drawings. In most situations, drawing annotation items are displayed in the model.

In a 3D model, annotations can be created as independent features. Multiple annotation entities can also be created in a single Annotation feature. An Annotation feature does not create physical geometry in your model. It simply enables you to group specific non-geometric information (e.g., Notes, Symbols, or Geometric Tolerances) and display it on the 3D model. Once created, you can manipulate it by hiding, using layers, or creating simplified representations. You can also include role-specific parameter information for quick access.

Using annotation features enables you to communicate the relevance of references in a model. This helps to ensure that references critical to the design are maintained in the model throughout the design process.

Annotation features have been incorporated to support the ASME Y14.41 (Digital Product Definition Data Practices) standard. This supports manufacturing from the 3D models (Model Based Definition). If you create Annotation Features in a model/assembly with the configuration command **auto_show _3D_detail_items** in your config.pro file set to **yes**, the Annotation Features are automatically displayed in the created views in drawings when a drawing view is placed in the correct orientation.

General Steps

Use the following general steps to create detail items in a drawing:

1. Set the orientation reference.
2. Start the creation of the Annotation feature.
3. Select an Annotation element.
4. Define the Annotation element and its references.
5. Assign parameters to the Annotation element.
6. Rename the Annotation feature or any of its elements.
7. Complete the Annotation feature.
8. Pattern the Annotation feature, as required.
9. Display the Annotation feature in the drawing, as required.

Step 1 - Set the orientation reference.

How To: Define the Annotation Orientation

1. Select the *Annotate* tab.

2. Select a predefined reference plane in the *Annotation Planes* group as shown in Figure 11-1.

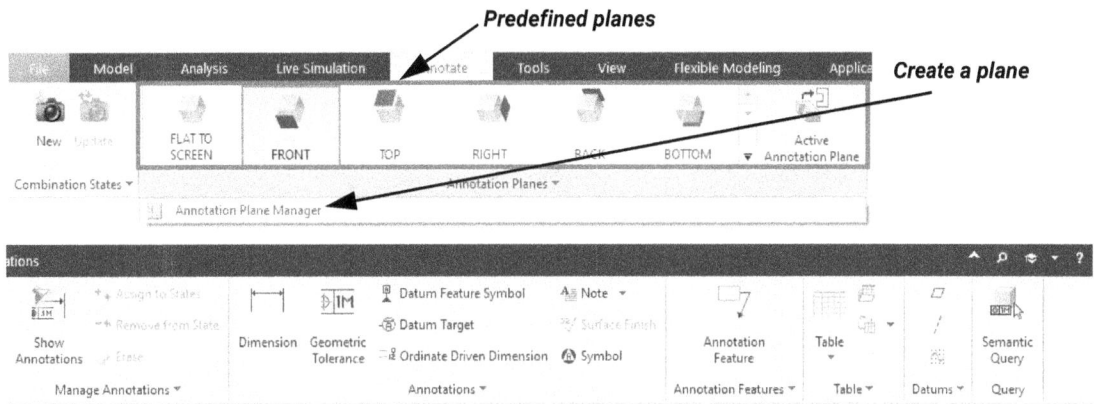

Figure 11-1

You can also create your own annotation plane by expanding the *Annotation Planes* panel and selecting **Annotation Plane Manager**. The *Annotation Plane Manager* dialog box lists the names of the available planes, as shown in Figure 11-2.

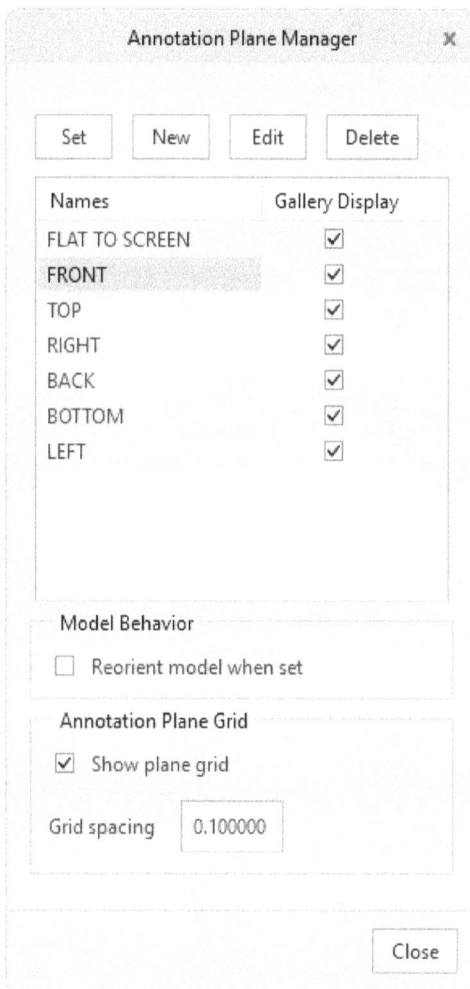

Figure 11-2

Click **New** in the *Annotation Plane Manager* dialog box to create a new orientation plane. The *Active Annotation Orientation dialog* box opens as shown in Figure 11–3 and enables you to create your own reference plane. Select **Reference Plane** and select a new planer surface or datum plane for the annotation reference orientation.

New reference plane

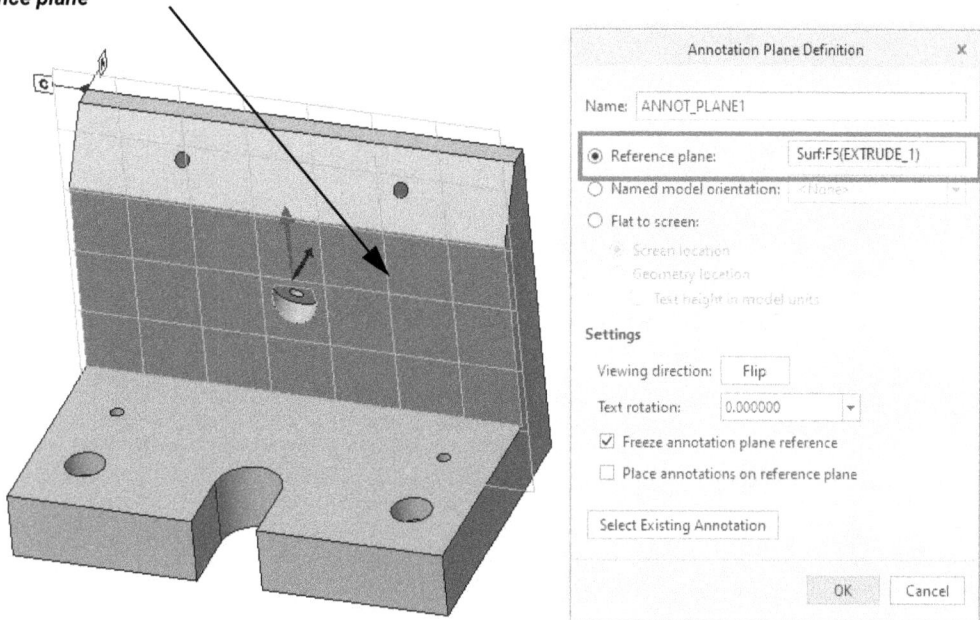

Figure 11–3

3. Click ⛶ (Active Annotation Plane) to set the model orientation to the active plane.

Step 2 - Start the creation of the Annotation feature.

Click ⍩ (Annotation Feature) in the *Annotation Features* group in the *Annotate* tab to create an annotation feature. The *Annotation Feature* dialog box opens, as shown in Figure 11–4.

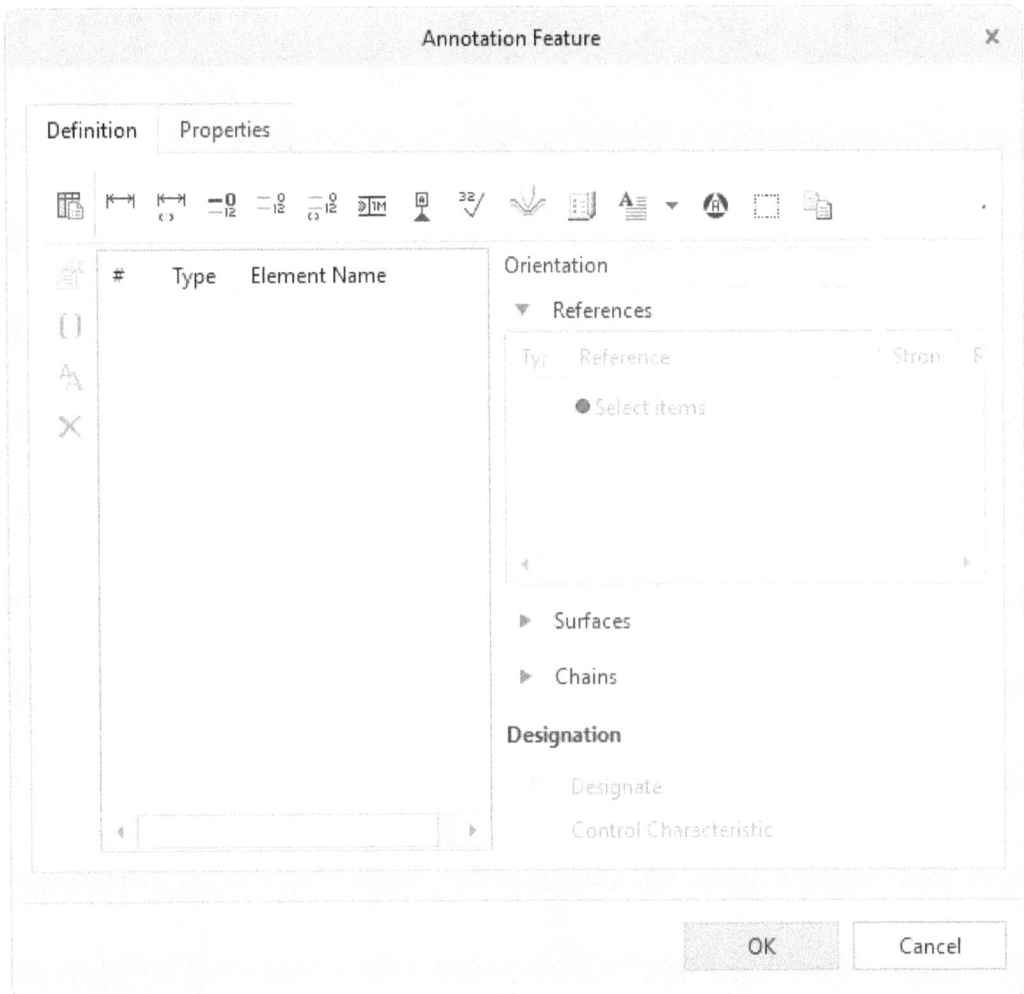

Figure 11–4

Note: *You can hide/show the annotation in the model by clicking* ⍩ *(Annotation Display) in the Graphics toolbar.*

Step 3 - Select an Annotation element.

An Annotation feature can consist of one or more elements. The available annotation elements are as follows.

Icon	Description
⊢⊣	Creates model dimensions.
⊢⊣ ( )	Creates reference dimensions.
−0 12	Creates ordinate baseline dimensions.
−0 12	Creates ordinate driven dimensions.
−0 ( ) 12	Creates ordinate reference dimensions.
⊅⌶M	Displays geometric tolerances.
⌷	Displays datums.
32/	Creates surface finishes.
⌄	Specifies sheetmetal punch model properties.
▤	Creates a manufacturing template.
A≡	Creates notes.
Ⓐ	Inserts a custom symbol.
⬚	Creates an empty annotation.
▤	Select an existing annotation to copy.

Select an element type in the *Annotation Feature* dialog box to add an element. A dialog box opens when you have selected the element type. The dialog box is the same as that used for creating any one of these items independently.

> *Note: Each element listed can also be created independently in the model to create independent annotation items.*

Step 4 - Define the Annotation element and its references.

Depending on the type of Annotation element that you select, you are required to select references and enter information to create the annotation. The information and references are consistent with creating any of the annotation element types independently.

Figure 11−5 shows the *Datum Feature* tab used to define a datum feature symbol on the top and the *Geometric Tolerance* tab on the bottom.

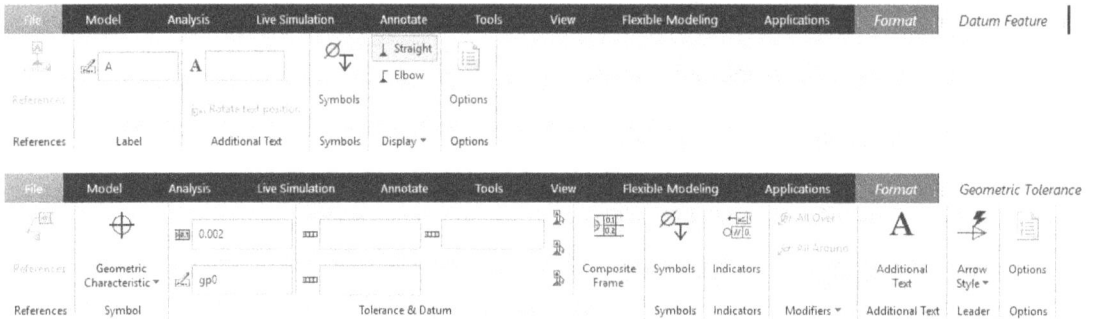

Figure 11−5

In addition to the references that are required to place each element, you must select a reference plane to which the annotation remains parallel, regardless of the model's orientation. This reference plane is called the annotation plane. You are prompted to define the front facing direction of the plane when selecting the annotation plane. The annotation faces the specified direction, parallel to the selected plane, and at the placement location for the element.

> *Note: Depending on the annotation element that you are creating, the reference plane can be created on the fly.*

Annotation references are classified as strong or weak, as follows:

* Strong references are verified during the regeneration of the feature. If missing, the Annotation feature fails.

* Weak references are verified at the end of the model regeneration. If missing, the Annotation feature does not fail regeneration. If the missing weak reference is used by an annotation leader, it becomes inactive and is not displayed on the model.

Depending on the type of reference created, Creo Parametric automatically assigns the reference as strong or weak. For example, annotation planes, reference entities for geometric tolerances, and dimension references are strong by default. However, leader attachments are weak. To change a reference classification from weak to strong or strong to weak, select or clear the checkbox in the *Strong* column in the *References* area for the element, as shown in Figure 11–6.

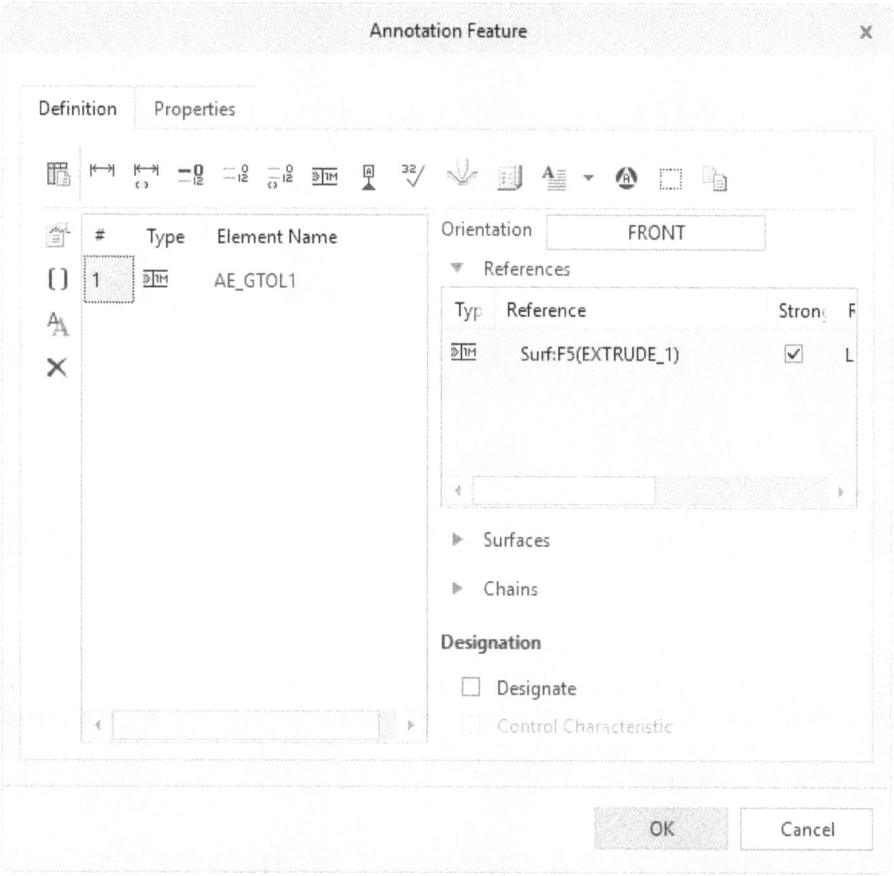

Figure 11–6

Step 5 - Assign parameters to the Annotation element.

You can assign parameters to individual elements once you have created and placed the Annotation on the model. To activate one of the elements and assign a parameter, select it in the Element Name list and click [] (Parameters).

The *Parameters* dialog box for the selected element opens as shown in Figure 11−7.

Figure 11−7

You can add parameters in the same way as in Part mode. Alternatively, you can use an external parameter file to populate parameters for an Annotation feature. To use an external parameter file, set the **auto_ae_param_file** configuration option as the full path to the file. For details on the syntax for this file, refer to the Creo Help Center document: *Example: Automatic Creation of Annotation Element Parameters*.

Step 6 - Rename the Annotation feature or any of its elements.

Each Annotation element is assigned a default name, which indicates the element type and a sequential number that depends on the number of this type of element in the model. To rename the element, double-click on the Element Name in the *Annotation Feature* dialog box and enter a new name.

As with all features, you can rename the Annotation feature in the Model Tree by double-clicking on it and entering a new name. Alternatively, you can select the *Properties* tab in the *Annotation Feature* dialog box and enter the name.

Step 7 - Complete the Annotation feature.

Once all of the Annotation elements have been created, you can complete the Annotation feature by clicking **OK** at the bottom of the *Annotation Feature* dialog box.

Step 8 - Pattern the Annotation feature, as required.

If an Annotation feature has at least one reference to an existing pattern in the model, it can be patterned using ⬚ (Pattern). The pattern is created as a Reference pattern.

All of the elements are patterned when an Annotation feature with multiple elements has at least one element referencing a pattern. The elements that do not reference the original pattern are duplicated. However, they still reference their original entities.

Step 9 - Display the Annotation feature in the drawing, as required.

Annotations created in the 3D model can be automatically displayed in the drawing view that has the same orientation and direction as the annotation plane, as shown in Figure 11–8. To disable this functionality, set the **auto_show_3D_detail_ items** config option to **no**.

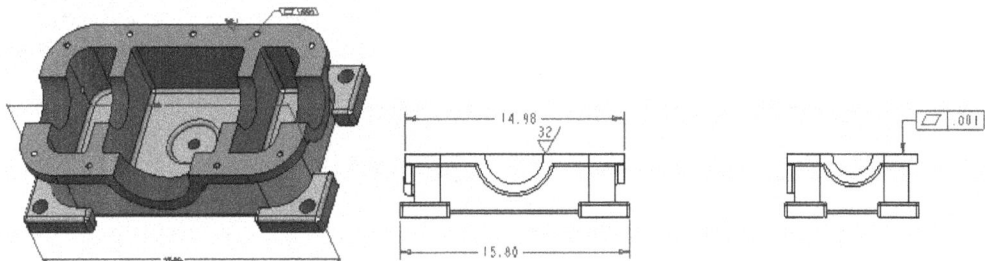

Figure 11–8

11.2 Manipulating Annotation Features

Selecting

An Annotation feature does not create geometry in your model. Therefore, the only way to select it is to use the Model Tree if the default **Smart** filter is active. Alternatively, you can select directly on the model if you select the **Annotation** filter. All of the independent annotations are listed at the top of the Model Tree and all of the Annotation features are listed in the order in which they were created.

Once an Annotation feature has been selected in the Model Tree, all of the annotation elements and their references highlight in the graphics area.

Model Tree Display

As with all of the features in Part mode, Annotation features are displayed in the Model Tree by default. Independent annotations and the expandable list of annotation elements in a feature are not displayed. The default behavior is for Annotations to be enabled, however if you are unable to expand Annotation features in the Model Tree, click $\stackrel{\theta}{\downarrow}$ (Tree Filters)**>General** and enable **Annotations** in the Model Tree Items dialog box. Figure 11-9 shows the Model Tree with the option enabled and disabled.

When the Annotation option is disabled, you cannot identify individual elements.

When the Annotation option is enabled, you can identify individual elements.

Figure 11-9

When the *Annotate* tab is selected the Detail Tree opens and displays the annotations created as shown in Figure 11-10.

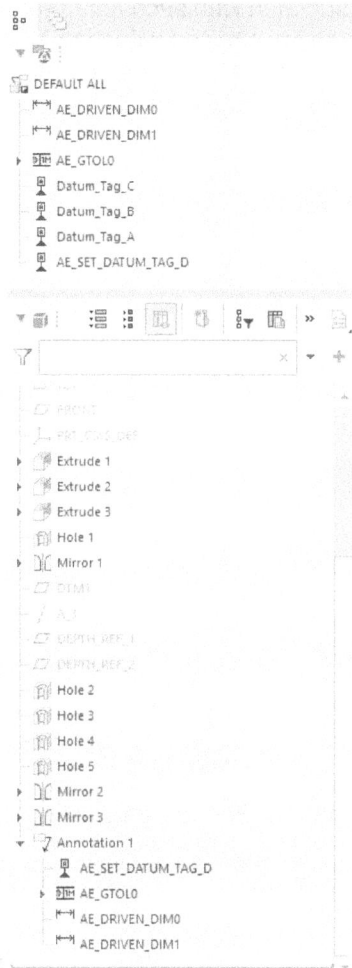

Figure 11-10

Editing

You can make changes to the elements of an Annotation feature using the ✎ (Edit Definition) option. You can also use the ✎ (Edit Attachment) option to modify any reference in the Annotation feature without opening the Annotation Feature dialog box.

For surface finish and geometric tolerance elements, you can edit the values associated with these elements by right-clicking on them in the Model Tree and selecting **Value**.

Text Style

You can change the Text Style associated with each annotation element by right-clicking on the element in the expanded Annotation feature and selecting **Text Style**. The standard Text Style dialog box opens (as shown in Figure 11−11), for you to make changes to the annotation element.

Figure 11−11

For Notes, simply select the note and the *Format* tab displays as show in Figure 11−12.

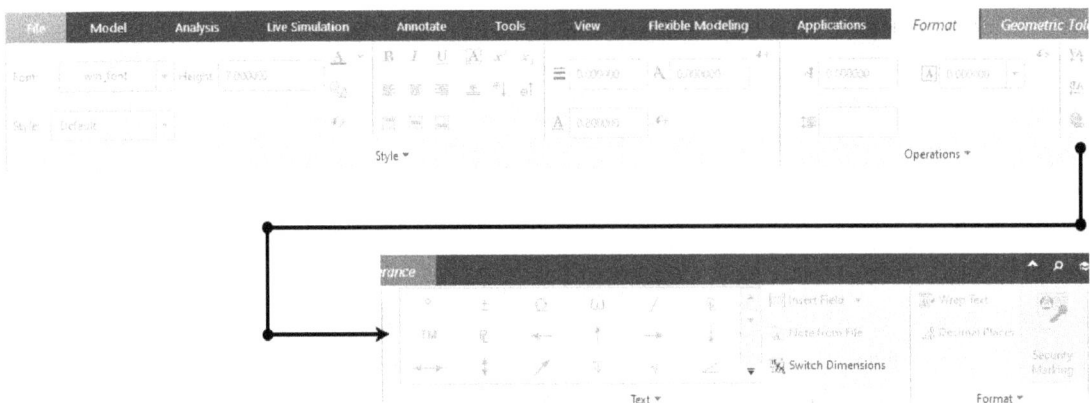

Figure 11−12

Deleting

As with all feature types, you can delete an Annotation feature by right-clicking on it in the Model Tree and selecting **Delete**. Alternatively, you can press <Delete>. Any references that were selected when defining the Annotation feature are not deleted from the model, because they exist as separate features and have only been used as references in the Annotation.

Disassociating Elements

All elements in the feature are deleted when you delete an Annotation feature. It is possible to disassociate elements before deletion, so that they are added to the model as independent annotations (i.e., at the top of the Model Tree).

To disassociate elements, edit the definition of the annotation feature, select the cell in the *Type* column for the required element, right-click, and select **Make Non-Graphical**, as shown in Figure 11–13. You can remove the element from the Annotation feature once it has been made non-graphical.

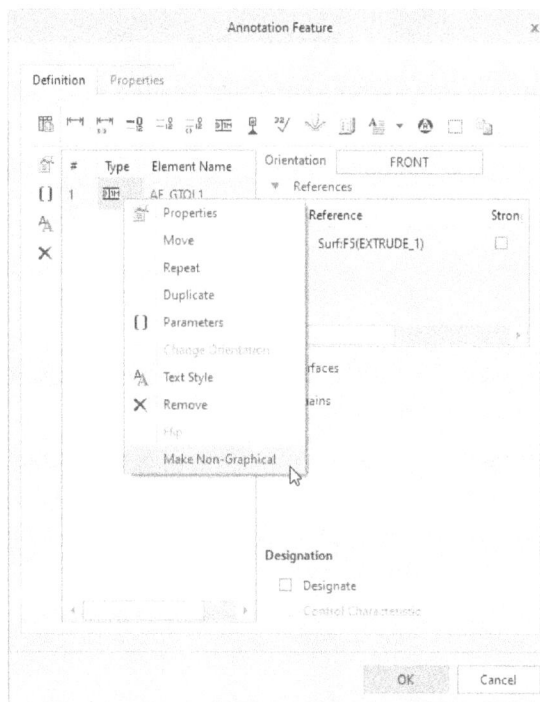

Figure 11–13

Once an element has been made non-graphical, you must create a new element using the **Existing Annotation** type to re-add it to an Annotation feature.

Reordering

As with all other features, you can select an Annotation feature in the Model Tree and drag it as required in the feature list to reorder it. Reordering can help you avoid failures due to missing strong references when you create additional geometry. You can reorder the Annotation feature back to a location in the model where the reference still exists. Remember that you cannot reorder a feature before any of its references.

Controlling Display

As required in the ASME Y14.41 standard, you can control the display of all of the annotations in your model. This can be accomplished using any of the following options:

* Hide/Show

* Suppress/Resume

* Layers

Hide/Show

The **Hide** option enables you to remove an Annotation feature from display in the model, but it updates in the regeneration sequence. To hide an Annotation feature, select the feature in the Model Tree and click ✎ (Hide) in the *mini* toolbar. A hidden Annotation feature is identified by

⬚ in the Model Tree. To return the feature to the display, select it again and click ◉ (Show) in the mini toolbar.

Suppress/Resume

The ▪ (Suppress) option enables you to remove an Annotation feature from display in the model and from the regeneration sequence.

To suppress an Annotation feature, select the feature in the Model Tree and click ▪ (Suppress) in the *mini* toolbar. By default, suppressed features are not displayed in the Model Tree. However, you can customize the Model Tree to display suppressed features using the tree filter. A suppressed Annotation feature is identified by ⬚ in the Model Tree. To resume the feature, if it is displayed in the Model Tree, select it again and click ⬧ (Resume). Otherwise, select **Operations>Resume>Resume** in the *Model* tab.

Layers

As with all other features, you can add Annotation features to layers and hide the layer to control the display. Layers maintain the Annotation feature in its regeneration sequence.

Practice 11a
Create Annotation Features

Practice Objectives

- Create a new annotation reference plane and create an annotation note in the model.
- Change the active annotation plane and create a geometric tolerance in the model.
- Copy existing surface finish annotations as new elements in the annotation feature and modify the style.
- Create a new geometric tolerance element in the model.
- Create a new drawing and change the configuration option to automatically display annotations.
- Create views in the drawing that display the newly created annotation elements.

In this practice, you will create annotation features in a part model, as shown in Figure 11–14. This practice highlights the similarities and differences between the two techniques.

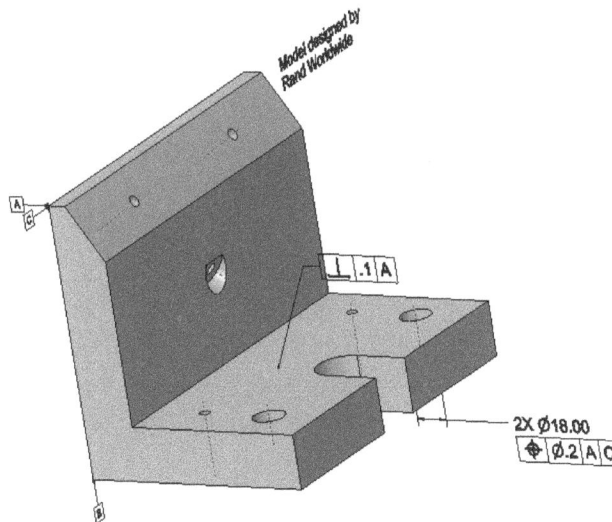

Figure 11–14

Task 1: Open a part file.

1. Set the working directory to the *Annotation_Features* folder.
2. Open **bracket_final_2.prt**.

3. Set the model display as follows:

- $\overset{x/}{\vphantom{x}}$ *(Datum Display Filters)*: All Off

- ⤳ *(Spin Center)*: Off

- ▢ *(Display Style)*: ▢ (Shading With Edges)

Task 2: Create an Annotation feature and add the first annotation element.

1. Select the *Annotate* tab.

2. Select the Annotation Plane **RIGHT** in the *Annotate* tab, as shown in Figure 11–15.

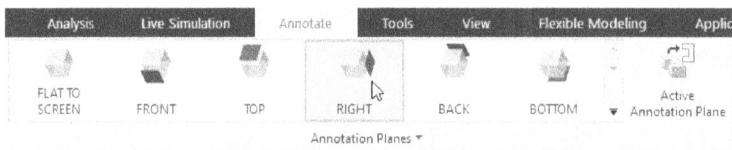

Figure 11–15

3. Click ▽ (Annotation Feature) to create an Annotation feature. The *Annotation Feature dialog* box opens as shown in Figure 11–16.

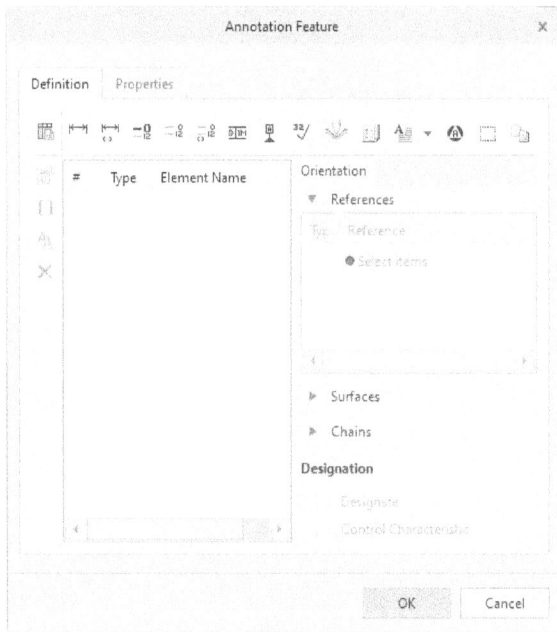

Figure 11–16

4. Click ⁴≡ (Note) in the *Annotation Feature* dialog box.

5. Select a location for the note, as shown in Figure 11–17, type **Model designed by**. Then, press <Enter> and type your name. You will modify the style of the note and its orientation later.

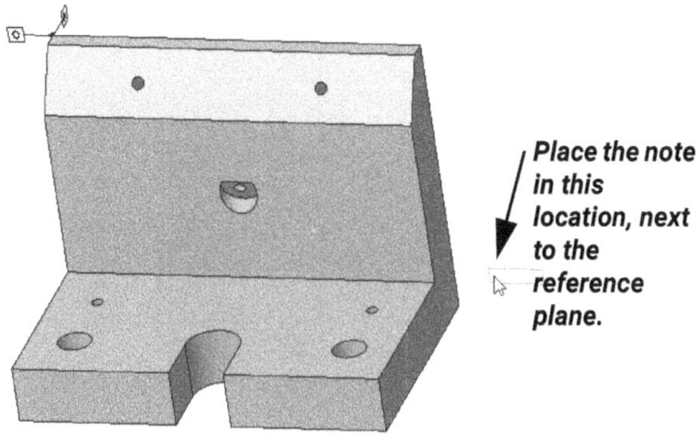

Place the note in this location, next to the reference plane.

Figure 11–17

6. Click on the screen to complete the note creation.

7. Select the **Element Name** cell in the *Annotation Feature* dialog box and set the name to **Designer_Info**. The dialog box updates as shown in Figure 11–18. Note that datum plane RIGHT is listed as the *Orientation* reference.

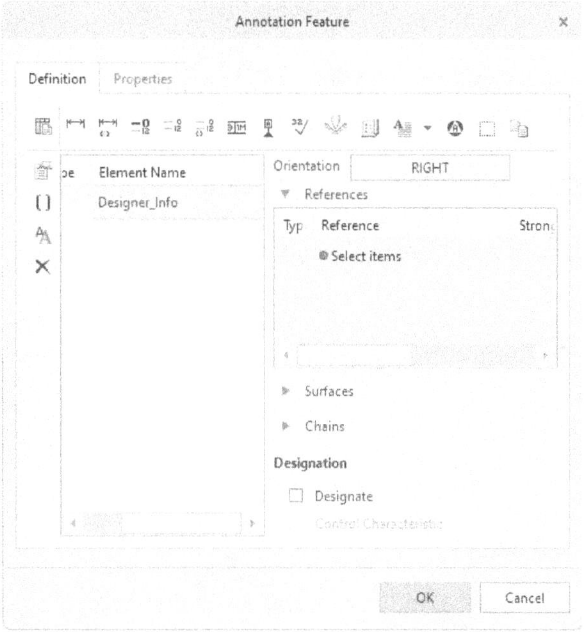

Figure 11–18

8. Click **OK** to complete the annotation feature.

Task 3: Move the annotation feature.

1. Select the **DESIGNER_INFO** annotation element in the Detail Tree.

2. Drag the note to the location shown in Figure 11–19.

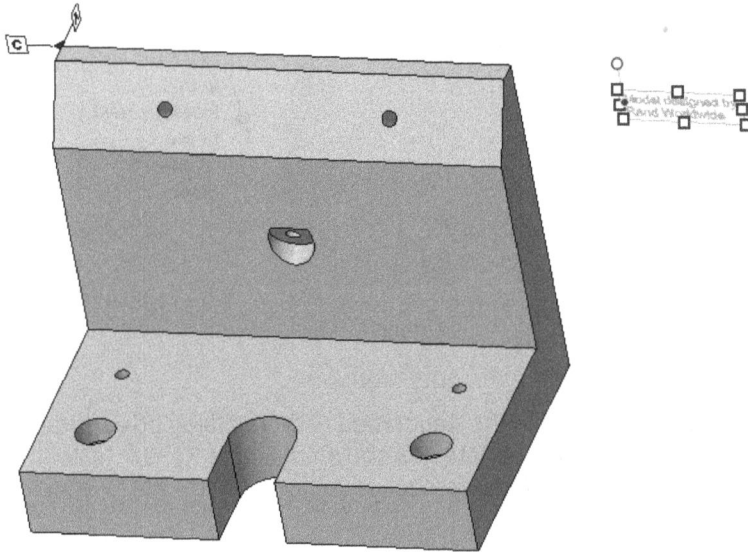

Figure 11–19

3. Click on the screen to finish moving the note.

Task 4: Create a geometric tolerance annotation element.

1. Select **FRONT** in the Annotation Plane group, as shown in Figure 11–20.

Figure 11–20

2. Click ⍍ (Annotation Feature).

3. Click ⍔ (Geometric Tolerance) in the *Annotation Feature* dialog box.

4. Select the surface shown in Figure 11-21.

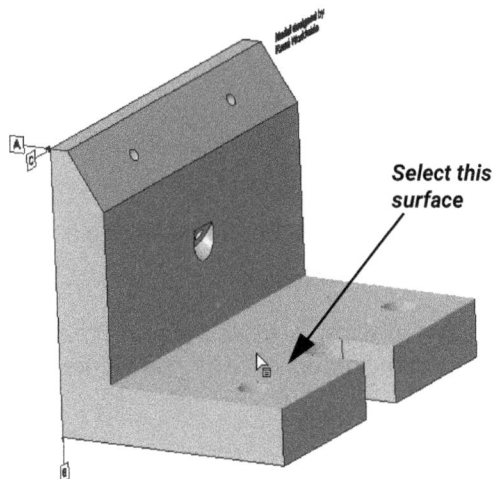

Figure 11-21

5. In the *Annotate* tab, click ⚙ (Active Annotation Plane).

6. Press the middle mouse button and select a location similar to that shown in Figure 11-22 to place the geometric tolerance.

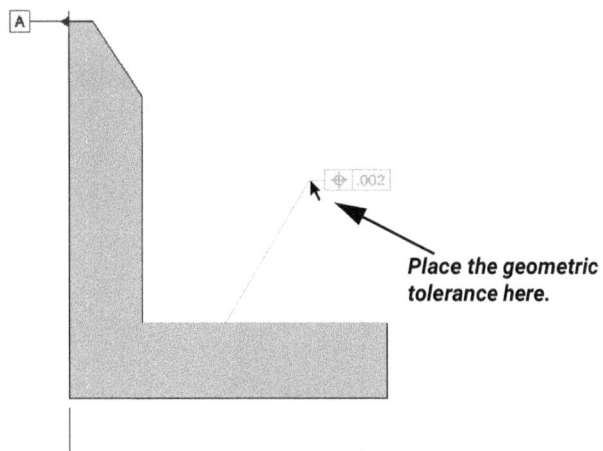

Figure 11-22

7. The *Geometric Tolerance* tab displays as shown in Figure 11–23.

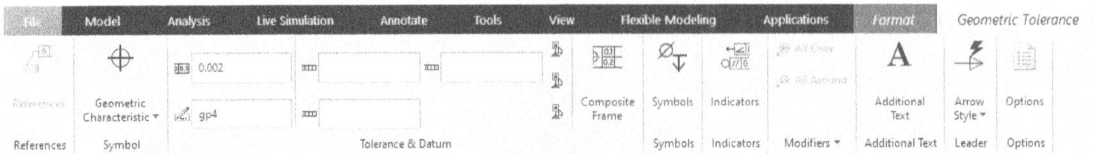

Figure 11–23

8. In the *Symbol* group, expand the *Geometric Characteristic* drop-down list and select ⊥ (Perpendicularity) if not already selected.

9. In the *Tolerance & Datum* group, click 🔖 (Select Datum) that is associated with the primary datum reference at the top of the group, as shown in Figure 11–24.

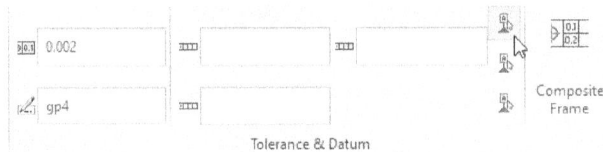

Figure 11–24

10. Select Datum Tag A and click **OK** in the *Select* dialog box.

11. In the *tolerance* value field, edit the tolerance to **0.1** and press **<Enter>**. Note that the geometric tolerance updates, as shown in Figure 11–25.

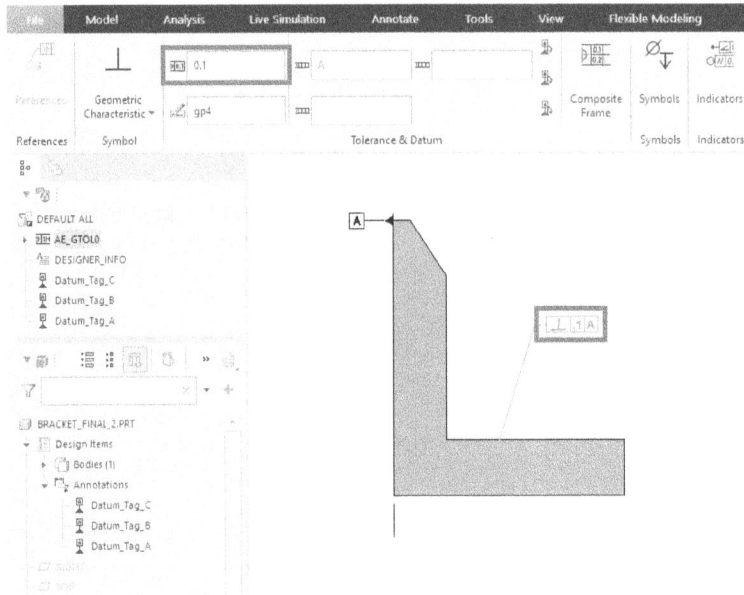

Figure 11–25

12. Click anywhere on the screen to close the *Geometric Tolerance* tab. The model and the *Annotation Feature* dialog box display as shown in Figure 11–26.

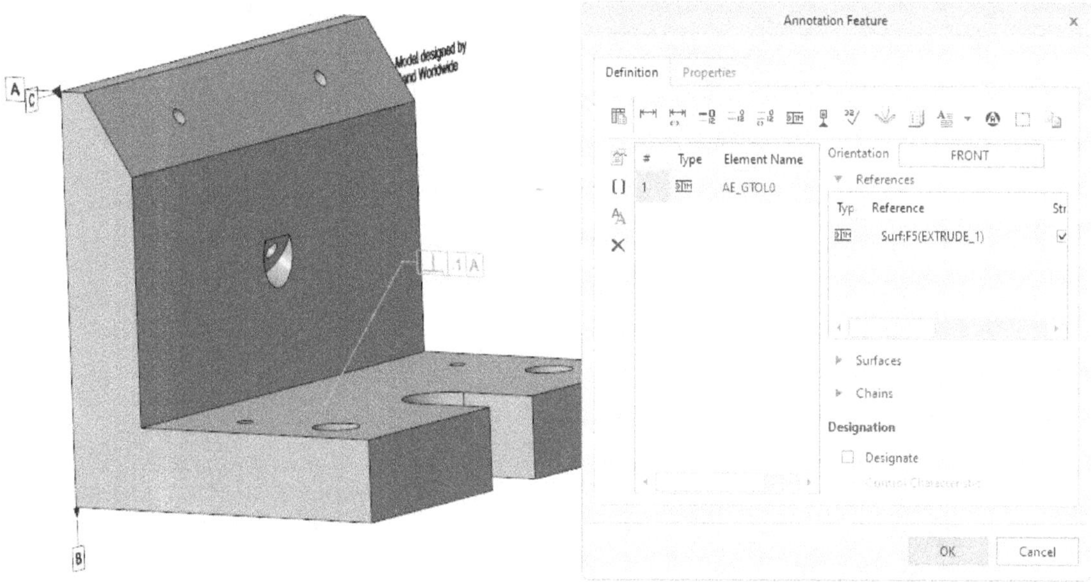

Figure 11–26

13. Click **OK** to complete the annotation feature.

Task 5: Edit the text style and properties of annotation elements.

1. Expand the **Annotation 1** feature in the Model Tree.
2. Select the **DESIGNER_INFO**. The *Format* tab opens.
3. In the *Height* field, enter **7**, as shown in Figure 11–27.

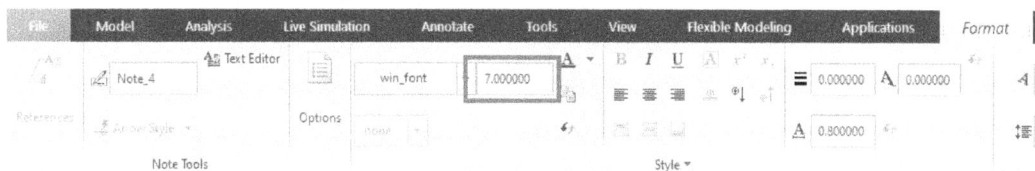

Figure 11–27

4. Press **<Enter>**. The note displays as shown in Figure 11–28.

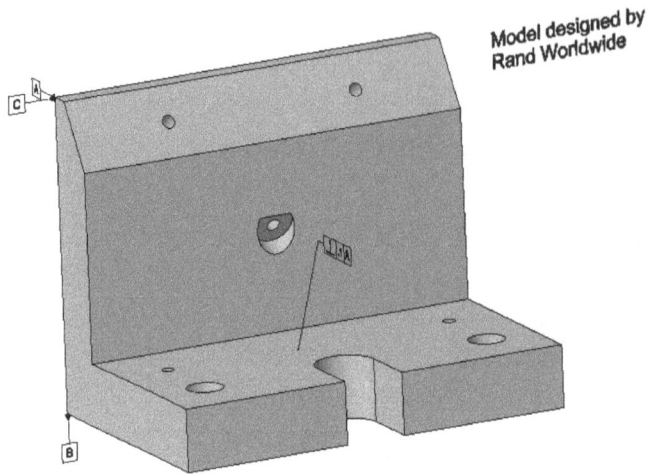

Model designed by
Rand Worldwide

Figure 11–28

5. Select the geometric tolerance on the model, right-click, and select **Text Style**. The *Text Style* dialog box opens.

Note: Instead of selecting the annotation element in the Model Tree, you can select directly on the model.

6. To the right of the *Height* field, clear the check next to **Default** and set the *Height* value to **7**.

7. Click **OK**. The geometric tolerance displays as shown in Figure 11–29.

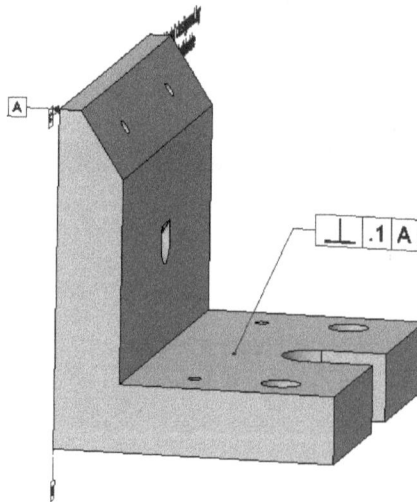

Figure 11–29

Task 6: Create an additional geometric tolerance annotation feature.

1. Click ⬚ (Annotation Feature) to create an annotation feature.

    *Note: You might need to change the selection filter back to **Smart**.*

2. Click ⊢⊣ (Dimension) in the *Annotation Feature* dialog box.

3. Double-click on the edge of the hole shown in Figure 11−30 and place the dimension by pressing the middle mouse button.

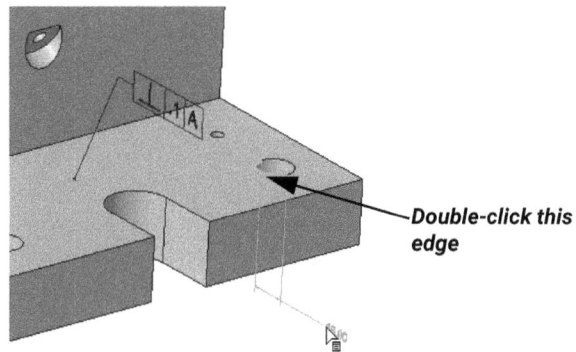

Double-click this edge

Figure 11−30

4. In the *Dimension Text* group in the ribbon, click ⌀¹⁰⁰ (Dimension Text). The *Dimension text* panel expands as shown in Figure 11−31.

Figure 11−31

5. In the *Prefix* field, type **2X** and press <Space>.

6. In the *Symbols* area, click the ⌀ symbol. The *Dimension Text* panel updates as shown in Figure 11–32.

Prefix/Suffix:

⌀10⊘	2X ⌀	⌀10⊘	

Exclude Prefix/Suffix from Basic box

Dimension Text:

@D

Symbols:

Figure 11–32

7. Click anywhere on the screen to finish editing.

8. Press the middle mouse button to complete the dimension.

9. In the *Annotation Feature* dialog box, click ▣™ (Geometric Tolerance).

10. Select the dimension you just created to place the geometric tolerance. The geometric tolerance attaches to the dimension as shown in Figure 11−33.

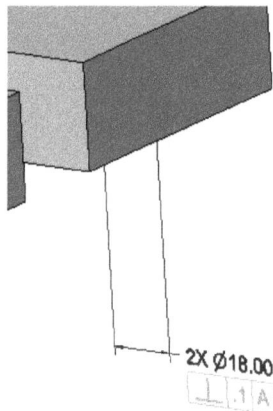

Figure 11−33

11. In the *Symbol* group, expand the *Geometric Characteristic* drop-down list and select ⊕ (Position).

12. The primary datum reference is automatically set to the datum tag **A**.Note that alternatively, you can type the datum tag letter in the appropriate field.

13. Click (Select Datum) that is associated with the secondary datum reference field located in the middle of the group, select the datum tag **C**, and click **OK**.

14. Edit the tolerance value to **0.2**.

15. In the *Tolerance Value* field, click in front of the tolerance value, then click ⌀⊤ (Symbols) in the ribbon.

16. In the *Symbols* area, click the ⌀ symbol. The tolerance updates as shown in Figure 11−34.

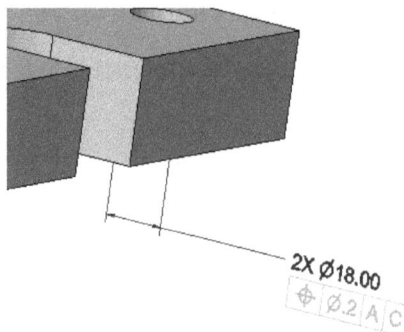

Figure 11−34

17. Click anywhere on the screen to finish editing the geometric tolerance.

18. In the *Annotation Feature* dialog box, click **OK**.

19. Select the dimension and geometric tolerance, right-click, and **Text Style**.

20. In the *Text Style* dialog box, change the text height to **7** and click **OK**. The completed model displays as shown in Figure 11–35.

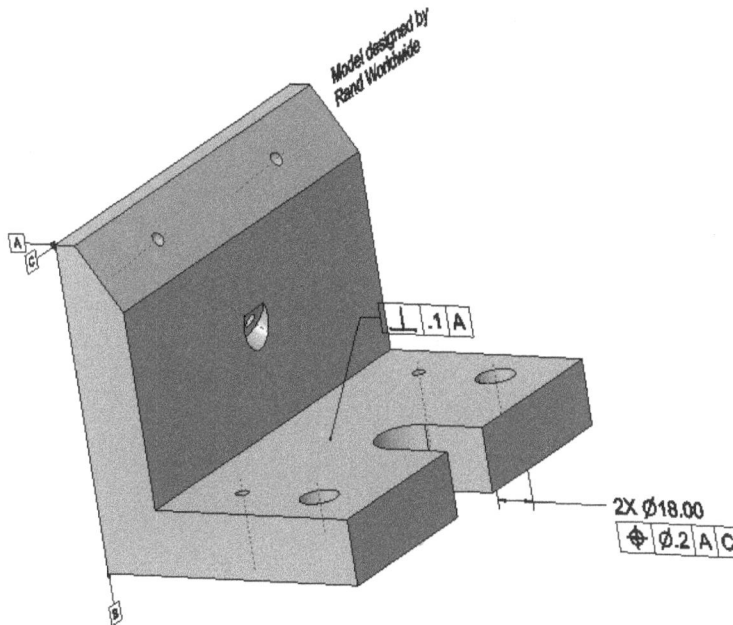

Figure 11–35

Task 7: Create a new drawing and select the format and sheet size.

1. Click ☐ (New) in the *Quick Access* Toolbar to create a new drawing. The *New* dialog box opens.

2. Select **Drawing**.

3. Clear the **Use default template** option to create an empty drawing.

4. Enable the **Use drawing model file name** so the new drawing has the same name as the part.

5. Click **OK**. The *New Drawing* dialog box opens.

6. Select **A** in the **Standard Size** menu.

7. Click **OK** to create the drawing.

Task 8: Place a General view.

1. In the *In-graphics* toolbar, select ⬜ (Hidden Line).

2. In the *Model Views* group, click ⬒ (General View).

3. Select **No Combined State** and click **OK**.

4. Select the location shown in Figure 11–36.

5. Select **RIGHT** from the *Model view names* list and click **Apply**. The model orients as shown in Figure 11–36. Click **OK**.

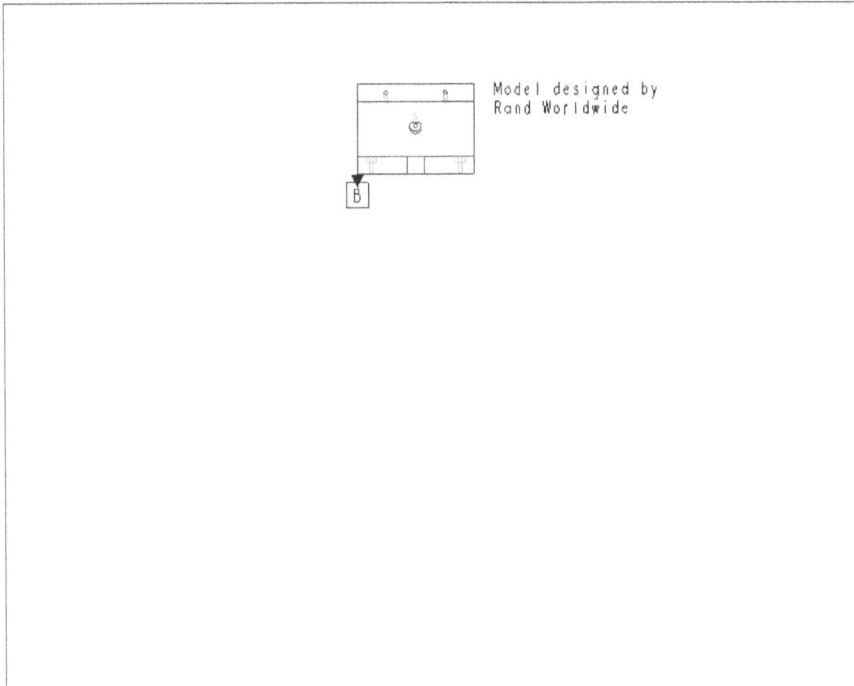

Figure 11–36

Task 9: Modify the scale value for the drawing.

1. Change the scale value to **0.01**.

    Note: *You can double-click on the scale value to modify it.*

Task 10: Create projection views in the drawing.

1. Select the view you just created and select ⬚ (Projection View) in the *mini* toolbar.
2. Click the location shown in Figure 11−37.

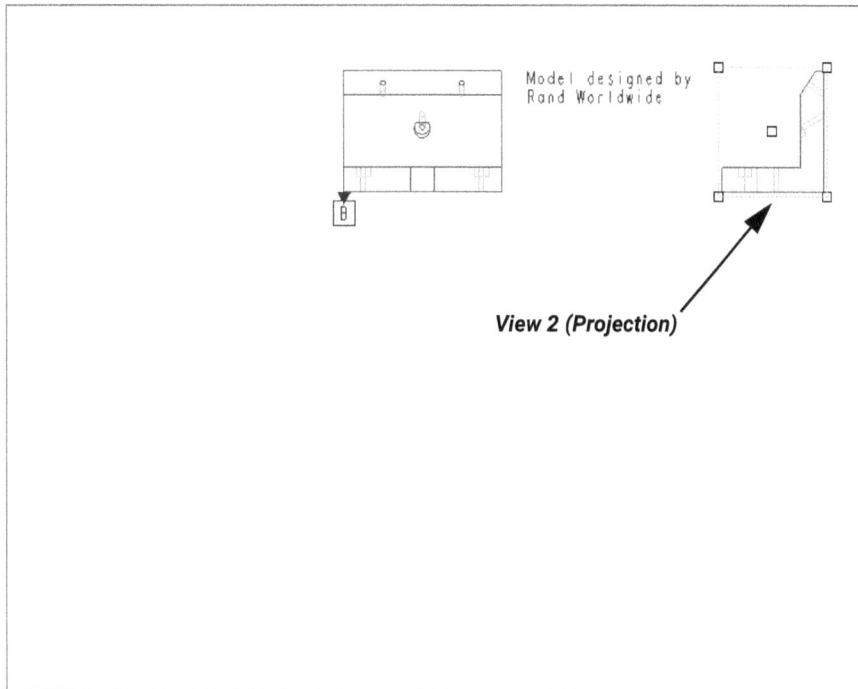

Figure 11−37

Note: *Because of the location of the projected view, you might experience a conflict in determining the parent. Select the oriented General view as the parent.*

3. Select the first view you created and select ⬚ (Projection View) in the *mini* toolbar.

4. Click the location shown in Figure 11-38.

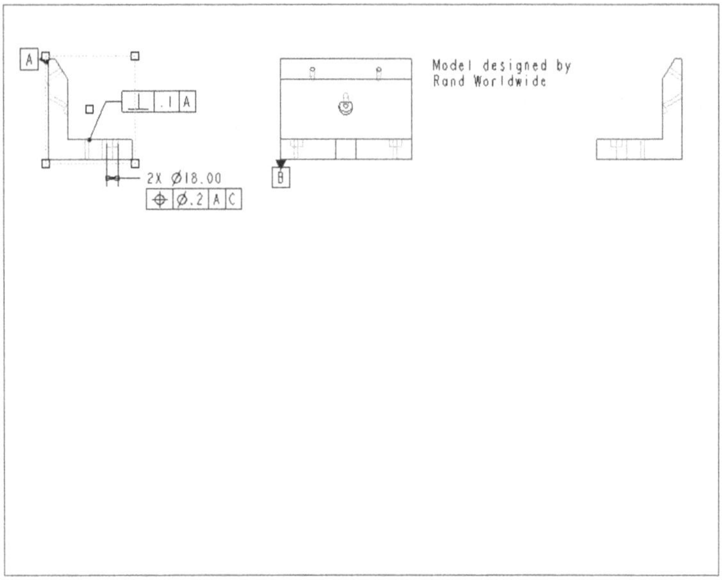

Figure 11-38

5. Move and modify the 3D details as shown in Figure 11-39. You might need to unlock the views to be able to move them.

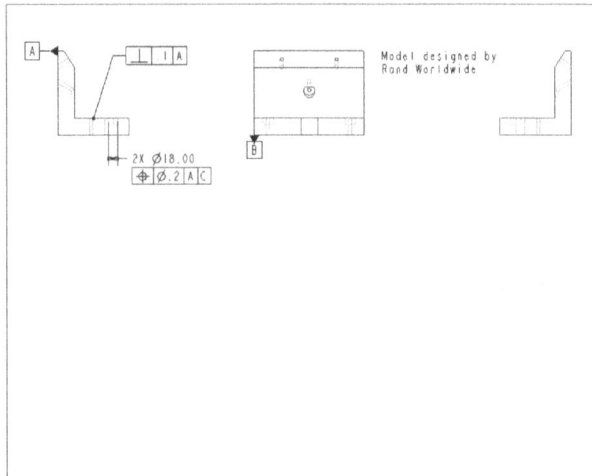

Figure 11-39

6. Select datum tag **B** and select ✎ (Erase) in the *mini* toolbar.

7. Select the *Annotate* tab.

8. In the Model Tree, expand the **Design Items** and **Annotations** branches as shown in Figure 11–40.

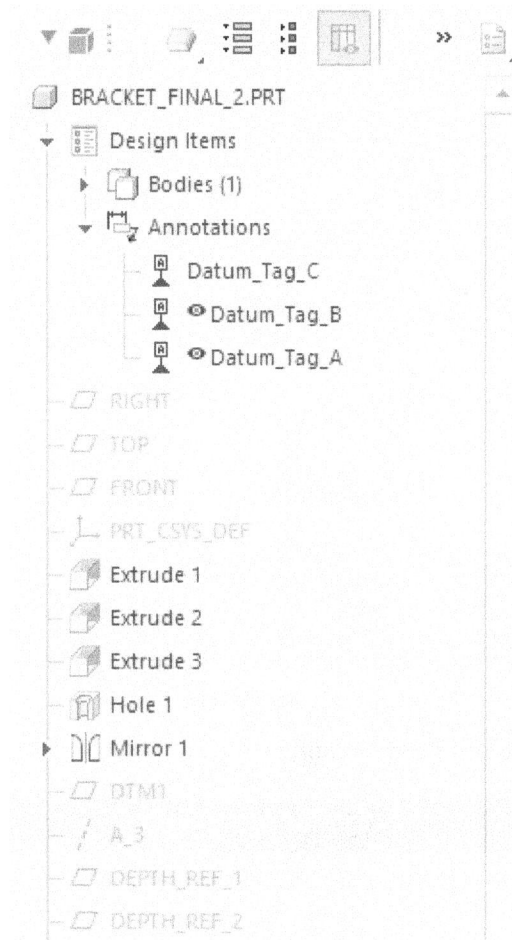

Figure 11–40

9. Right-click **Datum_Tag_C** and click **Show**.

10. Select the datum tag **C** in the left and right projected views and select ✏ (Erase) in the *mini* toolbar.

11. Click on the screen and the drawing updates as shown in Figure 11–41.

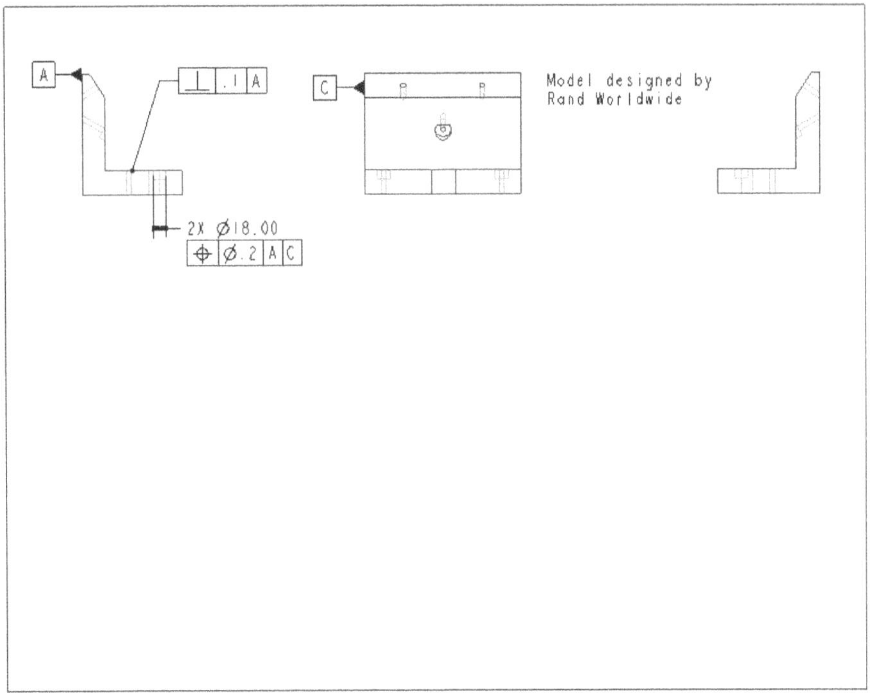

Figure 11–41

12. Save the model and erase it from memory.

End of practice

Chapter Review Questions

1. Which types of annotations can you create? (Select all that apply.)

    a. Notes

    b. Symbols

    c. Geometric Tolerances

    d. Dimensions

2. The creation of an Annotation feature adds geometry to your model.

    a. True

    b. False

3. An Annotation feature can consist of one or more elements.

    a. True

    b. False

4. Annotations created in the 3D model can be automatically displayed in a drawing view.

    a. True

    b. False

5. Independent annotations and the expandable list of annotation elements in a feature are not displayed. How can the annotations be displayed in the Model Tree?

    a. Click ⬚ **(Tree Filters)>General** and enable **Annotations**.

    b. Click ⬚ **(Tree Filters)>General** and enable **Annotations**.

    c. Select **File>Options** and change the **annotations_show** config option to **Yes**.

    d. The annotations cannot be displayed in the Model Tree.

6. It is possible to disassociate elements before deletion, so that they are added to the model as independent annotations.

    a. True

    b. False

Customizing Creo Parametric

Customizing Creo Parametric enables you to adjust the system's default appearance and options to fit your needs or preferences. Settings can be company-wide or user-specific, improving workflow efficiency. This chapter covers basic customization requirements.

Learning Objectives

- Use categories in the *Options* dialog box to globally customize the modeling environment.
- Customize the graphic and geometry colors using the *Creo Parametric Options* dialog box.
- Assign command aliases using keyboard keys for commonly used commands.
- Customize the ribbon using the shortcut menu or the *Creo Parametric Options* dialog box.
- Customize and add commands to the *Quick Access* Toolbar.
- Customize the system to meet preferences and requirements.
- Search the configuration options using keywords.
- Implement the changes set in the Configuration Editor.
- Modify the appearance and colors of parts, assemblies, and surfaces.
- Customize the Model Tree by specifying what items are displayed and by adding columns.

A.1 Customizing the Interface

You can customize almost any part of the Creo Parametric interface, including the window display, toolbar icons, and the tabs. The icons in the toolbars and ribbons provide shortcuts to commonly used commands. These commands can be added or removed to customize the toolbar or ribbon area. You can also place user-defined icons representing mapkeys.

- To customize the Creo Parametric interface, select **File>Options**. The *Creo Parametric Options* dialog box opens, as shown in Figure A−1. The dialog box enables you to customize toolbars, commands, navigation options, browser settings, and other interface options.

Figure A−1

- The *Creo Parametric Options* dialog box is divided into multiple categories for customization.

Favorites

The *Favorites* category enables you to add and remove frequently used configuration options, as shown Figure A–2.

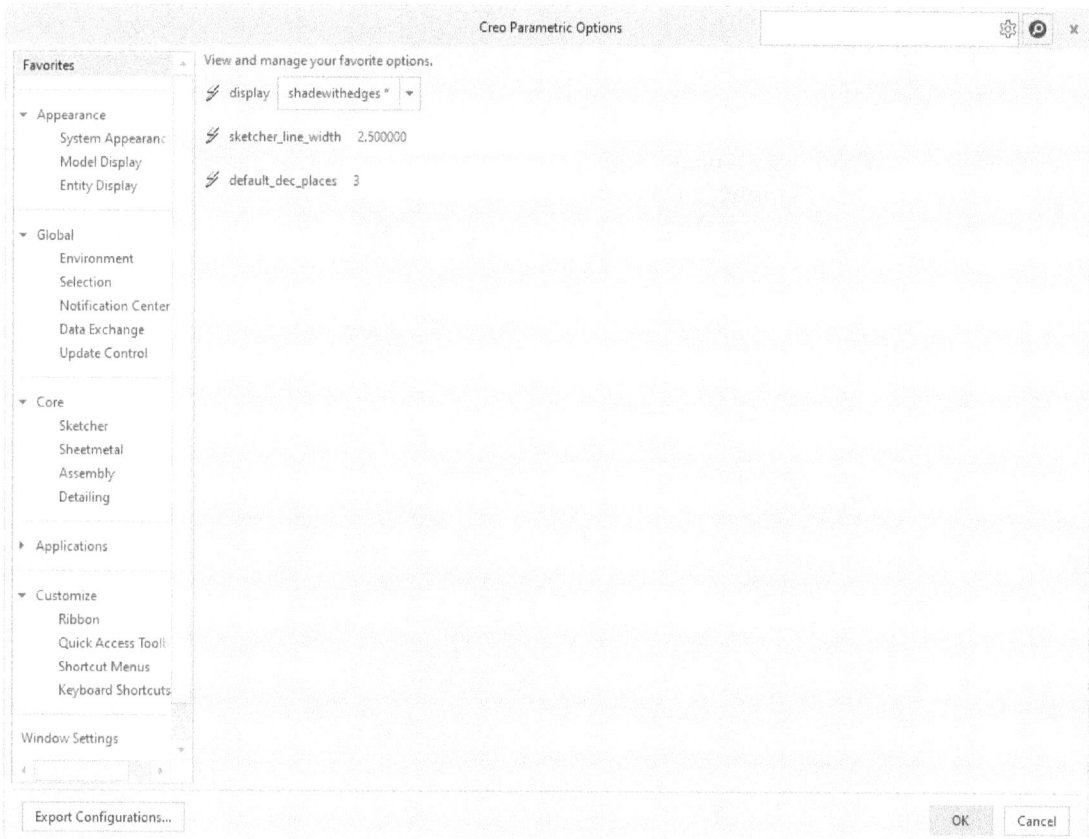

Figure A–2

How To: Add the Configuration Option to the Favorites Category

1. In the *Creo Parametric Options* dialog box, select **Configuration Editor**.
2. Select the configuration option, right-click on the option, and select **Add to Favorites**.
3. Click **Export Configurations** to save the changes.

System Appearance

The Creo Parametric software has assigned specific colors to entities, but you can customize the default system colors. This ability is useful for adding contrast and definition to presentation materials and other purposes. You can modify the overall color scheme, interface colors, or individual feature types.

Model Display

The Creo Parametric software enables you to customize the orientation, display, and rendering of the model in the *Creo Parametric Options* dialog box, as shown in Figure A–3.

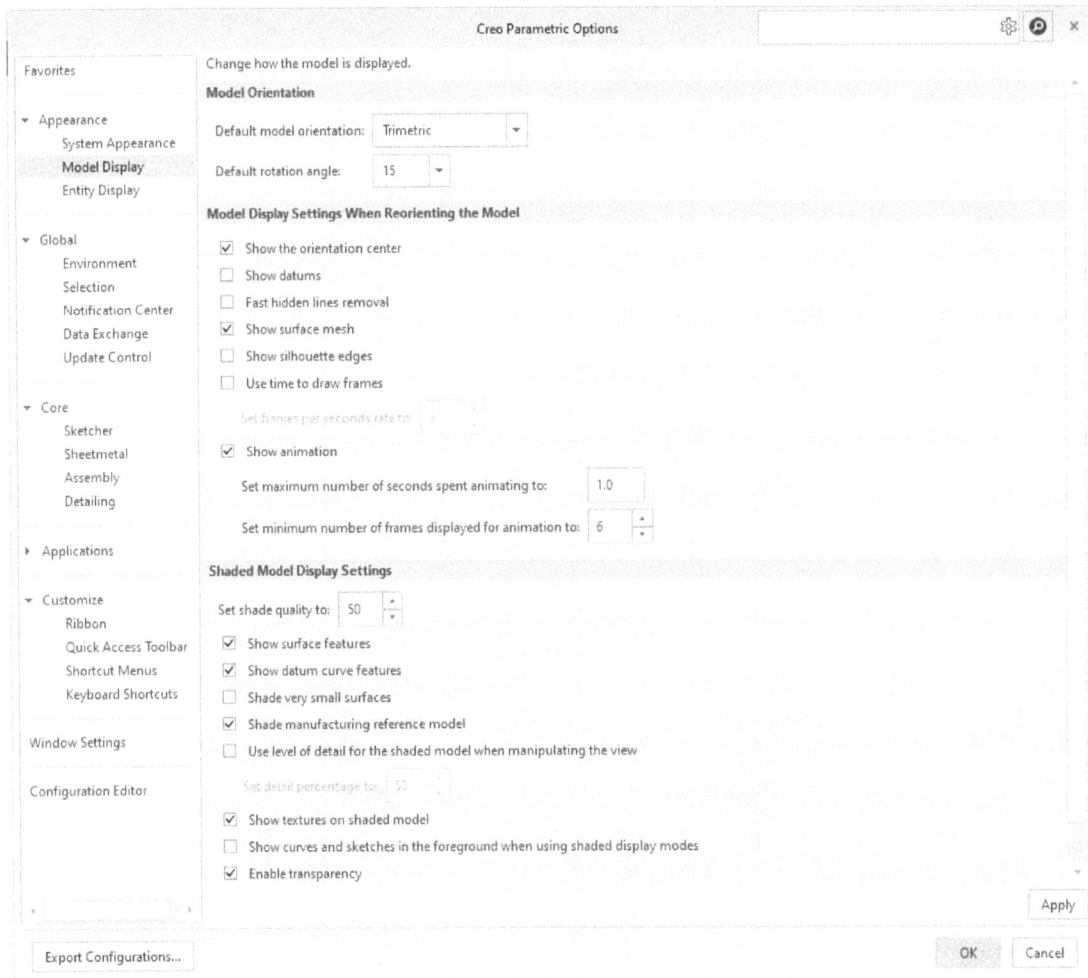

Figure A–3

Entity Display

The **Entity Display** option enables you to change the display of geometry, show/hide datums, and show/hide annotations. These options, along with several others, are shown in Figure A–4.

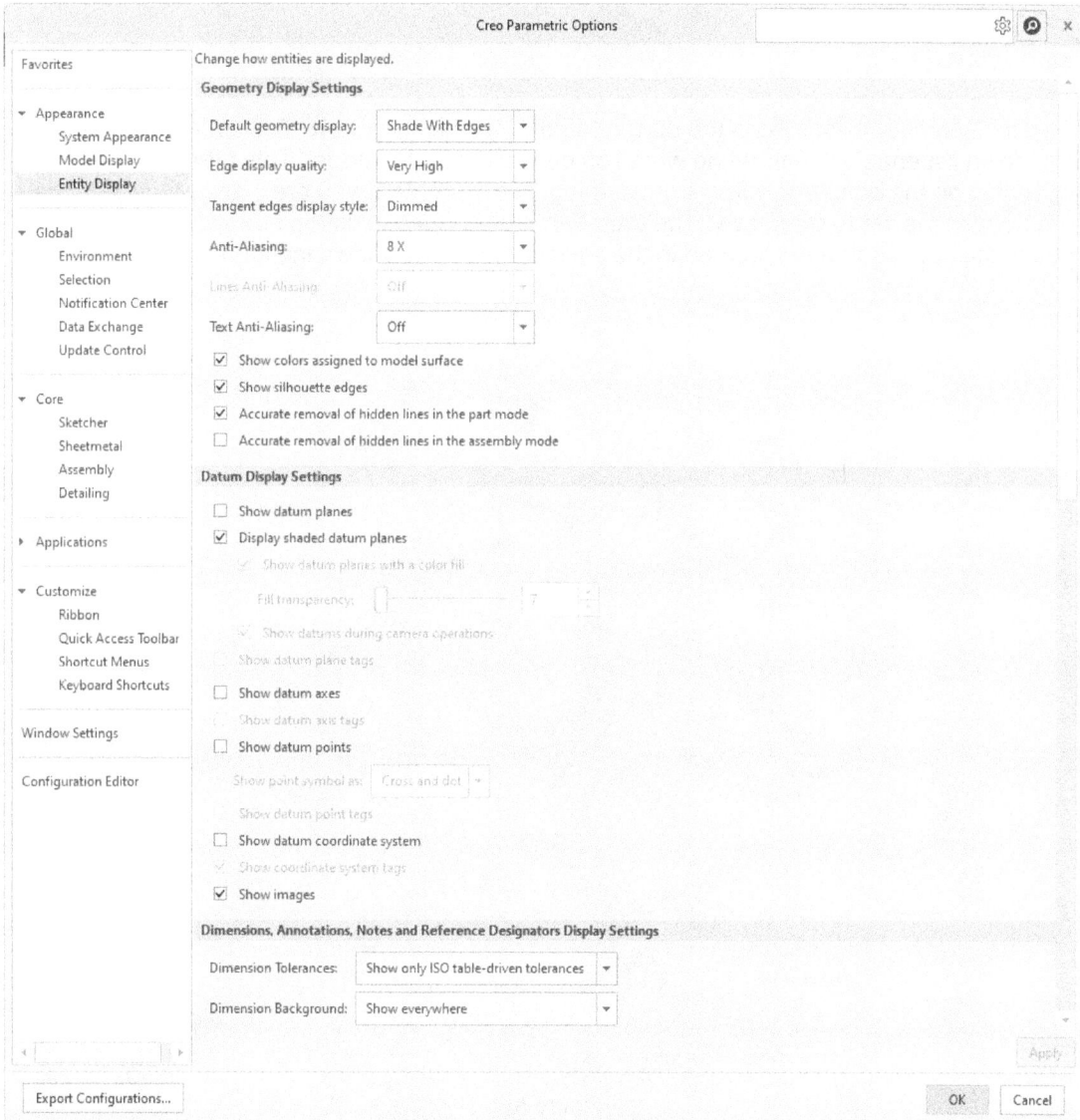

Figure A–4

Environment

The Environment options in Creo Parametric enable you the apply various settings. For example, you can set the working directory, save the display with the model, and create mapkeys.

Selection

The selection filter is located in the bottom right of the view window. The options in the Filter drop-down list enable you to refine what you can select in the model. This filter changes depending on the operation you are performing. For example, if you are in the *Model* tab, the default option is set to **Geometry**. The *Creo Parametric Options* dialog box enables you to specify the options that are located in the selection filter, as shown in Figure A–5.

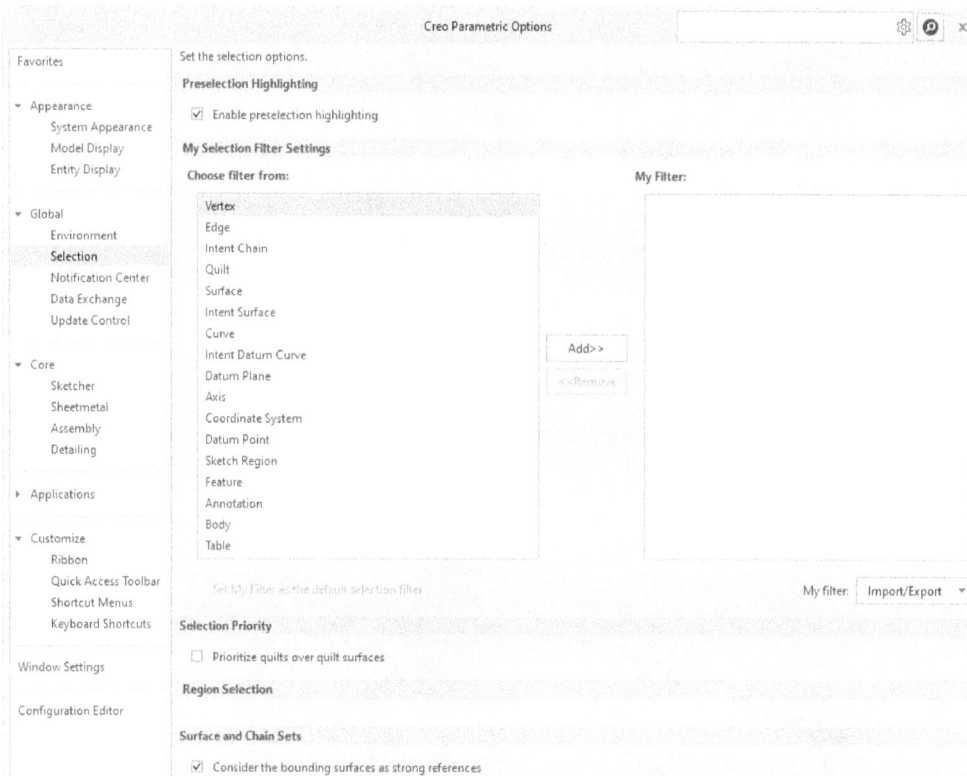

Figure A–5

The changes that you make to the settings are only used for the current session. The default settings are defined by the configuration file. To save the changes that you have made to the configuration file, click **Export Configurations**, specify the location, and click **OK**.

A.2 System Appearance

You can change the colors of parts and/or features to easily distinguish them from one another and to add contrast and definition to presentation materials. The Creo Parametric software enables you to customize the default system colors for such purposes and to modify the overall color theme, interface colors, or individual feature types.

- To customize the colors, select **File>Options**, and under the *Appearance* category, select **System Appearance**. The System Colors options are available, as shown in Figure A–6. The options enable you to customize the colors of datum features, geometry, graphics, sketched features, and/or the interface.

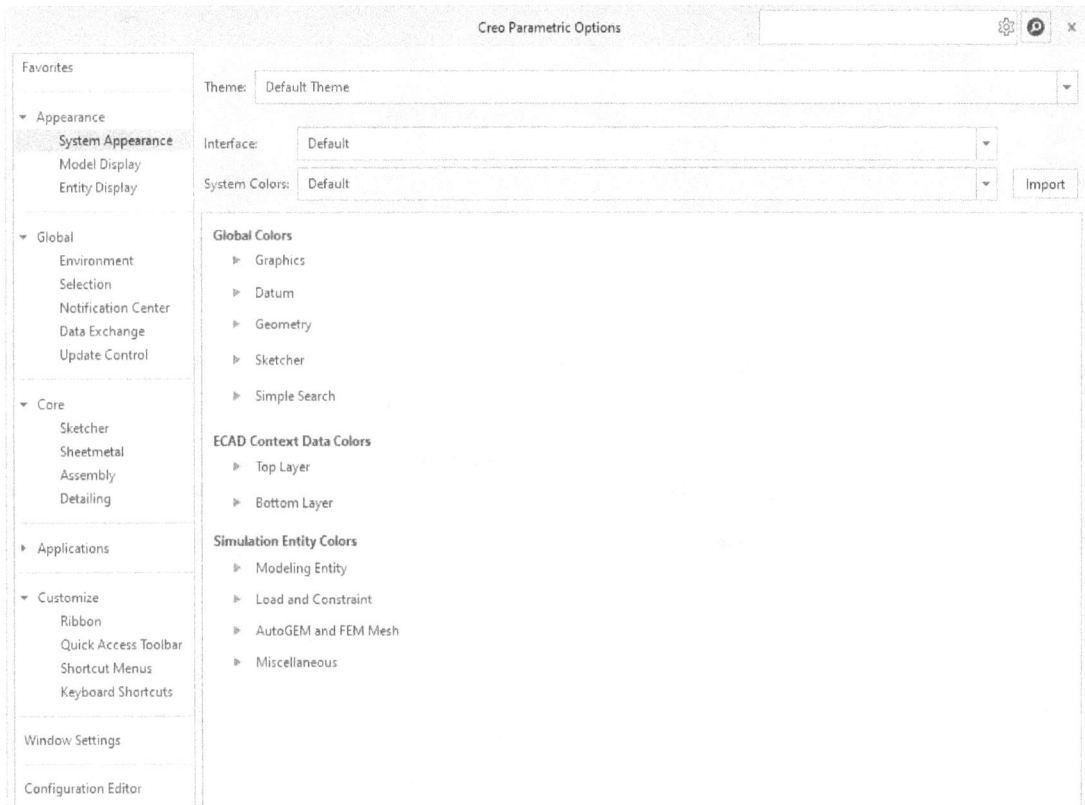

Figure A–6

- The *Global Colors* section of the *System Appearance* group is divided in various categories for customization.

Themes

You can save changes to the system colors as themes. In addition, Creo Parametric comes equipped with three predefined themes:

- **Default Theme:** Primarily gray theme with light gray background.

- **Light Theme:** Light gray colors with a near wight background.

- **Dark Theme:** A dark gray theme with near black background.

- **Midnight Theme:** Another dark theme.

Figure A–7 shows an example of the **Midnight Theme** selected.

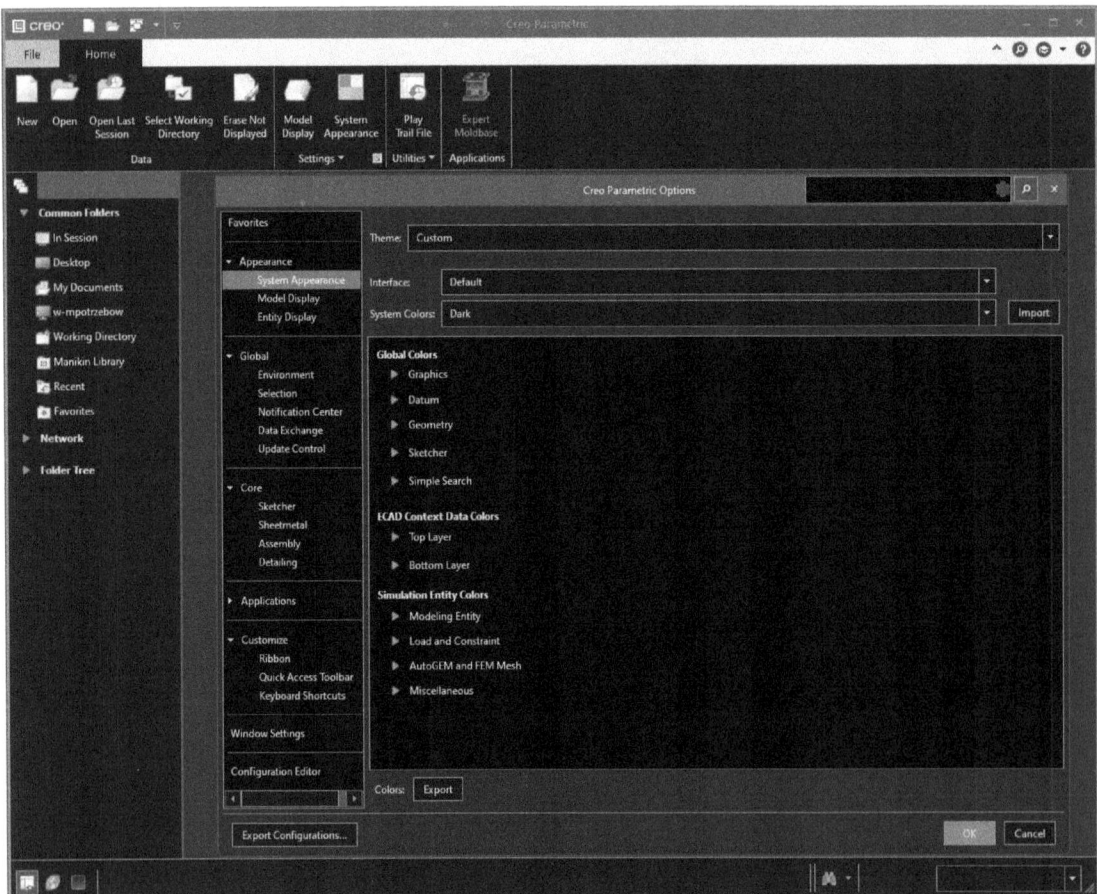

Figure A–7

Each predefined theme has been designed to ensure that 2D and 3D geometry and all other entities display with high contrast between them.

You can also define and change the system colors to your personal preference, which automatically creates a custom theme.

Graphics

The *Graphics* category enables you to modify the colors of certain features on your models. Click **Graphics** to expand and show the items in the *Graphics* category as shown in Figure A−8. Click a color swatch to change the color of any item.

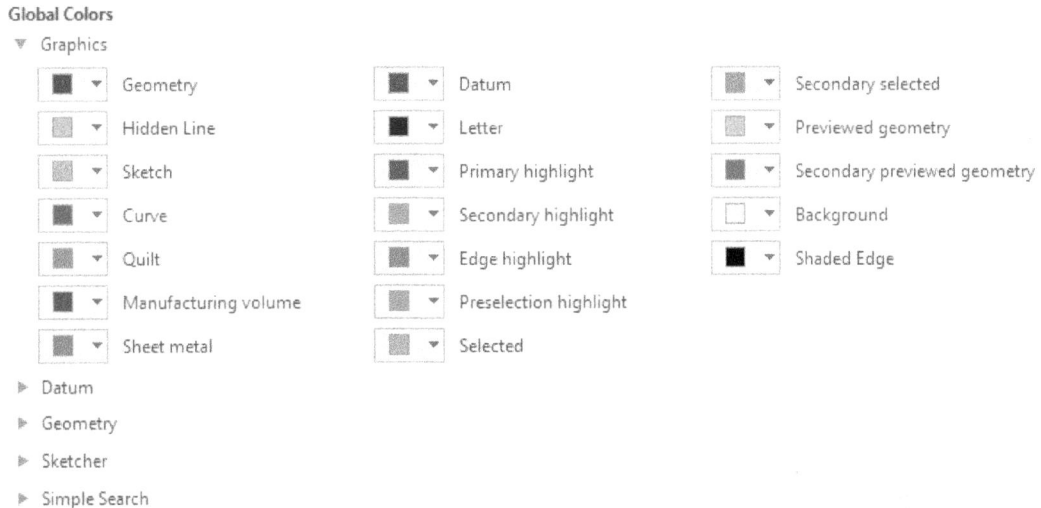

Figure A−8

Datum

The *Datum* category enables you to modify the colors of all of the datum features, including datum planes, axes, points, and coordinate systems.

Geometry

The *Geometry* category enables you to modify the colors of sheetmetal geometry, surface geometry, cables, model and cast surfaces.

Sketcher

The *Sketcher* category enables you to modify the colors of all the sketched features, including centerlines, construction geometry, and dimensions.

Simple Search

The *Simple* search category enables you to modify the colors of miscellaneous items including failed items, frozen components, and packaged items. To save your changes, click **Export**. The Creo Parametric interface displays with the new selected colors for the duration of the session. If you want to apply your new settings to the following sessions, you must point to the file with the saved settings in the config file option **system_colors_file**.

A.3 Command Shortcuts

Mapkeys

A mapkey is a keyboard macro that executes a series of menu selections. For operations that are used regularly, a mapkey is useful instead of going through multiple menu selections.

How To: Create Mapkeys

1. Select **File>OptionsMapkeys Settings**. The *Mapkeys* dialog box opens as shown in Figure A–9. The dialog box enables you to create, modify, delete, and save mapkeys.

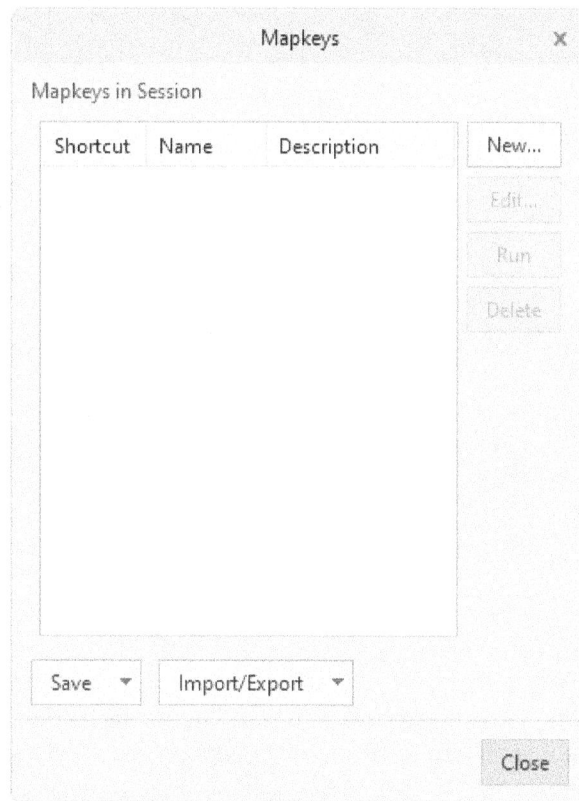

Figure A–9

2. Click **New** to create a new mapkey. The *Record Mapkey* dialog box opens, as shown in Figure A–10. Then, select a key sequence in the top drop-down list, to be used to activate the macro. It can be a sequence of numbers or letters or a function key. Select **$F#** to use a function key, where # is the required function key number.

The name and description are optional. However, it is useful to name the mapkey if it is going to be added as a toolbar option. Naming the mapkey also enables you to remember its functionality at a later date. For example, in Figure A–10 a mapkey is being defined that advances you to sketching an extruded feature by pressing <F2>.

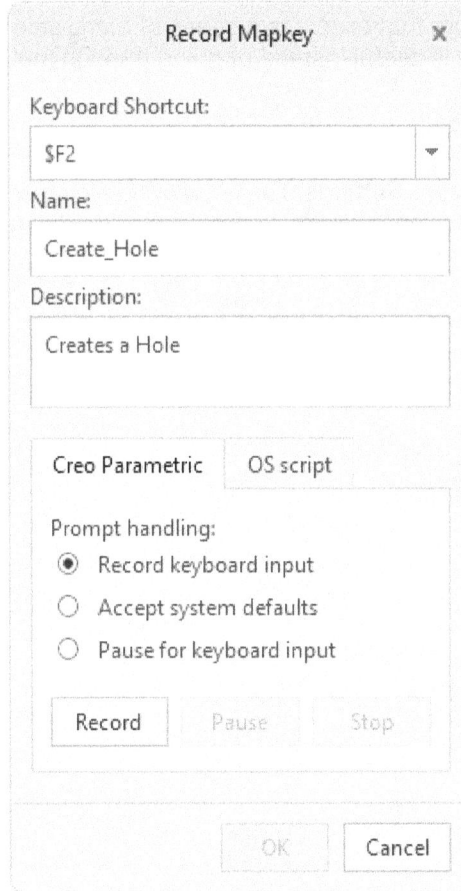

Figure A–10

3. You can begin recording the mapkey once the key sequence, name, and description have been defined. For details on how to record a sequence, follow the steps further below.

4. A mapkey initially only applies to the current session. However, when saved, it is stored to the **config.pro** option and can be used when the **config.pro** is loaded.

   To save any individual mapkey, select it in the *Mapkeys* dialog box and click **Save**. To save the selected mapkeys or all changed mapkeys, click **Save Selected** or **Save Changed**, respectively. When saving, you are prompted to select the configuration file to which you want to save the mapkeys.

   Note: The Mapkeys dialog box also enables you to modify, run, or delete existing mapkeys.

How To: Record the Sequence

1. Click **Record** to start recording and select the required menu options. Additional options enable you to pause the recording and customize how the mapkey handles keyboard entry and operating system commands. For example, to create a mapkey that opens the *Creo Parametric Options* dialog box, select **File>Options**.

2. Click **Stop** to stop the recording. You can resume the mapkey creation by clicking **Resume**.

3. Once you have completed the mapkey, click **OK**.

   Note: When recording a mapkey, it is recommended that you only select the required options, to create as efficient a mapkey as possible.

Keyboard Shortcuts

There are multiple out-of-the-box keyboard shortcuts available that provide access to common commands.

Click **File>Options** to open the *Creo Parametric Options* dialog box and click **Customize> Keyboard Shortcuts** to assign new keyboard shortcuts to commands, as shown in Figure A–11.

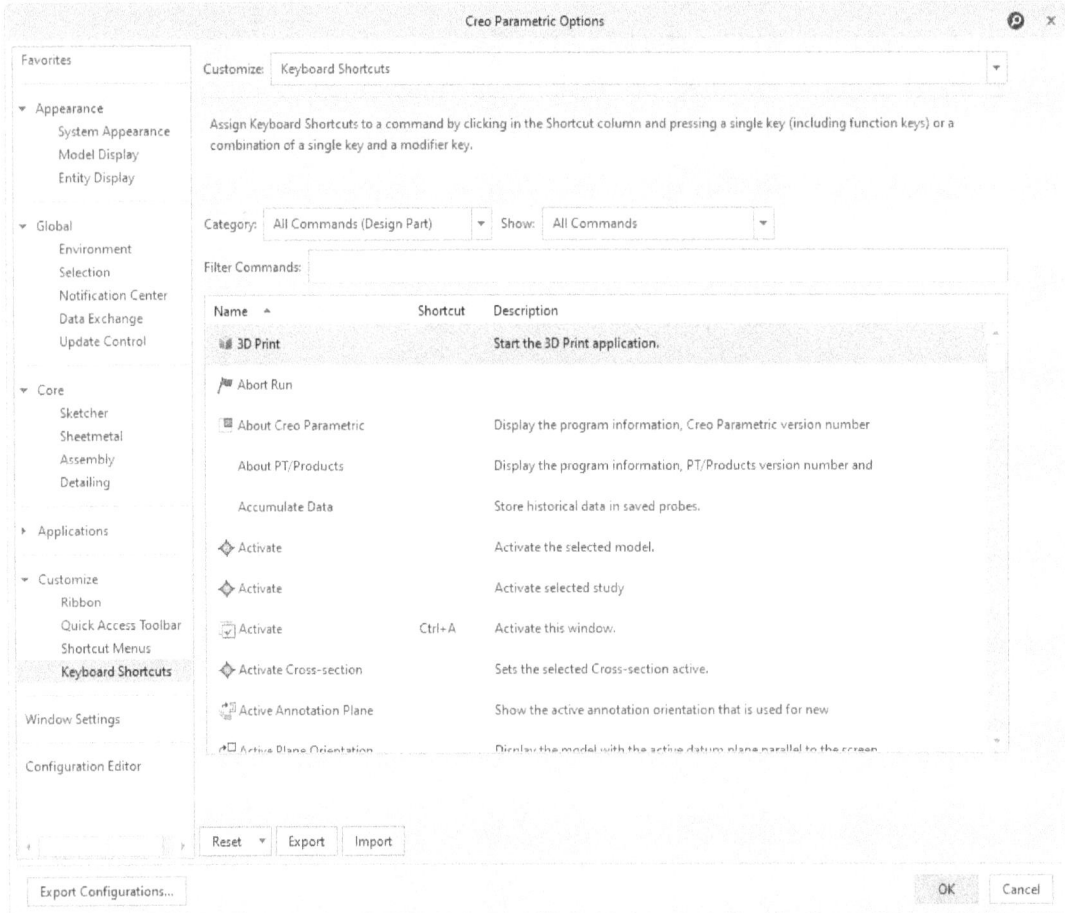

Figure A–11

You can define keyboard shortcuts with a single character or combination of a single character and an accelerator (Control, Shift) or function key.

You can use the Category and Show drop-down lists to narrow down the available commands, then select the command to which you want to assign a keyboard shortcut and define the new shortcut.

There are several predefined shortcuts available, as follows:

Command	Keyboard Shortcut
Close	<Ctrl>+<W>
Edit Definition	<Ctrl>+<E>
Extrude	<X>
Full Screen	<F11>
Open	<Ctrl>+<O>
Plane	<P>
Round	<R>
Sketch	<S>
View Normal	<Shift>+<N>

A.4 Customize the Ribbon, Toolbars, and Window Settings

You can customize the toolbars and ribbons in the Creo Parametric software. Customizing your interface provides shortcuts for accessing commonly used commands. These commands can be added or removed to customize the ribbon and toolbar area. You can also add and remove tabs and place user-defined icons representing mapkeys.

You can use the *Customize* area in the *Creo Parametric Options* dialog box to customize the commands found in the Ribbon, *Quick Access* Toolbar, and Shortcut Menus.

Ribbon

For the ribbon, you can define a customization for the following modes:

- **All Modes:** Shows all commands organized by mode.

- **Current Mode:** Only shows commands for the current mode (Design Part only, Design Assembly only, Sheetmetal Part only, etc.)

- **Popular Modes:** Commands organized by commonly used modes (Design Assembly, Design Part, Drawing, Layout, Section, Sheetmetal Part).

Figure A–12 shows the **Popular Modes** selection accessed from Part mode.

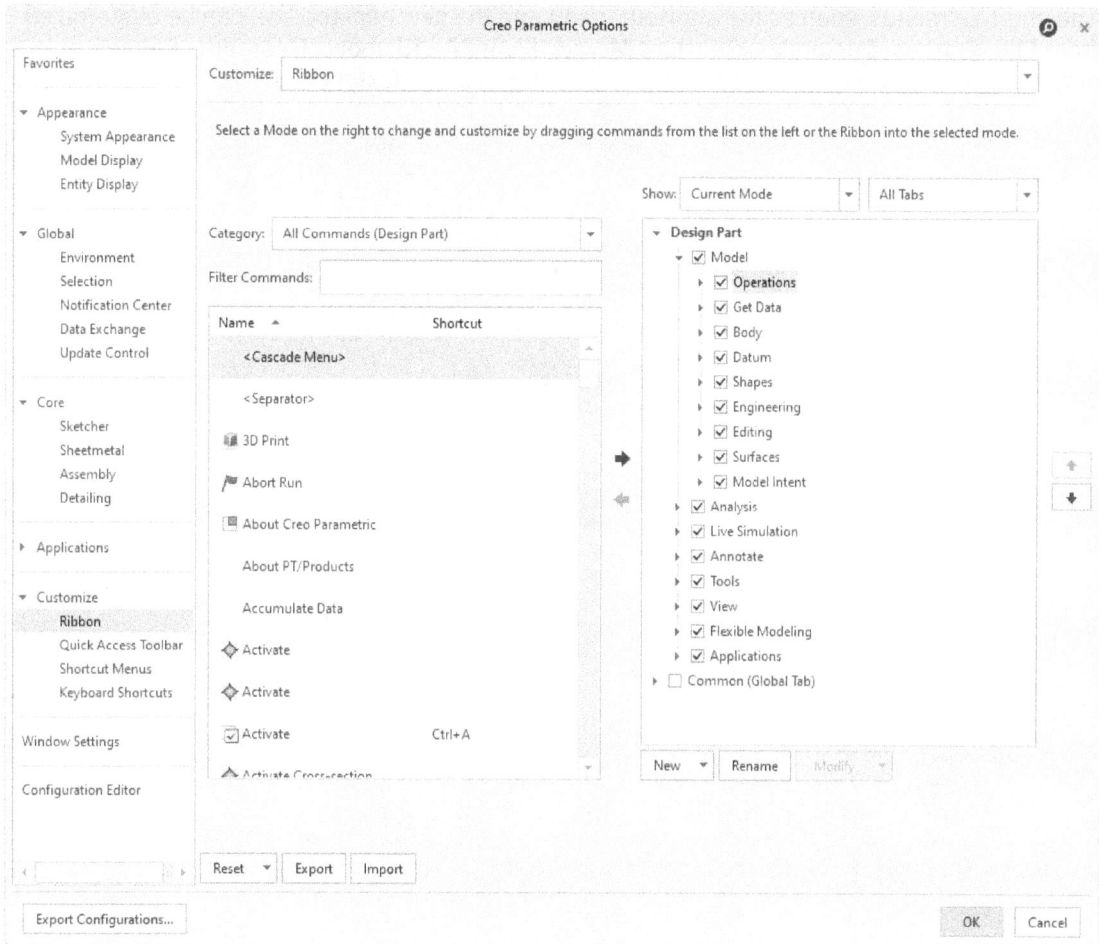

Figure A–12

You can customize the standard groups and propagate changes to other modes. To return to the default setting, expand **Reset** and select either:

- Reset only selected Ribbon tab

- Reset all Ribbon tabs and Quick Access Toolbar Customizations

A *Common* tab is now available, which is visible in the ribbon in all modes. This ensures that any command added to it will always be available.

Shortcut Menus

The shortcut menus, such as the shortcut menu and the new *mini* toolbar, can be customized from **File>Options>Customize>Shortcut Menus**. Figure A–13 shows Geometric Entities selected and the default options for the *mini* toolbar and context menus.

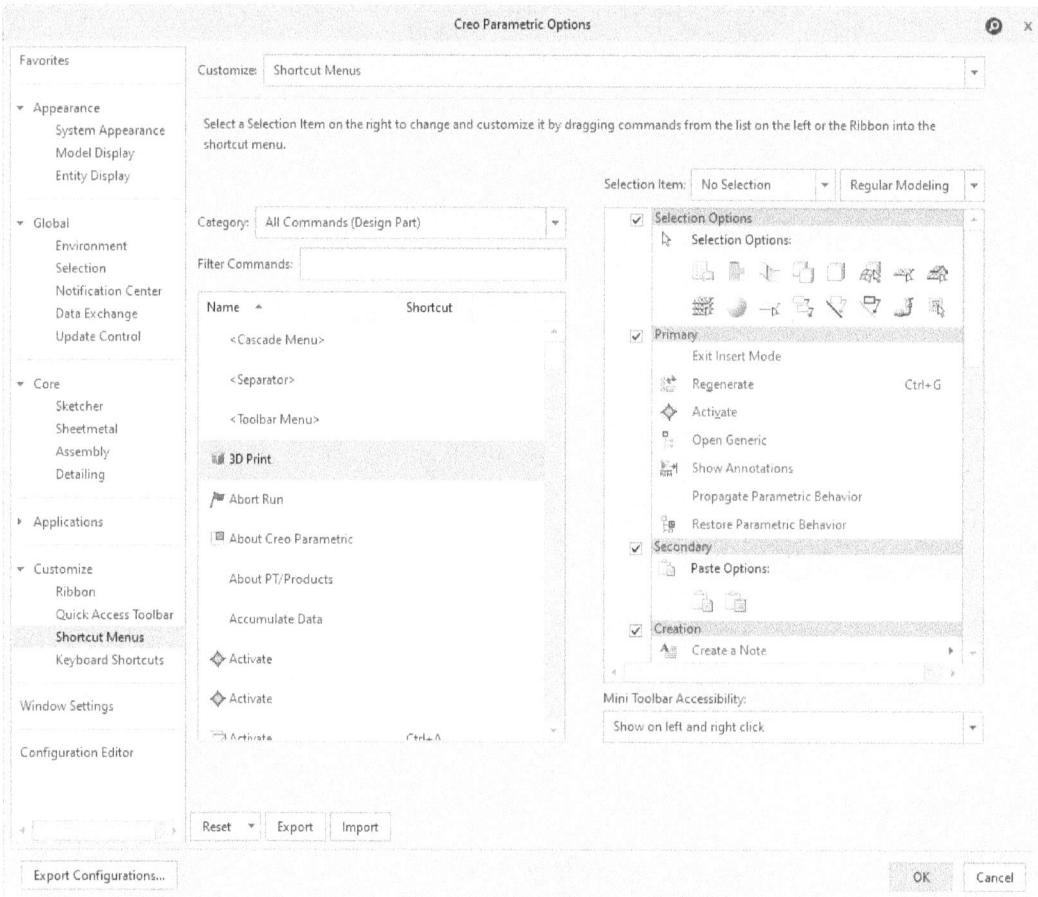

Figure A–13

You can drag commands on or off of the *mini* toolbar or menus. You can also reorganize the commands by dragging them to new locations. To return to the default setting, expand **Reset** and select either:

- Reset selected Shortcut Menu

- Reset All Shortcut Menus and corresponding *Mini* Toolbars

You can export the customized environment by clicking **Export** and saving the **creo_parametric_customization.ui** file. Place this file in the loadpoint directory and set the configuration option *load_ui_customization_run_dir* to **yes** to automatically load the configuration on startup

Quick Access Toolbar

The *Quick Access* Toolbar option enables you to customize the command in the toolbar by adding system- or user-defined icons, as shown in Figure A–14. You can also specify to display the toolbar below or above the ribbon. You can open the dialog box using the following methods:

- Select **File>Options>Quick Access Toolbar**.

- Right-click on the toolbar and select **Customize Quick Access Toolbar**.

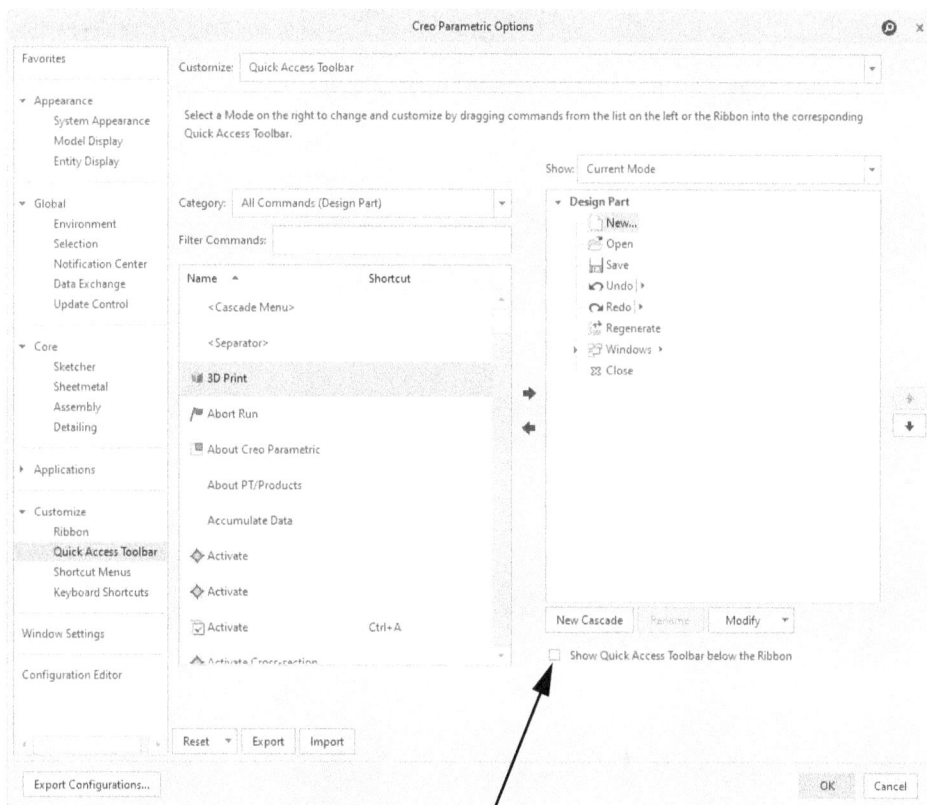

Toggle to display the toolbar below or above the ribbon

Figure A–14

Note: The shortcut menu also enables you to remove the toolbar and display it below the ribbon.

The commands are listed alphabetically and sub-divided into categories based on their function. You can sort them using the flyout menu at the top. By default, some of these commands are already located in the toolbar or the tabs.

How To: Add Additional Commands to the Quick Access Toolbar

1. Select the category to locate the command.

2. Press and hold the left mouse button over the required icon.

3. Drag the icon to the required location until the vertical or horizontal sash is displayed and release the left mouse button to place the icon.

   Figure A–15 shows a command being added to the toolbar.

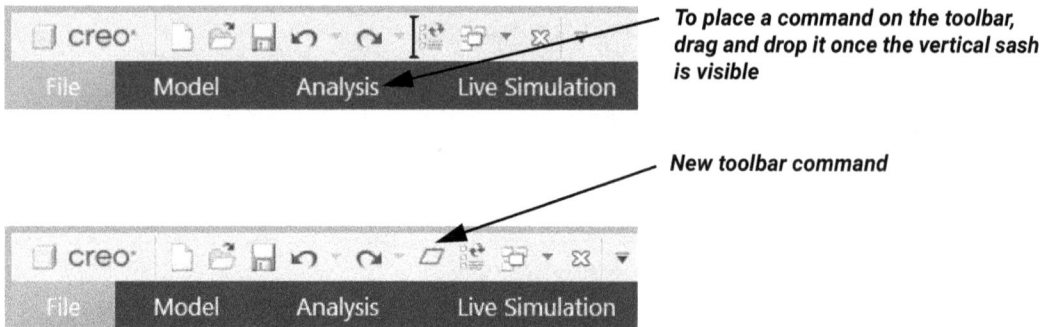

To place a command on the toolbar, drag and drop it once the vertical sash is visible

New toolbar command

Figure A–15

To delete a toolbar icon or menu bar option, select the item, right-click, and select **Remove**. You can also remove the icon by dragging it out of the toolbar or menu.

Mapkeys Category

Once created, a mapkey displays as an icon in the *Mapkeys* category. The default icon image for all mapkeys is identical and can be customized to better identify their intent. As with all other icons, mapkeys can be added to the toolbar using drag and drop. Add the mapkey to the *Customize Quick Access Toolbar* area and use the options in the *Modify* drop-down list to customize the mapkey image, as shown in Figure A–16.

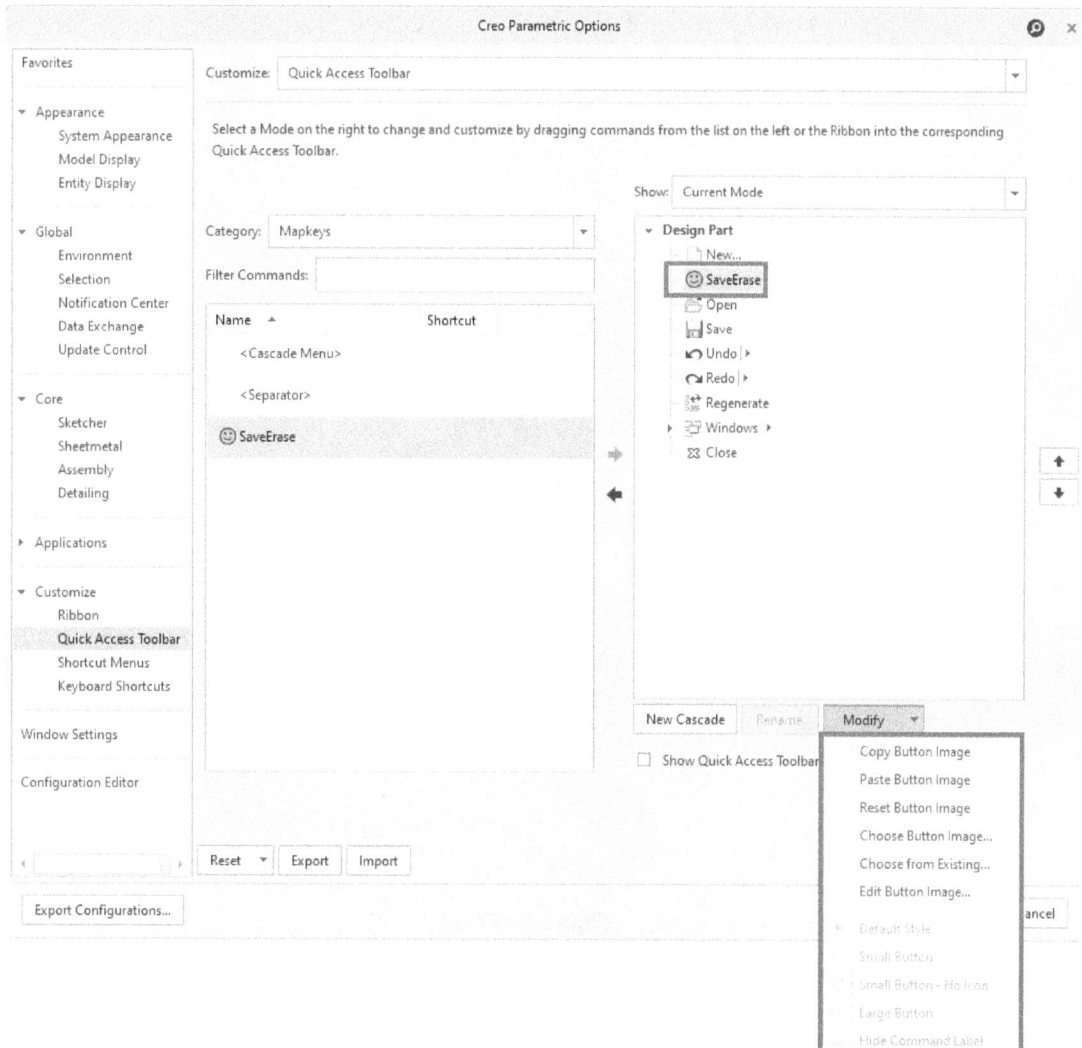

Figure A–16

Window Settings

The *Window Settings* category enables you to configure settings for the *Navigation* tab, Model Tree, Browser, Accessory Window, and *In-graphics* toolbar, as shown in Figure A–17.

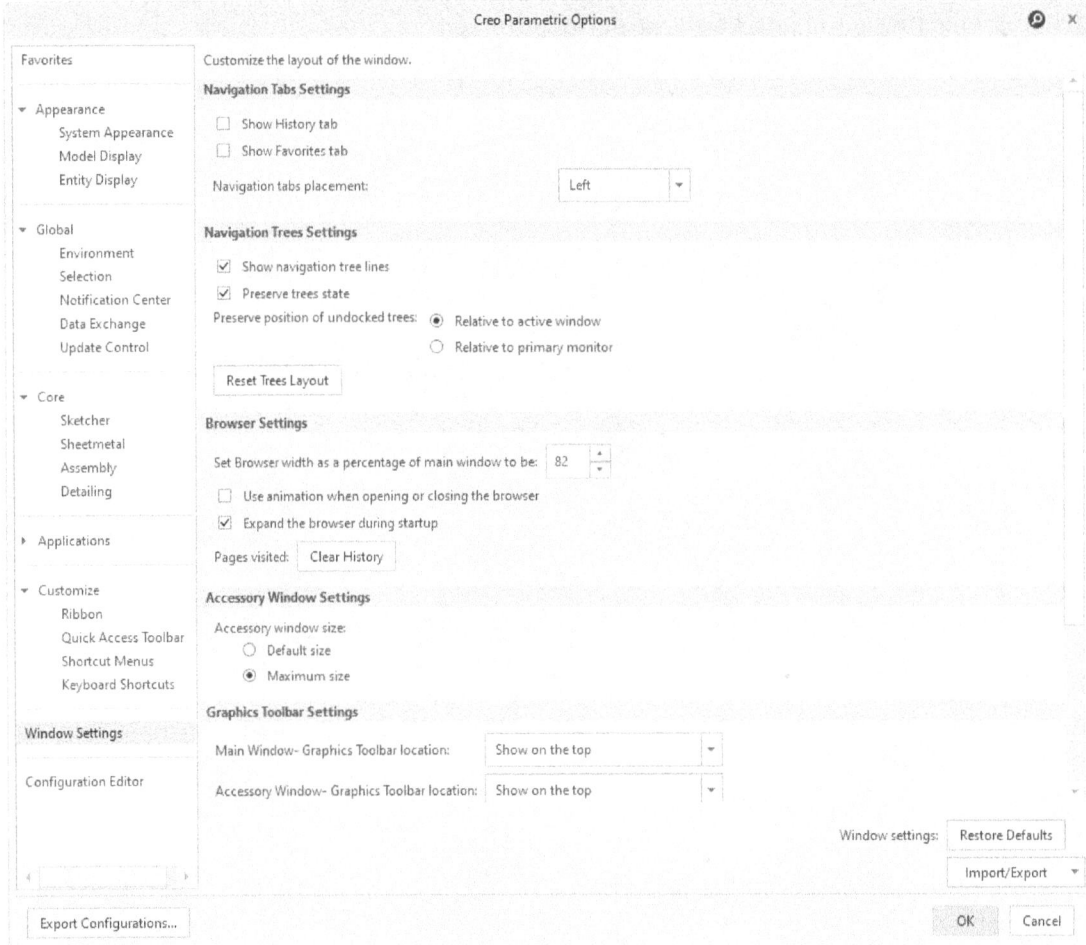

Figure A–17

- **Navigation Tabs Settings:** The Placement drop-down list enables you to place the window on the left or right side of the *Graphics* area. To access the *History* tab in the Navigator, enable the **Show History tab** option.

- **Model Tree Settings:** Enables you to customize the Model Tree display so that it is part of, or separate from, the navigation window. The default setting for the Model Tree is to be a part of the navigation window. If separate, the Model Tree can be placed above or below the graphics area and its height can be set to suit you requirements.

- **Browser Settings:** Enables you to customize the size and settings for the web browser.

- **Accessory Window Settings:** Enables you to specify your preferences for the secondary windows and menu icons.

- **Graphics Toolbar Settings:** Contains icons that control the display of the model. You can move the toolbar to various locations, add and remove icons, resize the icons to be small, medium, or large. You can customize the toolbar in the *Creo Parametric Options* dialog box, or by right-clicking and selecting options as shown in Figure A–18.

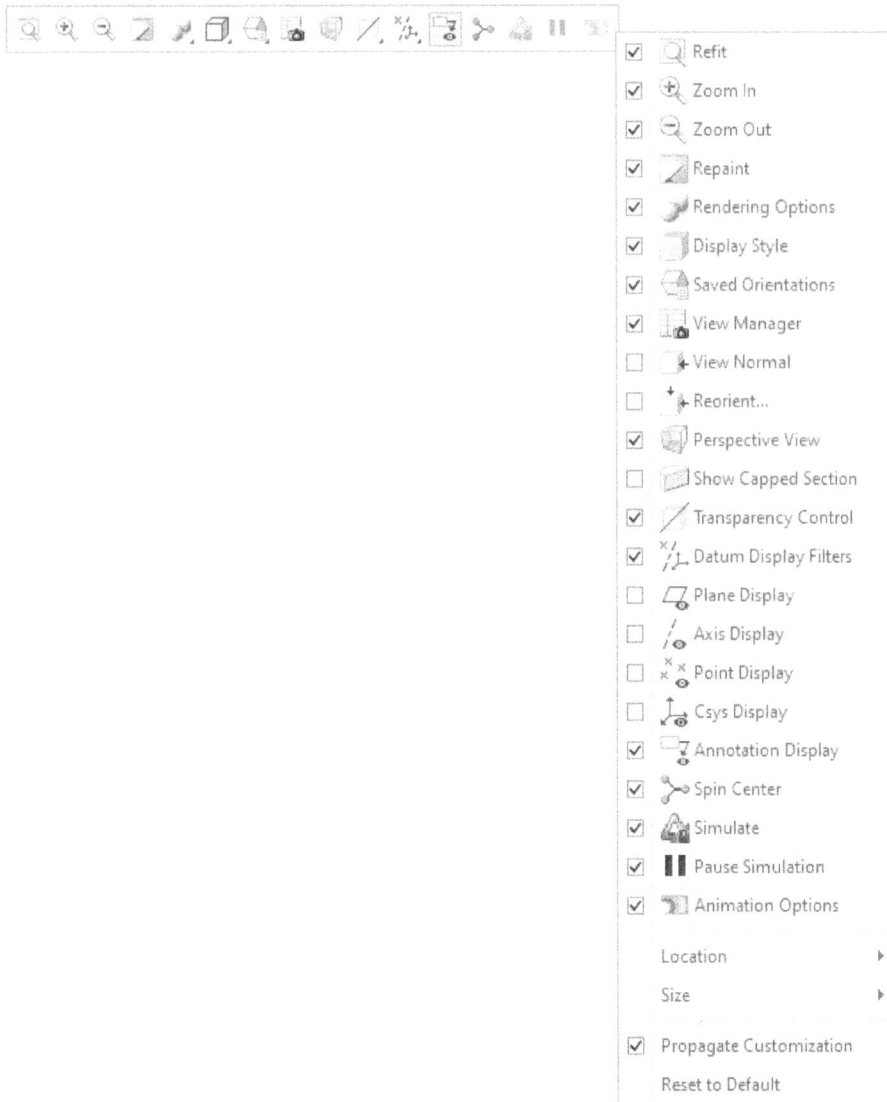

Figure A–18

- **General Settings:** The panels in the dashboard for any feature type can be dragged and undocked from the dashboard so they can be located anywhere in the graphics area, as shown in Figure A–19.

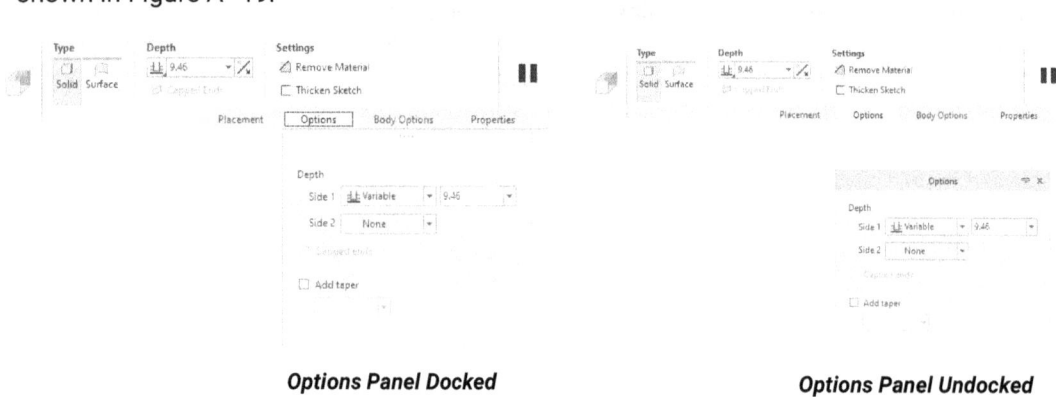

Options Panel Docked   *Options Panel Undocked*

Figure A–19

A.5 Customize the Configuration File

The main configuration file that is used in Creo Parametric is **config.pro**. It is used to customize the system to meet your preferences and requirements. A significant number of options can be customized in **config.pro**, which can save you modeling time and help to ensure the use of modeling standards. The most frequently customized settings include display settings, model decimal places, model standards, and file storage and retrieval standards.

The **config.pro** file can be accessed by selecting **File>Options>Configuration Editor**. The *Creo Parametric Options* dialog box opens, enabling you to set your preferences in the **config.pro** file, as shown in Figure A–20.

The dialog box consists of two frames:

• The left frame, which contains all of the options.

• The right frame, which contains the value, status, and description for each option.

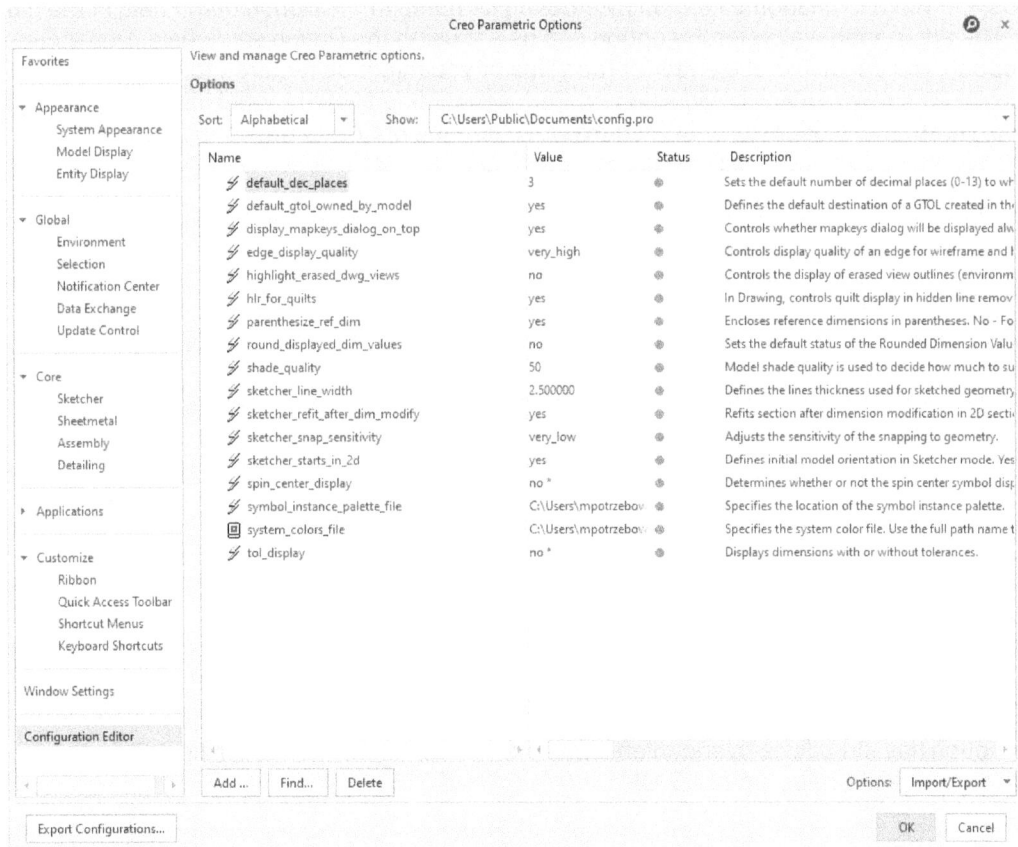

Figure A–20

By default, only the options that exist in the current file are displayed in the *Creo Parametric Options* dialog box. To display all of the options, click the *Show* drop-down list and click **All options**. It is recommended to use the **Sort** options to group the options, when reviewing them.

When Creo Parametric is launched, the system automatically looks for a **config.pro** file in the following locations:

* The */loadpoint/text* directory in the Creo Parametric software.

* Your home directory.

* Startup directory of the Creo Parametric software.

If an option is listed in more than one configuration file in any of these directories, the last value loaded is the one used by the system. Therefore, it is important to know the **config.pro** file that is being displayed in the *Creo Parametric Options* dialog box.

Changes are made to the **config.pro** file by adding options or changing the value for the options that are currently set. An option can be added by clicking **Add**. The *Add Options* dialog box opens and you can change an option by entering its name in the *Option name* field in the dialog box. The appropriate value for the option can be set using the *Option value* field. Depending on the option, you can select the entry for the value or you might be required to enter a value. Figure A–21 shows a value being selected from a predefined list of model display settings (e.g., **shade**, **wireframe**, **hiddenvis**, or **hiddeninvis**). To add the option to the configuration file, click **OK**.

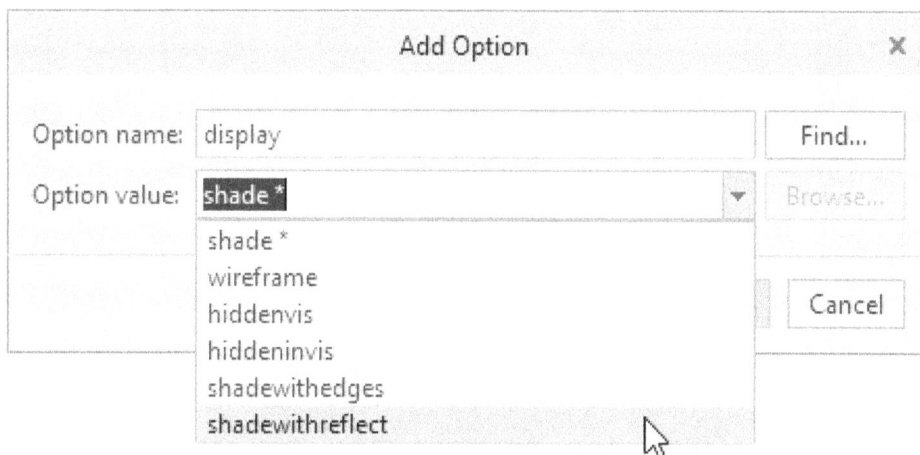

Figure A–21

If an option has already been added and only the value is to be changed, select the value from the list, change the value, and click **OK**.

Searching for Configuration Options

If the name of the option is not known, you can search for it by clicking **Find**. The *Find Option* dialog box opens, as shown in Figure A–22.

Figure A–22

To search for an option name, enter the keyword and click **Find Now**. The system searches all of the option names and descriptions (if enabled) and returns a list of results. Select the required option in the *Choose option* area, set the value and click **Add / Change** to add it to the **config.pro**. To narrow your search results, consider selecting a category in the *Look In* drop-down list.

When all of the required options and values are set, the **config.pro** file should be applied to the current Creo Parametric session. To apply the option(s), click **OK**. The status symbol changes from ✳ to a ● . A dialog box opens, as shown in Figure A–23. It enables you to decide whether the changes are only applied to the current session or if they are saved and applied in the next session.

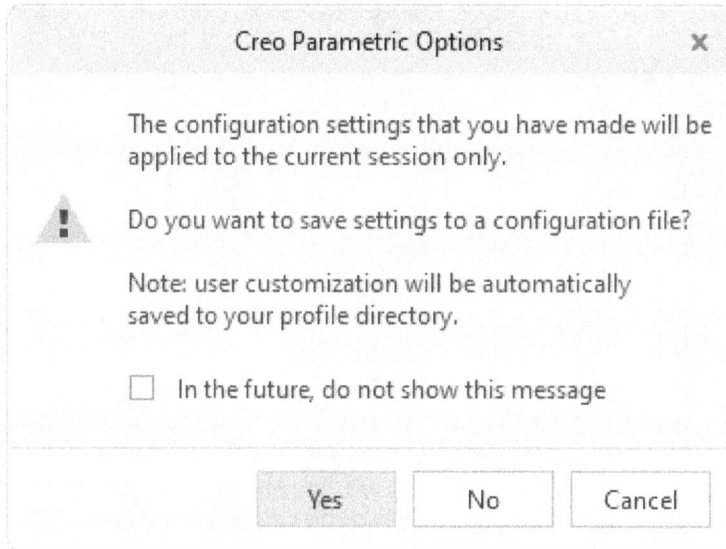

Creo Parametric Options   ✕

⚠ The configuration settings that you have made will be applied to the current session only.

Do you want to save settings to a configuration file?

Note: user customization will be automatically saved to your profile directory.

☐ In the future, do not show this message

Yes   No   Cancel

Figure A–23

- Click **Yes** to save the settings in the *Creo Parametric Options* dialog box. This applies the changes that were made. If you click **No** instead, it applies all of the changes that were done, but does not save the changes.

- The **Import/Export** option at the bottom of the *Creo Parametric Options* dialog box enables you to import or export the **config.pro** file in the current location or store it in a new directory.

- For example, if the software is started from */USER/PEOPLE/ TRAINING*, and the **config.pro** in the *TRAINING* directory is used. If the working directory for Creo Parametric is changed to */USER/PEOPLE*, the **config.pro** in the *PEOPLE* directory must be manually loaded. Otherwise, the file in the *TRAINING* directory still applies.

In most cases, changes to the configuration file are applied to the current session immediately. However, options that affect the graphical display of Creo Parametric require you to restart the software to implement them, as shown in Figure A–24. It is recommended that you restart the session as soon as it is convenient to ensure that all of the options are being used.

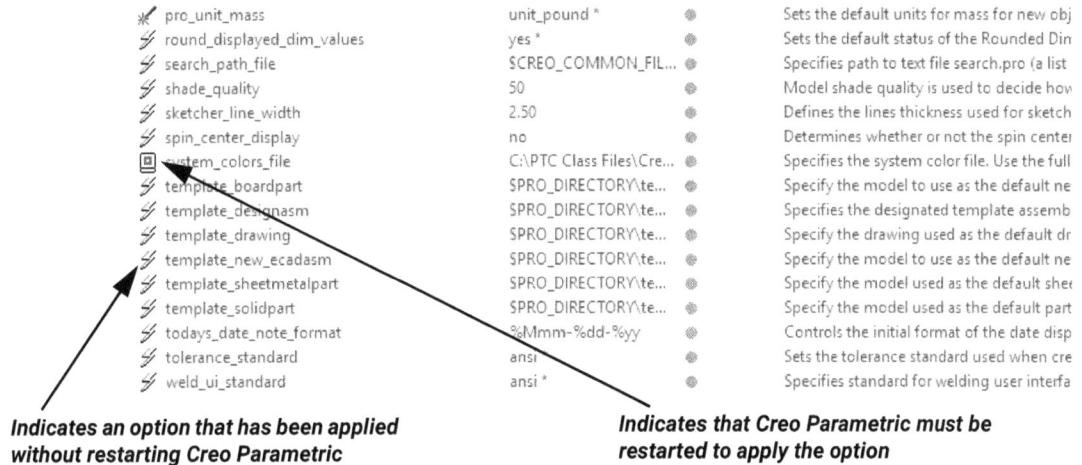

pro_unit_mass	unit_pound *		Sets the default units for mass for new obj
round_displayed_dim_values	yes *		Sets the default status of the Rounded Din
search_path_file	$CREO_COMMON_FIL...		Specifies path to text file search.pro (a list
shade_quality	50		Model shade quality is used to decide how
sketcher_line_width	2.50		Defines the lines thickness used for sketch
spin_center_display	no		Determines whether or not the spin center
system_colors_file	C:\PTC Class Files\Cre...		Specifies the system color file. Use the full
template_boardpart	$PRO_DIRECTORY\te...		Specify the model to use as the default ne
template_designasm	$PRO_DIRECTORY\te...		Specifies the designated template assemb
template_drawing	$PRO_DIRECTORY\te...		Specify the drawing used as the default dr
template_new_ecadasm	$PRO_DIRECTORY\te...		Specify the model to use as the default ne
template_sheetmetalpart	$PRO_DIRECTORY\te...		Specify the model used as the default shee
template_solidpart	$PRO_DIRECTORY\te...		Specify the model used as the default part
todays_date_note_format	%Mmm-%dd-%yy		Controls the initial format of the date disp
tolerance_standard	ansi		Sets the tolerance standard used when cre
weld_ui_standard	ansi *		Specifies standard for welding user interfa

Indicates an option that has been applied without restarting Creo Parametric

Indicates that Creo Parametric must be restarted to apply the option

Figure A–24

Creo Configuration Options Search

This search tool is found in the upper right corner of the *Creo Parametric Options* window as shown in Figure A–25. This tool allows for Creo options to be quickly located within the Creo Parametric Options without having to know its exact location in the window. Options can always be changed by navigating through categories on the left, but when looking for a setting and not knowing if or where it exists, a key word can be typed into the *Dialog Search* field.

Select the Dialog Search icon to reveal the text field to its left

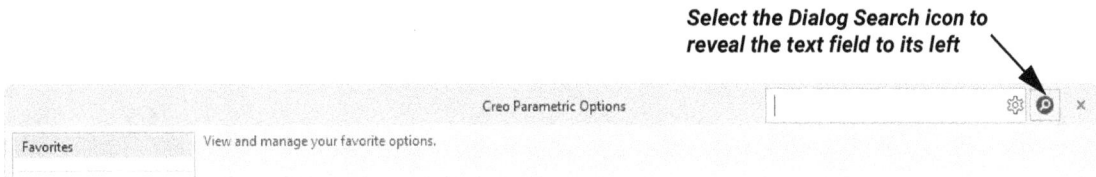

Creo Parametric Options

Favorites

View and manage your favorite options.

Figure A–25

Figure A–26 shows the use of the key word **Color,** used in order to find settings related to changing the color of something within Creo. By hovering over the listed options Creo will automatically hight the categories and locations within the Creo Parametric Options that contain that setting. This will also locate and allow for the change of settings found within the Configuration Editor so the Config.pro file can be modified as needed.

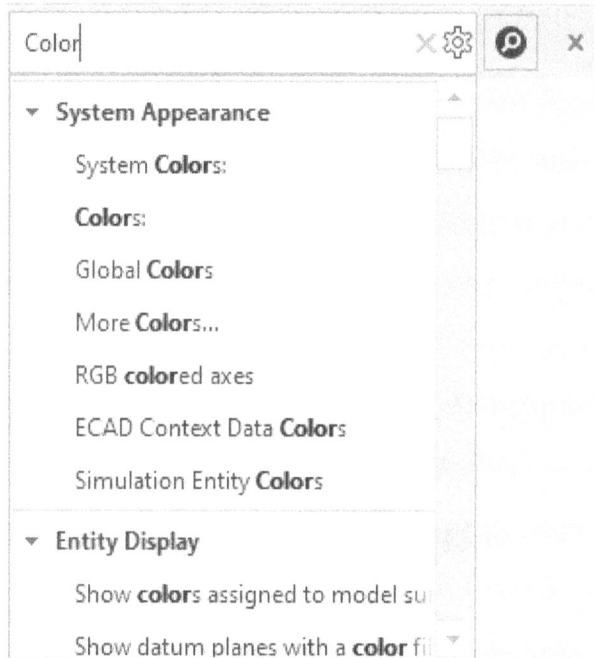

Figure A–26

A.6 Assigning Colors to Parts and Surfaces

For complex assemblies, you might want to change the colors of parts and/or features to distinguish them from one another. Creo Parametric enables you to customize the default system colors for such purposes. The **Appearance Gallery** icon is used to create, delete, save, and modify the appearance of parts and surfaces.

- Select the part in the Model Tree or individual surfaces on the model to apply the color.

- Select the **Appearances** icon flyout in the *View* tab to pick a color as shown in Figure A–27.

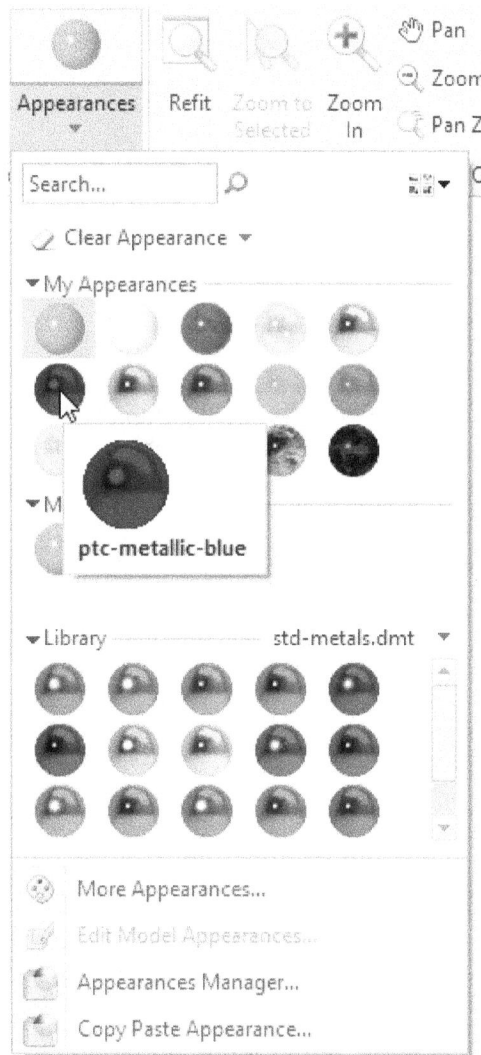

Figure A–27

A.7 Configuring the Model Tree

In an earlier chapter, you looked at controlling the items and columns that are displayed in the Model Tree. This section will focus on how changes made to the Model Tree load automatically. To change the Model Tree settings, expand the ⊞ (Model Tree Settings) flyout at the top of the Model Tree, then select **Settings**, as shown in Figure A–28.

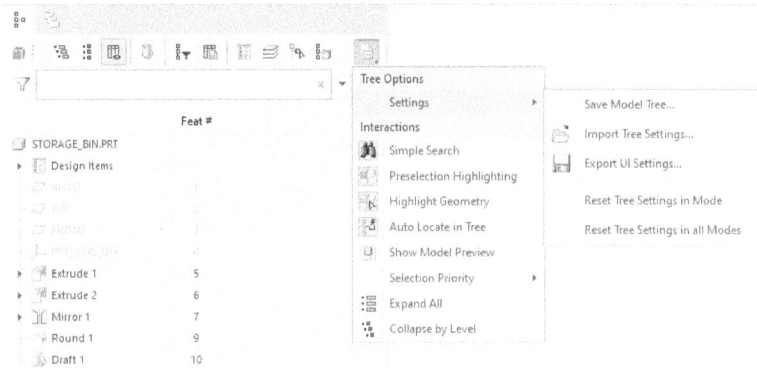

Figure A–28

As a quick review, you can use ⊞▼ (Tree Filters) and ⊞ (Tree Columns) to control the Model Tree settings. Select ⊞▼ (Tree Filters) in the Model Tree. In the *Tree Filters* dialog box (shown in Figure A–29), clear or select items to customize the display of items in the Model Tree.

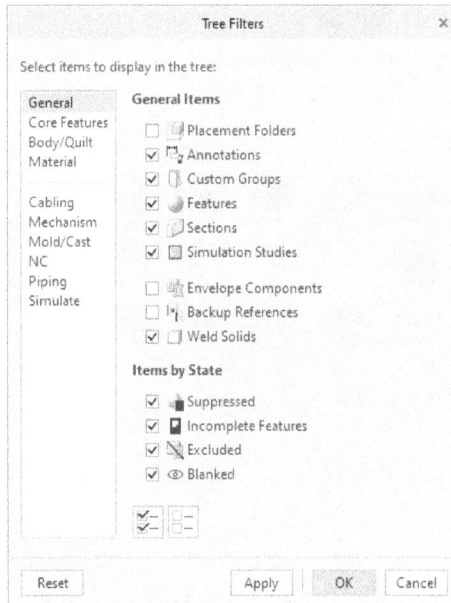

Figure A–29

The Model Tree can also be customized to include additional columns of information. To manipulate columns in the Model Tree, select ▦ (Tree Columns). The *Model Tree Columns* dialog box opens, as shown in Figure A–30.

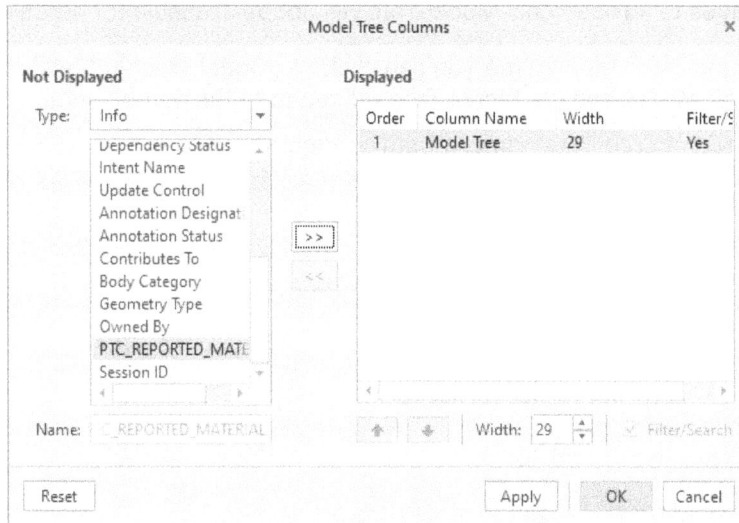

Figure A–30

Add columns to the Displayed list. Figure A–31 shows a Model Tree that is configured to display the feature number and feature ID columns.

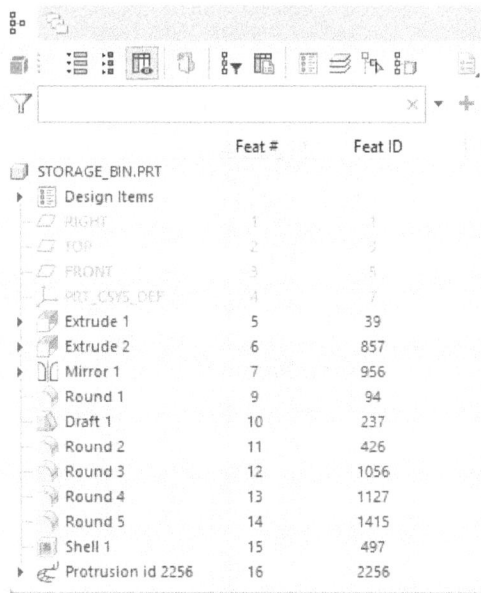

Figure A–31

Once changes are made to your Model Tree configuration, they are automatically stored in a *.ui configuration file. The settings are mode specific, so if you make changes to the Model Tree in part mode, those changes will be in place for any subsequent parts you open. The changes will not be in place when you open a different type of model, for example an assembly. Conversely, changes to an assembly Model Tree will not be available for part files.

To reset the options in the Model Tree, you can click ⌐ (Model Tree Settings)**>Settings>Reset Tree Settings in all Modes** and the Model Tree will return to the default setup.

In previous releases of Creo Parametric, a *.cfg configuration file was used. You may currently have one setup on your system. If you do, then you may receive the warning shown in Figure A-32 when opening models.

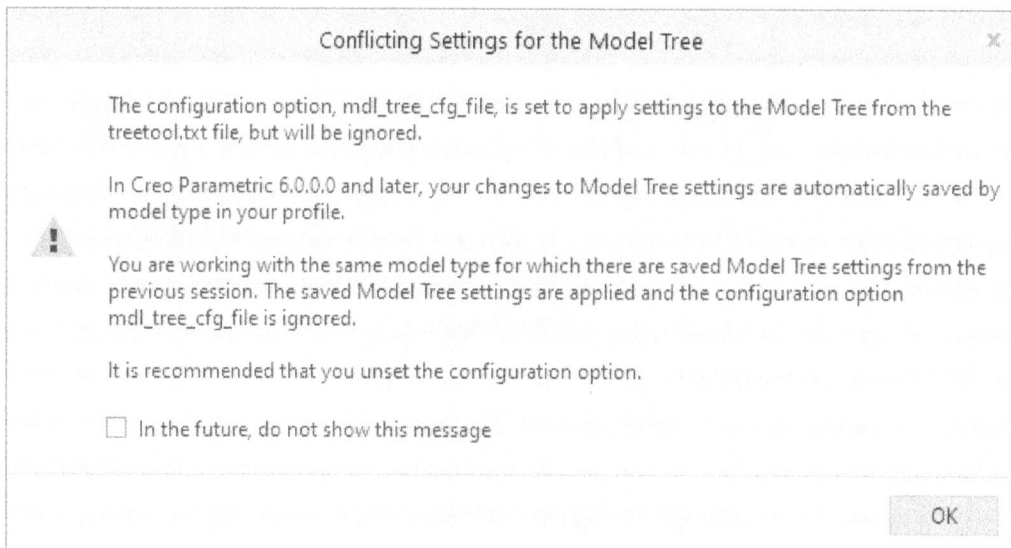

Conflicting Settings for the Model Tree	×

The configuration option, mdl_tree_cfg_file, is set to apply settings to the Model Tree from the treetool.txt file, but will be ignored.

In Creo Parametric 6.0.0.0 and later, your changes to Model Tree settings are automatically saved by model type in your profile.

You are working with the same model type for which there are saved Model Tree settings from the previous session. The saved Model Tree settings are applied and the configuration option mdl_tree_cfg_file is ignored.

It is recommended that you unset the configuration option.

☐ In the future, do not show this message

OK

Figure A-32

This warning indicates that the settings found in the *.cfg configuration file will be ignored and those found in the *ui file will be used.

The older style configuration file is loaded using the configuration option **mdl_tree_cfg_file** set to the path for the file's location. Although the warning in Figure A-32 recommends that you unset the **mdl_tree_cfg_file** option, you should leave it in place for now, since the configuration file may be used for older releases of Creo Parametric that do not use the *.ui file.

Practice A1
Customization

Practice Objectives

- Set and save the configuration options for the Creo Parametric system.

- Assign and test a command alias, referred to as a Mapkey, using keyboard keys to save and erase a file with one click.

- Customize the *Quick Access* Toolbar and the Model Tree with user preferences.

In this practice, you will customize the system's default settings to be user-specific.

Task 1: Make changes to the config.pro file.

1. Set the working directory to the *Customization* folder.

2. Select **File>Options**.

3. Select the *Configuration Editor* category.

4. Click **Add**. The *Add Option* dialog box opens.

5. In the *Option name* collector, type **display**. Note that you do not need to type the entire name. When the system matches an option, it completes the collector. If the provided option is not correct, continue typing.

6. For the value, select **hiddenvis** as shown in Figure A–33.

7. Click **OK** to apply the option to the list.

8. Click **OK** in the *Creo Parametric Options* dialog box.

9. A dialog box opens, as shown in Figure A–34. Click **Yes** to save the settings.

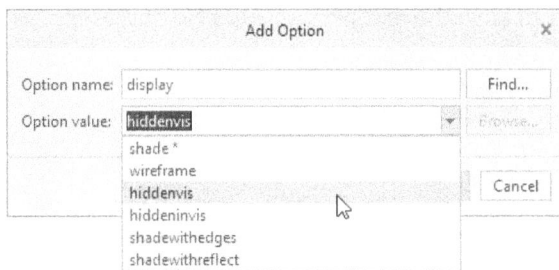

Figure A–33

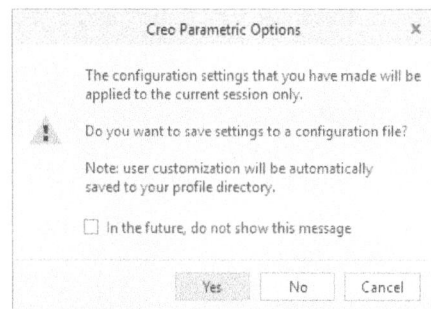

Figure A–34

10. Maintain the default name of **config.pro** and click **OK**.

11. Open any model and note that the model has now been set to **Hidden Line**. This is now the default display setting. Erase the file from session.

Task 2: Set another config option.

1. Select **File>Options>Configuration Editor**.
2. Click **Add**. The *Creo Parametric Options* dialog box opens.
3. Enter **prompt_on_erase_not_disp**. This configuration option prompts you to save the files that are to be erased when you select **Erase>Not Displayed**.
4. For the value, select **Yes** and click **OK**.
5. Add another configuration option. Enter **prompt_on_exit** and select a value of **Yes**. This option prompts you to save the files in session when you exit.
6. Click **OK**.
7. Click **Yes** to save the settings. Maintain the default name of **config.pro** and click **OK**.
8. Click **OK** to close the *Creo Parametric Options* dialog box.

Task 3: Test the config.pro options.

1. Create a new part and set the *Name* to **test**.
2. Select **File>Close**. **Test.prt** is still in session but has not been saved.
3. Click ✎ (Erase Not Displayed). **Test.prt** is now in the list of objects to be erased.
4. Click **OK**.
5. Press <Enter> to save the file. You might be prompted a few times if you have other files in session. The *Message* area now displays the *All the objects which were not displayed have been erased* prompt.
6. Create another new part and name it **exit**.
7. Select **File>Exit** and select **Yes** to exit.
8. The *Message* area again displays a prompt to save the **exit.prt** file. Type **No** and press <Enter>.

Task 4: Create a mapkey.

1. Open another session of Creo Parametric.
2. Open any part, then click **File>Options** and select **Mapkeys Settings**.

   *Note: Make sure to click **Options** only once to expand it and select **Mapkeys Settings**. Do not click **Options** twice, as it will take you to the Creo Parametric Options.*

3. Click **New**. The *Record Mapkey* dialog box opens. Set the following, as shown in Figure A-35:

    • *Keyboard Shortcut*: **$F3**

    • *Name*: **SaveErase**

    • *Description:* **Saves the current file and erases it**

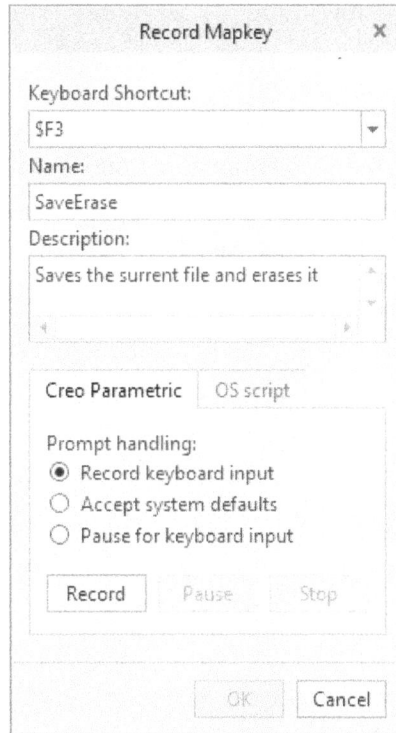

Figure A-35

4. Click **Record**.

5. Select **File>Save** and press <Enter>.

6. Select **File>Manage Session>Erase Current** and click **Yes**.

7. Click **Stop** to finish the mapkey creation and click **OK**.

8. Click **Save>Save Selected** to save the mapkey.

9. Click **Close** to close the *Mapkeys* dialog box.

Task 5: Test the mapkey.

1. Open any part.

2. Press <F3> to activate and test the mapkey.

Task 6: Investigate the default user interface themes and create a custom theme.

1. Open **NA200.prt**.

2. Set the model display as follows:

   - ⁂ *(Datum Display Filters)*: All Off

   - ⅀ *(Spin Center)*: Off

   - ▢ *(Display Style)*: ▢ (Shading With Edges)

3. Select **File>Options** to open the *Creo Parametric Options* dialog box.

4. In the *Creo Parametric Options* dialog box, click **Appearance>System Appearance**, as shown in Figure A–36.

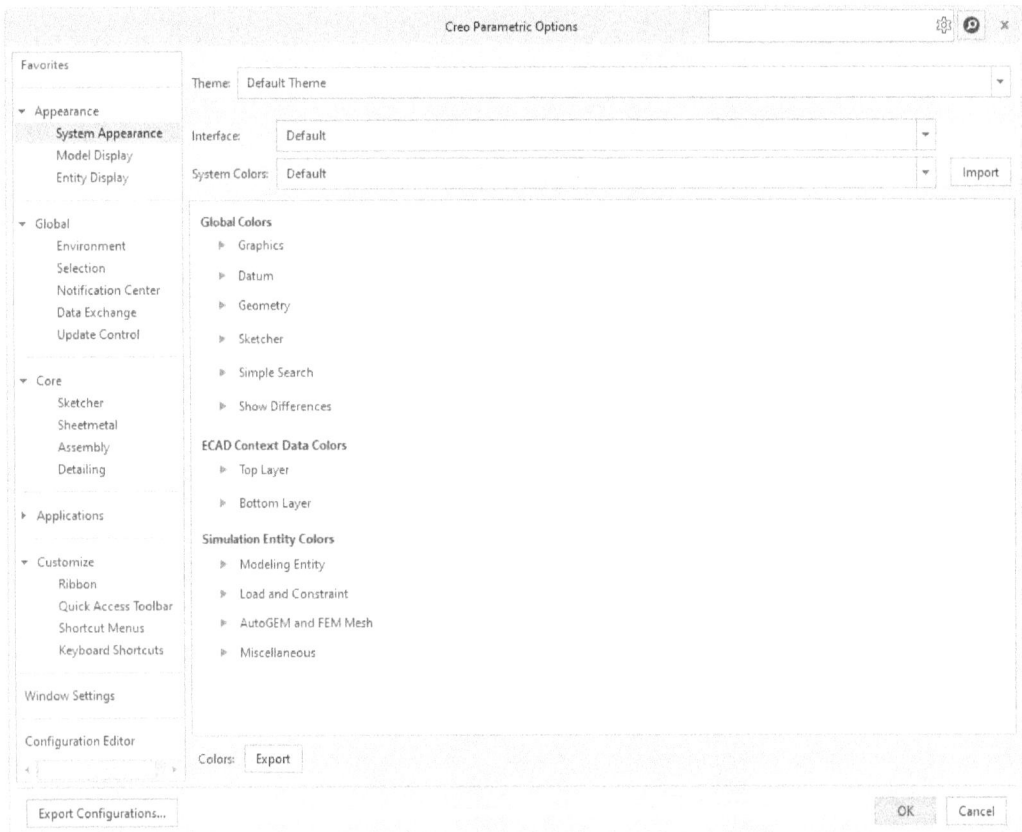

Figure A–36

5. From the *Theme* drop-down list, select **Dark Theme**.

6. From the *Theme* drop-down list, select **Light Theme** and click **OK**. The background, ribbon and window colors update, as shown in Figure A–37.

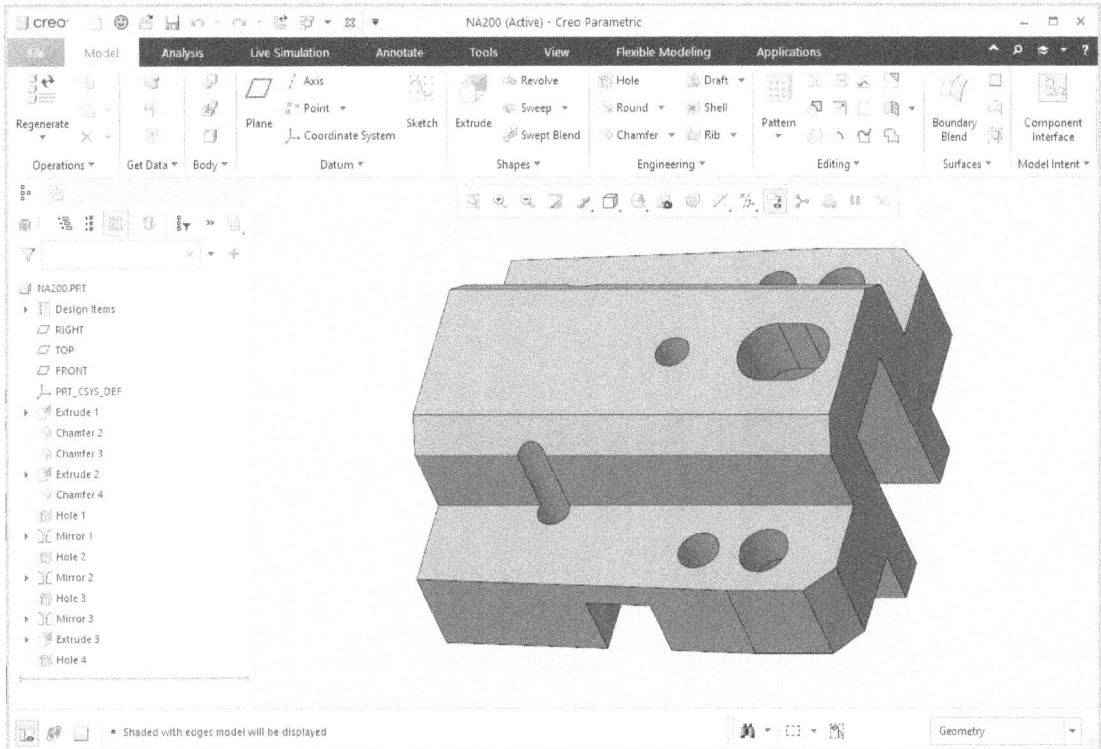

Figure A–37

7. Select **File>Options>Appearance>System Appearance**.

8. In the *Global Colors* area, expand **Graphics**.

9. Expand the **Preselection highlighting** color swatch and select the color shown in Figure A-38.

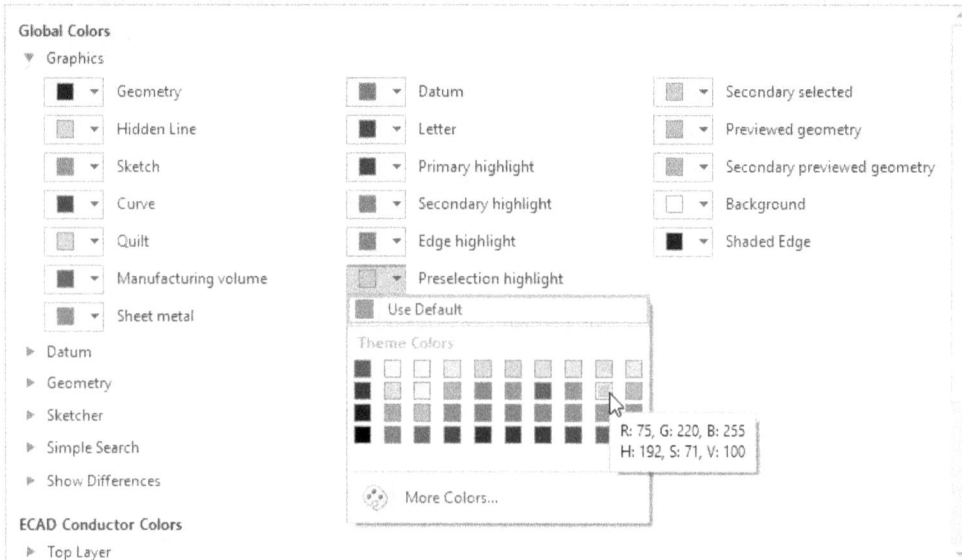

Figure A-38

10. Expand the **Background color** swatch and select **More colors**.

11. Edit the background to white by setting each of **R**, **G** and **B** to **255**, as shown in Figure A-39.

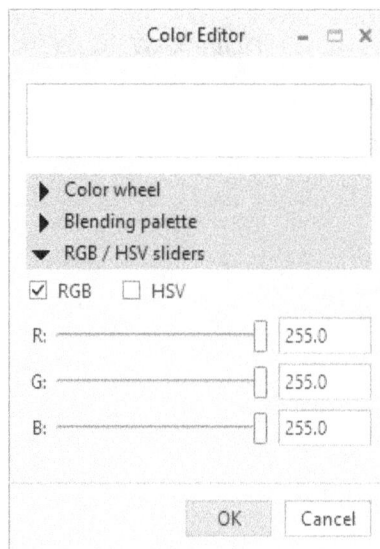

Figure A-39

12. Click **OK** in the *Color Editor*.

13. Click **OK** in the *Creo Parametric Options* dialog box.

14. Hover the cursor over objects in the model to show the change to prehighlighting, as shown in Figure A–40.

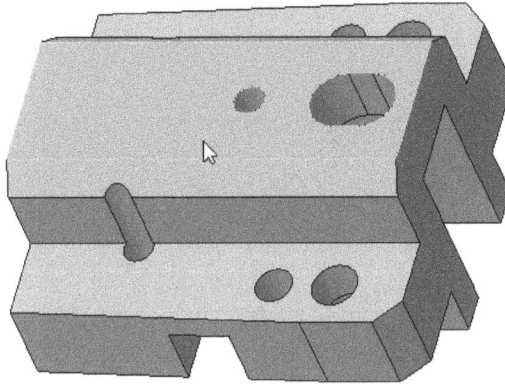

Figure A–40

Task 7: Investigate keyboard shortcuts.

1. Select **File>Options** and in the *Creo Parametric Options* dialog box, expand **Customize** and select **Keyboard Shortcuts**, as shown in Figure A–41.

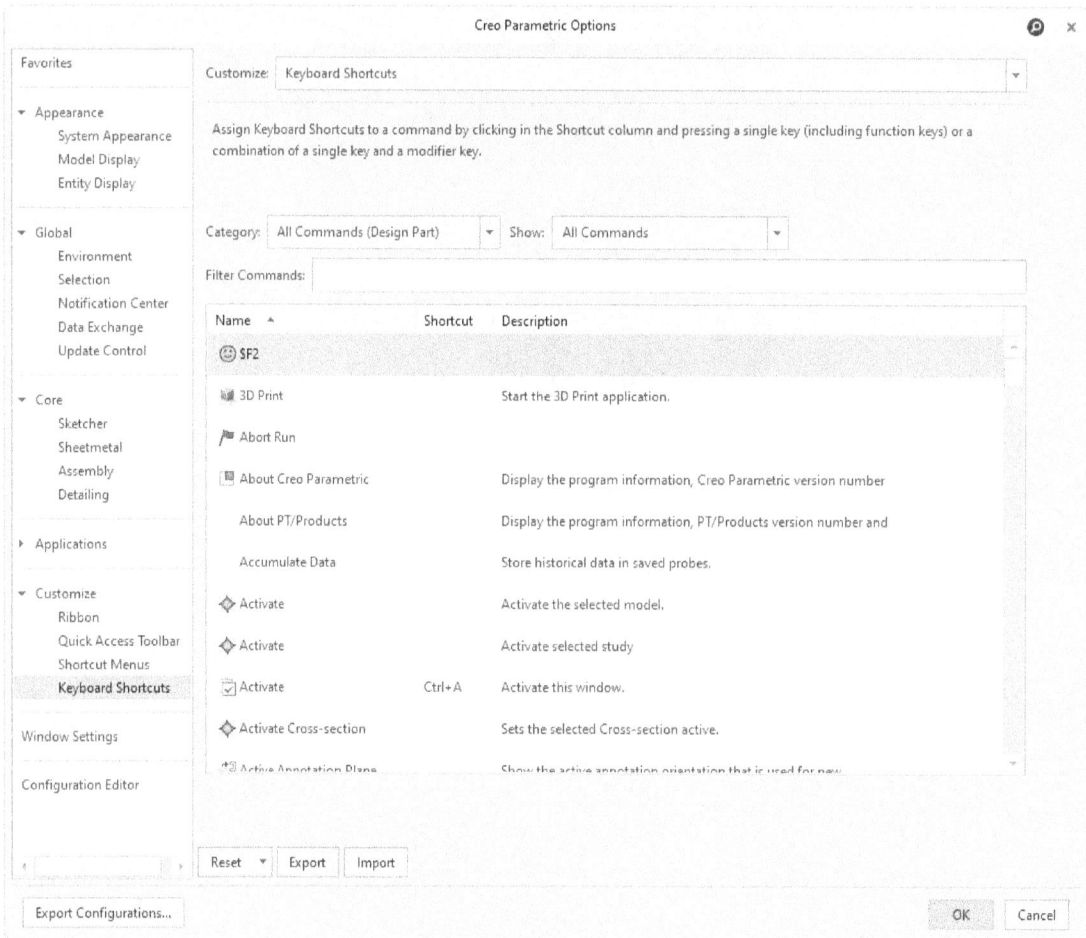

Figure A–41

2. Scroll down in the list and select **Angle**. Then, press <F6> to add the shortcut, as shown in Figure A–42.

Name ▲	Shortcut	Description
▦ Align Left		Align text to the left.
▦ Align Right		Align text to the right.
⊞ All Border		Draw all border for the selected cells, rows, columns, or a table.
Ambient occlusion		Toggle the ambient occlusion effect on or off.
✗⁄ Analysis...		Insert an analysis feature.
◿ Angle	F6	Measure an angle.
◁ Animate Deformation		Show animated deformation
Animation Options		Animation Options
Animation Options		Show Animation options
Annotation and Table		Toggle the display of 3D annotations and tables.
Annotation Feature...		Create an annotation feature.

Figure A–42

3. In the *Filter Commands* field, type **ex** and note that the commands list changes to only show those commands starting with or containing *ex*, as shown in Figure A–43.

Filter Commands: Ex

Name ▲	Shortcut	Description
▸ Extend...		Extend a contiguous one-sided edge of a quilt to a specified distance
External Analysis...		Perform an external analysis. Use an external application to perform a
Externalize Rounds		Externalize All Rounds
Extrude...	X	Create three-dimensional geometry by projecting a two-dimensional
Extrude...	X	Create three-dimensional geometry for an unattached wall by
A Copy Text Style...		Change the style of individual texts.
⠿ Flexible Pattern...		Create a pattern of the selected surfaces, curves, and datums.
FlexNet Publisher License		FlexNet Publisher License Administration Guide
Flip Text		Flip Text.
Move text		Move text location.
Open MS Excel file		Open MS Excel file computed by this feature

Figure A–43

4. Scroll down and note that **x** is assigned to ⬚ (Extrude).

5. Click **OK** in the *Creo Parametric Options* dialog box.

6. Press <F6> and the **Angle** tool activates.

7. Press and hold <Ctrl> and select the two surface shown in Figure A–44. The angle of **45** degrees displays.

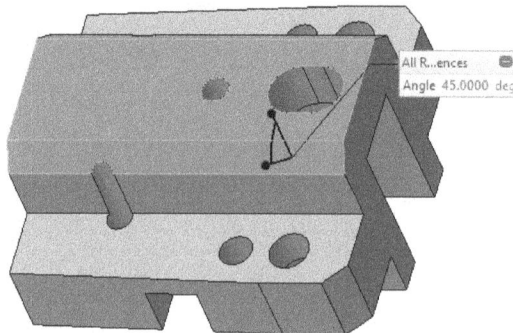

Figure A–44

8. Close the *Measure Angle* dialog box.

9. Press <X> to create an extrude.

10. Select the surface shown in Figure A–45.

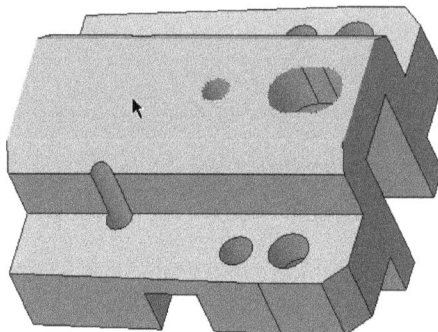

Figure A–45

11. In the *Setup* group, if required click ⬚ (Sketch View).

12. Create the sketch shown in Figure A−46.

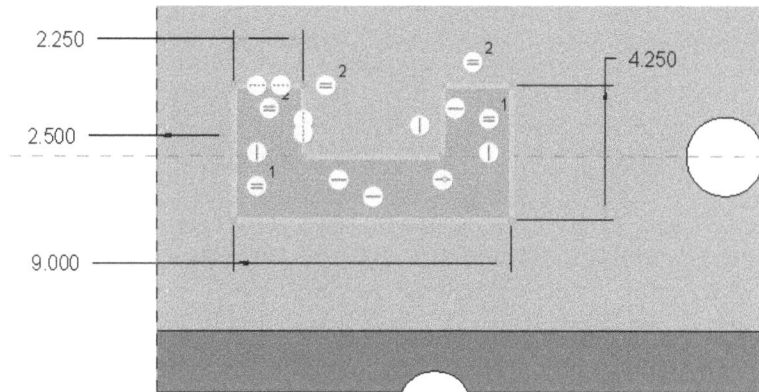

Figure A−46

13. Click ✓ (**OK**).

14. Press <Ctrl>+<D>.

15. Click the end of the direction arrow to flip the feature's direction.

16. If required, click ▱ (Remove Material) to create a cut. Depending on your configuration options, this may activate automatically.

17. Hover over the depth dimension and select ᴴ ᴱ (Through All).

18. Click ✓ (**OK**) and the assembly updates, as shown in Figure A−47.

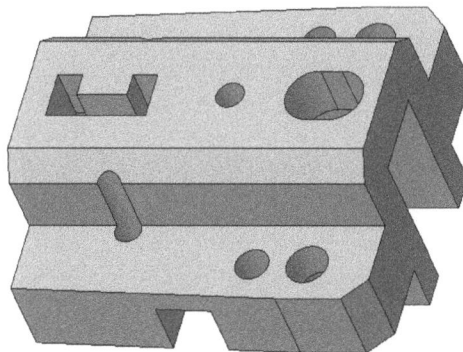

Figure A−47

19. Select **File>Options** and in the *Creo Parametric Options* dialog box, select **Customize>Keyboard Shortcuts**.

If you have made edits to the keyboard shortcuts you want to keep, do not complete the next two steps. Simply find the <F6> keyboard shortcut and delete it.

20. Click **Reset** and select **Reset all Keyboard Shortcuts**, as shown in Figure A–48.

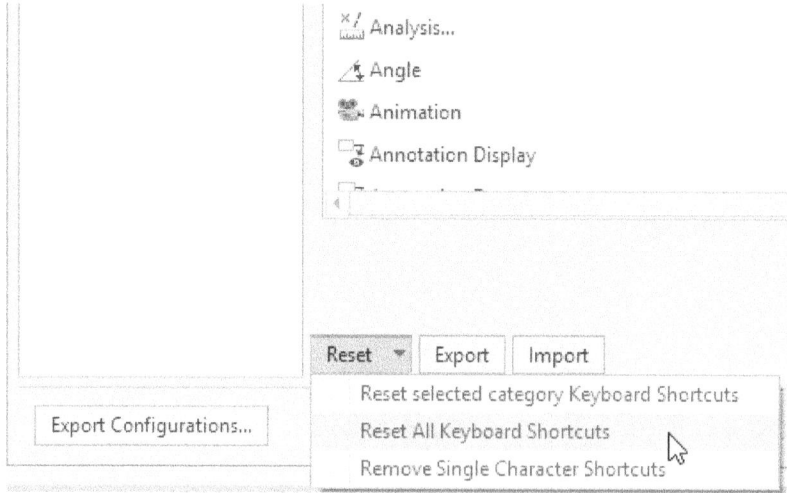

Figure A–48

21. In the *Reset* warning dialog box, click **Reset**.

22. Note that the <F6> shortcut has been removed for *Angle*, as shown in Figure A–49.

Figure A–49

23. Click **OK** in the *Creo Parametric Options* dialog box.

Task 8: Customize a shortcut menu.

1. Select **File>Options** and in the *Creo Parametric Options* dialog box, select **Customize>Shortcut Menus**.

2. In the *Selection Item* drop-down list, select **Geometric Entities**, as shown in Figure A–50.

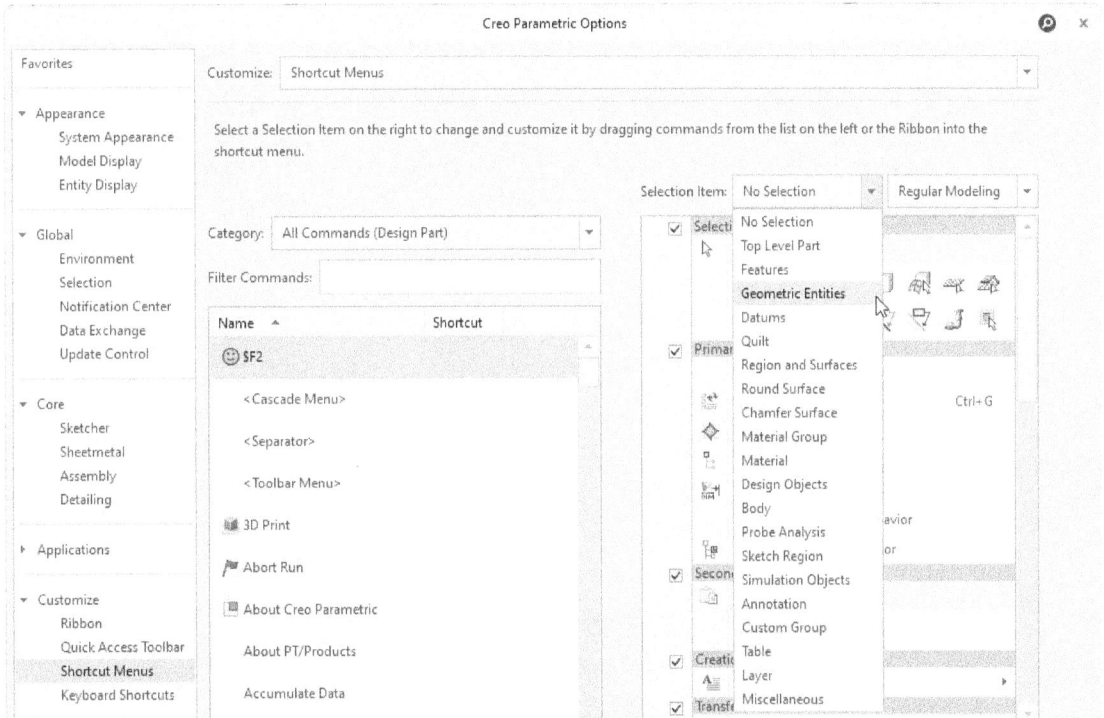

Figure A–50

3. The menu shows the default shortcut menus for when model geometry is selected, as shown in Figure A–51.

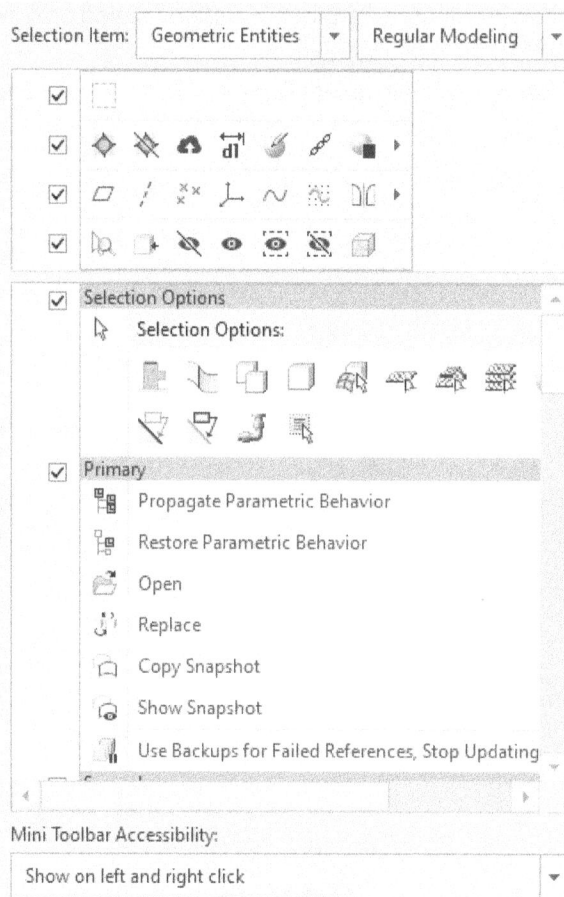

Figure A–51

4. Select ✕ (Delete) and drag and drop it to the location shown in Figure A–52.

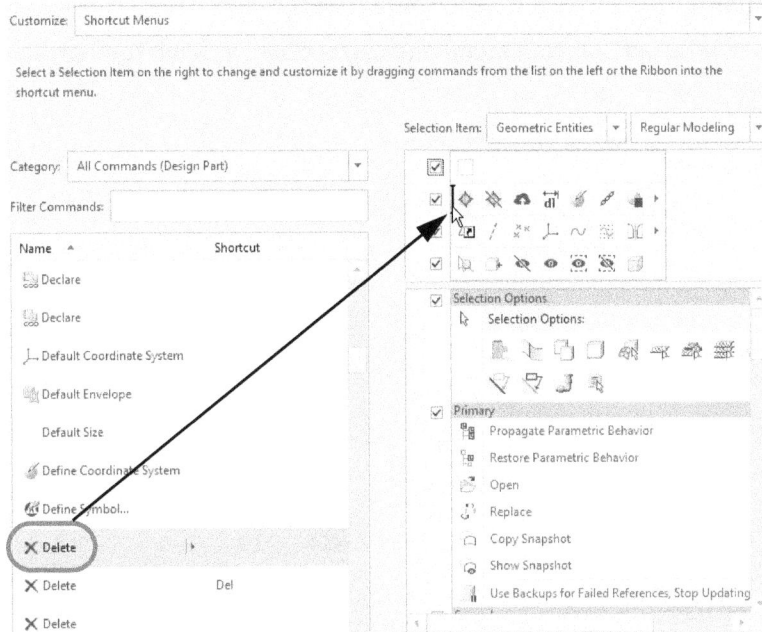

Figure A-52

5. Click **OK**.

6. Select the hole shown in Figure A-53 and note that ✕ (Delete) is now added to the *mini* toolbar. Click ✕ (Delete) to delete the hole.

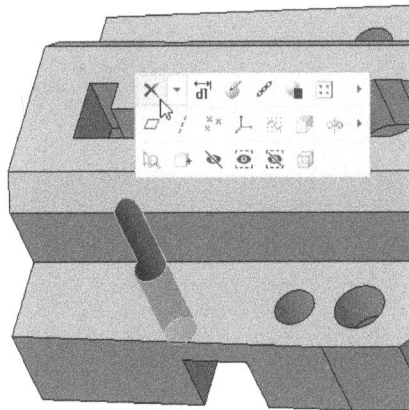

Figure A-53

7. Select **File>Options** and in the *Creo Parametric Options* dialog box, in the *Appearance* category, select **System Appearance**.

8. In the *Theme* drop-down list, select **Default Theme**.

9. In the *Customize* category, select **Shortcut Menus**.

10. Select **Reset selected Shortcut Menu and corresponding Mini-Toolbar**, as shown in Figure A–54.

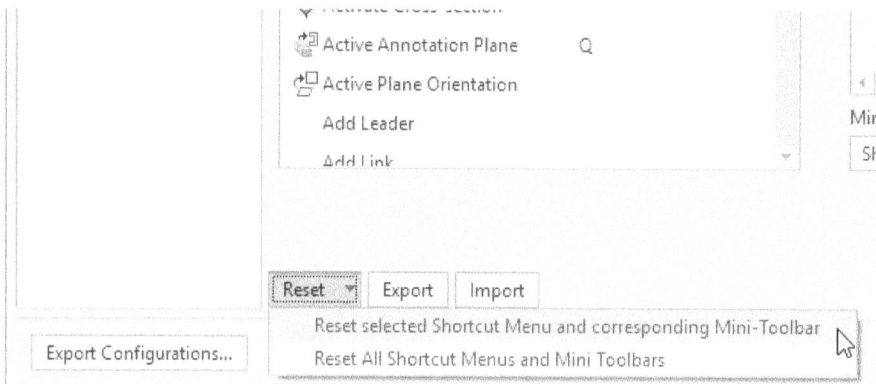

Figure A–54

Task 9: Customize the Model Tree.

1. Expand `»` in the Model Tree if needed and select (Tree Columns).

2. In the Not Displayed list, select **Feat #** as shown in Figure A–55.

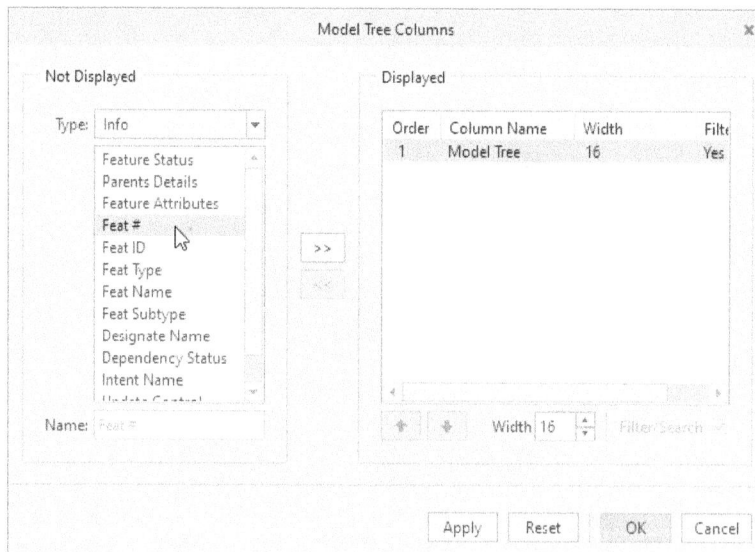

Figure A–55

3. Click `»` (Add Column) to move it to the *Displayed* area.

4. Repeat the steps to move **Feat ID** and **Feat Name** to the *Displayed* area.

5. Click **OK**. Note that the three columns have been added to the Model Tree.

6. Open the file **vise_final.asm**.

7. Note that the customizations to the Model Tree are not present. Changes to the Model Tree are mode specification and the previous changes were made in part mode.

8. Open the file **pin_final_vise.prt**. and note that the customizations to the Model Tree are present.

9. In the Model Tree, expand ⬚ (Model Tree Settings)**>Tree Options>Settings>Reset Tree Settings in all Modes** to return the tree to its default settings.

10. Close **vise_final.asm** and **pin_final_vise.prt**.

Task 10: Add configuration options to Favorites.

1. Select **File>Options**.

2. Select the *Favorites* category. Note that there are no current options in the dialog box.

3. Select the *Configuration Editor* category. There are several config options that are changed often. It is recommended to list these in the *Favorites* category for quick access.

4. Click **Add**. The *Creo Parametric Options* dialog box opens.

5. In the *Option name* collector, add the configuration options that are listed as follows:

Configuration Option	Value
sketcher_starts_in_2d	yes
show_axes_for_extr_arcs	yes
allow_move_view_with_move	yes
spin_with_part_entities	yes
auto_add_remove	yes

6. Select the **auto_add_remove** configuration option, right-click and select **Add to favorites**, as shown in Figure A–56.

7. Repeat Step 6 for the configuration options listed in Step 5.

8. Select the *Favorites* category. Note that the options are now added to the list as shown in Figure A–57. You can quickly change their values by selecting and clearing the option.

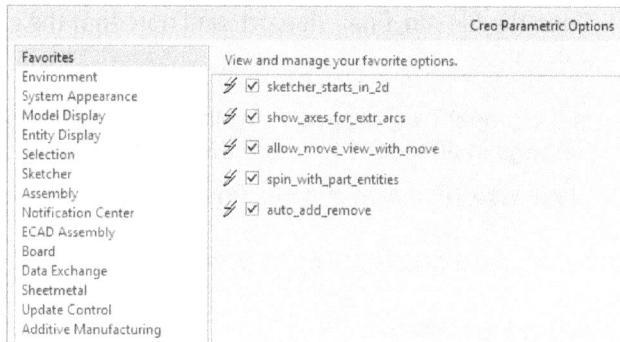

| **Figure A–56** | **Figure A–57** |

9. Click **OK** in the *Creo Parametric Options* dialog box.

10. Click **Yes** to save the settings. Maintain the default name of **config.pro** and click **OK**.

11. Save the model and erase all files from memory.

End of practice

Practice A2
Apply Colors to Geometry

Practice Objective

*   Add color to model geometry.

In this practice, you will add color to different model geometry.

Task 1: Open a part.

1. Set the working directory to the *Applying_Colors* folder.
2. Open **block.prt**.
3. Set the model display as follows:

    *   ✕ (*Datum Display Filters*): All Off
    *   ⊱ (*Spin Center*): Off
    *   ⬚ (*Display Style*): ⬚ (Shading With Edges)

Task 2: Create an extruded cut.

1. Select the top surface of the model and click ⬚ (Extrude) in the *mini* toolbar.

2. In the *Setup* group, if required, click ⬚ (Sketch View). Select the appropriate references and sketch the section as shown in Figure A–58.

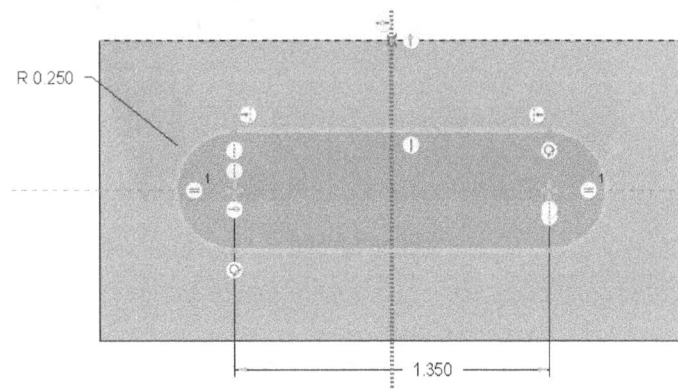

Figure A–58

3. Complete the sketch.

4. Drag the depth handle into the model, then set the *Depth* to **.2**, as shown in Figure A–59.

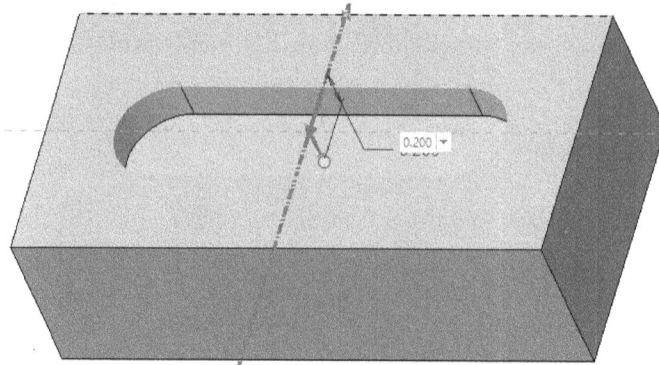

Figure A–59

5. Complete the feature.

Task 3: Change the color of the model and of individual surfaces.

1. Select the *View* tab.
2. Select **BLOCK.PRT** in the Model Tree.
3. In the *Appearances* group, click the ⊙ (Appearance) drop-down list.
4. Select the ⦿ (ptc-painted-red) color swatch. The model updates, as shown in Figure A–60.

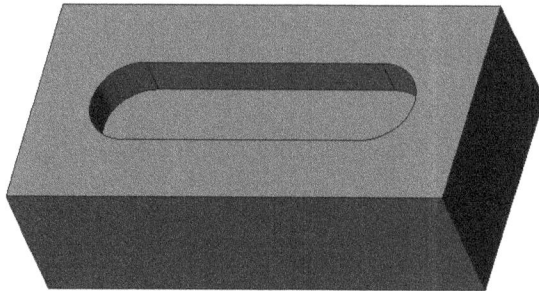

Figure A–60

Note: If the indicated color swatch is not available, select another color of your choice.

5. Select the internal surfaces highlighted in Figure A−61.

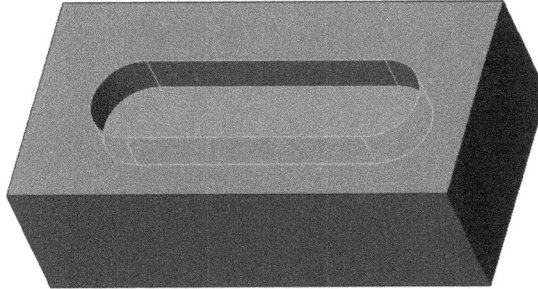

Figure A−61

6. Click ⚬ (Appearance Gallery) and select the ⚬ (ptc-painted-green) swatch. The model updates, as shown in Figure A−62.

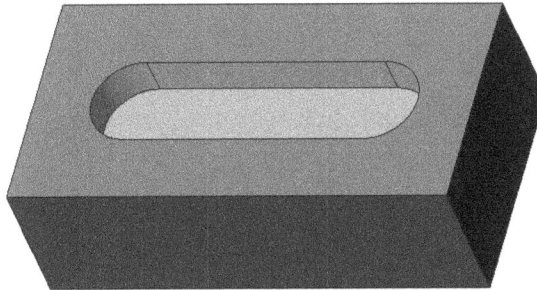

Figure A−62

7. Save and erase the file.
8. Exit Creo Parametric and restart it, so that it no longer loads the customizations made.

End of practice

Chapter Review Questions

1. What is the name of the configuration file that is used to customize your user preferences?

    a. configuation_file.pro

    b. config.pro

    c. preferences.pro

2. The Configuration Editor is divided into two frames. The left frame defines the _____ and the right frame defines its value, status, and description.

    a. Favorite

    b. File

    c. Name

    d. Location

3. Values for the configuration file options can be selected or entered in the value collector.

    a. True

    b. False

4. The color of Datum planes can be changed in the *Creo Parametric Options* dialog box.

    a. True

    b. False

5. Which of the following statements are true regarding mapkeys? (Select all that apply.)

    a. To create a mapkey, select **File>Mapkey**.

    b. Mapkeys enable you to record a series of menu selections that can be executed together as one keystroke.

    c. Function keys cannot be used for the key sequence of a mapkey.

    d. Mapkeys can be paused during definition.

6. Which of the following statements are true regarding customizing the Creo Parametric interface? (Select all that apply.)

   a. The *In-graphics* toolbar can be displayed at the top, left, or right side of the main window.

   b. Command icons can be added to the Quick Access Toolbar.

   c. Mapkey icons cannot be added to the Quick Access Toolbar. You must activate the mapkey using the assigned keystroke.

   d. Tabs can be added and removed.

7. The display of the Model Tree can be independent of the Navigation window.

   a. True

   b. False

8. Which of the following statements are true regarding customizing the Model Tree? (Select all that apply.)

   a. All changes made to the Model Tree are stored in the **config.pro**.

   b. Changes are automatically saved to a *.ui configuration file.

   c. The **Tree Filters** option enables you to filter the display of feature types.

   d. The **Tree Columns** option enables you to customize the display of columns in the Model Tree.

www.ingramcontent.com/pod-product-compliance
Lightning Source LLC
Chambersburg PA
CBHW080347220326
41598CB00030B/4630